The New York Times

SUNDAY CROSSWORD OMNIBUS VOLUME 10

The New York Times

SUNDAY CROSSWORD OMNIBUS VOLUME 10
200 World-Famous Sunday Puzzles from the Pages of *The New York Times*

Edited by Will Shortz

ST. MARTIN'S GRIFFIN ❧ NEW YORK

THE NEW YORK TIMES SUNDAY CROSSWORD OMNIBUS VOLUME 10.
Copyright © 2009 by The New York Times Company. All rights reserved.
Printed in the United States of America. For information, address
St. Martin's Press, 175 Fifth Avenue, New York, N.Y. 10010.

www.stmartins.com

All of the puzzles that appear in this work were originally published in *The New York Times*
from June 15, 1997, to January 11, 2009. Copyright © 1997, 2005, 2006, 2007, 2008, 2009 by
The New York Times Company. All rights reserved. Reprinted by permission.

ISBN 978-0-312-59006-2

ACROSS

1 Georgia state wildflower
7 Georgia neighbor
14 1970s–'80s singer Ronnie
20 Fixes, as a bow
21 Product usually used at night
22 New York lake
23 Puts to the test
24 Girls at the playground?
26 Word before and after "by," "on," or "to"
27 Subsist
29 It may be relative
30 Wheat ___
31 Rear parts of an article of radio equipment?
36 Big atlas section
38 Party person
39 Kind of race
40 "No way"
44 Hero
45 Rest on
47 Assails
50 Journalist Kupcinet
51 More than just a jaunt
53 Barely beats
54 Slow dance with quick turns
55 Provision of the Natl. Security Act, 1947
56 Grand ___ (wine appellation)
58 Golf club resembling an inverted V?
60 ___-Tiki
61 Retainers
63 Ones with potato peelers, for short
64 Break time
65 Shipping dept. stamp
66 First-aid item
68 "___ takers?"
69 Fume
71 Distillery items
72 Milk-related
76 2001 album with the #1 hit "Ain't It Funny"
79 Mass offering
80 Time ___
81 Metallic restraint on Baryshnikov?
83 Architectural feature
84 55-Across relative
85 Northeast tollroad option
86 Emasculate
88 Catty comeback
91 Symbol of slipperiness
92 Vikings' foes
93 Wore briefly
95 Map abbr.
96 Take out
98 Alliance
99 Con men often use them
101 The Baltics, once: Abbr.
103 Ball bearing on a spaceship?
105 Spot for a spare tire
108 Sister of Rachel
110 Cartoon dog
111 "Skip me"
112 Beneath a pendant opener?
117 Pretenses
120 Witnessed in the area of
121 What's left
122 Prom date
123 TV ratings period
124 Experimented with drugs, say
125 "National Velvet" star

DOWN

1 Ernst colleague
2 Time to attack
3 Present for your communication with an English saint?
4 Occupy
5 Like a really big shoe
6 Hired gun
7 Long suit
8 Range setting
9 "But who ___ to . . . ?"
10 Coal holder
11 2002 World Series champs
12 Hills without peaks
13 Good fellers
14 Den ___
15 First-move maker
16 "When Your Child Drives You Crazy" author
17 "Sure thing" for Speedy Gonzales
18 Mideast's Gulf of ___
19 Part of a wagon train's route
25 Garden party, maybe
28 Order more of
32 ___ Arc, Ark.
33 Homers, slangily
34 Sprang up
35 Squirt
37 Ghosts or goblins
38 Presidential monogram
41 When some insects are cited for biting?
42 Sweet roll
43 Boxer Holyfield
46 Quickly, briefly
47 ___ de combat
48 Dismounted
49 Golfer Ballesteros
52 Maynard G. ___ of "The Many Loves of Dobie Gillis"
54 Annual celebration, for short
57 "The good ol'" place
59 "The Things We Do for Love" rock group, 1977
61 Perceived intuitively
62 Miraculous cry at a revival meeting
65 Empire
67 One who may improve your outlook
68 Isles
70 Manchego cheese source
73 Food in bags or cans
74 The Kennedys, e.g.
75 1979 Nastassia Kinski title role
76 Tony's sister on "The Sopranos"
77 Mexican beer go-with
78 Impetuously, maybe
81 Car seat securer
82 Impresario Sol
87 Only in the past
89 "Psst!"
90 Unseld of the N.B.A.
93 Lots of hugs, in brief
94 Lowest score
97 Ancient Palestinian
98 "La ___" (opera)
100 Magnet alloy
102 Traffic caution
103 Landscapers' tools
104 Assignation
105 Weak one
106 All over
107 Creation of un philosophe
109 Sandy hue
113 Mil. titles
114 Little bit
115 Laotian money
116 1970s Bowie collaborator
118 Show presenter, for short
119 Farm area

by Joe DiPietro

2 ALL IN THE PAST

ACROSS

1 Scandinavian royal
5 Basilica area
9 Psychologist's study
15 Growler
18 If successful, they're laughed at
21 1970s White House name
22 Which card to pick, according to a magician
23 Films shown at dentists' conventions?
25 Bygone Ford
26 Handles
27 Captain Queeg's creator
28 Unloose
29 Make stuff up
30 Criteria: Abbr.
32 Shipper of Natalie's records abroad?
36 Common bonds
40 See 17-Down
42 To be, to Henri
43 "How obvious!"
44 Shalom
46 Feel fluish
47 Comprehends
48 N.B.A. star who starred in "Kazaam"
51 Disposition of a regular sort of person?
54 Accessory for the Penguin, in "Batman"
56 Allegro and vivace, e.g.
57 Bitter end?
58 Tyler of "Armageddon"
59 Court plea, for short
60 ___ curiam (by the court)
61 Waterfall feature
62 Buenos ___
64 Like an anode: Abbr.
65 Painter who makes a fast substitution?
70 "The Santa Clause," for one
71 South Pacific carvings
72 Bullwinkle, e.g.
73 Muscle movement
74 Number two
76 A few: Abbr.
77 "Fargo" director
78 Home cooker
81 Forward thinker?
83 Commuter train eschewed by Dracula?
87 Bacon bit
88 Hollywood's Grant
89 "___-La-La" (1974 Al Green hit)
90 Seasons to be merry
91 Go downhill fast
92 Wilbur Post's horse
93 Union member
95 Dish eaten with a spork
96 1960s presidential candidate living overseas?
100 Small fry
102 Born, in Bretagne
103 Posterior
104 Title mom in a comic strip
106 Head home
111 Cape ___
112 Pain caused by adding onto a house?
116 Snappy '60s dresser
117 Pungent sandwich slice
118 Angling gear?
119 Power brokers
120 Burn up
121 ___ milk
122 Carved

DOWN

1 Makes accessible, old-style
2 Sumptuous
3 Chip on the table, maybe
4 Some RCA products
5 19th-century author whose father founded a utopian community
6 Band's place on Broadway
7 Sledder's protection
8 Architect Saarinen
9 "Now ___ theater near you!"
10 Swiss canton
11 Knights in competition
12 Winter chipper
13 Breakfast table staple: Var.
14 Tusked animal
15 "Get help!"
16 Loose
17 With 40-Across, a popular rental
19 Boaters and such
20 Baffled
24 "Top Hat" film studio
31 "Phooey!"
33 West Yorkshire city
34 Kitchen addition
35 Kind of sentence
36 Copy
37 Barber shop call
38 Rustic locale
39 Shrimp ___
41 Intense teaching programs
45 Anticipate
47 Taste-related
49 Prorate
50 Late July babies
52 Oscar night greeting
53 Radio host John
54 Sorvino of "Mighty Aphrodite"
55 Go heavy on the levy
58 Legal safety net
61 1014, in history
62 One struggling
63 Half of a cartoon pair
65 Angry teacher's cry
66 Is frugal
67 Barely earns, with "out"
68 Song by candlelight
69 In myth he flew too close to the sun
70 Not fail
75 Eleniak of "Baywatch"
77 Deck units
79 Dickens heroine
80 Off the coast
82 Campaign smears
83 Food critic Greene
84 British afternoon TV fare
85 ___ lot (gorge)
86 Brisbane-to-Sydney dir.
88 Least refined
92 Sleeveless cape
93 Buttinsky
94 Whodunit awards
96 As a friend, to François
97 Element #54
98 Tinker Bell, for one
99 ___ Lilly & Co.
101 Bubbly drink
105 About
107 "Sheep May Safely Graze" composer
108 Entr'___
109 Vittles
110 "Show Boat" composer
113 Research org.
114 Montreal street sign abbr.
115 Berlioz's "Nuit d'___"

by Elizabeth C. Gorski

ACROSS

1 Regis Philbin or Kelly Ripa
7 Related on the father's side
13 Benefactor
19 "Forward!" in Italy
20 Number 1, e.g.
21 Distillate
22 Unmask
23 Supper at home before unpacking from a move?
25 "You're ___ friend"
26 Guinness superlative
27 Pipe contents
28 Founding Father listed on a popular computer?
33 Vinland pioneers
37 Suffix with Caesar
38 Cartoon dog
39 Rove
40 Constitutional
41 Old ___ (Satan)
43 Mild swearing competition?
49 Steps on the scale
50 Farrier's tool
52 Bargain repository
53 Connect with
54 American magazine founded in France
55 Old Colgate rival
57 All-Star team, with "the"
59 Part of E.E.C.: Abbr.
60 Divine one, to Dante
61 Shelters
64 Willa Cather's "One of ___"
66 Cuckoo bird
67 "This one's ___"
69 Prize for Coronado
70 Hurry up, as one decorating Christmas gifts?
74 Actress Scala
75 Red Cross inventories
77 Bill passer: Abbr.
78 Work on, in a way
79 Fire sources
81 Frequent abbr. in BBC announcements
82 Not give ___
84 1987 Pulitzer-winning critic Richard ___
86 Compact contents
87 Jack-in-the-pulpit, e.g.
88 Automaton of Hebrew lore
90 Art collector/ philanthropist ___ Broad
91 Working without ___
92 Latin American agreements
93 Like a test with a properly corrected score?
96 Guideline: Abbr.
98 Inner selves
100 Recommendation from a C.P.A.
101 Fed. overseer
103 Magazine exec in pj's
105 River to the Rio Grande
106 Improper trade of a St. Louis N.F.L. player?
112 Safarigoers may get a charge out of it
114 Think box
115 Quebec underground
116 Guests who jabber incessantly?
122 Less sweet
123 Haloes
124 Immediately
125 Box up
126 Undercover jobs
127 Use a straw
128 Experts

DOWN

1 Wine order
2 Flooded
3 What the Beatles were able to do?
4 Early hr.
5 Like yesterday's news, to today's
6 Three Dog Night hit "___ the World Ends"
7 Wing
8 Mill stuff
9 Beethoven's symphony with "Ode to Joy"
10 Bird: Prefix
11 First in double figures
12 Joule fraction
13 Jr.'s test
14 Balloonists' trips
15 Eloise was a little one
16 Messenger with a code
17 Natl. Pretzel Mo.
18 Maiden-named
21 Carrier with blue-striped jets
24 Punch alternative
26 "Flash Gordon" villain ___ the Merciless
29 Take in
30 I problem?
31 Bonkers
32 "Frasier" terrier
34 Positioning the Trojan horse in front of Troy?
35 Zigzag activity
36 On the other hand
40 Less emotional
42 Philosopher Kierkegaard, e.g.
44 Old ___ (Civil War eagle)
45 Cat's cry
46 Guarantee
47 Go over
48 Sought absolution
51 Ratted
54 Last shogunate capital
55 They're said before a kiss
56 Swift falcon
58 Exchange (as A and R in this puzzle)
62 Pharmacists' concerns
63 Unsaturated alcohol
65 Brown recluse, for one
68 Comfort
71 Guilty ___ counts
72 Marked pillar
73 Get rid of holes
76 Bank letters
80 Functions
83 An undesirable thing to be in
85 Divest
87 Quickly, quickly
89 Paltry
91 Garden party?
93 Ablution
94 [That's awful!]
95 Former New York cardinal
97 Honey
99 Longtime CBS/CNN newsman Bruce
102 "Hey Girl" hitmaker, 1971
104 Spanish blooms
106 Kansas-born playwright
107 Place: Abbr.
108 Ruffle
109 Slow in scoring
110 Material in tire cords
111 Tied score
113 Much may follow it
116 Desktop items, for short
117 Bunk
118 He was the "O" in Jackie O
119 Special ___
120 X-ray relative
121 Spirit
122 Mermaid's home

by Con Pederson

ACROSS

1 Club charges for nonmembers
10 One-named singer
14 Straight man of comedy
20 P.O. address of 75-Down
21 Lit ___ (college course)
22 Athlete in a crease
23 2003 action movie . . . or a 75-Down attraction
26 Party person
27 Where to find a story online
28 Not ___ many words
29 Sensitive
32 Some people who send I.M.'s
34 Rich soils
38 Reformer born in Denmark
40 Trap
42 Armstrong on wheels
43 Join, with "in"
44 Part of S.A.S.E.: Abbr.
45 Pull off
48 Filled up
50 Yours, in Italy
51 Properly lined up
53 Certain dweller on the Danube
55 Statute: Abbr.
56 Beach sight in W.W. II: Abbr.
57 Ratio marks
58 Presumptions
59 Bring up, as a grievance
62 "Aladdin" role
64 Musical with the song "Rainbow Tour"
65 Kind of party
66 One of the baseball Boones
68 Have value
69 Dreamcast game maker
70 Mata ___ (spy)
71 "You betcha"
72 Bias
74 Aromatic herb used by the ancients
76 To ___ (perfectly)
77 Movie shot
78 Mediterranean cruise stop
79 Mealtime plea to junior
81 Part of Lombard Street in San Francisco
82 Gray matter?
83 Astronaut Collins
84 Nod, maybe
85 ___ Locks
87 2004 sword-and-sandals flick
89 Took by force
90 Eggs in water?
91 Observant one
94 Torch carriers?
96 Sung syllable
97 Avril is part of it
99 Famous fountain
101 Old Mideast grp.
102 ___ hall
103 Bacon piece
104 Offering relief
106 Eponymous doctor who studied hypnosis
109 Diner side
111 Movie chameleon of 1983
113 "Cultured insolence," according to Aristotle
114 Any story in a certain movie serial . . . or a 75-Down attraction
123 Scout's interest
124 Auberges
125 Original price of admission to 75-Down
126 Overeater's plateful, sometimes
127 "I'll ___ brief as possible"
128 Age category of most college entrants

DOWN

1 Break
2 Valve opening?
3 Word with candy or drops
4 Works, as wet clay
5 ___ Range, in the West
6 Specialty
7 Miami duo?
8 "Baudolino" author
9 Call with outstretched arms
10 High ___
11 Ring of color
12 Sydney Carton's creator
13 Traveler's request: Abbr.
14 Averse to, in dialect
15 Matterhorn rider at 75-Down
16 Dogfaced primate
17 Flamenco dancer's shout
18 Actress Carrere
19 Wallet item
24 Not yet scheduled, in schedules
25 Meet
29 Amusement park that was a model for 75-Down
30 It doesn't rain but it pours
31 ___ room
33 DVD player maker
35 TV personality who co-hosted the opening of 75-Down
36 Group that made their first TV appearance at the opening of 75-Down
37 Turnstile feature
38 Works more to get the swelling down
39 Technology-based 75-Down attraction
41 Pay for some rides
45 Dame from Down Under
46 Deletes, with "out"
47 Most irritable
49 Work unit
52 Traffic circle
54 It may be dribbled
58 Steamed
60 "Roger"
61 English novelist Charles
63 Some speech sounds
65 Large mtge. insurer
67 After-dinner serving in France
73 Funny Sykes and others
75 Notable opening of 7/17/55
78 Architect ___ van der Rohe
80 Extremely
83 Drop a brick
84 Aberdeen hillside
86 Capital city on a river of the same name
88 Dry
89 Used to be
92 Verdi's "___ tu"
93 Gridiron area near the goal line
95 Farm-made butter
98 Not as strenuous
100 Schönbrunn Palace site
102 Pluck
105 Army members, for short
107 King Carl XVI Gustaf, e.g.
108 North Dakota city with an air force base
110 Army members
112 Cooler overseas
114 Old telecom inits.
115 "Fuhgedaboutit!"
116 Sixth-century year
117 Triangular sail
118 Lab exam subject
119 Lab examiner
120 Suffix with glob
121 Took off
122 Where IV's may be administered

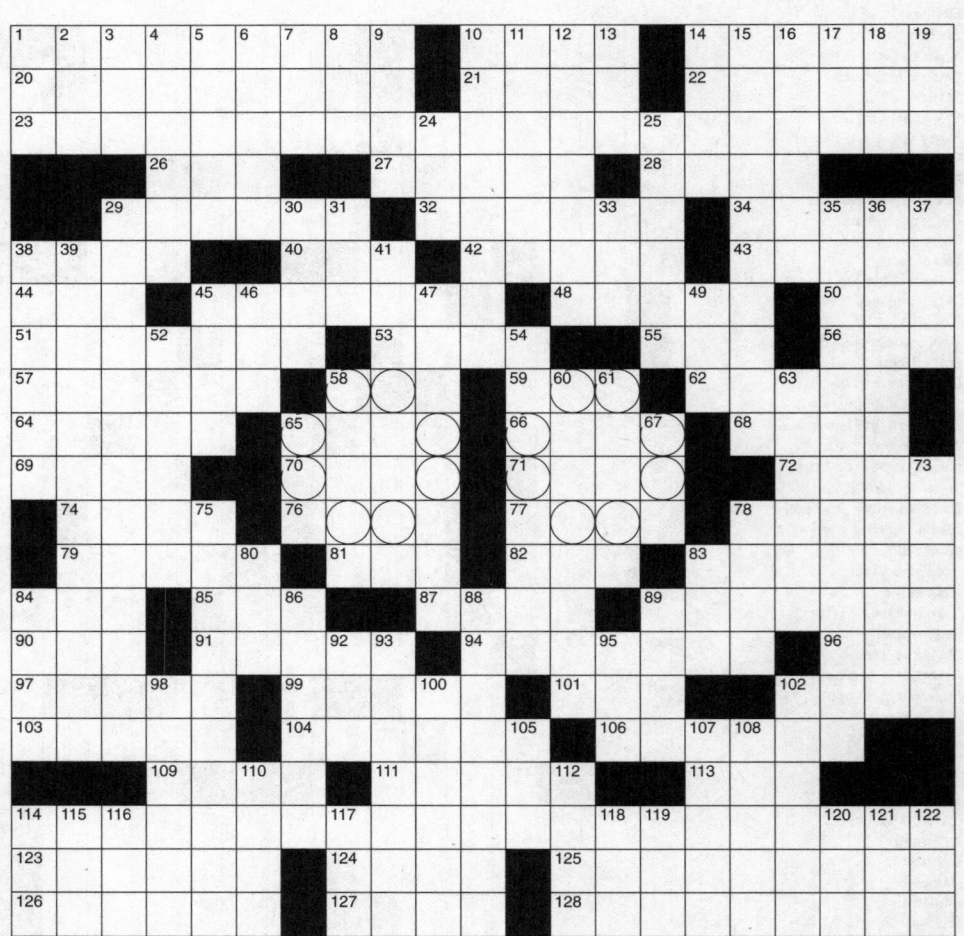

by David J. Kahn

ACROSS

1 Euripides heroine
8 Soyuz cosmonaut Makarov
12 Tending to radiate
20 Snow-white dog
21 Part of N.B.
22 Got going
23 Risky marketing of sports jackets on a city's outskirts? [Chevrolet]
26 It comes out in the wash
27 "This guy walks into ____ . . ."
28 Apollo mission vehicle
29 Cowpoke, often
30 More than a sip
32 "Bad Behavior" star, 1993
34 Result of teasing?
38 Understanding of how to keep peace in the community? [Honda]
45 Fell
48 Dance springily
49 "Rock and Roll, Hoochie ____"
50 His "Parade" included parts for typewriter, foghorn and rattle
51 Suffix with planet
52 Western native
53 Storting meeting place
55 Locale of some hangings: Abbr.
57 Zippo
58 Some underwear
59 Aura surrounding a black mountain lion? [Mercury]
64 One option for Hamlet
65 Garage supply
66 Deck material
67 N.H.L.'s ____ Trophy
70 Some claimants
73 Shooter Adams
75 Token
76 "Bewitched" witch
77 Harsh call
78 "Third Watch" actress Texada
80 Exiled African leader
81 Search for poetry in the Old West? [Nissan]
86 Its point is guarded
88 Sitter's acquisition
89 Volume 1 heading starter
90 Astronomer's study
91 Eavesdropping org.
92 Story
93 Hotel employee
95 Subj. for U.S. newcomers
97 Half seas over
98 Deck (out)
99 Fearless group of traveling sheep? [Dodge]
104 Moralistic declaration
105 Simile part
106 Prefix with cop, in a film title
109 Grandma at a bar mitzvah
112 Noted apple pie baker
114 Stretch
117 Daughter of Saturn
119 Accompany a horse researcher? [Ford]
125 Lobster may be served in it
126 Blue hue
127 Glimpses
128 Lake Michigan arm
129 Georgetown athlete
130 Baptisms of fire

DOWN

1 Petrol brand
2 Heaps kudos on
3 Form into an arch, old-style
4 TV personality with a voice in "Shark Tale"
5 Norse war god
6 Musical McEntire
7 Not much at all
8 Temporarily punched out
9 Cyber-chortle
10 Card catalog abbr.
11 Shady resting place
12 Labyrinth locale
13 Early 12th-century year
14 Resident: Suffix
15 Daily event
16 Zen goal
17 "Give ____ for . . ."
18 "Billy Budd" captain
19 Pulitzer-winning critic Richard
24 Figure in a bust
25 Mideast parley attenders
31 Fatigued action figure?
33 In ____ (really out of it)
35 Polish part
36 Number-starting cry
37 Kind of dye
39 Baron's superior: Abbr.
40 Homes with domes
41 Judiciary
42 "The whole of ____ consists in the art of being honest": Jefferson
43 Lay low
44 Lions' goals, briefly
45 Get the lead out
46 ____ shrdlu
47 Goose steppers?
54 Not non
56 Barrie buccaneer
58 42-Down division
60 Poe poem
61 Hostile look
62 Big Three meeting site
63 Shiite center in Iran
68 "Yea"
69 Writer Susan
71 Treasure of the Sierra Madre?
72 Worked out at the track
74 Japan's first capital
75 Big name in oil
77 Humans, e.g.
79 Travel guide listing
82 Actress Shire
83 Fictional diva Floria
84 Tel ____
85 Doha's land
86 Y sporter
87 One with a sticking point
93 Experienced
94 Pares
96 Layered dish
100 Biochemical sugar
101 Amount to turn it up?
102 Endangered
103 "Really!"
107 Anatomical sac
108 Best Supporting Actress for "Paper Moon"
109 Big chip off the old block?
110 Pusher's target
111 Four after the first?
113 Waldorf salad ingredient
115 Big show
116 Monkey
118 Crumbs
120 It has a certain ring to it
121 Longtime Elton John label
122 Driver's 180
123 Demurral
124 Fronted

by Frank Longo

ACROSS

1 Ballpark figures
5 Tourer with Carreras and Domingo
14 Genesis event, with "the"
18 Notarized doc., e.g.
19 Egg drop?
20 Lower small intestines
21 Kowtow
23 Doesn't cry uncle
24 Basketry material
25 One who's far from a fan
27 Like shrinking violets
28 Cordovan and kid, e.g.
30 Camaraderies
32 French mathematician Marin ___
33 Image depicted by this puzzle, after it's solved
34 Throng
38 Some cosmetics
40 Conseco Fieldhouse team
41 Bidding doers
43 One with a nice bod
44 It has moles: Abbr.
45 While getting there
46 Calendar mo.
47 Not practiced
50 Bit of workout gear
52 Symbols of happiness
54 "Huh-uh"
56 Something noticed at a fish market
57 Essential nutrient
59 Primrose variety
62 Sniff around
63 Refuse receptacle
67 Day's end: Abbr.
68 Spreadsheet fill
70 Fair feature
71 Vane dir.
72 Agnus ___
73 Come out of denial
76 Gershwin musical
78 Env. content
79 Joule parts
81 Slight irregularities
83 Ran while wet
84 Clown's cover-up
88 Really roughs up
89 Dignity restorer
92 Thin mug with sharp features
94 Bill of Rights subj.
95 Compact things
97 Giant of a Giant
98 Hand holder?
100 It's not necessarily the real worth
102 Go for the gold?
103 Helmsman's headache
105 Was in a meet, maybe
106 Take ___ (drop off briefly)
107 Bean source
108 Hair feature
110 Memorable times
112 Senior airman's superior: Abbr.
113 Hindu wonder-worker: Var.
114 Heroine in Bizet's "The Pearl Fishers"
115 Ones in charge: Abbr.
116 Conference start?
117 Regular
118 Novelist O'Brien and others
119 Out-of-commission cruisers: Abbr.
120 Operates
121 Feels dizzy

DOWN

1 School in La Jolla: Abbr.
2 She might cite you
3 Commonplace
4 Cork up
5 Look that says nothing
6 Forestall
7 Somme sight
8 European river source
9 Ill-considered
10 "Our Gang" affirmative
11 Wee warbler
12 Transparent linen
13 Communicate (with)
14 Stocking stuff
15 Unpleasant sort
16 Jack Lemmon's "Days of Wine and Roses" co-star
17 Metallica drummer Ulrich
22 Proverbial payee
24 County whose seat is Alamogordo
26 Tamari sauce and the like
29 "The Nazarene" novelist
31 Stands out significantly
32 Like some blocks
33 Provider of creature comforts?: Abbr.
35 Cloverleaf component
36 Water cannon target
37 Twice
39 Goes down
41 Litter box cry
42 "D-OH" person, e.g.
48 Those with clout
49 Title type, often
50 Anatomical dividers
51 Finished off
52 Be humiliated
53 Antenna holder
55 Singer called "The Little Sparrow"
58 First name of "America's Mayor"
59 Give up
60 Afflicted with root rot, perhaps
61 Repeatedly raise the bar?
64 Period of high artistic development
65 Ethnically diverse
66 Mathlete, stereotypically
69 Oberhausen outburst
70 "Angels of mercy," briefly
74 Broadway lyricist Rice
75 Gangster moniker
76 Not in profile
77 Airborne Express alternative
80 Quotation qualification
82 Nod, maybe
83 Letters on undies
85 Marijuana's chief intoxicant: Abbr.
86 Aquatic zappers
87 Smallish items on rods
89 Surrounders of light switches
90 Extra horsepower, slangily
91 Electrify
92 Limp
93 King and queen
95 Formation between two edges of a polyhedron
96 Pound sounds
99 Target alternative
101 Glad supporters
104 ___ monster
107 Matter for a judge
109 107-Down assignees, for short
111 Lottery-running org.
112 Three-time World Series of Poker champ ___ Ungar
113 Warm covering

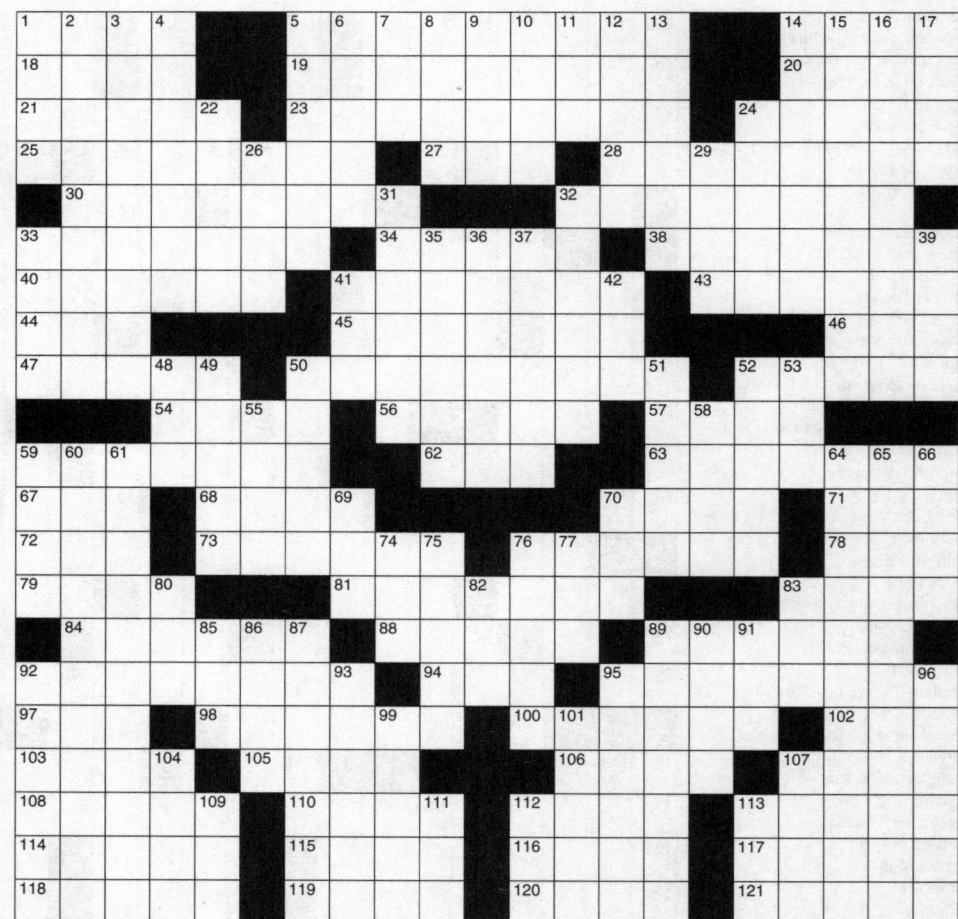

by Mark Feldman

ACROSS

1 Court case?
8 Friendly correspondent
14 Toy that goes "bang"
20 Rocket stage
21 Develop
22 Melodic
23 Protection in the city?
25 Cut with the grain
26 Playwright O'Casey
27 Keep out
28 Surfer stops
30 Work unit
31 Traditional brain doctor?
37 Thingums
39 Singer Jarreau and others
40 Take in
41 Pique
42 Nantes-to-Paris dir.
43 Brood
45 Convention V.I.P.'s
48 What Indian cooks play?
53 Tide competitor
54 Mystique
55 California river named for a fish
56 Major injustice
59 Historic plane
62 Home of a '69 "miracle"
64 Decent fellow
68 PC display
69 Federal government connections?
73 Sob syllable
74 Australian lass
76 Mavens
77 Try to snow
79 Sheet fabric
82 Iranian ayatollah Sayyed ___ Khamenei
83 Panhandle migrant
84 Work for eds.
86 Schedule at a Vegas chapel?
91 George Washington University athletes
94 Backside
95 Indivisible
96 "Double Fantasy" singer
97 Producer of its.
98 Tokyo carrier, for short
99 Adam and Eve, presumably
103 Sodom or Gomorrah?
109 Cry of wonder
110 Goes first
111 Thimbleful
112 Swing around
113 Scanty, in Scarborough
115 Result of wearing high heels?
120 Get to
121 Be upset by, say
122 Purified, as water
123 Cordwood units
124 Like slander
125 "Timon of Athens," e.g.

DOWN

1 Was addicted to
2 Lord of the ring?
3 English-speaking island in the Caribbean
4 ___ aside
5 Smoker's purchase: Abbr.
6 "___ let us in, knows where we've been" (Beatles lyric)
7 Cavern on the way to Hades
8 California's San ___ Bay
9 Modern music genre
10 ___ Tamid (synagogue lamp)
11 Some scampi
12 Infamous 1972 hurricane
13 Don't bother
14 Desert parade
15 Thank you, in Tokyo
16 Lab tube
17 Dirt spreader
18 Can. neighbor
19 "I said ___!"
24 It might go for a dip in the ocean
29 Wolf or shark
31 When repeated, Mork's TV sign-off
32 Linda of "Jekyll & Hyde"
33 ___ Andy ("Show Boat" role)
34 First name in fashion
35 Miles of film
36 Some warriors in "War of the Worlds"
38 Transfer
43 "As if!"
44 Salad topper
45 Where "South Pacific" was filmed
46 CPR giver
47 Bar mitzvah boy, for one
48 Asian weight units
49 Suspicion
50 Lose ground?
51 Behind
52 Busy people
57 Singing brothers' name
58 Daring deed
60 Fit
61 ___ gum (thickening agent)
62 More likely
63 Where to dig "Six Feet Under"
65 Plumed hat
66 Quinn formerly of "S.N.L."
67 Contrived
70 Highest mark
71 Key of Prokofiev's Piano Concerto No. 1
72 Way to go
75 ___ facto
78 Marisa of "Alfie," 2004
80 Opposite of loose
81 Big mail deliverer
82 Org. for lifesavers
84 Like old recordings
85 It's far off the record time
87 Future atty.'s hurdle
88 Canine cry
89 Win in a walk
90 1980s movie hero, informally
91 Camp sack
92 Unchanged
93 Chill
98 In no other way
99 Tries to bite
100 Sugar in coffee, e.g.
101 Barnstormed
102 "The Breakfast Club" co-star, 1985
104 River through Mali
105 Makes better
106 Lowest deck
107 Hit with, as a pickup line
108 Free
112 Like some shows
113 More, in Mexico
114 Outside: Prefix
116 Reaction to a rodent
117 AAA idea
118 Prescription notation
119 Altar in the sky

by Lee Glickstein and Nancy Salomon

ACROSS

1. Mathematical fig.
5. Whistler, e.g.
11. Cargo platform
15. Chatter
18. ___ pneumonia
19. Stephen Foster's dream girl
20. Pro's opposite
21. Arapaho foe
22. Lifesaver?
25. French law
26. Puzzles
27. "Survivor" sight
28. Sonar pulse
29. "Is that so?!"
30. King of England in 1700?
36. "Lord, is ___?"
38. Without interruption
39. Perfume amounts
40. Critical tennis situation
45. Bygone nuclear agcy.
46. Monstrous
48. Stingers?
51. Money substitute, for short
54. Timeline divisions
55. Prop for the Acad. Awards
56. Supreme finale
57. Launch sites
59. "Stay!"
62. Waterfall jumper
66. Rustic couple
68. Sidekick of old children's TV?
71. Idle talk
74. Jawaharlal Nehru's daughter
75. Nearby
79. Flour cake
80. Like NyQuil: Abbr.
82. Actress Gardner
84. Stick in a dish
85. Tahoe, for one
86. Plant expert?
93. Proofers' catches
95. Nashville-based awards org.
96. Watch
97. Hurting
99. Horseshoe-shaped wear
101. Delta wing craft
102. Duke Ellington classic?
106. Ballerina Karsavina
111. Big hands often take them
112. Musician Brian
113. Waters
115. First name in despotism
116. Tanning agents?
121. ___-mo
122. 33-Down's home today
123. Sister of Erato
124. Lace tip
125. Natural incubator
126. Masked one, informally
127. Bible parts
128. Diner in "Alice"

DOWN

1. His last words were "Thus with a kiss I die"
2. Critic with a Hollywood Walk of Fame star
3. ___ diem (motto of Horace)
4. 13-figure figure
5. Sophocles drama
6. Extend
7. Putts out
8. Pasta suffix
9. Failing
10. Shatner's "___ War"
11. Run one's fingers over
12. 1997 treaty city
13. ___ agent
14. Bashes
15. 1960s–'70s PBS star
16. Now
17. Considers
18. "Lethal Weapon" force: Abbr.
23. Like the fire goddess Brigit
24. Famed political hanger-on
28. Female swans
31. Soil layer
32. Actor ___ Cobb
33. Ancient people
34. Stronghold
35. Powerful
37. Court case title phrase
40. It's involved in many spills
41. Architect Saarinen
42. Certain fraud investigator, informally
43. Daily neighborhood sight
44. Ex-lax?
46. Some nods
47. "You'll never ___!"
49. Cupidity
50. Not extreme
52. "Alley ___"
53. Letters on a stamp
58. Briefly
60. Care, slangily
61. Suffix with verb
63. KO insert?
64. 50-Down: Prefix
65. Clandestine maritime org.
67. Baseball club designation
69. Brookie or laker
70. Diner cupfuls
71. Mail addenda, for short
72. Prefix with pressure
73. Aphrodisiac
76. ___-Seltzer
77. Waxing alternative
78. French illustrator Gustave
81. La-la lead-in
83. Some Dada works
87. Author Grey
88. Roman year with "two pair"
89. Monarchy since 1744
90. Caper
91. White terrier's nickname
92. Eight-pointed star
94. Exposure units
97. Mischievous
98. Noggin
99. Old draft deferment category for critical civilian work
100. Ones who are worlds apart
103. Hardly modern
104. Ski jump downslope
105. "Nancy" cartoonist Bushmiller
107. One of the Simpsons
108. Ever
109. California's Point ___ National Seashore
110. Office title abbr.
114. Info on grocery pkgs.
116. It's often below an ISBN
117. Late July delivery
118. Word on a Valentine candy heart
119. Exist
120. Dict. listing

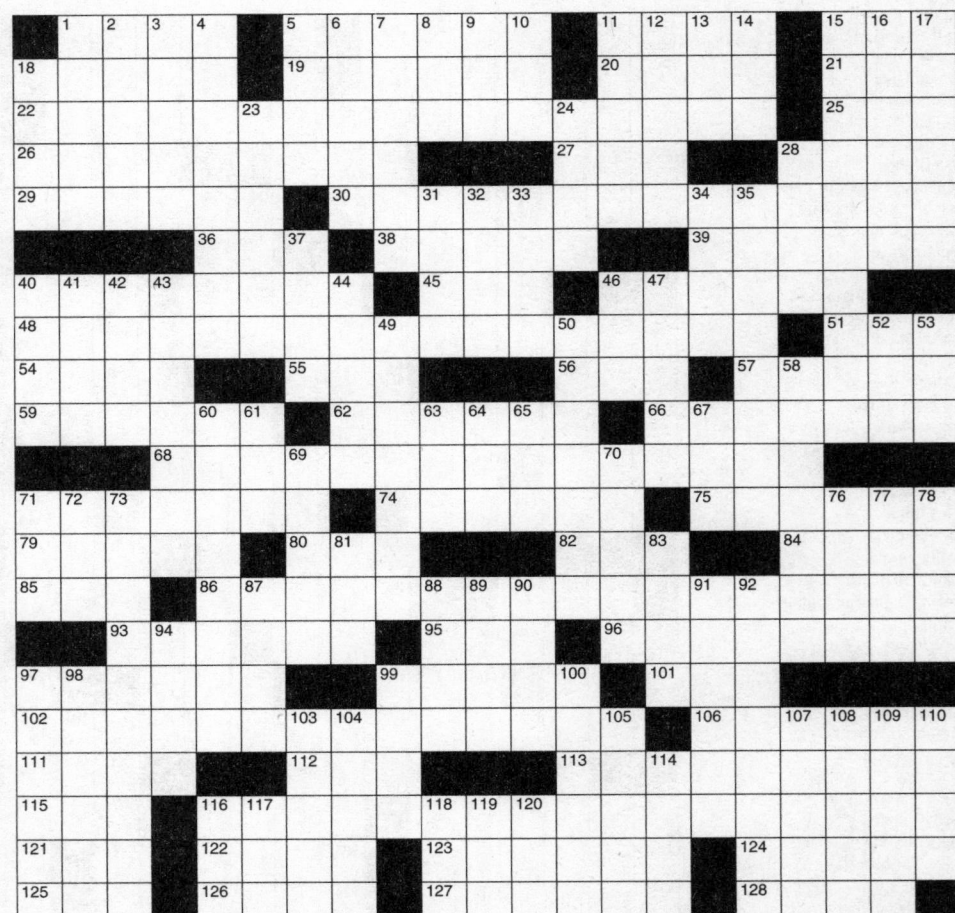

by Patrick Merrell

ACROSS

1 It's the top
5 Medieval chest
9 Energy ___
13 Ideally
19 Puts in one's place
21 Rwandan people
22 Place to store food
23 Hardly snug attire
25 Take offense
26 1967 war participant: Abbr.
27 Harley, slangily
28 Walruses and whales
30 Marker
32 Alternatives to lattes
34 Messenger ___
35 Hawaiian bigeye
37 Dove, for one
46 Some are hidden
49 "If ___ you . . ."
50 Light into
51 The City of Churches
52 Basketball commentator Dick
54 Face trouble
55 Lustrous fabrics
56 What major retailers do
59 Discomfit
60 Ram
61 Suffix with cine
62 Effeminate
63 Dramatic medium
66 Car that won the 1939 and 1940 Indianapolis 500
69 Journal ending
71 National symbol of Wales
72 Whittle
73 Brown shade
76 Works on a car's alignment?
80 Arc producer
82 Impertinent one
83 Friend of Peppermint Patty
84 Slip out of class
85 Striped African animals
88 Like the mumps
89 Trials
90 Store overseers
93 Title of respect
94 Actress Meyers
95 "Mighty stream so deep and wide," in song
98 To be, to Brutus
101 Sleepovers
109 Morgue, for one
111 Bill producer, for short
112 Literary critic Trilling
113 Tabloid nickname for Sydney Biddle Barrows
116 Largest city on the island Fyn
117 AOL and others
118 Remote power source?
119 "The Kingdom and the Power" author
120 "Out!"
121 Article II subj.
122 Requires

DOWN

1 Glaze for fish dishes
2 Go at it
3 Mr. Right, say
4 Grp. setting standards
5 Not standing
6 Approximate
7 100 lbs.
8 Shortage of punch
9 Blacken
10 Tribe noted for its silver and turquoise jewelry
11 Env. directive
12 Stratagem
13 Neighbor of Macedonia
14 Places for taking off
15 Cup part
16 Source for Wagner's "The Ring of the Nibelung"
17 Leave the shelves
18 "___ intéressant"
20 P.T.A. concern
24 Coat, as metal, to reduce its chemical reactivity
29 Actor who played Santa with Nancy Reagan in his lap
31 Flogging
33 Abbey area
36 Emotionally withdrawn
38 See 101-Down
39 Subject heading in a hotel brochure
40 Composer Khachaturian
41 Disappointing return
42 "The hour ___ hand"
43 Community abutting Santa Monica
44 Swedish taxonomist Carl von ___
45 Gray lines?
46 Very little
47 Cartoonist Browne
48 Pitches
51 Computer pioneer Lovelace
53 Film director ___ C. Kenton
56 Schnoz site
57 Plop preceder
58 Case studies, e.g.
60 Treat with honey
64 Poivre's partner
65 Crawl (with)
66 Even out
67 Boston-accented Harvard dropouts?
68 Left over
69 Derby locale
70 Name with instant brand recognition?
72 Peter O'Toole's role in "Troy"
74 Cat sound
75 The difference between what he said and what she said
77 G.E. product: Abbr.
78 Bluenose
79 Spread unit
80 Camel hazard?
81 Fossilized
84 Lanford Wilson's "The ___ Baltimore"
86 Declaration before washing up
87 Hillshire Farm's parent company
91 Just beat
92 "Sorry, Charlie"
96 Loonlike bird
97 Superstars walk around with them
99 Grim
100 Tube top honors
101 With 38-Down, common device on "The Twilight Zone"
102 "O patria mia" source
103 Follower of Hosea
104 Poet Sexton
105 "Yellow Dog" author Martin
106 Itch cause
107 Toys for Tots, for example
108 In case it's true
110 911 responder: Abbr.
114 Kind of cabinet
115 ___ clip

by Byron Walden

ACROSS

1 Turkic people
7 Series of movements
13 Patient form info
16 Baron von Trapp
21 It may be folded for breakfast
22 Part of Isabella I's realm
23 Sch. in Kingston
24 Connecticut or Delaware
25 How this answer is situated
27 Nothing
28 "Gladiator" setting
29 Cookout aid
30 Eyelid afflictions
32 Eventually
34 Thatching material
36 Irene __ ("A Scandal in Bohemia" woman)
38 Seventh-century Arab caliph
39 March cry
40 Paul Anka #1 hit
43 Must
46 Flighty sort?
48 Fuel suffix
49 Up
50 How this answer is situated
52 Purplish
53 Water carrier
54 Cassini and others
55 Some mil. careerists
56 Decorative fabrics
58 Basilica feature
59 Shave
60 How this answer is situated
63 Beer bash need
64 Like Nehru jackets
66 Made known
70 Possible backache cause
74 "Dies __"
75 Shepherd's pie ingredients
77 It gets a licking
78 Goof-offs
79 Out of memory?
81 Rennes resident
83 Gaze dreamily
84 Sight from Taormina
86 Messieurs' mates: Abbr.
87 Belly-dancers' accouterments
88 "Heat" co-star, 1995
91 Gounod opera
92 "If the __ is concealed, it succeeds": Ovid
93 How this answer is situated
96 Long
98 Certain sorority member
102 Summer Olympics racers
105 Wannabe, often
106 Got up
107 "What a pity!"
108 Normandy river
109 How this answer is situated
112 Time
113 Topper
114 Faculties
116 Finish second
117 Resembling a beanpole
118 Suffix with Capri
119 Identify
120 Prefix with comic
122 Reference book for a writer
125 Charles who founded an investment firm
127 Start of many sequel titles
129 Derelict
132 "That's an __!"
133 Oneself
136 How this answer is situated
140 Weeper of myth
141 Pal of Rover
142 Prayer
143 Two-timing
144 Thick novels
145 Censor's target
146 African scourge
147 Ostensible

DOWN

1 Boatload
2 Actor Leon of "Life With Father"
3 Sermon's basis
4 Sub
5 Camp David, e.g.
6 Curling item
7 __ Paulo
8 Leftover morsel
9 Casual turndowns
10 Hurried, musically
11 "Leave It to Beaver" actor
12 Sweetheart
13 Barbarian
14 Diagnostic aid, for short
15 Wick holder
16 Au __
17 Limerick locale
18 How this answer is situated
19 Give up
20 Scholarship winners
26 Doze
31 Rap session?
33 __ maison (indoors): Fr.
35 Farrier
37 Severity
40 1910s--'20s movement
41 Live __
42 Fundamentals
44 Zouave, by birth
45 Some Mercedes-Benzes
47 Seller of Alaska, 1867
50 Ernest who designed Washington's Corcoran Gallery
51 Fascinated by
52 Goes through
54 Starts the betting
56 Cask control
57 Reproductive cells
60 __ impasse
61 Ex-con
62 __ Bounty
63 Red apéritif
65 Columnist Bombeck
67 Haul
68 Organic compound
69 Vulpine abodes
70 City founded by Pizarro
71 Teen __
72 Dog
73 Not easily debunked
75 Burlesque props
76 Transported
80 Feeling superior
81 Revealed
82 Q-U connection
84 Musician Brian
85 Holy scrolls
87 Western resort area
89 Cartoonist's medium
90 Suppositions
91 Negotiator at Vladivostok, 1974
94 Sports equipment waved in the air
95 Lets
97 Rising star
98 Mexican rebel
99 Carolina university
100 Yachter's heading
101 Far from flushed
102 __ seal (six-pointed star)
103 Yardsticks
104 How this answer is situated
106 "Come __?" (Italian greeting)
109 Reel people
110 Willing interviewees, say
111 Tart: Var.
112 Copper or nickel
114 Oxford's "dreaming __"
115 It may be smoked
121 One with abs of steel?
123 Colombian gold
124 Trivial Pursuit edition
126 Sitcom about the Hart family
128 One pounder
130 Muralist José María __
131 Swing around
134 Ten C-notes
135 Tic-tac-toe loser
137 Couple in Cancún
138 Springfield-to-Boston dir.
139 Satiated

by Nancy Nicholson Joline

ACROSS

1 Toot one's horn
5 Make run smoothly again
10 Cellar container
14 Calculating folks?
18 See 65-Across
19 Turned up
20 Helm position
21 Used cars
22 French artist's vacation spot?
24 Masculine principle
25 Holly plant
26 Long in movies
27 Ecclesiastical setback?
28 Track of a sort
30 Formal response to "Who's there?"
31 Really blue
34 Browning work?
35 Bigoted bunch
37 Go-ahead
38 Prestige of Jay's predecessor?
40 Medical tube
41 Elaborate entertainment
44 Social register word
45 Actress Thurman
46 Tums alternative
49 Kneecap
53 Rural horse-drawn conveyance
57 Fancy fabric for Darius the Great?
60 "The Simpsons" creator Groening
62 They sit on the dais
64 1972 top 10 hit going over seven minutes
65 With 18-Across, Tijuana goodbye
66 Went at it
67 Dress style
69 "Hey . . . !"
70 Started a hole
71 Bird for the table
73 Stockpiling
75 Time long past
76 Dr. Jekyll's flooring?
79 Opposite of exo-
80 Ann or Andy
82 Mosey
84 ". . . boy ___ girl?"
85 Palm Sunday mount
88 Score unit
89 Forgets about
94 Fish surgeon?
99 1964 Hitchcock film
100 Apple pie order?
101 Be in misery
102 Part of a flight
105 Young Turk
106 Not presto
108 Like beds, at times
109 Leaving after lunch
110 Long-toed bird with a harsh cry
111 Attired
112 Pasta that will make you really sick?
116 White-tailed eagle
117 Coil in the yard
118 Record
119 Admiral's command
120 The Big Board, for short
121 Still-life subject
122 Seeder name
123 Buffalo Bill

DOWN

1 Adjective for Atlanta's Hartsfield-Jackson Airport
2 Backslide
3 Time of one's life
4 Sticky stuff
5 Deadens acoustically
6 Not leave one's mark
7 Brushed (up)
8 Bring to bear
9 Irritates
10 Hot pepper
11 Presidential middle name
12 One whose speech is halting
13 One tapped for a fraternity
14 Important pool shot?
15 Buff
16 Carol opening
17 Discriminatory, in a way
18 Blair and Hamilton
23 Firmly secured
29 "High Hopes" lyricist
30 "Veni," translated
32 Chihuahua on TV
33 ___'acte
36 Intense
38 Council member in "Star Wars"
39 Where the so-called "Roof of the World" is
41 Beat it
42 Toreador's reward
43 Frank McCourt memoir
47 Not a news piece
48 City near Monterey Bay
50 G.P. grp.
51 Part of LIFO, in accounting
52 Be there
53 Not quite legit
54 "Scream" genre
55 Soft wool
56 Welcome words to a fight promoter?
58 Tandoori-baked bread
59 Soapmaker's need
61 "Adios Muchachos," e.g.
63 Riddle-me-___
65 Many e-mail starts
67 Big hairy one
68 Prune
69 Subject to a fine, maybe
71 Engine part: Abbr.
72 Ike's opponent, twice
73 Polly, to Tom
74 Distribute
76 Not distribute
77 Go ballistic
78 "___ Vadis?"
81 Need a bib
83 MGM sound effect
86 Defamation
87 Skirt feature
90 Miss after marriage
91 Said without feeling
92 "Laura" star, 1944
93 Many a swing band
94 "T. J. Hooker" actor James
95 Notorious cow owner
96 Some motel accommodations
97 Academy member
98 Left via ladder, say
99 Bearing
102 Strike down
103 Electric dart firer
104 Love lots
107 Let up
111 "Evita" role
113 Bottom of some scales
114 Sgt.'s underling
115 "Evil Woman" band, for short

by Richard Silvestri

ACROSS

1. Much-used engine
7. Spring from a bed
12. "Twin Peaks" victim ___ Palmer
17. Nose-puckering, in a way
18. See 37A
21. Lay concern?
22. Pulmotor's purpose
25. Diplomatic successes
26. Comerica Park team
27. Ab ___ (from the beginning)
30. Some Ouija answers
31. Unhuman
35. Dog in Francis Barraud's painting "His Master's Voice"
37. With 59A, 18D and 18A, what these answers show
41. "___ Enchanted" (Newbery-winning book made into a 2004 film)
42. Troubled
43. No longer reliant on mother
44. Where many barrels are seen
47. Greases
48. Pained reaction
49. Within walking distance
51. Fix a track
52. Practicing grp.
53. Somewhat, slangily
54. "Goodness Had Nothing to Do With It" autobiographer
56. Many a computer icon
59. See 37A
61. See 62D
65. "Stop that!"
66. Overly glib
67. Borrower
68. With 27D, what these answers show
69. See 92A
74. Crave
75. Drank some coffee, say, with "up"
77. Long arm
79. Yossarian's tentmate, in "Catch-22"
80. Mgr.'s holding
83. "Two Women" star
84. "À ___ santé!"
85. Educator Montessori
87. Sandwich's title?
89. Enter all at once
90. Ancient Mexican
91. ___ function
92. With 69A and 69D, what these answers show
95. Certifiable
96. Musical wingding
99. Marvin Gaye's "___ That Peculiar"
101. Old Ford
102. Window flankers
103. No longer with us
107. Disaster coverage?
114. "Almost Famous" director, 2000
115. Confirms
116. Knit up again
117. While away
118. "In dreams begin responsibility" writer
119. Hose

DOWN

1. Student's stat.
2. Lord's Prayer starter
3. Giant at Cooperstown
4. Photomap overlay
5. Firefighters hold them outside windows
6. Correctional worker?
7. Preside over
8. Galley's many
9. Sport ___
10. Artemis, to Apollo
11. Debate club fodder
12. Pick up
13. More nervous
14. German-speaking Swiss canton
15. Young 'un in the Hundred Acre Wood
16. "Roman Holiday" princess
18. See 37A
19. Plant chewed in Arabia
20. Sleepwear
23. Semicircular shape
24. Stephen of "FeardotCom"
27. See 68A
28. Another name for retinol
29. One whose working days are numbered
31. Air or field starter
32. Ignoramus
33. Baseball's Felipe
34. Souvlaki meat
36. Calculator part
38. Good to have around
39. Bivouacked
40. Percentage of a legal settlement
43. La Belle Époque ender: Abbr.
45. Serviceability
46. Unlikely Scottish sight
49. Berkeley university nickname
50. Tropical wreath
53. Speedometer reading: Abbr.
54. Cell phone brand
55. Consequently
57. Coffeehouse crockery
58. Antediluvian
60. Be up
62. With 61A, what these answers show
63. Turn to a new setting
64. Like Mayan pyramids
67. Clog remover
69. See 92A
70. Smelter input
71. ___-X
72. Gunpowder ingredient
73. Language once known as Cape Dutch
76. [Bad call!]
78. Football's Dawson
80. Go well together
81. Scott of "Happy Days"
82. Ligurian Sea feeder
84. High spirits
85. 1967 music festival site
86. Unser and son
88. Anticlimax
89. Show unseemly curiosity
93. At some point
94. Where it's at
95. By agreed order
97. Guessed wrong
98. "Apocalypse Now" locale
100. Org. headquartered on Constitution Ave.
103. Not all there
104. Some Ivy Leaguers
105. Goodie to be divided
106. Arlene of "Here Come the Girls"
107. Intro deliverers
108. Dada pioneer
109. Everyman
110. The World Factbook publisher: Abbr.
111. Art movement prefix
112. Deep-six
113. Commuter carriers

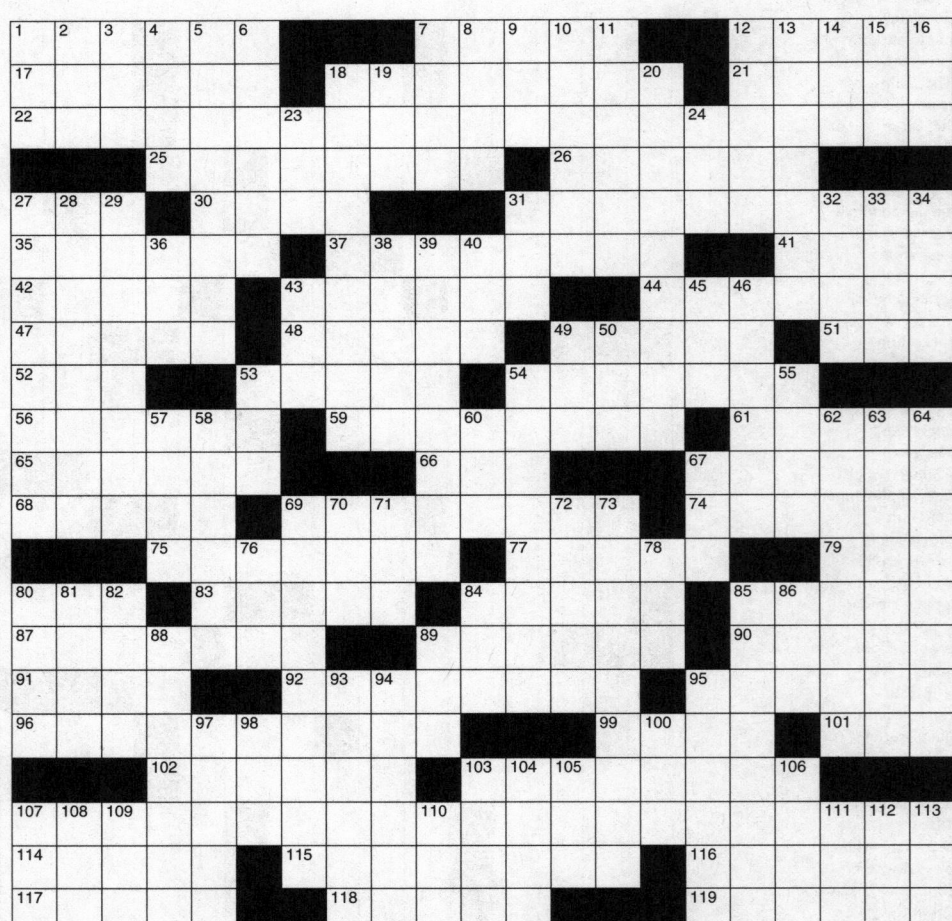

by Patrick Berry

ACROSS

1 ___ lab
4 Drunk
8 Whole lot
12 Pluck
18 One may be overhead or underfoot
19 Holding
21 Cut back
22 Greetings from the Far West?
23 Judge's cry?
26 Edit
27 Like some winter wear
28 Hides from view
29 Manicotti ingredient
30 Ignores
32 Coastal raptors
33 One making lots of money
34 Kind of grass
35 Envier's cry?
39 Informal evening
40 Came of age
43 "___ enough . . ."
44 Knowing
45 Titter
46 One might be a pull-out
50 F on a questionnaire, e.g.
51 Head of l'Académie
52 Unit of fat
53 Parishioner's cry?
58 Computer unit, informally
60 Door part
61 Antitank weapon
62 Miss, e.g.
64 Recluse's cry?
69 Beauty
70 Hole in the head
72 Deprive of courage
73 School basics, initially
75 New York sports fan's cry?
79 "My bad"
82 Place where there might be a mess
83 Card player's declaration
84 Coachmen : horses :: bullwhackers : ___
86 Brazen one
87 Richard of "Chicago"
88 A school might be found using it
90 Latter-day Aristotle
92 Nonstarters
93 Detroit sports fan's cry?
97 Outdoor sealant
98 Move, in real estate
99 Create, as a CD
100 Game sites
104 Single
106 Molded, as metal
109 Comedy Central's "The ___ Show"
110 Be a go-between
111 Racer's cry?
113 Printer type
114 One of the Waughs
115 Sexy Beatles lady
116 Certain Beatle's lady
117 Stop
118 Cotton fabric
119 ___ room
120 Dashiell Hammett character ___ Beaumont

DOWN

1 Whimsical
2 Peep show picture
3 Contract bridge?
4 Uncovered
5 Service arm: Abbr.
6 Onetime French fleet
7 Dastardly laugh
8 Other halves
9 Tout
10 Transgresses
11 Soaked
12 Corps member
13 Pick
14 Hurly-burly
15 Valley girl's cry?
16 Make milk
17 Home with a groundskeeper, maybe
20 ___ incognita
24 1991 Madonna hit
25 Quadrennial polit. event
29 Frost-covered
31 Suffix with butyl
33 Centennial of the Selma civil rights march
36 Fingers, so to speak
37 Window part
38 Ancient theaters
39 Explosion maker
40 Listing on a business sched.
41 ___ Lingus
42 Fatalist's cry?
44 Rock group with the 1995 hit "Buddy Holly"
47 Actress Lena
48 Roman, e.g.
49 Medea rode on it
51 Eliot Ness, for one
54 Society event
55 Black
56 Scratch (out)
57 Often-candied vegetable
59 Clear the throat?
60 Blessed
62 Venue for the Not Ready for Prime Time Players, in brief
63 Bladed tool
65 Fretted instrument
66 Laura's "La Gioconda" lover
67 Discover competitor
68 Do some modern surgery
71 Peter and others
74 "The Social Contract" philosopher
76 As much as you please
77 Roger Maris's number
78 Little biter
80 Last Greek consonant
81 Op opener
85 Eggy beverage
86 Highlight providers
87 Type of nucleotide
88 "You've got yourself a deal"
89 Kirstie's "Cheers" role
91 Colt fan's org.
92 Unexcitable
93 Old humorist ___ Burgess
94 Greatly
95 Coal cars
96 Clothing line
98 Blush alternatives
101 Coolpix camera maker
102 Deserted
103 Church council
105 Pacific island nation
106 "Burning Giraffe" painter
107 Couple
108 Motion in the ocean
111 Oil well feature
112 Underwater steerer

by Joe DiPietro

ACROSS

1 Dog's owner
7 Crit. condition areas
11 Go (for)
14 Famed Chicago hotel
19 Station number
20 Injured, in a way
22 Like an apartment
   with new tenants
23 Dislodging boats that
   have run aground?
25 Runs for no purpose
26 Long stretch
27 Go for the gold?
28 Actress MacDowell
29 Beehives, e.g.
30 One calling at peak times?
33 Salon worker
35 "Horton Hears ___"
37 Advice to a husband seeker?
42 "Lowdown" singer Boz ___
45 Photo ID?
46 Chinese philosopher Chu ___
47 Respecting
48 Goddess of agriculture
49 Warm wool
52 Presidential monogram
54 "Don't ___ dumb"
55 Karaoke?
61 TKO caller
62 Get
64 Stairstep measure
65 Spots
67 Dart
69 Medical worker in
   a billfold picture?
74 Mex. miss
75 Glass component
77 It may follow a def.
78 The CW predecessor
80 One of the Ewings,
   on "Dallas"
81 Selective Service
   System, once?
86 Be bombastic
88 Hellenic vowel
89 Shows homage
90 First airline with commercial
   trans-Pacific passenger flights
91 Lee foe
95 Football linemen: Abbr.
98 Melbourne-to-Brisbane dir.
99 [Not again!] and [I can't!]
100 Procrastinator's pick-up line?
105 Like venison
106 Annual Sunday night
    event, with "the"
107 Insignia
111 Bruce who appeared
    in "Suspicion"
113 Travis who sang "Here's a
    Quarter (Call Someone Who
    Cares)"
115 Comfy footwear
116 Shade of green
117 "We Help Heal" sloganeer
118 Where to store extra chandeliers?
122 Teacher's note on a test
123 Subject to change in size, as a
    picture on a screen
124 Famous Indy 500 family
125 Neil Armstrong's middle name
126 Halifax hrs.
127 Crosswalk users, for short
128 Shirley who sang "Goldfinger"

DOWN

1 Walk leisurely
2 Blessing preceder
3 Lose a lap
4 1960s chess champ Mikhail
5 Blow-up: Abbr.
6 Goes back into business
7 Library cataloging
   datum, briefly
8 PC "brain"
9 ___ Minor
10 Hélène, for one
11 Mark of a ruler
12 Money replaced by euros
13 QB stats
14 Icicle feature
15 1984 Patrick Swayze film,
   the first movie released with a
   PG-13 rating
16 "I'll do that"
17 Original Clarabell
   the Clown player
18 Brief strangers?
21 Its national anthem is
   "Jana Gana Mana"
24 Imperfection
29 Modern address
31 Beats (out)
32 Accesses the Web
34 Hebrew name meaning
   "He is my God"
36 Can. province
38 Kind of skirt
39 Kitchen item: Abbr.
40 Perfume holder
41 They make people
   raise their hands
42 Gobbles (up)
43 Historical novelist Holland
44 Fellini or Godard work
49 Acronymic pop group name
50 Teamster
51 Tennis score
53 Expensive
56 Big Ten inits.
57 Poetic preposition
58 VCR speed meas.
59 Absolute bliss
60 Turn dark
63 Look toward
66 R. J. Reynolds pack
68 Bow
70 Rustic setting
71 Capts.' inferiors
72 Flemish painter Jan van ___
73 Dines
76 Angler's basket
79 "Easy as pie!"
82 Grant and others
83 TV comic who wrote
   "If Roast Beef Could Fly"
84 Lorgnette piece
85 1997 Peter Fonda role
87 Humanitarian Wallenberg
91 Foreign flier
92 Common temple name
93 In high repute
94 Half of a double-header,
   maybe
96 Certs competitor
97 Menace
99 Place to work out
101 Joke response
102 Diner feature
103 Woman's shoe style
104 Fair-hiring grp.
108 Some blades
109 English distance
110 Smart
112 Place of bliss
114 "That is ___ expected"
115 Fr. ladies
117 Civil War inits.
118 Troop grp.
119 Outmoded
120 ___ whim
121 Sound of a leak

by Matt Skoczen

ACROSS

1 A pinch, maybe
6 Provide food for many
11 Some dance records, for short
14 Musical Young
18 Snouted animal
19 Of service
20 Double-crosser
21 "Lay it ___!"
22 1996 Helen Fielding book made into a film starring Renée Zellweger
25 Assault with a grenade, as a commanding officer
26 Move, quickly
27 Space chimp of 1961
28 Memo abbr.
29 Olympic rings, e.g.
30 Absorb the cost of
31 Suffix with social
32 Best-selling 2003 Alice Sebold novel
36 Three of ___
38 Capital of Hubei province
40 Israel's Weizman
41 1995 Ellen DeGeneres best seller
48 Very pleasant
49 Like some translations
50 Alternative to oil
53 Larry McMurtry novel made into an Emmy-winning TV series
57 Pharmaceutical giant
58 Longoria of "Desperate Housewives"
59 A thief might take one
60 Salad ingredient
62 Part
63 Not clerical
64 Battle reminder
65 2003 Bill O'Reilly political best seller
70 "Christ of St. John of the Cross" artist
71 "Wheel of Fortune" request
72 Bad party guest
73 Kennel cry
74 Made up one's mind about
75 Grazing spot
76 Imperiled
79 1994 semi-autobiographical novel by Anna Quindlen
83 Son of Prince Valiant
84 Heroic deeds
86 Monopoly maker
87 1939 Agatha Christie classic
92 Pakistani tongue
94 Early American diplomat Silas
95 Nine: Prefix
96 1929 Virginia Woolf title
101 Place for a team's insignia
103 Atlantic catch
104 Winter Palace resident
105 Sibilant talk
106 Dr. Pavlov
108 Author Jaffe
109 Stay too long on the beach
110 2000 essay collection by David Sedaris
115 Protected, at sea
116 Before
117 They give people big heads
118 Key
119 Sale site
120 Filch
121 Lilac, e.g.
122 Bonnie's beau

DOWN

1 Like poorly washed windows
2 Something a maid might break
3 Many a prom coif
4 Cookie fruit
5 Springs
6 Stephen King canine
7 Squares things
8 "___ the season . . ."
9 Trains in Chicago
10 Signal to stop
11 Poet's inspiration
12 Last of a Monday-to-Friday series
13 "Let It Snow, Let It Snow, Let It Snow" composer
14 Restricted area
15 Dress
16 "This looks verrry bad for me!"
17 Kids' blocks
22 Silver-scaled fish
23 Big bang cause
24 Suffix with proverb
31 Subject in foreign language class
32 Sem. degree
33 Applaud
34 "The ___ near"
35 Actress Sobieski
37 "Uh-uh!"
38 Baylor's home
39 Odd
42 Pilot's dir.
43 Rx instruction
44 Capri suffix
45 George of "La Cage aux Folles"
46 Spanish rice
47 Actor Raf of "The Italian Job," 1969
50 Fancy ice creams
51 Toyota model
52 Saw
53 [I can't remember the words to this song]
54 Henny Youngman specialty
55 Apelike
56 It may need gratification
61 Fed. property manager
65 Schlepped
66 Longtime photographer for Vogue
67 Author Segal
68 Disposed
69 Kind of logic
70 Take away the defenses of
72 Famed huckster
74 Actress Meryl
77 Take to court
78 Japanese martial art
80 Exceptional
81 Operate
82 "Charlotte's Web" monogram
85 Fret
87 Dolled up
88 Chinese dynasty
89 Impossible to read
90 Nursery arrival
91 Vitamin dosage
92 Author Le Guin
93 Lion
96 Held off
97 Ancient Mexican
98 1980s Pontiac
99 Ragtime dance
100 Massage locale
101 Bebopper
102 Marx Brothers-like
106 Press
107 A piece of a three-piece
108 "Tarzan" actor
111 Vegas opening
112 Fast food inits.
113 Grand ___, Nova Scotia
114 Fashion inits.

by Randolph Ross

ACROSS

1 Was in a blue state
6 "Hold on!"
12 "You go, ___!"
16 Dr.'s order
19 Eyes
20 Infrequent political event
21 1998 Sarah McLachlan hit
22 Asian capital
23 Spanish dancers' residence?
25 Hit the links
27 Shore sights
28 Jerk
29 Honey
31 Chin-ups and pull-ups develop them
32 Charlemagne's domain: Abbr.
34 ___ time
35 Monkey business
36 Author LeShan
37 Israeli leaders?
42 Words to a bride and groom
43 Take in
45 Lodge fellows
46 Removed
48 Shopper's aid
50 Captain of literature
51 To-do
55 Not close gently
57 Big name in antacids
60 Island settled by shipwrecked colonists in 1609
62 Run-in
63 Classic sports car
64 Old-fashioned education
66 Zapper
67 Sniffler's keepsake?
72 Melodious
73 Astin of "Lord of the Rings"
74 Keep out
75 Aid in solving the disappearance of the Thin Man
76 Car dealers' offerings
78 Member of a blended family
81 Trident-shaped letters
82 One side of a debate
83 Some tax advisers, for short
85 Danger for sailors
87 Symbol of strength
89 Movie roll
91 Go in all directions
94 ___-American
97 Photogenic cats?
100 Lush
102 Snaky swimmers
104 Lines of praise
105 Suffix with tank
106 Bygone royal
107 Square
110 Danger for sailors
112 Blue, perhaps
114 Romeo or Juliet
115 Aging Nintendo icon?
118 Football stat.
119 Newton, e.g.
120 Went smoothly
121 ___ being
122 Some batteries
123 Domain of the goddess Tethys
124 Go above and beyond
125 Perfect, e.g.

DOWN

1 City in 84-Down
2 Whence the line "The True North strong and free"
3 Can opener
4 Women of Paris
5 Purposely try to lose
6 Mercury or Saturn
7 Put in order
8 Brown family member
9 Puppeteer Tony
10 Collegiate Bulldog
11 Where some think monsters live
12 Rubberneck
13 Waiting
14 It can be thrown from a horse
15 Let have it
16 Optometrist's concern
17 Some museum displays
18 Overrun
24 Souvenir buy
26 "You're crushing the watch!"?
30 Itsy-bitsy
33 Oscar winner Benigni
34 "That was bad"
37 Camera attachment, informally
38 Happy ___
39 Pond plant
40 Pompom waver's cry
41 Crypt cover
44 Gas pump's place?
47 Moon of Uranus
49 Gentlemen they're not
50 Regarding
52 Star of "Scared to Death," 1947
53 Men and women
54 One that "eats shoots and leaves"
55 Encourage
56 Animal catcher
58 2000 Renée Zellweger title role
59 Dwarf with glasses
61 Displayed fear
62 Milan's La ___
63 It weighs on astronauts
65 Put in prison
68 Sugar suffix
69 Hardy character
70 ___ trick
71 Headed toward
77 Blueprint detail
79 "Give me another chance," e.g.
80 Toots
81 Sharpies, e.g.
84 1-Down's state: Abbr.
86 Hall of Fame football coach Tom
88 It has a giraffe mascot
89 Rudolph's feature
90 'Fore
92 Herald
93 Bootlickers
94 First name in aviation history
95 Roman Catholic period of prayer
96 Hall-of-Famers
98 "The Simpsons" bartender
99 "Amen to that!"
101 Symbol of sovereignty
103 Keith Richards, e.g.
106 Past its prime
108 Director Kazan
109 Fact-checks
110 Bank letters
111 Make eyes at
113 Latin 101 word
116 Hardly thorough
117 Tag on

by Kyle Mahowald

ACROSS

1 "Meet John Doe" director
6 Wooden shoe
11 PIN spotters?
15 Realize
19 Weaving willow
20 Softly
21 Bigmouth
22 Relieve
23 Dullish
24 Layabout
25 Poor actor staying sober?
27 "Yeah, we've got that," e.g.?
30 Aligned
31 Longtime "Today" co-host
32 Olin of "Chocolat"
34 ___-Magnon
35 Philosophy of the "Chuang Tzu"
38 Extra-base hit, probably?
44 Solo
45 Et ___
48 Like tea
49 F.D.R.'s wiring program
50 Doesn't own
52 Fancy home features
55 ___ powers
56 Now it's Thailand
57 Review of fall fashion accessories?
61 Skate part
62 Ticket
63 Astrological point
64 Trawlers' nets
65 Fetter
69 Sat
70 Agitation
71 Humiliates
72 Decision points
73 First name in court fiction
74 Official denial
75 Excused from saving a sinking boat?
81 "Casablanca" role
82 Obscured
83 Having nothing obscured
84 Balderdash
85 Like
86 Given to glad-handing
89 Double-bonded compound
91 Not forgetting
92 Fouled in basketball, in a way?
96 Prayer
98 Undisguised
99 Pianist/composer Dohnányi
100 Beau
102 Barren
107 Fake molding in a room?
112 Guidebook for golf greens?
114 Mideast potentate
115 Butterfly in youth
116 No, to Natasha
117 Make a long story short?
118 Like fur coats
119 City north of Cologne
120 Familiar truths
121 Try again
122 Rectangular paving stones
123 Was very bright

DOWN

1 Italian silk center
2 Wise ___ owl
3 Tropical helmet material
4 Practice tit for tat
5 Venues
6 Skyline pointer
7 Ambulance attendant, often
8 Aloe, naturally
9 Low tie
10 P.G.A. Tour site, ___ Pines
11 Oberhausen cry
12 Catch-22
13 Where "Guernica" was hung during W.W. II
14 Day in a heat wave
15 Run again
16 Tupper of Tupperware fame
17 Start of a sowing adage
18 Leave in a hurry, with "out"
26 Got along
28 Russian assembly
29 Channel changer
33 Part of the Old World: Abbr.
35 Tongue-curling
36 Blueprint datum
37 Farm sound
38 Can
39 Decreasing numbers of
40 It's in the past
41 European launch vehicle
42 Hard to lift
43 Most contrived
46 Drink from a machine
47 Spillane's "___ Jury"
51 Game with a yellow card
53 Skip
54 Dweller on Cape Prince of Wales
56 Insignificant
58 1912 Physics Nobelist ___ Dalen
59 Site of a historic 1905 revolt
60 Film, briefly
61 Suffering a loss
64 Ego
65 Out-of-control
66 Woolen cloak of ancient Rome
67 Long Island county
68 Toucher of the Pacific Rim
69 Vote seeker
70 Ring bearer
72 Gave, as wood to a wood chipper
73 Garden site
75 Antimob acronym
76 Managed, with "out"
77 Indoctrinate
78 Afflicts
79 ___ facto
80 City NNW of Madrid
82 Big trouble
86 Will of the Bible
87 Archaeologist's reckoning
88 Hang around
90 Hang around
93 Fills, as cracks between tiles
94 Archive documents
95 Dormmate
97 Ransacks
100 Trapshoot
101 Lyrics
102 J. R. R. Tolkien and C. S. Lewis, at Oxford
103 "A Day Without Rain" singer
104 Gush
105 Rush
106 Cherokee Strip city
108 Least change
109 Approximately
110 Dutch ___
111 Hamlet, e.g.
113 1964 Ronny and the Daytonas hit

by Con Pederson

ACROSS

1 Recovers, with "up"
7 Delibes opera
12 Wrinkle, maybe
19 Noted support group
20 Gibson gamish
21 Caffeine source: Var.
22 A man goes for a walk and . . .
25 Bird: Prefix
26 "Let's not go there"
27 Mother of Pollux and Helen
28 ___ cheese
30 Break
32 Like Bruckner's Symphony No. 7
33 Upper hand
36 Activists
37 When he pops the cork, a genie appears and says, ". . ."
43 2004 biopic that was a Best Picture nominee
44 Pronunciation difficulty
45 Like the sugar in cotton candy
46 Piedmont wine city
48 Lorelei Lee's creator
50 Have a hunch
51 Some health info ads, for short
55 The man says, "I want to see . . ."
60 Kind of leather
61 Fighting Tigers' sch.
62 John
63 Totaled
64 2003 Will Ferrell title role
65 He then hands the genie . . .
71 Springy steps
72 It's measured by the meter
74 Big-league
75 Scoundrel
76 One who's out of touch
77 The genie studies it for a while and finally says, "This is impossible. So . . ."
84 ZIP code 10001 locale: Abbr.
85 Radiation units
86 Above, in Aachen
87 Support, in a way
88 Composer ___ Carlo Menotti
89 Rye alternative
91 Fretted strings
92 The man says, "I always wanted to see . . ."
102 See 50-Down
103 Starting
104 "Sweet!"
105 Go bonkers
106 "Three Sisters" sister
107 Exertion
110 Grab some chow?
113 "The Waste Land" monogram
114 The genie replies, ". . ."
119 See 94-Down
120 Double order, perhaps
121 Conjured up
122 Some terriers
123 Jones of the Miracle Mets
124 Scares off

DOWN

1 Bush activity
2 Big Turkish export
3 Outlaw
4 Put a stopper on
5 "Mahogany" star, 1975
6 How some rivers proceed
7 Sewing machine gizmo
8 Con
9 Coyly playful
10 Small particle: Abbr.
11 Dir. of I-64 going up Ky.
12 Tough problem to face?
13 Push
14 Noted exile site
15 Papua New Guinea port
16 How shoelaces are often tied
17 Central parts
18 Bygone numbers
23 Cherry variety
24 Spread out on a table?
29 Seat, slangily
31 Highlander pattern
34 Sot's problem
35 Swindle
36 Remote location
38 Like some church matters
39 Stacks
40 Brought into play
41 Kind of column
42 Invalid
46 Fight stopper
47 Branching marine growth
48 Phoebe's player on "Friends"
49 "Movin' ___"
50 With 102-Across, London-New York time difference
51 ___-green
52 City in a 1968 Dionne Warwick top 10 hit
53 Comparably tense
54 Smelly smoke
56 Popular street name
57 John of England
58 ___-jongg
59 Eisenhower years, e.g.
60 Beat again in wrestling
65 Writer Rand
66 Work
67 Man in an order
68 Masseur's target
69 One having second thoughts
70 Not set things right
73 By the way
76 Threads
78 Chicago daily, with "the"
79 Parliamentary nods
80 Old Dodge
81 Old
82 Mountain lift
83 Bring around
88 Astronaut Grissom
89 ___ de trois (dance)
90 W.W. II battle site, familiarly
91 Like a horseshoe
92 Granting that, in brief
93 Meaningless
94 With 119-Across, 1920s literary couple on Cape Cod, with "the"
95 Jalopies
96 "Six Feet Under" role
97 Lumberjacks
98 "___ Flor and Her Two Husbands"
99 Food
100 Not as strenuous
101 Lays out
107 Place for a counter claim?
108 14-Down, for one
109 Good ending?
111 Art patron Kahn
112 Macadamize, e.g.
115 Benjamin Netanyahu's alma mater, for short
116 Mom's forte, quickly
117 Movie computer
118 Contracted

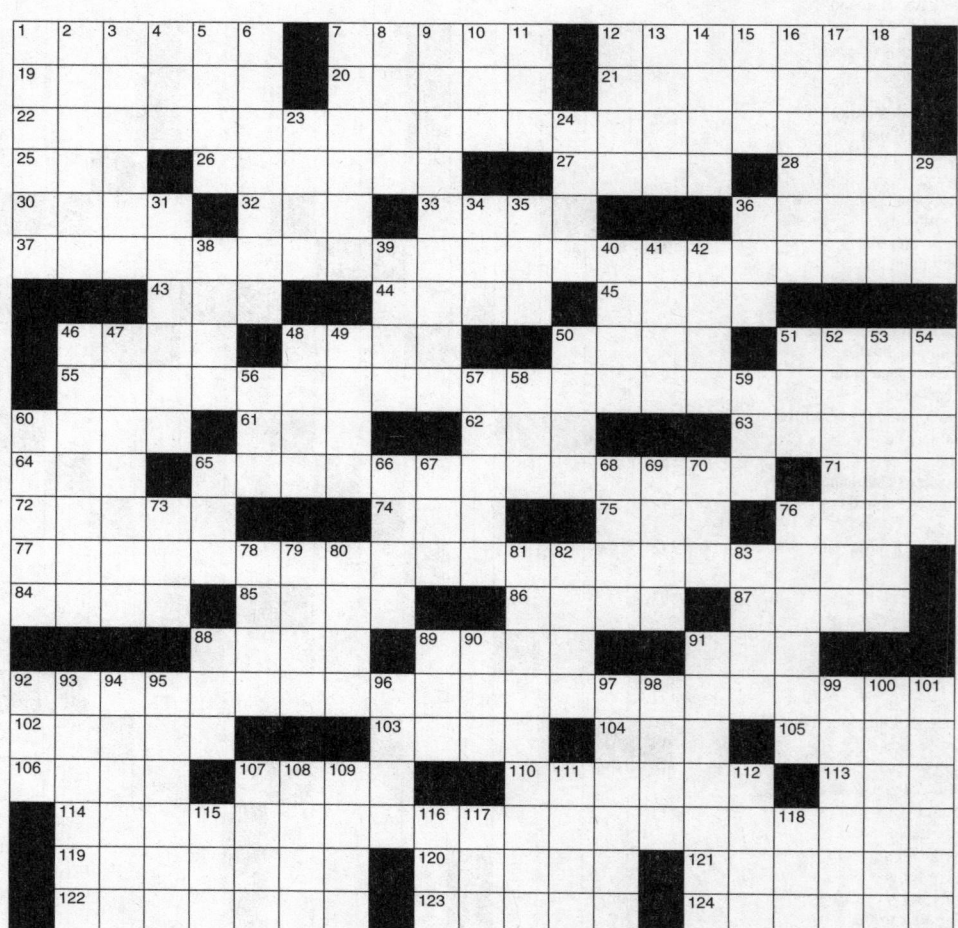

by David J. Kahn

ACROSS

1 Act high-handedly?
7 Kind of film
11 Having gone through a flood, say
17 Opposite of away
19 Boxers alternative
22 Neaten (up)
23 Sudden shock?
25 Precise
26 Abstain
27 1910s film star known as "The Vamp"
28 Interdicts
30 Père's frère
31 Farmer's prayer
33 "Batman" fight scene word
34 Book after Ezra: Abbr.
35 Durango domicile
39 Halloween expense?
43 French concern: Abbr.
46 Recreating
48 Beethoven dedicatee
49 Curious one
51 Creepy neighborhood?
54 Bobbing for apples, e.g.
55 Watchmaker's sci.
56 Weight lifters' units
57 Not only that
59 Laughing matter
60 Indecipherable
62 Onetime home of Kit Carson
63 Knows about
65 Apparition on a "Concentration" board?
69 Philatelic design on an envelope
73 Bats
74 Shouted encouragement
79 Tuning note instrument
80 Iris holder
81 College QB, maybe
83 1998 BP purchase
84 Prop for Quasimodo
87 Study of ghouls and goblins?
89 Grandmotherly type
90 Angler with pots
92 Provocation, metaphorically
93 ___ Halles, old Parisian market
94 Tuneup for a Halloween conveyance?
98 Spanish direction
99 Alphabetic trio
101 Grab ___
102 Puts
104 Sponge mushroom
106 Italian painter Guido
107 Poker declaration
109 Architectural projections
114 Singer of the aria "Dio! mi potevi scagliar"
116 Periodic Halloween sight?
119 Ahab, for one
120 Computer letters
121 Long green
122 Bedouins and Tuaregs
123 Future atty.'s hurdle
124 Made a haunted house sound

DOWN

1 Public relations effort
2 River of Tuscany
3 Riga native
4 Not mint
5 114-Across, e.g.
6 Recent U.S.N.A. grad
7 Good buddy
8 Astronomical bear
9 M.D.'s requirement
10 Brewers' needs
11 Worrying sound to a balloonist
12 Other side
13 Military reconnaissance tool
14 Group of cacklers in wooden shoes?
15 Biol. branch
16 Protected state bird
18 It's found above the ankle
20 Cold drink
21 What to call the barber of Seville
24 Airport shuttles
29 Cops
32 Tan and others
33 Work with needles
35 Kid's Halloween candy, e.g.
36 One of a French trio
37 Vice president before Gerald
38 Give out
40 Maintain
41 Parts of la Polynésie
42 Receptacle for some Halloween contributions

44 "___ my case"
45 Have an ___ the ground
47 Maintain
50 Martial arts place
52 Barbershop request
53 Not kick off
54 Land-clearing device
57 Nail site
58 Explorer's need
61 Snitch
62 Best
63 Neighbor of Jor.
64 Attack by plane, in a way
66 Jacksonville-to-Daytona Beach dir.
67 Mao's successor as Chinese Communist leader
68 Response to a bad pun
69 Cousin of Fortran
70 White poplar
71 Terrifying cry?
72 Didn't break
75 Potassium ___
76 Workers in rows
77 Fanfare
78 Caravan, e.g.
80 Hubbub
81 ___ Rabbit
82 Versatile nuke

85 Didn't take it any longer
86 Flat-ended instrument
87 Run for it
88 Two topper
90 "But I'm still white, sometimes I just hate life/ Somethin' ain't right . . ." singer
91 Like early dawns and late sunsets
95 Packing way too much
96 Tennis's Nastase
97 Lock site
100 Street of mystery
103 Handled
104 Cut
105 First-century Roman emperor
107 "To Live and Die ___"
108 Popular game set on an island
110 Kind of bread
111 Leave open-mouthed
112 Old Roman cry
113 Garden adjunct
115 Stitching posts: Abbr.
117 Rhein blocker
118 "Stand" rock group

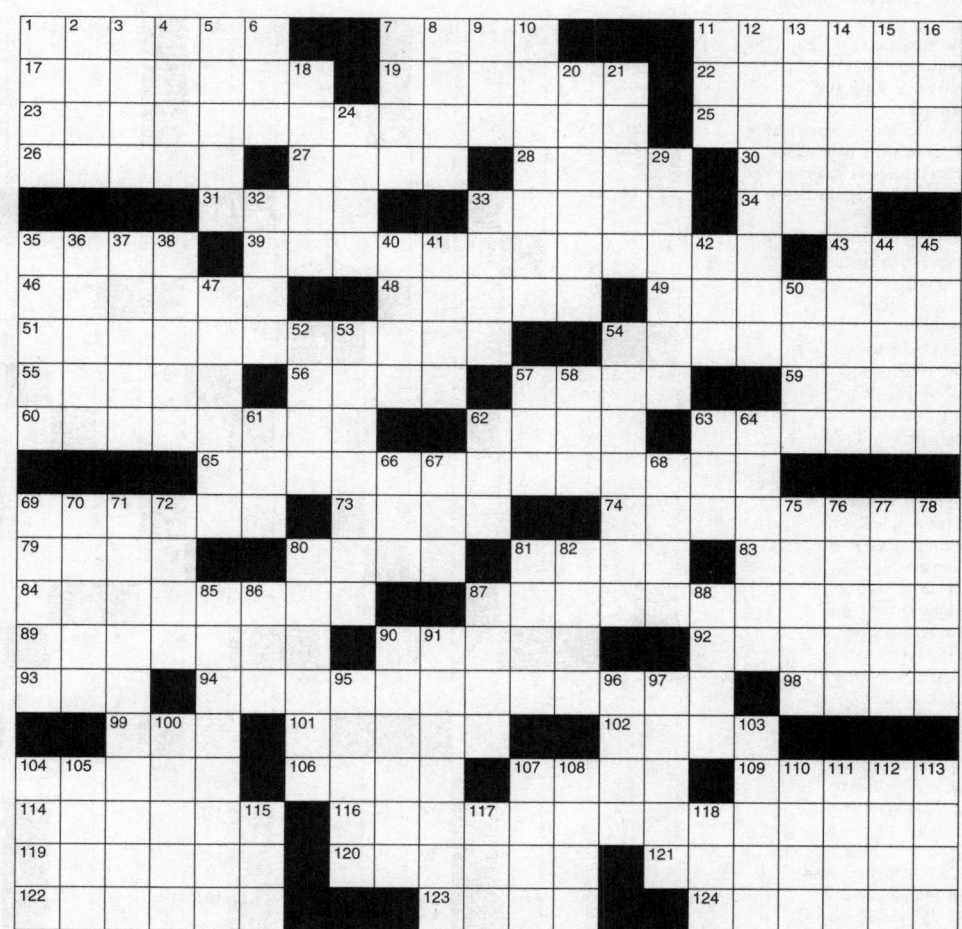

by Maxwell H. D. Johnson Jr.

ACROSS

1 Scientific research center
7 Belittling sort
11 Bills, e.g.
15 Two of fifty
18 Brush aside
19 Feeling
20 Italian province or its capital
21 Sharp-penned Maureen
23 Strong-arm
24 "___ Apart," 2003 Vin Diesel flick
25 Low in fat
26 Person seen in court
27 Free service started in 1905
31 Nobel Prize subj.
32 AT&T acquisition of 1991
33 Travel between the poles?
34 Irving Berlin's "___ a Piano"
35 Calendar abbr.
36 Popular 1970s–'80s vocal-harmony quartet
42 1930s–'50s actor J. ___ Naish
44 Nastase of tennis
45 Cross
46 Is beholden to
48 Reacts to, as a joke
51 More than exasperation
54 1993 Robert De Niro film
59 Military joes
60 The Supreme Court, e.g.
63 Snorkeler's interest
64 First prize at the 1992 Olympics
65 One who's an -ologist, maybe
66 Major industry of Madeira
67 What thousands do on the first Sunday of every November
72 Best way to drive
73 Do some carbo-loading, e.g.
74 Printer problem
75 Bird call
76 Best, as advice
77 Furtive
78 Teens with tiaras
81 Laugh sound
82 "C'est magnifique!"
85 "___ cost you!"
86 Ingredient in Cookies 'n Cream ice cream
87 Bowed, in music
90 Fixes up, as a ship
94 What people follow when they 67-Across
101 Turndowns
102 Month in Madrid
103 Nancy Drew's guy
104 Advanced degree
105 Bern's river
106 Classic best seller by Betty Smith
113 Bullwinkle, for one
114 1890s veep ___ P. Morton
115 "David Copperfield" wife
116 Sight from Turkey
118 ___-Soviet relations
119 Goons
120 Opposin'
121 Works with the hands
122 Shooting marble
123 Ready to come out of the 109-Down
124 Boxer's punch
125 Regret

DOWN

1 Lighter handle?
2 Prankster's cry
3 TV drama length
4 "Two Women" Oscar winner
5 Musical ties, essentially
6 ___ greens
7 Big name in ad agencies
8 I, for one
9 North African port
10 It can be found step by step
11 Talk radio feature
12 Between ports
13 "South Park" boy
14 Female deer
15 Collectible Fords
16 :56, timewise
17 Try to avoid hitting
22 Place for a tumbler
28 Politico Richards
29 Calypso kin
30 Fivers
31 Mail Boxes ___
36 Cut
37 1959 Wimbledon winner ___ Olmedo
38 Buster Brown's dog
39 Turn's partner
40 Translation material
41 Not your ordinary film director
43 Beam at the very top of a house
47 Expressionless
49 Operatic prince
50 Cable channel for kids
51 Apart from others
52 Work on more, as a farrier might
53 Irish runner Coghlan
54 Ornate wall hanging
55 1950s sitcom starring Ethel Waters
56 Go back
57 Don't just seem
58 Merrimack River city
61 New Deal agcy.
62 Cathedral bell sounds
65 When said three times, finale suggesting uncertainty
66 Singer Terrell
68 Shaker ___, O.
69 Combatant in una arena
70 "Divine Secrets of the ___ Sisterhood"
71 He wrote "Political power grows out of the barrel of a gun"
77 "Git!"
78 Green piece of Paris
79 Bowl parts: Abbr.
80 1997 Peter Fonda role
83 Anthem contraction
84 Fancy-schmancy
86 Wind up on stage?
88 With vigor
89 Surpass
91 12 months from now
92 Siren's cause
93 Storm course: Abbr.
94 Exploits
95 Rapt
96 "Romeo and Juliet" setting
97 Heretofore
98 Stupid
99 Some TV sets
100 P
105 "Risen From the Ranks" writer
107 Garden bloom, informally
108 Defaulter's loss
109 See 123-Across
110 Forbidden
111 Sturdy ones
112 Gambling game
117 Australian state: Abbr.

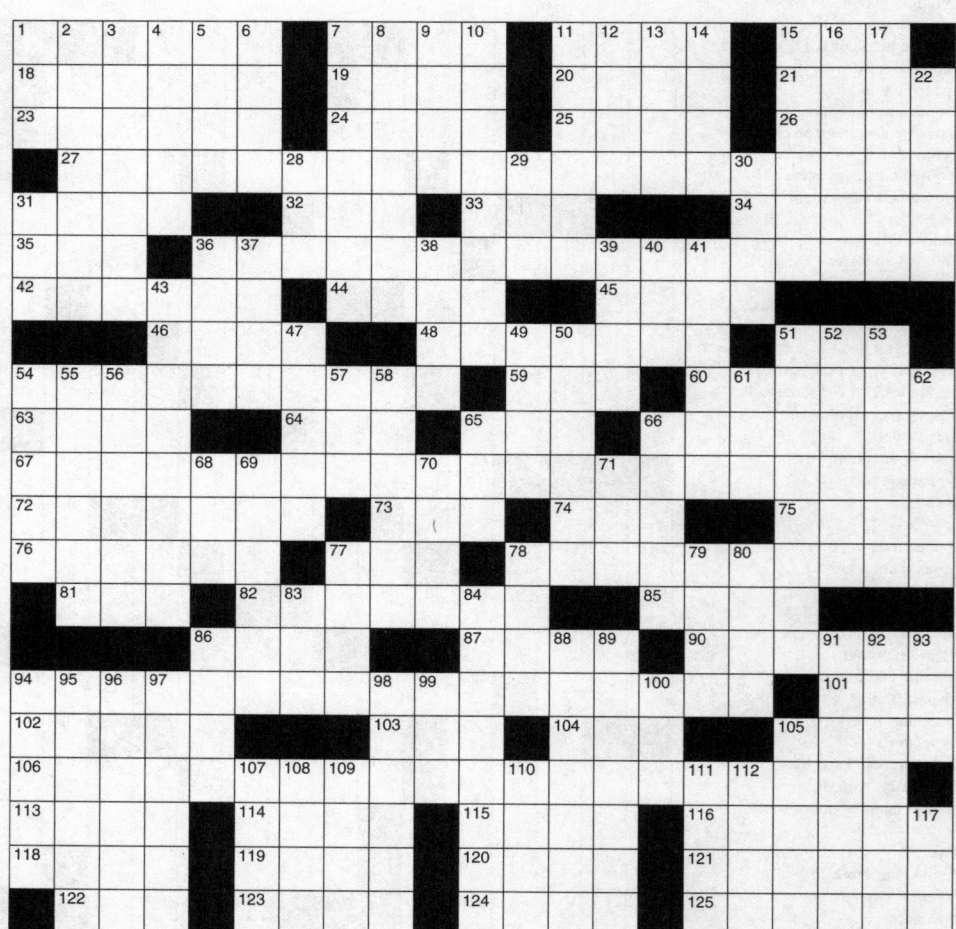

by Elizabeth C. Gorski

ACROSS

1 "A Passage to India" actor, 1984
9 Cultivation
16 Game divs.
20 Water, colloquially
21 They haven't any definite forms
22 Cover up
23 The SS Manhattan was the first commercial ship to cross it
25 Rain collector
26 N.Y.C. subway line
27 It may precede a nickname
28 Buenos ___
29 "Hooray for Love" composer
30 Scrap
32 Post-9/11 slogan
36 Take down the aisle again
38 Big name in Fox News
39 Made sport of
42 The Father of English History
45 Historic town on the Vire
46 "___ Cried" (1962 hit)
49 Place to get links
50 Macaroni dish with ground beef and a little tomato sauce
55 Come together
56 Neuter
57 After-dinner drink
58 Sculptor James ___ Fraser
59 Get a sense something's up
62 Doesn't just throw off
66 Engine measures: Abbr.
67 Warm winter wear
70 Novelist O'Flaherty
72 Anorexic's aversion
73 Stealthy activity
76 They get pins and needles
78 Do
80 Depilatory brand
81 "Your point being . . . ?"
82 Entertainer accompanying a slide guitar and harmonica, maybe
87 Son of Leah
88 10 cc, e.g.
89 Something that may be on a house
90 "Star Trek: T.N.G." counselor
91 Actor Quinn
92 Palestinian nationalist group
95 Ear inflammation
98 1977 Toni Morrison novel
103 Jim Backus provided his voice
107 U-shaped piece of wood
108 "Uncle Vanya" woman
109 18-Down writer
110 Coastal flier
111 Baloney peddler
112 Earthquake cause
117 Concert halls
118 Malleable
119 Utterly lost
120 Withered
121 Operatic tenor ___ Alagna
122 Place to stretch

DOWN

1 Arlo's partner in the comics
2 Festoon
3 Radio ___, broadcasting service to Cuba
4 One with a time-sensitive job, for short
5 Like some hooks
6 Guy from England
7 Soap ingredient
8 Marks (out)
9 Golf gimme
10 Japanese porcelain
11 Get crushed by
12 Minor
13 Court org.
14 Skit part
15 A foot wide?
16 Kind of keyboard
17 Refrain part, perhaps
18 See 109-Across, with "The"
19 Devote, as time
24 Overdrawn?
29 Pitched
31 Feed facts to, maybe
33 Family tree listing: Abbr.
34 Plus
35 Greenwich greeting
37 Temporarily suspended
39 Spirited dances
40 "Your slip is showing"
41 Bar challenge
43 Decline
44 Green
46 "Is that what you expected?"
47 Command position
48 Surveys
50 Take ___ from (copy)
51 1957 song that begins "The most beautiful sound I ever heard . . ."
52 Seed covering
53 Underground experiment, for short
54 Eastern wrap
56 Camera inits.
60 Cap
61 ×2
63 Manage to succeed
64 Home that may have painted designs on it
65 Old drive-in fare
68 Lennon's in-laws
69 Day care charge
70 Mother of Clytemnestra
71 Point
74 Big star
75 "How's it ___?"
77 Sick-looking
79 Oregon ___
83 "Back to the Future" bully
84 Areas between woods
85 "___ Me? I do not know you": Emily Dickinson
86 Columnist Peggy
87 Sen. Murkowski of Alaska
91 Targeted
92 Ancient marketplaces
93 Doorway jamb
94 More pious
96 Render helpless, in a way
97 Fairy tale baddies
98 Plays by oneself
99 Rust, e.g.
100 Hornet, e.g.
101 ___ work
102 Bridge opening, briefly
104 Mind: Ger.
105 "Ecco pur ch'a voi ritorno" opera
106 Available
112 It'll help you breathe
113 Spanish riches
114 Head
115 Seafarer
116 Defensive linemen: Abbr.

by Brendan Emmett Quigley

ACROSS

1 Crows
6 "A Passage to India" character
11 Popular player since 2001
15 Kids
20 Baker, of a sort
21 Bulb unit
22 Exclusive of anything else
23 Author Sinclair
24 Of last month
25 Incarnation
27 Best-selling Hasbro toy introduced in the 1960s
28 Mascot #1
31 Seafood selection
32 Feeling
33 It might make the torso seem moreso
34 Hypo meas.
35 One taking advantage of a long arm
37 Q.E.D. part
38 Ka ___ (Hawaii's South Cape)
40 Former German president Johannes ___
41 Duel personalities?
42 G.P.S. heading
43 Off-land lander
47 Gray head?
50 Lights (into)
51 Mascot #2
54 Rising times
57 Things best let be, proverbially
60 Symbols used in Navajo and Mayan art
62 Nut
63 Heavy
64 Barracks locale
66 "In excelsis ___"
67 Mail-sorting ctr.
69 Genetic inits.
70 M. Hulot's player, in films
71 Galoot-like
73 Street coat?
75 Mascot #3
81 Name-callers, maybe
84 One of 12 tiles in mah-jongg
85 Existence, to Claudius
89 Eight-time Norris Trophy winner
90 First thing Iowa State cheerleaders ask for?
91 It used to be pitched
94 Uffizi display
95 Best of the best
97 Landlocked land
99 Rising
102 Agog
103 Writer Carroll
105 Mascot #4
108 Theo. Roosevelt Natl. Park site
110 End in the Bible?
111 Shell carrier
112 CD burners
115 Tagged
118 Country singer Joe
120 QB's gains
121 Show appreciation
122 Acquisitive sort
123 Mideast org.
124 Scrap
126 Petach Tikva resident
129 Armory grp.
130 Mascot #5
134 1960s TV actress Stevens
136 Tries to trap something
137 One rolling with the Stones?
138 Skilled
139 "Smooth Operator" singer
140 Win by ___
141 Mooring spots
142 Clipped
143 List abbr.
144 Forlorn one
145 Union general

DOWN

1 Swindlers
2 Laser surgery targets
3 In the center of
4 Kind of ray
5 Hardly one of hoi polloi
6 "Hard ___!" (nautical order)
7 Airhead
8 Imprison
9 Hotelier Helmsley
10 Bandleader's start
11 Neat as a pin
12 Henhouse sounds
13 Caen's river
14 Prevents
15 Corked vessel
16 Like George Washington's church
17 Mascot #6
18 Decorated, as leather
19 Bad looks
20 Kitties
26 No fan of Pizarro, certainly
29 Devices in electrical networks
30 Act the ogler
36 Burn cause
39 Urgent transmission, for short
40 Country star's sitcom
43 Compos mentis
44 Roulette bet
45 2000 Olympics host
46 Most up-to-date
48 Basso Pinza
49 Startled interjection
51 "Sorry, Charlie!"
52 Narc's haul
53 Sweater style
55 A doofus might do it
56 It makes clothes close
57 Short order in a diner
58 Voice vote
59 Rod
61 Springs
64 Farm calls
65 Rear
68 Illogically, not the eighth mo.
71 Monstrous
72 Cement holder
73 Lodge letters
74 Large fish, maybe, to a fisher
76 Suffix with pay
77 River through Siberia
78 Like many Ping-Pong balls, nowadays
79 Dentist's target
80 Driver's lic. info
81 Take it easy
82 Latin hymn "Dies ___"
83 Mascot #7
86 Squealer's spot
87 Match in chips
88 Rear
91 Left
92 Fair and square
93 Metered praise
95 Inner tubes, topologically
96 Store sign
98 Avoids
100 Prompt
101 Having a goatee and beret, say
102 Digestive juice
104 "Do the Right Thing" pizzeria
106 Shoe salesclerk's urging
107 Ate
109 Sharply focused
112 Made, as a case
113 Stalagmite makeup
114 Volleyball putaways
115 Rodeo ring?
116 ___ honorable (formal apology)
117 Drift off
119 Prospector's find
121 Scriptural interpretation
123 Fashionable bag
124 Muscat resident
125 Taken back, as territory
127 Gauzy material
128 Wine region
131 Milker's handhold
132 Rush!
133 Prefix with mensch
135 Hwy. sign no.

by Patrick Merrell

ACROSS

1 Peter ___
7 Awakens
14 Hot coffee hazard
19 Queen of mystery
20 Bits of shells
21 Advice-giving sort
22 One who may give you fits
23 Upper crust of the N.B.A.?
25 Mideast capital
26 They may carry antibodies
27 Cold one
28 "Hot" one
29 One cautioning about opening a soda can?
33 Made heroic
35 Sports stat
36 "You don't say!"
38 Big lug
39 Antlered animal of the Old World
42 Mail-in for a toy ninja?
48 "___ Little Girl," Shirley Temple film
49 Football officials, slangily
52 Makes even
53 Wine holder
54 As ___ resort
57 Prefix with reading
58 Borden who founded the Borden Co.
59 High-performance Camaro
60 One who opts for a convertible?
64 Thrown together
67 Fast Eddie's girlfriend in "The Hustler"
68 Prefix with centric
70 It has a nut on each end
71 Tossed
74 Playwright in rare form?
78 About
79 Pronoun with "sommes"
81 Symbols used in angle measurement
82 Jim Henson gave him voice
83 "Fantasy Island" prop
84 Plaintiffs
86 Order member since 1534
89 Baseball C.E.O.'s
90 Part of Santa's team on a computer?
93 Papal court
96 Scrap for Rover
97 I.R.S. worker: Abbr.
98 Future ferns
100 Hot dog
105 Waikiki ringmaster?
110 Afghan makeup
111 Tennyson work
113 Sound heard through a stethoscope
114 Tools with teeth
115 Miss Road Pavement?
119 Hocked
120 ___ ease
121 "Star Trek" directive
122 Handles
123 Villainous looks
124 Serious scoldings
125 Furthest out there

DOWN

1 Draw on again
2 Budget rival
3 It's often seen over a bowl
4 After the fact
5 Magnetite, for one
6 Norse god of war
7 Cricket sounds
8 Club publication
9 ___-jongg
10 Capable, jocularly
11 "Superior" one
12 Dakota dwelling
13 The ___ twins of "New York Minute," 2004
14 League for L.S.U. and Mississippi St.
15 Socialite wannabe
16 "You've got ___!"
17 "I'll help!"
18 Woods nymph
20 Wind phenomenon
24 Baroque
26 Talked a blue streak?
30 W, for one
31 They may clash among titans
32 Mardi Gras royal
34 Work
37 Kett of the comics
39 Den din
40 Faulkner's femme fatale ___ Varner
41 Rubber-burning area
42 Jazz scores
43 "___ my flesh of brass?": Job
44 Bar exercise
45 Important info for advertisers
46 Mekong River locale
47 Delineate
50 Ascap alternative
51 On easy street
55 It may be fixed
56 Famous Amos
58 Vise
59 Slugabed
61 Shock absorber
62 Dropped a dime, so to speak
63 Judge in I Samuel
65 Blood classification
66 Corn cake
69 Man's name meaning "One who hears well"
71 Underwater breathing apparatus
72 Most likely to be called up
73 Places of open discussion
75 Buckeye sch.
76 Cola additive
77 Suffix with Congo
80 Inst. for midshipmen
84 Gather on the surface, chemically
85 Able
86 Knight at the movies
87 Start of a wish
88 One of the Monkees
91 Chauffeur's vehicle
92 Newbie
94 Sagelike
95 Like a slingshot
98 Situation
99 Surgery target
100 Emmy-winning role for Sally Field, 1976
101 Luscious Berry
102 Papal attire
103 Southwestern home
104 Competitive and impatient, say
106 Orphanage fare, once
107 Imperial pronouncement
108 Earthworm eaters
109 Words following "often"
112 Iron brace
116 Gold units: Abbr.
117 Band with the 1991 #1 hit "Unbelievable"
118 Asia's ___ Darya river
119 Prefix with metric

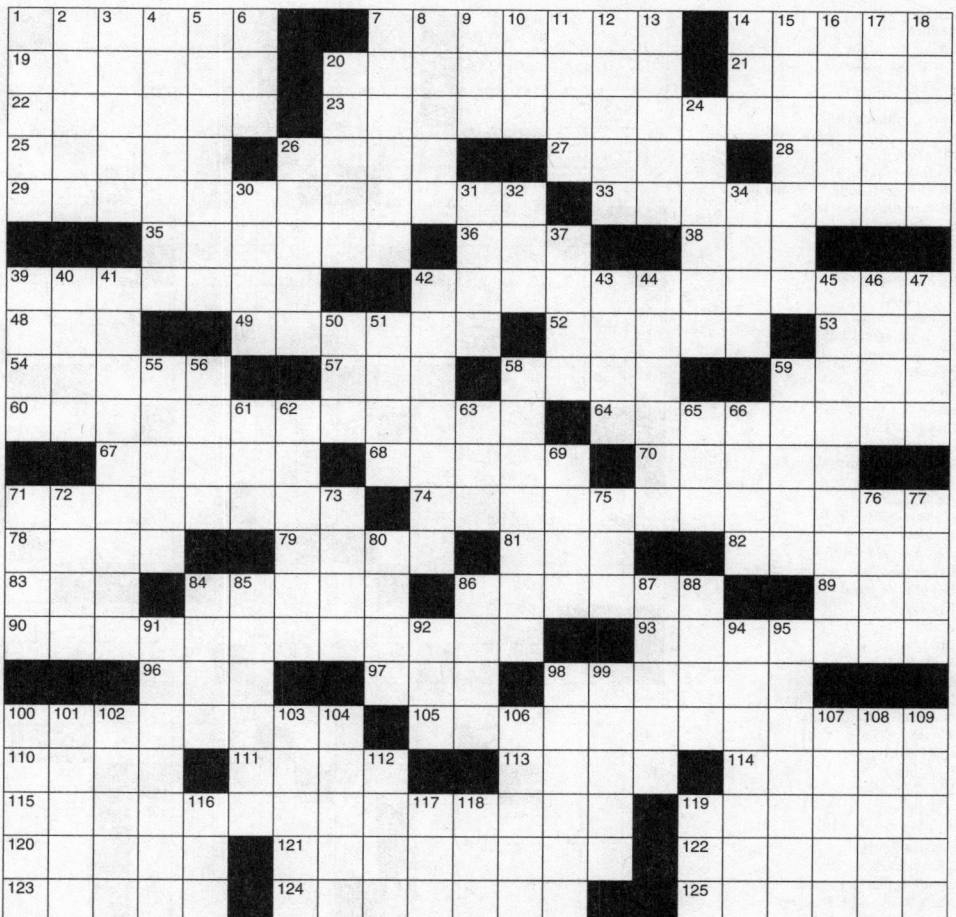

by Peter Abide

ACROSS

1 Diner option
6 Rice University mascot
9 Place to perform
14 Top of the line
20 Certain scholar
21 Top of a clock dial
22 Puts into action
24 Nobelist Sakharov
25 First-stringers
26 Football amts.
27 Mrs. John Quincy Adams
28 Do worse than
29 Solidify
30 "Now ___ it!"
31 Monopoly quartet: Abbr.
32 Tire holders
34 Sellers's foil, in the Pink Panther movies
35 Give life to
38 1966 film western set in Texas
40 Cassio's rival
41 Ripped
42 143A + 144A
47 Grp. with eligibility requirements
49 Certain supports
50 Unloading site
51 Fast-moving piano piece
52 14A + 6A
57 Completely
58 Old video game inits.
59 Channels: Abbr.
60 Many of the Marshall Islands
64 "Follow me"
67 Slowly
71 Sixth-grader, usually
72 Craggy peak
73 Amtrak train
74 Called across the field
77 You might shake on it
78 146A + 9A
83 Percolate
84 Tricky billiards shot
85 "L'Arlésienne" composer
86 "The One I Love" group
87 Stadium parking lot habitué
89 Some French wines, informally
91 Bests at the dinner table
95 Caught a glance of
96 "Take one"
98 Where a water mint grows
99 Sound of support
100 1A + 145A
108 Sounds of satisfaction
109 Rank above viscount
110 Classic theater
111 Percolate
112 20A + 142A
118 ___ Point Lighthouse, on Buzzards Bay
119 Abbé de l'___, sign language pioneer
120 Instruction to an equestrian
121 Séance holders
125 Mad. ___
126 Moonshine mix
127 Buddy
128 Acronym since 1960
130 Lake Okeechobee's state: Abbr.
131 Bought out the store, say
133 Eyepiece
136 Rattle
137 Lift
139 Withstand
140 Gary of "CSI: NY"
141 Louisville museum subject
142 Outpouring from ducts
143 Movie preview
144 Bad habits
145 "___ bite!"
146 Hood's place

DOWN

1 Actress Sonia
2 Like granola
3 Symbols marking spurious passages in old manuscripts
4 Not yet decided: Abbr.
5 Half of an everyday duo
6 About 21% of the atmosphere
7 Off, as a pitch
8 It's just one thing after another
9 M.p.h.
10 Head-turning experience?
11 Synapse neighbor
12 "Trinity" author
13 Some characters in "The X Files," for short
14 Gravlax base
15 Spanish ones
16 A.P.B. broadcasters
17 By and by
18 Many a zinger
19 Ecological units
23 Crusaders' enemies
30 "Lord, is ___?"
33 Stravinsky and others
36 Future doc's exam
37 Queequeg's captain
38 Crib cry
39 "East of Eden" woman
40 Suffix with exped-
41 Old White House scandal
43 Has a temperature, say
44 Toronto media inits.
45 Perfectly illustrate
46 Played out
47 Court plea, for short
48 Carbonated choice
52 Rage
53 Perseus' wife, in myth
54 Writer Rosten
55 Pressure unit: Abbr.
56 Achieved through great effort
61 What a rake may do
62 Little hole, maybe
63 NBC offering, in brief
65 They turn at busy intersections
66 Super ending?
67 German cries
68 Postponements
69 Taking after
70 "___ Talks" (1984 movie)
71 Capital of Poland
73 Ashcroft and Reno, e.g.: Abbr.
75 Snake eyes
76 Mich. neighbor
78 P.I.'s
79 Pile
80 Former Mideast inits.
81 German article
82 Even so
83 Burlington-to-Brattleboro dir.
88 Inherently
90 5-Down's partner
91 Ref. staple
92 London Bridge's home now: Abbr.
93 Poet laureate of 1700
94 Short
96 Junkings
97 High nest: Var.
98 Helvetica is one
101 Number twos
102 Entrance frame
103 "___ idea!"
104 Straight, or straightened
105 Slip on
106 Long periods
107 Checked item
108 Extras
112 For money
113 Ted of "Monk"
114 Column one story
115 Leaning to the right
116 Food Network name
117 Home of Times Sq. and Columbus Cir.
122 "Alas . . ."
123 University in Worcester, Mass.
124 Lively dance
126 Insignificant
127 Tax-free bond, briefly
128 City east of Santa Barbara
129 Gloomy atmosphere
132 Gloomy guy
134 Kind of engr.
135 ___ gestae
137 Racing car product
138 Sri Lanka export

by Eric Berlin and Craig Kasper

ACROSS

1 Tailors anew
7 Swami accessory
13 Year "As You Like It" debuted
16 Ticker tape letters?
19 Italian composer ___ de' Cavalieri
20 Frozen potato producer
21 Complete miss
23 Bulb-buyer's personal concern?
25 Country founded by King Tomislav in A.D. 924
26 Lawn game
27 Estab. with closed-circuit TV
29 Seconded
30 Whence daybreak
31 Growth rate?
34 Mil. branch
37 Having intervals
40 Way to go
41 Lion's den?
45 Left homes
50 Fool's gold
51 Dressing ingredient
54 Enamelware
55 Drop
56 NASA craft
57 "Give ___ go!"
58 Dog-eared piece
60 Manhattan component
61 Brazilian hot spot
63 Split bit
64 It's not clear
65 Underwear and socks inventory?
71 Kind of relationship
73 ___-bodied
74 "Cribs" network
75 One with a pole position?
78 Rush
79 Get going
80 Sets
83 Thick fur
85 Emmy winner Falco
86 Tony Clifton, to comic Andy Kaufman
88 Endeavor
89 Celebraciones grandes
92 [Insert your least favorite politician's name here]?
94 Historic 1972 hurricane
97 You can say that again
98 Rap's Dr. ___
99 Police contest?
104 Actor Tamiroff
107 Produces
108 Late ___
109 Turn off
113 Knobthorns and wattle trees
115 What a magazine subscriber may await?
119 Rainy-day resource
120 Joined the mob, maybe
121 Trial balloon
122 Summer quencher
123 Lush
124 "Why is this night different . . . ?" nights
125 Young chickens

DOWN

1 Jainism, e.g.: Abbr.
2 Title from which "admiral" is derived
3 Poodle's handle
4 "Mr. Belvedere" actress Graff
5 New York county whose seat is Owego
6 Dancing style
7 Kids' stuff
8 They may be bookmarked
9 Portuguese king
10 Famous
11 Not permanent
12 Go on and on
13 Jobs output
14 Tells how to act
15 Kind of hook
16 Use, as plates
17 Movie light
18 Sylvan locale
22 ___ Men ("Who Let the Dogs Out" band)
24 Wallpaper design
28 Cousin of a raspberry
31 Hard hats' lunch holders
32 Oscar nominee for "The Aviator," 2004
33 Feed
34 Word with house or hand
35 On the quiet
36 Radioactivity pioneer
38 Recess
39 Piccadilly Station sight
42 El ___
43 Going on and on
44 One of TV's Bunkers
46 Places for indoor plants
47 Speechless
48 ___ sch.
49 Some injections
52 Tribe related to the Missouria
53 Foot
56 Reed in music
58 Legal writ, for short
59 Each citizen's right, in a democracy
62 ___ of Skye
63 Downed
66 N.L. pitcher Shawn
67 Comic Mort
68 Something of yours you can't see
69 Fugitive
70 Followers of wells?
71 Caterer's associate
72 BMW competitor
76 Actor Burton
77 Partner, maybe, in a French firm
80 Insinuate
81 One of the Ghostbusters
82 Toss up
84 Taste
86 "This should come ___ surprise"
87 Avatar of Vishnu
88 Lose
90 Entertainment innovation of the 1920s
91 Way, way back
93 Follow
95 Worst grade
96 Removers of locks
99 Swahili sir
100 Rainbowlike
101 Fluff, in a way
102 Delicacy
103 Haunting
105 Draw
106 Swab's sobriquet
109 State
110 Boys
111 Terra-cotta piece
112 Part of E.M.T.: Abbr.
114 P.D. rank
116 Old-fashioned punishment
117 Suffix with suburban
118 TV drama sites, for short

by Ben Tausig

ACROSS

1 Takes off
6 Blurted (out)
10 Track runner?
14 Mona ___ smile
19 Parts of hearts
20 Docent's offering
21 Sarah Josepha ___, who wrote "Mary Had a Little Lamb"
22 Seven-time French Open winner
23 Melodramatic
24 "The Aviator" actor, 2004
25 Marine killer
26 The Beatles, once
27 "Have a nice weekend . . . heh-heh"
31 Cousin of Muhammad
32 Babealicious
33 E'en if
34 Part of a speller's clarification
35 Having four sharps
36 Cry of success
37 Pound with a metric system?
39 First name in modeling
42 Cantillated
44 "You, in the front row!"
47 Cracked
50 Family
51 Stamp letters
52 Controversial '50s event
56 Element in magnetic alloys
59 Caesarean delivery?
61 Apples can be compared to them
64 Quadrennial White House administration
65 "My lecture's done, but we still have five minutes"
68 Crowd attractor
70 Riddle-me-___
71 Like some effects
72 Last lines
74 The lonely goatherd, in a "Sound of Music" song
76 Feminine suffix
77 Slate, e.g., for short
79 "I can't read your handwriting!"
81 Track event
83 Record problem
85 Behind
86 Listening to Muzak, maybe
87 German coal city
89 Uncle ___ rice
91 Inlet
93 Some bills
94 "Your grades aren't what they should be"
100 Inhuman
103 Meatloaf serving
104 50-Across's partner
105 Father or son Joad in "The Grapes of Wrath"
108 It lacks 93-Across
109 Port container
111 Its musical ID is just the notes G, E and C
113 Brian of rock
114 Govt. org. with a flower in its logo
115 "If I could digress for a moment . . ."
121 Diplomat Deane of early America
122 Start of a decision-making process
123 "Good ___!"
124 Netanyahu's successor
125 Sharp
126 Philosopher Descartes
127 Ending of many toothpaste names
128 Steamed
129 Heads of états
130 River of W.W. I
131 Ziegfeld Follies costume designer
132 Spaced (out)

DOWN

1 Proceed nonchalantly
2 "High Spirits" star, 1988
3 Literary dueler
4 Opportune
5 Pourer's request
6 Successful film franchise starting in 1979
7 San Francisco street named for a president
8 Not take for credit
9 Certain guilty pleasure
10 Ten Commandments word
11 "For the ___ and radiant maiden": Poe
12 Reynolds Wrap maker
13 Isn't joking
14 Sore throat remedy
15 One of six Russian rulers
16 Submit
17 French satellite-launching rocket
18 Was a good dog, perhaps
28 Go through slowly
29 "Dig?"
30 Dig
38 Cutting down, after "on"
40 Old literary inits.
41 Car maker whose name is Latin
43 "___ take arms against a sea of troubles": Hamlet
44 Like some Bedouins
45 Like Charlie Chaplin
46 Gets
47 Professors' environs
48 Objects of envy
49 Black holes, e.g.
53 In the initial phases
54 Index fingers, in a children's hand game
55 Great American Ball Park team
57 Siren
58 Is multitudinous
60 Any of TV's Simpsons
62 Polite question
63 Technique for viewing some slides?
66 Neb. neighbor
67 Old German duchy name
69 Fall locale
73 Best replacement
75 Set of values
78 Ridicule
80 Trojan horse
82 Hardy girl
84 Some have black eyes
88 Bottom lines
90 Vikings' org.
92 Turn off
95 Verve
96 Open case
97 Good time to collect seashells
98 27 for 56-Across, e.g.: Abbr.
99 "That's ___!"
100 Serenades, as the moon
101 Le soleil, par exemple
102 It works like a charm
105 W.W. II conference site
106 Endorphin, e.g.
107 Like raccoons
110 Cap sites
112 Spy's gizmo
116 Beard
117 Feminine suffix
118 Appraiser
119 County of Dover, Delaware . . . or Dover, England
120 Relative of a potato

by Ethan Cooper and Michael Shteyman

ACROSS

1 A list of the A-list
6 Polish port
12 Footwear name
19 Gazetteer data
20 With freedom of tempo
21 "Dunno"
22 Source of a little laughter
24 Nether world
25 General breakout
26 Off course
27 Old propaganda source
28 List
29 Driver's opportunity
31 People aren't usually drawn to this
33 Make out
34 Yule decorations
40 Place in a Robert Redford flick
41 Foofaraws
45 Godiva product
46 One working close to Washington?
48 Breakfast cereal ingredient?
49 Learn via a third party
50 Berth place
52 Excessive suavity
54 Off
56 Doo-wop syllable
59 Virginia, once
60 Terse truths
63 Drew on
64 Coeur d'___
65 Almond Joy nuts, perhaps
67 Waiting for a pickup
68 Diner on "Alice"
69 Backyard game
70 Red and blue
71 Big Ten inits.
72 Makes right
73 Unwrap impatiently
75 Son of Mary Stuart
77 "Good grief!"
80 Give a little
81 Luc Sante is a Belgian writer of "Low Life" (1991)
82 Free
84 Paris pops
85 Start of a 1940s–'60s world leader's name
86 Vehicles that may be under the Yuletide tree
90 With 81-Across Belgian author of "Low Life"
91 Blowing away
92 Not even
97 Cultural character
99 Creaky, maybe
100 Prepares, as chestnuts
105 History chapters
106 Prepares for a ride
108 Season's greetings
110 Laments loudly
111 Capital of Somme
112 Render helpless
113 Old dinero
114 Fly with a long proboscis
115 Pounding parts

DOWN

1 Attended
2 Poet who wrote "I have executed a memorial longer lasting than bronze"
3 Saint-Germain's river
4 Drops off
5 Multitude
6 Cubism pioneer Juan
7 Way in or out
8 Can't take
9 Simba's love in "The Lion King"
10 Doesn't touch again
11 Levels, briefly
12 Thistlelike plant
13 Winter frosts
14 Mohawk-sporting actor
15 Hurdle for future docs
16 Present seeker
17 Juju and mojo
18 Popular drink mix
21 Stable place
23 Cold war side
27 Chevrolet model
30 Quoits pegs
32 Sports org. north of the border
35 Chief Jack House and others
36 Foie ___
37 "Ben-___"
38 West Coast airport inits.
39 Fishermen bring them back to shore
40 Suffix with Ecuador
41 Bum place to stay?
42 1983 World Series winners over the Phillies
43 Handel bars?
44 About half of table salt, chemically
47 "Capeesh?"
49 "Get your hands off me!"
50 Richie's mother, to the Fonz
51 Sights
53 Calgary-to-Edmonton dir.
54 Director ___ C. Kenton
55 New York City park name
57 Greek
58 Sum parts
60 Breezed through
61 Get by
62 Merry sound of the season
63 Strip
65 Mus. increase in volume
66 First name in Egyptian politics
67 "It is the night of ___ dear Savior's birth"
69 Course for course preparers
70 Speaker systems, briefly
72 Invoice no.
73 Garb for 2-Down
74 "I kiss'd thee ___ kill'd thee": Othello
76 Nickname for the young Darth Vader
77 Some credit card security features
78 Snake in the grass
79 Elementary school trio
81 Sink
82 Biting
83 Ending with tele-
84 Ltr. afterthoughts
85 Lies low
87 Heroes
88 1936 Olympics star
89 Pelé's org., once
93 Mantel
94 Hold forth
95 Contribute
96 Lots of sissies?
98 16-Down's desire
99 Fictional wirehair
101 Mayberry kid
102 In ___ (worked up)
103 Assn. and org.
104 "Just hear ___ sleigh bells jingling . . ."
107 Too rehearsed
108 Santa has a red and white one
109 Restaurant chain since '58

by Nancy Salomon and Harvey Estes

ACROSS

1 Failures
7 Strolled
13 Mob action
20 Foothold facilitator
21 Annual October event, with "the"
22 "That really touched me"
23 Scene of some disgraceful one-nighters?
25 Traffic caution
26 Longtime Syrian president
27 Singer Redbone
28 Business honcho Perelman, who was once the richest man in America
29 Bad testimony
30 Headline about a philanthropist's settled loan?
37 Several periods
40 Bribe
41 Vacationer's destination
42 Rudy's coach in "Rudy"
43 Take off (on)
45 Wife of Saturn
47 Like a piece of cake
49 "That'll do, thanks"
53 "I'll say it again—I'm outta here"?
58 A
59 Slows
60 Slow
61 Largest island in the Cyclades
62 It may blow when it's hot
63 Prefix with angular
65 Pour
67 Made privy to
69 Darning some smelly socks?
75 Early French settler in the Maritimes
76 "Oxford Blues" star, 1984
77 Fitness centers
78 Meticulousness
79 "Julius Caesar" role
83 When repeated, a South Seas getaway
85 Tattered Tom's creator
88 D.C. setting
89 Item on a busboy's to-do list?
92 Donne, for one
94 Spent
95 Behind
96 Bygone time
97 Notebook maker
99 Can't stand
102 Diving bird
104 Grp. with some crack staff
105 Retrieves a phone message again?
111 Had something
112 Kicks
113 Ill-gotten gains
114 Old Russian ruler known as "The Moneybag"
118 Big cheese?
121 Drive Dali back?
125 Occupied, as a saddle
126 Irish P.M. Ahern
127 Calm
128 Running out of gas
129 Vital ratings period
130 Password preceder

DOWN

1 Bologna bread, once
2 First-rate
3 Perks (up)
4 Skater Hughes
5 Moving experience?
6 It makes waves
7 Bloodless
8 Recounted account
9 "The Professor: A Tale" novelist
10 Turned on
11 Clown's foot spec, maybe
12 Cable alternative
13 Wisconsin college town
14 Egyptian god of the universe
15 Mid-millennium year
16 Curse
17 Walled city near Madrid
18 Contents of lamps, maybe
19 Just beat
24 Played pat-a-cake
28 Blue
31 Secure
32 ___ mgr.
33 Actor Atkinson, player of Mr. Bean
34 "The Faerie Queene" character
35 Faerie land
36 One of TV's Ewings
37 Work units
38 Go wild
39 Opening-night celebration
44 Md. town near Baltimore
46 Reject
48 Fairy tale character
50 "O.K. by me"
51 TV journalist David
52 Minute
54 PC character system
55 Slate, e.g.
56 Put ___ on (go for at auction)
57 ___ directed
62 "It's about time!"
64 Bit of evidence
66 Frequent English football score
68 Late name in rap
69 Toy on a track
70 Online shoppers might use it
71 Unsuitable
72 Gen. ___ E. Lee
73 Old draft category
74 ___ Buena, Calif.
80 Came home dusty?
81 "Put it here," basically
82 Prefix with nitrile
84 Farm plant also called lucerne
86 To be over there?
87 Mother of Hades
89 Country name
90 Place at the start
91 Pin holder
93 .001 inch
98 "Ri-i-i-i-ight!"
100 City connected to the Sunshine Skyway Br.
101 Nickname of baseball's Leo Durocher
103 Hibachi chef's pride
105 1969 Hoffman role
106 Novelist Canin
107 Senior Tour golfer Calvin
108 Bright
109 Someone ___ problem
110 Dodge
115 Purim month
116 Denier's comment
117 Hot
119 Queen ___
120 Across the street from: Abbr.
121 N.F.L. ball carriers
122 "That's gross!"
123 School opening?
124 The Fighting Tigers, for short

by Joe DiPietro

ACROSS

1 Quakers or Shakers
5 Old film magnate Zukor
11 Bill collector?
15 Low-___
19 1940s–'50s actress Raines
20 State bordered by the Colorado River
21 "It is my suggestion . . ."
22 Baseball star born in Santo Domingo
23 The marijuana dealer tried to . . .
25 Confidentially
27 Wasted
28 The veterinarian tried to . . .
30 Goes off
34 Title for a 50-Across
35 Clinton or Dole, once: Abbr.
36 Crosstown rival of the Bruins
39 Store outside a city?
41 "When I was young . . ."
44 What markers may represent
48 Actress Vardalos
49 Bette Midler and others
50 All-wise one
52 Bird feeder fill
53 Canasta plays
56 Budapest-born conductor
58 Flattens
60 Core of a PC
61 Radiant
62 Almost too much
64 Awestruck
66 Bottom line figure
69 The arsonist tried to . . .
71 Shades of red
73 Srs. may take it
74 Shakespearean term of address
75 The demolitions expert tried to . . .
79 Fuel
82 Use over, as tea leaves
83 Sonata finales
84 Tragic figure in Greek myth
85 Ending with rest or fest
86 Wheel on a spur
88 Slip by
91 All-purpose connector
92 Baklava ingredients
94 RCA competitor
96 Give a lift
98 It may get into deep water
99 Old-fashioned adventure
101 Food for thought?
102 Forward
104 Urban gridwork: Abbr.
105 42-Down users, for short
107 "Now I get it"
109 Baseball Hall-of-Famer Fox
111 The artist tried to . . .
117 Keyboard commands
121 National park in Colorado
122 The hair stylist tried to . . .
126 Angle (off)
127 Patient wife of Sir Geraint
128 Big bookseller
129 Somalia-born supermodel
130 Louver feature
131 Somewhat, to Salieri
132 Counters
133 Miss

DOWN

1 1999 war combatant
2 Ben-Gurion arrival
3 Sister in myth
4 Refinement
5 Bowl over
6 Cry made with a head-slap
7 What I will always be?
8 Prune
9 T.A.'s superior
10 Is averse to
11 Related to
12 "___ It Time" (1977 hit)
13 Plaster base
14 Instruments played by 3-Down
15 Denture parts
16 Tremendously
17 50–0, e.g.
18 In use
24 Verb origin of suis and sont
26 Scratched (out)
29 One who takes a bow?
31 Electric flux symbols
32 Modern subscription service
33 Zigzag
36 Frighten
37 War tactic
38 The telemarketer tried to . . .
40 One of the ones waiting in "Waiting for Godot"
42 Manuscript marks
43 Offshoot of punk rock
45 The rodeo rider tried to . . .
46 Crow's home
47 Gives an electric jolt
51 Supplement
54 Place marker
55 More stylish
57 Go where one's not welcome
59 Title girl in a 1979 #1 hit
63 Start of a full house declaration, maybe
65 Luke Skywalker's father
67 Paired up
68 "No dice"
70 Part of H.R.H.
72 Big name in women's tennis
75 Raise, with "up"
76 Song-and-dance special
77 "Unbelievable!"
78 Alternative education institute since the 1960s
80 W.W. II menace
81 Salon jobs
87 Ton of money
89 Broad
90 List ender
93 Popular late-night host
95 Home of the superhighways H1, H2 and H3
97 Actresses Fulton and Brennan
100 Ron Howard flick of 1999
103 "The Mod Squad" role
106 Wolf's prey
108 "And the ___ goes to . . ."
110 Web biz
111 Auto lic. bureaus
112 Part of a Hollywood archive
113 Fishing, perhaps
114 ___ Laszlo skin care products
115 It helps prevent runs: Abbr.
116 Philosopher David
118 First name in newspaper humor
119 Vitamin bottle info, for short
120 Personal ID's
123 Keyboard key
124 China's Lao-___
125 In

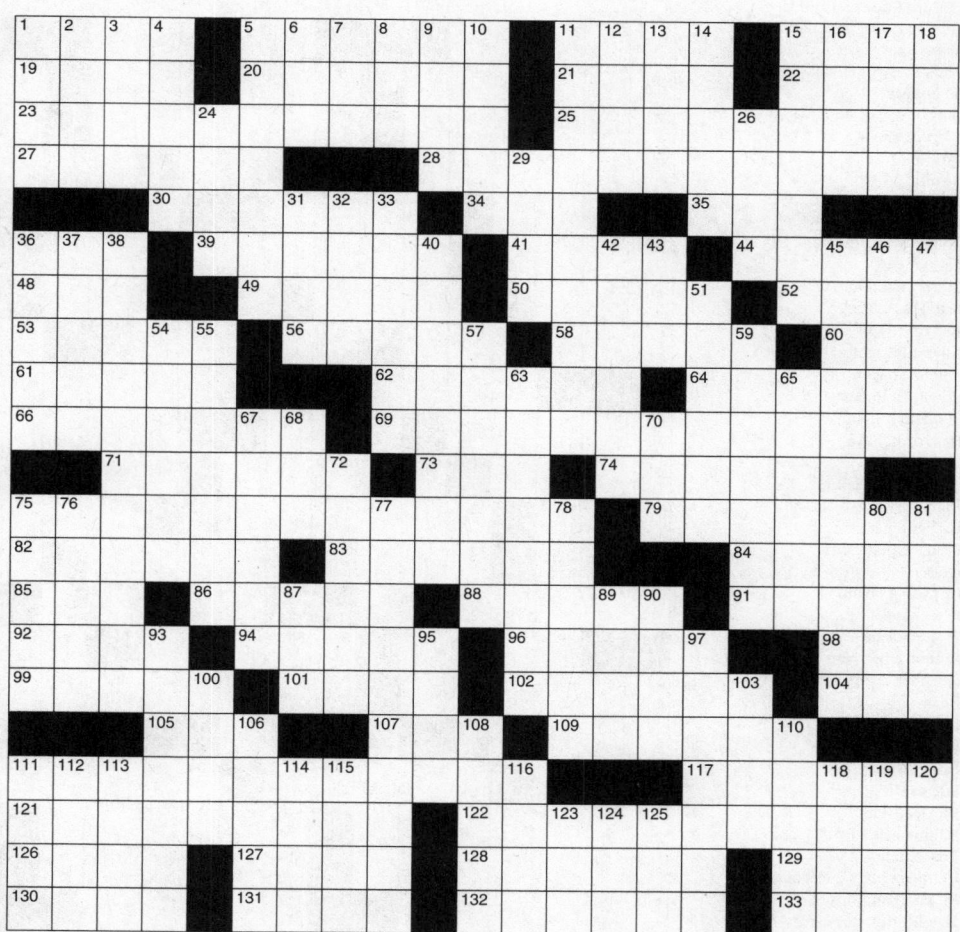

by Michael Ashley

ACROSS

1. ___ once
6. Blood-related
11. Spot on a horse
17. Not as nice
19. Oscar winner who made his film debut in "Me, Natalie," 1969
20. One who works on walls
21. Chant
22. Patch type
23. Go from worse to bad?
24. Female competitor in springboard competition?
26. Personal points of view
28. Pouchlike part
29. "House of Incest" author
30. Smidgen
31. Breathing space?
32. Cooped (up)
33. Decree
34. Where the smoke rises in a sty's chimney?
37. Sounds of impact
39. Cardboard pkg.
40. Suit to ___
41. Walmart rival
42. Normandy city
43. One of the Borgias
45. Film role played by both Vincent Price and Bill Cosby
47. They have quarters downtown
50. Newspaper no.
52. Without carrying charges?
55. Be-bopper
56. Start of the second quarter
59. It fits in a lock
61. On a high
62. Notable #4 with a stick
63. Lionize
64. Cashew family member
66. Contents of a diamond bag
67. Theater org.
68. Cross promotion?
69. Fellini's "La ___"
70. Part of T.G.I.F.
71. Not quite right
72. Solo in space
73. Where Brahmans build their houses?
76. Hard to believe
78. Get moving
80. Addition symbol
82. Imp
86. Barbering area
87. Produce plays, say
89. Grate
91. Corrosive chemical, to a chemist
92. Protractor measurements
94. A choice between cinnabar and galena?
96. Rush
97. One and only
98. Fraternal letters
99. School since 1440
100. Puerto Rico hrs.
101. Mexican Mrs.
102. Baltimore's Enoch ___ Free Library
104. Command to a gardener?
108. Maximilian, for one
110. Handle an F-15, e.g.
112. It may zip out
113. Chefs, at times
114. Gave birth on a farm
115. Sound setup
116. Underhanded, to put it nicely
117. President born in Charles City, Va.
118. It may be rolled up in a bun

DOWN

1. In the thick of
2. Early Russian Communist
3. Modern-day inhabitants of old Livonia
4. Apply chrism
5. Home of Ft. Donelson Natl. Battlefield
6. Author Ellison
7. Green subj.
8. Go for the gold
9. She rescued Odysseus
10. Topographic map feature
11. British title
12. Computer programs, briefly
13. In accordance with
14. What you'll find at a prison library?
15. Mediterranean region
16. Puts up
18. Make an impression
19. Devout acts
20. Toll road
25. Heavyweight champ Riddick
27. Lover of Aphrodite
31. Appointment book
32. Bargaining factor
33. TV overseer: Abbr.
35. Last word of Missouri's motto
36. Alarm
37. Show in theaters
38. Roughly measured (off)
40. Seed coat
44. 91-Across, e.g.
46. Wear away
47. Oil worker
48. What Shakespeare called "the little O"
49. Leave the straight and narrow
51. Student's selection
53. Kay Thompson character
54. Firmly secured
56. Kind of star
57. Song of joy
58. Miler's mistake?
60. Latin 101 word
64. Union members
65. Chalk or marble
67. Needs a doctor
69. Land's end?
71. Uproar
74. Word of honor
75. Leaves home?
77. Weapons collections
79. ___ bonding
81. Stepped lively
83. Cheese type
84. Some solvents
85. Letters after a barrister's name
87. Shed tears
88. Reading to the unruly
90. Lined up
92. Stocks and such
93. Everyday
95. One who's lying
96. One of the original Not Ready for Prime Time Players
98. Components of some codes
102. Veep's boss
103. Calhoun of TV's "The Texan"
104. Mental power
105. Overhang
106. "Norma Rae" director
107. Vanity cases?
109. Greek vowel
111. "Oy ___!"

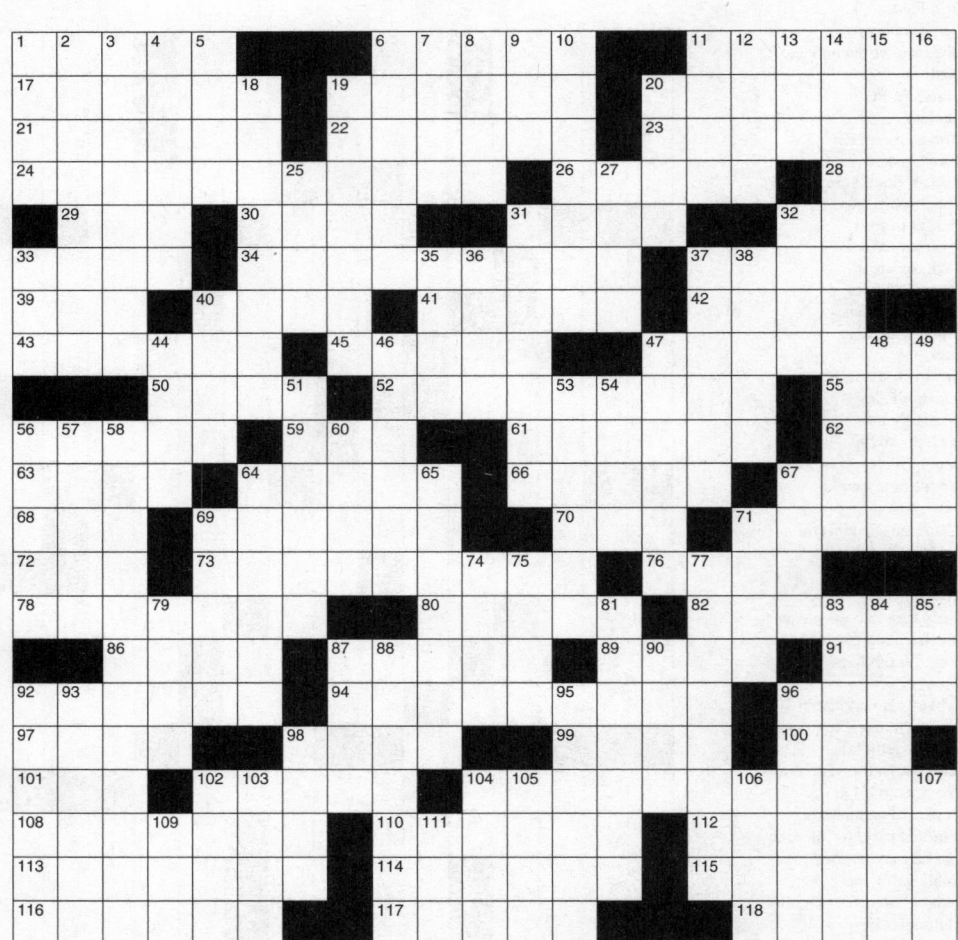

by Richard Silvestri

When this puzzle is completed, the circled letters, read in order from left to right (column by column), will reveal the name of a Mystery Person.

ACROSS

1 Oliver Twist, e.g.
5 Little fight
10 Squawker
14 Advanced
18 Some chorus voices
19 Run ___ of
20 Father-and-son name in football coaching
21 Modeler's need
22 As a toddler visiting a farm, Mystery Person heard a pig squeal and . . .
26 Dorothy's transport to Oz
27 Aardwolf features
28 Puncture
29 "Comin' ___ the Rye"
31 Blunderbuss
32 Francis, e.g.
33 After a single hearing of a sacred piece in the Sistine Chapel, Mystery Person . . .
44 Continental money
45 One of Alcott's "Little Men"
46 Privy to
47 Concept embodying yin and yang
48 Founded: Abbr.
49 Jawbreaker?
51 Less loco
53 Mythical creature
55 Mystery Person once composed a piano piece that, to be performed correctly, required the . . .
59 One pole: Abbr.
60 Hematite component
61 Song from on high?
62 Med. specialty
63 Use for support
65 Massenet opera
66 Jewish sect
70 Back
71 Trowel wielder
72 Uncommon
73 Singer with a palindromic name
74 Mystery Person would sometimes compose symphonies . . .
80 Assailed
81 Revere
82 Well
83 Cars once advertised as "The Gold Standard of Value"
84 Loosen up, maybe
85 Org. with an acad. near Colo. Spr.
86 ___-mo
87 Country north of Tonga
88 Scholars believe that "A Musical Joke" by Mystery Person was . . .
95 Tribe with a state named after it
96 Part of l'année
97 Carrier whose name means "skyward"
98 G-rated
101 Whine-making?
105 Throw
110 Mystery Person once wrote a waltz in which the choice of measures played was determined . . .
113 Suffix with switch
114 12 on a cube
115 "Whole ___ Love" (1969 hit)
116 Gusto
117 Buzzed
118 Gregor Mendel research subjects

119 Northernmost county of Massachusetts
120 Cuts off

DOWN

1 "Hold it!"
2 Fashion executive Gucci
3 Path of Caesar
4 Spender of markkas, once
5 Greeted informally
6 Pains
7 Vous, familiarly
8 January 27, 1756 (Mystery Person's birthdate), e.g.
9 Chicago district
10 Bloke
11 Deceit
12 "___ the heavy day!": "Othello"
13 Catch
14 Celebratory toast
15 Gusto
16 Buster?
17 Family
20 Working ___
23 "Soap" family
24 Part of Bush's "Axis of Evil"
25 ___-eyed
30 Favored
32 He outpolled H.H.H. in '68

33 Tots
34 Brown shade
35 Sandinista head
36 List heading
37 Swear words
38 Finished cleaning
39 Youngest Oscar winner in history
40 Poetic time of day
41 1931 Medicine Nobelist Warburg
42 Some stingers
43 Days of ___
49 1960s TV series set at Fort Courage
50 Exuberant casino cry
51 Ice treat
52 Simple arithmetic
53 U.S.-born grandchild of Japanese immigrants
54 Nay sayer
56 Act antsy
57 Reply to a captain
58 So very much
64 Simba's mate, in "The Lion King"
65 Furlough
66 Campus building
67 Long green
68 Away from the elements
69 Israeli intelligence group
71 Letter salutation

72 Five-carbon sugar
74 "Hold your horses!"
75 Locks
76 Furloughed
77 Use a surgical beam
78 "Road" picture destination
79 ___-American
85 One-eighty
86 Doctor's signboard
87 Canonized fifth-century pope
89 Edible clam
90 Minneapolis-based magazine
91 Old Dodges
92 Game stopper
93 Missouri feeder
94 Swab target
98 "Good buddy"
99 Neighbor of Draco
100 ___ jacket
101 Fashion
102 "Eugene Onegin" girl
103 Pub quaffs
104 Gunks
106 Chisel-like tool
107 It means nothing to the French
108 Golden State sch.
109 Understands
111 Agt.
112 Basketball stat.

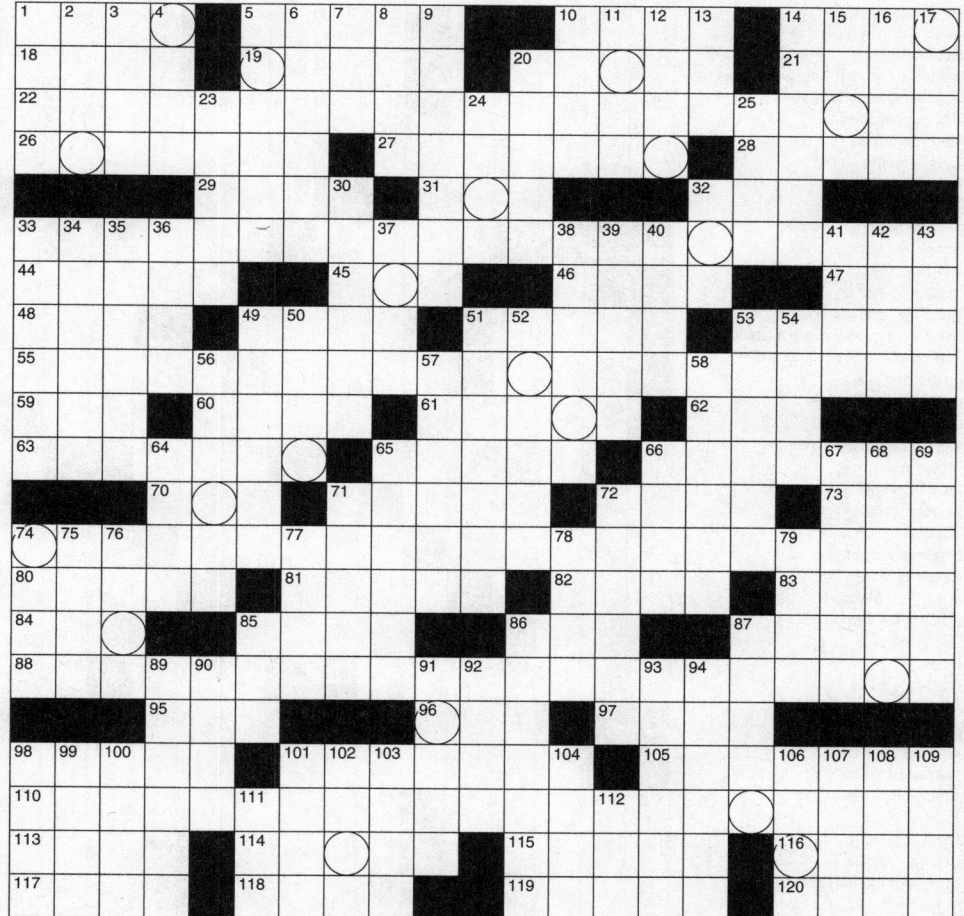

by George Barany and Michael Shteyman

SOUNDS OF NEW ENGLAND

ACROSS

1 Printing array
6 Eats
10 Not very bright
14 Eighty-six
18 Like tinned fish
19 Pointer's pronoun
20 Sommelier's prefix
21 Fixes holes, say
22 Important part of mayo
23 Site for stretchers
25 U-shaped river bend
26 Raise money using heavenly messengers?
29 "Romanian Rhapsodies" composer
30 Something may be taken in it
31 TNT alternative
32 ___-Seltzer
35 Defense grp. formed in Bogotá
36 Farm workers
40 Like a phobic longshoreman?
45 Suffix with ranch
46 Mid-seventh century date
47 Tip, in a way
48 Appetizer or entree
49 Geiger with a counter
50 Here, in Juárez
51 Cross inscription
52 Close encounter
54 Tax check
55 Portrait of an explorer with his timepiece?
58 One expressing the same thoughts
59 ___ Clemente
60 Kind of pass
61 Agcy. spawned by the Manhattan Project
62 Brewpub staple
63 F.D.R. program
64 Erasers?
66 Force a physician and a "Star Trek" officer into a plane?
71 "Stand and Deliver" star, 1987
72 Hydra, for one
73 Dash
74 Can. money
75 Sangre de Cristo Mountains resort
76 "It's Impossible" singer
77 Middle: Prefix
78 "Rocks"
79 Onetime Jeep mfr.
80 Result of wires down in a blizzard?
85 Prepare for firing
87 Cock and bull
88 Restrain
89 Québec's Côte-St.-___
90 Works together
93 Not fooled by
98 Brews in an elm instead of an oak?
102 The Wall Street Journal visual
104 Draft, basically
105 "Them" author
106 European capital, in song
107 ___ B'rith
108 Alternative to Breyers
109 Surgical tube
110 Blown away
111 Short pans
112 Secretary, for one
113 Wiesbaden's state

DOWN

1 Archives unit
2 Bagel flavor
3 Time being
4 Seconds on a watch
5 Toy racer
6 It's found on a lid
7 "Whoops!"
8 House gofers
9 Begin
10 Akin to Ken?
11 Check the total
12 Looped handles
13 Cap'n's underling
14 Accountant's concern
15 Planets, to poets
16 ___-Globe (common paperweight)
17 Jacksonville-to-Tampa dir.
21 Makes out
24 One of diamonds?
27 Guadalajara greeting
28 Deep ravine
33 Take illegally
34 Sew on sequins, say
36 Fancy-schmancy
37 Herd containment device?
38 1944 Pulitzer-winning journalist
39 Cosa ___
40 Ridicule of a foreign speaker?
41 It might be only a scratch
42 "The Wizard ___"
43 Cabinet dept.
44 Poker chip, e.g.
46 1989 Peace Prize recipient
49 "Say what?"
51 "The fix ___"
52 One may replace an oath
53 Fabled fliers
54 Super-duper
56 "Concord Sonata" composer
57 Encrusted
58 Sommer of "The Prize," 1963
59 Like clay pigeons
62 Buttonhole
65 Calendar pages: Abbr.
66 N.Y.C. cultural center
67 Like crazy
68 ___-à-porter (ready-to-wear)
69 Havens
70 Bank regulating org.
72 Work with feet
76 Pain in the neck
77 1960s TV show set on a farm
80 Lacking tact
81 Thingy
82 Author/screenwriter Ben
83 Chopped down
84 Valley Girl exclamation
86 Chose the window instead of the aisle?
90 Giving a line to
91 Book club name
92 Nobel, for one
94 Condition
95 Some Deco works
96 Cold temps
97 270° from norte
98 Stripped
99 Indian-born actor in "A Tiger Walks," 1964
100 They're caught at the shore
101 City on the Irtysh River
102 Univ. stat
103 Damp and chilly

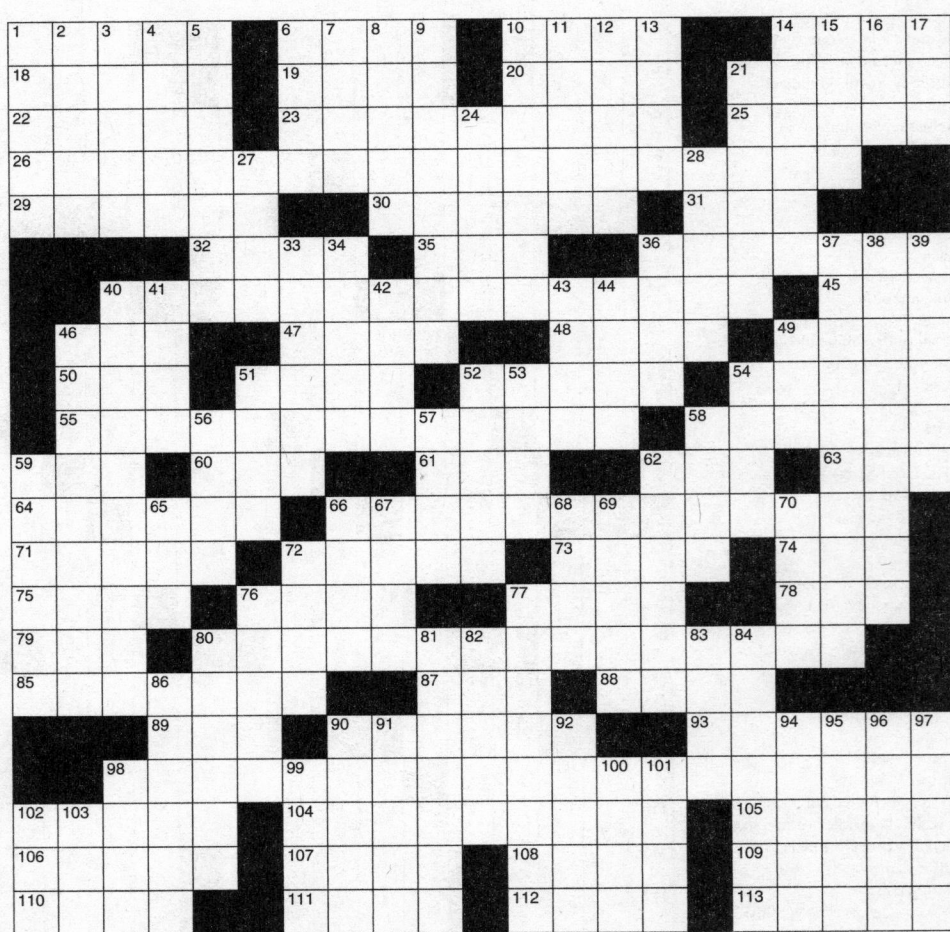

by Rich Norris

The eight theme answers in this puzzle are clues to common words. When the grid has been filled, guess these missing words and enter them on the numbered dashes shown. Then transfer each letter from a dash to its correspondingly numbered square in the middle of the grid. Every letter in the middle will be used twice in the missing words. When you're done, the 25 squares, in order, will reveal a bit of advice about getting ahead.

ACROSS

1 Father of Magnus the Good
5 "Uh-huh"
8 Pressure: Prefix
12 "There ___ goes . . ."
15 Mrs., in Madrid
18 Auto with a trident logo
20 Far from home, perhaps
22 "If only ___ listened . . ."
23 $\overline{17}\,\overline{20}\,\overline{24}\,\overline{12}\,\overline{8}\,\overline{9}\,\overline{13}$
25 Latin 101 word
26 Suffix with violin
27 Radio advice-giver
28 "Outta here"
29 Quarrel
30 Corp. bigwig
31 5% of a C-note
32 Like many adherents to 55-Down
34 $\overline{17}\,\overline{9}\,\overline{19}\,\overline{10}\,\overline{2}\,\overline{12}\,\overline{22}\,\overline{7}$
39 Loonies
40 Smells
41 Charlemagne's realm: Abbr.
42 English exclamation
43 Foot soldiers: Abbr.
44 Classic gas brand
45 Level
46 Baby kisser, maybe, in brief
47 Hard times
51 Fraction of a min.
53 Parisian article
54 "___ Baby" ("Hair" song)
55 Suffix of approximation
58 Seize
60 Like many sports interviews
62 Place for Us and Them
64 How bananas are bought
65 Breaking news
66 Mighty boss's opposite
67 River at Ghent
68 Actor Guinness
69 "Brat Farrar" mystery writer
70 Turning point?
72 Place on a TV?
74 Woman in a personal ad: Abbr.
77 Hang
79 Road ___
83 Good times
84 Code in which many Web pages are written: Abbr.
85 Suffix with Capri
86 Bit of Gothic architecture
87 Bite-the-bullet type
89 $\overline{1}\,\overline{15}\,\overline{6}\,\overline{11}\,\overline{5}\,\overline{22}$
92 Followers of philosopher René
94 Make like
95 Youngster
96 Common conjunctions
97 Joker, e.g.
98 Roils
100 Lawyer: Abbr.
103 Original "King Kong" studio
104 $\overline{25}\,\overline{14}\,\overline{2}\,\overline{19}\,\overline{7}$
107 Hosp. readout
108 Ethiopian river
109 Discharge into the air
110 Crown maker: Abbr.
111 Mormons: Abbr.
112 Restaurateur Toots
113 Like some ears
114 Leisure

DOWN

1 Popular hotel chain
2 Vientiane's land
3 Secy.
4 Whimsical
5 Peter who wrote "Puff the Magic Dragon"
6 Elec., e.g.
7 Garment worn like an apron
8 Ludlum protagonist
9 Reebok rival
10 Lawyer's thing
11 Something that gets copied
12 Fishing nets
13 ___ cow
14 Compass point
15 $\overline{24}\,\overline{8}\,\overline{20}\,\overline{16}\,\overline{11}$
16 Observation
17 Prettifies
19 Places for clowns
21 Hip's opposite
24 Arrow's place
29 It started about 2½ million years ago
30 Storage medium
32 Japanese soup
33 It may leave its mark
34 The "vey" of "oy vey!"
35 They often have photos
36 Rebuffs
37 Red squirrel named for the sound it makes
38 Upholstery problem
45 $\overline{4}\,\overline{23}\,\overline{14}\,\overline{10}\,\overline{3}\,\overline{18}\,\overline{25}$
47 How many proposals are delivered
48 $\overline{15}\,\overline{21}\,\overline{13}\,\overline{1}\,\overline{18}\,\overline{6}$
49 British tar
50 Burpee product
52 Slow-cooked meal
53 Start of Superman's catchphrase
55 See 32-Across
56 Reach the top of
57 $\overline{4}\,\overline{23}\,\overline{16}\,\overline{21}\,\overline{5}\,\overline{3}$
59 Vortex
61 "___'clock scholar"
63 New members
71 Weave
73 Some time ago
74 Subs
75 One rationale for the 2003 invasion of Iraq: Abbr.
76 "Alice" waitress
77 Baked entree
78 Kind of cable for a computer
80 Stomach muscles, for short
81 Day-___
82 Poetic time of day
84 Car known for its storage space
86 Staples of annual reports
87 One way to run
88 Bloody drunk
89 Break
90 "Our ___ . . ."
91 Connect, in a way
93 Say "tsk" to
98 Historic Normandy town
99 California's ___ Valley
100 Three oceans touch it
101 Ring wins, briefly
102 Actress Daly
104 Two-bagger: Abbr.
105 Biomed. group
106 Lao-___

by Eric Berlin

ACROSS

1 Staff
5 Test group?
10 La Scala cheer
15 Germ jelly
19 "I smell ___!"
20 Financial mogul Carl
21 Indian bread
22 Plain and simple
23 Nostalgic person's utterance
24 Why the convent's head couldn't find information on the nun?
27 Basilica of San Francisco site
29 "Er-r . . ."
30 First step in addicts' treatment
31 Kind of school
32 Merged coastal access?
36 Gives more than a licking?
38 Social sort
39 Wall protector
40 Victory: Ger.
42 Staple of Italian cuisine
44 Unilever?
47 Mexican Mrs.
49 Reason for school cancellation
50 "Ouch!"
51 Canadian Club and others
52 Henhouse sounds
54 Iceland is part of it: Abbr.
57 Pops
60 Accepts oppression no longer
63 Reason to lube a tube?
69 Certain canine
71 Tape, for short
72 Surrender
73 Artist's board nearby?
76 Circular
77 Cast
78 Word said with a tip o' the hat
80 Stomach and intestine, e.g.
81 View from the Gulf of Catania
85 Speaker of the line "Help me, Obi-Wan Kenobi; you're my only hope"
87 Spanish flower
90 French connections?
91 Cabaret singer in the style of an old pope?
97 Square things
98 "Cut it out!"
99 "___ take arms against a sea of troubles": "Hamlet"
100 Knock over
103 Second-stringer
104 Top knot?
107 Mil. address
108 Washersful
112 Accelerate, for short
113 Lesser hit locations
114 Rubber mania?
119 Stakes
120 Moscato d'___ (Italian wine)
121 Lion's home, to Hercules
122 Dander
123 "Waiting for the Robert ___"
124 Sound before "Your fly's open"
125 Dagwood and Blondie's dog
126 ___ Foods, Fortune 500 company
127 Cat with tufted ears

DOWN

1 Winter melon
2 Up
3 Bothers
4 Standard of living?
5 They're easy to park
6 "Baudolino" author
7 Time out?
8 Fuchsia, e.g.
9 Belief of many Africans
10 Cold comment
11 Felt sorry about
12 Area with a curved wall
13 Flak jacket, e.g.
14 Like some exercises
15 Cinemax competitor, for short
16 Class of planes?
17 One in handcuffs
18 Funny Foxx
25 "___ vincit amor"
26 Have a place in the world
28 Citi field replaced it
33 It takes the cake
34 Quark-plus-antiquark particle
35 Counting-out starter
37 See the sights
41 Kind of room
42 Unfair treatment
43 Surgeons' sites, briefly
44 Philip Seymour Hoffman title role
45 Substitute
46 Pays, as a bill
47 "Bye"
48 Make merry
52 Princeton Review or Kaplan study
53 Exertion aversion
55 Modern recording option
56 It's addictive
58 ". . . so long ___ both shall live"
59 Crouch
61 Carry
62 Enter quietly
64 "So Big" author Ferber
65 In chains
66 Acclaim
67 Smart guys?
68 Etta of old comics
70 "___ heart" ("Be kind")
74 Power to control
75 Put in stitches
79 Tool along
81 Ingredient in a flip
82 Poach
83 Bases from which profits are figured
84 Golden or teen follower
86 Isn't naturally
88 Novi Sad resident
89 High-speed roadway
92 Seed-to-be
93 Get well fast
94 Time of operation
95 "Bon ___!"
96 Propagates
100 In many places
101 50 to two
102 Setting for many Thomas Hardy novels
105 Part of EGBDF
106 Defamation
107 "Do I need to draw you ___?"
109 Well off the coast
110 Half: Prefix
111 "___ Gotta Have It"
115 Do nothing
116 "Way to go!"
117 Bradbury's "___ for Rocket"
118 Prefix with morphic

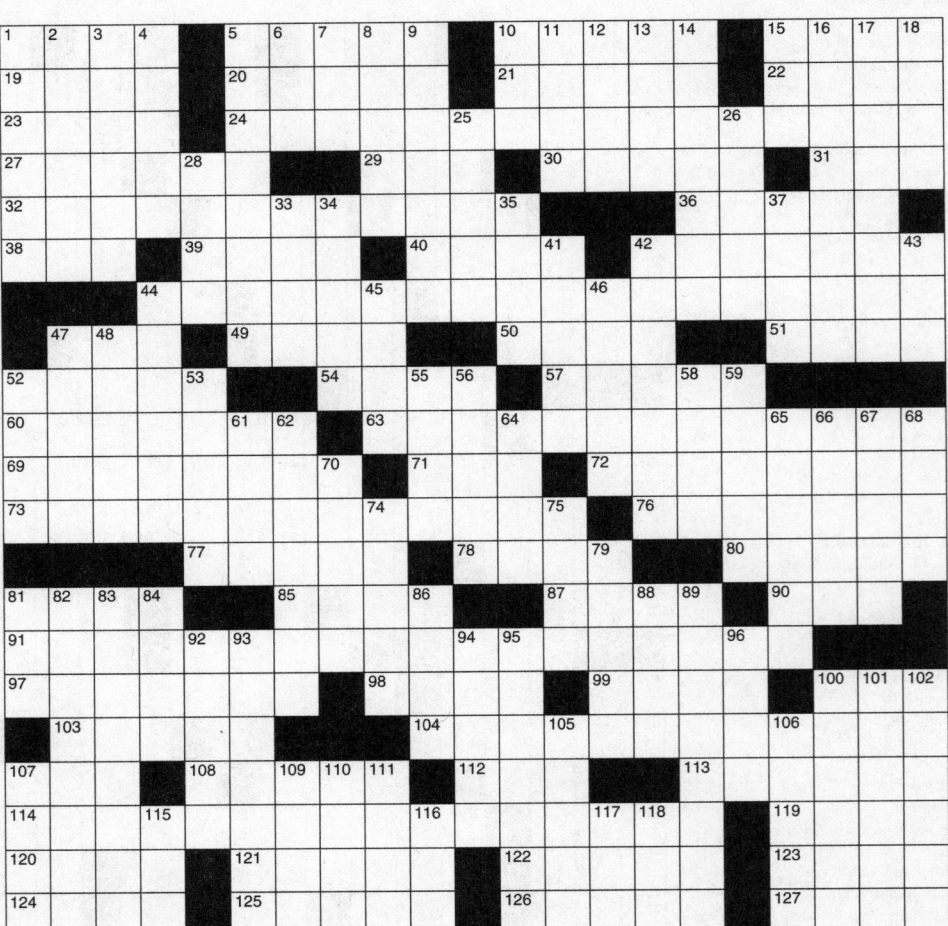

by Manny Nosowsky

ACROSS

1 Small turnover
7 Careless
15 Gut feeling?
20 Preener's partner
21 Color similar to turquoise
22 Shades
23 "Now!"
25 Make into law
26 Stephen of "Breakfast on Pluto"
27 Thought some more about
28 Gas company known for its toy trucks
30 Gas company known for its tiger slogan
31 Tiny ___
32 Ceremonial burner
33 Gob
34 Crescent point
36 "A Passage to India" woman
38 Bawdy
40 One way to chop peppers
42 For one
45 Certain turtle
48 One with a thin skin?
50 "I'm not impressed"
53 Jacket style
54 "Make ___ away"
55 Vice
56 Cry of distress
60 What the connected may have
62 The D.A. probably took it once
63 Dear ones
65 Graph component
66 Pension recipient
68 Afternoon hour in Italy
69 Puts on a coat
71 Bother
72 Cartoon collectible
75 Worked up
77 It may be met or filled
78 2002 Olympics venue
80 Musical opening
82 Gran Canaria, for one
83 Support
85 Blood designation, for short
86 Old sports org. featuring the Minnesota Kicks
87 Florida Rep. ___ Hastings
89 Theseus abandoned her
91 Fugard's "A Lesson From ___"
93 Not just lean
96 Shelters
97 "Yeah, right"
99 Angelo's instrument
100 Trac II alternatives
104 Off-white
105 It has nine figures: Abbr.
107 Markets of yore
111 Greeting of yore
112 Carl Sagan's subj.
114 Popular insulator
116 Dyemaking material
117 Raiders' org.
118 Old war story
120 Debt cause
123 Describes
124 "Just a little bite?"
125 Crumbly Italian cheese
126 Symbol of strength
127 Certain math sign
128 Staggered

DOWN

1 Ancient military hub
2 Work recounting Dido's suicide
3 Butterfly, e.g.
4 An omega stands for it
5 Specialty of Russian painter Aivazovsky
6 A joint that's hopping?
7 Short cuts
8 Leaves something behind
9 Loser
10 ___ Station
11 Under the name of, as a co.
12 Part of many stars' names
13 A-one, or one living in 1-A, perhaps
14 Attention getters
15 Had a beef?
16 Declined
17 Instantly
18 P.I.'s
19 Concerning
24 Poetic time of day
29 Genetics, e.g.: Abbr.
33 Use keys
35 Afternoon hour in Italy
37 Dish out the beans?
39 Punishes, in a way
40 Healthful dessert
41 Eastern discipline
43 Alliance created in 1948: Abbr.
44 Not take risks
46 Ikhnaton, for one
47 Automaker Maserati
49 "Hardly"
50 Swig
51 Actor Novello
52 "Be a little more patient"
57 & 58 Common cake ingredient
59 Fire starter?
61 Nothing that plays a prominent role in this puzzle
64 Resting place
67 Ad salesman, informally
70 "___ was saying . . ."
71 March word
73 Knotted up
74 Ticket choice
76 Character on "Frasier"
77 Quite odd
79 Not just poke fun at
80 Santa in California
81 Cartel city
84 "___ Day" (1993 rap hit)
88 Dash
90 Just partly
92 It's 94-Down for south
94 See 92-Down
95 The Arrow constellation
98 Coke's partner
101 Michelin offering
102 Get payback for
103 Neptune, e.g.
105 Display
106 Vaults
108 Football Hall-of-Famer Merlin
109 Splitting image?
110 Something lent or bent, in a phrase
112 Hurts
113 Opening
115 Object of worship
116 Room to swing ___
119 Cable alternative
121 Letters within the theme entries that are, literally, next to nothing
122 Quit working

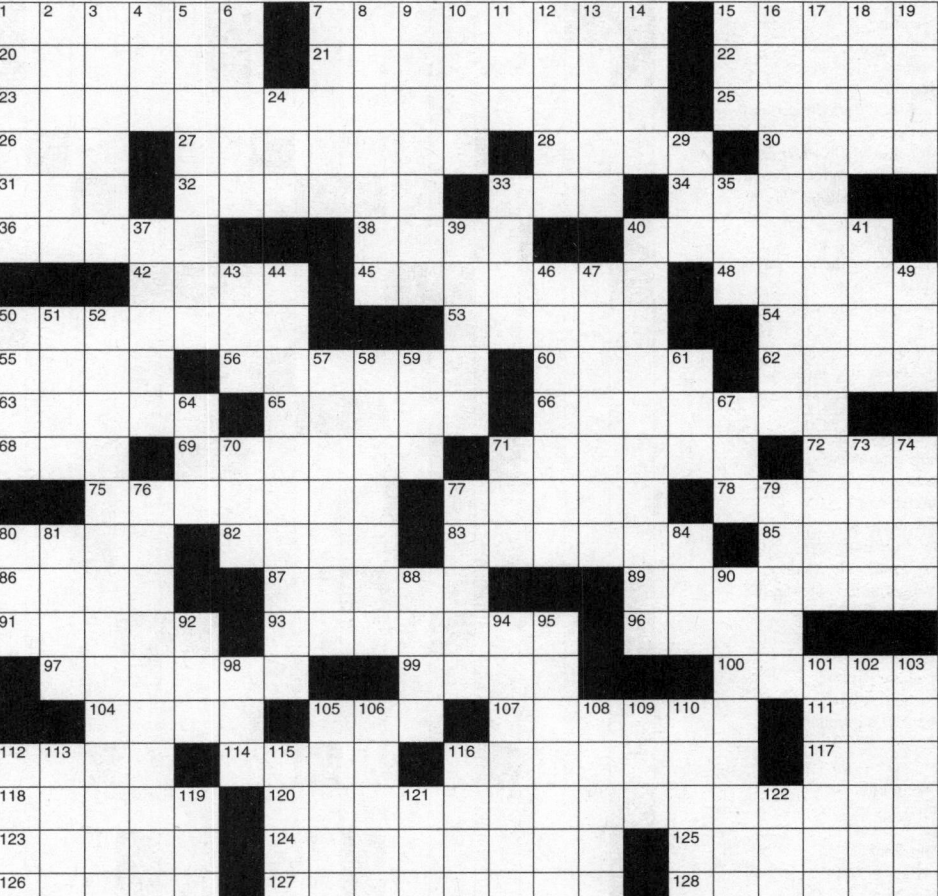

by Joe DiPietro

ACROSS

1 Constitution
8 "___ '70s Show"
12 Operating
17 "How dare they?!"
18 Darn it
19 Uranium-exporting country
20 Infinitives . . . it's ___
23 Word we share
24 Daily Planet worker
25 Reach
26 Beverage served with le dessert
27 More, in music
29 Big fish, to a fisherman
31 Paleontologist's discovery
32 Frat party detritus
34 The passive voice ___
38 Agcy. once involved with fallout shelters
40 Carrier with HQ in Tokyo
41 Gift on "The Bachelor"
42 N.F.L. linemen: Abbr.
43 Ambiguity ___
49 Trip planning org.
51 Pub order, maybe
52 Rhetorical questions . . . ___
57 Fantastic
58 Author's desire
59 Pope after John X
60 Org. that rates members of Cong.
61 C-worthy
64 Cold capital
66 Latin foot
67 Meshlike
70 ___ Life ("Porgy and Bess" character)
74 1997 title role for Demi Moore
77 Subject-verb agreement ___
79 One in the fast lane?
81 Deface
82 Contractions ___
84 Show whose theme song is "Who Are You"
86 Shortstop Chacon of the 1962 Mets
88 Malodourous room?
89 84-Across airer
90 Prepositions are not good ___
97 Sad poets
98 Creator of "All in the Family"
99 Mule alternative
103 Outworn
104 Scratch (out)
105 Not much
106 Daydreaming, say
108 Word said with a salute
109 Exaggeration is among the ___
114 Put back at zero
115 Ticked
116 Toughened
117 Macho types
118 Proceed slowly
119 Reporter's purchase

DOWN

1 Vacuuming, e.g.
2 Setter
3 Perspectives
4 Comeback
5 Adviser of Capt. Picard on "Star Trek: T.N.G."
6 When to call, in some ads
7 M.L.K. Jr., e.g.
8 Seat of power
9 Inexpensive place to stay
10 Brand in a can
11 Bus. card info
12 Ahead
13 Bistro, informally
14 "I don't like it"
15 Overlook, as someone's weaknesses
16 Fine furs
17 Steadfast
20 Bowl-shaped pan
21 They may be stroked
22 Receipt listings
28 Mt. Rushmore State sch.
30 Apparel company Evan-___
31 Round end?
32 Part of a talk show staff
33 Work for a museum
35 Spanish eyes
36 Restaurant waiting areas
37 Lecture badly
38 In pieces
39 Abu Dhabi, e.g.
43 Creature in a Tennessee Williams title
44 Cellular stuff
45 Elusive swimmers
46 Member of the flock
47 Doo-wop syllable
48 Piece of property
50 Communication for the deaf: Abbr.
53 Night school subj.
54 Not hoof it, perhaps
55 Planes
56 Lowest state?
58 Tree trauma
62 Jardin zoológico attraction
63 Trainers treat them
65 Meanie
68 Comic's asset
69 Singer Sumac
71 "The Facts of Life" actress
72 Spike TV, formerly
73 Cousin ___ of "The Addams Family"
75 Collection agcy.
76 Heifetz heard at Carnegie Hall
78 Media handouts
79 Big suits
80 "Don't have ___!"
83 Pgh. Pirate, e.g.
84 Nabs
85 Tiny start
87 Wings hit "___ In"
90 Formula One driver Fabi
91 Lost on purpose
92 What a picador pokes
93 Got warm
94 Bad boyfriends
95 "Perhaps"
96 Do some fancy footwork
100 Counterfeited
101 Spotted
102 Hi-___
105 What a soldier shouldn't be
106 "___ Angel" (Mae West movie)
107 Force
110 Baton Rouge sch.
111 Medium ability?
112 Whip
113 ___ king

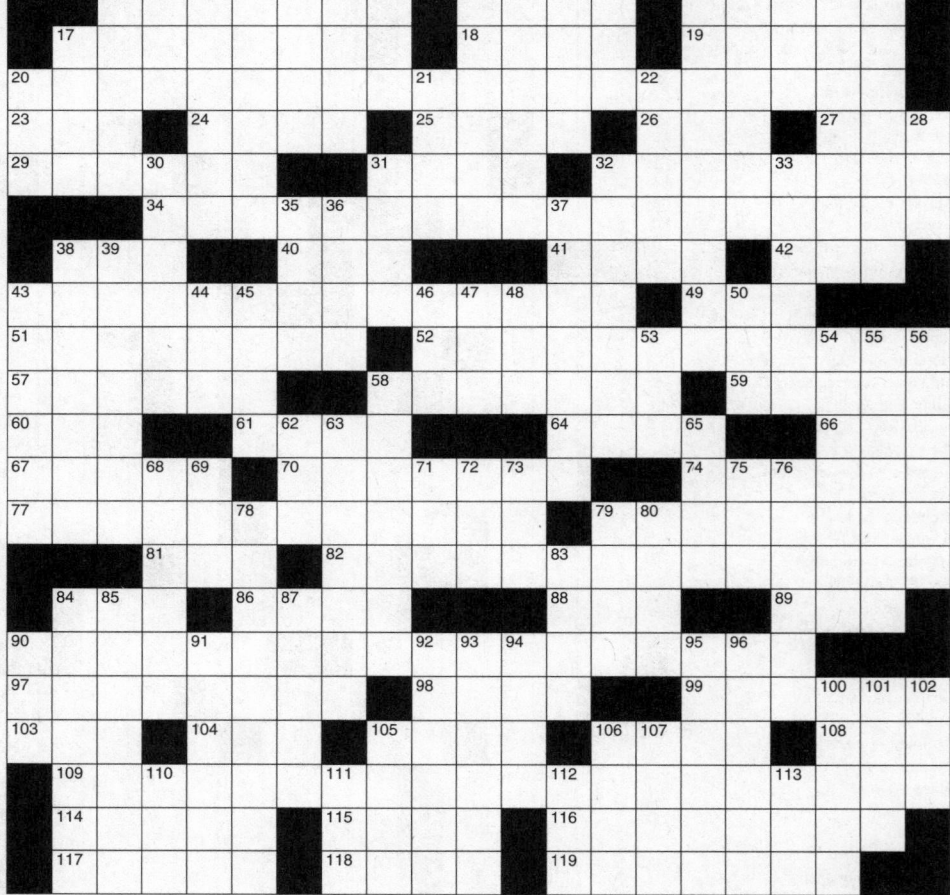

by Randolph Ross

ACROSS

1 Country that won its first Olympic medal in 2004
8 1959 Ricky Nelson hit
15 Summons
20 Nay sayers
21 Tennis star Zvereva
22 Essence
23 Shady accountant's April 15 work?
25 Allied (with)
26 Saxophonist Al
27 Racer Al
28 Director of "Chicago" and "Dancin'"
30 Hula hoop
31 Connects with
34 Chinese "way"
36 Smash hits
38 G.R.E. takers
39 Caroler's reward?
44 Kind of D.A.
45 Rolodex no.
46 Pad site
47 Handy-andies
49 Unsmiling
51 Slip in a pot
53 1940s–'50s All-Star Johnny
55 Pilot announcements, for short
57 "Little Shop of Horrors" dentist
58 Persistent photographers?
61 Sorority letters
63 Main entrances?
65 Wisecracker
66 Analyze
68 Turkey part
69 Mischief makers
73 Deep Throat, e.g.
74 Owls
76 Vandal
77 Comparatively small
79 Late '80s sitcom
80 Unfolding view for a hapless hang glider?
84 Summer cooler
85 Summer coolers
87 Art containing 4-Down
88 Elvis or Madonna
89 Honeyed drink
90 Tens, e.g.
92 Cry of eagerness
94 Et ___ (following)
95 Asunción assent
97 "Faucet drips ahead"?
101 Nutrition info, for short
104 Graffitist's addition to a face
106 Org. that drafts guards
107 School zone requirement
109 Goals in 106-Across, quickly
110 "Cool!"
113 Runner
116 Served past
117 Dull
119 Roller coaster inventor?
123 Top guns
124 Waist reducer, perhaps
125 Current contraption
126 Comic Lewis
127 Sits atop
128 Fancy parties

DOWN

1 Puts out
2 "La Loge" artist
3 Feels irritated
4 Kids' TV staples
5 Like some sleep, for short
6 ". . . ___ he drove out of sight"
7 Not dull
8 "Need You Tonight" group, 1987
9 Weight allowance
10 Catch off-guard
11 Ontario, par exemple
12 Request
13 Dutch filmmaker ___ van Gogh
14 Packs away
15 Old Toyota
16 Jackie's "O"
17 Concern for Rev. Falwell?
18 Gulf State V.I.P.'s
19 Tormentor
24 Soon
29 Sports venue once seen from the Grand Central Parkway
32 Twosome
33 Kings' org.
35 Hairy Halloween costume
37 Fountain order
40 '30s migrant
41 M.D.'s who may cure snoring
42 "Got it"
43 Like city land, usually
45 Soldier's helmet, slangily
48 Instruction unit
49 Nutritious nosh
50 Where the ice skater fell?
51 "Evita" narrator
52 English pianist who was made a dame
54 Works of Michelangelo
56 Follow
57 Hold 'em variation
58 Mild cigar
59 Part of the 1992 Olympic Dream Team
60 Knolls
62 Metric measure
64 ". . . and I mean it!"
67 1968 hit with the lyric "I like the way you walk, I like the way you talk"
70 Dr. ___
71 Shoos
72 W.W. II site
75 Projecting part at the foot of a wall
78 Dark time in poetry
81 City south of the Salt River
82 Stylish gown
83 Yearn
86 Get to work on Time?
89 Former players at 29-Down
91 One way to turn
93 Rural valleys
94 Liverpool-to-Plymouth dir.
95 Military V.I.P.
96 Halogen salt
98 Comic Don
99 Staff leader
100 Main lines
101 Say poetry, say
102 Political pundit Myers
103 Puff ___ (Old World menaces)
105 Other side
108 Kitchen implement
111 Way off
112 Yarn
114 Chocolaty treat
115 No-no on office computers
118 Salt
120 Plenty steamed, with "up"
121 Wellness grp.
122 Recording giant

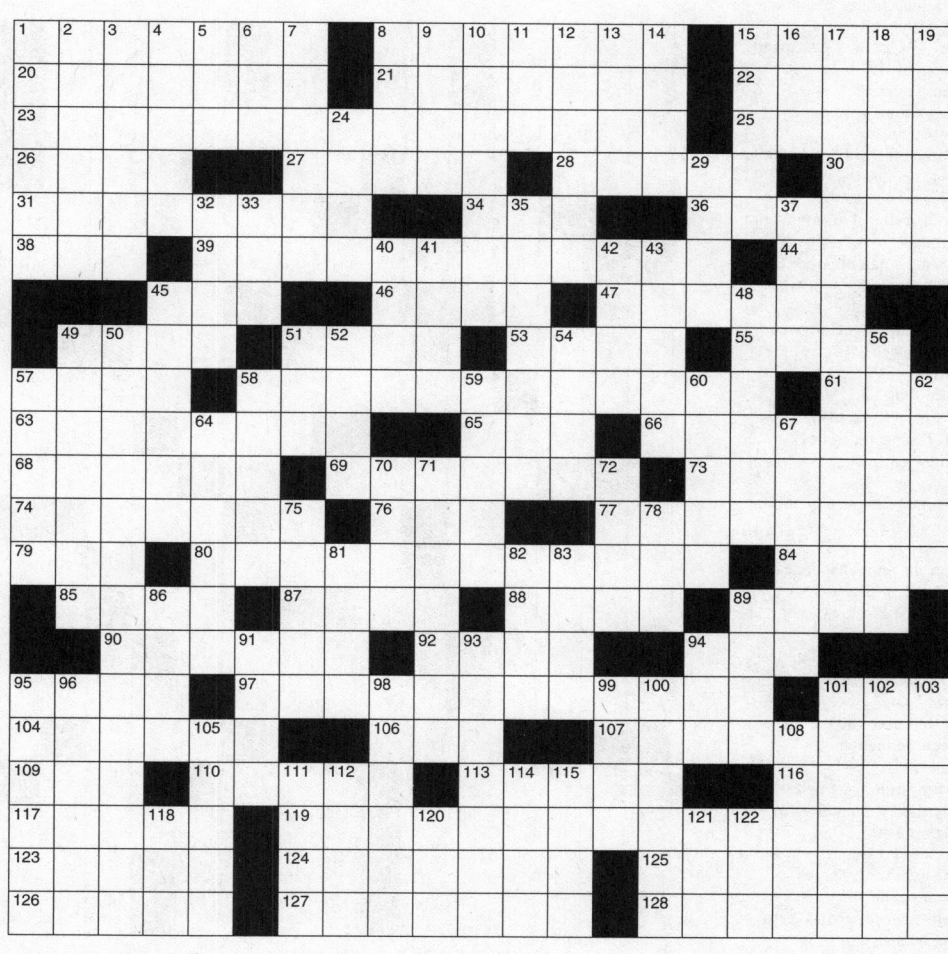

by Ashish Madhukar Vengsarkar

ACROSS

1 Professional bouncers' org.
5 "Chicago" star, 2002
9 Ne plus ultra
13 Significance
19 Omelette ingredient
20 Lena of "Havana"
21 Gymnast's worry
22 Charlotte ___, Virgin Islands
23 Rabbit cliques?
26 "Phèdre" playwright
27 Caffeine-free drink
28 Foreign title of respect
29 Poker prize
30 Elect
31 "The Godfather" actor
33 Word before "dear" or "sir"
35 Parenting author Eda
37 Training with building strips?
40 Ex followers
44 Desktop feature
46 "Scram!"
47 Prairies
48 ___-kiri
49 Old troupe member
52 Dr.'s order?
53 Autobiographer of "Speak, Memory," 1951
55 Did lunch, say
56 Extreme admirer of a Poe poem?
60 "Oh, really?"
61 Way to address a sweetheart
63 Saturn model
64 Saturn model
65 More fitting
66 Closet feature
69 Spacecraft that began orbiting Saturn in 2004
71 "This time ___ me"
74 Basis of illegal discrimination
75 Disperse, with "out"
76 Driving a nail obliquely
80 1953 film or the last word spoken in it
81 Pics featured at Dollywood?
85 "." follower
86 Certain NASA craft
88 According to
89 Pharmaceutical plant
91 1947 romantic comedy "The Egg ___"
92 Times up
95 National League city: Abbr.
96 Rug source
97 Imbroglio
98 Fees for removing dead animals?
102 Not caring anymore
104 Site for 125-Across, with "the"
105 Sleep: Prefix
106 Money may be held in this
109 Prefix with system
111 Speed
113 He was cast into the lion's den by Nebuchadnezzar
117 Bowls
118 Permit from the Nuclear Regulatory Commission?
121 Very much
122 Within: Prefix
123 Gunfight time, maybe
124 Concessions
125 Performances at 104-Across
126 Saxophone, e.g.
127 Bygone fliers
128 Graceful fliers

DOWN

1 Blows away
2 Tide type
3 Vice president under Jefferson
4 Just over 6% of U.S. immigrants nowadays
5 Attacked
6 Trickster
7 Shore indentations
8 Make secret
9 "___ was saying . . ."
10 Walking sound
11 Olympus competitor
12 Brian who managed the Beatles
13 Italian noblewoman
14 Creighton University site
15 Cry of joy in Georgia?
16 Bush and Kerry, once
17 Small square
18 Adolescent
24 Conseil d'___
25 Class
32 Israeli desert
34 Author Rushdie
36 Wall fixtures
37 Filleted
38 West ___ virus
39 Ones sharing a crest
41 Siberian people
42 Weaken
43 Relish
44 Prayer leader
45 Washington or Madison
50 Apprentice
51 "Bloody"
52 One way to have gone
54 Close
57 Warmer and sunnier
58 Several czars
59 Part of the E.U.: Abbr.
62 Commotion at an English school?
67 Tupac, for one
68 Turkish title
69 Marriage site in a Veronese painting
70 "Sock ___ me!"
71 Submission, literally
72 Feudal aristocrat
73 Bygone Las Vegas hotel
75 ___ Prison, setting for the 1979 film "Jericho Mile"
77 Ones who take the cake?
78 "A Doll's House" wife
79 Fed
82 Comical Jacques
83 "Hell ___ no fury . . ."
84 Southwestern crocks
87 Harness tracks
90 Like some waltzes
93 Intelligence officer, at times
94 Classy French theater
95 Behavior
99 ___ Corp., former name for Royal Crown Cola
100 "The Thinker" and "The Kiss," e.g.
101 Auto financing co.
103 "There!"
106 Old station name
107 Period in English literature
108 Kind of package
110 Bone: Prefix
112 Slaughter in Cooperstown
114 "___ out?"
115 ___ Zone
116 Minus
119 It has roots
120 Builder's purchase

by Daniel C. Bryant

ACROSS

1 Item on a chain
7 Deep water
14 Microwaveable lunch sandwich
18 3½ million square mile expanse
19 Lapse
20 Antarctica's Prince ___ Coast
21 Diethyl ether, to butanol
22 Medium, maybe
23 Bone: Prefix
24 Whizzes (by)
25 "Go!"
26 Prepare, as leftovers
28 Authorize
30 Renaissance family name
31 Playground retort
32 ___ given
34 1998 British Petroleum acquisition
36 It has frozen assets
42 Constellation next to Telescopium
43 1969 N.H.L. M.V.P., familiarly
47 Tree with pods
48 Undo, as binder rings
51 Hua's predecessor as Chinese premier
52 Many
54 Starting
55 Recliner feature
57 Brand X
59 Hit, in Variety slang
61 Not far from
62 Bit of editing
64 Big name in construction
66 One making calls
67 Powerful handheld electronic devices
70 Game played on a 49-Down
72 Avalanche victim's salvation
73 Spectra maker
74 Radiate
75 Popular candy since the 1780s
77 Like King Gyanendra
79 "Quién ___?"
81 "Aha"
85 Place to see a camel
87 Scandal
89 Must
90 Spore producer
91 Aunt Chloe's husband, in literature
94 Ethelbert who composed "Mighty Lak' a Rose"
95 Classic brand whose symbol is a tiger
96 "___ bad"
97 Kitchen fixture
99 "Understand?"
101 O's predecessors
102 Simple itinerary destination
106 Interstate sign
109 Old 280Z's and 280ZX's
115 Covered
116 Temperatures
118 Capital that's the home of Lenin Park
119 Distant
120 Lecture
122 Blasted, with "at"
123 See 103-Down
124 Exposed to oxygen
125 Object in le ciel
126 Subtle thieves
127 Big fish, say
128 Lint collector?

DOWN

1 Miniature
2 Had a base in baseball
3 "What ___!"
4 1960s singer Terrell
5 Procter & Gamble brand
6 Laugh sound
7 Vintner's prefix
8 Turn out
9 Some Art Deco works
10 Tokyo airport
11 Road atlas part
12 Port. is part of it
13 Language that favors "sedans" to "saloons"
14 To-do
15 Half of a 1930s vaudeville duo
16 Byes
17 Presidential prerogative
25 Mojave Desert vista
27 Green: Prefix
29 Family pooch
33 Actress Karina who played Scheherazade
35 City SSW of Moscow
36 Heroin, slangily
37 Anemic-looking
38 Coll. major
39 Judges
40 Longtime Lone Ranger player
41 Old section in Algiers
43 Prophet who led Jews back to Jerusalem
44 L.P.G.A. star ___ Turner
45 Campaign need
46 Like some expenses
49 Image this puzzle grid is supposed to suggest
50 Mistaken
53 Quick timeout
56 Prefix with centric
58 Early second-century year
60 Lacking sparkle
63 Cpls.' superiors
65 Morlocks' prey in "The Time Machine"
67 Handy-dandy tool
68 Shares
69 Tricks
71 Farm cries
72 Complimentary closing
74 Roth who directed the 2005 horror flick "Hostel"
76 Silas ___, emissary of the Continental Congress to France
78 River to the Ligurian Sea
80 Half of a noted 1955 merger: Abbr.
82 River that flows by the Hermitage
83 Suffix with neur-
84 Overstudious sort
86 Rope expert's favorite radio station?
88 Poet who wrote "To err is human . . ."
92 Do
93 Smart set?
98 Org. for Va., but not Md.
99 Sporty Pontiac
100 Kicker's aid
102 "Fingersmith"
103 With 123-Across, pleading, perhaps
104 Lazybones
105 Lymphatic system parts
107 Like quaking aspen leaves
108 Stop
110 Angle denoter, in math
111 Permanent site?
112 Pitch-black
113 Seasonal music
114 Start of 67-Across or end of 72-Across, literally
117 Some roulette bets
121 Low mark
122 Rural affirmative

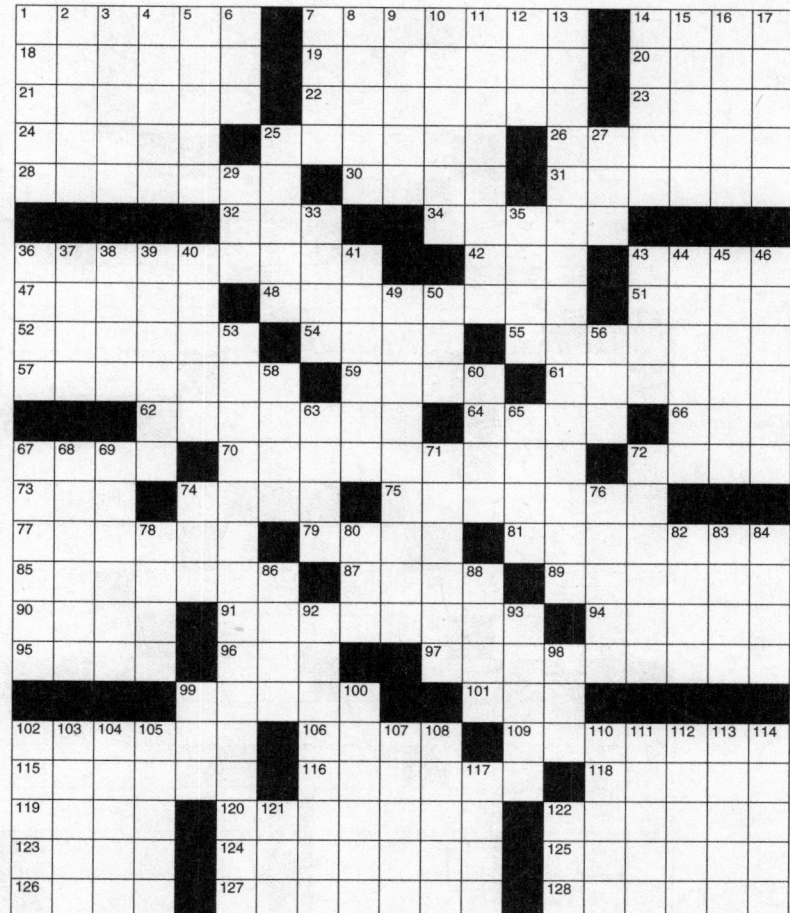

by Michael Shteyman   ℗ = POCKET

ACROSS

1 Military academy freshman
6 Cowbell sound
11 Fingerboard ridge
15 Weaken
18 "___ Gets Drafted" (1942 Disney cartoon)
20 Much-climbed Alpine peak
21 Actor Jared
22 Hamas rival grp.
23 California, compared to Kansas?
25 Kiss
27 Call's companion
28 ___ Ark
29 ___ polloi
30 Jeweler's unit
31 Tweak
33 Silk undies, compared to cotton undies?
37 White-collar worker?
39 Dance to 1920s–'40s jazz
40 Big time
41 "We've been ___!"
42 1990s sitcom based on the British series "One Foot in the Grave"
45 Having seniority
47 Claim valuables
51 Strong suit
52 A waistcoat worn in summer, compared to one worn in winter?
54 In addition
56 Subject in religion class
58 Hero of Tom Clancy novels
59 Jai alai basket
60 Some H.S. math
61 Clinton cabinet member Hazel
63 Dolly of Dollywood
64 Naval base?
65 A one-milligram tablet, compared to a five-milligram tablet?
70 Employee of M
71 Chevrolet sedan
73 Land created by C. S. Lewis
74 "QB VII" novelist
75 Froth
76 Small indentation
80 Go ___ length
81 Formal vote
82 Potatoes and cucumbers, compared to apples and eggplants?
85 Rows on a calendar page
87 Actor Omar of TV's "House"
88 Hang it up
89 1996 Olympic gymnast Strug
90 Spoon-___
93 ___-pitch
94 Tribe of the Amistad slaves
96 Intense, as a gaze
98 Dog show winners, compared to dog show also-rans?
105 Africa's largest country
106 Benefit
107 Wise actions
108 Get the better of
110 Novelist Jaffe
111 Measureless
113 SpongeBob SquarePants's pants, compared to Humpty Dumpty's?
116 Dead heat
117 Stylist's creation
118 Cliff's edge
119 Pass on
120 Airport checkpoint needs
121 Palindromic girl's name
122 Napster downloads
123 Some Southwest scenery

DOWN

1 Pseudonym of musician Peter Schickele
2 Gossipy Parsons
3 Passed
4 Televangelist paroled in 1993
5 Priest in I Samuel
6 French film award
7 How ballerinas dance
8 Tennis star with a shaved head
9 Human cannonball's destination
10 Test for M.A. seekers
11 Elevator stop
12 Is an integral part of
13 "You know the rest" abbr.
14 Bird on a Kellogg's Froot Loops box
15 Slash on a scorepad
16 Here comes the bride
17 They're "born, not made," according to an old saying
19 TV room
24 Pistol, slangily
26 Scientist's formulation
29 Prime
32 Puerto ___
34 Winter blanket
35 Do-nothing
36 Fixed course
38 Spanish city where Seneca was born
43 Pricey vodka, for short
44 Produce
46 H, in Hellas
47 Goes on a spending spree
48 Fix up
49 Where kroons are spent
50 Doesn't take a hit
51 Low-aimed headlights
52 Bollywood film costume
53 Camcorder brand
54 Fabricate
55 Crankcase device
57 One sitting on the porch
60 Pyramus lover, in myth
62 Hunger
63 Actors or athletes
66 "Darn!"
67 Tennis club teacher
68 Stupefied
69 Protective covering
72 Hawaiian band?
76 Fate
77 Natl. Adopt-a-Dog Mo.
78 Hampers
79 "M*A*S*H" setting
83 ___ Stanley Gardner
84 Colonial ___ (insurance firm)
86 Litter contents
89 Banshee sound
90 Zoot suit hats
91 Hyundai model
92 Rulers who inherit their power
93 Flint is a form of it
95 Toxic compound found in cigarette smoke
97 "When Paris sneezes, ___ catches cold"
98 Leafless plants
99 Like planetary orbits
100 Attorney's workload
101 Kipling novel about an orphan boy
102 Musical syllables
103 Vichyssoise vegetables
104 California's Big ___
109 Abbr. on a boiler's gauge
112 Yardbird
113 Air rifle ammo
114 It's sought by conquistadores
115 "That's curious . . ."

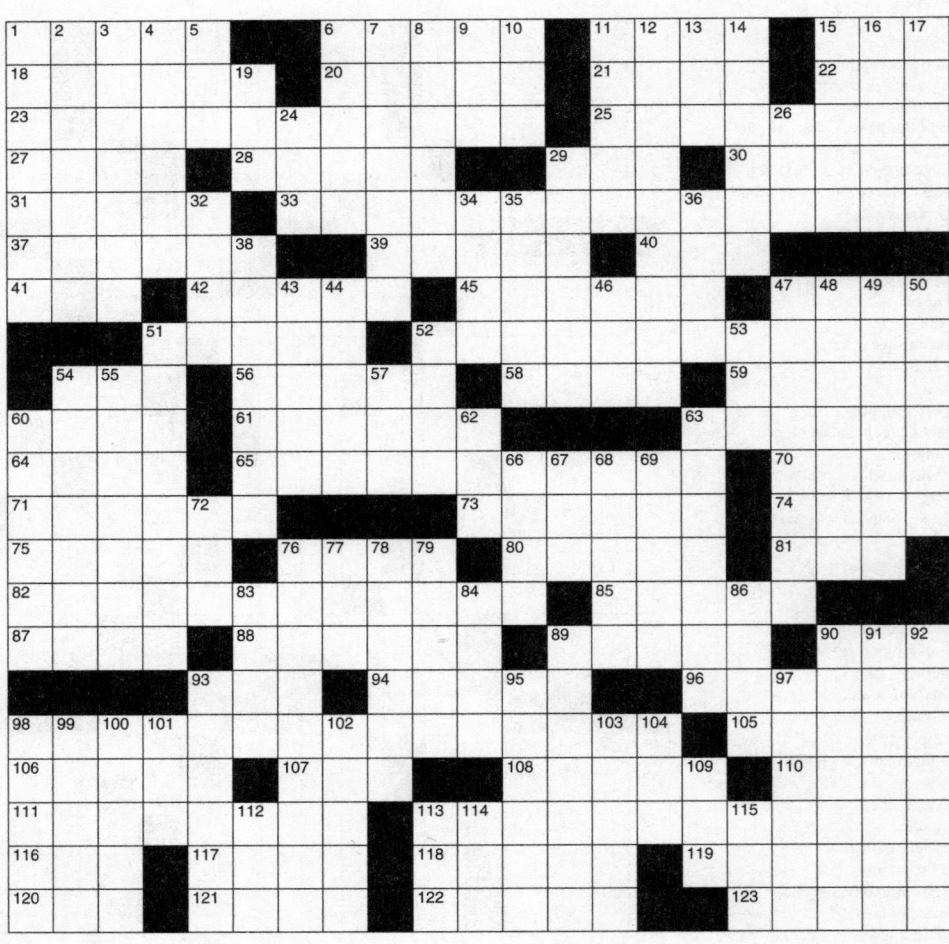

by Patrick Berry

ACROSS

1 Mistress of the spirit world?
8 Was an Orly arrival?
14 "The Old Man and the Sea" catch
20 Handles differently?
21 Historic Honolulu palace
22 Beethoven symphony
23 Writer Fleming as a two-year-old?
25 Ibsen's "Hedda ___"
26 Ring count
27 Sweet 16 org.
28 Yevtushenko poem
29 Shark pools?
30 J.F.K. advisory
32 Playground retort
34 Scrubbed
35 Puzzling
36 Scotland?
41 Sprinkling
42 Talk like a baby
43 "Winnie-the-Pooh" baby
44 Estrous
46 Picture on a $5,000 bill
50 Country with a pentagonal flag
54 View
57 Onetime capital of India
58 One lacking bucks?
61 Austin of TV's "Knots Landing"
62 Actress Meyers
63 Game sometimes called "bucking the tiger"
64 French entree
65 Unwelcome twist
67 Far from loaded
69 Burdensome bird
73 Prepares for a Masters?
74 Lose track?
76 It may need a big jacket
77 Cartoonist Addams
79 Wasted
80 Frost lines
81 Bar owner's job on "The Simpsons"?
85 Prefix with -gon
86 Catalan is its official language
88 Fast ___ Felson, real-life hustler portrayed in "The Hustler"
89 Mister
91 Release
93 With 107-Down, Westerner with an oxymoronic-sounding name buried on Boot Hill
95 Forever and a day
96 Doctor's bag?
98 Guillotine?
103 Heads overseas?
106 Mine transport
108 Flambé
109 Take the course
110 ___ Tzu (dog)
111 Well-armed predator?
114 You can be in it and out of it at the same time
116 Indo-Iranian language
119 John Glenn, e.g.
120 Warning on court testimony?
122 "Star Trek: T.N.G." engineer
123 It was named for the infant Jesus
124 Playroom threat
125 One of the Gallo brothers
126 Actress who starred in two Hitchcock films
127 Emergency situation

DOWN

1 Bach bit
2 Listed
3 The Muses, e.g.
4 40, 60, 75 or 100, commonly
5 Chat room initialism
6 Stocking stuffers
7 Treasure
8 Oregon's state tree
9 Desolate
10 Provoke
11 Part of the Illinois/Indiana border
12 Arriving home after curfew
13 "When Schweine fly!"
14 Prefix with millions
15 ___-American
16 Early bird
17 Comedian Tomlin as a bowler?
18 The Pleistocene Epoch, familiarly
19 Shoe specification
24 Door sign
28 Ape's home
31 "One never knows, ___?": Fats Waller
33 Robe fastener
36 Jolly sounds
37 Alley Oop's girlfriend
38 Grendel and Beowulf
39 W. C. Fields affirmative
40 Special request at a shoe store
42 9/11 Commission subj.
45 Nolan Ryan, for most of the '80s
46 The folks
47 Mutually approve
48 Course for a Maytag repairman?
49 Mrs. James Joyce
51 Foreshadow
52 Marc Antony's love
53 Jared of "Panic Room"
55 Opening
56 Sheriff's badge in the Old West
59 Nick name?
60 Hustler's hangout?
63 Just so you know
66 Some film ratings
68 Devoted friend of Greek legend
70 Shade of white
71 In the heart of
72 The Beatles' "___ Leaving Home"
75 Old global positioning system
78 Destination in the movie "Dumb and Dumber"
82 Bearcats
83 Coolidge Dam river
84 Rodents, playfully
85 Judo ranking
87 Baseball scorecard letters
90 Certain buck
92 Distinction, slangily
94 Tenuous
96 Second fiddle
97 Bow pro
99 Cartoonist Hollander
100 Pulverized
101 Moss Hart's "Act One," e.g.
102 Biased writing?
103 Kvetch
104 There's simply no end to it
105 Ozone layer, for one
107 See 93-Across
110 Clobbered
112 Launch sites . . . or crash sites
113 Complex part?
115 Tyler who wrote "Breathing Lessons"
117 Storage space
118 Didn't break
120 Mumbled assent
121 Chaney Sr. or Jr.

by Bob Klahn

ACROSS

1 Cab Calloway catchphrase
7 Another time
14 Deep-sea diver's worry
22 Tiger cat
23 Not your normal imports
24 After-tax investment choices
25 Elevators . . .
27 Deferential
28 Bar in court
29 Sounds at doctors' checkups
30 Reduced by
32 Owner of the Biography Channel
33 Dumb bunny
35 Diet centers . . .
40 N.Y.U., e.g.
43 Harbor tower
44 ___ test, given to newborn babies
45 Plains tribe
46 Anvils . . .
49 Mice and men, e.g.
54 Pop singer Lavigne
55 Media of exchange
57 Stable baby
59 Cut for a column
60 Settle, for one
61 ___ example
63 Short dash
65 Bride, in Bari
66 Caterpillars . . .
70 Guillotines . . .
72 Paris-to-Lyon dir.
73 Study grant named for a senator
74 Outburst from Homer
76 Ottoman governor
77 Overdoes it
78 Very cool, in '50s slang, with "the"
79 Patio grills . . .
81 Two caliphs
82 Like Sartre's "No Exit"
85 Part of the W. Coast
86 Peace, to Pedro
87 Spanish snack
88 Dernier ___
91 Pace cars . . .
94 Nails . . .
97 Brewery fixtures
98 Make like crazy
100 Department that is home to the Parc Astérix amusement park
101 ___ speak
102 Hilarity
103 Embargoes
104 "Ecce homo" utterer
107 Computer acronym
108 Chews out
110 Real estate developers . . .
113 Minotaur's home
116 Utah lilies
117 NASA vehicle
118 Saint, in Portuguese
119 Cattle . . .
124 "La classe de ___" (Degas work)
126 Make disappear
127 Folk tales
128 Singer Anderson of Jethro Tull
129 Ford competitor, although not in autos
133 Hitchcock specialty
136 Freight trains . . .
141 Boarding school crowd
142 First name in popcorn
143 Typical downtown sign
144 Rasta's messiah
145 African pests
146 Runners' aids

DOWN

1 Julia ___, first woman elected to the American Academy of Arts and Letters
2 Cold treats
3 Ding
4 John of pop
5 Place to wear a gown
6 Polo Grounds slugger
7 Longtime Vermont senator
8 ___ of Evil
9 Dress (up)
10 Biblical verb ending
11 Slowing, in music: Abbr.
12 Visual
13 Barbers brush them
14 "To your health!"
15 Burgle
16 Monet's "Vétheuil en ___"
17 Alternative to reflexology
18 Rough rug fiber
19 Heavens: Prefix
20 Shoemakers' strips
21 Opera singer Simon ___
26 A to Z, e.g.
31 ___-mo
34 Center
35 Self-serving slant
36 Lambs: Latin
37 Conducts
38 Cheer at Gillette Stadium
39 It may be raised at a party
40 Equilibrium
41 Inquisition targets
42 "Dulce et decorum est pro patria mori" writer
44 Make up (for)
47 Friends and neighbors
48 Menotti opera character
50 Prints
51 Pass
52 Stocking material
53 Collar inserts
56 Tanning lotion letters
57 Seafood entree
58 "Members ___"
61 Carol starter
62 Highway department supply
64 Nixon friend Bebe
65 Dr. Seuss's green eggs and ham offerer
67 Times to remember
68 Nutrition author Davis
69 Palme ___ (Cannes award)
71 "SOS!"
75 With it, once
78 Fisher-Price's owner
79 Goes on strike, informally
80 Unlikely pageant winner
81 Penlight batteries
82 Science
83 Author Zora ___ Hurston
84 Son of Henry and father of Henry II
85 Scott of "Ocean's Eleven," 2001
87 Last president of South Vietnam
88 Orangish yellow
89 Acne cream ingredient
90 Enthusiastic assent
92 Violent, perhaps
93 Poodle's cry
95 Hauls around
96 Canadian pump name
99 Bruce of old films
103 Prepared to streak
105 Italy's ___ di Garda
106 State categorically
107 Frequent subject of government approval
109 Hauls around
111 Dallas suburb
112 Mil. commander
114 "Thy Neighbor's Wife" author
115 Rock's Brian
116 Says with a raised hand
119 Godfather's utterances
120 Habituate
121 Photographer Adams
122 Soho serving
123 Grain disease
124 French face cards
125 Counting word
128 Asleep, say
130 Mount SW of Messina
131 ___ Belt
132 CPR pros
134 Serbian city, birthplace of Constantine the Great
135 Six, in Siena
137 "___ had it!"
138 Minor carp
139 Noisy rollers
140 250th anniversary of the incorporation of Los Angeles

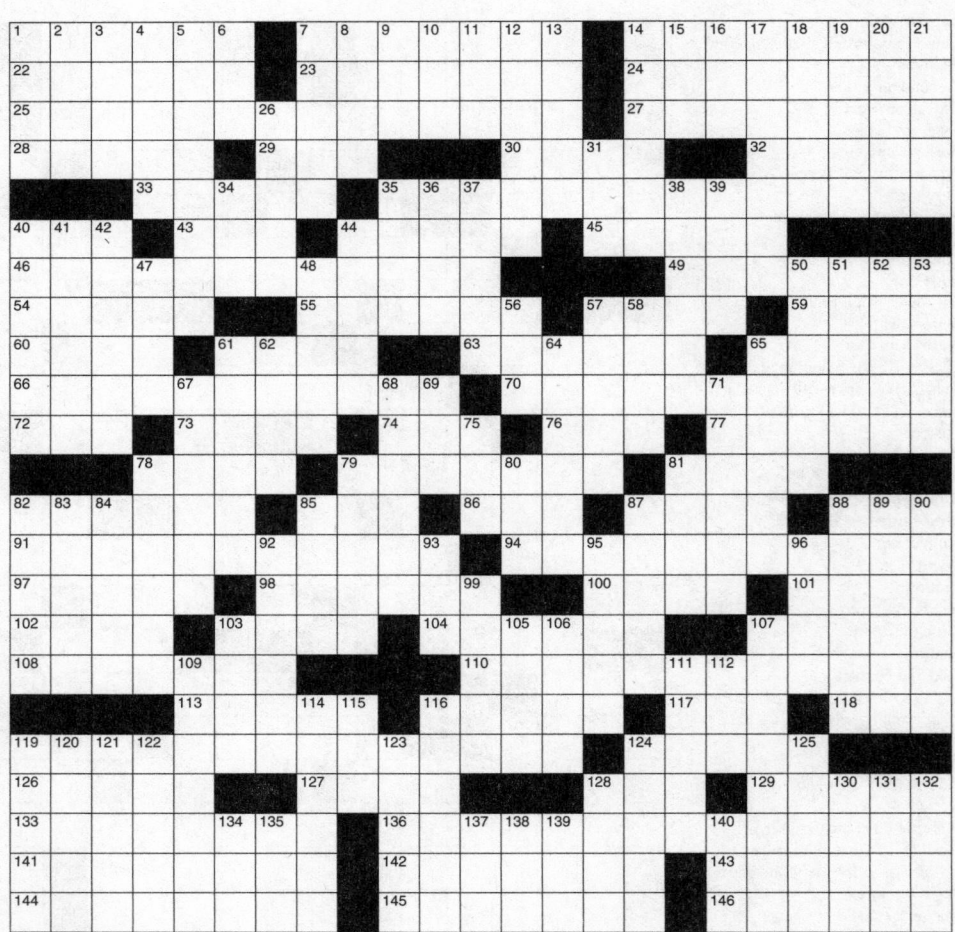

by Paula Gamache

ACROSS

1 Berates
8 Customary manner of doing things
13 Orbital extremes
20 City near Fort Roberdeau
21 Smooths
22 Live it up
23 Tornado abhorrence?
25 Nice 'n Easy maker
26 "___ Isn't So" (Hall & Oates hit)
27 Merry-go-round music
28 Change, chemically
29 Where a prince might work at a hospital?
37 Sounds of understanding
40 These, in Madrid
41 Thicket
42 Mekong River land
43 Never
45 Swabs
47 Foreign, to an American, briefly
48 Lesson from Jack Nicklaus?
51 Cargo on the ill-fated Edmund Fitzgerald
53 Close
54 Nike competitor
55 Fakes it
56 Plunder
57 Road warnings
59 Met highlights
60 Homily about gymnastics?
66 Dye-yielding shrubs
67 Oozes
68 Ballet move
70 Forsaker of the faith
74 "___ here"
75 "Peter Pan" dog
76 Users of barbells, e.g.
77 Losers on "The Apprentice"?
82 Coin words
83 Brings in
84 Wore
85 Onslaught of cold weather
86 Kind of princess
88 K. T. of country music
90 Cockney residence
91 Place for unhappy diners?
96 Schools for engrs.
97 Greek theaters
98 Represent
102 Recent reputed spy organization scandal
105 Red Cross sales strategy?
109 Like a size 8 blouse vis-à-vis a size 10
110 "It's déjà vu all over again" speaker
111 Capitol feature
112 Anarchists, sometimes
113 Fresh
114 Extreme joy

DOWN

1 Dosage units
2 Inter ___
3 Tiny, informally
4 This makes sense
5 Boston area, with "the"
6 Response: Abbr.
7 Make lace
8 Goes up against
9 Grammy winner Lou
10 Disciple's query
11 Cariou of Broadway
12 Dropped stuff
13 Entry
14 Camelot sight
15 Spinachlike plant
16 Solo
17 Where Lux. is
18 Inner: Prefix
19 French seasoning
24 Spicy stew
28 Tears
30 Fungal spore sacs
31 Numbered rds.
32 Mark Harmon action drama
33 Ninny
34 Babbled
35 Noggin
36 Tough turns
37 Uneasiness
38 Uproars
39 "The beloved physician"
44 More frequently, old-style
45 One of five
46 Makes a mess of
47 "Untrue!"
49 King of music
50 Pizza places
51 Maya Angelou's "And Still ___"
52 Opens up a hole in
55 Self-congratulated
57 Deep-sea fishing aid
58 Some O.K.'s, for short
59 "What ___!" (famed Bette Davis line)
61 Defeated, in a way
62 Boards
63 Cousin of radial
64 Close by
65 Two-seater
69 ___ basque (dance step)
70 Elite
71 Feather, zoologically
72 Gift ___
73 Traffic control
77 Actress Garr
78 They can be caught at the beach
79 Vacation destination
80 Political slant
81 Spies' info
83 Relieves (of)
86 Nourish
87 Dessert, in Dover
88 Sometime in the future
89 Native South African village
92 Related on a mother's side
93 Maker of Zima and Killian's Irish Red
94 Locker room emanations
95 Recon, perhaps
99 Kind of steak
100 Added conditions
101 "Don't go!"
102 Municipal facility: Abbr.
103 The "Rocky" film with Mr. T
104 In the past
105 Kids' ammo
106 Grazing area
107 Anger
108 Assn.

by Mike Torch

WHAT'S THE STORY?

ACROSS

1 Picks up
6 Sea lettuce, e.g.
10 Wide open
15 15-Down rival, once
19 Taxing time
20 Attends
21 They're towed away
22 See 98-Across
23 Footwear eaten by an animal?
26 Tumults
27 Page
28 Instant
29 General ___ chicken
31 Old-time welcome
32 Clue that helped convict a movie snack thief?
38 Wretched
39 Get all lovey-dovey
40 Police car maneuver, slangily
41 Cell, e.g.
42 Like the ans. to this clue
43 One in a six-pack
44 N.Y.S.E. and Nasdaq, e.g.
46 Like some fishing hooks
48 Stubborn person getting on another's nerves?
53 Black
54 ___ weight
55 Built
56 Weed
59 Went after
61 Shot up
62 Rub the wrong way
63 Home to some Mongolian nomads
64 Thug whose books aren't selling?
68 Dust Bowl refugee
69 Mitsubishi competitor
70 Vandals
71 Famed Georgia football coach Vince
72 Sparkle
73 Tuna salad ingredient
74 River isles
75 Thick
76 Nicholson negotiating with Stiller and Affleck?
81 Less than explanatory parental explanation
84 Bowls over
85 H.S. class
86 Call from a meadow
87 Cousin of a cobra
88 It must be in the genes
89 B. A. Baracas portrayer on TV
90 Starting to get blue?
92 Supreme rulers blow up a major hardware store?
98 With 22-Across, movie hero of 1977
99 Hot
100 Mortar mixer
101 Acute
102 Twin sister of Ares
104 Cousins of a disheveled wading bird?
111 Going ___
112 Spots on a graph
113 One of the Waughs
114 Priest's urging
115 "Only Time" singer
116 Annual parade honoree, for short
117 Point
118 Sound at the front of East Hampton

DOWN

1 Buddy of the Clintons, e.g.
2 Apple had one in 1980: Abbr.
3 Funky do
4 Called
5 Due for a drop-off?
6 "Like that matters"
7 Actor Cariou
8 Bugs
9 Leftovers at a barbecue
10 Hedge fund whiz, for short
11 "Whaddaya know"
12 What two palms up may indicate
13 Hoop star's entourage
14 Prevent
15 Traditional Olympics powerhouse
16 Sugary quaff
17 Eastern European
18 Like some provocatively colored lips
24 Pencil holder
25 System start-up?
30 William Styron title heroine
32 Kind of support
33 "This should get you started . . ."
34 Unelite, in London
35 Eccentric
36 Singer/radio host John
37 "___ Lap" (1983 film)
38 Did nothing
43 They don't provide outlets
44 Stuck
45 Be acquainted with Vanna?
46 Diplomat Boutros Boutros-___
47 Tear-jerkers often have one
49 Try
50 Biblical shepherd
51 Shepherd's concern
52 Radiates
56 It has six holes
57 Peter and the Wolf's "duck"
58 Like some sums
59 Horse sound
60 Long walk
61 Andrea Doria's domain
62 Wash out
63 Write (for)
65 Columnist Mike
66 ___ Chris Steak House (restaurant chain)
67 Saturn and Mercury, for two
73 House keepers
74 Negative campaign feature
75 Water, perhaps
76 Be in harmony
77 Billionth: Prefix
78 Intruder's deterrent, maybe
79 Chaps
80 Starr of song
81 "Count me in"
82 Arid
83 Extra
88 Dusty floor cleaner
89 Breakfast cereal
90 Ungodlike
91 Must pay
93 Station house figures
94 Jump for joy
95 Ship over there?
96 Show agreement with
97 Pint-sized, downsized
103 Irish ___
105 Elhi org.
106 Mil. transport
107 Knockout of knockouts
108 ___-Tiki
109 Beethoven's "Minuet ___"
110 Once

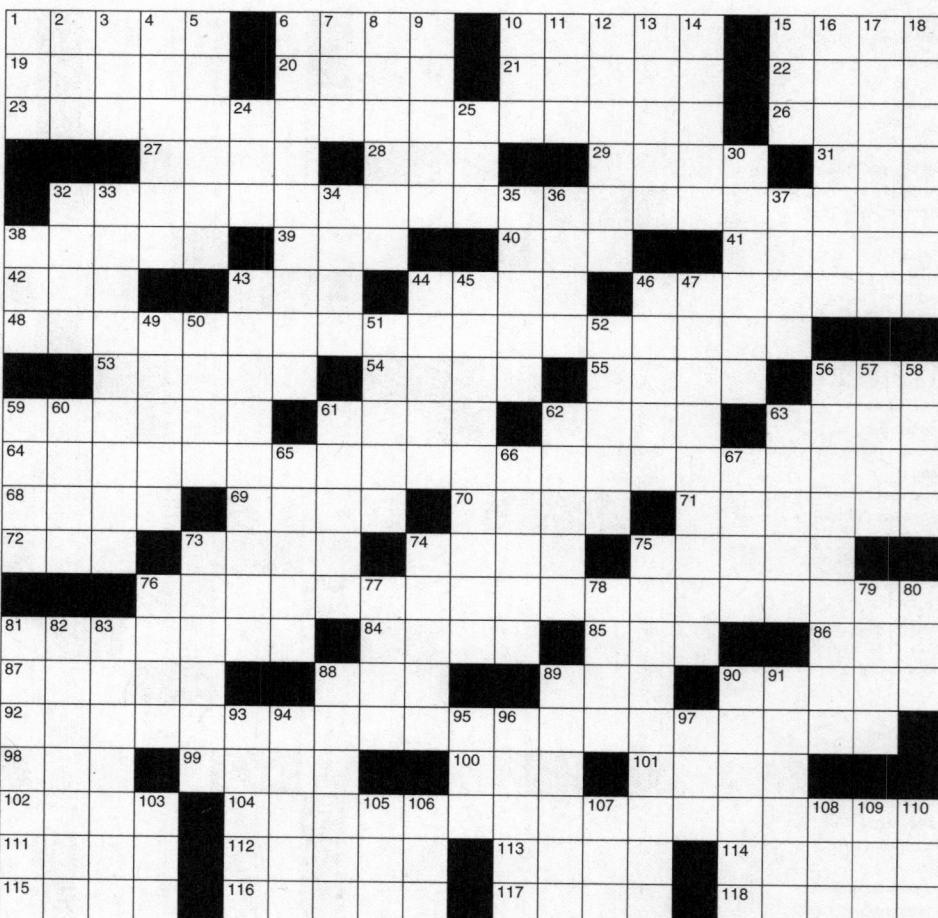

by Joe DiPietro

ACROSS

1 "Exodus" hero
4 Film director Petri
8 "Pow!"
12 Chicago's ___ Aquarium
17 Novel by Toni Morrison
19 Coquette
20 View from Mauna Kea
21 Frighten away
22 Winning it is a sweet victory
25 Many an archaeological site
26 Lock, stock and barrel
27 Overdoes it
28 Eats at home
29 Goes over again
31 River in Irkutsk
32 Meddle
33 Big name in ice cream
34 Cheapskate
36 Latin case
40 Lo-___
41 TV show since 1/6/75
43 Treasury
45 Imported wheels
48 D.C. bigwig
49 "À votre ___!"
50 Signature piece?
51 Emulated a cat burglar
53 West Indies isle
55 Deflected
59 Gradually decline
61 Car wash sight
62 Stern who saved Carnegie Hall
64 Whopper
65 Music producer Brian
66 Add light, or not (and do this 13 more times to solve this puzzle)
69 Ocean State sch.
70 Put down, on the street
71 Gushes forth: Var.
72 Owns
73 Criminal
75 Not in the middle
77 Something's brewing here
80 Accompanies to the airport
81 Film buff's cable choice
82 Nut tree
84 Never, to Mozart
86 Followers: Suffix
87 Sweeping
90 Concealable weapon
93 Prefix with friendly
94 1960s TV western
95 Lowermost ship deck
96 Abbr. in a personal ad
99 Like some student housing
102 Subject of a May tribute
104 License
106 Bad state to be in
107 Security holder
110 Bacteriologist's study
111 Sound of a willow in the wind
112 End-of-meal serving
114 More beloved
115 Make up for
116 Needlepoint shop purchase
117 One of two bath towels
118 Popular mixer maker
119 Commuter map points: Abbr.
120 Some 20th-century art
121 Aug. clock setting

DOWN

1 Have big plans (to)
2 Like an imploded soufflé
3 "Well, here goes . . ."
4 Personifies
5 Lucy of "Ally McBeal"
6 Regarding, to counsel
7 Deafening silence, e.g.
8 "Bummer!"
9 Word just before a snap
10 Orders at McSorley's
11 Skylight?
12 Barely enough
13 More strapping
14 Elimination
15 Judge
16 Quality of cooking
18 Spiky plant
21 Resoluteness
23 Hospital danger
24 ___ choy (Chinese vegetable)
28 Intentional loss, in boxing
30 Trapshooting
35 Where gringos live
37 "___ cost to you"
38 King in 1922 news
39 Follower of Paul?
41 Use a towel
42 Show Me State river
43 Pieces of cake
44 How Elvis albums are rereleased
45 Followed, as advice
46 Pertaining to element 92
47 Boot out
50 Statue of Liberty attraction
52 "I'm not making this up!"
54 Skeptics' remarks
55 Corpulent
56 Dodges
57 Most hopeless
58 Little-used clubs
60 How many magazine articles are written
62 "As ___ saying . . ."
63 "Yes sir!," south of the border
67 Land on the other side of the Atl.
68 Figures in Iranian history
74 "No, mein Herr!"
76 Badger
77 Shepherd
78 Commerce department staffers
79 "The Da Vinci Code," e.g.
82 High jump need
83 Collie's charge
85 "I" trouble
87 "Portrait of a Musician" artist, familiarly
88 Earns over time
89 Loudly enjoys, as a joke
90 Freshness
91 Hit one out of the park
92 Raised
94 Siren
96 Reacted to a heartthrob
97 Works of artist Max
98 Least restricted
100 Oxford measure
101 Needing more sun
103 Hurrah for El Farruco
105 N.Y. Philharmonic, e.g.
107 Trump
108 Voyaging
109 Singer James
112 Gets into
113 Place for a meeting: Abbr.

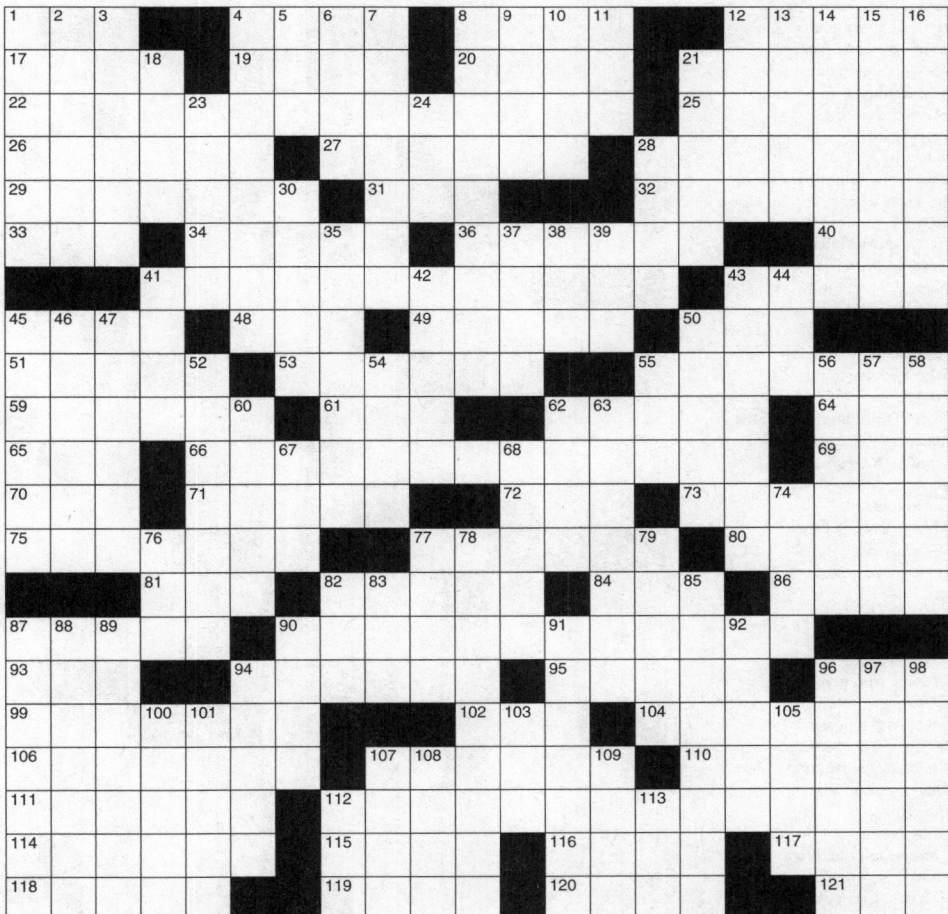

by Elizabeth C. Gorski

ACROSS

1 Long narrative poem
7 Outlaw Kelly
10 Uses a ring, maybe
17 Camp Pendleton group
19 Summer treats
21 Brand of sports drink
22 Long time that just flies by?
24 An Easter egg hunt may have one
25 Long bones
26 Nickname of a boxer who converted to Islam?
28 Board member: Abbr.
29 3 for 2 and 4: Abbr.
30 A camera may be set on this
31 Matter to the jury
32 Mao's grp.
33 Wing, say
36 Supermarket checkout action
39 It gets in the groove
42 Bee product?
47 Befalls
50 Enjoys a hammock
51 Slip into
52 Whom bouncers might bounce
53 Law firm aide, for short
54 Not just approximately
55 Conventioneers' place
57 Duo that might review films based on arcade games?
62 In a workable manner
67 Most fibrous
68 Like some siblings
69 Water color
70 Ticks off
71 What King Arthur's men would like to have seen more of along the way?
73 Offensive basketball position
75 Where a haircut may end
76 Claim of a sort
77 ____ for the long haul
81 Don't chug
82 Stage after pupation
84 Monte ____
86 "Therefore, I have proven the existence of jalapeños!"?
90 With 40-Down, a 1975 horror novel
91 Some crockery
92 Director's second try
96 1940s spy grp.
97 Sound made with outstretched neck
99 Rings of islands
101 O.A.S. member: Abbr.
102 Sitarist Shankar
104 Grizzlies who give great interviews?
108 Movie with a posse
110 Photographer's setting
112 Possible response to "My boss is leaving and I hate his replacement"?
114 Fitting into a joint
115 Phrase usually before a colon
116 1972 U.S. Open champion
117 Stew
118 Cartoonist Avery
119 Got behind, with "for"

DOWN

1 Printer's unit
2 Pope of 1963–78
3 Rubber gaskets
4 Printer's unit
5 Speed-skating gold medalist Karin
6 Common Market letters
7 Angina treatment, for short
8 O.A.S. member: Abbr.
9 "Citizen Ruth" actress, 1996
10 Senators' wear
11 "Trainspotting" star Bremner
12 Short-finned ____
13 Uncommon delivery
14 It's used with some frequency
15 Singer Brickell
16 Where scenes are seen
18 Title with a number, perhaps
20 Heroine of TV's "Alias," for short
21 Cut back
23 Kook
27 Brunch buffet items
30 Father-and-daughter fighters
32 Small brain size
34 Places for fish
35 Forest sticker
36 Part of a heartbeat
37 Cool ____
38 Stubborn one
39 Where God sent Jonah
40 See 90-Across
41 Officer with a half-inch stripe: Abbr.
43 Stepped
44 Substantiate
45 Outhouse issue
46 Simple bunk
47 Part of "The Alphabet Song"
48 Italian-born explorer of the New World
49 Blintz relative
54 Destructive stuff
55 Grass and such
56 Disbeliever's cry
58 Sub
59 Hockey stat
60 Mag. staff
61 Grabs some chow?
63 Put a stop to
64 King Louis XII's birthplace
65 "Network" director, 1976
66 Kind of question
69 Sault ____ Marie
71 Letter before resh
72 Each
74 Trader ____
77 Test results, sometimes
78 United Feature Synd. partner
79 Warm assent
80 Joan Collins's villain on "Batman"
82 U.N. agcy.
83 With, in Wiesbaden
84 Non-dean's list grades
85 Reading and the like: Abbr.
87 Chanted sounds
88 Device with a scroll wheel
89 Con junction
93 Surpass in gluttony
94 Ominous-sounding phrase
95 Put down roots?
97 Reims's department
98 Universal donor blood type, for short
99 Skintight material
100 Tomfool finish
102 Hindu avatar
103 Fat as ____
104 Classroom handout
105 E.P.A. pollution meas.
106 Batter's ploy
107 The Auld Sod
108 "In that range"
109 About
111 Plane heading?
113 Onetime Mideast union: Abbr.

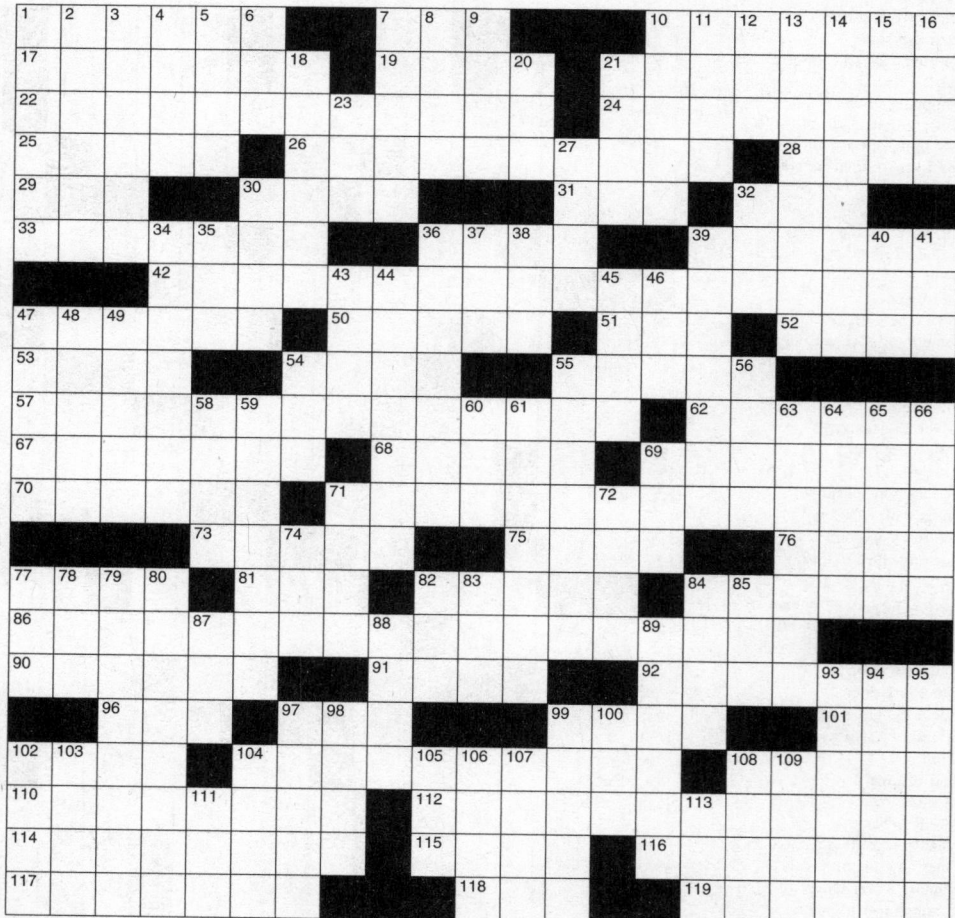

by Trip Payne

ACROSS

1 White-collar position
6 Big guy
10 "Did you ___?!"
14 Moo goo gai pan pan
17 Sonata movements
18 Not the most reliable set of wheels
20 Little-known
22 It surrounds the Isle of Man
23 "New Look" pioneer
24 Eastern way
25 Half-German/half-Indian film hero
27 Cymbal in a drum kit
31 3-D figures
32 "I hope to see London once ___ I die": "Henry IV, Part 2"
33 Cognizance
34 Carnegie's cronies
36 Comment made after jumping in a pool, maybe
38 State strongly
41 Faultfinders
44 Throaty sound
46 Eye sockets
48 Certain ID check
49 Cross shape
50 Obstructor of congress?
54 ___ Sunday, the fourth Sunday in Lent
55 Farm pitcher
56 "The Time Machine" race
57 Agatha and Dahlia, in P. G. Wodehouse books
58 What this puzzle's circled spaces represent
64 Subject of a Michelangelo sculpture
67 Westminster area
68 L. L. Bean competitor
72 Made fun of, in a way
73 Ring duo
77 Hairstyling need
78 2000 Elton John/Tim Rice musical
79 Fluoroscope inventor
81 Traditional Christmas Eve meal in Germany
82 Drink served in a tall glass
84 Hoof handlers
86 Rtes.
90 Startled cry
91 Reuters competitor
93 Refresher
95 Casino fixture
101 Hunter slain by Artemis
102 Gillette brand
103 "What ___ care?"
104 Five or ten, say
105 Unsuccessful, as a mission
110 Bear in mind
111 Appropriate
112 Blubberless marine mammals
113 Leftmost digital watch no.
114 Recycle bin fillers
115 Tap sites
116 Boon to Scottish tourism

DOWN

1 Fuddy-duddy
2 1988 De Niro thriller
3 Under a false name, briefly
4 G
5 Sleeping sickness carriers
6 Sports ___
7 Cereal grass
8 Schindler's business partner in "Schindler's List"
9 Sonatas, e.g.
10 Like some mushrooms
11 Florida's ___ Beach
12 "Hostel" director ___ Roth
13 1950 film that retells the same events four times
15 Mountain nymph
16 "Beauty is truth, truth beauty" writer
18 Potsherds
19 Passed (away)
21 "What nonsense!"
26 Intersected
28 Grp. involved in "the Troubles"
29 Flavor lender
30 Ludicrous
31 M.I.T.'s ___ School of Management
35 Ending with defer or refer
36 "Goldberg Variations" composer
37 Daughter of Uranus
38 Count
40 Super-duper
42 Big ___
43 Appeals to
45 Out of sorts
47 The place of one's fodder?
48 Does a run
51 Snakes with vestigial limbs
52 Escort's offering
53 Lettuce type
54 Country
57 "Son of ___!"
59 It serves many courses: Abbr.
60 Juicer
61 Former Hong Kong leader Tung ___ Hwa
62 Lacking sense
63 One of the Bobbsey Twins
64 Star followers
65 Group that includes the U.A.E.
66 Picks
69 Girder with flanges
70 It may come with a gift
71 European peaks
73 Render unavailable
74 First of all
75 Molière comedy, with "The"
76 Became an item
80 Brother of Ham and Japheth
83 Honored alumni, usually
85 Rest cure destination
87 Bugs that live in trees
88 Actress Merkel
89 Ancient Turkish dynasty founder
92 Mini-maps
93 Whistle wearer
94 Garden spot
96 Shabby treatment
97 Soirees
98 Pillbox quantities
99 ___ ware (Japanese porcelain)
100 Clipped
102 Hot room, colloquially
106 Gilbert & Sullivan princess
107 Carry with effort
108 Collection agcy.?
109 Took in

by Patrick Berry

ACROSS

1 Codger
5 Mischief maker of myth
9 1945 news, in headlines
14 "Amerika" author
19 Part of the Dept. of Labor
20 Option for heads
21 Indian queen
22 It begins "Sing, goddess, the wrath of Peleus' son . . ."
23 Seasonal salutation
25 "Jeopardy!" phrase
27 Start of quote
29 Column of boxes on a questionnaire
30 Failing grades
31 Shipboard cries
32 Nursery cry
35 Column of boxes on a questionnaire
38 Of a heart chamber
42 New at the beach, maybe
43 Part 2 of quote
49 Very wide spec.
50 Command to a dog
51 -like
52 Geometry figure?
53 Of a certain hydrocarbon group
54 Crew alternative
57 Bombay-born dancer Juliet
59 Lao-tzu follower
62 "The Return of the Jedi" girl
64 Latin 101 verb
65 Montgomery of jazz
68 Part 3 of quote
73 Originally
74 Carry
75 Drug drop, maybe
76 Goolagong of tennis
77 Sight for sore eyes?
79 Capital of Meurthe-et-Moselle, France
82 Trials
83 Like some cats
86 ___ minimum
88 Langston Hughes poem
90 ___ the finish
91 Part 4 of quote
96 Zero
97 Shark, e.g.
98 Postpaid encl.
99 Suffix with lact-
100 Cup holder
102 Alternative to gov or edu
104 Related maternally
108 End of quote
115 Time to grow rice
117 Pictorial
119 Kind of acid
120 Dock site
121 Tongue site
122 Slick
123 Actress Graff
124 Goes a mile a minute
125 Cache contents
126 Fill

DOWN

1 Shipping option, for short
2 Words on a medicine bottle
3 Opposite of hog
4 Closet contents of a 21-Across
5 Trysts
6 Admits, with "up"
7 Acquaintances
8 Very impressed
9 Ray, Klee and Millais
10 Thai money
11 "That's ___ haven't heard!"
12 Willfully tightening the screws, say
13 Calcutta native
14 Wellington natives
15 Architect William van ___
16 Computer protection
17 Chiang ___-shek
18 Pop-ups, e.g.
24 Pad user
26 Slippery
28 Miles away
33 Jai ___
34 Drove
36 1999 Ron Howard comedy
37 Nine inches
39 Robert, for one
40 Police dept. employee
41 Guru habitat
42 Purple shade
43 Colorful wrap
44 Fictional donkey
45 Oliver's love in "As You Like It"
46 "___ the Needle" (1981 movie)
47 Like some acoustic music
48 Composer Mahler
49 Stationery brand
55 Something to pop
56 Nobel-winning economist Lawrence
58 Medical suffix
60 Rodney Dangerfield's "I don't get no respect," e.g.
61 Like the arrangement of gems in some bracelets
63 "The Shelters of Stone" heroine
65 A Ryder
66 The Supreme Court, e.g.
67 View for Shakespeare?
69 Eur. land
70 Undo
71 One of the Gandhis
72 "Holy cow!"
77 Grabber's cry
78 People: Prefix
80 Cig. purchases
81 Film character who says "Do, or do not. There is no 'try'"
83 Fifth-century year
84 2003 A.L. M.V.P., to fans
85 Go-getter
87 1977 double-platinum Steely Dan album
89 Checks out
92 Exclamation at the end of a trip
93 Résumé parts
94 ___ Mix
95 Actress Zellweger
100 Utah's ___ Canyon
101 Literary inits.
103 Bright circle?
105 Bushes rarely seen nowadays
106 Leg part
107 Glorify
109 "Come ___!"
110 Fall off
111 Madonna's "La ___ Bonita"
112 No bystander
113 Physicist with an element named after him
114 ___ Penh
115 Diamond stat.
116 MSN competitor
118 Burn cause

by Ashish Vengsarkar

ACROSS

1 Voyaging
5 Hitchhiker
10 Percentage
15 Somewhat
19 Writes quickly
21 Plaque, e.g.
22 Volcanic formation
23 Show a Woody Allen feature?
25 Heart
26 Mangy mutt
27 Medical research org.
28 Not a substitute
29 Thomas Paine, for one
30 Magazine supply
32 Certain spawner
34 Quick trip
35 Bryologists' study
36 What ageists do?
41 Sad
44 One side in a debate
45 Kung ___ chicken
48 Off the mark
49 Razzes
53 Ties up
55 3.26 light-years
57 Abandon the Centennial State?
59 Sound from a hot tub
60 Yellow flag
61 Env. science
62 Night school subj.
65 Not-so-Big Apple?
72 Lead-in for long
73 Abbr. on an envelope
75 Words of concession
76 Airline abbr.
78 Cut an awful demo?
84 Sot's state
88 Saw
89 Feel extreme discouragement
91 Sports page news
92 Show featuring many alumni of L.A.'s Groundlings comedy troupe
93 Mineral residue
95 Made multiple
97 Drink at a Kyoto reunion?
101 Certain Arab
104 Each
105 Book before Phil.
106 Make a mad dash
110 On the range, say
111 Summertime quaffs
114 Like about half the world's pop.
116 God, in Roma
117 Insipid
118 What a hypnotist might do for help?
121 Construction financed by a hedge fund?
122 Eastern European
123 Happens
124 Tavern selections
125 To the point
126 Köln or Nürnberg
127 Like a spent campfire

DOWN

1 Org. for pound watchers?
2 Flu fighter
3 Vast, in verse
4 Descriptive wd.
5 Most spicy
6 Wrapped up
7 Monk's title
8 Greek vowels
9 Best Musical of 1996
10 Experts, slangily
11 Babe or fox
12 Alternative to a dish
13 Big laugh
14 West end?
15 Public ___
16 Czar in a Mussorgsky opera
17 Busy
18 Transcripts
20 Capitol Hill abbr.
24 Biblical verb
29 Crunchy chip
31 The Pearl of the Black Sea
33 Like ears
35 Traveler's stop
37 It runs down the leg
38 Peter Fonda title role
39 Actor Beatty and others
40 Completely
41 Baby's resting spot
42 G.P.'s grp.
43 45-Down in Russian
45 43-Down in English
46 Fire
47 "___ Mio"
50 One-pointers
51 First name in courtroom drama
52 Stay up nights
54 Charlemagne's realm: Abbr.
56 A.L. or N.L. Central city
58 Ejaculate
62 Tombstone brothers
63 Place for an outboard motor
64 Maj.'s superior
66 Just a bite
67 Suffix with form
68 Mary in the White House
69 Longtime Ferrara family name
70 Places for forks: Abbr.
71 Where something may be brewing
74 Mo. with topaz as its birthstone
77 Precisionist
79 Automaker's bane
80 Donald Duck, e.g.
81 Stove or washer: Abbr.
82 How you may know something
83 All-American name
85 La ___, Bolivia
86 Ben Jonson wrote one to himself
87 Like Twizzlers, usually
90 Hospital hookup
94 Unknown element
96 Emily Dickinson's home
97 Bidding card game
98 Cultural entertainment
99 Spin
100 Candid
101 Kind of queen
102 Acoustic
103 Cup, maybe
107 Best and Ferber
108 Common aspiration
109 Grier of the gridiron
111 Memo starter
112 Makes a move
113 Politician's goal
115 Star athlete, briefly
118 Outer: Prefix
119 Reggae relative
120 In the manner of

by Timothy Powell

ACROSS

1 Wide-eyed
6 "Help wanted"
9 Bass productions
13 Big name in cards
18 Kind of spray
19 Investment mgr.'s subject
20 Exasperated cry in a 1950s sitcom
21 "Wake up!"
22 Gold gathering dust?
25 Shish kebab need
26 Tested in a fitting room
27 Lower oneself
28 It has wings but doesn't fly
29 On Soc. Sec.
30 Deportment on the Discovery?
32 One having a ball at the circus?
35 "Don't make such ___!"
37 Prefix with phobia
38 Hi-___
39 Rear ends, slangily
41 One slightly higher in a tree
44 Very, very soft, in music
46 Supersized marathon?
50 Attacked, in a way
54 Summer cooler
55 Not agin
56 Target
57 Hit musical with the song "Razzle Dazzle"
59 Kind of badge
61 Mix
62 Spread dirt
63 What Edmund Hillary had?
68 Advertising "spokesman" since 1916
71 Oscar ___ Hoya
72 Strepitous
76 Model
77 1945 Robert Mitchum war film
79 Datebook abbr.
81 Old home loan org.
82 Shorthand taker
83 "Let's try e-tailing!"?
87 Dress (up)
89 Snoopy
90 Lets go
91 Trouble
94 Place for a stream
96 Like some buggy drivers
98 Sudoku and others
99 Pre-trial blunder?
104 "Concentration" pronoun
106 Struck out
107 Turn red, maybe
108 She may be off her rocker
112 Outdid in
113 Neigh?
115 Diner
116 Really digging
117 It may be inflated
118 Bait
119 Comics canine
120 Role for 45-Down in "Angels in America"
121 Spotted
122 Some hook shapes

DOWN

1 Acad.
2 Product that comes as a cream or wax
3 City ESE of Turin
4 Ignominious end
5 Pass over
6 Ink
7 Venus or Mars
8 Allies in the Gulf war
9 "___ lost!"
10 Dramatist Pirandello who wrote "Six Characters in Search of an Author"
11 Low-budget prefix
12 Dict. listing
13 Ruthless attitude
14 Thalassographer's study
15 Tankard material
16 State capital since 1889
17 Pressure
21 Only key Irving Berlin composed in
23 What a lover of kitsch has
24 Marked down
28 HBO competitor
30 Deliberate
31 Turkey club?
32 Split
33 ___ Cologne
34 Li'l Broadway role for Peter Palmer
36 Longtime baseball union head Donald ___
40 Strong out of the gate
41 Hershey bar
42 Diminutive suffix
43 Little louse
45 See 120-Across
47 ___ fide (in bad faith)
48 Sundial hour
49 Ones getting base pay?: Abbr.
51 High fiber?
52 Sensitive subject, to some
53 Strauss's "___ und Verklärung"
58 Philosopher Chu ___
60 Words from a backpedaler
61 12-time baseball All-Star, 1934–45
62 Fed. property overseer
64 Game with a seven-card draw
65 Trevor who directed "Cats"
66 Low hand
67 First Hebrew letter: Var.
68 AWOL chasers
69 Backstabber
70 Opposite of post-
73 Red leader?
74 Drew back
75 Eastwood's "Rawhide" role
77 It was "really lookin' fine" in a 1964 pop hit
78 "___ for Innocent" (Sue Grafton novel)
79 Dos follower
80 In the sky, maybe
84 "Dedicated to the ___ Love"
85 Russian poet ___ Mandelstam
86 Transgressions
88 High spirits
91 Building blocks
92 Put down
93 Sleep inducer
95 Part of a U.K. business name
96 On the calm side
97 Playful creatures
100 Playful creature
101 Home of the Black Bears
102 Last inning, usually
103 Secretly watch
105 Refuse
108 Wax
109 Turns down
110 Brood
111 Army members?
113 Quick shot?
114 Org. for drivers

by Patrick Blindauer

ACROSS

1 Where to stick a pick
5 Stay-at-home dad
10 Volunteer's words
14 Spanish eyes
18 Seller of Kenmore appliances
20 Belly button type
21 Well-known
22 Chianti or Orvieto
23 Horoscope Writer
25 Hostlers
27 ___ kwon do
28 "Two eggs over easy," e.g.
29 Look
30 Illegal lighting?
31 Hardly a hipster
33 Puzzle Editor
37 Rainbow component
38 Fifth word of the Gettysburg Address
39 Bakery offering
40 The son on "Sanford and Son"
42 Foreign Affairs Editor
46 "Jurassic Park" terror, for short
48 Soldiers of Saruman, in Tolkien
49 Connecticut collegian
50 Go over again, in a way
52 Like a prima ballerina
54 Nickname for Dartmouth
58 Peak in Thessaly
61 Pince-___
62 Washington city on Puget Sound
63 "Handyman's Corner" Columnist
67 Survivor
68 Sicilian seaport
69 Debonair
73 Obituary Writer
75 Start eating
76 Clear (of)
77 Survive
78 Dogs that rarely bark
79 Lettuce
81 Sparkle
85 A as in Amiens
86 Coin in Cancún
87 Nero's love
90 Book Reviewer
94 Some are blessed
96 Opposite of kick
98 One way to go
99 It may be run up
100 Travel Editor
102 Fruit with a pit
106 Like the stone that slew Goliath
108 It's just over a foot
109 Cockpit need
111 Isaac Asimov mystery "Murder at the ___"
112 Lost one?
114 Weather Page Editor
117 Shamu, for one
118 Bounder
119 News in sports
120 Traditional Sunday fare
121 Oom-___ (tuba sounds)
122 Something that's struck
123 Alternative to stamp
124 Cinematic beekeeper

DOWN

1 Send an invitation for
2 Untamed
3 Like the crown of the Statue of Liberty
4 Places for M.D.'s and R.N.'s
5 Antiquated
6 Any of TV's Clampetts
7 Turkey's highest point
8 Quaker State, e.g.
9 Tillis who sang "I Ain't Never"
10 Viewable
11 Party professional
12 Maytag acquisition of 2001
13 Colo. neighbor
14 [continued on the other side]
15 High School Sports Reporter
16 Perfume quantity
17 14-liners
19 Butt of jokes
24 Element whose name comes from Greek for "inactive"
26 Holy man
29 Non-PC?
32 Away's partner
34 "Good shot!"
35 Present time in France?
36 A year before the Battle of Hastings
39 Fats Domino's "I've ___ Around"
41 Velvety cotton fabric
42 Physicist with a unit named after him
43 Ticking
44 Star in Orion
45 ___ à manger (ready to eat, in France)
47 Morales of "N.Y.P.D. Blue"
51 "M" star
53 Hire
55 Area between posts
56 Change, as part of a computer program
57 Accusatory phrase
59 British actress Sylvia
60 "No seats left"
63 Pantry stock
64 Put on cloud nine
65 Race
66 Spanish cubist Juan
68 Org. whose members' lies are discussed on TV
70 Twain's ___ Joe
71 "Goosebumps" author R. L. ___
72 Canadian lout
74 Light
75 See
76 Gardening Columnist
78 The N.B.A.'s Elvin Hayes, to fans
79 First Irish P.M.
80 Ski wear
82 Hurl everywhere
83 Number's target?
84 Person living along a large stream, informally
86 Litter site
88 Lover of Eurydice, in myth
89 Gold watch recipient, maybe
91 Animal with a flexible snout
92 Turmoil
93 King, in Portugal
95 Air Force noncom: Abbr.
97 Shell game
101 Schoolyard retort
102 Chicago's ___ Planetarium
103 Lock site
104 Scale-busting
105 Discrimination
107 Peeples and Vardalos
110 White House worker
113 Dadaist Jean
114 NCR product
115 Ante-
116 Slip in a pot

by Maxwell H. D. Johnson Jr.

ACROSS

1 Trumps
6 Frame part
10 Thrill
14 Slaves
19 Ring around the collar?
20 Copycat
21 Tones
22 Like some monuments at night
23 Dear old dad the comedic foil always told me to ___
26 Châteauneuf-du-Pape locale
27 This may shock you
28 Scottish turndowns
29 German crowd?
30 Whine
31 Tower, often
34 The first place
35 "Quit dreaming"
36 Peace, in Russia
37 Common connections
39 Period
41 Supermarket chain with the slogan "Hometown Proud"
42 Dear old dad the umpire always told me to ___
47 Termite clearer?
49 Oxlike antelope
50 Windflowers
52 [That punch hurt!]
53 Brooklyn-born rapper
54 The Seven Dwarfs, by profession
56 Tropical ornamental
61 Blaster
62 Hatha and others
63 Hick
64 Horse/donkey cross
65 Extend, as a line
67 Clinch, with "up"
68 In
70 Traffic director
71 W.W. II aircraft
74 One making a pit stop, maybe
76 New Test. book
77 Hollywood setting
79 Like some sects
80 Bygone polit. cause
81 The Maurice Podoloff Trophy is awarded to its M.V.P.
82 "Green Acres" co-star
84 Tony winner Uta
86 Learn about through books
90 Dear old dad the builder always told me to ___
92 Commuting options
93 Impala, e.g.
95 Booster grp.?
96 Fairness-in-hiring abbr.
97 Marine bioluminescence
99 Stay in line
101 Honeyed pastry
105 This clue has two of them (for short)
106 Eats
107 Big name in faucets
109 Wallace who wrote "Ben-Hur"
110 Habituate
111 Dear old dad the sharpshooter always taught me to ___
115 They're easy to catch
116 Support, with "up"
117 Jackie Robinson's alma mater
118 An emirate
119 Panda hangouts
120 Itches
121 Turn off
122 Economize

DOWN

1 More lowdown
2 Woman's name that sounds like two consecutive French letters
3 Sell outside the stadium
4 Great deal
5 Regular: Abbr.
6 Modern name for old Cipango
7 Place for icons
8 Queens subject?
9 "It's a cold one!"
10 Bilbo's home
11 City NW of Crater Lake
12 Old pop
13 Reason to reset the clocks: Abbr.
14 Dear old dad the cosmetic surgeon always told me to ___
15 Wealthy biblical land
16 "Fantastic!"
17 Extraction
18 Out of this world
24 Pacify
25 Supplements
30 Pie chart part
32 A sultanate
33 Dear old dad the C.E.O. always told me to ___
34 Coated Dutch exports
35 Geometry suffix
37 Problem in bed
38 Braves, but not Indians, briefly
40 Out
42 Prime
43 South American cowboy
44 Hunting times, for kids
45 Three Gorges Dam site
46 Fund, as a museum
48 From south of the Mediterranean
51 Cry at the sight of 107-Down
55 Marker
57 Spider-Man foe
58 Busy
59 Lip curler
60 Aid for the blind
63 Thumbs-up
66 ___ behold
67 "'Tis a pity"
69 Island chain
72 Alexander's wife in "Uncle Vanya"
73 Gun on the street?
74 Keeler and Dee
75 Hello or goodbye
78 Wowed ones
79 Procter & Gamble soap
83 Of yore
85 Baseless?
86 1967 #1 hit whose title is spelled out in the lyric
87 Noted Roosevelt
88 Generally
89 Words of praise
91 Was serious, with "it"
94 PC protection brand
98 ___-lance
100 Removes from the schedule
101 Joy of daytime TV
102 Out
103 One with a strict diet
104 At all
106 People's 1999 Sexiest Man Alive
107 See 51-Down
108 Look like a creep
111 Person with intelligence
112 Yukon or Xterra
113 '60s grp.
114 Word repeated before a hike

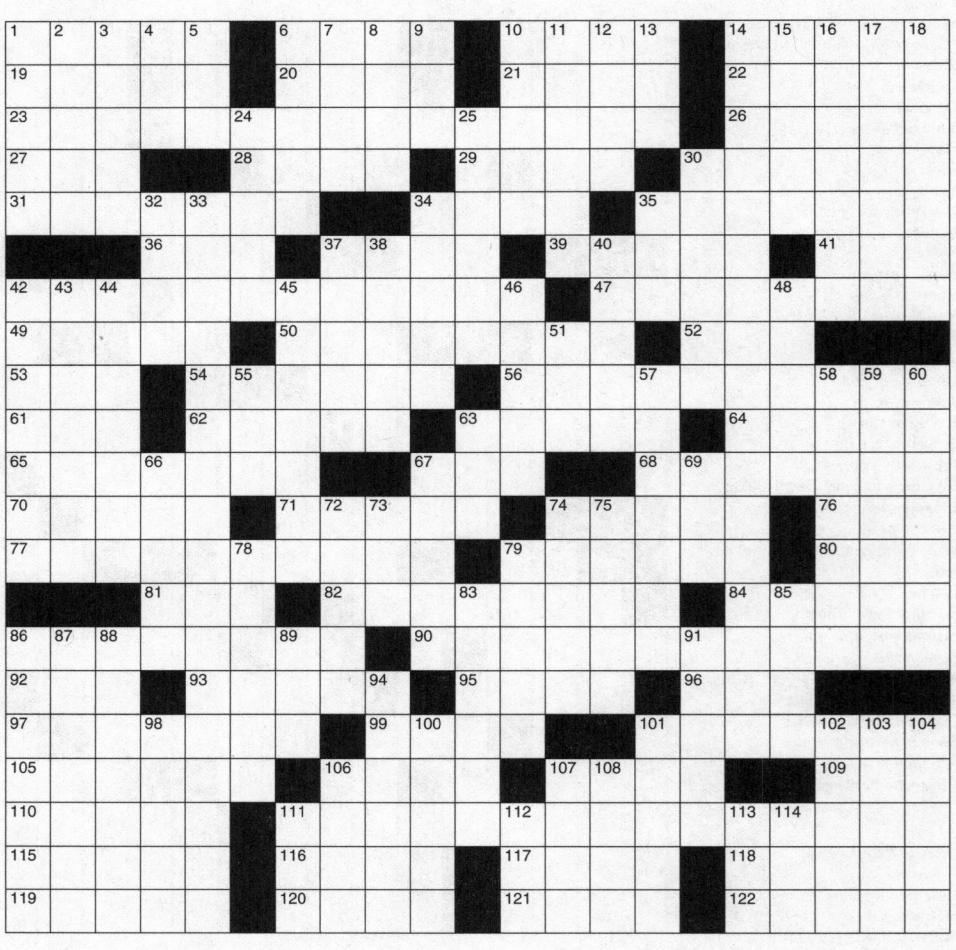

by Ben and Mark Tausig

ACROSS

1 Day-___
4 Hat trick trio
9 Envelope opener
14 Racket
17 Race
18 Greenwich Village resident of a hit 1980s sitcom
19 Low clouds
20 Ponte Vecchio's river
21 Enzyme suffix
22 Pastel shade
23 Jeweled pieces
24 Hand holder
25 "The Sound of Music" role
28 Channel bought by TV Guide in 1999
30 Many new corp. hires
31 Flock member
32 Stout relatives
33 Comparison shoppers
34 Capital of Pas-de-Calais
36 Lab vessel
37 Preflight ritual
38 Fixing up a house in Britain
42 See 7-Down
43 "No problems here"
44 Wear
46 Not the most maneuverable ship
49 Endorse
53 Series of shocks?
54 Come across as
55 Epoch 50 million years ago
58 Month after Shevat
59 Toothpaste tube abbr.
60 They're out of reach
61 National flower of Mexico
62 Home of golf's Blue Monster
64 Asian country in which English is an official language
68 Puts (away)
69 Clothed
71 Too smooth
72 2002 champion at 62-Across
74 Da-dah, da-dah, da-dah, poetically speaking
75 Cocktail with 108-Down
76 Cold spot
77 ___ were
78 Overthrows first, e.g.
79 "Love is my ___ . . .": Shak.
80 Lose badly
82 Lei Day greetings
84 Become active
87 Ones with guns put away
92 Shut (up)
93 Heroic verse
94 Bouncing off the walls
95 Noisy censure
96 In the past
97 Fox dialect
100 Dealer in futures?
101 Chemical "twin"
102 Former western English county
105 Prep exam, for short
106 Capital city captured by Mussolini's forces in 1939
109 Heads-up
110 Edible South American tuber
111 Mark of a ruler
112 Toughens
113 Item often stored upside-down
114 Pro ___
115 "Ixnay"
116 Set, as a price
117 Lady love?
118 Help-wanteds, e.g.

DOWN

1 What this clue ain't got?
2 Former Buick
3 Kind of pitch
4 Inaugural ball, e.g.
5 It may be stuck in a bar
6 Sanction
7 With 42-Across, an NPR host
8 Part that's broken off
9 Leaflet appendage
10 Tourist hazards
11 ___ candy (pop music)
12 ___ loss
13 Like some highly collectible paper money
14 Quick deposit receiver
15 Successively
16 Jottings
19 Year-round camp
20 Don of "Cocoon"
26 Golfer ___ Aoki
27 Monsoonal
29 Truck stop stoppers
33 Tree in a Christmas song
35 Reagan program inits.
36 It has two jaws
37 Maine radio station whose call letters spell a pronoun
39 Rachel's baby on "Friends"
40 Phoned-in info
41 Tropical porch
44 Like land not drained
45 Baja bread
47 One that makes one
48 Wild things
49 Noted German spa
50 Hebrew title for God
51 Arizona football V.I.P.
52 Reuben ingredient
54 Musical exercise
56 Intl. assn. created in 1948
57 Make sore
60 Like a tightrope walker
63 Herd hangout
65 Breakfast place
66 Fix, as a golf green
67 Root of diplomacy
70 "Laugh-In" host
73 Yds. rushing, e.g.
76 Golf course feature
77 Melmac alien et al.
81 No-goodnik
82 Up to, in poetry
83 ___ orch.
85 Friendliness
86 Caen confidante
87 "Lakmé" and "Lulu"
88 Alternative to plastic
89 The tiniest amount
90 Like some ears
91 Begs (for)
92 Company that makes the Skyhawk
93 Smoothed
95 Use, as one's savings
96 Tony-winning actor Denis
97 Kind of panel
98 Combat zone
99 Info holder
103 Not fancy
104 One foot forward
107 ___ panic
108 See 75-Across

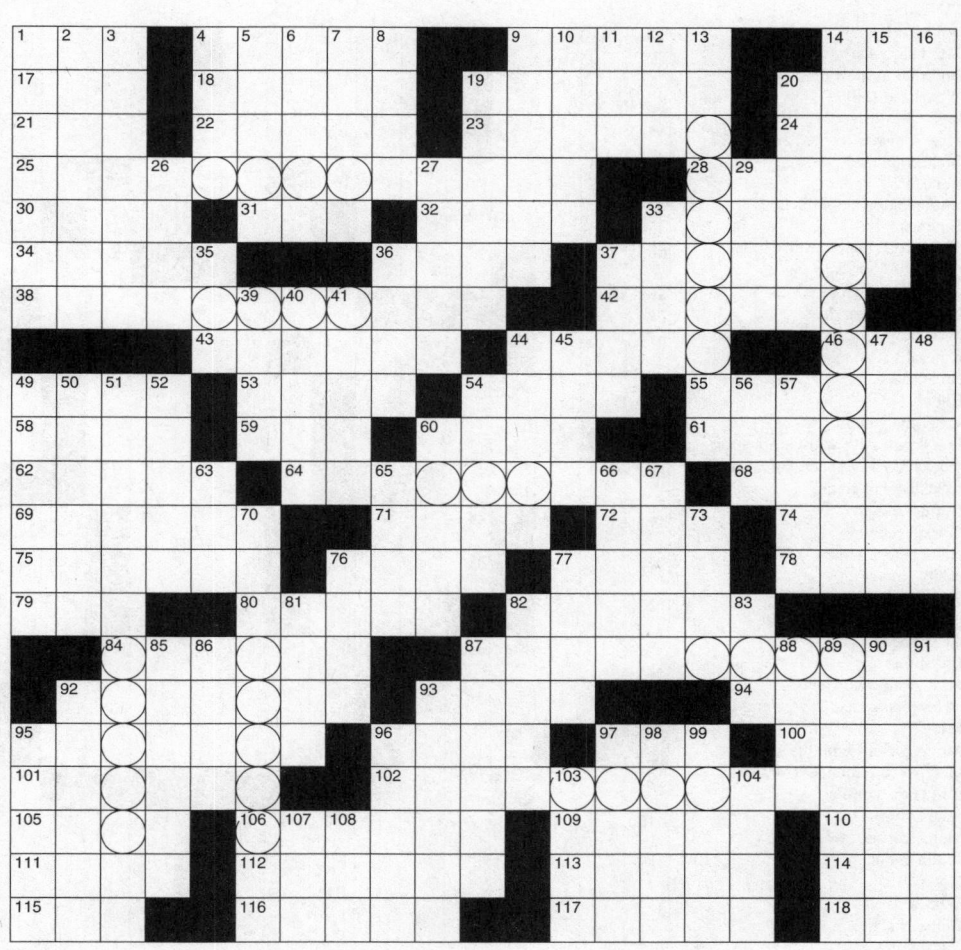

by Jim Page

ACROSS

1 Some radio dispatches, for short
5 Album feature
10 ___ Popular
15 Small handful
19 "George of the Jungle" elephant
20 Historic symbol whose shape can be found hidden in this completed puzzle
22 ___'acte
23 Southern side?
24 Made better
25 French noodle product?
26 Shot by a doctor
28 1776–1876: Abbr.
29 Guitarlike Japanese instruments
31 Better set
32 Hypodermics
34 Alexander Hamilton's place, informally
35 It's filled with bills
36 Allegro ___ (music direction)
38 Grps.
40 Prefix with dermis
41 Lateral lead-in
42 Takes power away from
46 Henpeck
47 Bard's nightfall
48 Shavings
51 TV canine
52 Old washing machine feature
56 34th U.S. pres.
57 Opposite of blow up
59 "I beg to differ!"
61 Neat
63 Stage elevator
64 Bighearted one
65 Out
66 Ones making amphibious landings?
68 They go all out at beauty shops
69 Center of Florida?
72 Coulter who wrote "Godless: The Church of Liberalism"
73 Mention
77 Kind of I.R.A.
78 Broadcasts
81 Big bird
82 U.S. atty. gen. in 1962
83 In a Weird Al Yankovic song, he "looks like a Muppet, but he's wrinkled and green"
84 Get-up-and-go
85 Certain fungus
86 Book before James: Abbr.
87 "Cool" amount
88 Saturate, in dialect
89 "Sweet as apple cider" girl
90 Cheesehead
91 Ballantine, e.g.
92 First group of invitees
95 "Consider it done!"
98 More fit
100 Moving away from the sides
102 German auto pioneer Gottlieb
103 Carpentry supplies
104 Like Saturn
105 Skin cleanser component
106 In the middle of
107 Not dis
110 Whirler
112 Comedy shtick
113 Twisty turn
116 Within reach
121 Savory French appetizers
125 "Tell me about it"
126 Much-photographed White House area
127 Accent
128 Misses the wake-up call

DOWN

1 Like many T's and P's
2 Emergency calling plan
3 Image that appears with the 20-Across on an old half dollar
4 Go over the limit?
5 Groups that run
6 Olympic officials
7 Still snoring
8 Actor Gibson
9 Like a Rolls-Royce
10 Talking Heads co-founder David
11 Legal org.
12 Pulls in
13 Baseballers' wear
14 Graybeards
15 Houdini's real name
16 Longtime setting for 20-Across
17 Things needed around dictators
18 High reputes
21 Ornament that may be worn with sandals
27 Org. with operations
30 Pulls
32 Original ___
33 Hang
37 Mozart's birthplace: Abbr.
39 From Phila. to Miami
43 Hard stuff
44 Repeated phrase in Martin Luther King Jr.'s "I Have a Dream" speech
45 Like a juggernaut
48 Elapse
49 Polished off
50 Fraudulent contestant
53 Welcome, as the new year
54 Green: Prefix
55 Check over
58 Hat, slangily
59 Top-secret grp.
60 Sounds of woe
62 It often gets glossed over
66 Airport area
67 Previously recorded
70 Dish prepared in a skillet
71 Rutabagas, e.g.
74 Starr and others
75 Japanese noodle product
76 Temple with curved roofs
78 Put forward
79 Muslim leader
80 Call
93 Series
94 Rocks
96 June honorees
97 Author Deighton
98 Direct contact
99 Routine
101 Domestic Old World birds
103 Creme-filled chocolate treats
107 Talking point?
108 I.R.A. part: Abbr.
109 "There's gold in them ___ hills!"
111 Oil producer
112 Afrikaner
113 Earth, to Mahler
114 Flight segment
115 Payroll dept. ID's
117 Follower of Benedict?
118 Pastoral cry
119 P.O. box item
120 Comics shriek
121 Granada gold
122 Natl. Novel Writing mo.
123 British verb ending
124 It may follow you

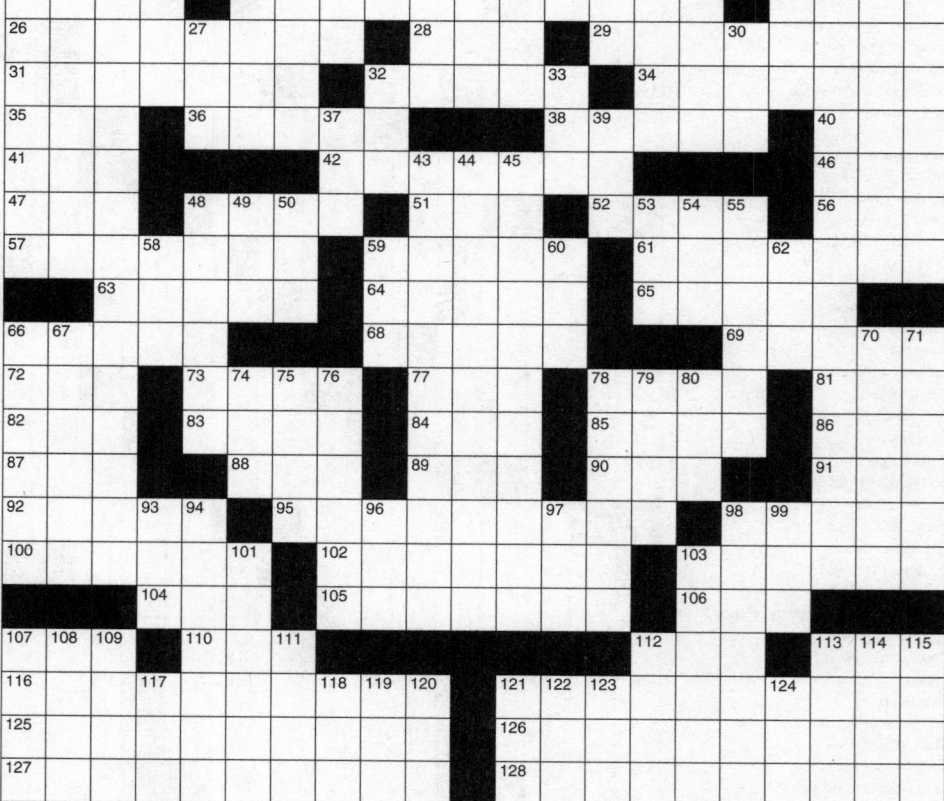

by Elizabeth C. Gorski

ACROSS

1 Makes sticky
7 Old Spanish gold
14 Plato dubbed her "the tenth Muse"
20 Turkey's highest peak
21 Buddy
22 Served the drinks
23 It means "strained" in drink names
24 Author of "The Fall of the Horse of Usher"?
26 Mad cap?
28 Dudgeon
29 "Dinner and a Movie" airer
30 Prefix with friendly
31 Caring grp.
32 Coal byproduct
33 Hard slog
35 Arthur and others
36 It may be legally beaten
37 Accomplish flawlessly
39 Essential part
40 American representative to France during the Revolutionary War
41 Love hate?
46 Iron man?
49 If things go well
50 Cry with a pompom
51 What golf pencils lack
54 Brand of craft knives
55 Cubes
59 Unable to make "Ocean's Thirteen," maybe?
62 Actress Olin
63 Break down
64 Professionals' earnings
65 From scratch
68 Exotic means of suicide
69 Brewed beverages
71 Organ that can perform martial arts moves?
78 Writing set?
81 Alprazolam, more familiarly
82 Femme fatale, often
83 Progressive ___
84 Quick-change artists?
86 1983 Nicholas Gage book
87 Ex-wife's refrain?
93 Products with earbuds
94 2004 spinoff show
95 Lip-puckering
96 Long ride?
99 Recording device
100 Blue
101 All for
104 "___ dien," motto of the Prince of Wales
105 Specialist M.D.
106 Reason to retire
107 Monstrous bird of myth
108 How a diaper is removed?
111 Cry to a lunch sandwich before it's eaten?
115 Set off
116 Arctic natives
117 "Eureka!"
118 "Is this a ___ which I see before me": Macbeth
119 Salary after deductions
120 Sequoias and Siennas
121 Whiles away

DOWN

1 Angel
2 Beethoven's Third
3 Hurry on horseback
4 River through Kazakhstan
5 Jotted down
6 Alien
7 Three-sided blade
8 Mubarak's predecessor
9 Company with the motto "A Business of Caring"
10 Old carrier name
11 Have the gumption
12 ___ roll
13 Roman Helios
14 Catalyst
15 Top-notch
16 Spot early on?
17 Able to change shape
18 Unwanted plant in farmyards
19 Spacecraft orbiting Mars
25 Mislead and then some
27 Hook worm
33 Pan coating
34 Off-color
35 Hebrew for "house of God"
38 Wahine accessory
39 Very, to Verdi
40 Horror movie figure, informally
41 British bludgeon
42 Year that Spenser's "The Faerie Queene" was published
43 Set of rings?
44 Food item that can be soft or hard
45 Historic Swiss canton
46 Prepare to give what you received?
47 Brooks Robinson, for 23 years
48 Secure tightly, with "down"
52 Lament
53 Chooses to leave
55 Units of force
56 Late wake-up call?
57 Seemingly not there
58 Ancient manuscripts
60 Black layer found in Morbier cheese
61 Put dishes away
66 Stretch (out)
67 Pull ahead yet further
70 Small suit
72 Left
73 Actress Bates
74 Ending with sever or suffer
75 ___ avis
76 It'll turn you around
77 In a proper manner
79 Shaw's "___ and the Man"
80 Research center
84 On-the-water front
85 Wildean quality
87 Drug taken mostly by kids
88 Inferior imitator
89 Pack up and go
90 Deplane dramatically
91 Common street name
92 Nero Wolfe's obsession
96 Not harmful
97 Together
98 They're rounded up in a roundup
100 Punk
101 Utah County seat
102 Big name in reference books
103 ___ vincit amor
107 Nino who composed the music for "The Godfather"
108 Scold severely
109 Feedbag's fill
110 "Splendor in the Grass" writer
112 Currency of Laos
113 It may come straight from the horse's mouth
114 "Now the truth comes out!"

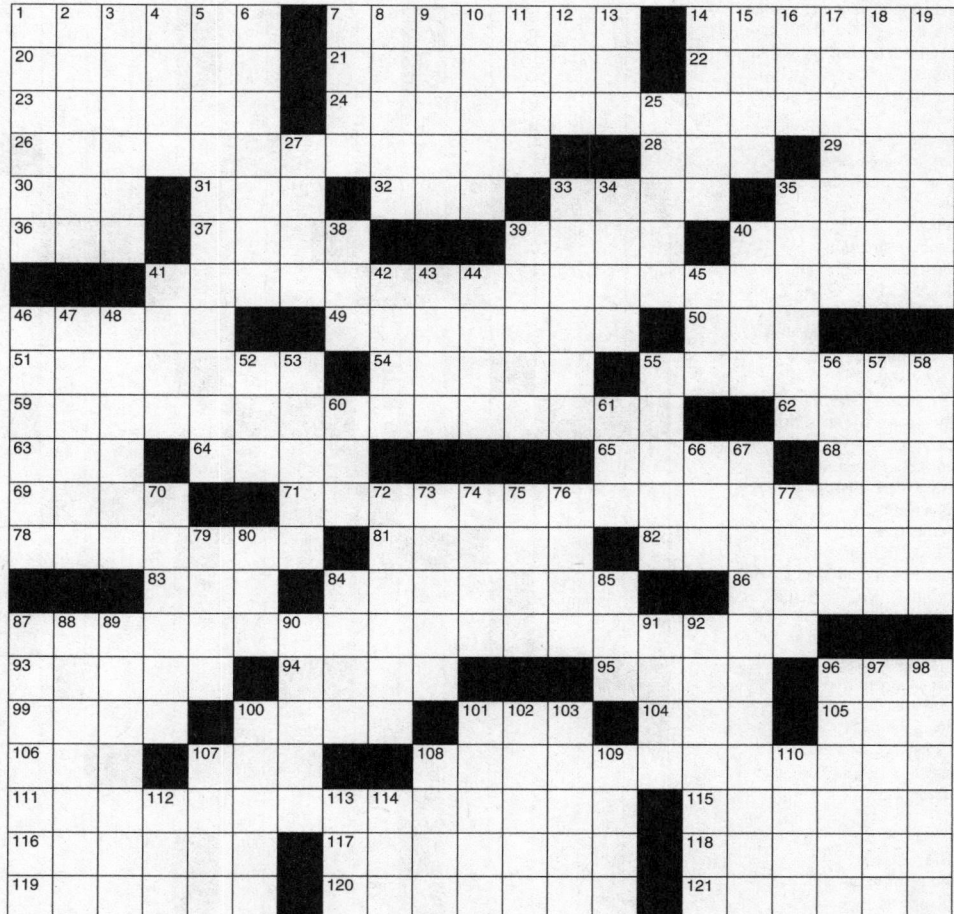

by Patrick Berry

ACROSS

1. Pelvic
6. P.M. times
10. Fast feline
14. They don't do Windows, as a rule
19. Sheryl Crow's "All I ___ Do"
20. Goggle
21. City south of Moscow
22. Lollygag
23. EVIL BRAT IN THERE
26. Muchachas: Abbr.
27. Part of the refrain before "hey hey hey" in a 1969 #1 song
28. ___ League
29. Absorbed
30. CANNY OLDER AUTHOR
34. Notches, usually
38. Honk
39. Frown
40. School for King's Scholars
41. Not manual
42. Signs
44. Passers, briefly
47. TO APPEAR ON ELBA, NON?
52. Diminutive suffix
53. Nevada county
54. Sharper
55. P.O. items
56. 1940s–'50s All-Star Johnny
57. Old cars with 389 engines
58. Secretary of state before Shultz
59. Diet doctor
61. EAGER TO USE LYRICAL MOLD
68. Benedict XV's successor
69. Vault
70. Narc tail?
71. Playfully roguish
72. Jason ___, longtime Denver Bronco
73. Touch
76. Recipe instruction
79. Sci-fi drug
80. SEEN ALIVE? SORRY, PAL!
84. Co. founded by Perot
85. Old-fashioned contraction
86. Good buddy
87. Abbey area
88. Like some Fr. nouns
89. God whose wife had hair of finely spun gold
90. Storyteller's challenge
93. EVER THE CRISP HERO
98. Taos sight
99. Picnic hamperer
100. "Clever thinking"
105. Esther of "Good Times"
106. I VALUE NICER ROLE
109. Affaire
110. Some wings
111. B'way showing
112. Part of a platform
113. Carryalls
114. Dying words?
115. It's usually slanted
116. Pete ___, 1970s–'80s General Motors chief

DOWN

1. "Bingo!"
2. Source of basalt
3. ___ uproar
4. Tolstoy heroine
5. Short break
6. Operatives
7. Al ___ (Mideast group)
8. Philosopher Mo-___
9. Sun. talk
10. Herculean literary character?
11. Concentrated, in a way
12. Peach ___
13. Cask contents
14. "I give up"
15. St. Stephen, in the Bible
16. Soviet cooperative
17. One doing heavy lifting
18. Meth.
24. Hopper
25. Nocturnal animal: Var.
29. Start of a refusal
31. Part of an instrument measuring fluid pressure
32. Kind of blade
33. Pirates and Cards
34. Kind of diagram in logic
35. Dog command
36. Word before and after "against"
37. "Wheel of Fortune" buy
41. Industrious one
42. Some nerve
43. Pulitzer-winning critic Jefferson
44. Dennis of "The Alamo"
45. Hip-hop jewelry, in short
46. Pick up
48. Glove material
49. Potentially dangerous strain
50. Boot
51. Winged
56. Their tips turn up
57. Wax rhapsodic
58. Short flight
59. Race of Norse gods
60. Group of three
61. Rush
62. Was on
63. Goos
64. Texas hold 'em announcement
65. Catalytic converter?
66. Temple tender
67. Flight maneuver
72. Boot
73. Pergola
74. Baseball Hall-of-Famer Bobby
75. Dad's namesake: Abbr.
76. "Kubla Khan" river
77. First name in '50s TV
78. Salon supplies
80. Amazon.com and others
81. Stop from running, maybe
82. One-seeded fruit, botanically
83. Parked oneself
88. 1959 #1 hit by the Fleetwoods
89. Craving
90. Start a drive
91. Like Ford's logo
92. Garment size
93. 1980s–'90s New York governor
94. Spartan serf
95. Toothbrush handle?
96. 1945 Physics Nobelist Wolfgang ___
97. Madrid month
98. Something to fall on
101. Composer Charles
102. Force
103. Clown shoe width
104. Culture
106. August person
107. "Wait Wait . . . Don't Tell Me!" network
108. Bus. driver?

by Ashish Vengsarkar

ACROSS

1 Corp. honcho
5 Some Filipinos
10 Starter's need
13 TV alien
17 Storyteller of Samos
19 Virtuous sort
20 Duration of many a TV show
23 Wine that causes incoherent talk?
25 Vietnamese city painted in soothing colors?
26 Pseudopod formers
27 Capital on the Mississippi
29 "Missed it!"
30 Literary governess
32 Girl's name that's a Texas county seat
33 Second word of many limericks
34 What a dummy!
37 French priest born in early July?
41 Worry, it's said
45 Calif. hub
46 Not quite right?
48 Mint hardware
49 Fillet
51 Poppy derivative
53 W.W. II-era enlistee
55 They're trident-shaped
57 Dries, in a way
58 Popular British society magazine
59 Steamed
61 Authorize
63 Life of ___
64 Monologist of note
65 Start of Montana's motto
66 Source of iron
67 Defeats regularly, in sports lingo
69 Cracker spread that's a little sparse on top?
74 Shook down
75 Game with matchsticks
76 Yearbook sect.
77 Brownie, e.g.
78 ___' Pea
80 Dasher, to Dancer
83 Gave in
84 Haberdashery item
87 Put out
88 It melts in your mouth
90 Journal add-on?
91 Attire
92 Bungled, with "up"
94 Common order, with "the"
96 Bit of sports news
98 Foreign exchange option
99 Kind of engr.
100 Discontinued investigative series?
103 Chanson de ___
105 Some choristers
107 Spot in a Manilow tune
108 Ad headline
110 Centers of squares, maybe
113 Brute
116 Deli offering
120 Expert in ornamental fabrics?
122 Rate at which a personnel manager works?
124 Orchard starter
125 Cream
126 "Not my problem!"
127 1940s first lady
128 Rehabilitated, in a way
129 Boxer-turned-actor
130 Ring

DOWN

1 Jumper, briefly
2 Enlarge, in a way
3 Salinger dedicatee
4 Lamenting one
5 Common Internet letters
6 Bireme gear
7 Sidesplitter
8 With no guarantees
9 Was of use to
10 Make it big
11 ___ corda (music marking)
12 Trojan War sage
13 Like pure gold
14 Dept. of Labor div.
15 Romp
16 Place for a pad
18 After-school arrangements
21 Punished, in a way, in the Bible
22 Fair-hiring org.
24 U.S. ally since '48
28 Green
31 Old five-franc coin
34 Place on the schedule
35 Auto parts giant
36 Trick shot that knocks the balls off a French pool table?
38 Freely
39 Drew nigh
40 Old "public diplomacy" org.
42 Enthusiastic cheering section at a bullfight?
43 Unbroken
44 Just back from vacation, say
47 They do the thinking
50 River whose delta is Cape Tortosa
52 [sigh]
54 "Please?"
56 St. Andrews golf club member
60 Pacific kingdom
62 Like a cardinal
67 Promptly
68 Peace Nobelist called a "messenger to mankind"
70 Concerning
71 "Had enough?"
72 Lively tempo
73 Catkin bearers
74 Kind of blast
76 J. M. Barrie pirate
79 Flute, e.g.
81 Sweet after-dinner drinks
82 Additionally
83 "You've got to be kidding!"
85 Lend support to
86 ___ Coty, predecessor of Charles de Gaulle
89 Simple, pretty songs
93 Grandparents, often
95 No longer good
97 He hoped to succeed H.S.T.
101 Authorized to travel
102 Actress Anderson
104 Fishing gear with fine mesh wire
106 Garage job
109 Enzyme suffix
110 Simple headstone
111 Put on record, but not actually on a record
112 Intensifies, with "up"
114 Clarifying phrase
115 Rink leap
117 Sleek, for short
118 Jazzman Saunders
119 Tranquil scene
121 Suffix with front
123 Apology starter

by Fred Piscop

ACROSS

1 Carousel contents
5 Life may be spent here
11 Ones whose work isn't picking up
16 Flightless birds
21 Nabisco brand
22 Against
23 Country/rock singer Steve
24 "Anybody home?"
25 Start of a comment by 3- and 126-Down
28 Oil holder, maybe
29 Wig wearer
30 "It's ___ to the finish"
31 Overhead bin, e.g.
33 Dearie
34 Kia model
36 Yellow or gray
37 Popped
38 1914 battle line
39 Comment, part 2
46 Brim
47 La-la lead-in
48 Trike rider
49 Some racehorses
50 Puffed up
54 Library Lovers Mo.
55 Natural pump outlet
57 Former U.N. chief U ___
58 Comment, part 3
61 Proctor's call
63 Cabinet dept.
64 "So ___ to offend . . ."
65 Phone book abbr.
66 Where many Sargents hang, with "the"
68 When repeated, an old TV sign-off
70 Spanish pronoun
71 Drink sometimes flavored with cinnamon
72 Whiz
74 Dirt in a dump truck, maybe
76 Isle of Mull neighbor
78 "The Torch in ___" (Elias Canetti memoir)
79 & 81 Landmark 1972 album by 3- and 126-Down
83 Actress Van Devere
87 TV series featuring the war god Ares
89 D-Day transports: Abbr.
91 Very narrow, in a way
92 Football Hall-of-Famer Herber
93 Dated
96 Russian assembly
98 Spanish eyes
100 Damone of song
102 Land on Lake Chad
103 Swear
105 Lexicographer's study
107 Comment, part 4
110 Sloughs
112 Cape in the Holy See
114 Colorful moths
115 Piña ___ (drinks)
116 Monetary unit of Panama
118 Where the Snake River snakes: Abbr.
119 Constellation near Cancer
120 Put out
121 Comment, part 5
125 Seventh-century year
129 Opera singer Mitchell of "Porgy and Bess"
130 Strand material
131 Afrique du ___
132 Had in view
133 Most dear
136 Ken and Lena of Hollywood
138 Belt and hose, e.g.
141 "I'm ___ here!"
142 End of the comment
145 Kind of call
146 Publication that clicks with readers?
147 Helping hands
148 A Sinatra
149 Some Romanovs
150 Honey bunch?
151 Entertain, as a child at bedtime
152 Real lulu

DOWN

1 Base for the old British East India Company
2 Indo-Europeans
3 With 126-Down, a noted humorist
4 Not so pleasant
5 Some hallucinogens, for short
6 Really clobber
7 Temporary
8 Recipe direction
9 Places for R.N.'s
10 Bubkes
11 Waste
12 Judge in 1990s news
13 Kill ___ killed
14 R&B singer Cantrell
15 Establishes
16 Electrical resistor
17 Subject of many a sad ballad
18 Couturière Schiaparelli
19 Something to break or shake, in phrase
20 Unduplicated
26 Up to, in ads
27 Slangy commercial suffix
32 Activate, as a switch
35 String group, maybe
37 Put oneself where one shouldn't
39 "Beam ___ . . ."
40 "___ no?"
41 Ride around
42 Order
43 "The Family Circus" cartoonist
44 Cousins of ospreys
45 Minute Maid Park player
46 Barely got along
50 One begins "The Lord is my light and my salvation"
51 Anthem start
52 Con game
53 Favoring bigger government, say
54 Kind of conservative
55 Bit of tomfoolery
56 With full force
59 Circus trainee
60 Butterfingers
62 Brian of early Roxy Music
67 Cinders of old comics
69 Straighten
73 Station along Route 66
75 Basis of a biblical miracle
77 Exuberant cry in Mexico
79 Now you see it, now you don't
80 NW Missouri city, informally
82 Cry one's head off
84 Opening for a coin?
85 Tuscany cathedral city
86 Ranch stock
88 Wrench's target
90 Sequel title starter
93 Latin dance
94 Feathered, say
95 Tulsa daily, with "the"
97 Show up
99 Trash pads?
101 Drink that's stirred
104 On-site supervisor?
106 Concocted
108 Night calls
109 What's expected
111 Midwest harvest
113 Noncellular phone
117 Wall St. figures
119 Lists
120 Led astray
122 Flexible reply
123 Plays peacemaker for
124 Bantu language
125 Not hearing
126 See 3-Down
127 Chant
128 Battle cry
132 Radar fig.
133 Toll
134 Baseball Hall-of-Famer Aparicio
135 Not this or that, in Spain
136 Medical suffix
137 Shoot up
139 Acerb
140 Italian bone
143 ___ dye
144 Golfer Michelle

by Victor Fleming and Bonnie L. Gentry

ACROSS

1 See 131-Across
4 Root holders
10 End of "Lohengrin"
16 Minor player
19 Manning the quarterback
20 Good to go
21 Perfume bottle
22 Itinerary info: Abbr.
23 Yo-yo
24 Demonstration against a Miss America pageant?
26 Riddle-me-___
27 One making calls from home
29 Off one's feed
30 Tourist's aid
31 Fingerprint feature
33 Multiplying rapidly?
38 Legendary elephant eaters
40 Sinuous swimmer
41 It maddens MADD
42 Italian innkeeper
43 Loose rope fiber used as caulking
45 Ruckus
47 Shoebox letters
50 Grant-giving grp.
51 Collection of publications about historical advances?
58 Rush violently
59 Interstice
60 Northern Ireland politician Paisley and others
61 Dog it
63 Follower of Shakespeare?
65 Matter of aesthetics
66 Honored Fr. woman
67 Fab Four forename
68 One who accidentally blurts out "I did it!"?
75 De ___
76 Do-do connector
77 In excelsis ___
78 Perp prosecutors
79 ___ B'rith
80 Is indisposed
81 Use as a resource
82 Nobel-winning poet Heaney
87 Nose-picking and belching in the White House?
92 L.A.P.D. part
93 Work for eds.
94 Untilled tract
95 Coil inventor
96 Where people travel between poles?
100 "Little Birds" author
103 Twisted letter
105 Person who's not straight
106 Competitor's dedication to hard training?
111 Shaded spots
112 Carnation or rose
113 Gray spray
114 Come back again
117 Bird ___
118 Item to be checked on a census form?
123 Bit for an accelerator
124 Considerably
125 Taking prescription drugs, informally
126 Put something on
127 Ki ___ (Korea's legendary founder)
128 Antigua-to-Barbados dir.
129 What to see in a Chevrolet, in old ads
130 Got as a result
131 With 1-Across, an agreeable guy

DOWN

1 Course offerer
2 '06 class member, e.g.
3 Hairsplitter
4 One born on a kibbutz
5 "Splitting Heirs" actor
6 Patterned after
7 Tiger Stadium's sch.
8 Minor, at law
9 Like some hair
10 Recipient of much intl. aid
11 Opposite of tiptoe
12 Turkic language
13 Fruity frozen treat
14 Cyclades island
15 Unwelcome visitor
16 Healthful exercise, informally
17 Home of the John Day Fossil Beds National Monument
18 "The Quiet American" author
25 Bulldoze
28 Dig
32 4-Downs, e.g.
34 Really run
35 "Jenny" co-star, 1970
36 Feudal estate
37 Canines to beware of
38 "Zuckerman Unbound" novelist
39 Locale of Interstate H1
44 Teatro alla Scala locale
46 Players for prayers
48 Like some sees
49 Sister of Thalia
52 Contorted
53 Sometime sale site
54 Decided one would
55 Continuously
56 Male issue
57 Starchy foodstuff
62 In place of
64 With great strength
67 Take as an affront
68 Flyboys' hdqrs.
69 Pow!
70 Leave a mark on
71 Drain of color
72 Faith of fakirs
73 V.I.P. at V.P.I., say
74 Burkina ___
80 Stubborn sorts
83 Penguin variety
84 Nashville nickname
85 Where Lew Alcindor played
86 Critic's award
88 Touchy subject
89 Fails to be
90 Garlic relative
91 Whodunit title word
96 Gibes
97 Down Under denizens
98 Have covered
99 In
101 "___ robbed!"
102 More prone to pry
104 Flash light?
107 Pot-___ (French meat-and-vegetables dish)
108 Must have
109 Lyon is its capital
110 Under a spell
115 Watering aid
116 Some till fill
119 Abbr. after Sen. Judd Gregg's name
120 Nine-digit ID issuer
121 Org. that publishes American Hunter
122 Knock

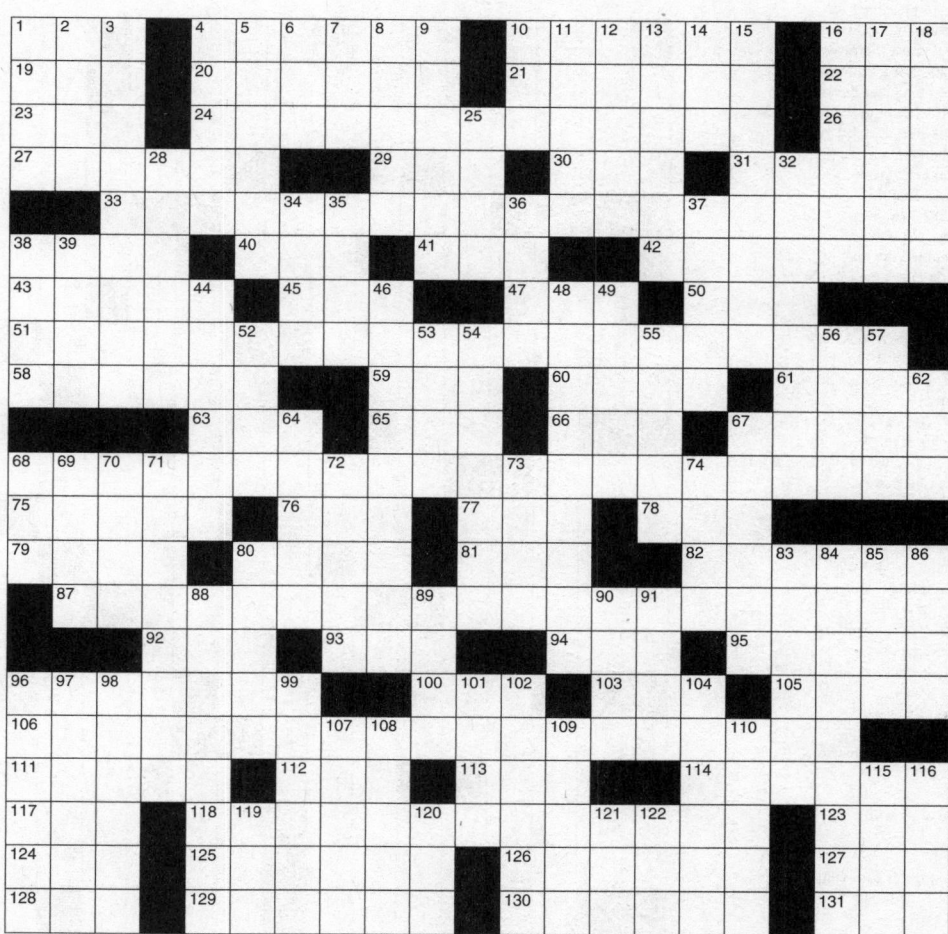

by Mark Feldman

ACROSS

1 Pitch in
7 Sight near an igloo
11 Show utter disrespect to
17 Something in France
19 Plastic surgeon's target
22 *Discount brokerage formed in 1996
23 *Site of a famous drawing?
24 Scorch
25 My dear man
26 Run the show
28 Ratio phrase
29 Hardly raining?
32 *Writer who coined the word "booboisie"
35 Wane
38 Fee follower
39 Biological rings
40 Satellite counterpart
41 *Deceased writer whose work was the basis for a hit 2005 film
44 Kiss, in "Harry Potter"
45 Former Span. money
48 Something a bride may have
50 Newsman Potter and others
52 Doll
54 Old man of the sea, to Homer
55 Pop
57 How 265-pound football Hall-of-Famer Larry Little was named?
59 Legal hearing
60 Bonus
61 1939 Best Picture nominee banned in the Soviet Union
63 Year Chaucer died
65 *Kids' cookie makers, informally
68 Folk duo ___ & Sylvia
69 Johnnycake
72 Porcelain piece
73 Alpine sight
76 Some takeout
77 Spy, at times
79 Damned doctor
82 First two words of "Waltzing Matilda"
83 Building contractor's study
84 These provide relief
85 ___ Kosh B'Gosh
86 Language whose name means "army"
89 *1970s–'80s TV villain
92 Knick rival
93 French West Indies isle, informally
95 Bit of a comic
96 Peter the Great's co-czar
98 *It was retired in 2005
101 Chestnut
103 Make ___ for it
104 Capital of Belarus
107 As well
108 Daily ___, "Spider-Man" newspaper
113 *QB who was the 1963 Player of the Year
116 *World order
119 Dumps
120 "Mission: Impossible" types
121 Skip
122 Seven ___
123 Treat as a villain

DOWN

1 Its logo is four rings
2 Iced, with "up"
3 Waste
4 *Measure of brightness
5 Attorney's advice
6 Breviloquent
7 Peewee
8 Record producer ___ Adler
9 Latin 101 verb
10 Regard
11 Barefoot
12 "Gotta catch 'em all!" sloganeer
13 Its logo is five rings: Abbr.
14 How Holmes beat Ali in '80
15 How chicken à la king may be served
16 Scandinavian language, to natives
17 Milk purchases: Abbr.
18 In the main
20 Fill up
21 University of North Carolina
27 Prot., for example
30 Some college staff
31 Tree that's a symbol of sorrow
33 "Don't Bring Me Down" grp., 1979
34 Pesters
35 Continental abbr.
36 *It provided tires for Lindbergh's Spirit of St. Louis
37 Good relations
39 "Just ___!"
40 French Dadaist
42 Ones getting coll. counseling, maybe
43 Harry Bailly, in "The Canterbury Tales"
45 *Not for everyone
46 ___ blue streak

47 Kind of race
49 Go with
51 Setting for part of Kerouac's "On the Road"
53 Kind of symbol
55 Precipitate
56 What Indiana once pursued
57 River to the Danube
58 "A seductive liar": George W. Ball
60 Grp. with balls and strikes
62 Ending with cash
63 Singer Marilyn
64 Film executive Harry and others
66 #26 of 26
67 Fall behind
70 Brussels-to-Amsterdam dir.
71 Nice ones
74 Neighbor of Rom.
75 Lab safety org.?
78 Hot and heavy, e.g.: Abbr.
79 Crosswords, say
80 The Runnin' Rebels, for short
81 Mach 1 passer
83 Like Larry of the Three Stooges, surprisingly
84 Healthy amount
87 Football positions: Abbr.
88 Pioneering German auto
90 ___ boost

91 Barbara on the cover of 15 TV Guides
93 "Apollo 13" actor
94 Symbol of perfection
97 *Beetles
98 Lee of the old Milwaukee Braves
99 Look inside
100 Quiet, now
102 Truth, old-style
105 Figure (out)
106 Common arthroscopy site
109 Mountain West Conference team
110 Actress Gershon
111 1990s Senate majority leader
112 Nav. designation
114 Zenith
115 Singing syllable
117 Zenith rival
118 Chou En-___

by Derrick Niederman

ACROSS

1 Pop group with a hit Broadway musical
5 "Dido and Aeneas," for an early English example
10 Three-time Masters winner
15 Smack
19 Pastelería offering
20 Had
21 Challenger's quest
22 Agitated, after "in"
23 Affectionate aquarium denizen?
25 Opposed to getting more angry?
27 Changes a mansard
28 Popular women's fragrance
30 Force in the Trojan War
31 French department
32 Glyceride, e.g.
33 Hatched
34 Monty Python member
37 Two-time L.P.G.A. Championship winner Laura
39 Grime fighter
40 Dark suit
42 Hub of a wheel
43 Grade enhancer
44 Does one's part
45 "Invasion of the Body Snatchers" invaders?
49 Trombonist Winding
52 Tiny amount
53 Preceder of Peter in a phonetic alphabet
54 Ear flap?
55 Listing
57 Less taxing
60 They're all that matter
62 A little flat?
63 At a slow pace
65 Evening thing
66 Sub
67 Wannabe surfers
68 Pluvial
69 Cot on wheels
70 "There's ___ for that"
71 Rhine feeder
72 Peach or beech
73 Panama, e.g.
76 "Miss Pym Disposes" author, 1946
77 Lettuce in the spring?
81 It's long in fashion
82 Actress Long and others
83 Beef cut
84 Discharged
86 Stink
90 It might raise a stink
92 ___-length
93 Ranchero wraps
94 Sine or cosine
95 Author of "Chaim Lederer's Return"
97 One offering compensation, maybe
98 Fit
99 Calm
102 Very scared insect?
104 Tainted tapioca?
107 Start of the Order of the Garter's motto
108 Bring down
109 Not done as well?
110 Switch attachment?
111 Puts on
112 Beat
113 Sty sound
114 Home, informally

DOWN

1 Patriots' grp.
2 Memory, sometimes
3 Invited
4 Sci-fi figures
5 Concert hall
6 Made pants?
7 Certain Prot.
8 Low-___
9 Stuff on tape
10 Union members
11 Number in C.B. lingo
12 Suffix with novel
13 Iran's Ayatollah ___ Khamenei
14 Actor William of "My Three Sons"
15 Desperado
16 Newscast segment
17 Sowing machine
18 Cremona product, for short
24 TV's Michaels
26 Stretch
29 Part of many a Civil War statue
32 Get out of
33 Blockhead
34 It's administered in H.S.
35 Capital whose Parliament house is called Fale Fono
36 The best time to elope?
38 Choice words
39 First or economy
41 Loot
43 Feather in one's cap
46 Hypnotist's directive
47 Deceiving
48 Old Nick
49 Young warmonger?
50 Others, in the Forum
51 Pour ___
56 Lyricist's need
58 Faithful servant in "As You Like It"
59 Lesser cut, usually
60 Not native
61 It fades in the fall
62 Play up
63 Pointer's reference
64 Primo
65 Oenone's husband, in myth
66 Like a defendant in court
68 Police car feature
69 Purplish
71 "So long"
72 Beat
74 Bit of skating practice
75 Marigraph activator
78 Take in too little
79 Rub the wrong way
80 Cubans' locations
81 Cousin of a herring
85 Went back and forth
86 Kind of acting
87 Near
88 Tour de France cyclist Floyd
89 Newspaper piece
90 Like Captain Kidd
91 Modern-day rhymer
93 Olympic skater Cohen
94 Awaken
96 End of many a race
98 Way up
99 ___-Asiatic
100 King
101 Hazzard County lawman
103 Category in baseball's Triple Crown: Abbr.
105 Athletic supporter
106 Caught on to

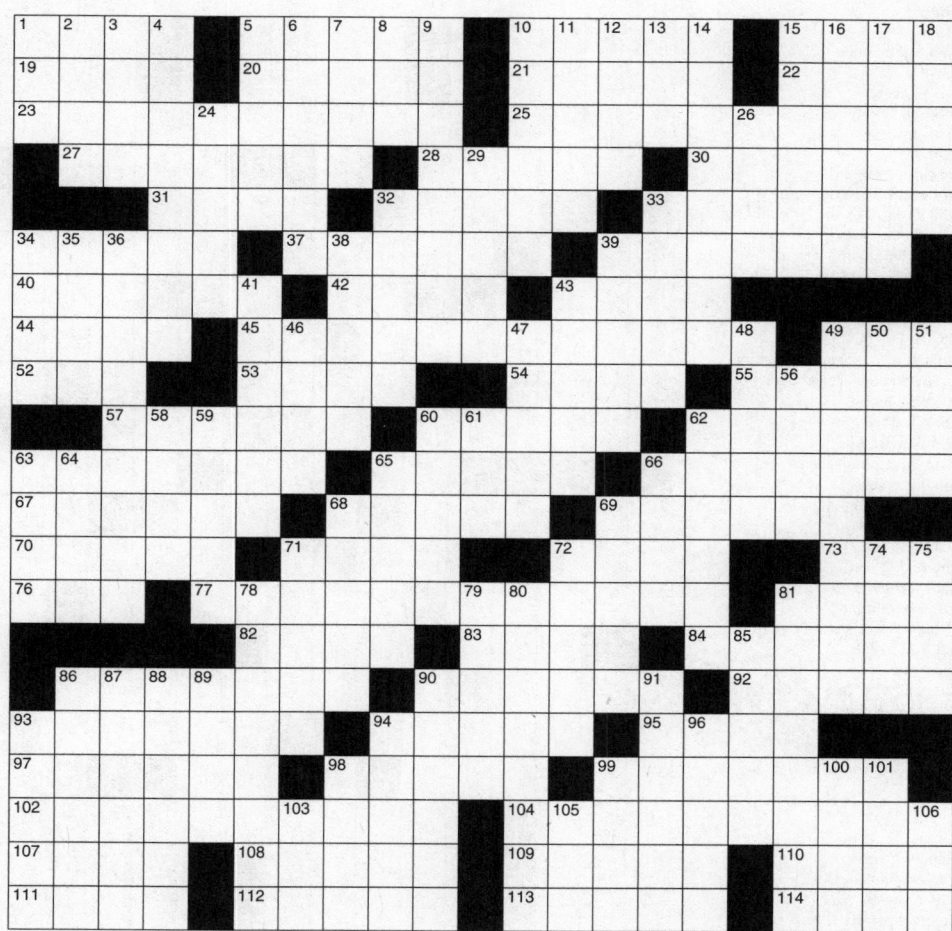

by Richard Silvestri

ACROSS

1 Not generic fashion
6 Hurry
11 Complaints
16 Soldier's fare, for short
19 Accustom
20 Appropriate
21 Full-length
22 Anthem contraction
23 Parent's admonishment
26 Records that are easily broken
27 Greets
28 Catchers
29 Drink with a three-leaf logo
31 Water source
32 26-Across, e.g.
35 Disorder
36 Landon of 1930s politics
39 1986 Pulitzer-winning novel set in a cattle drive
43 Computer-animated hit film of 1998
44 Vein holder
46 "In principio ___ Verbum"
47 Hot, in Vegas
49 Delta hub
52 They're hooked
55 Satisfy
58 Paul Theroux novel made into a Harrison Ford film, with "The"
60 Hebrew name meaning "Hill of spring"
62 Biased
63 Solid South, once
65 Thus far
66 "___ my case"
69 Cheering loudly
71 Snap, e.g.
76 ___-free
78 Dangerous place
84 Painting and printing, e.g.
86 1982 #1 hit with the lyric "living in perfect harmony"
89 Nixon commerce secretary Maurice
90 Dickens boy
92 Certain book addendum
93 Zip
95 Rossetti's "___ Ancilla Domini"
97 ___ II, first man-made object to reach the moon
98 Baker's stock
100 Sign of affection
105 Form W-9 datum: Abbr.
106 Initial progress
108 Response to "am not"
109 Canon camera
111 Black ice, e.g.
112 About
114 Goes for the bells and whistles
119 Suffix with infant
120 TV announcer's exhortation
124 U.S.S.R. successor
125 Reds, once
126 Host of TV's "In Search Of . . ."
127 New Mexico county
128 Salon job
129 Candymaker Harry
130 Sends to Hades
131 Spring

DOWN

1 Gifts of greeting
2 One-two connector
3 Water mark?
4 Young's partner in accounting
5 Devastating
6 Un plus sept
7 Invite to one's home
8 Lyon who played Lolita
9 Word of encouragement
10 Gabriel Fahrenheit or Anders Celsius
11 Actor Young of the "Rocky" films
12 Specialist M.D.'s
13 Prefix with system
14 Causing more laughs
15 Strengthen
16 Soft rock?
17 Evangelist's cry
18 Imitation
24 Slimming procedure, briefly
25 One of two rivers forming the Ubangi
30 Personal, often
33 180-year-old in Genesis
34 Avoid
35 "Halt!"
36 Something to remember
37 Reveal
38 Two-timing
40 More trim
41 Adulterate
42 Minn. neighbor
45 Common Web site content
48 Olympics city after St. Moritz
50 Rapa ___ (Easter Island)
51 More trim
53 Pat
54 Puerto Rico, e.g.
56 Paramedic's need
57 Seth and Abel's mother
59 Pablo Neruda's "___ to Common Things"
61 Online brokerage since 1993
64 ___ Nostra
67 Curtain raiser?
68 Mug in a pub
70 Founder of the American Shakers
71 Duplicates, briefly
72 Bran material
73 Marmalade ingredient
74 Home of Carthage College
75 Superlative suffix
77 Little squirt
79 "Kid-tested, mother-approved" cereal
80 It can't be good
81 Part of a magical incantation
82 Smooths
83 Ronan ___, "God Bless America" singer at Yankee Stadium
85 Didn't lie?
87 Flower girl, sometimes
88 Some pool sites
91 Bookkeeper's mailing: Abbr.
94 Through
96 Salad morsel
98 Law school class
99 One interested in net savings?
101 Grp. founded in Washington on 4/4/1949
102 Pulverized
103 Creator of Genesis
104 Somewhat
107 Where a person might get into a habit
110 "___ say . . ."
112 Bill producers
113 Site for sore eyes?
115 Sci. class
116 Lord in France
117 Net
118 Part of a piggy bank
121 Originally
122 Kind of operation
123 "Let me think about that . . ."

by Seth A. Abel

ACROSS

1 Thwacked but good
7 Come to one's senses
13 Trial case
20 Needing crackers, say
21 Spotted cat
22 More than tanned
23 Is acquainted with a quartet of wildebeests?
25 Consummate skill
26 Have coming
27 Poetic contraction
28 Religious sch.
30 Clears for liftoff
31 What is that in Mexico?
33 Community character
36 Drill one more time
38 Early run?
40 Booby-trapped nudist resort?
43 Soul buddy?
46 Skin ___
48 Cornmeal creation
49 Like 60% of people
51 Prudent time to get to the airport
54 ___ Dinh Diem of Vietnam
55 Old guy, slangily
56 Young guy, slangily
57 Subject of some gossip
61 Busy
62 Poet ___ García Lorca
65 Had plenty
66 "Once in Love With ___"
69 Vegetarians' supermarket protests?
73 "Um" cousins
74 Sulking more
76 One who's fallen
78 Home of the world's second-oldest written constitution, after America's
79 Make it big
82 Traveling
86 Old Olds models
87 Record producer Brian
88 Belief in disbelief
91 Contractions
92 Outskirts of the outskirts
96 Italian, e.g.
97 ___-wolf
98 Transported a couple of Porta-Potties?
101 C.S.I. evidence
102 Zoom in on
105 Sought morays
106 Foolish talk
108 "Fanny Hill," supposedly
110 Hockey's Tikkanen
112 Fifth and Mad.
114 Skip it
117 City on the Smoky Hill River
119 Rose raised by a sardonic gardener?
123 Less considered
124 Title heroine of a hit 2001 French film
125 Diplomat Harriman
126 Emotional
127 Busybodies
128 Towers above

DOWN

1 Expressway
2 Trollope's "Lady ___"
3 Place for strikes or strokes
4 Dots on a map
5 Salon workers, for short?
6 Nimble
7 Pointed
8 Main threat?
9 Calc. prerequisite
10 Blood sharers
11 Old French coins
12 Results of piercing pain?
13 1972 treaty subj.
14 Available on the stock exchange
15 "And they went ___ in a Sieve": Edward Lear
16 Robin Williams-esque
17 Eastern European guy who loves both sexes?
18 Word turned into its own opposite by putting a T in front
19 Big name in ice cream
24 Shy person?
29 Candy billed as "The Freshmaker"
32 Heed
34 She was famously married 3/20/69 at the Rock of Gibraltar
35 Initials for two Belushis
37 Bagged leaves
38 Horizontal, perhaps
39 Oktoberfest serving
41 "Exodus" hero
42 Word on a wall, in the Bible
44 Vulture, e.g.
45 Beginnings
47 Symbol on the front of some bars
49 Halt
50 Mideast capital
52 Campaign dirty trick
53 Trumpeter on the "Kill Bill" soundtrack
55 "___ go!"
58 Sis, e.g.
59 Horned Frogs' sch.
60 Kind of pain
63 Key of "The James Bond Theme"
64 List for St. Peter
65 Fidgety
66 Horrifies
67 Cabbage
68 Christmas quilters' haze?
70 Number cruncher, for short
71 Ad follow-up?
72 "Wait ___!"
75 Poi source
77 Individually
79 One-spot
80 En route
81 Oval-shaped loaf
83 Alternative energy source
84 Speller's phrase
85 Community ctr.
89 Prefix with realist
90 Teeny, slangily
92 Manhattan, for one: Abbr.
93 Follower of Manhattan
94 Milk source
95 Convalescent sites
98 Noble partner
99 Current resisters
100 Had too much
103 "The Prince of Tides" co-star
104 Certain '60s protest
107 Bouquet
108 When repeated, a dolphinfish
109 Abba of Israel
111 French weapon
113 Calif. force
115 Ill-gotten gains
116 Mound stats
118 Poetic preposition
120 Long
121 Place for a toothpick
122 Postgrad field

by Lee Glickstein and Ben Tausig

ACROSS

1 Major-league team with the most season losses, 120, in the 20th century
5 Fills positions for
11 A mouse moves over it
14 "Get ___!"
17 Former enemy capital
18 Kind of wrestling
19 House painting attire, maybe
22 Electrolysis particle
23 Whining from execs?
25 Be slightly turned on?
27 "Son of Frankenstein" role
28 Mint family plant
29 Rock guitarist Barrett
30 Flight
32 Pens and needles
35 "Summer of Sam" director
36 Day ___
39 Laid up
41 "Yikes!"
42 Fashionable gun?
47 Lose resilience
49 Ringside shout
50 Regard
52 Cheesy snack
53 Engineering project begun in 1898
55 Usher to, as a table
57 Princess of Power
58 Money in the bag, maybe
59 "Well, this pays the rent"
61 Bug
62 Whit
63 Deletes
66 "Then join you with them, like ___ of steel": Shak.
67 Assistants at a Kate Spade factory?
71 Valle del Bove locale
72 ___ Park, N.J.
74 NASA vehicle
75 Part of a winning combination
76 Irish-born actress McKenna
78 Washer setting
80 Like James Brown's music
82 Snoops
83 Someone sexy
85 60 shares, e.g.
87 Cordial
88 The Wildcats of the N.C.A.A.
89 New England hockey hero
90 Unit amount of sunlight seen?
92 Knotted up
94 Central
96 Suffix with Ecuador
97 Accident
100 Missouri city, briefly
102 Flit (about)
103 Equi- equivalent
106 Motivated
109 As recently as
111 Reunion no-shows?
115 Hemlock?
118 Go blading
119 Literary orphan
120 Swimming
121 Glacial ice formation
122 Three of a kind, in poker parlance
123 Suffix with bass
124 Scenic vistas, briefly
125 African antelope

DOWN

1 Stick
2 Isolate
3 Play garden produce like a horn?
4 New York's Mount ___ Hospital
5 No-no's opposite?
6 Letter-shaped fastener
7 Mine entrances
8 In a proper manner
9 Braved
10 High-hatter
11 Beer can feature
12 ___ right
13 W.W. II event
14 Shaggy sponsor of a sort?
15 Lodge
16 N.Y.C. arena
17 "The Laughing Cavalier" artist
20 Sprightly dances
21 Brief online message
24 A. A. for children
26 Place trailers are in
31 Wires
33 ___ land
34 Footnote word
37 Grenade part
38 Santa ___ (hot winds)
39 To whom "We'll always have Paris" was spoken
40 Time for crowing
43 Key with three sharps: Abbr.
44 Separation
45 "Voilà!"
46 Examination of an English royal house?
48 Phazyme alternative
50 Raison ___
51 Relieving knee pain?
53 Uninteresting
54 Cat's sniffer?
55 Kingdom of Broadway
56 Beat
60 Long jumper
62 Inconstant
64 Prevent from making a hit?
65 Gets some color
68 Wreck site
69 Supermarket chain
70 Nurse
73 Able to see right through
77 "Say as he says, ___ shall never go": "The Taming of the Shrew"
79 Gang land
80 Farm young
81 Old
83 "Gilligan's Island" dwellings
84 Attending to a task
86 F.D.R. plan
90 They meet in the middle
91 ___-European
93 "Go, and catch a falling star" poet
95 City connected to Philadelphia by the Benjamin Franklin Bridge
98 Where kites may be found
99 Canon competitor
101 Sommer in the cinema
103 Ishmael's half-brother
104 Rap relative
105 Ready to be drawn
107 "One Good Cop" actress
108 Tiny time period: Abbr.
110 Jerk
112 ID's with two hyphens
113 It may be given from father to son
114 PC screens
115 Station personalities
116 Actress ___ Dawn Chong
117 Back again

by Joe DiPietro

ACROSS

1 Outstanding football player
7 Keep after further changes
13 Indian-related
19 Letter-shaped tesserae
20 Little sucker
21 He wrote "Even the worthy Homer sometimes nods"
22 Store I most like to shop at?
24 Ready for publication
25 Comic Auerbach
26 2600, 5200 and 7800, gamewise
27 Photo ___
29 Site of July 1944 fighting
30 Jack who hosted the 1950s game show "Dotto"
32 Mouse catcher, in Madrid
34 Actress Aniston, to friends
36 Missing from 22-Across
37 Melee in a Dumpster?
42 Fix up, as old floors
45 "Too bad"
46 1957 hit for the Bobbettes
47 Combine
48 Hang around
51 Missing from 119-Across
52 ___ Corner, Va. (Washington suburb)
53 N.R.C. forerunner
54 What you will
55 Cabbie's call
57 Worked (up)
58 Missing from 73-Down
59 Clothing retailer beginning in 1969
60 Flipper?
62 Most calm
65 Discounted by
66 Rouses
68 Seasonal beverage
69 Perennial best-seller subjects
71 Medieval chest
74 Dr. Egon ___ ("Ghostbusters" role)
77 Imagine
81 Signals
83 Missing from 13-Down
84 Busy travel day, typically
86 East German secret police
87 Baseball Hall-of-Famer Al
88 Actress Gardner
89 Glacial ridges
91 Missing from 61-Down
92 Where Zaragoza is
93 Blue Stater, more likely than not
94 Pioneering weather satellite
95 Federico of Clinton's cabinet
96 Novel
98 Place to wash clothes in old Rome?
100 U.S. News or YM
102 Gold units: Abbr.
103 Vater's boy
105 Memorable 1966 hurricane
106 "I Ain't Marching Anymore" singer
108 Cry of surprise
110 Overflowed
113 Arab capital
117 Senator's locale
119 Droid in an oil container?
122 Looked like Groucho
123 Some T-shirt designs
124 Arose
125 Pitcher's quote
126 Cops' weapons
127 Tone deafness

DOWN

1 Soprano Gluck
2 Astronomical meas.
3 Good news on a gloomy day, e.g.
4 Objections
5 Exhibit
6 Baja bruin
7 Missing from 37-Across
8 Forces
9 Apelike
10 Starbuck's order?
11 Dictionary abbr.
12 Prefix with -derm
13 A particular bit of typography?
14 Casting need
15 It's usually blue, green or brown
16 Certain eligibility requirement for Little League?
17 Amtrak service
18 Deceived
20 Where Kofi Annan received an M.B.A.
23 Finely honed
28 Attire with pics of sheep, maybe
31 ___ Martin (cognac)
33 Source of spices for old traders
35 Charlie Chan player on TV
37 Soaks
38 Thrown for ___
39 Super Bowl XXXVII winner, for short
40 Sheet of ice
41 Leanings
43 Go over
44 Communications orbiter
47 Get by
49 Pilots' info
50 Sales crew
52 Bolt holder
56 "Maybe this is fate"
58 "Be ___" ("Help me out")
61 Heeds humorist George?
63 Memory trace
64 Across
67 Jon with the 1992 hit "Just Another Day"
70 "___ of the D'Urbervilles"
71 "Lonely Boy" singer
72 Crowd sound
73 What you hear on a Chris Rock recording?
75 Faux "buttons"
76 Hoist again, as a sail
78 Whiz
79 Not abstaining
80 Type measures
82 Actress Aimée
85 Missing from 16-Down
89 Expiate
90 Airer of many games
95 Founder of Lima
97 Show to a seat, informally
98 1992 Elton John hit
99 Postgame productions
100 Cabbage
101 Functioned
104 Four Holy Roman emperors
107 Missing from 98-Across
109 Passing mention?
111 Range: Abbr.
112 Quizzical sounds
114 OPEC member
115 Italian artist Guido
116 Saint from Kiev
118 Dripping
120 Mouths, zoologically
121 Org. receiving royalties for "God Bless America"

by Brendan Emmett Quigley

ACROSS

1 With 126-Across, author of the quip starting at 27-Across
6 Kind of race
10 "Come Back, Little Sheba" playwright
14 Modern home of the 10-Down
18 Product sold with a bag
20 "Hop ___!"
21 Tyros
23 Bill Clinton memoir
24 Nasty sort
25 Effecting a release
26 Blue
27 Start of a quip from Court and Society Review, 1887
30 V.I.P.
32 Literature Nobelist Morrison
33 What "Lucy in the Sky With Diamonds" may or may not be about
34 Quip, part 2
38 Edit
44 "An Affair to Remember" star, 1957
45 Berlioz's "Les nuits d'___"
46 Man of mystery
47 Layered
48 Project completion?
49 King Minos, for one
52 Site for Franklin Roosevelt
54 Matter of debate
55 Pageant prize
57 Quip, part 3
60 "It's about time!"
62 Lucre
63 Energizer or Duracell option
64 Low-value wad
65 Quip, part 4
70 "The Thief of Bagdad" actor, 1940
73 Ramallah grp.
74 Mystique
75 W.W. II wolf pack
79 Quip, part 5
83 "Rubber Duckie" singer of children's TV
84 See 112-Down
85 Winter pear
86 Brynhild's beloved
90 Granting grp.
91 It can be found in a tree
93 Cry with eyes lit up
95 4×4
96 Cold war winner
97 Huge, to Hugo
98 Quip, part 6
102 Lao-___
104 Dutch export
105 Dia's opposite
106 End of the quip
113 Try to win, in a way
116 Like a Swiss Army knife
117 One of a sailing trio
118 Time competitor, informally
120 Used a crowbar on, maybe
121 Election day: Abbr.
122 Fish that may someday spawn
123 Call after a hammer is hit
124 Agrippina's slayer
125 Prize since 1949
126 See 1-Across

DOWN

1 ___ law
2 Nutritious bean
3 Breakfast in a box
4 Flying start?
5 Common ink purchase
6 Tittle
7 It's read word for word
8 Fun house item
9 "Revolution From Within" author
10 Old inhabitant of 14-Across
11 With every hair in place
12 Ones dressed in black
13 F.D.A.-banned supplement
14 Match player?
15 Dramatic rebuke
16 Scout leader?
17 S O S responder: Abbr.
19 Satisfied subscriber, apparently
22 Part of a manger scene
28 Stem
29 Poet with the longtime NPR program "A Word in Your Ear"
31 Pencil holder, sometimes
34 Muscular watchdog
35 Sparked anew
36 "But on the other hand . . ."
37 Early sixth-century year
39 Put out
40 Stain
41 Actor Williams of "Happy Days"
42 Revolution, for one
43 Hammock supports
47 Sic on
49 Bills, e.g.
50 Exactly, after "to"
51 Court plea, briefly
53 Anne of comedy
56 Bygone Crayola color
58 Black piano key
59 Pearl City setting
61 Imbibe
62 Brigham Young University site
66 "Let's ___ There" (1980s NBC slogan)
67 Dim responses
68 ". . . ___ saw Elba"
69 Retired
70 Tired
71 Mark Twain/Bret Harte play
72 Game of chance
76 "Black Beauty" author
77 Link with
78 ___ Tranquillity
80 Offer that seems too good to be true, probably
81 Birthright seller
82 Lug
87 Floor (it)
88 Knoxville sch.
89 Get back on track
92 Begin something, in slang
94 Just firm enough
96 Lofty degree
98 It's a test
99 Element that quickly oxidizes in air
100 Artist with the 2002 #1 hit "Lose Yourself"
101 Winter fishing tool
103 Not attack head-on
106 Family viewing mark
107 "My ___!"
108 March slogan word
109 Dawning response
110 "Way cool!"
111 Strange: Prefix
112 With 84-Across, very simple
114 Had to settle
115 Bone head?
119 Application form abbr.

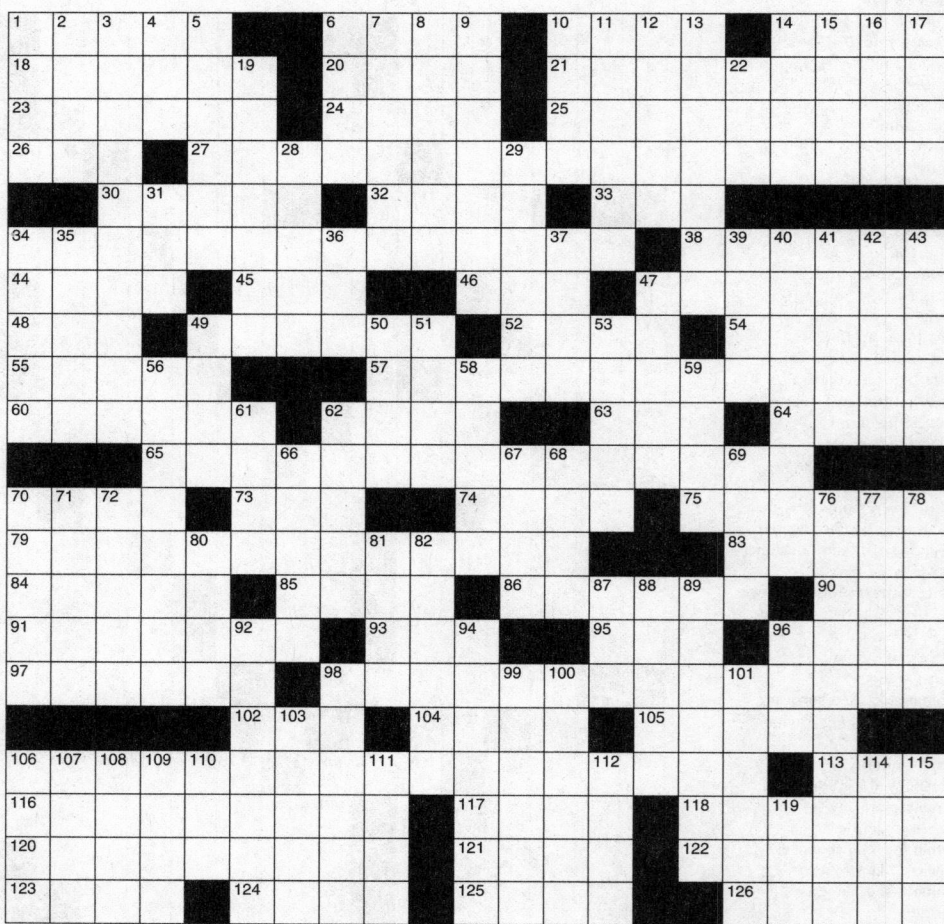

by Mark Diehl and Kevin McCann

ACROSS

1 Mitsubishi S.U.V.
8 Knocked their socks off
15 Earth
20 Wake-up call, e.g.
21 It may be said after kissing the tips of one's fingers
22 Healing plants
23 What the peddler owes?
25 B-ball
26 Bust ___
27 Construction material in King Solomon's temple
28 National rival
30 Driver's aid
31 Maker of the first walkie-talkie
34 "All My ___ Live in Texas" (1987 #1 country hit)
36 Berate
38 Lt.'s subordinate
39 Top Tatar's tattler?
44 Jellied dishes in England
45 Place for a father-to-be: Abbr.
46 First name in gossip
47 Passes
49 Squad leaders: Abbr.
52 Way to the top
54 Shirt tag info
56 Not knowing what to do
59 "You're ___!" (Archie Bunker comment)
60 Advice for an understaffed yachtsman?
63 ___ seul (solo dance)
64 Change for a fin
66 Net alternative
67 Close pitches
69 Kind of acid
70 Unable to get loose
74 Site of a 1797 Napoleon victory
75 Cause of some spots
77 Screwball
78 Apple holder, maybe
80 St. Martin, e.g.
81 Result of whipping?
85 Architect William Van ___
86 Simmons competitor
88 Suffix with flex
89 Cartoonist who drew the Shmoo
90 Mimics
91 Some hotel visits
93 Summer coolers
95 Clamor
96 Spanish for "are"
98 Best-selling baseball equipment?
102 Sec
105 Neverland
107 Common street name
108 At no charge
110 Classic New Yorker cartoonist ___ Irvin
111 100 centimes
114 ___ set (group of tools)
117 Early Beatles, affectionately
118 "The Goat, or Who Is Sylvia?" writer
120 Packer fan's angry cry after an interception?
124 Massey of "Rosalie"
125 Slimmest election margin
126 Cupidity
127 Cake part
128 Balcony's edge
129 Gifts

DOWN

1 ___ Defarge of "A Tale of Two Cities"
2 Hells Canyon locale
3 "Quit your excuses"
4 All, in music
5 That, to Tadeo
6 Call
7 Ouija, e.g.
8 Blue dye
9 Dancing girl in "The Return of the Jedi"
10 "The ground ___ she trod": Milton
11 Urban carriers
12 Patterned fabric
13 Operation Exodus participant
14 "Every ___ king"
15 Literally, "big water"
16 Grp. with the 1977 platinum album "Out of the Blue"
17 Hoboes by nature?
18 Anti-Prohibitionist's cause
19 Ledger column
24 Burn
29 Repetitive sort
32 Delivery lines: Abbr.
33 Law man?
35 Unknown
37 Riga native
40 Show horse
41 Ring figure
42 Ox-eyed queen of myth
43 Means to ___
45 Fla. vacation spot
48 Black currant flavor in wines
49 Bush activities
50 Skeletal support in a sponge
51 Muppet seller's gender guideline?
52 Lao-___
53 1940s first lady
55 Woeful words
57 Flashback caption
58 Transfers
60 Cry made with one's arm behind one's back
61 Less than right?
62 Real-life boxing champ who appeared in "Rocky II"
65 Lubrication channel
68 VCR insert
71 Bottom-of-letter abbr.
72 Panpharmacon
73 Insomnia cause
76 O'Connor successor
79 Alley ___
82 Recipe abbr.
83 Fast server?
84 Island that's part of 90-Down: Abbr.
87 Big fat mouth
90 See 84-Down: Abbr.
92 Clash (with)
94 Floor wiper
95 Elevs.
96 Overseas train service
97 ___ Artois, beer from Belgium
99 "Mr. Belvedere" co-star
100 Hit man
101 Pawed
102 Attract
103 Blue-pencil
104 Impatient agreement
106 Start to a bit of bad news
109 Blaze
112 Opposite of under
113 Kid watcher
115 Suffix with electro-
116 Sarcastic comment
119 Little Rock-to-Memphis dir.
121 Seductive Longoria
122 New Deal inits.
123 Chess champion Mikhail

by Ashish Vengsarkar

ACROSS

1 Slanted
7 Silly smile
13 "Le Rhinocéros" playwright
20 Protracted prayer
21 Relative of a rhododendron
22 Start of a hole
23 Job for a ballroom dance instructor?
25 Refuse to help in the garden?
26 Is in the Vatican
27 Sing ___ Daily, major Hong Kong newspaper
28 Altar in the sky
29 "Nonsense!"
31 Internet message
32 Discovery accompaniers
34 Job for a lingerie salesclerk?
38 Popeye, for one
39 Divine
41 Jimjams
42 Sainted pope called "the Great"
43 No. of People, say
44 Start of Idaho's motto
45 Anatomical enclosure
47 Banks on
50 Vegetable with sushi
52 Officer who may not be in uniform
55 Elects
56 Bus. runners
59 Job for a coffee shop employee?
64 Base approval
66 Shrinks' org.
67 Modern music genre
68 Blocks
70 Mucho
71 Mass. summer setting
72 "Family ___"
74 Decorate, as a 54-Down
75 It rolls on a Rolls
77 127-Down grp.
78 PC user's shortcut
80 Fearsome weapon
83 Martinmas's mo.
84 Grind
85 Miscellany
87 Job for a high school teacher?
90 Diamond of note
91 Bite
93 Suffix with super
94 Info at SFO
95 "Forget it"
98 Sermon subject
100 Man chaser?
103 Fix
105 "___ take arms . . ."
106 Queen of the fairies
109 Rosencrantz or Guildenstern, in "Hamlet"
112 Least bit
113 Job for an architect?
116 Roughly
117 Yawning
119 What a keeper may keep
120 Poetic ending with how
121 Idled
123 The Divine, to da Vinci
124 "With All Disrespect" essayist
126 Job for a business tycoon?
130 Supremely spooky
131 Skirts
132 Putter's near-miss
133 Jilts
134 Mixture of many spices, in Indian cookery
135 Ties a no-frills knot?

DOWN

1 Green
2 It has a tip for a ballerina
3 Rama and Krishna, e.g.
4 Was up
5 Quick approval: Abbr.
6 Appetite whetter
7 Baseball's Maglie
8 "The Compleat Angler" author Walton
9 Siege site of 1936–39
10 Flexible
11 Extra-wide spec
12 Farriers' tools
13 Most eager to go
14 Antipoverty agcy.
15 Moriarty, to Holmes
16 X Games airer
17 Job for a film photographer?
18 Multi–Emmy-winning NBC sportscaster
19 Bewhiskered animals
24 Subject heading for strategizers
30 In a tizzy
33 Party prep
35 Worrisome mechanical sound
36 Prime meridian std.
37 Kids' jumping game
40 Absolutely fabulous
46 Italian sweetheart
48 Farm measures
49 "___ Excited" (Pointer Sisters hit)
51 "This one's ___"
53 More cordlike
54 See 74-Across
57 Flub
58 Development sites
59 Subordinate deity, in classical myth
60 Modernize
61 Job for a dating service counselor?
62 Ascend
63 "You can't get out this way"
65 Lift
69 Harmony
73 Where some major arteries go
76 Medea, for one
79 Move, in Realtor-speak
81 Box
82 Certain specialty docs
86 See 108-Down
88 Competitor of State Farm
89 Handled
92 Disgraces
96 Hobbyist with toy trains, e.g.
97 J.F.K. debater in 1960
99 Chinese restaurant sign
101 Help from on high
102 What's left
103 Steamy, maybe
104 "Hear, hear!"
107 Early NASA rockets
108 With 86-Down, popular serial comic strip beginning in 1940
110 Functional
111 Settles down for the night
114 Against a thing, legally
115 Cantilevered window
118 Dancer's dip
122 It might make you a sweater
125 Suffix with spiritual
127 The Cavaliers of coll. football
128 Hush-hush grp.
129 Mil. mail depot

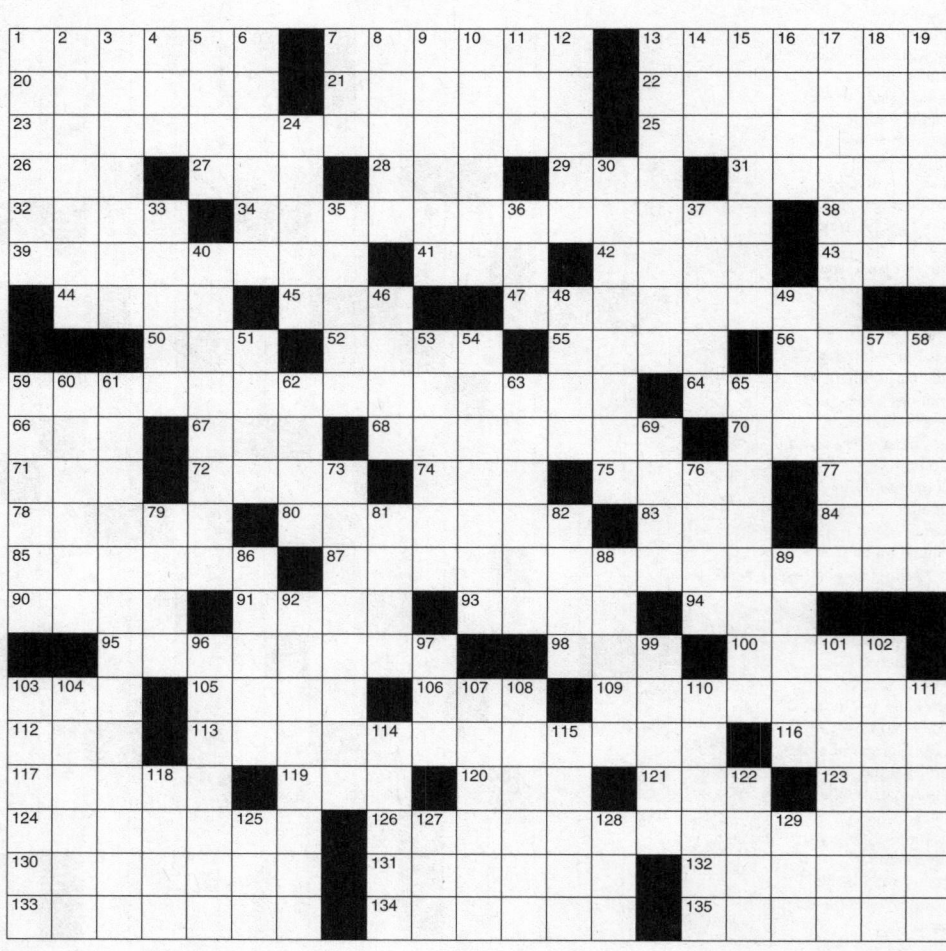

by Norma Johnson & Nancy Salomon

ACROSS

1 How sale goods may be sold
8 Hardy bulbs
13 Hockey game starter, often
20 Contract
21 Even if, briefly
22 Humbled
23 Ann Landers, e.g.
24 Further shorten, maybe
25 Fooled around
26 Dirty coat
27 Hollywood stars, e.g.
29 Hang loose
31 Swim routine
32 Chaps
33 Henna and others
34 Helgenberger of "C.S.I."
38 Heroine of a Gershwin opera
39 Horse course
41 Swing around
45 Praise from a choir
47 "Here ___"
49 "Holy mackerel!" and others
51 Utilizes fully
53 Where to find an eBay listing
54 It's often left hanging
55 ___ Brazzi, star of "South Pacific"
56 Harvester ___
57 Personae non ___
60 Cur
61 Conforming to
65 Sympathetic
66 Hands down
67 Williams with a crown, once
74 Hits hard
75 Mr. Big, e.g.
76 High points
77 Suffix with Ecuador
78 Bilingual Muppet
81 Legendary
85 Soldier's accessory of old
86 Actress Gardner
87 Precisely
88 Hymn pronoun
89 Small racer
90 Honks off, so to speak
91 B. D. ___ of Broadway's "M. Butterfly"
92 Staff note
94 Henley who wrote "Crimes of the Heart"
95 Hopper
99 Irish revolutionary Robert
100 Had dinner at home
102 Natty sorts
106 Vulnerable to fire
108 Product label abbr.
110 Teases
112 Kind of family
113 Masonry, for one
114 Shows
115 Hands out, as homework
116 Some HDTV's
117 Haifa money

DOWN

1 Hieroglyphic figures
2 Huxtable boy, on "The Cosby Show"
3 Florence is on it
4 Trap contents
5 Some ducts carry them
6 Highway behemoth
7 Heavy hitters
8 "Haven't Got Time for the Pain" singer, 1974
9 Like non-oyster months
10 Some score notations, for short
11 Leafy green
12 "Thanks, pal"
13 Ancient
14 Soft-soap
15 Leather sticker
16 Carter of sitcomdom
17 Part of a score
18 Heavy
19 Interjects
28 Heave-hos
30 Go after, as a rebound
34 Hepburn, Garbo and Gable employer, once
35 Huntsville's home: Abbr.
36 Seoul soldier
37 Rocky Mountains line
38 Tip of Manhattan
40 Very expensive contest prizes?
41 Hera, to Persephone
42 Drug once available under the commercial name Delysid
43 Emma player in "The Avengers"
44 Fancy name appendage
46 Hebrew of old
48 Diamond cutter?
49 Series terminal
50 Macho way to fight
52 Old atlas abbr.
57 Former high-tech co.
58 "Citizen X" star, 1995
59 Response: Abbr.
62 Cousin ___ of "The Addams Family"
63 Name separator
64 Dept. store stuff
67 Ad ___ (how tariffs may be assessed)
68 Homes, for some
69 Norse goddess of fate
70 Heckler's missile
71 "I ___ bad moon rising"
72 Hand cleaners at the dinner table
73 Phoenician fertility deity
78 Bit of sch. writing
79 "How exciting!"
80 Halmstad's locale: Abbr.
82 "How was ___ know?"
83 Place for a duck
84 Hosp. readout
93 County with the White Sands National Monument
94 Blue
95 Howe who wrote "Pride's Crossing"
96 Weight
97 Hyperbola parts
98 "Hallucinogenic Toreador" artist
99 New York cardinal
101 First name in a dictionary
102 Hall-of-Fame catcher Carlton
103 Plains native
104 Apostle who wrote "Ye see how large a letter I have written"
105 Heathrow sights, once
107 Photog's image
109 Spank
111 Heavy-duty cleanser

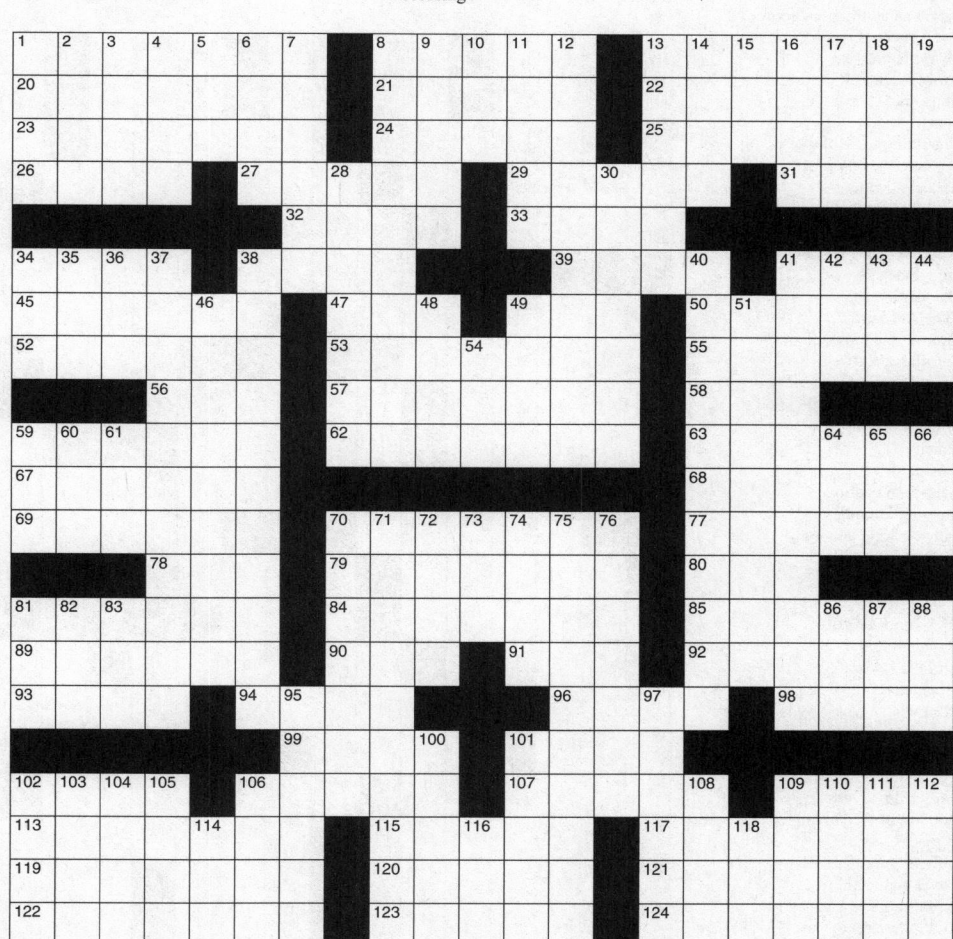

by Harvey Estes

SANDWICH MAN

ACROSS

1. Modern wall hanging
5. Military letters
9. Kind of case in grammar: Abbr.
12. Fruit of a flower
19. Place
20. Water carrier
21. Shetland turndown
22. Nail polish remover
23. Cheery fellow in the neighborhood?
26. One for the books
27. "You got that right!"
28. Slowly ascended
30. Class clown, e.g.
31. More furtive
32. Actress Kelly
33. Empties (of)
35. Bit of tax planning, for short
36. Excellent portrayal of a Gary Cooper role?
39. Hitch
40. Brainy
45. Work periods
46. Fireplace
47. Social breakdown
48. Turkish title
49. Answer men
50. "Let me repeat . . ."
51. Tattoo an anonymous source?
56. Dried coconut meat
57. Charlotte ___
58. "Holy mackerel!"
59. Night spot
60. Clears
61. Something to "call me" per an old song . . . or a hint to this puzzle's theme
65. Tin Man's malady
68. Let up
70. Turn red or yellow, say
71. Impermissible
72. Flat storage site
73. "The A-Team" actor on the cover of GQ?
76. Lines on a staff
77. Presenter of a likeness?
78. Start of a Latin conjugation
79. Minnesota college
80. Match
81. "Enough!"
84. Gemstone quality
86. Running in circles?
87. Father's song about a 79-Down character?
89. Bard's "before"
90. Pull (in)
91. "It's Too Late Now" autobiographer
92. All in ___ work
97. Mountain climber, e.g.
99. Saint whose feast day is December 25
102. 1969 hit by the Who
103. Nuts
105. Get a bald advertising icon out of the slammer?
107. In pieces
108. Father figures
109. Cover girl Heidi
110. Razor name
111. AOL alternative
112. Sheffield-to-London dir.
113. Big name in games
114. Outdoor wedding rental

DOWN

1. Returnees from Mecca
2. Not laugh-out-loud funny, perhaps
3. Place for a programme
4. Dance in France
5. "This is right ___ alley"
6. Mediterranean isl.
7. Keep from overheating, in a way
8. Rococo
9. Recipe amount
10. Starr of the N.F.L.
11. Bach's "___, Joy of Man's Desiring"
12. Campus figs.
13. Candles in a menorah, e.g.
14. They may go under the arms
15. Response to a backstabber
16. Putting up a guy in the bath?
17. Among other things
18. Aristocracies
24. "Babi ___" (Yevtushenko poem)
25. They may make you sick
29. Kind of income
32. Extinct flightless bird
34. Security needs
36. Test before further studies, for short
37. Geom. line
38. Many a NASA employee: Abbr.
39. Showy bloom
40. Stone heap
41. Come after
42. Honored a monocled man at the Friars Club?
43. Diplomats
44. Wait
46. Game player's gleeful cry
49. View by computed tomography
51. Noted polar explorer
52. Charles, for one
53. Natural bristles
54. Wyo. neighbor
55. John on a farm
59. Angled
61. Attention-getting cry
62. Open ___ . . .
63. Typing test stat.
64. Election closer?
66. RC's, e.g.
67. Fashion plates, in British lingo
69. Low part of a high top
71. Place for a béret
72. Havana's home
73. Column material
74. "Typee" sequel
75. Idiotic
77. Pitcher
79. See 87-Across: Abbr.
81. Turn red or yellow, say
82. Dunk
83. Singer Lopez
84. Achieve through trickery
85. ___ St.-Louis, Paris
87. Mabel who sang "Fly Me to the Moon"
88. Lighthouse signals
90. Aptly named author Charles
92. Film buff's channel
93. Key of Prokofiev's Piano Concerto No. 1
94. Mountain ridge
95. Pine
96. Overseas assembly
98. Mozart's ___ Symphony (No. 36)
100. Mail letters
101. College application nos.
102. "Joy of Cooking" author Rombauer
104. Sign of success
106. Kisser

by Elizabeth C. Gorski

ACROSS

1 Fooling (around)
8 Open, in a way
13 7, on modern phones
17 Alternatively
21 "Way to go!"
22 Weeping daughter of Tantalus
23 Perfectly, after "to"
24 Must have
25 White ___ House
27 Moved to and fro
29 Adds to the pot, say
30 Each
31 "The Sound of Music" name
33 Hunting canine
34 Intermittently, after "off"
35 Small spray
37 Muse of mimicry
39 Singer Mann
40 Big name in faucets
41 N.L. East team, on scoreboards
42 Double ___ play
45 Sun. talks
46 Loop loopers
47 Streamlined
49 Some E.M.S. cases
50 Address
52 U.S. 1, for one: Abbr.
53 Ultrapatriot
55 Ole Miss rival
56 Postgrad degs.
59 Orange ___ Bowl
66 Sign of love . . . or rejection
68 Heavenly hunter
69 Bruin
70 One given "unto us," in Isaiah
71 Sundae topper
72 Spur (on)
73 Defeater of R.M.N.
74 Latin twinklers
75 Monocle part
76 Easter ___ bunny
85 Airline rarity, increasingly
86 Had a lame-duck session, say
87 Part missing from a vest
88 Poet laureate before Southey
89 Fails to
91 Attending to the matter
92 Too, in Toulouse
95 Skater Slutskaya
97 Had
98 e ___ Bay
101 Comprehend
102 Answer to the riddle "The higher
    it goes, the less you hear it"
104 Stand
105 Early third-century year
106 Alternatives
108 Engine part
109 Nada
111 F.B.I. facility
114 Thickening agent
117 New ___ Latin
120 Head's opposite
121 Only: Fr.
122 Fanatical
124 Fab Four name
125 Whacks
127 Part of MGM
128 Tropical fruits
130 Like many benefit tournaments
132 Computer file suffix
133 University in Greenville, S.C.
134 Like the 1915 San Francisco
    Mint $50 gold coin
136 Flag ___ Day
139 Exhausted
140 Seconds
141 Words after "put an" or "see no"
142 Fit for consumption
143 Time long past
144 Cornerstone abbr.
145 "The Exorcist" actor, with "von"
146 :-) :-) :-)

DOWN

1 It's tied up in knots
2 Tractor powerer, maybe
3 Progress
4 Printemps, par exemple
5 Norwegian playwright
6 Relatives of AND's and OR's
  in Boolean logic
7 High school class
8 Big name in auto racing
9 Kind of acid
10 Where streets meet: Abbr.
11 Support
12 Noblewoman
13 Contents of some patches
14 i ___ Pod
15 Gas station abbr.
16 Darns
17 Body ___ language
18 Lentil or bean
19 Petitioner
20 Whirlpools
26 Big ___ time
28 Bond rating
32 MGM motto opener
35 Start of many Québec place names
36 Former Patriots QB Steve
38 Mountain nymph
41 Pub offerings
43 Something carbon monoxide lacks
44 Rep.'s opposite
47 Render speechless
48 German canal name
51 Nut in mixed nuts
52 Varig destination
54 Hush-hush govt. org.
56 Abdominal pouches
57 Down's opposite: Abbr.
58 Blue shade
59 Average guys
60 Spur (on)
61 Bone connector
62 Take into custody
63 Beauty queen's wear
64 "The Thin Man" pooch
65 Actress Martin, star of TV's
   "National Velvet"
67 Tape, say
71 Dollar, slangily
73 Shock
74 It's the law
77 Suffix with Congo
78 Bit of beachwear
79 Setting for part of
   "King Henry VI, Part 2"
80 Mideast bigwig
81 Himalayan sighting
82 Hindu titles
83 Harmony
84 Furniture wood
89 Follow relentlessly
90 Show a deficit
92 Reproducing without
   fertilization
93 Letters at sea
94 1956 trouble spot
95 Desire
96 Goal for a D.H.
98 Trivial Pursuit edition
99 Kind of tide
100 Latin "behold!"
103 Former CBS military show
106 Buck ___ eye
107 In a tangle
108 Chianti containers
110 Part of L.A.
111 "Go away!"
112 With respect to hearing
113 Lightheaded people?
114 Fleet of ships
115 Bola user
116 One who suspends an action, at law
118 Leandro's love, in a
    Mancinelli opera
119 Urban renewal target
121 Soap format
123 Hammarskjöld of the U.N.
126 U-shaped river bend
127 Civvies
129 A portion
131 When repeated, a top five hit
    of 1968 or 1987
133 Deception
135 Turndowns
137 Like 9 or 5
138 Former defense secretary Aspin

by Derrick Niederman

ACROSS

1 Big rays
7 A little dirty
11 Fly nets?
15 Deer hunter
19 Golden Crinkles maker
20 Product in a tub
21 Mosque overseer
22 A part of
23 Bare
24 In a ___, there's at least one fluid ounce of ___
27 In a ___, there's a volume of ___ that keeps it firm
29 Designer Alvar
30 Symbol of Ireland
31 "Sixteen Tons" singer's workplace
32 In a ___, there's plenty of sweet ___ to be harvested
36 Nonexistent
37 Come by
39 Root used in perfumery
40 In a ___, you can periodically catch a ___
46 Entry need, maybe
48 Part of FWIW
49 Stackable snackables
50 Burst of energy
51 See 5-Down
52 Pounding
53 In ___, you might see some ___ hanging around
55 The America's Cup trophy, e.g.
56 Trueheart of "Dick Tracy"
57 "Foucault's Pendulum" author
58 Kind of bran
59 Region holding ancient Ephesus
62 Nuptial agreement
64 Scattered
66 In a ___, there's no shortage of ___ to drink
68 Targets
72 Red, white and blue letters
73 Mend a seam, say
74 Sutcliffe of the early Beatles
75 Stage sign
76 Onetime host of "The Morning Show" and "The Tonight Show"
79 Iran-Iraq war weapon
81 In the ___, there's the greatest concentration of ___
85 Latin word on a cornerstone
86 That isn't it
87 Actress Kelly
88 Grim, as a situation
89 Dogfight enclosure
90 "Get Smart" group
91 In a ___, many a ___ is rolled
93 Rejecters of modern technology
95 Advance again
97 Co. that created the term "Buddy List"
98 In a ___, there's lots of ___ in the machinery
100 Lengthy time units
102 Spritzer mixer
106 R&B singer Marie
107 In ___, plenty of ___ is growing
111 In a ___, many a ___ is standing
114 Two-syllable unit
115 Aftershave sold in green bottles
116 Needle holder
117 Animal on Sri Lanka's flag
118 Stone used by pedicurists
119 Philosophies
120 Some Hindu music
121 Items sometimes seen on car tops
122 Sets forth

DOWN

1 Go from person to person?
2 Team building
3 When pigs fly
4 Occupy
5 With 51-Across, Caped Crusader portrayer
6 Site on St. Paul's first missionary journey
7 Violinist's need
8 Role in Verdi's "Falstaff"
9 Copper
10 He's flexible
11 Use a paper towel on
12 Punk music subgenre
13 Rule out
14 Bit of negative campaigning
15 Supporting structure
16 Measure of one's worth?
17 Easter Island mysteries
18 Oscar winner Lee
25 Bad lighting?
26 Setting of Margaret Mead's first book
28 Attacks with a lance
33 Collapse
34 Plant resembling Queen Anne's lace
35 Double curves
36 Missing persons
37 He-men's opposites
38 Cartoon feline
40 Looks hangdog
41 Burp
42 Tone
43 "Arabian Nights" monster
44 Mo. of Paul Revere's midnight ride
45 Nickname of Lincoln's youngest son
47 Make furrows in
51 Dam in a stream
52 Bit
54 Card game that uses jokers
60 Have bills to pay
61 Like fresh hay
63 Active from dawn to dusk
65 Guilder's replacement
66 Tough guy
67 Wine list column
69 Dark expression
70 War hero Murphy
71 Trifling
74 Nostalgic 1970s variety show
76 Large oval fruit
77 Short drawers?
78 Immunity provider
80 Onerous duty
82 Refinery input
83 Prefix with city
84 Chat room abbr.
87 Extinct kiwi kin
90 Turkic tribal leaders
91 Animals used as food on "Lost"
92 Dishes the dirt
94 Some linen
96 Raven-haired heroine of a Poe tale
99 Eye site
100 End of a ballade
101 Starts off
102 Highest, as honors
103 The way of the world?
104 Two in one's hand
105 Fools
108 Wrigglers
109 Composer Satie
110 Stretched
111 Grp. in TV's "Criminal Minds"
112 Sch. group
113 Prayer ___

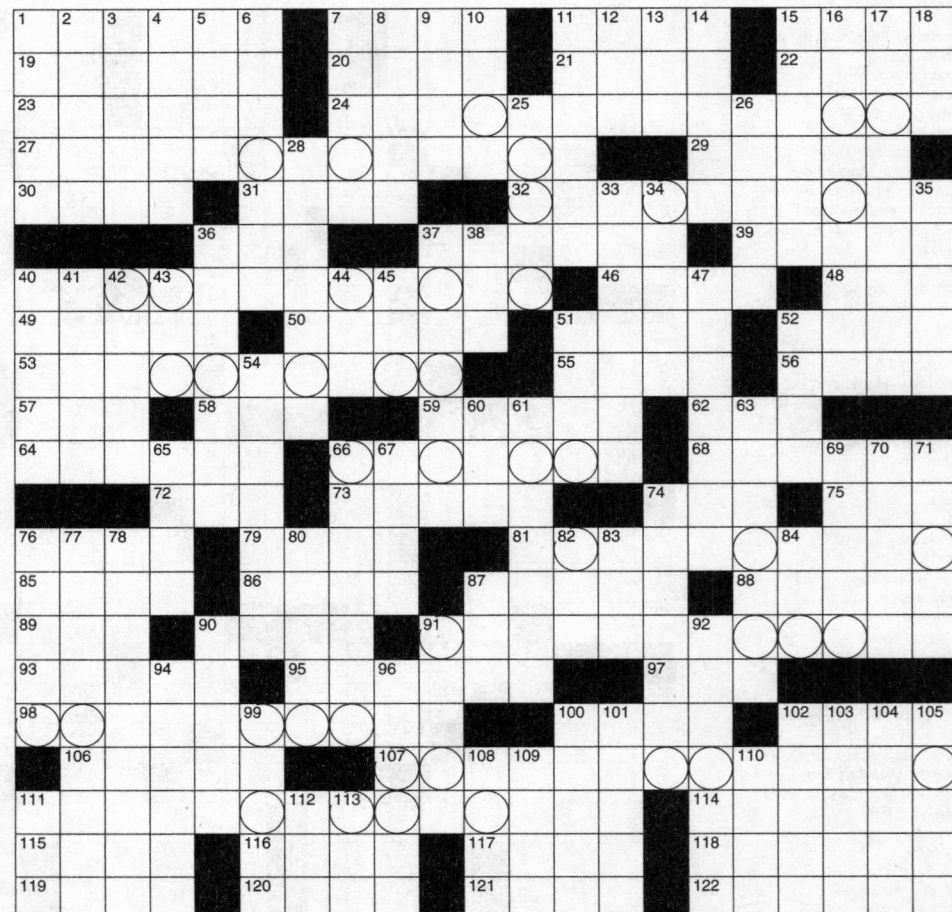

by Patrick Berry

ACROSS

1 Most distant
7 Big Twelve team
13 Last of the Minor Prophets
20 First Ford
21 Philippine port
22 Nonrecurring publication
23 33.8 ounces?
25 Some honky-tonk music
26 Stephen of "The Crying Game"
27 Decoy site, maybe
28 Boil
30 Screen figure
31 Singers James and Jones
33 Friend of Dorothy, on "Sesame Street"
35 Disconnect
38 Stalwart plumber's credo?
43 Pharmaceutical chemist ___ Lilly
46 [Wham!]
47 End
48 Father of the Titans
50 Special attention, for short
53 Al ___
56 Ratchets (up)
57 Spoken
58 Pros
60 Teetotaling nun?
63 Straight
64 Saint in Brazil
66 Pops
67 Prefix with comic
69 Lawn tool
70 Long ago, long ago
71 Fur, e.g.
74 ___ Blaster (classic arcade game)
77 "Se ___ inglés?"
79 Make a bad copy of?
80 Winner's cry
81 Fiddle (around)
83 Oddly colored shoe?
88 Tide type
89 One line at passport control
91 U.S. highway with a ferry connection between Delaware and New Jersey
92 Language of India
94 Parts of apts.
95 Karate teacher
96 San ___, Tex.
98 Neth. neighbor
100 ___ rose
101 What the wet, baggage-laden passenger might take at the train station?
108 Former British royal
110 Newcastle's river
111 Old print
112 Actress Lena
114 And others
118 Calls a game
120 Western setting: Abbr.
121 One on the left
124 The ram in "A ram walks into a bar . . ."?
127 Rich green
128 Abet, in a way
129 Contract-negotiating pro
130 Garments at a 44-Down
131 Certain smokes
132 Chargers

DOWN

1 Eastern inn
2 Approaches in the Bible?
3 Think
4 Ending with how
5 Sloppy
6 Kind of shell
7 Light
8 Word before, after—or both before and after—"in"
9 Harmful
10 Spot
11 On the safe side
12 Kind
13 Oscar winner for "West Side Story"
14 Something to give an Alabama cheerleader?
15 Race part
16 John of "Freaky Friday," 1977
17 Rooster?
18 Human genus
19 Highway damaged by hurricane Katrina
24 Again
29 Most imposing
32 Venom carrier
34 Film character whose first name is Longfellow
36 Home of "Winged Victory"
37 About
39 Is into
40 Home of the N.C.A.A.'s Minutemen
41 California's ___ Valley
42 Recipe amts.
44 Outdoor party
45 Place for a 44-Down
49 Craftsperson
50 Enter
51 Aid for a detective
52 Like some C.S.I. evidence?
54 Game show contestant's option
55 Way to the top
59 Dirtbags
61 No-goodnik
62 Respect
65 Venus or Mars
68 Unit of hope?
71 Whisper sweet nothings
72 Dais delivery
73 Film company
75 Stray
76 "Not good!"
78 Behind
79 & 81 Quick
82 Title apiarist of film
84 Peeved
85 Soave or Orvieto
86 Bldg. planner
87 World capital on a gulf of the same name
90 At hand
93 Healthful food claim
97 1970 #1 song and album
99 Rd.
102 Investors' info
103 Hardens
104 Captain of the Nautilus
105 Fight
106 Put on the line
107 Mums
109 Month before febrero
112 Praise for toreadors
113 Home of the oldest university in the continental Americas
115 Lincoln and others
116 ___ Park, old Coney Island attraction
117 Emphasized: Abbr.
119 NCO's charges
122 Tore
123 Some H.S. math
125 American ___
126 Mr. Average

by Tony Orbach

74 ENERGY CRUNCH

ACROSS

1 Prefix with -drome
5 Mogul
9 Philippine seaport
15 Mug
19 Low part of a hand
20 Pickup shtick?
21 "Haven't a clue!"
22 Duck: Ger.
23 Base leader
25 Parisian entertainment since 1869
27 "Likewise"
28 Shackles
30 Juicy, tart apple
31 It may be pushed before starting
32 Homestead Act unit
34 Sponsor at Indy
36 1 + 1 = 3, e.g.
37 River of Hesse
38 British ___
39 Western Hemisphere grp.
41 ___-Foy, Québec
42 "Time to go now!"
47 Pause that refreshes
50 Phrase of nonspecific attribution
52 Leaked, as from a container
54 Nashville-based awards org.
55 Diamond baron Cecil
56 1998 animated bug film
57 Nymph pursuers
59 "___ the ramparts . . ."
60 Tasting of wood, as some wines
63 Itch cause
67 Like some cottage cheese
68 Friend in a sombrero
71 Household scare
73 Natural sparkler
74 Bakery order
75 Hells Canyon locale
76 Not to mention
78 Tuneful city "by the sea-o"
79 Brought up the rear?
81 Stir up
83 Guiding light
86 Prince Valiant's firstborn
87 Directional aid
91 Teeth, slangily
93 L.A. hours
94 Slicker, umbrella, galoshes, etc.
96 Opening sound?
99 It's in the genes
100 Places for laces
101 Lure
105 Elevator stop
107 MoMA's home
109 Lifts
110 "Amadeus" star Tom
111 Steamed dishes
113 Place of sacrifice
115 "Ulysses" setting
116 Christmas decoration site
118 He was no dummy
121 Trojan ally in the "Iliad"
122 Sci-fi weaponry
123 Jean ___, creator of 56-Down
124 ___-majesté
125 Plain and simple
126 Does a dog trick
127 "This is going to get ___"
128 ___'acte

DOWN

1 It's worn
2 Worn
3 Rest
4 Place for pearls
5 Classic Liz Taylor part
6 President of Pakistan, 1978–88
7 Lily Tomlin's Edith ___
8 Many a Floridian
9 Skinny
10 Nutcases
11 Heater with a storage tank
12 Exiled Amin
13 Historic Virginia family
14 Kilns
15 Edvard Grieg work
16 Quick-acting intl. military unit
17 Dogie
18 Witnessed
24 Rye fungus
26 Raises a howl
29 Lean against
32 Screened terrier
33 White-collar workers?
35 No longer owed
38 Linda Ronstadt's "___ Easy"
40 ___-Cat
43 See here!
44 Some bedtime reading
45 Nelson in reruns
46 Onetime American Communist leader ___ Hall
48 Uncommon sources of music nowadays
49 Stick to
50 Setting for some Sherlock Holmes mysteries
51 Combining of companies making the same product
53 Zest
55 Travel guide
56 "The Clan of the Cave Bear" heroine
58 One little piggy
61 Bee: Prefix
62 On the canvas, informally
64 Lab vessel
65 Immigrant's course: Abbr.
66 Network on a 55-Down: Abbr.
69 Atty. ___
70 They're easy to dial on a rotary phone
72 Chuck
77 Winds in a pit
80 "What's the ___?"
82 Lake that's a source of the Mississippi
84 Big time
85 Potential lifesaver for a drowning person
88 Mars or Mercury
89 Ex-senator Sam
90 Site of swings and a sandbox
91 Restaurant chain founded in 1958 near L.A.
92 Edges
95 "Nothing is so much to be feared as fear" penner
97 Croaking
98 Boring result
102 It may lead to a breakout
103 Least friendly
104 Two fins' worth
105 Three-time N.F.L. M.V.P., 1995–97
106 Staggers
108 Bob Cratchit, in "A Christmas Carol"
110 "Ben-___"
111 Mets, Jets or Nets
112 Spur-of-the-moment
114 "___ of the D'Urbervilles"
115 Big John of golf
117 Literary monogram
119 Grooved on
120 Set

by Manny Nosowsky

ACROSS

1 Percussion instrument
5 Hive makers
11 Easily passed
15 Junket
19 "Oh, uh-huh"
20 One with a mortgage
21 Dark region of the moon
22 Do followers
23 Meat, lettuce, cheese and tomato in a foot-long bun?
25 Huge
26 Destructive 1995 hurricane
27 Glare reducer
28 Graffiti on a jail wall?
31 Traffic monitors
36 O.K.
37 "P.U.!"
38 Actor Charleson of "Chariots of Fire"
39 Poplar tree
40 Lifeguard's purview
43 Like some penguin feet
45 Social activity on a military base?
47 Pastor who pitches?
49 Prefix with light
50 Irritated with
52 Nascar circuits
53 Early second-century year
56 Something struck
59 Legal
63 Support payment query?
70 Cataract site
71 Refrigerator brand
72 "Finding ___"
73 Cinnamon source
74 Tidewater collector
75 Director Gus Van ___
76 Amounts owed at a diner?
79 "CHiPs" star of 1970s–'80s TV
82 Snowmobile steerer
83 Obsessed with
84 Defense initiative, for short
86 Bad musician's "body part"
91 Draft org.
94 Part voting aye?
99 Headwear for a building chief?
102 "S O S"
103 Bottle size
105 Cat-___-tails
106 Maria preceder
107 Dockworkers' org.
109 Shine, in product names
110 Island hoppers
112 Junk mail a trucker might get?
116 Auto needs
117 Killarney's land
118 Drink mixer
119 Where we be?
125 Insurer's calculation
126 Bygone despot
127 One who's left
128 Big source of corn
129 Legis. meeting
130 Radio, e.g.
131 Judge's declaration
132 Run things

DOWN

1 Dogfaces
2 Big Ten powerhouse, for short
3 Homestead Natl. Monument locale
4 Unified whole
5 Looie or hooey, e.g.
6 Approached
7 "Then what?"
8 Food label fig.
9 Chicago futures exchange, for short
10 Arizona tourist town
11 Changed
12 Pitch-raising guitar device
13 Verdi aria
14 Having all angles equal to 144°
15 Counselor on "Star Trek: T.N.G."
16 Fix, as brickwork
17 "Somehow everything gets done"
18 Footed glass
24 Clichéd
29 Romance novelist Roberts
30 Electrification
31 Totally consumed
32 "Take ___" ("Congratulations!")
33 Extra capsule in a pill bottle
34 Film style
35 Loudness measure
41 N.Y.C. landing site
42 Latin 101 word
44 Not quite rhyming
46 "Just ___ about to . . ."
48 Trump daughter
51 Robert Burns's "___ Louse"
54 "The Sound of Music" family name
55 Philanthropist Hogg
57 "What'll ___?"
58 When repeated, start of a child's taunt
60 Where the first Ringling Brothers circus was staged, 1884
61 Nobelist Wiesel
62 Places to put your feet up
63 Facility
64 Kind of tree
65 Having parts to be filled
66 "The Matrix" hero
67 Radio iconoclast
68 Bop
69 Ball
74 Outlaw
77 Small songbird
78 One way to the Hamptons, for short
80 The first letter in 84-Across
81 Bums
85 Uruguayan uncle
87 "Woe ___" (humorous grammar book)
88 Loco
89 Sport with arm-waving
90 Bubble makers
92 Fish throwaway
93 God with a crested helmet and spear
94 Sci-fi weaponry
95 It might end with a start
96 Rebels of the Southeastern Conference
97 Wary
98 Dudley Do-Right's love
100 Vital Russian route
101 Agitated
104 Stevedore
108 Emerged
111 Things counted by the second?
113 Signs
114 Genealogist's study
115 Nature film?
120 [per the original]
121 Size bigger than med.
122 It might be called in
123 Wise one
124 Rob Roy's refusal

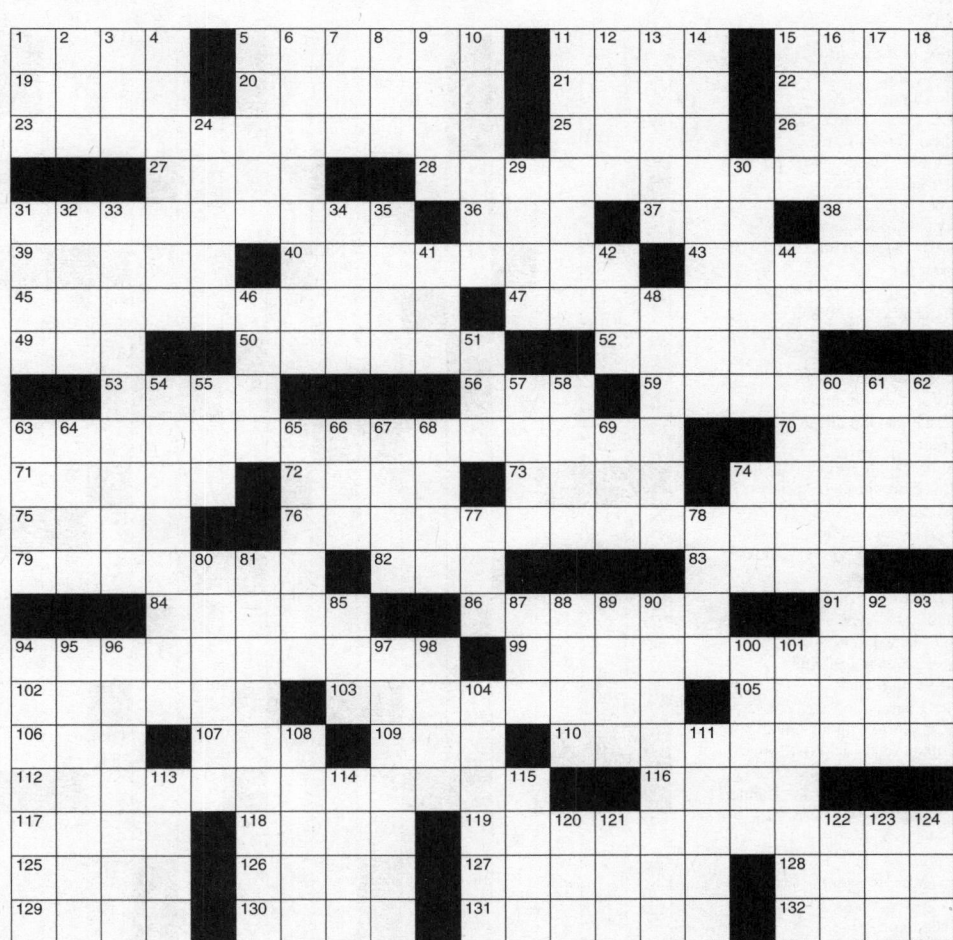

by Patrick Merrell

ACROSS

1 Many applications
5 Miss
9 Tudor queen, informally
13 Rafting area
19 Final, e.g.
20 To be played in unison
21 Horse ridden by Hotspur in "King Henry IV, Part I"
22 Shrewdness
23 Jazzy James
24 Breakdown on a Hyundai assembly line?
27 Edit for TV, say
29 Birthplace of 41-Across: Abbr.
30 Reason for a flood of calls to the police dept., maybe
31 "Wheel of Fortune" purchase
32 Rev. Jesse on Sundays?
38 ___ florentine
39 Author Bagnold
40 Till bill
41 "Nemesis" novelist
45 Stickers
47 Old Roman's boast after a deer hunt?
52 Town north of Anaheim
53 Seat of Washoe County, Nev.
54 Runners at the corners, say, in baseball
55 Chow
56 Long in the tooth
57 Go on stage
59 Bluish gray
62 "Oh, give ___ home . . ."
63 Check for typos, e.g.
65 Some of Shakespeare's income?
69 Astroturf alternative
72 Truss
73 Popular vodka, informally
74 Newly mortared bricks and stones?
79 Decrees
83 With 74-Down, unanimity
84 Grisham's "___ to Kill"
85 Obstruct
88 Become unhinged
89 Words of confidence
91 Go ___ (start fighting)
94 Person making unauthorized reports
95 Oscar-winning Irene
96 November through April, to vacationers?
100 World Series game
101 Decorate with pointy figures
102 Unveil, in poetry
103 Instance
105 Mad staff: Abbr.
106 One needed to bestow a blessing on a golf club?
112 Leaves at a luau
114 Mad., e.g.
115 1950 World Cup host, with a stadium for 180,000+ people
116 Musical with the song "N.Y.C."
117 Advice to Claudius, in "Hamlet"?
123 Memorable 2004 hurricane
125 Spoke in a poke?
126 Spoils
127 Dubai or Houston
128 TV part
129 Gets rid of
130 Big petrol seller
131 Chop ___
132 Formerly, once

DOWN

1 "Is that a fact?!"
2 Supersized
3 Phase of life before retirement
4 Buss
5 "Beauty and the Beast" role
6 Words said with a raised hand
7 Reward for going home?
8 Pick up
9 Most insolent
10 Volkswagen model
11 Took notice
12 State of confusion
13 Far out
14 Coolers, for short
15 Commonly accepted as such
16 Comment after looking at one's cards
17 Submarine base?
18 NBC inits.
25 ___-frutti
26 Cambodia's Lon ___
28 Applications
32 N.B.A. legend Kareem Abdul-___
33 Oscar winner for "Separate Tables"
34 Driver's lic., e.g.
35 Adequate, old-style
36 Tablet
37 See 117-Down
42 Home of El Nuevo Herald
43 Wedding band, maybe
44 Travel items
46 Dishonest sort
48 Rejections
49 Jet part
50 Battery number
51 Out of place
53 Pharaoh, for one
58 ___-Rooter
60 Company on the move
61 Yellow ball
64 "Di quella pira," e.g.
66 Palindromic writer
67 Eggheady sort
68 Flop
70 Hit hard
71 Where "yes" is "ioe," pronounced in three syllables
74 See 83-Across
75 Like the emperor Atahualpa
76 Backs
77 Like baseball covers
78 Thanksgiving dishes
80 It starts in Yellowstone National Park
81 Barrel-shaped marine mammals
82 Meager
86 Sponge
87 Long bones
90 Splits hairs
92 On and after
93 Be under, as an officer
97 Ewe said it
98 Cold response?
99 High point
100 V.I.P.'s opposite
104 Meager
107 Africa's ___ Tomé
108 Future seed
109 ___ Circus (ancient Roman arena)
110 Big name in trading cards
111 Put together
112 Hidey-hole
113 10,900-foot European peak
117 With 37-Down, popular book on grammar
118 Laugh syllable
119 Tailback's stat: Abbr.
120 Call for help
121 Symbol of worthlessness
122 It's found in seams
124 Celtic rival

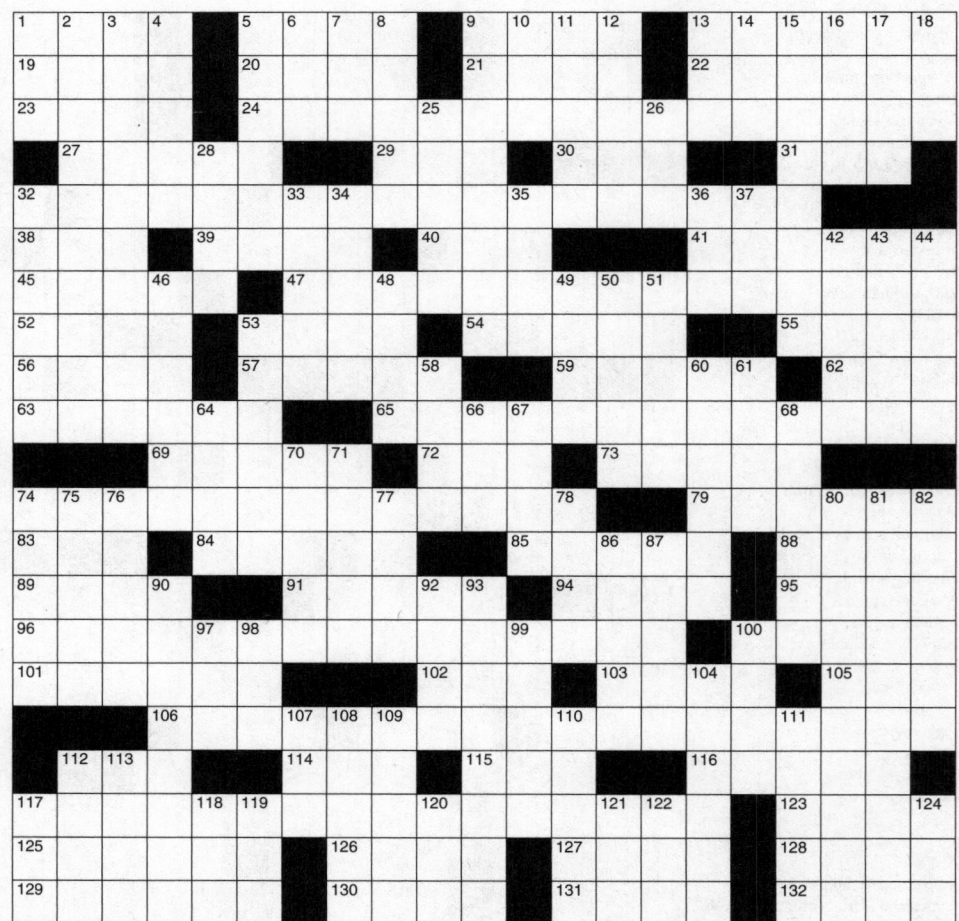

by David J. Kahn

ACROSS

1 Sharp cheese quality
4 Center of emotions
9 Mountain top?
15 ___ Club of old TV
18 Big record co.
19 Many, many
21 This puzzle's northern border?
22 Be in a hole
23 Access code?
25 Stockpiles
26 Fired up
27 Scruffs
28 Its clue reads "Unstable subatomic particle"
30 Treater's words
32 Key-signature preceder
33 Family subdivisions
34 Opposite of post-
36 Drying chamber
37 With 33-Down, quickly
38 More than devotion
40 Sine ___ non
41 Gary ___, Pultizer-winning Beat poet
42 Kind
43 Plays
44 Abrasive stuff
46 Spot for slop
47 Prevent from escaping
49 Breaches of faith
51 With 97-Across, bearer of edible triangular nuts
53 Land with monsoons
54 Not monaurally
58 Meat, in Madrid
61 Count with many titles
64 More faithful
65 Congresswoman Abzug and others
67 Vulnerable point
68 "Awww"-inspiring
69 It may be indicated by a stroke
70 Hot
72 An Untouchable
73 Mosaic flooring
75 Restaurateur Toots
76 Newport Beach sight
78 Where a bell ringer may stand
80 Ibsen play
83 Like some carol apparel
86 Within reach
87 Receiver's counterpart
90 Gave birth to
92 Drops
94 Fourth of 12: Abbr.
95 Eye openers?
96 Clark of country music
97 See 51-Across
98 Provided, as a line
99 ___ haddie (smoked fish)
100 Run for dear life?
102 Cold war draft
104 Williams's "Popeye" co-star
105 Attacked in a rage
106 Unpaired
107 Missed a golden opportunity
110 Disagrees
113 In shape
114 This puzzle's southern border?
115 Antarctica's ___ Coast
116 French pronoun
117 "___ bad!"
118 Hot
119 Water falls?
120 "___ a chance"

DOWN

1 It may glow in the dark
2 Crater creators, e.g.
3 Makeshift Frisbee
4 One taking a big bow
5 Suffix with Capri
6 Message in a bottle, maybe
7 Already chosen for play, say
8 Mass × velocity measurements
9 Sound in the middle of Italy
10 Unstable subatomic particle
11 Minute opening?
12 Beetle, e.g.
13 Hall-of-Fame pitcher Joss
14 Onetime
15 Spots for some shirts
16 Matching pair
17 "Here, maybe I can do it"
20 They're often dinged
24 Once called
29 Suffix with direct
31 RCA competitor
33 See 37-Across
34 Big name in sneakers
35 Like baba
39 Bay windows
40 Ancient Roman financial officer: Var.
41 Targeted, as with a mailing
44 Boom
45 Firms: Abbr.
48 "Sic et Non" author
49 Discuss business at a social occasion
50 Mansion staff
52 Bay
53 Hater
55 Rustic
56 Often-smoked fish
57 Metallurgists' supplies
58 Explorer at Labrador in 1497
59 French conductor Leibowitz
60 Red or Card
62 Satellite of 1962
63 Approval on "The Little Rascals"
66 Strong women
68 Licentious man
70 Blood carriers
71 Has trouble swallowing
74 Place of chaos
77 Cow annoyers
79 Org. in TV's "Nash Bridges"
81 Adds as a bonus
82 State capital on the Tietê River
83 Started to melt
84 Home of many talk shows
85 Opposite of dominate
87 Supplier of candy and toys for kids
88 "Shane" actor
89 Lion, at times
91 It's used to check septic systems
93 Asian observance
95 Shareholder's income: Abbr.
98 Steakhouse selection
99 Cot alternative
101 Guitar great ___ Paul
103 They were once cloned
104 Chop up
108 Prefix with skeleton
109 Actor Wheaton
111 Yalie
112 Take in slowly

by Joe DiPietro

YULE LAUGH

ACROSS

1 Relaxed
8 Co. that makes Band-Aids
13 Pivots
19 Dish ladled out hot or cold
20 Draw out
22 Dominant dogs
23 In myth, killer of his own mother, Clytemnestra
24 Chinese symbols on Santa's vehicle?
26 Do some tailoring
27 Snooker need
28 Fortuneteller's opening
29 Baseball's Moises
30 Paleontological wonder at a natural history museum
31 Part of old French Indochina
33 Punching devices
35 "March of the Penguins" director ___ Jacquet
36 8-Down, with "the"
37 Rolling rock
38 Itsy-bitsy door decoration?
43 Like some chiefs
45 Variety
46 Second string
47 Refuges
49 Spoke at great length
52 1994 sci-fi writer's memoir
56 Makings of a coup
57 Some 1960s coupes
58 "Get ___ get out"
60 Chemical ending
61 Home's counterpart
63 Sold out, in a way
67 In use
69 Hearst's San ___ castle
70 Delay
71 Scratch
72 Tremor
73 Relief provider
74 Dispatch boats
75 Spigot site
76 Common green house gift
77 A long, long time
79 "___ Rollo" (popular Mexican variety show)
80 Big test
83 Opposite of should
87 Whitish
88 "Don't get any ___"
90 ___-Caps
91 Hot dog
93 Sunburnt Santa?
97 Greek height
98 Dandy
101 River of Devon
102 Kind of terrier
103 ___ speak
104 Bog down
105 Big top?
107 Sight from Messina
109 It might leave tracks
110 "Peter Pan" writer
112 Santa reindeer-turned-zombie?
116 Fetch
117 Three in one
118 Celebrates
119 Woman in Sartre's "No Exit"
120 Texas city
121 Goodwill
122 Sauntered

DOWN

1 Cancels
2 One who might grab the bull by the horns
3 Gifts you only think about giving?
4 Hedingham Castle locale
5 Court minutes
6 Place to get a reaction in school?
7 Venusians, e.g.
8 Manger figure
9 Everyone, on the Ems
10 Never, in Nürnberg
11 Early seventh-century year
12 Christmas gift easily identifiable by shaking?
13 Away's partner
14 Suffix with form
15 Kraft Nabisco Championship org.
16 Spiny cactus
17 Expired
18 Per se
21 Amazon's home
25 Cross-out
27 Handler of gifts for the kids on the "naughty" list?
32 Call at sea
34 Attest
37 Fleur-de-___
38 Mincemeat ___
39 Corner piece
40 Stretch (out)
41 Dorm overseers, for short
42 Popular record label
44 Adjusts, as laces
47 Pogo, e.g.
48 Italian tragic poet Vittorio
50 Stern parent's reply
51 Played some songs, say
53 Throws a Christmas tree?
54 "Encore!"
55 Hunter's meat
57 Star wearer: Abbr.
59 Christmas quaffs set atop a board?
62 Dot follower
64 Film buff's cable channel
65 Thrice, in Rx's
66 Grp. with the 1977 hit "Do Ya"
67 "Mazel ___!"
68 Melodic pieces
71 "Law & Order" figs.
73 Sell to a new audience, say
76 Rescues
78 Military trial, briefly
81 "___ the season to be jolly"
82 N.J. summer setting
84 G8 member
85 Serengeti grazer
86 Christmas laughs
87 Tokyo-based carrier
89 Father Time prop
92 1962 Paul Anka hit
93 Precede
94 Stephen Hawking's alma mater
95 Comedian ___ Mac
96 Kansas City suburb
99 Brooks Robinson, e.g.
100 Squinted (at)
103 Like dishwater
104 1957 hit for the Bobbettes
106 Obligation
108 Genesis man
109 QB Hasselbeck
111 Hgts.
113 U.S.N. officer
114 Stephen of "V for Vendetta"
115 Samuel's teacher, in the Bible
116 Two qtrs.

by Brendan Emmett Quigley

When this puzzle has been completed, the following answers will form a progression: 76-Across, 10-Down, 112-Across, 22-Across, 51-Across, 15-Down, 37-Across, 86-Down, 97-Across, 62-Down and 131-Across.

ACROSS

1 Sharp competitor
4 "Do ___ to eat a peach?": Eliot
9 German link
12 Represent, as in legal matters
18 Ectomorphic
19 Worker with a chair
20 Be a make-up artist?
21 Red fluorescent dye: Var.
22 1954 film set in 16th-century Japan
24 Old cable inits.
25 They may get into a jam
26 Low digits
27 Elite groups
29 About
30 Many garden plantings
32 Most broad?
34 Wide shoe spec
37 1981 Alan Alda comedy, with "The"
42 Underground network
43 Diplomat Silas
45 Flip (out)
46 Jubilant
48 Barely beat
49 Director Welles
50 Stockholm flier
51 1982 Dudley Moore tearjerker
54 British gun
55 In a sardonic way
56 Blood line
57 Goldman ___
59 Pre-Q queue
60 Some accents
63 Bad beginning?
66 Prof.'s helpers
67 More manly-chested
70 Charged
71 "Yeah, that'll happen!"
73 "All the Things You Are" composer
74 Avian meat
75 Wordsworth works
76 1983 Charles Bronson thriller
79 Symbol
80 Fed. medical research group
81 Fey of "30 Rock"
82 Supremos
83 QB Favre
84 Child's activity?
86 Candy holder
87 Madrid Mrs.
88 Browns slowly
90 Roman man
91 "___ new?"
93 Fights
94 Pang
96 Tale
97 1990 sequel to "Chinatown," with "The"
101 Half of a 1955 merger: Abbr.
104 January 1 events
105 Colorado Indian
106 Ghost
107 Instruments with keys
109 Off
110 Christopher who wrote "Still Me"
112 1988 baseball flick
115 Emeritus: Abbr.
116 In an odd way
119 Magazine success
120 Cart
122 Subscription card option
127 Feminine suffix
128 The Caribbean's ___ Islands
130 Suffix with glass
131 1987 Peter Falk crime caper
133 "Quantum Healing" author
134 Some linemen: Abbr.
135 Heraldic silver
136 Towel embroidery
137 Reasons
138 Summer clock setting: Abbr.
139 Entangle
140 Gridiron figs.

DOWN

1 Incomes
2 Pause in verse
3 Cape ___, Mass.
4 "___ Said" (Neil Diamond hit)
5 Knock out, say
6 Start of a spell
7 Tail end
8 "Love Story" author Segal
9 Last month
10 1995 Hugh Grant farce
11 Rock stats
12 Auspices
13 With 81-Down, tradition suggested by this puzzle's theme
14 Bygone despot
15 1970 Jack Nicholson picture
16 ___ lark
17 Thing in court
18 Original title of Beethoven's "Fidelio"
19 Rafter's wood
22 Crooks
23 Dover delicacy
28 Not liquidy
31 Begins courting
33 Cable staple since 1979
35 Organic compound
36 Choosing-up word
38 "___ needle pulling thread" ("The Sound of Music" lyric)
39 Flamenco cheer
40 Rob Roy's refusal
41 Co. shares
44 Overthrowing, e.g.
47 Twisty curve
52 Temper
53 Old IBM PC's
54 Price reader
56 Turkish V.I.P.'s
58 Feuding (with)
59 Gas station adjunct, often
60 It may go for a couple of bucks
61 Dashboard feature
62 1932 romance with Maurice Chevalier
63 Actor with a mohawk
64 Kind of harp
65 Elegy
67 Laugh sound
68 Not play it straight
69 Peewees
71 Kind of test
72 War stat
73 Metric wts.
76 Baseball's Martinez
77 Part of E.S.L.: Abbr.
78 Bank offering
79 It's surrounded by white
81 See 13-Down
83 Some cricketers
85 Popular smokes
86 1999 film set in the Persian Gulf
88 ___ choy
89 Parisian way
91 Flamingo, e.g.
92 Speedway letters
93 Huge financial loss
94 It'll give you a lift
95 Instruction to a chauffeur
96 Gagarin in space
98 Golf's Michelle
99 ". . . ___ quit!"
100 Springy dance
101 Joint proprietors
102 Cold-blooded pets
103 Horse handler
106 Unload
108 Like a Cyclops
111 Most loathsome
113 1545 council site
114 No more than
117 Arm parts
118 Jewish orgs.
121 Concert gear
123 Bring in
124 Org. for women drivers
125 Copycat
126 Actress Daly
128 Junk bond rating
129 "I see!"
132 "___ me?"

by Elizabeth C. Gorski

ACROSS

1 Cross, maybe
6 Met expectations?
11 Refuge
20 Nitrogen compound
21 TV exec Arledge
22 Last czarina of Russia
23 "Absolutely, ambassador"
25 Colonies, e.g.
26 Frigid
27 Southern group address
28 Alliance dissolved in 1977
29 "Wonderful!"
30 Pulitzer Prize subj.
32 Continental capital
34 Starter: Abbr.
36 Island with a Hindu majority
39 Like some unpopular leaders
45 Computer pioneer Lovelace and others
48 The Huskies of the N.C.A.A.
50 Fraternity letters
51 Captivate
52 Antivenins, e.g.
53 Award-winning TV host
56 Charles Lindbergh, once
58 Buzzer
59 Blue-pencil
60 Advance
62 Academy head
63 Follower of mars
64 Modern greeting
66 Narrow the gap with
67 Marine mammal
70 Advantageousness
71 Fair fare
72 Friends
73 Went downhill
74 "___ ramparts!"
75 St.-Tropez's Place des ___
76 Bingo call
77 Cuneiform discovery site
79 Cartesian conclusion
82 "It's dark in here!"
84 x
86 Ad time
87 Main international airport of Japan
91 Width measure
92 Holy text
93 Raison d'___
94 1 + 1 = 2, e.g.
97 Great American Ball Park team
98 Death on the Nile cause, perhaps
100 "Brave New World" drug
101 Usher in
103 ___-Boy
105 Keep an ___ the ground
109 Some Wall St. deals
112 Daughter of Zeus
116 Claim
118 Weighty issue?
120 Scoots over
121 Prudential competitor
122 Female demon
123 Nickname for Tasmania
124 Waste
125 City on the Rhone

DOWN

1 "Apocalypto" subject
2 Like some profs.
3 Wink in tiddlywinks, e.g.
4 "Take your pick"
5 Sainted pope of 682
6 Airport sign abbr.
7 Classic theater name
8 Seat of Allen County, Kan.
9 Shaker leader
10 Shut off
11 Dirge
12 Natural balm
13 Relief provider, for short
14 Out
15 Capital once known as Thang Long ("Ascending Dragon")
16 Cuckoo bird
17 Streaming content
18 Composer Dohnányi
19 Ambassador or Statesman of old autodom
24 Campus 100 miles NW of L.A.
31 Hip
33 Oysters ___ season
35 Molotov cocktail component
36 Onion, for one
37 Teen trouble
38 Treasure-trove
40 Not built up
41 Tiny time unit: Abbr.
42 Capacitance measure
43 Richard of old westerns and action films
44 Pentagon fig.
46 Playground retort
47 It's a wrap
49 Most gutsy
54 ___ Circus (where St. Peter was crucified)
55 Enter
57 Fictional knight named for a bird of prey
60 Carriage
61 Fabulous monster
63 Property recipients
65 Do, re, mi
66 "I've ___ Strings" (Pinocchio song)
67 Like tears
68 Bring out
69 Rare ex-prisoner
70 Classic Jaguar
71 Some horns
73 Brooking no dissent
74 Lead-in to bow or hike
76 Show pride, in a way
78 Memory: Prefix
79 About
80 Just barely
81 Much of Colo.
83 "Mad TV" rival, for short
85 Marin and Sonoma's region
88 "I'll get this"
89 Chinese "way"
90 Two bags of groceries, say
95 Talk on and on, Down Under
96 Get wind of
99 Intrinsically
102 Ringlike formation
103 Priest of the East
104 "Pronto"
106 Longfellow's bell town
107 Paraguay and others
108 Cleaver or lever
110 Numerical prefix
111 RR stops
113 Sailor's saint
114 Ruhr refusal
115 Latin 101 verb
117 Reef dweller
119 Not abroad

by Ashish Vengsarkar

ACROSS

1 Eponymous physicist
6 Mary Kay rival
10 See 64-Down
14 Corroborator, maybe
19 Drink
20 Ill humor
21 Online initialism
22 Parts of a routine
23 Hat with a plume
24 Steady, say
25 Family-gathering time
26 One year's record
27 Like shoes made in St. Louis and finished in New Orleans?
31 "Bambi" character
32 Tops
33 2001's "Ocean's Eleven" and others
34 Matching
35 Bear witness
38 Fauna
40 Listing
42 Part of a parka
43 Detroit's Joe Louis ___
44 "Gr-r-ross!"
45 Old pigskin org.
46 Got a facial piercing?
51 Danger to divers
54 Birthplace of the Cyrillic alphabet
56 Dressing room door figure
57 "Funny Girl" composer
59 Dadaist Max
60 Flips
63 Acclaim
64 Got by
66 Crooks on golf courses
67 Kind of iron
68 Moon of Uranus
69 Diver's hose
70 "Blood and Fire" for the Salvation Army
71 Certain finish
72 Break
73 Bread-for-cake event?
76 Tie indicator
77 Played tenpins in officers' uniforms?
82 Good deal
83 ___ Falls
85 Hides a mike on
86 Fair shelter
87 Modern site of the capital of ancient Galatia
89 Pinkish yellow
92 Deepen
94 Home paper
95 Freshly consider
97 French word of approval
98 Sacrifice fly stat
99 Walking on hot embers?
105 Top
107 Bothers
108 Familiar sigh
109 Boy in TV's "Life Goes On"
110 Old war story
111 Tennis's Nastase
112 Jell-O flavor
113 Boring bit
114 To-do list
115 Org. in TV's "Adam 12"
116 Ankh feature
117 Novel content

DOWN

1 Chuck
2 Parrot
3 SeaWorld frolicker
4 Silt locale
5 Some terminals
6 Superior's title
7 Pleasant hotel room feature
8 Pearl Buck heroine
9 Elementary particle
10 Screening locale
11 Making no value judgments
12 Some oil barons
13 Work out
14 Close to closed
15 First name in horror
16 Comment about suddenly thinner mares?
17 Small topper
18 Easter, e.g.
28 Schedule-shifting syst.
29 Atlas, e.g.
30 Opera singer Simon ___
34 Pampering, for short
35 Starring role for John Barrymore and Gregory Peck
36 Good source of protein
37 Rang true?
38 Painter's calculation
39 Actor Beatty
41 They just scrape the surface
43 Made a touchdown
44 Knight's time
46 Place to get a grip
47 Estimator's phrase
48 City north of Cologne
49 Oater transport
50 Is off guard
52 Hydroxyl compund
53 ___-majesté
55 Say hey to
58 University of Massachusetts
60 "Blame It on the Bossa Nova" singer, 1963
61 Like some bodies on a beach
62 Samuel's teacher, in the Bible
64 With 10-Across, popular 1960s–'70s singer
65 Kazakhstan's ___ Sea
66 Combination lock feature
67 Cooking vessels
69 Part of a Lawrence Welk count
70 "Serpico" author
73 Writer Harte
74 Dragged out
75 Female name ending
78 Midwest transfer point
79 Causing wonder in
80 Line of soldiers needing medical attention
81 "My man!"
84 Little League coach, often
86 "Message received"
87 Nimble
88 Distant cloud
89 Fifth-century invader
90 Avant-garde composer Glass
91 Finished, as dishes
92 Game piece
93 Worker for tips
96 Sell online
97 Clean up, in a way
99 Mercury and Mars
100 Grant's birthplace
101 Magazine contents
102 Start of a conclusion
103 Barely gets, with "out"
104 Phoenician trading center
106 Former U.S. terr.

by Harvey Estes

ACROSS

1. Fly effortlessly
6. Bub
9. Unstable
14. Talks up
19. Raise the proof?
21. Think the world of
22. Muppet who sang "Rubber Duckie"
23. 1956 Oscar-winning title role for Ingrid Bergman
24. James Stockdale as running mate?
26. Terse account of what happened at the Raptor Petting Zoo?
28. Remained functional
29. Vest wearers
30. Tightens a piece, say
31. Golfer Ballesteros
32. Kind of bar
34. Attended without really belonging
36. "The child of Pride," according to Jonathan Swift
37. Badge awarder: Abbr.
40. "___ go bragh!"
41. Girl who wears hair clips in nonstandard ways?
46. Stimpy's TV pal
47. Poet/novelist Elinor
48. Like a crow or lark
49. Morales of "NYPD Blue"
50. Half of a longtime country duo
52. Impetuous quality
53. Forbidding
54. Quite often
55. Subtly suggest
57. Sows with salt, maybe
58. Work on logical proofs while dining out?
63. Historic Irish city
64. Bête ___
65. Player's chance to shine
66. External
67. ___ of Oxford
68. Oscar nominee for "Unfaithful," 2002
73. "You said a mouthful!"
74. Archive's contents
76. Subsided
77. Alternative to Rover
78. Practice sessions for coercion?
81. Sprout
82. Infiltrator
83. "___ says?"
84. Suspicious
85. Tries
86. One of Emma's lovers in "Madame Bovary"
87. Quonset hut material
89. Lickety-split
90. In more pain
93. Show contempt for yellow fruit?
98. The Kingdom of Heaven?
100. About whom Shakespeare wrote "Age cannot wither her, nor custom stale / Her infinite variety"
101. Two-time loser to Dwight
102. Jive, e.g.
103. Kind of hat
104. Tranquility
105. Deep gulf
106. Geared up
107. Isn't complete without

DOWN

1. Seven-time Wimbledon winner
2. River of Yakutsk
3. "High Sierra" actress
4. Sony introduction of 1984
5. Impedes legally
6. Other: Abbr.
7. Inter ___
8. Crimson
9. Accesses
10. Lead-in to further explanation
11. Summer sweaters?
12. Impel to action
13. So far
14. City on the Seine
15. Cropped up
16. Hand or foot
17. They're spotted in casinos
18. Some bird feed
20. Whips but good
25. Split
27. Underground film actress Sedgwick
31. Main character in Proust's "Remembrance of Things Past"
32. Cousin of a gull
33. Vicinity
34. General acknowledgment?
35. Like the Gobi
37. Split, in a way
38. Horror film's offerings
39. Claude who starred in TV's "Lobo"
41. "Here's a pleasant surprise!"
42. Fly from Africa
43. Ceremonial splendor
44. Sporty Mazda
45. Another name for vitamin A
47. More artful
51. 1984 Hollywood biopic
53. Like diplomatic pouches
55. Distinctive Rolls-Royce feature
56. Ending with profit or racket
57. Some reconnaissance craft
58. Foster, as enthusiasm
59. Bistro
60. Nonsensical
61. NBC newswoman O'Donnell
62. In a convenient way
63. Witches' familiars, often
67. "Conspiracy of Fools" topic
68. Cancels, as in an online order form
69. Steel grating component
70. "Metaphysica" writer
71. Swift production?
72. They've split
74. How things may get washed
75. Soup accompaniers
79. Ladylove
80. Go through volumes
81. Make larger or smaller, as a photo
85. Clavell novel set in Hong Kong
86. Pale purple
87. No-goodnik
88. Olympians Liddell and Heiden
89. Jumper
90. Order letters
91. Set of standards
92. ___ Bowl (postseason game)
93. Colorless
94. "Hard ___!" (sailor's yell)
95. Confined, with "up"
96. Walked along
97. ___-culotte
99. Cereal box abbr.

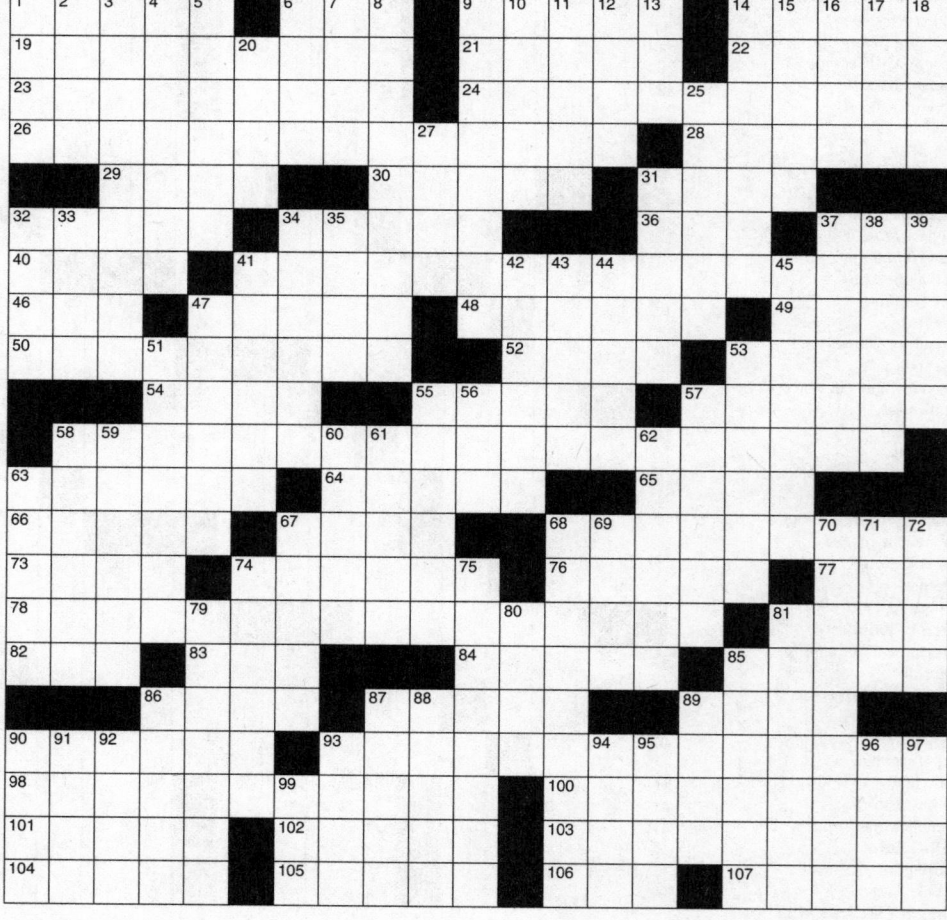

by Patrick Berry

ACROSS

1 Shoots
6 Wicker willow
11 Bee Gees brother
15 Cry from a butterfingers
19 Words sung "with love" in a 1967 hit
20 Band of fighters
21 ___ vez (again, in Spanish)
22 "Fudge!"
23 They may be pulled
25 It may be pulled
27 Visibly showed displeasure with
28 "Falstaff" and others
29 Contest of wills?
32 Member of the familia
34 Lady from Ipanema
38 Neutral shade
39 Half of a 1970s TV duo
43 Traveled (along)
44 Cookout staple
45 ___-mo
46 Goethe play
48 Cusp
49 One may be pulled
54 Scripture topic
55 Mil. mail drop
57 Appeared
58 Roasted snacks
60 Lincoln, maybe
63 Hibernation site
64 Water holder
65 Select group
67 Bank holdings
68 They may be pulled
70 Place for a beer and a bite
71 Stu of early TV
72 Dandy
73 She-demon
74 Like some Roman tragedies
75 Feature of many a hospital rooftop
77 Saw-edged
79 Day divs.
80 "___ see"
81 It may be pulled
85 Blockheads
87 Half of a 1980s TV duo
88 Sot's affliction
89 Lyndon Johnson, by birth
92 Fireplace receptacle
94 Brandy glass
97 Some jackets
98 Women's apparel department
100 "Count me out"
101 Convertibles
103 Fundamental figure in geometry
106 Tiger Beat topic
109 It may be pulled
112 They may be pulled
116 Pizazz
117 Always
118 Syrian leader
119 Grasshopper stage
120 Arab League member
121 Break off
122 Content of some rings
123 Far from enthusiastic

DOWN

1 Place to sell tkts.
2 Campaign pro
3 Immigrant's class: Abbr.
4 A hummingbird has a fast one
5 Country that styles itself a "democratic socialist republic"
6 Yellowish shade
7 Fill
8 Fingered, briefly
9 Text miscues
10 Not let settle
11 Kind of dancer
12 "Live ___!"
13 Highland hillsides
14 Hair clasps
15 Worthless loafer?
16 Sch. in Tulsa
17 Stroke
18 Dump
24 Hood's rod
26 Linda of soaps
29 Abbr. of politeness
30 Gradually slower, in mus.
31 It may be pulled
33 ___ as a fiddle
35 It may be pulled
36 University official
37 Gulf of ___, off the Horn of Africa
39 Diet
40 Worked out
41 "Krazy ___"
42 Desert bloomers
45 Chinese checkers board shape
47 Counterfeit
50 Some VCR's
51 Pushes off
52 They may be pulled
53 Köln's river
55 "Look ___!"
56 Oliver Twist's birthplace
59 Besides that
61 Pulitzer-winning writer Sheehan
62 Diogenes, for one
64 Put down
66 Major stretches
68 Posers
69 Prix de ___ de Triomphe (annual Paris horse race)
70 Kick
72 Strike out
74 Marie and others: Abbr.
76 Pilot, flight attendants, etc.
77 Lager holder
78 Observatory observer: Abbr.
80 Sharp rebuke
82 Diarist Anaïs
83 "Aha!"
84 1962 musical co-directed by Bob Fosse
86 Secretly watched
90 Econ. measure
91 C.I.A. ancestor
93 Swift's "A Tale of ___"
95 Mullahs' calls
96 Basic belief
99 Freedman, once
101 ___ Janeiro
102 Naval V.I.P.
104 Furniture retailer since 1943
105 Laura of "I Am Sam"
107 Petrol brand
108 Sask. neighbor
109 "Deadwood" carrier
110 Tentacle
111 Actress Long
113 Literary monogram
114 ___ Friday's
115 Brick holder

by Victor Fleming and Bruce Venzke

ACROSS

1 *Sweater option
6 *Choice cut
16 *Primo
20 ___ Nast magazines
21 "Hey, good lookin'!"
22 Prior work
23 ___-totsy
24 Construction toy
25 Rock music's Better Than ___
26 Serpent suffix
27 Mythical bird-woman
29 Works on
30 Roman fountain name
31 Executes
33 Acknowledge
34 Cheat
35 Some Ivy Leaguers
36 Philosopher Kierkegaard
37 Perfectly
38 Existing at birth
41 Always
42 Terse response to an interruption
46 Ties up
47 Symbol of speed
49 Author Silverstein
50 "___ not"
51 Section
52 Zero
53 Infamous innkeeper
55 Info on an electric bill
56 Rants
58 One doing the twist, e.g.
60 Deli order
61 What the answers to the 15 starred clues have
64 Summer hrs. in N.Y.
67 Lean
68 Biker's prop
72 Retired N.H.L. great Hull
74 Palm, say
75 Mock-scared cries
76 Mil. school
77 Years in old Rome
78 Inured (to)
79 Nonprofit?
80 Central courts
81 Sang on high?: Var.
83 Paramount
85 Unyielding
86 In order (to)
87 King or queen
88 Comedian Mort
89 "The Paper Chase" author John Jay ___ Jr.
92 Ill
93 Treat for a dog
97 Golf outing
98 Where St. Paul was shipwrecked, in Acts
99 Ballot listing
100 Quiz feature: Abbr.
101 Still
102 Period of future bliss
104 Motown singer Terrell
106 Scrubbed
107 Diet soda feature
108 Resting, say
109 *Backup for Dick Tracy
110 *Gridiron lineup
111 *Benjamin

DOWN

1 *Show stopper?
2 To whom a dictator answers
3 Word with an arrow
4 Cautious investments, for short
5 Places for Peeping Toms
6 Units of heat
7 Pats on the back?
8 Mind
9 Its slogan was once "Be there"
10 Diner sign
11 Trigger
12 Activate
13 Buddy of TV
14 Vigoda and Fortas
15 Kit ___
16 Campari and Cinzano
17 Goes slowly
18 Temerity
19 *In-box contents
28 Kalahari-like
30 Isley Brothers hit "___ Lady"
32 Its logo is a rearing horse
33 It's nothing
34 Shade of black
36 Like sororities, at times
37 Nowheresville
38 *Apple variety
39 Best-selling author Roberts
40 ___ War of 1899
42 Product in an orange box
43 Caulk
44 Villain who says "For I am nothing, if not critical"
45 *Natural history museum attraction
47 Some restaurant employees
48 Chosen
49 Umpire's call
52 ___ Kinnock, 1980s–'90s British Labour Party leader
53 *Saloon floozie
54 Author Rand
55 Modern addresses
57 Part of M.I.T.: Abbr.
59 Battle of Fair ___, 1862
62 Open field
63 Majestic
64 *Fortune 500 company based in San Jose, Calif.
65 Villain who says "That's a Dom Perignon '55. It would be a pity to break it"
66 Gravitate
69 Israeli port
70 It's right at your fingertip
71 *Critical time
73 Gets blitzed
78 ___ Bator
79 ___-white
80 Fit
82 Follower of "O"
83 Important exam
84 Home of Spelman College
85 Put (away)
87 Higher up
88 Gobs
89 *Certain gasket
90 Corot painting "The Burning of ___"
91 Dieter's problem
92 Md.'s largest city
93 Villain who says "So you don't like spinach?"
94 1980's Stallone role
95 Not fulfilled
96 *It's usually not played much
98 Upset
99 Acapulco approval
102 French month
103 D.C. baseballer
105 Common female middle name

by Paul Guttormsson

ACROSS

1 Shooting marble
6 Cradle call
10 What I will follow
14 Mystery writers' awards
21 Printing process, briefly
22 North Sea feeder
23 Dramatic solo
24 Observant Mormons, e.g.
25 Scottish hillsides
26 With gusto
27 Tendon injury
28 Emotional traumas
29 Full of compassion
30 Hit hard
31 Pitchers' places
33 From memory
34 Writer Gogol
36 Midwest and Plains states, e.g.
38 Old tar's shipmates
40 Siberian river port
44 No longer hungry
45 Where it's at
46 Endurance, informally
47 Whitecap formation
48 Maj.'s superior
49 French white wine
51 Reddish-brown gems
52 Relatively robust
53 Magnanimous
56 Washington's profile is on it
58 Prevented
60 Old Aegean region
62 Get ___ (be rewarded at work)
63 Stumble upon
64 Enthusiast
65 Mary Hartman's TV hometown
67 Screened, as a patient
68 Swing
69 "Gilligan's Island" castaway
70 "MADtv" alternative
71 Dirty
73 "Mr. Mom" co-star
74 East Lansing sch.
77 1972 #1 Neil Young hit
81 Deli delicacy
82 Depresses
86 Free
88 Break ground?
89 Grainy finishes
91 Physicist Fermi
92 One can be educated
94 Strong
95 Pregnant woman, in obstetrics
97 Feminine fiend
99 Pulitzer-winning biographer Leon
100 Pilotless plane
101 1938 #1 hit composed by Hoagy Carmichael
103 Physical sound?
105 Lee's men
106 Ending with ranch
107 Crash-investigating org.
109 ___'acte
110 Versatile vehicle
111 Work like ___
112 Dental damage
113 White-collar work
117 She married Dick twice
119 Not yet showing signs of wear
121 Founder of analytic psychology
123 "The Producers" extra
124 On a par with
128 Valentine symbol
129 Get shot in a studio?
130 Ply with drink
131 Better at stand-up
132 Still having a shot to win
133 Lead-in periods
134 Concertedly
135 Haberdashery buy
136 14 for Si or 102 for No: Abbr.

137 Joins
138 Player of Santa in "Elf," 2003

DOWN

1 Composer Berg
2 "The ___ Left Behind Me" (Civil War tune)
3 Have ___ with
4 Where "sage in bloom is like perfume," in song
5 Dawn deity
6 Oscar-winning "Titanic" song by Celine Dion
7 It touches three oceans
8 Get to people emotionally
9 Suffix with station
10 Be consumed with envy
11 Dream interpreter
12 Composer ___ Carlo Menotti
13 Lacking sympathy
14 In essence
15 Bee Gees brothers
16 "It's worth ___"
17 1917 Frank Lloyd film
18 ". . . made ___ woman": Genesis
19 Deluge refuge
20 Draft inits.
30 Eastern European pork fat dish
31 Of the morning
32 Coll. fraternity with a skull-and-crossbones symbol
35 Shakespeare's "The Rape of ___"
37 Andean capital
39 Rio de la Plata, e.g.
41 To a greater extent
42 In the dumps
43 U.K. distance measures
46 ___-da (pretentious)
48 Well-trained company?
50 Minimal money
51 Give rise to
52 After-dinner development
54 Ukr. neighbor
55 Sci-fi figures
57 Cell stuff that fabricates protein, for short
59 "Dr." with Grammys
61 Yonder
63 Very quick rotation meas.
66 Flub
68 eBay entry
69 Upper figure
71 "Help wanted" letters
72 Cosmonaut Makarov
73 Pays for oneself
74 Ravel's "___ Antique"
75 Fishhook line
76 Battleship inits.
77 1967 medical milestone
78 Drab shade
79 Meeting points
80 Like a mensch
81 Become smitten with
82 Blue state
83 Chemical suffix
84 Urban grid
85 Joseph Conrad classic
86 Stowe villain
87 Clothe
88 Sneaky laughs
89 Typing speed stat.
90 Tic-tac-toe win
93 Meat stamp inits.
96 Golden calf crafter
98 Jewelry designer Peretti
100 Sixers' #6
102 Where nairas are spent
104 Blood type, briefly
108 Quaint cry of surprise
111 Tenochtitlán resident
112 Slew
114 1980s screen slasher
115 Earth protector
116 Pernicious pet
118 Hip parts
120 Left
122 Like antiques
124 Immature newt
125 On the ___ vive
126 Évreux article
127 Sitcom planet
129 Church perch
130 Sound heard while shearing

by Mark Feldman

ACROSS

1 Treat for a dog
6 California's ___ Woods National Monument
10 Near eternity
15 Runner's place
19 Moses' brother
20 "___ cost to you!"
21 Civil War signature
22 Sinatra's "Meet Me at the ___"
23 Organisation des ___ Américains
24 Calls the shots?
25 Einstein's asset?
27 Acerbic rock/folk singer?
30 Plenty
31 Like some garages
32 Jim Palmer, notably
34 Graf ___
35 "___ Tu" (1974 hit)
37 Interminably
39 Shell alternative
43 Protest gone bad?
48 The Henry who founded the Tudor line
50 Faulkner character ___ Varner
51 Little ___
52 Manche's capital
53 15 minutes of tightrope walking and animal acts?
57 Sign up for more
60 By and by
62 1993 Super Bowl M.V.P.
63 Worked (up)
64 1986 self-titled soul album
66 Done in
68 Con
70 Magic words . . . or a hint to the other long answers in this puzzle
77 Fashion
78 Percolate
79 Heretofore
80 Doo-wop syllable
83 Copy illegally
86 Greeting with a salute
88 "Baloney!"
89 Certain NASA probes?
92 Not docked
94 In the know
95 Eastern royal
96 Way-off
97 Deer season hairdo?
101 End of an act, maybe
104 Person at court
106 France ___ (Parisian daily)
107 Library indexing abbr.
109 Engine capability, slangily
112 Not stay alert
116 Post-accident inquiry
120 Troupe of suspects from "The Fugitive"?
122 Tennessee offense and defense?
124 Lead-in to girl
125 "___ Dream" ("Lohengrin" piece)
126 Space: Prefix
127 Chocolate, e.g.
128 Fed
129 Fix, as a bow
130 Sore, with "off"
131 Ones picking up things?
132 Psychiatrist's appt.
133 Detect, in a way

DOWN

1 Modern workout system
2 Bring home?
3 Make a delivery
4 Saw
5 Tangle up
6 French film director Allégret
7 Unborn, after "in"
8 About to receive
9 "The Barber of Seville" composer
10 Sock pattern
11 Ending with ballad
12 Cooking staple
13 Certain tides
14 Cons
15 Airport worker
16 Cadger's request
17 Anthony Mann's "The Fall of the Roman Empire," e.g.
18 Any King Christian I-X
26 French flag color
28 Lady Jane and Zane
29 Blessings
33 Ballade ending
36 Onetime French fleet
38 Dagger
40 "Yow!"

41 Word in many a Nancy Drew title
42 Hops-drying oven
43 Boxer nicknamed "Hands of Stone"
44 Año starter
45 Good ___
46 Admission of defeat
47 "A Confederacy of Dunces" author
49 "___ come as no surprise . . ."
54 Title woman in a Woody Allen film
55 River rental
56 Sequentially
58 Dict. info
59 First name in comedy
61 Hammer user
65 Some German imports
67 Relative of -ian
69 Logical start?
71 Font feature
72 Where an echograph is used in measuring
73 Tricks are played in it
74 Words with house or move
75 Polite refusal
76 Soap time, maybe
80 Georgia and others, once: Abbr.

81 Sen. McCarthy ally
82 "___ of the Thousand Days" (1969 film)
84 Run ___ (owe)
85 Literally, "instruction"
87 Rings of plumerias, e.g.
90 Napa sight
91 Cut off
93 + part
98 Defeats, in a way
99 Beams
100 "No ___!"
102 ___ Society (English debating group)
103 Jumps
105 Hen cages
108 Tours can be found on it
110 Wonderland cake message
111 Sp. women
113 Devastate
114 Slowpoke
115 Citation of 1958
116 Rat follower?
117 Progress
118 Suffix with major
119 Orthopedic specialty
121 Staffs
123 What barotrauma affects

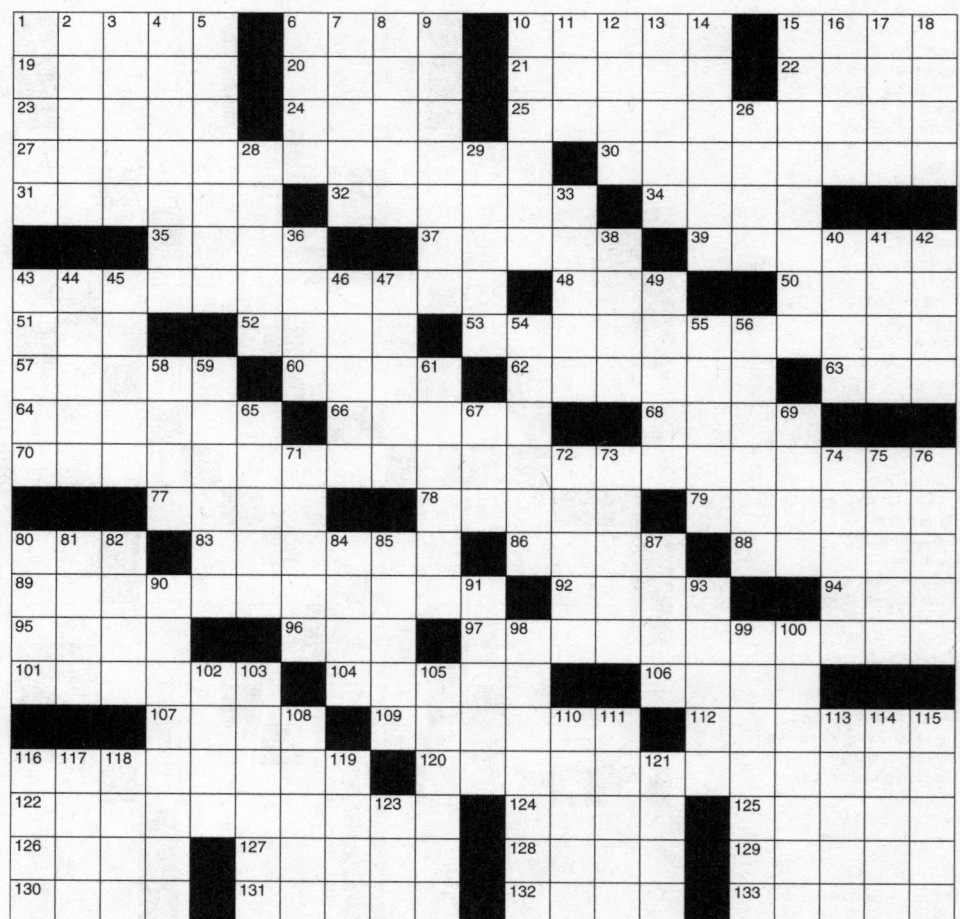

by David Kwong and Kevan Choset

ACROSS

1 Stick used to swat flies
6 Doesn't run
11 Senseless
15 Place to relax
18 Popular humor weekly, with "The"
19 Something to lay down
20 "___ Enchanted" (2004 movie)
21 Heap
22 Birdie beater
23 First mate's greeting?
25 Break off
26 Hawks
28 One after another
29 Jct. joiners
30 Sticker
31 "Wheel of Fortune" request
32 Actors Max and Max Jr.
33 Animal with a black-tipped tail
35 Tighty-whities
37 Word with "hand to hand" or "time to time"
39 Inventor's inits.
41 Show taped at Chicago's Harpo Studios
43 Ecdysiast Blaze and others
44 Charging, in a way
46 Reported mountain sightings
47 U.S. auditor
48 "Baudolino" novelist
49 Ahead
51 Layer of a bed
52 Year Constantine the Great became emperor
55 Family of things
56 First name in humor
57 Some Guggenheim works
59 Acoustic
60 Fed. health research agcy.
61 Many a Wall St. Journal subscriber
62 1970s HUD Secretary Hills and namesakes
65 C₈H₈
67 With 56-Down, start of eight answers in this puzzle
69 Fill up
70 St. Clare's birthplace
71 "The Facts of Life" actress
72 Post-op area
74 Navel type
75 "See ya"
76 Snick and ___
77 Attention
78 Weber State University locale
79 Greek group
81 Showed to the foyer
83 Abbr. after Lincoln or Kennedy
84 Iron-___
85 Misrepresent
87 Display on a tray
89 Shaw's "___ and Cleopatra"
93 Deposit in a depository
94 Code word
95 "See ya"
96 Corrida charger
97 Old computer
99 Beat
101 Court grp.
103 Pizazz
104 Häagen-___
105 Even though
107 Part of 60-Across
109 Master
110 Marvel Comics supervillain
113 Root beer ingredient
115 Tarnish
116 See 104-Down
117 Kind of inspection
118 Greenland settlers
119 Hesitations
120 Cornerstone abbr.
121 "Shall we go?"
122 Aquarium buildup

DOWN

1 The Axis, once
2 Together
3 Neighbor of Chad
4 Popular Bach work for keyboard (1994, 1996, 1999, 2002)
5 Having no depth, in brief
6 Arizona Diamondbacks ballpark (1988)
7 Had the advantage
8 Commercial suffix
9 Florida's ___ Trail
10 Wretches
11 Opening in the North Pole?
12 Ray of "Battle Cry"
13 Weak spots
14 Pompom holder
15 Birding capital of New Zealand (2006)
16 It's often tied with a rubber band
17 Common connectors
19 Some agents, for short
24 Company that merged with Lockheed in 1995 (2001, 2003)
27 Knot holder
29 Words from Pope's "An Essay on Man" (1940, 1942–43, 1960–62, 1965–68, 1978)
30 Some shot
32 Time magazine 2005 co-Person of the Year
34 Miniature
36 Least robust
38 Roasted fowl (2005)
40 Hollywood biggie?
42 President who created the N.S.C.
45 Sirtaki dancer in a 1964 movie
50 Tropical rodent
52 Zorro's house
53 Batters take them
54 Futurists? (1990–93, 1997–98, 2000, 2004)
55 "Rocks"
56 See 67-Across
58 Lucid
63 Break ___ (go into sudden death)
64 Public
66 Moviedom's Long and Vardalos
68 Composer Camille Saint-___
69 Big ___
73 Western capital (1979–82, 1984)
76 Sign of worry
79 "The Silence of the Lambs" org.
80 Alamo mission?
82 Put on
83 Mobile home?
84 Davy Jones's locker
86 Airport fig.
88 Transitional land zone
90 Eschewing accompaniment
91 Waters fed by the Amu Darya
92 Old White House nickname
98 Sale places
100 Harshness
102 Word with china or dry
104 With 116-Across, saucy Aussie
106 Advanced
108 "There!"
110 "Hmmm"
111 Youth org. since 1910
112 Top
114 Naut. heading

by David J. Kahn

ACROSS

1 Likewise
6 Chipped in
11 ___ II razor
15 Where to see "Monday Night Football"
19 Ryan of Hollywood
20 Big throw
21 One of the Castros
22 Pluck
23 *Where to find para in the dictionary
25 * . . . oatmeal . . .
27 Minnesota ___
28 History chapters
29 Restriction on children, maybe
31 4×4, for short
32 Exam for a future D.A.
33 Link with
34 Head-scratcher
38 Independent country since June 5, 2006
40 * . . . Suita . . .
42 Sneeze causers, for some
45 Plant openings
46 * . . . Hancock . . .
49 Not fully formed
52 Speed: Abbr.
53 Like some Keats works
54 Part of the Treasury Dept.
55 Rival of Cassio
56 Apprised
58 "The Man Who Knew Too Much" actress, 1934
61 Remark that might get one in trouble
62 When "Dallas" aired for most of its run: Abbr.
63 Dictionary source for each asterisked clue in this puzzle
69 Slate workers, for short
70 Actress Kimberly of "Close to Home"
71 Shooting match?
72 Big cavity
75 Course related to physiol.
76 Volga feeder
77 Fashion designer Saab
78 ___ Hill (R&B group)
79 Guidance system at sea
81 * . . . boar . . .
84 1981 German-language hit film
87 Talks monotonously
88 * . . . subscapular . . .
92 Model's job
96 "That's cheating!"
97 Daffy Duck and others
98 Spanish ___
100 Call to a calf
101 1989 high-school film based on a song title
103 Charades player
104 Farming prefix
105 * . . . war dance . . .
108 * . . . ZZZ . . .
111 Unhappy chorus
112 Lincoln, maybe
113 Rainwear brand
114 Fervor
115 Old flames
116 Stallone and others
117 Medgar of Mississippi
118 Hit the top

DOWN

1 Pinhead
2 There from birth
3 Show uncertainty
4 Running things?
5 ___ Miss
6 Now, in Nueva York
7 Unfamiliar with
8 A little night music?
9 Longoria of "Desperate Housewives"
10 Wrecks
11 Faithful about
12 Needed more
13 A3 maker
14 San ___, Calif.
15 "I" problem
16 Abbr. before a Spanish surname
17 Stomach part
18 Extraordinary degree
24 Writer of "Gil Blas"
26 Leader of the All-Starr Band
30 Shampoo form
32 Bad witness
33 Sondheim protagonist
35 Jelly flavor
36 High hat
37 Subtitle starter, sometimes
39 Fabrics with elaborate designs
40 Boggy lands
41 Terre Haute sch.
43 Rustling sound
44 Broad, in a way
46 Cape settler
47 Old mythological work
48 Trollope's "Phineas ___"
49 Assessor's figure
50 Votin' no on
51 Reverse
55 To wit
56 Take ___ (swing hard)
57 Mallard cousins
59 Physiques, for short
60 Modem termini?
61 ___ Games, quadrennial event since 1951
62 Monastic title
64 It's parallel to a radius
65 Opposite of yellow
66 Big do
67 Dignitary from Dubai
68 Lockbox document
72 Write a codicil
73 "Huzzah!"
74 Jazz's ___ Lateef
76 One of the winds
79 Frank Sinatra said he had "the silkiest chops in the singing game"
80 Handicapper's hangout, for short
81 Wall St. figures
82 Spots
83 Something to be thankful for
85 Without support, in a way
86 Basket material
87 Place for a small table
89 Turbulent
90 Real estate ad section
91 CD-___
93 "See ya!"
94 N.H.L. trophy honoree
95 Able to do well
98 Member of the track team
99 Stockpile
102 Get the goods on
103 Parcel (out)
104 "Suppose they gave ___ and nobody came?"
105 Former Japanese P.M. Shinzo ___
106 "America's Most Wanted" airer
107 Small digit
109 Kind of lane
110 Inits. for a film buff

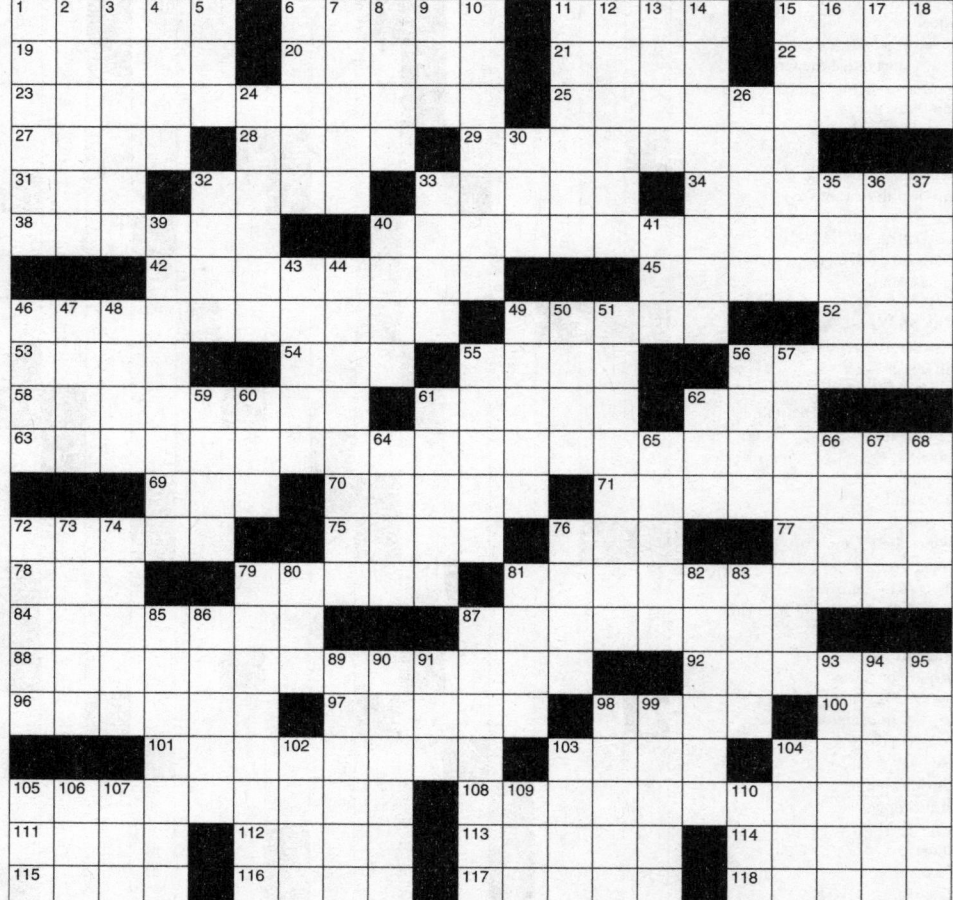

by Randolph Ross

ACROSS

1 Prefix with red
6 Denpasar is its capital
10 "Concord Hymn" writer's inits.
13 Green ___
19 Green, for instance
20 Christmas team
22 Trunk lines
23 Green 55-Down
26 "Me too"
27 Make messy
28 Enzyme ending
29 Gremlins and Pacers
33 Codger
34 Fella
36 Rat follower
38 A hero might have it
40 Box in many homes
41 Bracelet
44 Green 83-Down
49 Like
50 Trademarked chilled drink
51 Neighbor of Lanai
52 Live
54 Ding
56 Be listless
57 Lot of money
58 Channel for debates
60 Fast runners
63 Some socials
65 Corroding, with "into"
66 Green 58-Down
72 Cry from a balcony
73 Neat as ___
74 Legless creatures
75 Quarter of a deck
76 Skid row sounds
78 Yves's eve
80 Natural flavoring
84 His or her, to Henri
85 Computer connection
86 Destruction
89 The third of September
90 Green 8-Down
95 Cartoon character with a big nose
96 Mideast money
97 Old TV part
98 Map parts: Abbr.
99 Still
100 Kathryn of "Law & Order: Criminal Intent"
103 "Put it back in"
104 The sun
107 Utah city
109 Like turncoats
112 Green 13-Across
119 Tony-winning actress Martin
120 Inferior
121 Server of Norm, Cliff and Frasier, on "Cheers"
122 Not overdone
123 Stopover
124 Those caballeros
125 Cap sites

DOWN

1 "Eww!"
2 Dijon denial
3 Part of Dixie: Abbr.
4 Bird in the "Arabian Nights"
5 Sacred chests
6 Stomach settler
7 Correo ___ (airmail)
8 Green ___
9 About
10 Fix, as a rug
11 Early Chinese dynasty
12 Marine birds
13 First person indicator
14 Early colonizer of America
15 Great time
16 Mountain whose name in Greek means "I burn"
17 Hurdles for high schoolers, for short
18 Being, to Brutus
21 Furry-tailed rodents
24 Spa treatment
25 Tend to
29 Syrian president
30 Word before or after sugar
31 Scrub
32 Egg holder
35 Philosophical study of the universe
37 ___ Friday's
39 Bad start?
40 Mountain view
42 Not think things through first
43 Off course
45 Measure of light
46 Cold coat
47 Enemy: Abbr.
48 Start of many a city name
53 Some M.I.T. grads: Abbr.
55 Green ___
57 It's connected to a boom
58 Green ___
59 Hideaway
61 NASA's ___ Research Center
62 Old truck maker
64 Verdi's "___ tu"
65 ___ trip
66 Bone setters
67 End of an estimate
68 Close relative
69 Place with a moving line
70 Ship in 1898 headlines
71 Start of a supplication
76 Papal court
77 N.Y.C. subway line
79 One of the Wright brothers, for short
81 Center of entertainment
82 "The Cloister and the Hearth" author
83 Green ___
85 Kindergarten handicraft
86 Preparing for shipment
87 "Rah!"
88 E.E.C. part: Abbr.
91 Indian tourist destination on the Arabian Sea
92 They're not pro
93 Fade out
94 Loire laugh
100 Actress Lanchester and others
101 Repetitive musical piece
102 Storage units
104 Did laps
105 "Yikes!"
106 Actor Alan
108 Year in the middle of this century
110 Father
111 Need
113 One-fifth of quindici
114 Suffix with ball
115 Best-selling author Brown
116 "___ Sleep Comes Down to Soothe the Weary Eyes" (Dunbar poem)
117 "Rah!"
118 Points on a scale

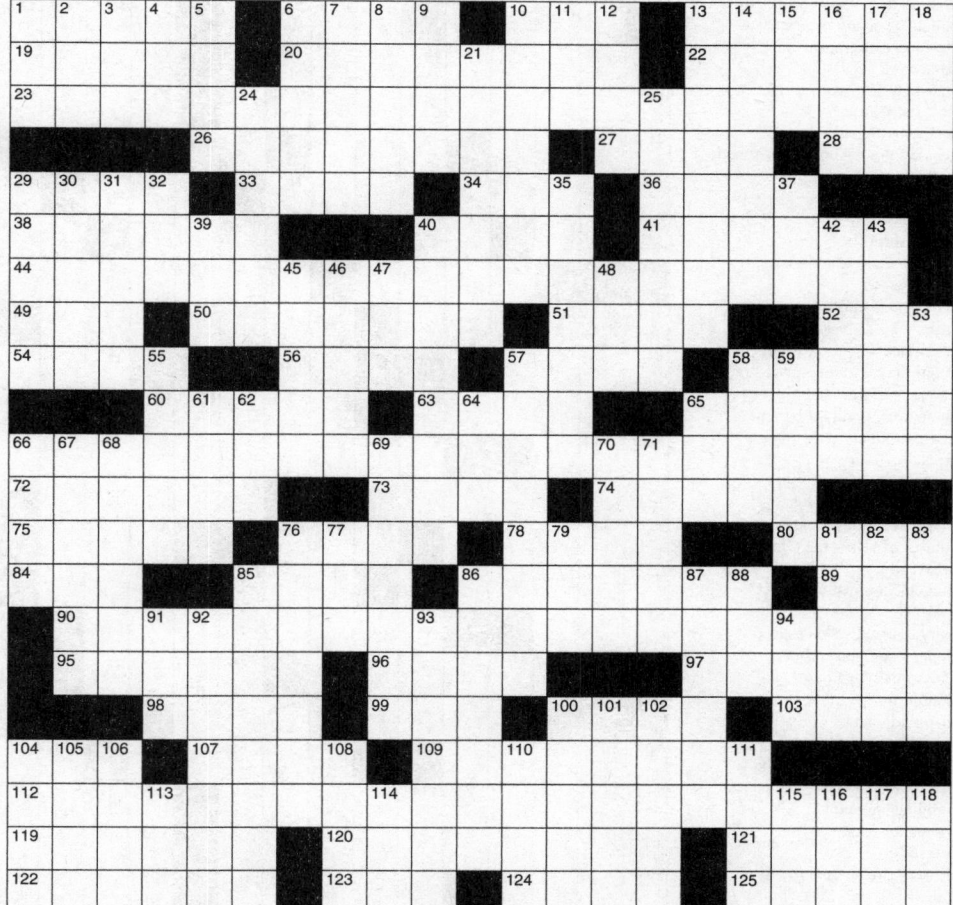

by Eric Berlin

ACROSS

1 Home of the Natl. Hollerin' Contest
5 Spicy cuisine
9 Beat ___ horse
14 Complain
18 Tenant's desire
20 Really rough
22 As a refutation
23 Acquirers of lost property
24 Part of New Eng.
25 Bit of cheer
26 Major source of the narcotic qat
28 Plain ___
29 Words under Washington's picture
32 "American Justice" network
33 International retailer whose name is an acronym
35 Stolen
36 Former German president Johannes
37 Major finale?
39 Desert attribute
43 Co-star of "Blow," 2001
44 Noisy celebration
46 Knock over
47 Writes without pen or pencil
50 Keys
51 Don who pitched a perfect game in the 1956 World Series
54 Lollobrigida and others
55 Tip for a calligrapher
56 Dandy
58 President who won by one electoral vote
59 Space shuttle supply
61 Locale for a vision of the Apostle Paul
64 Sicken
66 Candy treat
67 Basic infirmities
70 Cousin of a credit union
71 Friendly
74 Dimensions and tolerances, say
75 Taste
78 Tot minder
79 Major player in the movie biz?
81 Certain parallel: Abbr.
82 Some Sony computers
83 Apple product
85 Proclaims
88 Extends
89 The whole song and dance?
90 1999 "Star Wars" release
92 Subject of Cyrus the Great
93 Registers
96 Nickelodeon explorer
97 Fuss
98 Fairy queen, in Shakespeare
101 Underwriter's assessment
102 It's typically off base
103 Bottom line
106 Bistro adjunct
109 Round top
111 Long of "Boyz N the Hood"
112 Cease pleading
113 Building support
116 No matter what
119 Bruised
120 Nursery rhyme dish
121 "___ I!"
122 Theodore of "The Defiant Ones"
123 Subject of una sinfonia
124 Prosperity

DOWN

1 "You're doing it all wrong!"
2 Cream-filled pastry
3 Doctor
4 Music category
5 Calculate, as the bill
6 Kind of yoga
7 Parseghian of Notre Dame
8 Without thinking
9 First two
10 Old "Romper Room" character with bouncing antennae
11 Actor McGregor
12 Newswoman Compton
13 Game with orcs and half-elves
14 Like the labyrinth of Knossos
15 Graded materials
16 Suit to ___
17 Financial inits.
18 Japanese electronics giant
19 Sack materials
21 Was overly nice
27 Choice at a restaurant
30 Unfinished threat
31 Breathe
33 Cause of a red face
34 German port
38 E Street Band's leader, informally
39 Ones with incendiary ideas
40 Simple
41 Equal alternative
42 Beyond understanding
43 Neither hor. nor vert.
45 Barker's attention-getter
47 Legend in one's own mind
48 Sign at a store clothing bin
49 Imminently
50 One way to take it
52 Contented responses
53 Arctic explorer John
57 Go for the gold?
60 Snare
62 Store chain since 1859
63 Part of a bee
65 ___ Enterprise
68 Year in the reign of Antoninus Pius
69 Like Longfellow's Evangeline
72 King's longtime home
73 Assent
76 Photographer Richard
77 Locks in a stable
80 Hi-___
84 Part of a conference sched.
86 Fishing gear
87 Have great affection for
88 Punches a new number in
91 Commercial ending with Water
92 English royal known as the Empress Maud
94 "Cooks who know trust" this, in an old slogan
95 Tourist info spot
98 TV title role for Brandy Norwood
99 Beverage named for a Dutch river
100 Actress Blair
102 Idée ___ (accepted idea, in French)
104 Gird for battle, say
105 Oscar nominee for "The Insider"
106 Banned chemicals
107 1968 live folk album
108 Odious one
109 Shy
110 "The ability to describe others as they see themselves": Lincoln
114 Offerer of cozy accommodations
115 Baseball stat
117 Election day: Abbr.
118 Musical genre

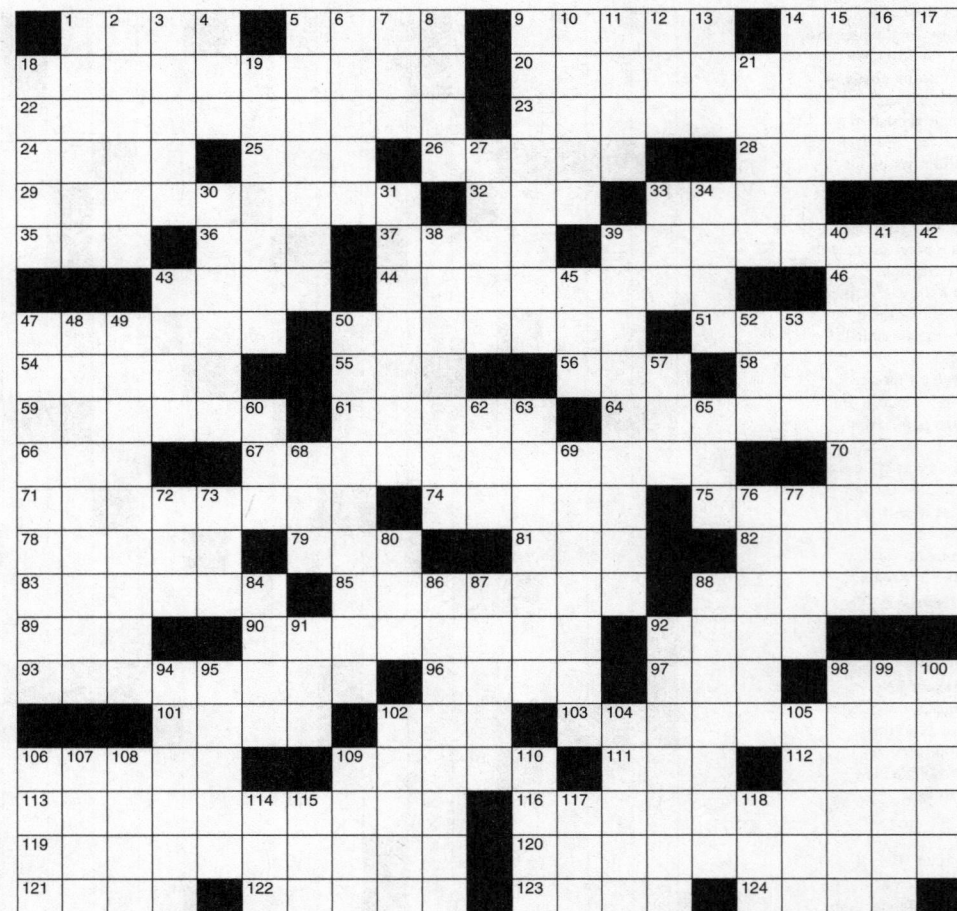

by Craig Kasper

ACROSS

1 Lays at the door of
7 One drawing sympathy
14 Tequila brand, for short
20 Any "Rock 'n' Roll High School" band member
21 Did some bookkeeping
22 Teamed up
23 Cuddly sheep?
25 Simple digs
26 TV remote, e.g.
27 Scout's find
29 Operatic prince
30 16th-century council city
31 Pen's end
33 Equinox mo.
34 Qum native
37 Eerie ability
39 Entre ___
41 Role-play, say
43 Those on the bench
46 Conservatives waiting in line?
50 Oater command
52 Wilhelm I ruled it
54 Pilot's vision problem
55 Idle, with "around"
57 A cabinet dept.
58 Blood: Prefix
60 Pro ___
61 Like a Miata
62 Expulsion from a court?
65 Treaty subject
68 Juilliard subj.
69 Necessitate
70 Mess up
73 Blasting aid
75 Carnaby Street types
77 Hillbillies' coif?
81 Hawkish
84 Test version
86 Biographer Leon
87 Ref. work with more than 300,000 entries
88 Be a fink
89 Lustrous fabric
91 Gave power to
93 Geom. solid
94 What van Gogh said regarding ears?
97 Reactor parts
98 Sinatra impersonator on "S.N.L."
100 Action film hero Williams
101 ___ Miguel (Azores island)
103 Cause of an intl. incident, maybe
104 Monokini's lack
106 ___ whim
108 Overshadow
112 Totally nuts
114 Taxco wrap
117 Edible spherule
119 Oscar-winning director of 2005
122 Sitting Bull being evasive?
124 Poverty-stricken
125 Downsize without layoffs
126 Timeless, in verse
127 Dedicated an ode to
128 Sonnet endings
129 Stopped arguing

DOWN

1 French port
2 Debussy opus
3 Go unhurriedly
4 State of increased quantity
5 Puts into effect
6 Shia, e.g.
7 Halloween activity
8 Clerical garment
9 Shoulder muscle, briefly
10 Vanilla-flavored treat
11 Cub leader
12 It may be found under a grate
13 Scene of a fall
14 1920s White House name
15 Kin of -kin
16 Lancelot lover
17 Calling the author of "In Cold Blood"?
18 Nix
19 Nose-wrinkler
24 Time on end
28 Makeshift swing
32 Nobelist Niels
35 Stays for another hitch
36 Really enjoyed
38 Druid, e.g.
40 In ___ (not yet born)
41 Wall Street option
42 Loses on purpose
43 Cross words
44 The munchies, for one
45 Swindle, slangily
47 2001 Sean Penn film
48 "___ chance"
49 Book size, in printing
51 Take a shot
53 Kick target
56 "Alfie" actress, 2004
59 Canton's home
63 Cereal box abbr.
64 Biddy
66 Pouty look
67 Insect-eating plant
71 Pool group
72 In ___ land
73 "The Sound of Music" name
74 Worthless African animal?
76 Genesis son
77 Novelist Binchy
78 Court plea, in brief
79 Thing to do
80 Some calculations
81 Carat divs.
82 Mrs. Theodore Roosevelt
83 New stylings
85 Rend
89 ___ Balls (Hostess brand)
90 Verne skipper
92 Chocolaty treats
95 Picks, with "for"
96 They're depressed during exams
99 Lost zip
102 Carol starter
104 Knuckle-dragger
105 Goes bonkers
107 Prince Valiant's son
109 Left on board
110 Alums do it
111 Sent, in a way
112 Journalist Sheehy
113 Ballerina Pavlova
115 History units
116 Jay Gould railroad
118 River of central Germany
120 Shoebox marking
121 Baseball Hall-of-Famer Roush
123 Polo Grounds legend

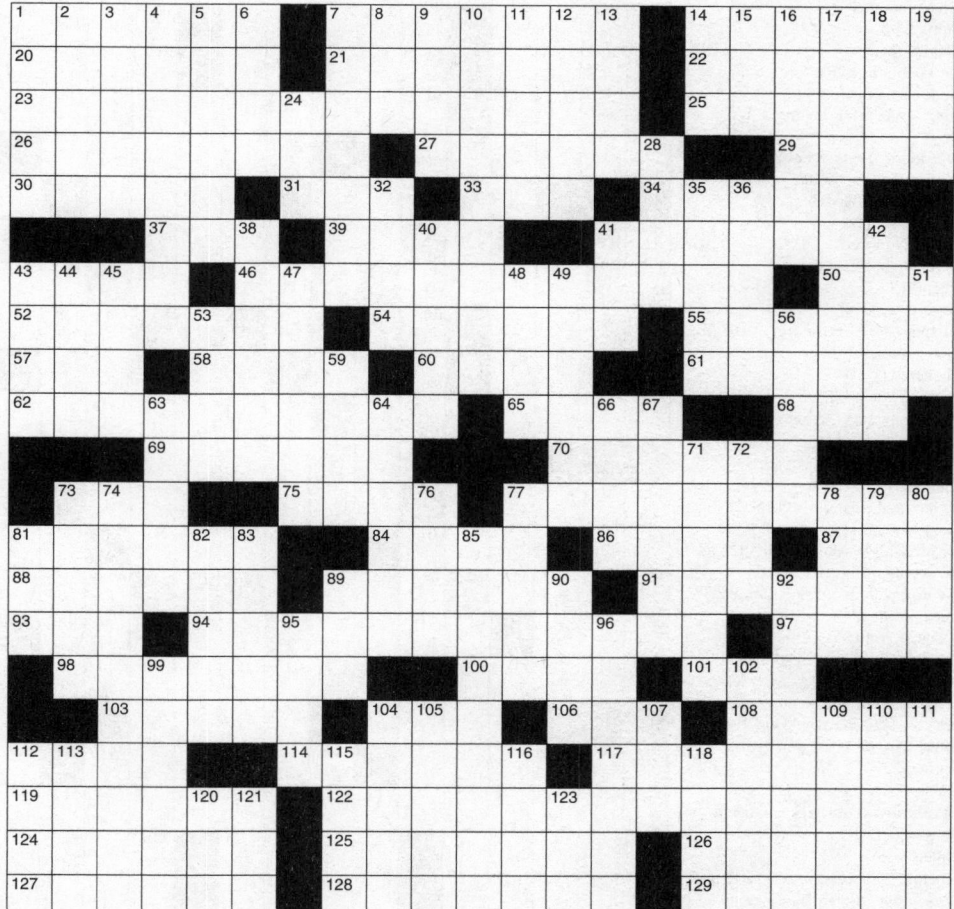

by Fred Piscop

ACROSS

1. Some people count by them
5. Potters' needs
10. Bits of Three Stooges violence
14. Instruction to a violinist
19. Overhead light?
20. Place for boats
21. Cut for a column
22. Ones undergoing transformation
23. Rock band whose first album was titled, appropriately, "High Voltage"
24. Announcer's cry at a hound race?
27. [Boo-hoo!]
29. Inconsistent
30. "___ Thou Now, O Soul" (Walt Whitman poem)
31. Jazz pianist Bill
33. Skirt feature
34. Flies, maybe
35. Minotaur's home
38. What priests on a space mission wear?
44. Pitch maker?
46. How sardines are often packed
47. Requirement for a hand, say
48. Receiver of donations
49. Take ___ (swing hard)
50. A celebrity carries one
52. Bldg. planner
53. Smart-mouthed
54. Prefix with -zoic
55. Classic Jaguar
56. Dr. Gregory of "ER"
59. Attack helicopter
61. King Frederick I's realm
63. Naps
65. Werner of "Ship of Fools," 1965
66. Mouthing off to police officers?
69. Informal head cover
72. Asylum seekers
73. Formally attired
77. Child actor discovered by Chaplin
79. Observe furtively
80. Atlanta-based health org.
81. Faux: Abbr.
82. Sheltered spot
83. They have big bills
85. Result of a slap, perhaps
86. ___ bean
87. Word with bitter or winter
88. Man ___
89. Abbott and Costello's "Here Come the ___"
92. Novelist Glyn who coined "It" as a euphemism
94. TV dog with its muzzle removed?
98. Teen problem
99. Chantilly seraph
100. "Norma Rae" director Martin
101. Consumer products giant, briefly
103. Fictional hero whose first words are "I was born in the Year 1632, in the City of York . . ."
106. Tissuelike
108. Tease
112. Marshes with libraries and opera houses?
115. Noted exile
116. Kitchen floor coverings, to a Brit
117. Fossey who did gorilla research
118. "The Wreck of the Mary ___"
119. Longtime NBC star
120. Dumb
121. Snafu
122. Turned up
123. Trails

DOWN

1. Sign of spring
2. City on the Brazos
3. ___ Towne
4. Debutante ball?
5. "Dreams From My Father" writer
6. Singer in the 1958 movie "Go, Johnny, Go!"
7. Night school subj.
8. His ___ (self-important man)
9. Stops daydreaming
10. "Hush!"
11. "Swan Lake" role
12. Terrible shame
13. Rte. parts
14. Lift
15. Habana or Cádiz
16. Grp. with lodges
17. Fall guys?
18. Horizontal thread in a fabric
25. Longtime Chicago Symphony conductor
26. Start of Kansas' motto
28. Cinematographer Nykvist
32. Common English place name ending
34. Big report
35. Surgical aid
36. Like triple plays compared to double plays
37. Aria that ends "O speranze d'amor!"
39. A, in Italy
40. Harvard student
41. ___ lit
42. Buckwheat groats
43. Drive . . . or part of a cattle drive
45. Horizontal line
51. Decree
52. Major extensions?
53. Backdrop for carolers?
56. "Wittle" toe
57. So out it's back in
58. Pasty
60. Foot specialist
62. Family history, e.g.
63. Short cuts
64. Stock market sell-off
67. "Without a doubt"
68. Word said with a hand behind one's back
69. 1983 Mr. T film
70. Alley Oop's girl
71. Vagabond
74. Cyberchatting
75. Wheels for big wheels
76. Windows button
78. Crystal user
80. ___ number (ID on all stocks and registered bonds)
84. Symbol of royal power
85. Driller's deg.
88. Worthless
89. Some sunglasses
90. Many a John Ford film
91. Spanish road
93. Curtsier
95. City where the Lehigh and Delaware rivers meet
96. Soap operas, e.g.
97. Ones at the feeding trough
102. "Long time ___!"
103. Third-century year
104. Archaeological site
105. Bone that means "elbow" in Latin
106. Balletic bend
107. River of Flanders
109. Guess
110. Little bite
111. Doctors' grps.
113. Two-inch stripe wearer: Abbr.
114. ___ Tomé

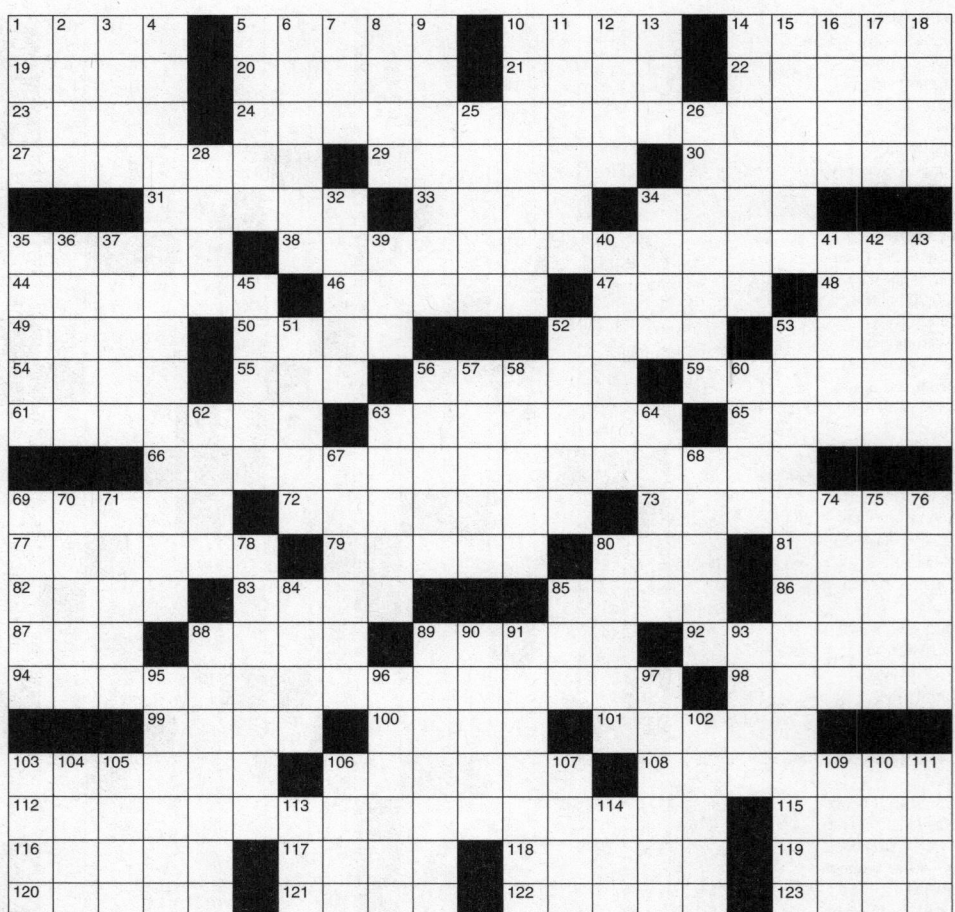

by Paula Gamache

ACROSS

1 Pot builder
9 Solitaire measure
14 Court marshal
21 Undying flower
22 Round window
23 Condition of the 85-Across
24 Peacemaker
25 Of yore
26 Boards
27 Something that goes for a quarter?
29 How Peter denied Jesus
31 The Marx Bros. left Paramount for it
32 Subj. of a library in Austin, Tex.
35 Opposite of protruding
36 Chaise place
38 Actress Andersson of "I Never Promised You a Rose Garden"
39 Delivered a stemwinder
41 Plant sci.
43 Unification Church member, slangily
44 Loaf
45 Threw out, as a question
46 Flip out
48 "Gold" Fonda role
49 Like Van Buren's presidency
50 123-Across or 96-Down?
53 It may be polar
54 Israeli political leader Peretz
56 Original finish?
57 Howe in the National Inventors Hall of Fame
58 Diana on the cover of "Sgt. Pepper's Lonely Hearts Club Band"
59 Snowboard alternative
61 Seize
62 Quadrille designs
64 Box ofc. buy
67 127-Across or 91-Down?
70 God who cuckolded Hephaestus
71 Seating areas
72 Cause of an explosion
73 Doofus
74 Put (down)
75 Old five-franc pieces
76 23-Across or 19-Down?
83 Not camera-ready?
84 1994 film with the tagline "Get ready for rush hour"
85 Really big
86 Bows
87 Wasn't straight
88 Mâcon's river
89 NNW's reverse
90 Big Southern department store chain
91 "The Trouble With Harry" co-star Edmund
93 24-Across or 5-Down?
97 Once across the Rio Grande?
98 Hamburger shack?
99 Caravaggio's "The Sacrifice of ___"
100 Neptune's closest moon
103 French textile city
104 Oxford lengths
106 Norse war god
107 Saloon habitués, slangily
108 Boarders board it
109 Bordeaux wine
111 On ___ (raging)
113 Wing
114 Tail
115 Like some stars
116 Reddish gem
119 Most drunken
121 Worth having
123 VX, e.g.
127 Secondary competitions, in some tennis tournaments
128 Piano's counterpart
129 Words before roof or flag
130 Tabasco and others
131 Let out
132 Course option

DOWN

1 Rude character
2 U.K. record label
3 Dorm leaders, for short
4 Smell ___
5 Wedded couples
6 Not forgotten
7 Flute parts
8 ___ Problem of celestial mechanics
9 Codger
10 Some toll units
11 Reverse mantra of "The Shining"
12 Salt agreement?
13 Circus props
14 "Don't fight"
15 It begins here
16 About
17 J.F.K. alternative
18 "Assuming it's O.K. with you . . ."
19 Impression of Count Dracula?
20 Second-largest city in Ark.
23 Cereal toppers
28 Leaf pore
30 Sharp fellow?
32 Cut (off)
33 Bud
34 "A Different World" actress
37 Candy bar fillings
38 Fake
40 Chinese bloomers
42 Person behind bars?
44 Some gowns
46 Welcome words to a hitchhiker
47 Dropped from the galleys
49 Undermine
51 Vandeweghe of the N.B.A.
52 Not final, at law
54 Strolls
55 Ancient deity mentioned 39 times in Allen Ginsberg's "Howl"
58 Slam
60 Serpentine signal
61 Overcaffeinated
62 "Six Degrees of Separation" playwright
63 Comedic spiel
64 A heart often has one
65 Place to keep toys?
66 "Shame!"
68 Nobel laureate between Hesse and Eliot
69 Heads to Harvard or Georgetown, maybe
70 It often features the quadratic formula
74 ___-10
76 An Ivy, briefly
77 Outlaw Kelly
78 Make rough
79 It's blown
80 Starbucks order
81 Unadorned
82 Rink athlete, informally
84 Trig ratios
87 Seesaw, e.g.
88 Flee like mice
89 Refurbish
91 Lack of gravity
92 Cry of relief
93 Months after Tebets
94 Real downer?
95 One-eyed leader
96 Makes a special invitation?
97 City on Lake Victoria
101 Tie indicator
102 Dial-up alternative, for short
104 Fancy homes
105 Land
107 Puppeteers Bil and Cora
109 Spanish sky
110 Liking
112 Dementieva of tennis
115 Texas metropolis nickname
117 Portland college
118 Maker of the game Dart Tag
120 Transfer ___
122 Pro
124 Indian state
125 What goes in your nose to make noise?
126 Pommes frites accompanier

by Byron Walden

ACROSS

1 Audibly shocked
6 Bar
11 Two-seaters, maybe
19 Quaint opening for a note
20 Google's domain
22 Sailing
23 First you . . .
26 Nav. rank
27 ___ kwon do
28 Bit of athletic wear
29 . . . which . . .
34 Longevity
37 Explosion maker
38 Sound off
39 Smith Brothers competitor
41 Music box?
44 Super Mario Bros. player
45 You may put something on it at a bar
49 ___ Today (teachers' monthly)
50 High-altitude home
51 Not subject to any more changes
53 Shortly
54 Kind of help
55 Depilatory brand
56 . . . that . . .
59 Sot's woe
60 Didn't play
61 Suffix with hip
62 Mai ___
63 After a while the . . .
72 ___ soda
73 "Dream on!"
74 Spanish pronoun
75 Geom. figure
76 . . . who . . .
83 House or senate
84 Med. plans
85 Sick as ___
86 Glaswegian : Glasgow :: Loiner : ___
87 Waits
88 Foreign pen pal, maybe
89 Oil tanker cargoes
91 "Looky here!"
92 Bring in
93 Ship-to-shore transport
95 "Café-Concert" painter
97 Special
98 Additional, in commercialese
99 . . . which . . .
106 Replacing
108 "___ who?"
109 QB Grossman
110 Next time . . .
117 Aesthete
118 Trojan War hero
119 Capital nicknamed "City of Trees"
120 Back-of-book feature
121 Classic Harlem ballroom
122 Story subtitled "The Yeshiva Boy"

DOWN

1 Stock phrase
2 1977 biographical Broadway play starring Anne Bancroft
3 "Ditto"
4 [as is]
5 Make-believe
6 "I Love Lucy" neighbor
7 Any ship
8 Concert souvenir
9 Pained sounds
10 Glimpse
11 Classic setting for detective pulp fiction
12 Win by ___
13 "Don't take ___ seriously!"
14 Antitheft device
15 Stunk
16 Part of a windy road
17 Crack team?: Abbr.
18 Bloody 2004 thriller
21 It comes with strings attached
24 Class
25 Songwriter Washington
30 Stoop feature
31 Ancient region bordering Lydia
32 Rock singer Reznor
33 Homes on the Costa del Sol
35 Subject of a makeup exam?
36 Fishhook line
39 Tall and thin
40 On base
41 Music genre, briefly
42 End
43 Do-or-die time
46 Couldn't stand
47 Año nuevo time
48 Start of the title of many an ode
51 Party
52 Lascivious
54 Men-only
56 "2001" computer
57 Nos. on a scoreboard
58 Source of an explosion in Italy
60 French town of W.W. II
64 Lip
65 Lead character on TV's "The Pretender"
66 Plains tribe
67 Kind of lic.
68 Jupiter's counterpart
69 Belief
70 Senate staff
71 Assignation
76 Mississippi senator Cochran
77 Blend
78 Modulate
79 Internet address suffix
80 Long stretches
81 Shorten, maybe
82 "What did ___ deserve this?"
83 Beginning
87 Defeat easily
89 Handel's "___ Anthems"
90 With 101-Down, unwrinkle
92 Areas next to a great hall
94 Subjects to cross-x
96 Pitching figures
99 Roughage
100 Cautious
101 See 90-Down
102 Asking too much of someone?
103 Utah senator Hatch
104 Nadir amount
105 Dismiss
107 58-Down output
110 Capture
111 Link letters
112 Lance in law
113 Indianapolis's ___ Dome
114 "Punk'd" airer
115 Resetting setting
116 Kicker?

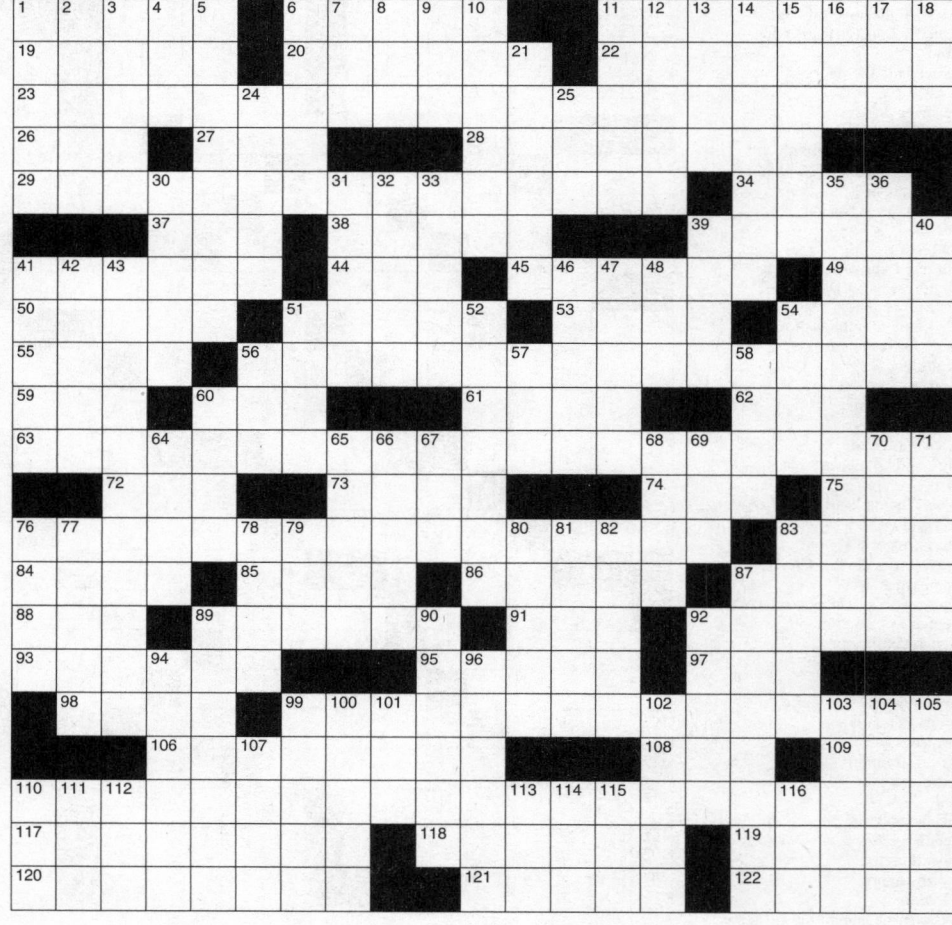

by Brendan Emmett Quigley

ACROSS

1. Student's declaration
6. Restricted part of a street
13. Paul of pet food
17. 1947 crime drama
21. Block in the Southwest
22. Golf club with a nearly vertical face
23. Love letters?
24. U.S. city in sight of two volcanoes
25. With 36-Across, "Poetry is . . ." (Osbert Sitwell)
27. Orange/yellow blooms
29. Feature of the villain in "The Fugitive"
30. Walk to the door
32. Single thread
33. Radisson alternative
36. See 25-Across
40. Hearty drink
43. Like the Uzbek and Kirghiz languages
47. Smog-watching grp.
48. Bagnell Dam river
49. Purplish
52. Ella of "Phantom Lady"
54. One way to be paid
58. Amount past due?
59. "Poetry is . . ." (Joseph Roux)
63. Oater locale
64. Where Springsteen was born, in song
65. Monte ___
66. Hyde Park stroller
68. Toil
71. Have on
75. Japanese band?
78. Like many pubs
81. With 89-Across, "Poetry is . . ." (Carl Sandburg)
85. Flat
88. Struggle
89. See 81-Across
93. QB Rodney
94. Banned spray
95. Russian city or oblast
96. Office gizmo
98. Soissons seasons
100. Baseball Hall-of-Famer Banks
104. Make an inauguration affirmation
107. Literary ending
111. "Poetry is . . ." (Edith Sitwell)
117. Took top honors
118. French city in W.W. II fighting
119. Title character in a "Sgt. Pepper" song
120. Grant maker
121. Hatch from Utah
123. 15 years before the Battle of Hastings
125. Dead Sea Scrolls scribe
127. "___ gratias"
128. "Poetry is . . ." (Pablo Neruda)
133. Verges on
136. Sing "Gladly the cross-eyed bear," say
137. Tyro
141. ___ Mae
145. Elderly
148. "Poetry is . . ." (E. E. Cummings)
151. English university V.I.P.'s
152. Punjabi believer
153. No more
154. #24 of 24
155. As a result
156. Besides
157. Fall field worker
158. Snooped (around)

DOWN

1. Bueno's opposite
2. Tennis edge
3. It may start with someone entering a bar
4. West Indian sorcery
5. Prepare, as a side of beans
6. Beantown, on scoreboards
7. Durham sch.
8. Half of doce
9. Energy
10. Singer India___
11. ___ this world
12. Nutrition drink brand
13. Belief
14. Up to one's ears (in)
15. Cuban patriot José
16. Go around
17. Beachwear
18. "Zounds," e.g.
19. Antiquity, quaintly
20. Denials
26. "This is where ___"
31. Halfhearted
34. Go bad
35. Red hair, e.g.
37. Arabian capital
38. Fairy-tale menace
39. G.P.A. spoilers
40. Mtn. stats
41. Trevi coin, once
42. Month after Ab
44. Friends
45. Not on the border
46. Poetic break: Var.
50. Sitting on
51. Tapas bar offering
53. Writer Sontag
55. Big spinner
56. Here, in Juárez
57. Camera inits.
60. Aligned
61. Main seating area
62. Namely
67. Perfect
69. N.C. State plays in it
70. Denny's alternative
72. Oklahoma city
73. Steinbeck's "To ___ Unknown"
74. Angry talk
75. Really, really
76. Physicist Niels
77. "Dies ___"
79. Arrived quietly
80. ". . . ___ great fall"
82. Exactly, after "to"
83. Parlor piece
84. Gridiron protection
86. Wasted gas
87. Inventor's place
90. Group of spies
91. Kind of check
92. Hundred Acre Wood donkey
97. Winter Olympics venues
99. It's raised on a farm
101. NASA homecoming
102. Tiny bite
103. "See ___ care!"
105. Two, in Lisbon
106. In many cases
108. Operatic Jenny
109. Early Nebraskan
110. Deli order
111. Old deferment classification
112. Beeper
113. Ticking off
114. Pulled in
115. Poe's middle name
116. Surrealist Magritte
122. Reply to "No way!"
124. Old-style hangover remedy
126. League division
129. Mighty big
130. Swing wildly
131. Corner office and others
132. Gettysburg general under Lee
134. Household health hazard
135. Sportscast feature
138. Peevishness
139. TV's Swenson
140. Fashion's ___ von Furstenberg
142. "Here ___ . . ."
143. "Bus Stop" playwright
144. "Yikes!"
145. "___ on Melancholy"
146. Swe. abutter
147. Ma'am or dam
149. K.C.-to-Duluth dir.
150. "___ the fields . . ."

by Victor Fleming

ACROSS

1 Rude awakening
5 Frequent abbr. on sheet music for folk songs
9 Compound number?
14 Without an out
19 1998 Andrea Bocelli operatic album
20 DeSoto or LaSalle
21 Concentration thwarter
22 Something that might be tucked under the chin
23 . . . and 25-Across have "canine" surnames
25 . . . and 41-Across sang with their siblings
27 Ignore the alarm
28 "With any luck"
30 Shamed
31 Save one's own neck, maybe
32 Poet with a seemingly self-contradictory name
33 Bundle of nerves
34 Barely perceptible
36 Reach a settlement
37 Healing aid patented in 1872
41 . . . and 52-Across are Mormons
43 Matches
44 No Westminster contender
45 Compass point suffix
46 Not at all certain
47 Contest that leads to a draw
48 Loyal pooch
49 Census stats
51 Agassi partner
52 . . . and 69-Across have affiliations with "Jeopardy!"
55 Museum employee
57 The King of Pop, in headlines
58 1980s–'90s N.B.A. star Danny
59 Belligerent deity
60 Branches
61 He reached his peak in 1806
62 "Everybody Loves Raymond" role
64 News exec Roger
65 Glockenspiels' kin
69 . . . and 80-Across have mythological creatures as surnames
71 Mmes., across the Pyrenees
72 Symbol in el zodiaco
73 "Zip-___-Doo-Dah"
74 Have an in (with)
75 Stimulate
76 Kia model
77 "Didn't I tell you?!"
78 Faith in music
80 . . . and 99-Across starred in musicals and share their first names with a classic sitcom couple
84 Comment following a lucky guess
86 Pin site
87 Slippery as ___
88 Taking care of the situation
89 France's Oscar
90 "The Most Happy Fella" song
91 Bailiwick of TV's Matlock
94 Country with a palm tree on its flag
95 Sophocles subject
99 . . . and 101-Across are known for their fancy footwork

101 . . . and 23-Across are Olympic gold medalists
103 Clan symbol
104 Makes
105 Xena's horse
106 Absence
107 Talked a blue streak?
108 Showed courage, old-style
109 In case
110 Caustic chemicals

DOWN

1 Fixes
2 Exam format
3 Erstwhile denaro
4 Cons
5 Access
6 Contrite
7 Long-distance letters
8 Exhibiting Ennui
9 Had fun with
10 Rogaine alternative
11 Cheryl of "Curb Your Enthusiasm"
12 Tongue's end?
13 Not totally disastrous
14 Flies
15 Strands in the winter?
16 This and that
17 Sheltered
18 Sale locale
24 Like hedgehogs
26 Bigger than big
29 Keratoid
34 Make a name for oneself?
35 Queen ___ County, Md.
36 Elizabeth Taylor's pet charity, for short
37 Mission ___, Calif.
38 Hockey infraction
39 Wink accompaniment
40 Asteroid discovered in 1898
41 Pricey
42 Donkeys, to mules
43 Discards
47 Casino supply
48 Police epithet, with "the"
50 Make fast
51 "The Female Eunuch" author
52 Singer/actress Akers
53 Performs perfectly
54 Puma rival
56 Before markdown: Abbr.
57 Half of Brangelina
60 Grant money?
61 Masterpiece
62 Jilted wife of myth

63 Staggering
64 "Is that ___?"
65 Truculent
66 Leader of the Mel-Tones
67 Typeface akin to Helvetica
68 Expeditiously
69 Like il but not elle: Abbr.
70 Sore
71 Round all around
75 March honoree, familiarly
78 George Eliot, e.g.
79 Uses a Moviola, in film-making
80 Showing the least resistance
81 Close-fitting garment
82 Georgia of "The Mary Tyler Moore Show"
83 Erythrocyte
85 U.P.S. staffer, at times
86 Memorizes
89 Cicada sound
90 Baffin Bay sights
91 P.M. periods
92 Think way back?
93 Actor Jared
96 Bob of the P.G.A.
97 It may be served in a bed
98 Shows curiosity
100 Sports org. for nonprofessionals
102 "Chances ___"

by Henry Hook

ACROSS

1 Tribe with a sun dance
6 Periods in contrast to global warming
13 Cuff
17 Rise and fall, as a ship
18 Team supporter's suction cup-mounted sign
19 Regardful
20 Where smart shoppers shop?
23 Ad ___
24 Lodges
25 Fake-out
26 Short-order cook's aid
27 A person doing a duck walk grasps these
29 Site of Napoleon's invasion of 1798–1801
31 Place for fish and ships
32 Tell
33 "___ me!"
34 Plight of an overcrowded orchestra?
38 Cat, at times
40 Computer file name extension
41 Camera inits.
42 Kind of sch.
43 Crew
46 Fit for dwelling
51 Blushing
52 Introduction to opera?
54 Epitome of blackness
55 Oodles
57 Frustrated
58 Gaynor of "South Pacific"
59 Common origami creations
61 Sought sanctuary, old-style
63 ___ "Inferno"
64 Lilylike plant
65 Actress Shire and others
66 Insider talk
67 Not exceeding
68 Locale of Hoosier beaches?
71 Bub
74 Leaving, slangily
76 Virus variety
77 "Essays of ___"
78 Bow
79 "___ now!"
81 Yes-men, maybe?
83 Bit of winter exercise?
89 Italian librettist Gaetano ___
90 Abbr. after many a military title
91 Match
92 Annual announcement from 13-Down
93 "Drink to me only with thine eyes" poet
94 Burmese gathering?
97 "Ciao"
98 Carolina university
100 Dog with a tightly curled tail
101 Geraldo rehearses his show?
105 Much-counterfeited timepiece
106 More run-down
107 Traction provider
108 ___ empty stomach
109 Mugs
110 Hopper of Hollywood

DOWN

1 Dish for an Italian racing champ?
2 Stimpy's TV pal
3 Most like a breeze
4 Dame Edith who was nominated for three Oscars
5 In stitches
6 "___ tree falls . . ."
7 Stephen King's first novel
8 Last
9 "Far out!"
10 Show fixation, maybe
11 Stowe girl
12 Composer Prokofiev
13 See 92-Across: Abbr.
14 French Bluebeard
15 Cultural/teaching facility
16 Una ___ (old coin words)
19 Calais confidant
20 Item on a chain, usually
21 Steers clear of
22 Passage
23 Nautical rope
28 Former Irish P.M. ___ Cosgrave
30 Québec traffic sign
31 Stole
34 ___ hammer (Viking symbol)
35 Show slight relief, maybe
36 Computer key
37 Kind of paper
39 Whoops
44 Basket material
45 Iowa and Missouri
47 A club, e.g.
48 Sandwich that can never be finished?
49 Be a couch potato
50 "___ Coming" (1969 hit)
52 Tiny annoyance
53 Gouges repeatedly
56 Overall
58 Jazz's Herbie
59 Thick-bodied fish
60 Cowboy's aid
61 Send out
62 Denver's ___ Gardens amusement park
63 Photographer Arbus
65 "Star Trek: ___"
66 German camera
68 Canine neighbor
69 Words often applied to 93-Across
70 Hen, at times
72 Freshens
73 Cover
75 Bug

77 School named in the Public Schools Act of 1868
80 Many urban dwellers
82 Like electrical plugs
83 Hall of Fame jockey Eddie
84 Become tiresome to
85 Loser at the Battle of Châlons, A.D. 451
86 Birthplace of Aaron Burr
87 "Happy Days" role
88 Lessener
93 Eponymous physicist
95 1932 skiing gold medalist Utterström
96 Bit of spelling?
97 King ___ tomb
99 ___ Lomond
102 Historic Heyerdahl craft
103 Prof.'s posting
104 Fooled

by Charles M. Deber

ACROSS

1 Like windows and geishas
7 Subject of a David McCullough political biography
12 Copper head?
15 Staying power
19 Chevy introduced in 1958
20 Time's 1977 Man of the Year
21 Strong draft horses
23 *What someone who looks at Medusa does
25 Act of putting into circulation
26 Private line
27 "___-La-La" (Al Green hit)
28 "A Lonely Rage" autobiographer
30 "Star Trek" series, to fans
31 Laws, informally
32 *1850 American literature classic
37 From ___ Z
39 Suffix with convention
40 Faulkner hero
41 Shakespearean question after "How now!"
42 *Demonstrate the method
48 Staying power?
50 Bus. card abbr.
51 Your highness?: Abbr.
52 ___-mo
53 Stuffs
54 Area of authority
56 It has gutters on each side
59 "The Lord of the Rings" creature
61 Mary of "Where Eagles Dare"
62 Cost of time or space
63 Without a break
65 Succeed
69 Agnus ___ (Mass prayers)
70 *Push aside
73 TV's "___-Team"
75 Meets, as a challenge
78 Kind of patch
79 Received, as a message
80 Eydie Gormé's "___ Es el Amor"
81 Hair-raising cry
84 Boxer Trinidad
85 Becker on "L.A. Law"
86 Verve
88 Run down
90 ___ 88
92 State with the fewest counties (three): Abbr.
93 John who hosted TV's "Talk Soup"
94 *Walk in the park, say
98 "Wouldn't ___ Loverly?"
99 House calls?
101 Battery size
102 High-school dept.
103 *Put at bay
108 Appointees confirmed by Cong.
112 Did not go fast?
113 Film noir, e.g.
114 ___ Schwarz
115 "Well, look ___!"
116 "Hamlet" setting
119 *Miami baseball list
122 British composer Robert
123 Have ___ in mind
124 Gertrude who swam the English Channel
125 Not included: Abbr.
126 9-1-1 grp.
127 Percolates
128 They may be light or free

DOWN

1 Relative of a mandolin
2 Tickle
3 Cutting
4 It goes back and forth in a workshop
5 Further
6 "Gimme ___!"
7 "Steady ___ goes"
8 Computer input
9 Big flap
10 Victorian roofs
11 Leather source
12 McMurry University site
13 Lays siege to
14 Mass transit choices
15 *Toothless South American animal
16 Seemed right
17 Money rival
18 Bisected fly?
22 "___ Nacht" (German words of parting)
24 Kyrgyzstan city
29 Support group
32 Diligent student, in slang
33 These: Fr.
34 Eases off
35 Head set
36 MapQuest request: Abbr.
38 English class assignment
42 Pricey strings
43 Attentive one
44 Sainted king called "the Stout"
45 Defeatees' comment
46 Son of Cedric the Saxon
47 Word of encouragement
49 Banjo-picker Scruggs
55 *Not so important
57 Opposite of paleo-
58 P.O. item
60 Place for a star
64 Girl in a gown
66 "Misty" composer Garner
67 "___ the Magician" (old radio series)
68 More chilling
71 Table scrap
72 Sundial hour
74 Gustav Klimt's "Portrait of ___ Bloch-Bauer I"
76 Start of Idaho's motto
77 Woody's partner
79 Sets upon
82 Kinetoscope inventor
83 Mrs. Doonesbury, in the comics
86 "___ life!"
87 Fair-minded
89 Modern and technologically advanced
91 Pricey
93 Smart
94 Lush fabrics
95 ___-tzu
96 Deerstalker fold-down
97 "Boston Legal" Emmy winner
100 Memory trace
104 Oversee
105 1980s major-league slugger Tony
106 Accomplishes perfectly, as a dismount
107 Lot of time
109 Fort ___, Fla.
110 Synthetic gem
111 Film extras, for short
115 Page, for one
116 Conductor ___-Pekka Salonen
117 Old Ford
118 East End abode
120 Fish eggs
121 Pentateuch book: Abbr

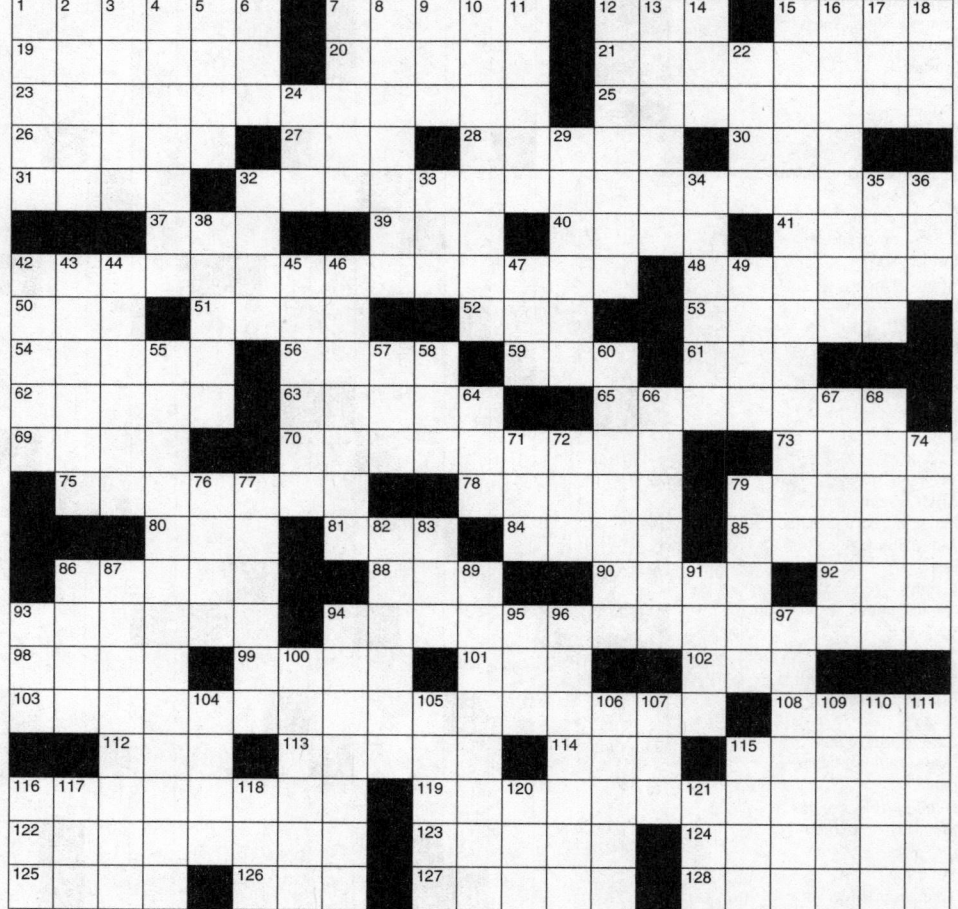

by Jim Page

ACROSS

1 Trick-taking card game
5 Yemeni port famous as a source of coffee
10 Former Connecticut governor Ella
16 Take in
21 Swenson of "Benson"
22 Saw
23 Comparatively flush
24 "No men allowed" area
25 Ambiguous headline about a man charged with killing his attacker?
29 Mystic
30 Level of care
31 Connected, in a way
32 Bright-eyed
35 Santa ___
36 Earth Day subj.
38 Retired boomer
39 Ambiguous headline about a protest?
48 Gone by
49 Parcel
50 Company with the slogan "born from jets"
51 Field protector
52 Sandwich rank
54 Take ___ breath
56 Hang over
59 "What ___?"
63 Ambiguous headline about school closings?
69 Oil-rich ruler
70 Dutch painter Jan
71 Hair-raiser
72 Fall setting
73 Was contrite
76 Break
78 Field stars
80 Early hrs.
81 Ambiguous headline about a California drug bust?
87 Rocky peak
88 One with a thick skin
89 ". . . ___ saw Elba"
90 Actress Sedgwick
91 JFK-to-TLV option
93 Peter and Paul, but not Mary
95 Sugar cube holder
98 Rating of a program blocked by a V-chip
101 Ambiguous headline about a vagrancy statistic?
106 Moonshine
107 Progress smoothly
108 Broom ___ (comics witch)
109 "___ & Stitch," 2002 animated film
111 Encouraging sounds
114 Cozy corner
117 Country singer Carter
119 McKellen of "The Lord of the Rings"
120 Ambiguous headline about attorneys' pro bono work?
125 Do-do connector
127 Jump in the rink
128 "___ of Destruction," 1965 protest song
129 Actor Morales
130 Words said with raised arm and glass
133 Word for word
138 Huge
142 Ambiguous headline about a stolen Stradivarius?
146 Kind of chin
147 Vast
148 Heavy metal bar
149 Like the rim of an eyecup
150 Earthenware pots
151 Kind of valve
152 Wild guesses
153 It's not held when it's used

DOWN

1 Sets (on)
2 In the ___
3 It'll douse a fuego
4 Frequent congestion site
5 "Welcome" offerer
6 Kitchen gadget company
7 Big name in credit cards
8 Blast maker
9 "The Bonesetter's Daughter" author
10 1983 U.S. invasion site
11 Narrow inlets
12 Dramatic opening
13 Quake
14 One of New York's Finger Lakes
15 E-mail address ender
16 Place for a guard, in soccer
17 Shaker formula
18 Word with scam or sketch
19 Means of control
20 Irish patriot hanged in 1803
26 Close
27 Elaine ___ ("Seinfeld" role)
28 One end of the Moscow Canal
33 Longtime staple of daytime TV
34 Popular air freshener
37 Dated
39 West of Hollywood
40 Playing marble
41 Composer Ned
42 Their service is impeccable
43 Mushroom cloud creator, briefly
44 Columbo portrayer
45 Duo in a typical symphony
46 Exhort
47 Sudden increase on a graph
53 Scottish estate owner
55 Prefix with dactyl
57 Muppet who lives in a trash can
58 Mazda model
60 "Myra Breckinridge" novelist
61 Abnormal plant swelling
62 Info that may be phished: Abbr.
64 Trounce
65 "Still Me" autobiographer Christopher
66 Some magazine ads
67 Schlock
68 In need of a washer, perhaps
74 Head of costume design
75 Lush
77 Palm readers?
79 Gaiety
81 Manuscript sheet
82 Muse with a wreath of myrtle and roses
83 Makes unwanted overtures?
84 Jazz pianist Chick
85 Breeze
86 Maritime
87 High-___
92 Sock fiber
94 Definitely no arm-twister
96 Father Sarducci of old "S.N.L."
97 Fifth-century pope
99 11th-century year
100 Company with a "spokesduck"
102 Newsman Bernard
103 "The Time Machine" race
104 "Do ___?"
105 Grannies
110 It's next to nothing
112 "Grand" hotel
113 Reason for a 98-Across
115 Not neat
116 N.F.L. running back Barlow
118 Rhett Butler's last words
120 Choo-choo name
121 Trust
122 Most cunning
123 Hip locale
124 MTV's owner
125 Transmission repair franchise
126 Silver quarters?
131 Film brand
132 Numismatists' goals
134 Author Janowitz
135 Composer Satie
136 It might get the brush-off
137 Home stretches?
139 Joe
140 Anthem starter
141 Move, in Realtor lingo
143 Poli ___
144 High ball?
145 "___ true"

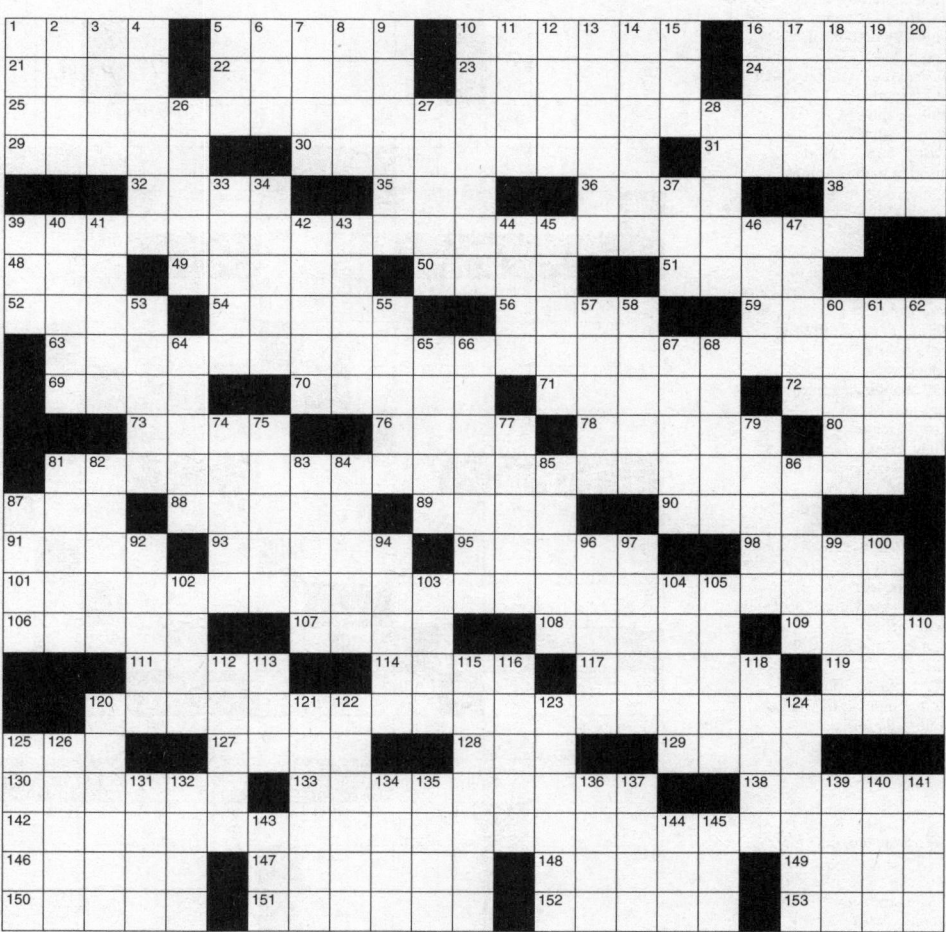

by Seth A. Abel

ACROSS

1 Lhasa ___
5 Breathing tube
12 Old cracker brand
16 Back on board
19 Pfizer product used before brushing the teeth
20 Tony winner Mike
21 Reason to shout "Eureka!"
22 Language along the Mekong River
23 Play about tenderizing meat with one's toes?
26 Beast with a bugling call
27 Patronize, as a hotel
28 "Let's Make a Deal" choice
29 Red spot on the skin
31 Drama about a butcher who sells deer meat?
37 ___ de Cologne
38 Honoree's spot
39 Gullets
40 Musical play set at McDonald's?
49 Dangerous place to pass a car
50 Pole, e.g.
51 Even
52 Actress Barbara Bel ___
54 In love
55 Blast
56 Windsor princess
58 Muppets' creator
59 Musical drama that tells the tale of a sausage casing?
61 Hat trick component
63 Ring holder
64 Musical drama about a man eating soup?
72 Mulling spice
78 Many baseball card stats
79 What you may call it
80 Business with net gains?
81 Tighten, say, as strings
82 1962 hit film whose climax is on Crab Key island
83 Conveys
84 Place in the pecking order
85 Play about a guy ordering beef from Dublin?
88 Martini & Rossi offering
89 Little fellow
90 Despite this
91 Play about swine intestines that are semidivine?
101 Miner's major problem
102 White sheet
103 Person who has something going on?
105 Allen Ginsberg's "Plutonian ___"
106 Play about meat that's good to eat anytime?
112 Elbow-bender
113 Brand name with an accent on its last letter
114 Character in many a joke
115 B.A. or M.A. offerer
116 Retired number of Dodger Tommy Lasorda
117 Goblet part
118 Juvenal work
119 Pageantry

DOWN

1 "Be on the lookout" messages, briefly
2 Oliver of "The West Wing"
3 "The Terminator" heroine
4 Common daisy
5 U.S. bond market purchase
6 Kia subcompact
7 Stage entertainment
8 N.L. and A.L. city
9 Passport maker
10 Mr. ___, scheming vicar in "Emma"
11 Take ___ at
12 Stylin'
13 Swearing-in phrase
14 Deity credited with inventing the lyre
15 Like Hoosier cabinets
16 Composer Scarlatti
17 Popular quarry for British hunters
18 Arcade game inserts
24 Relations: Abbr.
25 Worn away
30 Meant to attract
32 Possessed girl in "The Exorcist"
33 Town largely destroyed by the Battle of Normandy
34 "Ben-___"
35 Quite a ways
36 Using
40 Radio host John
41 "Dialogues Concerning Natural Religion" author
42 The Isle of Man's Port ___
43 Nonhuman co-hosts of TV's "Mystery Science Theater 3000"
44 Incumbent on
45 Attack once more
46 Sky light

47 Palette globs
48 Trapper's prize
49 Does a certain dog trick
52 Sickly-looking
53 Slovenly abode
55 Thermometer's terminus
56 Get stuck
57 Drink suffix
59 Fistfuls, say
60 Phaser setting
62 Missing broadcast channel
64 Scorecard heading
65 Dwarf
66 Compared with
67 Symbol of hardness
68 Talk, talk, talk: Var.
69 Memo header
70 Steinway & ___ (piano maker)
71 What, to Watteau
73 Five-Year Plan implementer, for short
74 "The Cosby Show" kid
75 Badlands landform
76 Bow-wielding deity
77 "Peer ___"
80 Diets drastically
82 Go from endangered to extinct
83 Slapstick missiles
85 First name in Objectivism
86 Bibliophile's love: Abbr.
87 Grain susceptible to ergot

88 Buttonhole
89 W.W. I helmet, informally
92 Inventive sorts?
93 Line at the dentist's office?
94 Main line
95 Sprung
96 Some mantel pieces
97 Mens ___
98 Get fuel
99 University of Maine's home
100 Shade of blue
104 Get back to
107 Gray
108 Closemouthed
109 Hula dancer's accessory
110 Common pg. size
111 "Didn't I tell you?"

by Patrick Berry

ACROSS

1 Key of Beethoven's "Für Elise"
7 Some trigonometric ratios
14 Sarcastic comment of sympathy
20 "Dr. Strangelove," e.g.
21 Parsnip, e.g.
22 Bewitched
23 Charles Schwab?
25 Service group
26 Cows
27 Vehicle on 30-Across
29 "This means business" look
30 See 27-Across
31 Annie Oakley?
34 Title girl in a 1962 Roy Orbison hit
37 ___ voce (quietly)
40 Others, to Pedro
41 Assimilate
44 Southwest chips-and-chili snacks
46 Viking landing site
50 Leonardo da Vinci?
52 Like one end of a battery terminal
54 "We the Living" author Rand
55 Equine
56 It has five pillars
60 Saffron's mom on "Ab Fab"
61 "My dear lady"
62 Place that's all abuzz
63 Sordid
64 Sigmund Freud?
69 Tiger Woods?
71 Rectify
72 Dish eaten with chopsticks
74 "___ would seem"
75 George Bush or Dick Cheney, once
76 Continental boundary
77 Easter Island is a province of it
79 It needs refining
82 Author/journalist Fallaci
84 Benjamin Franklin?
87 Illustrations: Abbr.
88 Cutting humor
92 "Lord Jim" star, 1965
93 Disney subsidiary
94 Gleans
96 Contemptuous expression
97 Bill Gates?
102 Seed cover
105 Cartoon mermaid
106 Construction company
107 Just make out
112 Bedtime for junior, maybe
114 Babe Ruth?
117 Country singer West
118 Nutty
119 Stranded by winter weather, perhaps
120 Initial stages
121 Sees about
122 Zeus' domain, in myth

DOWN

1 Second: Abbr.
2 SAT section
3 "Like ___ not . . ."
4 Court encouragement
5 Like Mork of "Mork & Mindy"
6 Front of a manuscript leaf
7 Smith who won the 1972 Wimbledon
8 Stirrup sites
9 Cruncher of nos.
10 Pendulum's path
11 Wrong
12 Skater's leap
13 Overlapping fugue motifs
14 See or call
15 Where hens sit
16 Grad school grillings
17 Starts in on
18 "Idomeneo," e.g.
19 Ursine : bear :: lutrine : ___
24 Chops
28 Awful
31 Mix up
32 Tout's offering
33 Pioneer org.
34 Eastern title
35 Silent auction site
36 Part of N.A.A.C.P.: Abbr.
38 Wastes
39 TV dinner holder
42 Set after melting
43 Panoramic
45 Legendary Gaelic poet
46 Classic flivver
47 Something to bid
48 Billboard chart category
49 Leaves rolling in the aisles
51 Faux gold
53 Agnostic
57 Ontario or Supérieur
58 "Chances ___"
59 Common muscle protein
61 Pokémon and the Beatles, once
62 Nutritionist Davis
64 ___ the dinosaur (extinction)
65 Japanese porcelain
66 1983 Woody Allen mockumentary
67 Backing
68 The Monkees' "___ Believer"
70 Shakespearean compilation
73 San ___, Argentina
77 Pet plant
78 Web address lead-in
79 Radio letter between Nan and Peter
80 Three strikes and you're out, e.g.
81 Hungarian spa town
83 "This won't hurt ___"
85 Tony-winning actress Verdon
86 "Leave It to Beaver" catchphrase
89 Skater's leap
90 Welsh cheese dish
91 Army outfit
93 Sermon site
95 Cutty ___ (clipper ship)
97 "No prob!"
98 Rigel's constellation
99 Breath fresheners
100 Quarterback Rodney
101 ___ Quinn, formerly of "S.N.L."
103 Make like new
104 Tchaikovsky's middle name
107 Tempt
108 Bowed, to a violist
109 Root beer feature
110 Estrada of "CHiPs"
111 Start of a counting-out rhyme
113 Enero, e.g.
115 Former name for Ben-Gurion Airport
116 N, E, S and W

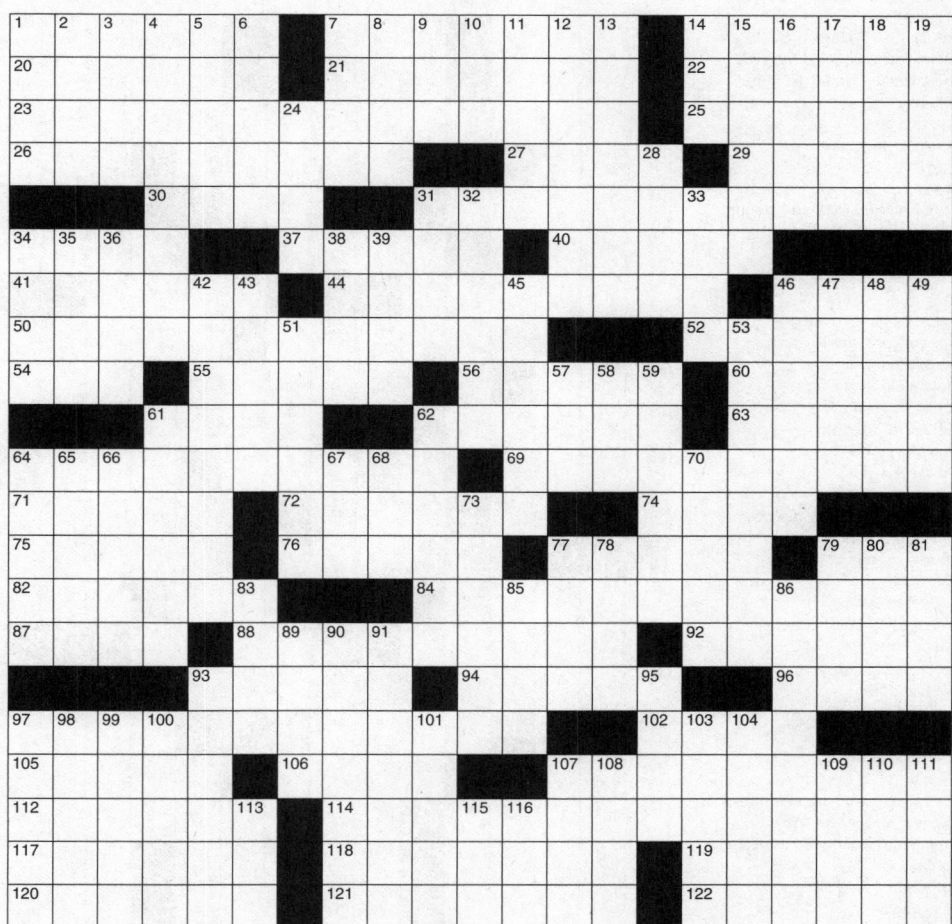

by Kelsey Blakley

ACROSS

1 Cause for a massage
5 K.G.B. predecessor
9 Crookspeak
14 Blog comments
19 Crony
20 Look
21 Risibility
22 Poet who wrote "Immature poets imitate; mature poets steal"
23 Tax relief, e.g.
26 Churchillian trademark
27 Chapter
28 Lies
29 Subject of a Boito opera
31 "Down ___" (Janis Joplin song)
32 Be too tight
34 Doc's wife in "Come Back, Little Sheba"
35 Timeline breaks
37 December laughs
38 "___ the morning!"
39 Mary Shelley subtitle, with "The"
44 Moved purposefully
46 Windsurfers' mecca
47 Using one's shirtsleeve as a napkin, e.g.
48 Big letter
52 Free, in a way
55 "Fish Magic" and "Twittering Machine"
56 Fig. in TV's "Third Watch"
58 TV star who directed the 1999 documentary "Barenaked in America"
61 Thingumbob
63 Consume piggishly
64 Piggy
65 Lhasa ___
69 "The End of the Affair" author, 1951
71 Miracle-___
72 "___ Crazy" (1977 Paul Davis hit)
74 Car body strengtheners
76 Answers, for short
77 Sot spot
79 Stately old dance
82 Father of Henry II
83 Fall event, usually
87 Doc bloc: Abbr.
88 Palatable
91 Live in the past?
92 World's biggest city built on continuous permafrost
94 Priority system
96 Short notes
98 Branch of Islam
101 Matter of W.W. II secrecy
107 Mindful of
108 Special ___
109 Rank and file
110 Dudley Do-Right's love
111 Permanently
112 CAT scan units
114 Cheese ___
116 Transverse rafter-joining timber
118 Reading and others: Abbr.
119 Comment made while crossing the fingers
121 Serigraph
124 Skyscraper
125 Batch of Brownies
126 Back then, back when
127 Bleu hue

128 ___ cards (ESP testers)
129 They're the pits
130 Short ways to go?
131 "The Mysterious Island" captain

DOWN

1 Countenances
2 Early racer
3 Contortionist
4 Ottoman, e.g.: Abbr.
5 Jump over
6 "Just a ___" (Marlene Dietrich's last film)
7 1914 Booth Tarkington novel
8 Disentangle
9 "Under the Pink" singer Tori
10 Circular edge
11 Put on a happy face
12 Lake that James Fenimore Cooper called Glimmerglass
13 First sign
14 Lifter's rippler
15 Salmagundi
16 Words of endorsement
17 Robert Burns poem
18 Italicizes, e.g.
24 Burning issue
25 Give up on détente
30 Barrel org.
33 It's for the birds
36 Stir up
39 Broad terrace with a steep side
40 World's smallest island nation
41 Castigatory
42 Fully ready
43 Flag raiser
45 Côte d'Or's capital
49 Chinese philosopher Chuang-___
50 Nonmechanized weapon
51 Boeing worker: Abbr.
53 European Union member since 2004
54 Car that "beats the gassers and the rail jobs" in a 1964 hit
56 Adam and Eve, at a diner
57 "Harlequin's Carnival" painter
59 Initial sounds of a relief effort?
60 Good name for a minimalist?
62 Handel oratorio
66 Russian literary award established in 1881
67 Glass bottom
68 Where the Storting sits
70 energystar.gov grp.
73 Slightly tainted
75 Bridge supports
78 Alternative to the euro: Abbr.

80 Pianist Rubinstein
81 Hair-raising cry
84 Mystery award
85 Kurt denial?
86 Sign of neglect
88 Swiss resort with the Cresta Run
89 Ally of the Cheyenne
90 Gets to commit
93 Capital of Valais canton
95 Where Huxley taught Orwell
97 Kind of barrier
99 It sticks to the ribs
100 The whale in "Pinocchio"
102 New wrinkles
103 Reach for the stars
104 Vocal opponent
105 Second-highest mountain in the lower 48 states
106 Q player in "Die Another Day"
111 Devilkin
113 Admiral who went down with the Scharnhorst
115 ___-eyed
116 Recipe measures: Abbr.
117 Social workers
120 Muff
122 Sent sprawling
123 Turned yellow, maybe

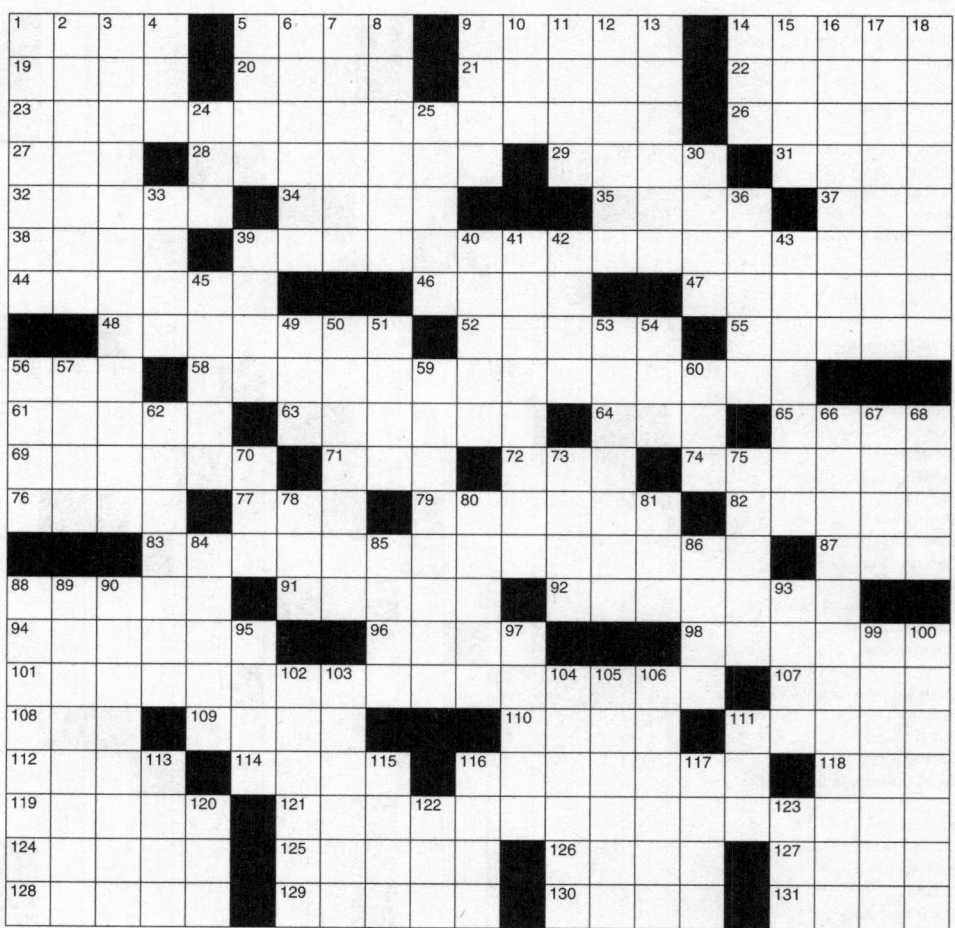

by Bob Klahn

ACROSS

1 Smears
7 Fells
11 Looks for help
15 1954 sci-fi movie with an exclamation point in its title
19 Arctic wear
20 "Il mio tesoro," e.g.
21 1980s fad item
22 Blood: Prefix
23 Yosemite Sam's cursing of Bugs Bunny's food?
25 That's a lot to do
27 Then preceder
28 Explanation for why some pillows do weird things?
30 Domingo, e.g.
31 Wash (out)
33 Photo lab abbr.
34 "Stupid," in Spanish(!)
35 Armpit, to a doctor
37 Oscar winner Helen
39 Psychiatrist's scheduling
41 Theological schools: Abbr.
43 Part of baking powder
46 Letters from Atlanta
47 Basic food choice?
55 Noontime service
56 Handi-Wrap alternative
57 Flavor tasted in some wine
58 Frees
62 [Knock], in poker
64 Mile-high world capital
66 Be the 4 in a 5-4 decision
67 Natl. Safe Toys and Gifts Mo.
68 Short-term worker who causes utter disaster?
73 Jackie's "O"
74 They're beside sides
76 Boat propeller
77 Singer K. T. ___
79 Walnut and others
80 Kind of tape
83 "Livin' on ___ time" (lyric in a #1 Don Williams country hit)
85 Lineman's datum
86 Jazz-loving young entomologist?
90 Bon ___
93 Imp
94 Slew
95 Precipitately
98 Artificial, in a way
102 Has-been
106 Puffball seed
107 Draft pick?
109 Puts up
111 ___ nuevo
112 Meal for the Three Little Pigs?
116 Lola, e.g., in "Damn Yankees"
117 Intrinsically
118 Work on analytical psychology?
121 Czech composer Janácek
122 Stretched out
123 Sports Illustrated 1998 co-Sportsman of the Year
124 Brown shade
125 Sea eagle
126 Abbr. at the bottom of a business letter
127 Too-too
128 "Ready to go?"

DOWN

1 Too-too
2 Stuck
3 Stuntwork?
4 As a result
5 Varnish ingredient
6 Some Jamaican music
7 Early casino proprietor
8 Beethoven's Third
9 Occult
10 N. Dak. neighbor
11 Do something about
12 Cover for a grandmother
13 Hot spot
14 Put (away)
15 "___ Company"
16 Pleasure-filled
17 Boston college
18 "Gilligan's Island" castaway
24 Way to go: Abbr.
26 ___ law
29 Car famous for its 1950s tailfins
31 Ran
32 "Falcon Crest" co-star
36 Measurers of logical reasoning, for short
38 Ballpark fig.
39 "How ya doin'?"
40 Designer Pucci
42 Winds
44 Narc's agcy.
45 Bug
47 "P.S. I Love You" and "Revolution," e.g.
48 "Be saved!"
49 Bet to win and place
50 "Darn it all!"
51 Naïf
52 Coin word
53 ___ girl
54 Floors
59 Experimental underwater habitat
60 "Lucia di Lammermoor" baritone
61 Like Limburger cheese
63 Position that's an anagram, appropriately, of "notes"
65 Providers of cuts
66 Water seeker
69 Announcer's call after three strikes
70 Numerical prefix
71 Dance seen on TV's "Hullabaloo"
72 Hello ___, shop frequently seen on Letterman
75 Tease
78 Certain NCO's
80 1953 Wimbledon winner Seixas
81 Small chuckle
82 Ran through, as a card
84 Rearward, at sea
87 College sr.'s test
88 1980's "Double Fantasy" collaborator
89 They're encountered in "close encounters"
90 Lose in one's drawers
91 Not oral
92 James who wrote "Rule, Britannia"
96 Melodic
97 "Note to ___ . . ."
99 Portuguese Mister
100 Swiss-American composer Bloch
101 Record keeper?
103 They do dos
104 Chant
105 Ogle
107 Stuffy spot
108 Rhone's capital
110 French wine classification
113 Site of Beinecke Library
114 Digitize, maybe
115 "___ girl!"
116 Biblical brother
119 Intelligence grp.
120 Poet/musician ___ Scott-Heron

by Tony Orbach and Patrick Blindauer

ACROSS

1 Dogs named for a region of Japan
7 Wrapped up
12 Jazz great Malone
16 Symbol for density
19 Dramatist Ibsen
20 Mrs. Gorbachev
21 Start a pot going
22 Ref. work with online subscriptions
23 Wall Street worker
26 Clavell's "___-Pan"
27 Sort of
28 Select
29 Party's nominees
31 Wasps' home
32 Catch in the West
34 Stretch out
38 Terre's counterpart
39 Broadway's "The Producers," e.g.
43 Some acids
47 Like wicker furniture
48 "The Matrix" lead role
49 Carpet choice
50 They might come back to haunt you
53 Blu-ray players, e.g.
54 Does dictation, maybe
55 Short pans
56 Island in the Aegean
57 Great Society agcy.
58 Game played with a ½- to ¾-inch ball
60 Kind of approval
61 One of the Trumps
64 Sotheby's domain
65 Alternative title for this puzzle
69 Elevs.
71 Put over high heat
73 High degree
74 Car that won the 1939 and '40 Indy 500
76 Might
77 Head honcho
78 Yemen's capital
80 Polynesian carvings
81 More than enjoyed
84 Appetizers served with sauce
87 Prosperousness
88 Subj. of many conspiracy theories
89 Symbol on a 6 key
90 "You sure got that right!"
91 It might go in a tank
94 Put one by
95 Political prisoner, e.g.
96 One way to be taken
98 Speaking spot
102 Language from which lemon and julep come
103 In ___ rush
106 Like beaches
108 Singer DiFranco
109 Elizabeth Dole once led it
114 Word with pack or pick
115 Israir alternative
116 Tempter
117 Pick of the litter
118 The, abroad
119 10-year prison sentence, in gang slang
120 ___ coil
121 Time out?

DOWN

1 Play co-authored by Mark Twain
2 City ENE of Brattleboro
3 Tawantinsuyu dwellers
4 Money you can't touch?
5 Frigid finish?
6 Like some hot dogs
7 Indians known as the Cat People
8 Refusal, in Renfrew
9 Coupon offerings
10 Mess of pottage buyer
11 Frontier name, for short
12 ___ Kan pet food
13 "___ takers?"
14 Some linemen: Abbr.
15 "C'mon!"
16 Gradually substitute
17 One way to argue
18 Comics canine
24 Early 1900s ruler
25 1960s British P.M. ___ Douglas-Home
30 Send up or put down
33 Overhead
35 Brings in
36 Plaza de toros sounds
37 It's below grade one: Abbr.
38 Cheese place
40 Finalize, with "up"
41 1966 Broadway hit with the song "My Cup Runneth Over"
42 "O.K."
43 Broadcast worker's union
44 Coolidge, Cleveland and Andrew Johnson, once
45 Ascribe
46 "O Sanctissima," e.g.
47 Not free
51 Strummed an old string instrument
52 Engine sound
53 Stinging jellyfish
57 Sheep's genus
59 "___ Say," 1939 #1 Artie Shaw hit
60 Co. with a Mercury logo
61 10-Down's father
62 Casual dress
63 Historic role played by Jack Palance and Anthony Quinn
66 Phone button
67 Superior
68 "___ Rappaport"
70 Playground taunt
72 Charms
75 Yemen's capital
77 Rub the wrong way
78 Some farm machinery
79 Sharp
81 "How cute!"
82 Afternoon event
83 Cafes
84 Priory of ___, group in "The Da Vinci Code"
85 "Whoo-ee!"
86 Starts
88 Letters before a colon, on TV
92 Burst in on
93 Mar, in a way
94 Prefix with phobia
97 Prudential competitor
98 Steak ___
99 Parisian priests
100 "___ My Heart in Monterey" (1927 hit)
101 Perfect Sleeper maker
102 Wash out
104 ___ Helens
105 Gaston's girlfriend
107 Sixth-century year
110 Film director Roth
111 Actress Grier
112 Ginger ___
113 First word of Dante's "Inferno"

by Eric Berlin

ACROSS

1 Suction devices
11 Pepper-upper
20 Knocked out
21 Many an Alessandro Scarlatti work
22 Cause of some baseball errors?
23 Texas ballplayer?
24 Modern organizer, for short
25 Castaway's call
26 Supported
27 Schmo
28 Just watched
30 Times of day, in classifieds
32 Kobe Bryant, e.g.
36 Bewhiskered fish lover
37 Where "Aida" premiered
39 Plane's N.Y.C. destination, maybe
40 "I see," kiddingly
41 Soldier's fare, briefly
42 1988 Best Picture, with the repeated line "I'm an excellent driver"
44 1980s Geena Davis sitcom
46 "The Race ___" (1965 hit)
48 Dweller along the Danube
50 Hägar creator Browne
51 More decayed
53 Hamburger's article
54 Gold standards
56 Gland: Prefix
58 Going according to plan
60 Crystal ___
61 Mrs., in Peru
62 Suffix with pamphlet
64 In myth, her tears created the morning dew
65 Nelson Rockefeller was its gov.
66 Commoners
69 Classic Abbott and Costello bit
72 "___ precaution . . ."
75 Round Table title
76 Shot spot
78 Unenthusiastic reviews
79 Beginning drawing class
82 "No way, no how!"
85 Turn
87 Cold-shoulders
89 "Blondie" tyke
90 Place for some bling-bling
92 Venusians, e.g.
94 Formula for "S"
95 Iron alternative
96 Lid irritation
97 Makes war
100 Sound from the rafters
101 Painter's subject
103 Suffix with morph-
104 Glassware ovens
105 "If you ___ . . ."
107 Pin holder
109 Some police officers: Abbr.
110 Beat badly
111 Sample
112 "Get out of here!"
113 Shade of blue
115 Florida senator Martinez
116 Diamond border?
121 Complaint about a baseball playing area?
125 Longish stories
126 It can be a relief
127 Haunts
128 Not yet ready to be deposited

DOWN

1 W.W. I military grp.
2 Racecar-generated air current
3 Temporary residence
4 White Rabbit's cry
5 Purge
6 On tenterhooks
7 South Seas staple
8 1970s N.F.L.'er Armstrong
9 Sales ___
10 '60s radical grp.
11 W.W. I French fighter plane
12 Thrice, in prescriptions
13 Get to
14 Actress Gibbs
15 Scream for the Dream Team
16 More protracted
17 Neighbor of Bol.
18 Never, to Nietzsche
19 Pothole patch
21 Unlocks, in verse
26 Peerless
29 "It's c-c-c-cold!"
30 Point
31 Part of a certain scorecard
32 Mystery writer Marsh
33 Lack of adornment
34 Hand out
35 Andy Hardy player, in 1930s–'40s film
36 Trans-Siberian Railroad city
37 LI doubled
38 Turkey heads can be found here
39 A hallucinogen
43 Show stoppers
45 Movie droid
47 Takes home
49 Precede the cleanup spot
52 MGM co-founder
55 "___ Eyes," 1969 Guess Who hit
57 Figures
59 "Piece of cake!"
61 Streaked
63 Perlman of "Cheers"
67 Web creations
68 So it follows that
70 Worrywart's words
71 New in theaters
72 Some
73 "Later"
74 British mail
77 Object of tornado destruction
80 Dash holders
81 Failed, as a pass
83 Awesome beauties
84 "I'm listening"
86 "John Brown's Body" poet
87 Atlanta-to-Miami dir.
88 Plant with dark purple berries
91 "Brokeback Mountain" director
93 Things made by Vikings, for short
98 Tape format
99 Kind of score
102 Isolate, in a way
106 Unsmiling
108 Some recesses
109 Ellipsis, basically
110 Ecclesiastics' assembly
112 Some coll. tests
113 Individual
114 Former baseball commissioner Bowie
116 Econ. yardstick
117 Pooh's pal
118 School media depts.
119 Some chess pieces: Abbr.
120 Mineral suffix
121 Sch. in Atlanta
122 ___ Tin Tin
123 Rock's They Might Be Giants, e.g.
124 Inserted, in a way

by Nancy Salomon and Bill Zais

ACROSS

1 Comfort
7 They're tapped in the woods
13 Cape Cod course
20 Transfer
21 Daddy Warbucks's henchman
22 Lowly digs
23 Remake about a red, white, and blue libido?
25 Now and then
26 Forklike
27 Dowel
28 Patriots' grp.
29 Rice-A-___
30 Boxer Marciano's given name
32 Remake about impiety during a storm?
37 Acapulco article
38 In position for a back massage
40 No dessert for dieters
41 Game co. that originated Dungeons & Dragons
42 Rhein residence
44 Pound sound
45 ___ soit qui mal y pense
46 ___ good turn
48 Ristorante suffix
51 Remake about a strip club?
55 Seepage collectors
57 Accept another tour of duty
58 Coll. hoops competition
59 Liberty
61 Time immemorial
64 Rib
66 It's cut and dried
67 To ___ (exactly)
68 Remake about a lecherous instructor?
74 Rodrigo ___ de Vivar (El Cid)
75 Diamond great Hodges
76 "Evil Woman" grp.
77 Pop singer Brickell
78 Claim
82 Stock page letters
84 Enter
87 Hold in the gym
88 Remake about a TV station/F.C.C. controversy?
93 Web address ending
94 What precedes 93-Across
96 Flight stats.
97 P
98 A lot of volume?
99 Union partner: Abbr.
101 Like a twice-used cigar
103 Following closely?
105 Fresh
106 Remake about a holy person's slip?
110 These, to Tomás
112 Wits' bits
113 Quick
114 Yale Bowl player
115 Seminal mainframe
117 Figures of speech?
119 Remake about a ribald watchman?
124 Pamper
125 Difficult
126 San ___ (Western mountains)
127 Represses
128 Night flight
129 Least interesting

DOWN

1 Part of R.S.V.P.
2 Tulsa sch.
3 It's not worth pursuing
4 Caper
5 Like some laundries
6 Feminine suffix
7 '70s sitcom producer
8 Actor Brian of "Juarez," 1939
9 President ousted in a 1955 coup
10 Buttered someone up big-time
11 PC key
12 Hot spot
13 Made
14 Come out of one's shell
15 Old Polo Grounds headliner
16 Fans' sounds
17 Japanese "thank you very much"
18 1983 Nicholas Gage book
19 Sticky stuff
24 Gather in a condensed layer
28 Tiny tunneler
30 Essen's basin
31 Transmitting
33 Just for laughs
34 Canonical hour
35 Lucky ones?
36 Much commerce nowadays
39 Arctic explorer John
43 Tight spots
45 Signal to start
47 Observed
49 "When hell freezes over!"
50 "Gotcha"
52 Familiar with
53 Many a Punjabi
54 Swinging London district
56 Rent
60 Olympic track great Johnson, familiarly
62 1998 Winter Olympics site
63 Clubs, e.g.
65 It won't run if it's fast
68 Floored, in a way?
69 Sense the unreal
70 Smooth
71 Trudges
72 Cadet's org.
73 Communicate silently
74 Great ___
79 Beckett's no-show
80 Toothbrush handle?
81 "This is on the level"
83 Wrist bones
85 "Whatever you want"
86 Where Hercules slew a lion
89 Where a whodunit is solved
90 Like gleaming shoes
91 Load
92 Leaves in stitches
95 Stumbles over
100 Marching together
102 Ballpark fig.
103 Zoo section
104 Counter creator
106 Logical Mr.
107 Atmospheres
108 Cuban national hero
109 "Seascape" playwright
111 Yemeni neighbor
116 "___ Blue"
118 Scrubs sites, for short
119 Rocky top
120 Realm of Otto I: Abbr.
121 Slingshot's shape
122 Children's author/illustrator Asquith
123 What to spring to when springing ahead: Abbr.

by Elayne Cantor and Nancy Salomon

ACROSS

1 Ancient Greece's Seven ___
6 Wrinkled melon
12 "Well, yeah!"
15 Doctrine
18 Team for which 1970 N.B.A. M.V.P. Willis Reed played
20 "Sense and Sensibility" sister
21 Axis, of a sort
23 Dire proof-of-purchase slip?
25 Annual celebration for a Catholic
26 Three-way joint
27 Complete circuit
28 What Dr. Frankenstein tried to do?
30 Not merely smoldering
32 ___ vivant
34 Jackie's second
35 Rep. of S. ___
36 Bored kayaker's movements?
43 Planned
44 Founder of General Electric
45 ___ Glue-All
49 Haughty mannerisms
50 Chilled garnish
52 Cut off
54 Battle of Hastings participant
55 Atlanta's ___ Center
56 Much-needed windfall?
60 Because of this
61 Unable to relax
62 Water bearer
63 Showing deep embarrassment
66 Water pipes
68 Less ripe
70 Old Germanic character
71 Tighten, as a corset, maybe
73 Drink in "Beowulf"
74 Like workers' salaries under a miserly boss?
79 Big prize on "The Price Is Right"
82 Portion of a flight
83 Roman sun god
84 Fleeting light
85 ___ of the Rock (Jerusalem shrine)
86 It's often put on paper
88 Missouri city
90 Actress Hayek
91 Hogwarts?
96 Nickname preceder
99 Theater sign
100 Just fine
101 Crown insets
102 Sharply focused Warsaw residents?
107 "Hellboy" star Perlman
108 Erwin of 1950s TV
111 One who's expected to deliver?
112 Clairvoyants' charges?
117 She plotted to kill Clytemnestra
118 Rugged mountain chain
119 All your work may go into it
120 H, to Hellenes
121 Datum sought by identity thieves: Abbr.
122 Rocky's girl
123 Writes a Dear John letter

DOWN

1 "Monty Python" segment
2 Queen Elizabeth's daughter
3 Care
4 Prefix with -cide
5 It takes up many chairs
6 Fortune subj.
7 Puppet show?
8 Grauman of Grauman's Chinese Theater
9 Consecrates
10 Big help
11 Shaw's "___ and the Man"
12 "The Good Shepherd" director, 2006
13 Dissimilar
14 Web programmer's medium
15 Sepoy Rebellion site
16 Wizard's prop
17 Gangster Lansky
19 Wolf (down)
22 Common sushi ingredient
24 Three-sided blade
29 Pitch
31 Cod pieces?
32 Shroud
33 In abeyance
36 Computer that originally came in "flavors"
37 Ja's opposite
38 Offering at a government auction
39 "Sayonara!"
40 Some government bonds
41 "Anything ___" (Woody Allen film)
42 Blotto
46 One who's done stretches?
47 Energize
48 Elvis impersonator's expression
50 Sweater material
51 Cream tea go-with
53 Significant degree?
56 Org. that requires schedules
57 Musical pitches
58 "I am the ___" (Beatles lyric)
59 Lease again
60 Retired professors
63 Like new bills
64 Make altogether
65 Atahualpa's people
66 Basque novelist Pío
67 Endangered wildcat
69 Fill up on
72 Aix-___-Bains
75 Poetic country name
76 White house
77 Creep furtively
78 "S.N.L." alum Fey
79 Structure finished during Titus' reign
80 Magazine's contents
81 Authentic
85 "The Witches" author
87 Potential Emmy nominees
89 Egyptian coin
90 Medically examined via machine
92 Book printer's no-no
93 Talk sweetly
94 "Tank Girl" actress Petty
95 Something that helps you follow the game?
96 Singer Mann
97 Showed obeisance
98 Befogged
103 Exit-the-program button
104 Lice-to-be
105 "I'm Not ___," 1975 #1 country hit by Jessi Colter
106 Geraint's wife, in Arthurian legend
109 Per diem worker
110 A Swiss Army knife has lots of them
113 William Tell's birthplace
114 401(k) alternative
115 Like camel's hair
116 Home of the Seminoles: Abbr.

by Patrick Berry

ACROSS

1 Ginger's friend on "Gilligan's Island"
8 Comic Kilborn and others
14 Lie on the beach
19 So-called "miracle plant"
21 Bag handler
22 Egyptian crosses
23 "Pardon me, are you from the Caribbean? Because . . ."
25 Catcher in the World Series' only perfect game
26 Humorist George
27 Better
28 Compass dir.
29 Hemingway's "___ Time"
30 "I know it's not my business, but if you were a laser . . ."
38 Coarse
39 Collins of '70s funk
40 Look (around)
42 First name in aviation
44 Middle mark
46 Letter-ending abbr.
47 Pres. Jefferson
48 "Say, is it hot in here . . . ?"
52 Key over Control
53 Free throw's path
54 Actor Cage, informally
55 Hip-shaking dance
59 ___ mind
60 N.B.A. coach George ___
62 Loser to R.M.N. in '68
64 Nobelist, e.g.
66 "Sorry to bother you, but do you work for NASA? Because . . ."
72 Dinosaur National Monument site
73 Dummkopf
74 Scottish refusals
76 Well-put
79 Rich with humor
80 Application datum: Abbr.
82 Suicide squeeze result, for short
83 Two-time losing Republican presidential candidate
85 "Excuse me, I seem to have lost my phone number . . . ?"
91 Press
92 Orioles' org.
95 Chop
96 Lemonade + ___ = Arnold Palmer
97 Doggie sounds
98 Title teen in a 1990s sitcom
101 NPR's ___ Simon
102 "I don't mean to pry, but are you from Nashville? Because . . ."
108 Conductor's aid
109 When Can. has Thanksgiving
110 Évian, e.g.
111 Sgt. maj., e.g.
113 Instruction for casual dress
114 "Even though we've never met, I'm sure your last name is Campbell. That's because . . ."
120 Make better
121 Den, often
122 It gets a licking
123 Catfish Row resident
124 Bridgewater of jazz
125 Like talkers at a movie

DOWN

1 Goya subject
2 Henry James's "The Portrait of ___"
3 Amorist
4 One voting for
5 Bird: Prefix
6 IBM competitor
7 "Piece" org.
8 Inched
9 ___ hall
10 Glandular prefix
11 Daredevil's retort
12 Montreal daily
13 Mole, e.g.
14 Peres's predecessor
15 About 11%
16 City that won the first N.F.L. championship, 1920
17 Doesn't get bothered by
18 Dweller in the Peterhof
20 Eager
24 Victim of Bart Simpson's prank calls
31 Doesn't let go to waste
32 Hero's place
33 Lure
34 Key of Bruckner's Symphony No. 7: Abbr.
35 "You must ___"
36 Publisher of All Hands magazine: Abbr.
37 Home of Roosevelt I.
41 Spanish pronoun
42 Host
43 Prefix with dot
44 CBS debut of 10/6/2000
45 Plus more: Abbr.
48 The A's, on scoreboards
49 O.K.
50 One ___ (kids' game)
51 "Never gonna happen"
52 Japanese who won the 1974 Nobel Peace Prize
56 Afghan airline
57 British tax
58 Orders to plow horses
61 Filmdom's Jean-___ Godard
62 Prefix with pad
63 Knee-slapper
64 Band with the 1999 hit "Summer Girls"
65 Coastal bird
67 ___-poly
68 Bathroom powder
69 Concert halls
70 Lash of westerns
71 Raymond's wife on "Everybody Loves Raymond"
75 Yucatán yeses
76 1998 Sarah McLachlan hit
77 Recipient of the first gold single awarded by the R.I.A.A.
78 Easy putt, say
80 ___-string
81 Any ship
84 Guaranteeing
86 Indian bread
87 #2, informally
88 H.S. course
89 Creature of legend
90 Slugger Mel et al.
92 Woman of la maison: Abbr.
93 Good deal
94 Serve well
99 Safe
100 Dragster's ride
101 Baffle
103 Like marshes
104 "I wanna try!"
105 Starchy food
106 Son of Cain
107 ___ des Beaux-Arts
108 Go postal
112 Did too much, in a way
114 From Jan. 1 till now
115 Help wanted abbr.
116 Jan. and Feb.
117 Radar reading: Abbr.
118 Big Ten sch.
119 Ones "over there"

by David Levinson Wilk

ACROSS

1 Basis for the first commercially successful video game
9 Just folks?
16 Mugger?
19 They may have smiles and frowns
21 Athlete's slump
22 Grosse-___, Québec
23 Somebody else's soaking dentures?
25 Tour stop
26 Outstanding
27 Aviation pioneer Eugene
28 Palm Beach County city, for short
29 One who might stand in front of a map
31 Prefix with sphere
33 Life stories
36 Yellowish brown
37 Ghost in a battery?
41 Experimental figures
42 Wing: Prefix
44 Their mascot is Handsome Dan
45 Was wistful
47 Thataway
48 Comedian Jay
49 Thin opening
50 Vegetarian's credo
52 Prefix with metric
53 Actress Barbara
54 Whence the phrase "Brevity is the soul of wit"
58 Love, in Livorno
61 Former pol. div.
62 Avoid being captured by guitarist Richards?
64 1986 Indy 500 winner
65 Neighbor of a Pole
67 Fluttering sound
68 Deity featured on California's state seal
69 Fed-up cry
70 Baby twins?
74 Bar fig.
75 Some NCO's
76 Isolate
77 Possessive on Chinese menus
78 One of the "Magnificent Seven"
79 Skywalker portrayer
81 Circle
82 Middles: Abbr.
83 One of the Bushes
85 Ballade endings
88 In a jiffy
89 Joyous sounds
90 Org. with the motto "The power to make it better"
92 Sherlock at the Space Needle?
95 Drub
97 "Unh-unh"
98 Repeated sounds in "Hey Jude"
102 Poet Omar
105 "Can that be true?"
106 PC linkup
107 ___ cit.
108 Magazine with a fold-in
109 Billionaire's last dollar?
114 "What Is ___?" (Tolstoy essay)
115 "Gather Together in My Name" writer
116 Get set
117 ___ degree
118 Start of a trip in a bathysphere
119 Made blue

DOWN

1 Remains undecided
2 Poker player's declaration
3 Observant one
4 Classic muscle car
5 Batter's material
6 Nocturnal feline
7 Too inquisitive
8 Vitamin supplements store
9 Farm animal, in kidspeak
10 Tabloid fodder
11 In the back
12 "The Eyes of ___" (public TV science show)
13 Bug spray ingredient
14 Cracker spread
15 Nirvana attainer
16 Good eating and clean living?
17 Not recognizable by
18 "You've Got Mail" co-star
20 Change, as a manuscript, in Britain
24 Quinces, e.g.
30 Heel
32 Great server
33 Character actor Alfred
34 Thor Heyerdahl craft
35 Official seal
38 Spiral: Prefix
39 Egyptian god of wisdom
40 Something that's turned up
42 Some residents, by census classification
43 Very detailed scope?
46 Shortages
48 Wife, colloquially
49 Its cap. is Regina
51 Asian nurse
53 Comment made with a shrug
54 Garden output
55 "A View to ___"
56 Ruckus
57 One of TV's Munsters
59 Highly opinionated sorts
60 Lifts up
63 Spitting sound
66 "La Dolce ___"
68 Above
70 Go (into)
71 Borrowed
72 "Becket" star
73 Route from Me. to Fla.
80 Connections
81 Gets bounced by
82 "Call Me Irresponsible" lyricist
83 Actor Hugh of "X-Men"
84 First woman to earn the Distinguished Flying Cross
86 "Am ___ believe this?"
87 Apostle known as "the Zealot"
88 Line of text?
89 Done
91 Reward
93 Left hurriedly
94 Not impressed
96 "Oops!"
99 Detective Pinkerton
100 Dark time in Italy
101 Suffered
103 Rook's spot on a chessboard
104 Board events: Abbr.
106 Fictional princess
110 P.I.
111 World Cup chant
112 Time sheet abbr.
113 Put away

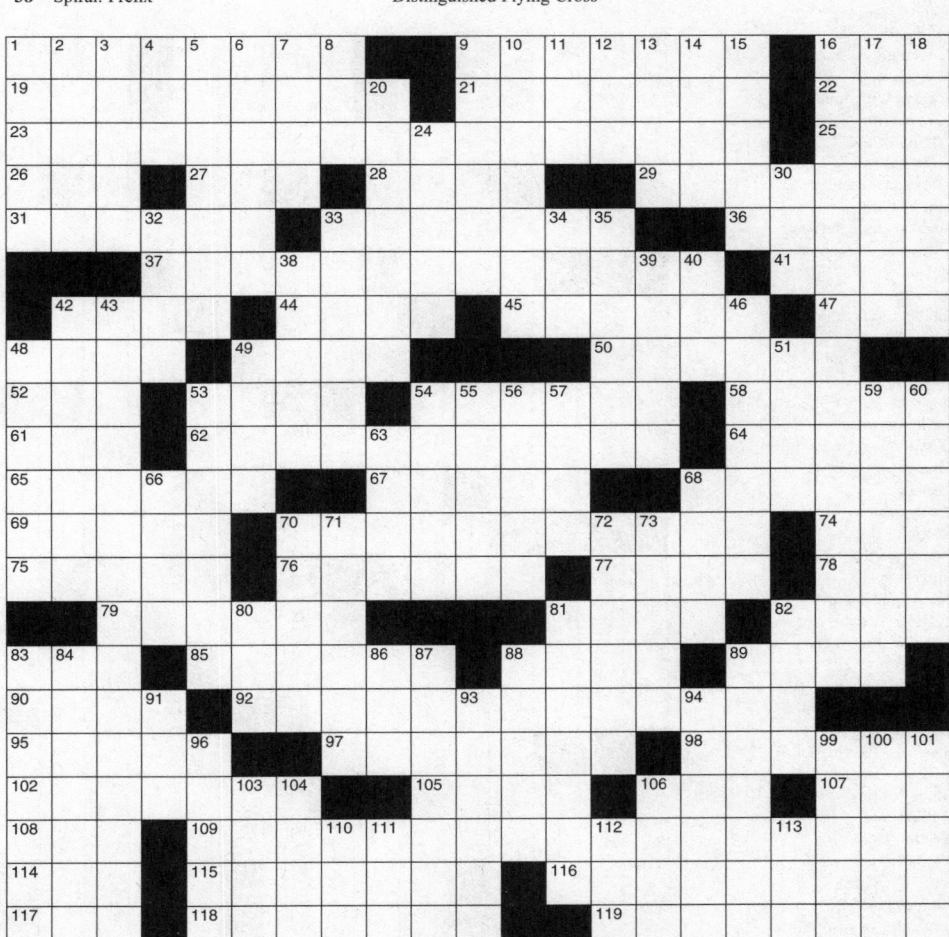

by Brendan Emmett Quigley

ACROSS

1 "Downtown" singer Clark
7 Wheat ___
11 Kohada, on a sushi menu
15 Ernst & Young employees, for short
19 Up
20 Kind of speculation
21 "___ fan tutte"
22 Actress Wood of "Diamonds Are Forever"
23 Nurse Florence sells adventures?
27 Crackerjack
28 French silk
29 Manual reader
30 Coca-Cola Co. drinks
31 Actor Steve repeats what geezers say?
35 T or F: Abbr.
36 "___ Wolf," Michael J. Fox film
37 Annual event celebrated outdoors
41 Croak
44 Hideaways
45 Smutch
47 Kansas county seat on the Neosho River
48 Bow site
49 Static
51 Designer Geoffrey
52 Hot flash
53 Ratiocinative
55 Play opener
56 Overate, with "out"
57 Lawyer Atticus avoids crazies?
62 "Anything ___?"
63 ___ fatuus
64 Word game popularized by James Thurber
65 Fund-raising letter, e.g.
69 Architect Christopher gobbles banisters?
72 Picks up
76 Cabinet member: Abbr.
77 Futile
78 Some military helicopters, familiarly
79 Cuts out
81 Plantation inventory
83 1970s–'80s supermodel Carangi
84 Smart ___
85 Acceleration
86 Siberian
87 Sound
88 Conversed
90 "Hold your horses!"
91 Early 10th-century year
93 Famed magician cheats chumps?
100 "Stop equivocating!"
103 Prefix with 94-Down
104 Go-___
105 Rapa ___ (Easter Island)
106 Disney's Captain Jack dupes church leaders?
110 A, in Austria
111 "Swell!"
112 "Monster" actor, 2003
113 Runs off (with)
114 Some stereos
115 Troubadour's inspiration
116 Indian titles of respect
117 Title hero of a classic western

DOWN

1 ___ Games
2 Longtime "All My Children" role
3 Go-getter
4 Show to a seat, briefly
5 Admits
6 Particles in electrolysis
7 Gourmand
8 Food packaging abbr.
9 Charms
10 "Les Misérables" star, 1998
11 Lasting marks
12 "Lord, ___ long?": Isaiah
13 Personal offer to help
14 Strip
15 School souvenir
16 ___ zoologique (French zoo)
17 "Lonely Boy" singer/writer
18 Guff
24 Chill in the air
25 Worked (up)
26 Actor Jared
32 Select
33 Payment in Monopoly
34 Lord Byron biblical drama
38 Snoop
39 How a ship may be turned
40 It may be behind a picket fence
41 Jamestown colonist
42 Bubbling
43 Some campaign expenses
44 40 days and 40 nights event
45 Turn unpleasant
46 Food writer Ruth
49 Freud's ego
50 Bottoms
51 Abbr. on top of some e-mails
52 Sue Grafton's "___ for Alibi"
54 Word before maker or breaker
55 How a rose by any other name would smell, according to Shakespeare
56 "Happy Days" boy
58 "The Situation Room" airer
59 Rejects, with "off"
60 Hootchy-___
61 Warren Commission subject
65 Familiar
66 Feudal lord
67 ___ Janis, star of Broadway's "Puzzles of 1925"
68 Tea-growing area of the Himalayas
69 Gen. Clark, informally
70 Window boxes, for short?
71 Abbr. in an apt. ad
72 Bygone monarch
73 Faulkner femme fatale ___ Varner
74 Straits
75 Graceful trees
79 Copyist
80 Norse deity of mischief
81 Musical credit
82 Ones with the motto "North to the Future"
85 Without exception
86 Voter, e.g.
87 Household member, for short
89 Australia's Northern ___: Abbr.
90 ___ apart
91 Like some tires
92 Capable of getting around, biologically
94 Voyagers: Suffix
95 Faith: Abbr.
96 Kind of exam
97 Not fitting
98 Mathematician who introduced the function symbol f(x)
99 Wuss
100 River in W.W. I fighting
101 Sweeping
102 Mideast capital
107 Fed. auditor
108 ___ de coeur
109 Rejections

by Caroline Leong

ACROSS

1 Illustrious
8 She wrote "Under the Sign of Saturn"
14 Body of precepts
19 Dow product
20 Country whose leader has competed in five Winter Olympics
21 Part of U.R.I.
22 Tarot reading, crystals, spiritualism, etc.
24 Arrive
25 Jack who played a sawmill worker in "Twin Peaks"
26 Mourn audibly
27 "___ yellow ribbon . . ."
29 U.S.N. noncoms
30 Wheel on a spur
33 Traditional English festival
36 Caladryl : itch :: Bengay : ___
40 Partner of music
42 Charlotte who played Mrs. Garrett on TV
43 Gaits out of the gate
44 Little John's weapon in Robin Hood legend
47 You are: Sp.
48 Does some file transfers
49 Break-even enterprise
51 Basic way up a slope
55 Comparable to a fiddle
56 Bootlicker
59 You might play something by it
61 A current flows into it
62 ___-deucy (game with dice)
64 Brooke Shields movie, with "The"
67 Bit of a snicker
68 Alma mater for Carol Burnett and Jim Morrison: Abbr.
70 Keyboard instruments
72 Some contraband
73 Fish that migrates from seawater to freshwater and back
74 Playmate of Piglet
75 Its roar is worse than its bite
77 It may be waved at the Olympics
79 Learning level
81 Language suffix
82 Overdone
84 One of the Spice Girls and namesakes
87 Northernmost borough of London
89 Well-planned
91 Elongated marine fish
93 Biathlon needs
94 Dinner bun
97 Exempli gratia, e.g.
99 Abbr. on Rockies skeds
101 "Pride and Prejudice" beau
102 Root canal, in dentist-speak
103 Hair removal site
106 Composer Franz
108 Seed cover
109 Mrs. Chaplin
110 Egg
112 "South Pacific" role
117 Nabisco's ___ wafers
119 1987 Kubrick film
123 Longtime Chicago mayor
124 Capital of France's Aube department
125 "Ta-ta"
126 Show awe, in a way
127 Fix firmly
128 Like a paradise

DOWN

1 Attorney William after whom a stadium was named
2 Given the ax?
3 Apple on a teacher's desk?
4 Neighbor of Chad
5 Sculpting medium
6 Sen. John Kerry served there
7 Sullen looks
8 Bob Hoskins's role in "Hook"
9 Zip
10 Salem-to-Portland dir.
11 Spiritual path in Hinduism
12 Off the injured list
13 Start of a referral
14 Work unit
15 Chaim Potok novel
16 Family-style Asian dish
17 See red, talk a blue streak, etc.
18 Perfume, in a way
19 Where Bernard Shaw was an anchor for 21 yrs.
23 African grassland
28 Space City baseballer
31 Had a bill, still
32 Most base
34 Pound sounds
35 Boring tool
36 Greenish-blue
37 Tarot suit
38 Proverbial portion
39 Beethoven's Third
41 Carpentry byproduct
45 London gallery
46 Alice of "Hollywood Cavalcade"
47 What "[sic]" may signify
50 Paradise
52 Ralph Kramden catchphrase on old TV . . . and a hint to this puzzle's theme
53 Ancient theaters
54 Dandelion or goldenrod, e.g.
57 They're blown in the winds
58 Nelson ___, author of "The Man With the Golden Arm"
60 Old Greek market
63 Singer Sumac
65 Tied surgically
66 Santana's "___ Como Va"
68 Press
69 Base of some ethanol
71 Opinion pieces
73 Always: It.
75 Quickly check (on)
76 Certain girder
78 Trapper's prize
80 Hiram Walker, for one
83 Parasite
85 "Should ___ acquaintance be forgot . . ."
86 French town on the Vire
88 Jive, e.g.
90 Outer: Prefix
92 Singer with the double-platinum album "The Memory of Trees"
95 French greeting
96 Burn at the end?
97 Dogie catcher
98 Underarm
99 Garden fertilizer
100 Zigzag, in a way
103 Airport screening equipment
104 Centaur's head?
105 The "Claudius" in Tiberius Claudius Nero
107 Page-turners are good ones
111 Life ___
113 Mid 12th-century date
114 Swedish retail giant
115 Province NW of Madrid
116 W.W. II arena
118 "___, captain!"
120 Alkali in cleansers
121 Response to a funny text
122 Procter & Gamble detergent

by Cathy Millhauser

ACROSS

1 As yet
6 Strands in a diner
15 March of ___
20 Mme. Tussaud
21 One who keeps a beat?
22 Opposition
23 Complete flip-flop
24 Mind
25 Just above average
26 With 113-Across, 1972 song lyric hinting at this puzzle's theme
29 Play group?
30 ___ Tomé
31 Besmirching
33 Scene
34 They're pitched
36 Victorians, e.g.
38 Patron saint of Norway
39 Outdoor shindigs
41 "Your mother wears army boots!," e.g.
44 Kristin ___, six-time swimming champion at the 1988 Olympics
45 Classic Atari game
48 Approaches
51 Mahler's "___ Lied von der Erde"
52 "Typee" sequel
53 First Shia imam
56 Latin 101 verb
57 Marie or Suzanne: Abbr.
58 "Homage to Clio" poet
59 Some shavers
61 Pianist Claudio
63 "Barnaby Jones" star
65 Set up
67 Thick
70 Check words
71 D.C. pol
72 Narc employer, for short
74 "The Baptism of Christ" painter ___ della Francesca
76 ___ Reader
77 Child-care provider
79 Capital city about an hour by plane from Miami
81 Campaign expense
82 End of a hammer
83 Music unlikely to be played at a party
84 Squeezing (out)
85 Weigh station sight
86 Prefix with valve
87 Delilahs
88 Lifework
90 White House advisory grp.
91 Snorkeling locale
93 Wide of the mark
95 "The best ___ to come!"
97 European air hub
103 "The Naked Maja" and "The Clothed Maja," e.g.
106 It's often "proud"
109 Sine or cosine
110 Two-year periods
112 Straight
113 See 26-Across
116 Solidarity symbol
117 Director Wertmüller
118 How ballerinas dance
119 Jalapeño feature
120 Tennis player Smashnova
121 Dairy aisle purchase
122 Detects, in a way
123 Slight difficulties
124 Typical Mad reader

DOWN

1 Laura Bush's alma mater: Abbr.
2 Nibble for Trigger
3 Tropical cave dwellers
4 Radiator part
5 Go back (on)
6 Person with binoculars, maybe
7 Glazier's stock
8 Mailing label abbr.
9 Facilitates
10 Bill who created the comic strip "Smokey Stover"
11 Missy ___ with the 2002 hit "Work It"
12 Some govt. investigators
13 Indicator of silence
14 Prefix with state
15 Some Martha Stewart Living photo displays
16 Locked up
17 Deep black garnets
18 Swift-running bird
19 Way: Abbr.
27 Lover boy
28 Overseas Mrs.
29 Burrito topping
32 Reach an understanding of
33 Mr. ___ of "The Wind in the Willows"
34 Letters from Greece
35 Mideast's House of ___
37 Peeved
39 Common symbol in heraldry
40 German-born Hollywood actor ___ Keir
42 Org. of which U.S. Grant was once president
43 Author Janowitz
46 Event where chaps may be seen
47 Warning, maybe
49 "Close"
50 Landing place
53 Constellation near Scorpius
54 Extol
55 Magician's name suffix
58 Author who wrote "One half of the world cannot understand the pleasures of the other"
59 Harmless
60 "Happy Birthday, Sweet Sixteen" singer
62 Independent examinations
63 All gone, in a way
64 Like 113-Across
65 Backside
66 1954 Jean Simmons movie
68 Atomic number of the special parts of this puzzle which, when connected, form a 113-Across
69 Toronto transports
70 Kind of platter
71 Politico Agnew
73 He played Grant on TV
75 Like some of Keats's work
77 Sound
78 Thing, in court
79 Big inits. in Japanese computers
80 Carpentry tool
87 Pepper and others: Abbr.
89 Frenzy
92 Son of Aphrodite
94 Like some yogurt
95 Basketry fiber
96 Parsley bit
98 Boo-boo
99 Microsoft man
100 Park Avenue, for one
101 Mountain climbers?
102 Sign on to a computer
104 French department in Picardy
105 "Paradise Lost" figure
107 "We got trouble!"
108 Painter Magritte
110 Whse., e.g.
111 ___ of March
114 ___ crossroads
115 Suffix with pay

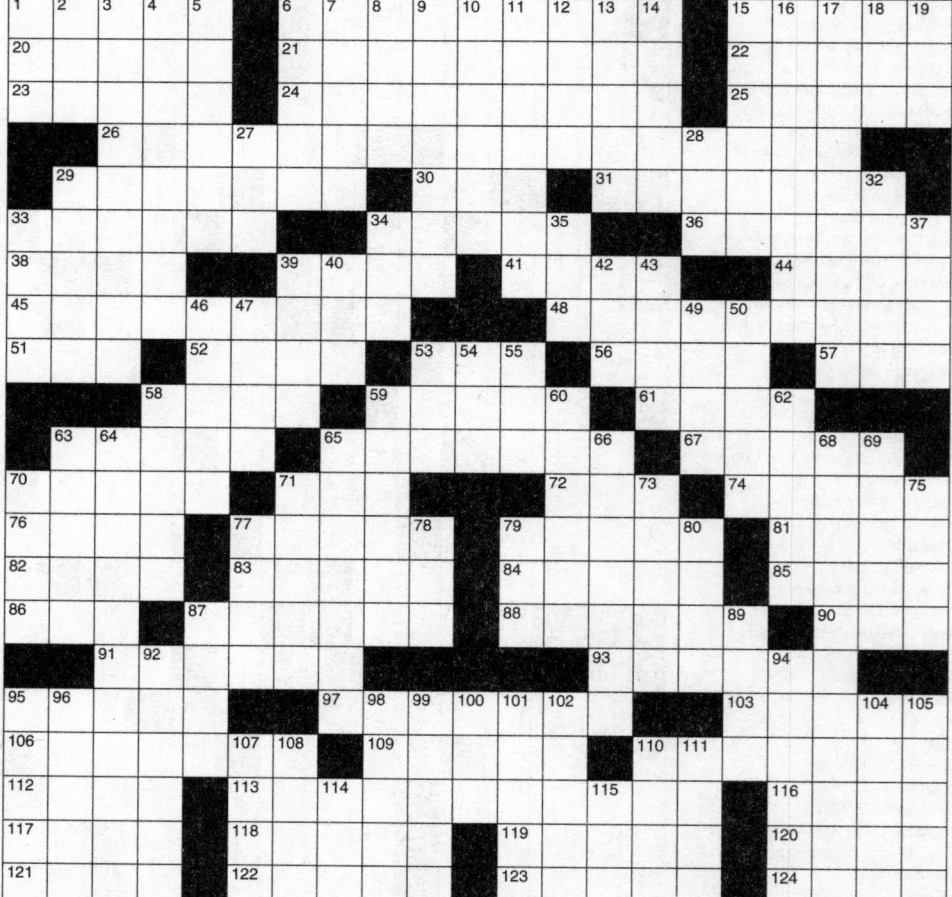

by Elizabeth C. Gorski

ACROSS

1 See 7-Across
7 Product whose 1-Across is a 61-Across
11 Posh part of Boston
18 Heavy-duty hand soap
19 Like some upset stomachs
20 Showed relief, in a way
21 Toddler's mealtime accessory
23 Ceramists, at times
24 Battle report?
25 Slam
27 Hatchery supply
28 Danger in a uranium mine
29 Quarters for a business, e.g.
35 Lorre's "Casablanca" role
37 Crew members
38 "It's been ___"
39 Defense contractor whose stock symbol is the same as its name
41 Alluring
42 Grinch disguise
44 Annual Pebble Beach tournament
45 ___-noir (modern film genre)
46 Place for a mud bath
47 Thanksgiving fare
49 Rough
51 Crawl space?
54 Safari, e.g.
57 Worrywart's cry
58 Idiot
60 Lacking a partner
61 Snack item
64 Persuaded with flattery
66 Noted explorer of Polynesia
70 1940s–'50s Dodger who was a 10-time All-Star
71 Particle created by a cosmic ray
73 A stone's throw away
74 Comedy show that once featured John Candy and Martin Short
76 Time in which light travels one foot, approximately
80 Sandal's lack
81 Creatio ex ___ (Christian tenet)
84 A few
85 ___ fix
86 Prayer opener
87 Put into effect
89 Nurse
91 Misstep
95 Entrance to the Medit.
96 Knight time?
97 "Quit your crying!"
98 Teahouse floor covering
100 Astronomical events that occur twice or more a year
104 Mark down, say, as a sale item
105 Univ. aides
106 Best
107 Filmed over
109 Minnesota's state tree
113 Nested set of containers
117 License
118 Yearned (for)
119 Tell
120 Stupidest
121 Relative of Rover
122 Begins

DOWN

1 Point of decline
2 Dock payment
3 Dungeons & Dragons weapon
4 Steve Martin romantic comedy
5 Like seven of Sophocles' 123 plays
6 Champagne name
7 First person in Austria
8 Italian possessive
9 Puma rival
10 Saint for whom the Russian alphabet is named
11 Panhandle
12 ___ Rose
13 Political asset
14 Skiffle instrument
15 Empathetic one, derisively
16 ___ Lingus
17 Dash units: Abbr.
19 Worth trying?
22 Org. with the motto "Per Ardua ad Astra"
26 In short supply
28 1904–'05 foe of Japan: Abbr.
30 Didn't move
31 Tool for many a homemade Mother's Day card
32 Bigheadedness
33 Trunk location
34 Dutch painter Jan
36 Dead Sea Scrolls sect
40 Kerfuffle
43 Certain emergency call, briefly
44 10 Downing St. residents
48 Knock over
50 First name in Israeli history
51 Outlawed pollutant, for short
52 http://www.myspace.com, e.g.
53 Be weighed down
54 Bouquet source
55 Reactor part
56 Bit of sunshine
59 ___ Fountain
62 Sports bar wall decoration
63 Subj. follower
65 Coin with kanji writing
66 Long-handled implement
67 Secret
68 "There's No Place Like ___" (old TV slogan)
69 Oven cleaner ingredient
71 Pop's partner
72 Goes through
74 It might produce a run
75 Polite
77 Mien
78 Part of N.A.
79 "Yes, I'm a Witch" musician
82 Save for later
83 ___-Eaters
88 Blast furnace material
90 Magazine no.
91 Leave
92 Rubbery compounds
93 Cry of triumph after "Whew!"
94 Truffle finder
97 Music of Kanye West
99 Suitable for farming
101 Kittens' "handles"
102 Fishing spots in Fife
103 French possessive
108 Shadows
109 "Mayberry ___"
110 Poetic preposition
111 They were worth $5 each on "What's My Line?"
112 911 responder
114 W.S.J. news item
115 Shrimper's aid
116 ___-Caps (candy)

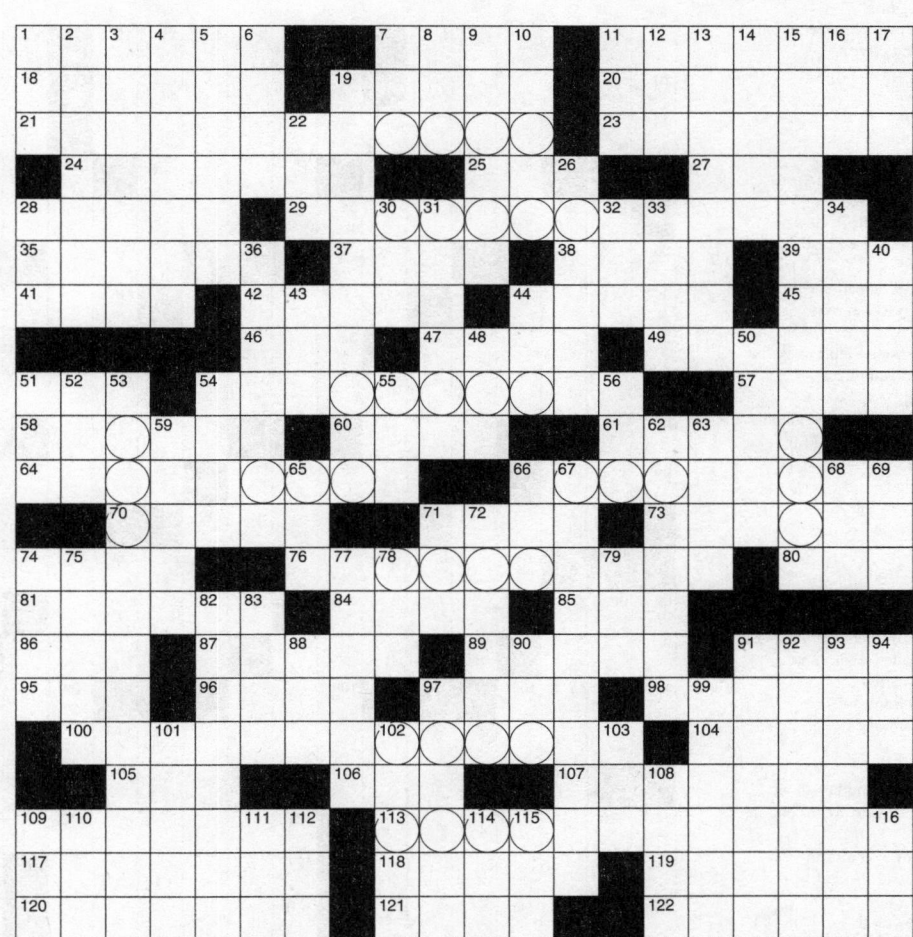

by Andrew M. Greene and Craig Kasper

114   PUT IT IN WRITING

ACROSS

1 Heart of a bus. district
7 High-end watches
13 Mexican state east of Veracruz
20 Squeezed at the ends, as leaves
21 Crumb catchers, often
22 Some unwritten rules
23 Quentin Tarantino paperback about a minister's stories?
25 Exposé
26 Bottom-of-letter abbr.
27 State where Geo. W. Bush was born
28 Became fully evident
29 Randy Shilts exposé of an outlaw musician?
35 Kind of boost
36 Deborah's "The King and I" co-star
37 "My dear fellow"
38 Get out
39 Prepare to frame again, maybe
42 Attack
46 Champagne grape
50 Car introduced in 1905
51 Warning signal, once
53 Triangular kerchief
55 "Just because"
57 Susan Howatch novel about protesting clergy?
60 Rescue squad V.I.P.
61 Years ——
62 Be down
63 Money maker
66 63-Across device
67 Mexican Indians
71 Composer Prokofiev
74 Hardly glowing reviews
76 Disney movie with a hacker hero
78 Paraffin-wrapped cheese
80 Old presidential inits
81 Bad news
82 Marlo Thomas storybook for liberated vampires?
89 Piddling
92 "In ——" (#1 Nirvana album)
93 Is out
94 Blowup: Abbr.
95 Rye malady
97 One way to think
99 Saucy dance
100 Love child?
102 "Frasier" role
104 Social type
106 "And ——!"
107 Grimm Brothers story about a sorry leader, with "The"?
116 Medal-worthy
117 "I don't think so"
118 He was chased by the Cowardly Lion
119 Copycat
121 Shakespearean play about a monarch who writes bad checks?
126 Owner of a stud farm
127 This second
128 Second
129 Goes downhill
130 Crowds, it is said
131 One way to live transsexually

DOWN

1 Big job for a barber
2 —— Ghraib, Iraqi prison
3 "—— bite"
4 Red-—— sapsucker
5 Be frugal
6 Peevish
7 Japanese band
8 Believer's goal
9 Stationery name
10 Rat race
11 Hunk
12 W-2 info: Abbr.
13 Wreck
14 Bowl
15 Obstinate
16 In something together
17 Doesn't just bad-mouth
18 Oriole Ripken
19 Symbol of Minerva
24 Bloom of Paris
28 One on the fast track?
29 Little League issue
30 "Don't sweat it"
31 Putting all the poker chips in the pot, maybe
32 Line just above the total
33 Table spread
34 City light
35 Did away with
40 Former White House press secretary Fleischer
41 Dell order
43 Petty peeve
44 Essen exclamation
45 Joyce Carol Oates novel
47 Japanese theater
48 Buried treasure
49 United places
52 Certain NCO
54 Alien craft
56 "Take me —— am"
58 Win in a children's game
59 Siamang, for one
64 City served by Indira Gandhi International Airport
65 Hunter of literature
68 Transiently brilliant
69 Union words
70 "Elephant Boy" boy
72 Miracle-——
73 Birds as big as people
75 Go one way, then the other
77 One-kind connector
79 Canon alternative
83 Where 84-Down is: Abbr.
84 Where London is: Abbr.
85 No. on a business card
86 Leandro's love
87 "—— has no age": Picasso
88 Grant grp.
89 Least complaint
90 Cross letters
91 One whose work may suit you
96 Best
98 Necrophobiac's fear
101 Some war plans
103 Climax
105 Study in multiplication and division?
108 Undermine
109 "Funny Face" director Stanley
110 Places to drop a line
111 Chopper part
112 Speak out
113 Cross swords (with)
114 Old lab burners
115 "—— Doone"
119 "Charlotte's Web" initials
120 Backing
121 Kit —— Club
122 Kenmore alternatives
123 Candied vegetable
124 —— quandary
125 Camper, e.g.

by Lee Glickstein and Nancy Salomon

ACROSS

1. Talk follower
6. Twinge
11. Bit of info
16. Memory unit, for short
19. Horse genus
20. Dantean division
21. About to explode, maybe
22. Botheration
23. "Marie Antoinette" star, 2006
24. Put the touch on
25. *One who gets beaten badly?
27. *Sticks in the medicine cabinet?
30. Crow's-nest sighting
31. Dodge pickup
32. Some R.S.V.P.'s
33. Hub-to-rim lines
34. Hammett's canine creation
38. Battle of Britain grp.
40. *Forbidding countenance
44. Roe source
45. Render difficult to find
48. High-quality
49. *Lacking compassion
52. Recharge one's batteries
53. Tire swing supporter
57. Holmes who married Tom Cruise
58. Typewriter brand
60. Song that Elvis's "It's Now or Never" was based on
62. Man in a sombrero
63. Baseball star Maglie
64. "Sketches by ___," 1836
66. Losing ground
67. Lid
68. *"It's true, like it or not"
72. ___ up (get dressed)
73. Former coeds, maybe
75. Blue expanse
76. Half of a cartoon duo
77. Practices for a bout
79. Inundating
81. Belgian painter James, known for bizarre fantasies with masks
83. Former N.F.L. QB Rodney
84. "Holy moly!"
85. Sonogram, e.g.
87. *British motorist's right?
90. Serve
92. "The Princess Bride" character ___ Montoya
93. Electromagnet component
94. *1999 romantic comedy based on "Pygmalion"
99. Doughnut shop qty.
100. They have guests
101. Moderated, with "down"
102. The Big Aristotle, in the N.B.A.
105. Key above Caps Lock
107. Part of I.M.F.: Abbr.
108. *It's taken by doctors
115. *Follow-up to a potential insult
117. Works magic on
118. Go further than
120. Tooth holder
121. Bug-repelling wood
122. Like noble gases
123. Near East hotel
124. Eyeball
125. Stops flowing
126. Brings in
127. The Process of Elimination: In the answer to each starred clue, cross out any letter that appears ___; then read the letters that remain

DOWN

1. Proof closer
2. Greenish-blue
3. 1970s–'90s senator Sam
4. Indoor settler
5. In motion
6. Underlying patterns
7. Poker holding
8. Unable to sit still
9. Blockhead
10. Down in the dumps
11. Worst-case scenario
12. "East of Eden" twin
13. Like vinaigrette
14. Mountain West Conference team
15. Ferrer of "Lili"
16. Site fortified by Herod the Great
17. Paradisiacal
18. Howe who was known as Mr. Hockey
26. Minnesota's St. ___ College
28. Minority member in India
29. Reference books?
33. Way to go: Abbr.
34. Volcanic output
35. "Hurry up!"
36. Fuzzy crawler
37. Increase
39. Jill's portrayer in "Charlie's Angels"
41. Jazz singer Laine
42. Late Jordanian king
43. Acquire by unsavory means
46. Items checked at an opera house checkroom
47. Casual greeting
50. In need of help
51. Expert, in England
53. Stayed in front
54. Made of paste
55. Studied on the side
56. Wade at Cooperstown
59. Head of England
61. Gamblers' setbacks
62. You'll find it under a tree
63. Letter-writing aid
65. Position the cross hairs (on)
69. 1960s–'70s Saudi king
70. Go steady with
71. Vehement
74. Disgraced one's name?
78. "Home Alone" actor Joe
80. Intl. commercial agreement first signed in 1947
82. Overseas title
83. Mood lifter
86. People who haven't a chance, in Britspeak
88. Their priority is number one
89. Loop circlers
90. Bank roll
91. iPod variety
94. "Sophie's Choice" narrator
95. Waugh's "Sword of ___" trilogy
96. Enter into a plot?
97. "Note to ___ . . ."
98. Computer whiz
103. Game site
104. Not as stringent
106. Leg up
108. Crusty piece of bread
109. ___-European
110. High school jrs. take it
111. Gull relative
112. All over again
113. Hatcher of "Lois & Clark"
114. Red Scare grp.
116. Org. overseeing decency standards
119. Pizza order

by Patrick Berry

ACROSS

1 Grand Ole Opry sight
6 "Huh?"
10 Style of Japanese writing
15 N.H.L. great from the Czech Republic
19 Buddy on TV
20 James Joyce's home
21 Be gaga (over)
22 Jai ___
23 Annual "Movie Yearbook" author since the 1990s
24 Bit of news at the aviary?
27 Nag
29 Settle (into)
30 Servings from a grill
31 "Love ___"
32 Cry from a selfish child
33 Chant at a basketball game
34 Notion of an underwater creature?
39 Load bearer?
40 Least populous U.N. member
41 Fluoride, for one
42 Pet in old cartoons
43 TripTik provider: Abbr.
46 Tombstone word
47 Fraternization on an army base?
53 East German secret police
55 Range part: Abbr.
56 Accumulate, with "up"
57 Speed
58 1980 N.F.L. M.V.P. Brian
60 Org. that established the Legends Tour in 2001
61 1992 Oscar-nominated title role for Robert Downey Jr.
63 How courteous swordsmen fight?
69 With geniality
70 Wagered
71 Elegance
72 Particular purpose
73 Regarding
74 Saturn, for one
75 Gwen ___, Spider-Man's first love
80 Farm young 'un with a blanket?
85 Inflammation reducer
86 Esq., usually
87 Jordanian queen
88 Veneration
89 Fishing with traps, maybe
91 Early ___
93 Local cutie pie?
96 Calf feature
99 Charges (up)
100 Je ne ___ quoi
101 Start of an itinerary
102 Superior
103 Junked
108 Capture of a Mafia runner, e.g.?
111 Ultraviolet filter
112 Midway attraction
113 Go from dawn to dusk
114 Early version
115 Tied, in a way
116 They may prevent passage
117 "Hägar the Horrible" dog
118 "Think big" company
119 Ethyl cinnamate, for one

DOWN

1 It should have a head and a good body
2 "Voulez-Vous" pop group
3 Small interval of time: Abbr.
4 Prolonged complaints
5 Injured, in baseball lingo
6 Bother
7 Cat's warning
8 Work of Michelangelo, e.g.
9 Leaves after dinner?
10 Singer who spells her name in all lowercase letters
11 Emanate (from)
12 Survey choice
13 Stir
14 Comment to a new friend
15 Go on and on
16 Crazy as ___
17 Get-ups
18 Instruction before "repeat"
25 Coachman's line
26 Sound's partner
28 Dishonor
32 Mouthwash flavor
33 Literary preceder of "Goldfinger"
34 Benchmarks: Abbr.
35 Renounce
36 Anatomical part whose name comes from the Latin for "grape"
37 Like many Scots
38 Cut above the flank
39 "No ___!"
42 "Knockin' on Heaven's Door" songwriter
43 What a train goes down
44 Bit of tomfoolery
45 One may be double or free
48 Hint at
49 Stuck on
50 Unforgiving
51 Kids go through them
52 Scandinavian native
54 Sanford of "The Jeffersons"
59 Feeling much less than 100%
60 Master
61 Primitive
62 Something bad that may be put on you
63 Comic actress Sykes
64 Poker declaration
65 Coloring
66 Succeed, with "it"
67 ___ artery (blood vessel of the arm)
68 Protected, as a surgeon's hands
73 Russian conductor/composer Markevitch
74 Order for Oscar night
76 What a specialist men's store may offer
77 Et ___
78 Fifth state to ratify the Constitution: Abbr.
79 One trying to find the right combination?
81 Gives the oath of office, e.g.
82 "Away in a Manger," for one
83 Field calls
84 Plot again
90 Part of a season
91 Zellweger and Adorée
92 Like some verbs: Abbr.
93 Lodger
94 Supervising
95 Amount paid on some out-of-state purchases
96 Reject
97 Land bordering ancient Lydia
98 Radio talker G. Gordon ___
99 "Copy that"
102 It might get your kitty going
103 Judge
104 "Dónde ___ . . . ?"
105 Delete
106 Suffix with insist
107 Bucks, e.g.
109 Singer Janis
110 Diamond stat.

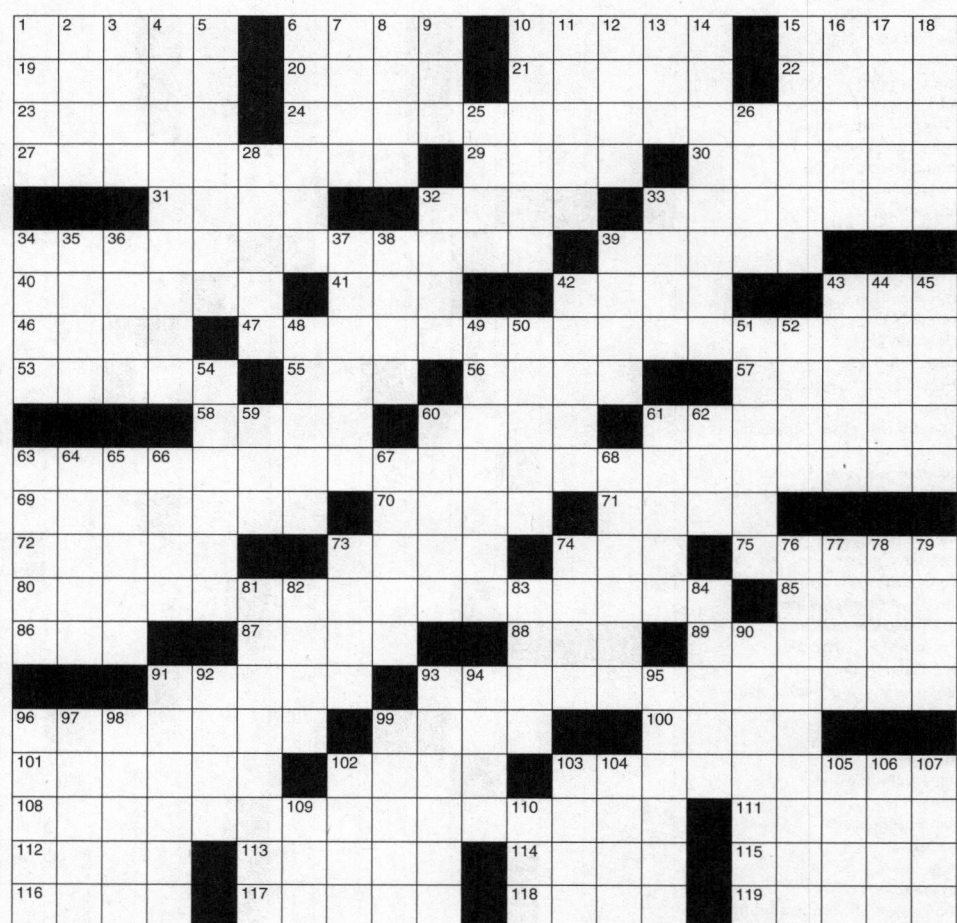

by Mike Nothnagel

ACROSS

1 Kicked off
6 Pill
10 Jacket-and-tie affair
14 Afternoon fare
19 Good, to Guido
20 Comedy Central's "___ 911!"
21 Jubilant cries
22 Unadulterated
23 Rolled sixes while on Water Works, in Monopoly?
25 552, on a cornerstone
26 Whirlpool alternative
27 Co-star on TV's "Taxi"
28 Doesn't throw away, as a stage prop?
31 Element that's liquid at room temperature
33 Remote
34 Kings' lands
35 What a sushi chef loves to hear?
41 "Say Say Say," say
42 Royal jelly maker
43 Hi-___
44 Nasdaq listings: Abbr.
47 Opposite of morn, to a poet
48 "8 Minute Abs," according to some?
56 Wilson of Tinseltown
57 BlackBerry nos.
58 Vatican emissary
59 Extra-large
64 Webster and Wyle
67 Canon competitor
68 Till
69 January 15?
72 Bond
73 Pull a ___
75 Unit of yarn
76 Historical separation
78 Dish
80 Volume by Horace
82 History
83 Was late to an appointment at the cosmetician?
88 Stroke
91 Flight attendant's announcement, for short
92 German name part
93 "Shine a Little Love" grp.
94 Arcade
95 What scientists working for Gatorade have?
103 Some moon rocks
106 Three-day holiday
107 Hero of Sophocles' "Electra"
108 Dylan not liking Dell computers?
112 Grosse ___, Mich.
113 Opera ___
114 Not closed all the way
115 Like pro bono work?
119 Part of TWA
120 "___ known then . . ."
121 Gladness: Fr.
122 Andropov and Gagarin
123 To date
124 Darkens, maybe
125 Let go
126 Actress Graff

DOWN

1 Fraud finder: Abbr.
2 Grand tour locale: Abbr.
3 A bird flying by on the right, to the Greeks
4 Disheveled
5 Words following see, hear and speak
6 For now
7 Start of many airline names
8 Like Mozart's Symphony No. 10
9 Cozy spot
10 Develop anacusis
11 Gridiron star
12 Rings of islands
13 "Like that'll ever happen!"
14 Indications of anger
15 Kind of band
16 One bit
17 The Beatles arrived in New York in 1964 on this
18 Does in
24 Done, in Dijon
29 40% of fifty?
30 Prayer
31 A following?
32 Wolf
36 Withdraw
37 Born as
38 Try
39 Basics of grade school learnin'?
40 Small number
44 Certain shell
45 "But of course, Monsieur!"
46 More than buzzed
48 Deuce
49 "___ Tramp," Peggy Lee song in "Lady and the Tramp"
50 Bagnold and others
51 Carpenter, at times
52 Spanish bloom
53 Honshu port
54 "Danger! Danger!"
55 Dungeons & Dragons figure
56 Mitch Miller, e.g.
59 What multitaskers do with things
60 Displace
61 Greek peak
62 Ringo's eldest
63 ___ newt (witches' brew ingredient)
65 With it
66 Hogwarts professor
70 Paul Bunyan's dog
71 Pulitzer-winning novelist Shirley Ann ___
74 Little complaint
77 Recipe amt.
79 Moves around
81 "Peter Pan" pirate
84 Cut (down)
85 8×10, say: Abbr.
86 TV character from the planet Melmac
87 "Rock and Roll, Hoochie ___"
88 Rear seating section in a theater
89 "What ___?"
90 B'way buys
94 Yearning
95 Al in Cooperstown
96 The Braves' div.
97 Online investing site
98 Ruins
99 Classic Ferrari
100 Laid some tiles
101 The Police, e.g.
102 Son of William the Conqueror
103 "No more, Luigi!"
104 Parrots
105 Nozzle choice
109 Late Saudi king
110 Any member of a 1970s R&B group
111 Low: Sp.
112 "Swan Lake" bend
116 Nova, e.g.
117 German article
118 Wind dir.

by David Levinson Wilk

ACROSS

1 Starting point
5 Wraps on stage
9 Org. that inspects factories
13 Frog's place
19 ___-pointe (ballet position)
20 Footballer-turned-politician Swann
21 Inn's offering
22 Hungry lion, e.g.
23 *Ice hockey penalty
26 Mame, e.g.
27 Motrin rival
28 They may be high before a competition
29 Purges
31 Companion of a spade
32 Surgically excise
33 Pod that's sometimes pickled
34 *Tongue-in-cheek
36 Côte d'___
38 Observed
40 *Somewhat in jest
46 Unbroken
50 Dinner spread
51 Food label abbr.
52 Rocky Mtn. highs?
55 Patron saint of metalworkers
56 Not skip a beat?
59 Go-go-go
61 Not go by one's own locomotion
62 Connections
63 Family V.I.P.'s
65 "Myself was stirring ___ the break of day": Shak.
66 Oiled, in a manner
68 *Sign of coming danger
72 To be handled by
75 ___-eyed
76 "TV Funhouse" show, for short
77 Key holder?: Abbr.
80 "Fantastic Mr. Fox" author, 1970
81 Upshot
85 Lack of variety
87 Special case?
88 Dan ___, former N.B.A. star and coach
89 Roman historian
91 Jazzy Anita
92 Sharp bend
94 *Drifter
98 Colorless, flammable gas
101 Imitator
102 *What "dele" means
105 ___ moss
108 Does just all right
113 Top-notch
114 Israeli statesman Barak
115 Actress/spokeswoman Belafonte
116 Ancient Greek region
117 Tin: Prefix
119 *Barnyard fixture
122 Former New Hampshire senator John
123 1965 movie "___ What You Did"
124 Give a come-hither look
125 Toy company whose name is an anagram of 124-Across
126 Corkscrew, e.g.
127 One-liners
128 General ___ chicken
129 Bygone U.S. gas brand

DOWN

1 Annual literary award
2 Silas of the Continental Congress
3 Thompson and Lazarus
4 Relative of 26-Across
5 Jewish crêpe
6 Exclamations of exasperation
7 Religious recluse
8 Derisive gesture
9 Periods in prison, e.g.
10 Old French coins
11 Ad follower
12 City of New Orleans operator
13 *Professional courtesy in pricing
14 First word spoken to Earth from the lunar surface
15 Dashed
16 Maker of Bug-B-Gon
17 Fivesome seen in order in the answer to each starred clue
18 Shady sorts?
24 Biotite and phlogopite
25 Home of "The Diane Rehm Show"
30 Put away for good
34 Christopher Morley novel "Kitty ___"
35 Future residents
37 Banquet holder
39 Designer Cassini
40 Some cliff dwellers
41 English playwright Ayckbourn
42 "I'm game!"
43 Backing
44 Landlord, e.g.
45 Development sites
47 Came down
48 Word with bar or color
49 One-to-one, e.g.
53 Card catalog abbr.
54 Chiantis, e.g.
57 Poet who wrote "The moving finger writes; and, having writ, moves on"
58 *Time during a graveyard shift
60 Tears to pieces
64 Arch sites
67 Nothing doing?
68 Sea of ___
69 Newts
70 Stephen Jay ___, author of "The Panda's Thumb"
71 Role in "The Color Purple"
72 Carded, say
73 Grp. conducting Operation Deny Flight
74 Repeated cry at a beer blast
77 Cousin of Spot
78 Beach bash
79 ___ nitrate
82 Lick again
83 Flair
84 Nielsens
86 To-___
90 Small bark
93 Saint-___, capital of France's Loire department
95 4-Down's brothers
96 Brings to naught
97 Feminist Germaine
99 Crossword solver, presumably
100 Philosopher Wittgenstein
102 Italian poet Torquato ___
103 Misbehave
104 "The Family Circus" cartoonist
106 Side flap
107 Rampaging
109 "A Confederacy of Dunces" author
110 Pivots
111 "American Pie" actor Jason
112 Uneducated boor
115 Unaccompanied
118 Novice, maybe
120 Simile's center
121 Day-___

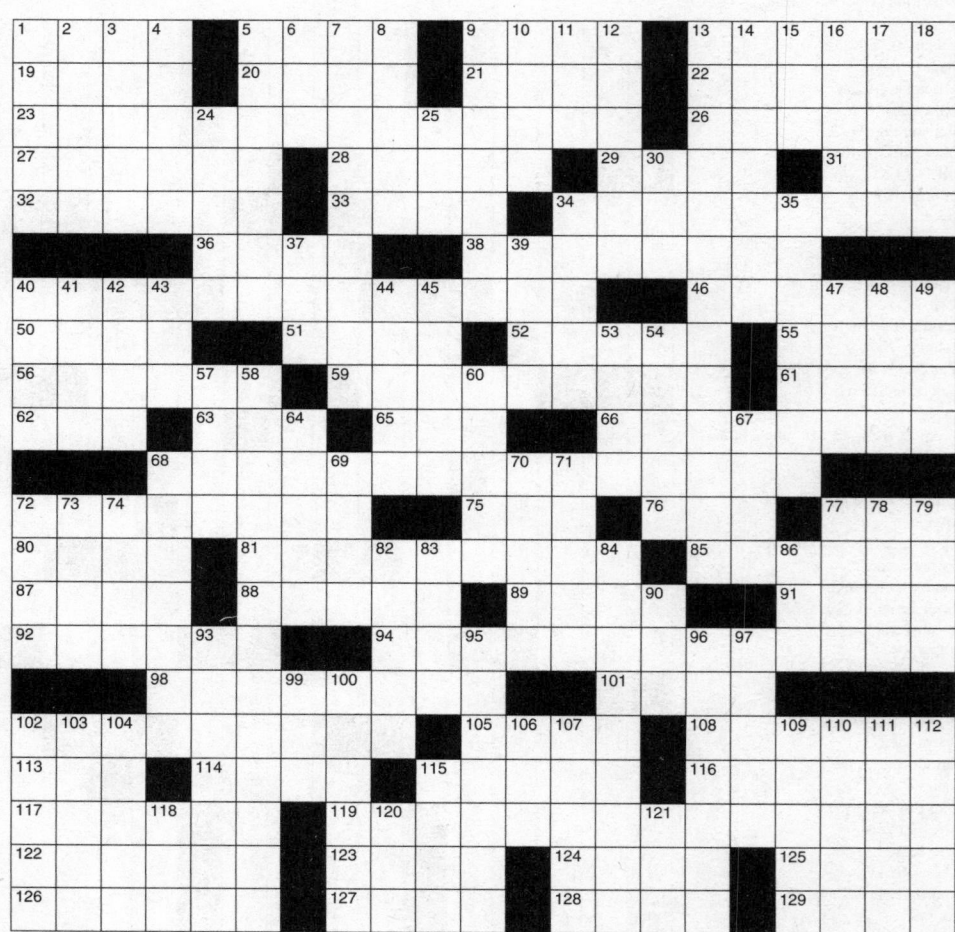

by Kelsey Blakley

ACROSS

1 Surgeon's instrument
8 Egg white
15 Having no master
20 Queued up
21 Sewing machine parts
22 Ex of The Donald
23 Sunflower seeds, botanically
24 Event where there might be burping
26 Set boundaries
28 Offends the olfactories
29 Cleans
30 Coming
32 Wait on
33 Poker player's gloat
38 Start on a stage
40 Vacuum tube filler
41 Bad ___ (German spa)
42 Students' gifts from home
48 Like Cain
51 Brought forth
52 Factor in a wine rating
53 Afternoon affair
54 Crew implement
55 Character size
57 Mogul
58 Kind of service offered at some cafes
60 Rain-___ (classic bubble-gum balls)
62 Simple housing
63 Cariou of Broadway
65 Response to "Want some?"
68 Somme time
69 Jazzman Jackson
70 Foolish sort
71 One present but not participating
73 Energy secretary under Clinton
75 Obstinate
77 Snaps
78 Delivery people, briefly
81 Food in Exodus
82 Slow mover
84 Feature of many modern computer monitors
87 Prize since 1928
89 Turnabout, slangily
90 Journalist ___ Rogers St. Johns
91 Specify
92 Help in checking calls
95 Wrist injury
99 Excite
100 Mum
101 Mottled mount
103 Junkyard supply
109 Candidate's "This isn't over!"
112 Smooth
113 Not so nutty
114 Obviously embarrassed
115 Like a skunk
116 Blown away
117 Has in mind
118 In quality?

DOWN

1 King topper
2 Foe of Pizarro
3 Cowardly Lion portrayer
4 Baldwin of "The Cat in the Hat"
5 Turner of records?
6 Like some trucks
7 Forward
8 Flight no.?
9 Pilgrimage site
10 Girl with a crook
11 Stimulant
12 Like a milquetoast
13 Goes off
14 Sydney's state: Abbr.
15 Sunken cooking site
16 Get around
17 ___ to go
18 Put chips in up front
19 Places
25 Story that's over one's head
27 Widow's inheritance
31 Scrap
32 Not much
33 Whole slew
34 Iroquoian language
35 Indian tourist mecca
36 Some records or cars
37 Chekhov who wrote "Uncle Vanya"
38 Rhine tributary
39 Brunch serving
42 Summons: Abbr.
43 Bandleader Kyser
44 Zodiac symbol
45 Leave home
46 Wax theatrical
47 Lacking, to Louis
49 Ball club come-on
50 Snacks often served with milk
51 Duke Ellington classic
56 Baguette, for one
57 Accepted criticism without complaint
58 Working together
59 IV givers
60 Life story
61 Parkinsonism treatment
63 Sachet scent
64 "Uncle Vanya" woman
66 Press coverage
67 Angle with artificial bait
69 N.Y.C. attraction
72 Brit in America, maybe
74 Light line
75 Show fully
76 A helping hand
78 Scott Turow title
79 ___ Fleck and the Flecktones
80 Put in stitches
82 Park lake denizen
83 Where many vets served
85 Lead-in to "pray"
86 Worker in the TV biz
88 Ekberg of "La Dolce Vita"
89 Like neglected muscles
92 Successively
93 Venomous
94 Approaching
95 Supporting instrumentalist
96 Primary strategy
97 Periodical plea
98 Physicist Ampère
99 Cybermemo
100 "You bet!" in Yucatán
101 Hammer's end
102 "Rhyme Pays" rapper
104 Loud noise
105 Have ___ with
106 Weapon in the game Clue
107 When to vote, usually: Abbr.
108 F.C.C. concerns: Abbr.
110 Swinger's stat
111 N.F.L. successes

by Nancy Salomon and Harvey Estes

ACROSS

1 Film character who says "Play it once, Sam, for old times' sake"
5 Clear furniture material
11 Doctrines
15 Having no cost, in Cologne
19 Arrive
20 Choirs may sing in it
21 On
22 Make over
23 Base for many French fries
25 "Are we finished?"
27 C_2H_4, e.g.
28 1987 Nicolas Cage/Holly Hunter film
30 Caterpillar competitor
31 One of two school colors (along with heliotrope) of New York's Purchase College
32 Beluga delicacy
33 French pupil
34 Ends of sandwiches?
36 Light, maybe
38 "Nearer the Moon" author Nin
40 Was really agitated
43 "The fix ——"
45 French way
47 Letters of compassion
48 Setting of Blackmore's "Lorna Doone"
49 Titles at A.B.A. mtgs.
50 Doesn't keep from
52 "Boola Boola" singer
53 Big car racer sponsor
54 1950 #1 hit for Patti Page
58 Tenor in "The Flying Dutchman"
60 Yuletide quaff
61 Time ——
62 Sounds of relief
65 Robert Redford film . . . and a hint to what occurs at 23-, 28-, 54-, 77-, 111- and 116-Across
72 "Buona ——"
73 Pops
74 85-Across, e.g.: Abbr.
75 Tiny fraction of a min.
77 Lead-in to "Show me!"
84 "Get it?"
85 AOL alternative
88 Tedious
89 Excellent, slangily
90 Ready for an emergency
92 Ear: Prefix
93 High fashion inits.
94 Like cotton candy
95 Works on, as a set of tires
96 Toscanini's birthplace
99 Anwar's successor
101 Florida snapper
102 She was wild about Harry
104 Rock's —— Fighters
105 Not showing one's age, in a way
107 Harding who made headlines in 1994
111 1915 song that popularized the phrase "Hail! Hail! The gang's all here"
114 Muscle relaxant
115 Party people?
116 Ice cream treat
118 Zodiac symbol
119 "Bee Season" star, 2005
120 Not unaware of the joke
121 Pugilist Spinks
122 Eye doctor's concern
123 "What are the ——?"
124 Soaks in water
125 Timeless Turner

DOWN

1 Poem that ends with the funeral of Hector
2 Scooper
3 Gem State stream
4 Follow
5 1966 hit "Little Latin —— Lu"
6 Card game with a draw pile
7 Kumquat, for one
8 Esau's father
9 Funny Fields
10 Genesis son
11 Retort to "You are a liar!"
12 They get props for their work on Broadway
13 1998 French Open winner Carlos ——
14 Church bell locale
15 Like some assets and smiles
16 Give a face-lift
17 Al Bundy player
18 A Siouan
24 Having no sequel
26 Grand Canyon State stream
29 Modern home of ancient Media
31 Walker, briefly
35 Composed
36 Volunteer State and Show Me State stream
37 Dance accompanied by a gourd drum
39 Astron., e.g.
40 Zaire's Mobutu —— Seko
41 Cast of thousands
42 Variety of apple
43 British verb ending
44 Geometric figs.
46 Pipe joint
49 Many a NASA worker: Abbr.
50 Georgia ——
51 Antler holder
55 Lillehammer's land: Abbr.
56 Med. specialty
57 Newswoman Paula
59 Soprano —— Te Kanawa
63 Treat as a villain
64 Political writer Shelby ——
66 Improvise
67 "Nothing —— sleeve"
68 "Platoon" setting
69 Laughfest
70 Big Ten sch.
71 Pull out
76 Toon pics
78 Stay too long at the beach
79 —— Hashana
80 Body of water seen in Munch's "The Scream"
81 Moo —— pork
82 —— Clemente
83 Altogether
85 Swab
86 Abruptly stop
87 "I'm serious!"
91 Supermodel on the cover of Sports Illustrated's 1982 swimsuit issue
94 Name-dropper, perhaps
95 Unit of light
97 Heart of Dixie stream
98 Gray matter?: Abbr.
100 Juicers
101 Author of "The Third Man," 1949
103 Friend of Carlos
105 Pitch
106 Orange ——
108 Child of Asian parents
109 The Last Frontier stream
110 Range maker
111 Alerts, for short
112 Opposite of blew
113 Cousin of a stork
114 Chocolate factory needs
117 Salsa or guacamole

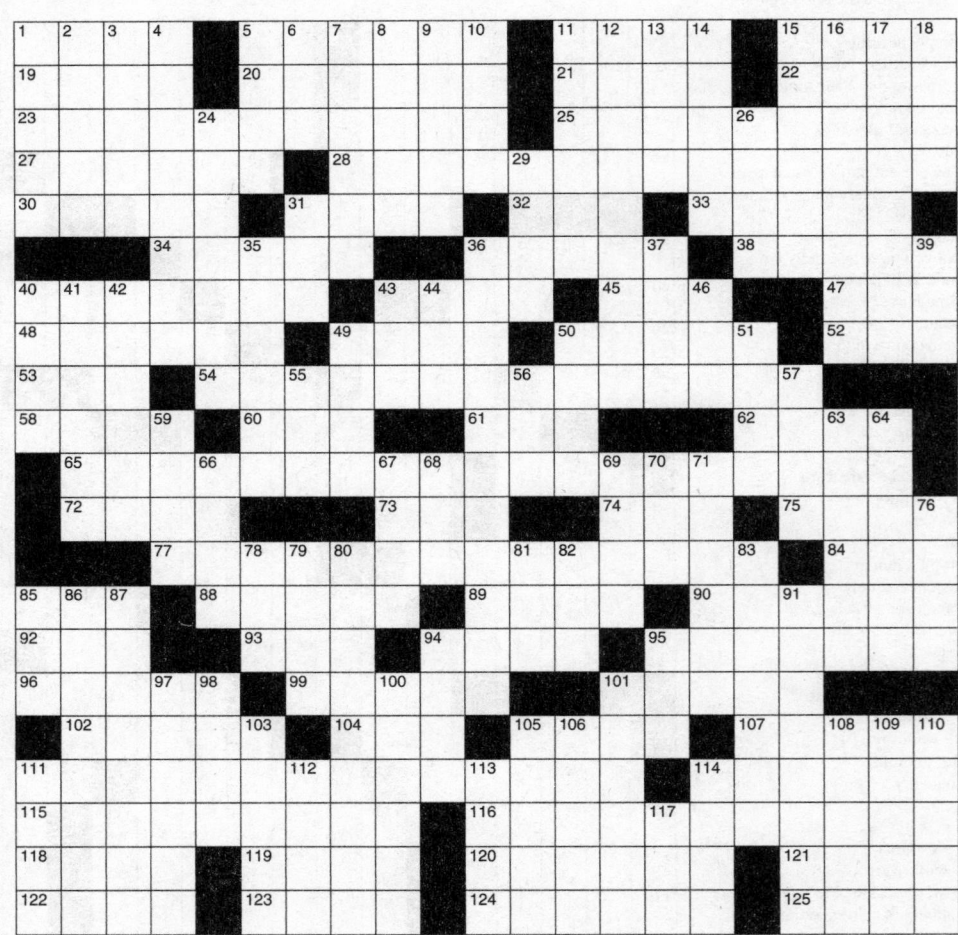

by Elizabeth C. Gorski

ACROSS

1 Drink with a straw
8 Resting places
13 Bit of congratulations
16 Nurse
19 Open-mesh fabric
20 "Day of ___" (what "Dies Irae" means)
21 Oil used in making polyurethane
23 Organization of easily frightened people?
25 Clambake item
26 Chuck
27 Unbending
28 Sensors
30 Heaps
31 Place to buy a hookah
33 Italian eyeglass
34 "The Treachery of Images" artist
38 Go for again
39 They're checked at the door
40 Result of not wearing rouge?
42 Seven ___
43 Psalm, e.g.
46 Right triangle figure
47 Football Hall-of-Famer ___ (Greasy) Neale
48 Part of a dash
49 It goes around at an amusement park
50 Some skirts
52 Cartoon character who amorously chases Penelope
54 Stand-up comedian Caroline
56 Former Israeli president Weizman
57 Jams
59 HBO founder Charles
61 For one
63 Modern prefix with village
64 Blood fluids
66 Wagner's Tannhäuser, e.g.
68 Radio no.
70 Nasty biter
73 Turns the other way
75 Freedom from government control, for short
77 Traveling
81 State
83 Object rising in a Van Gogh landscape
85 Brand of Lego bricks
87 "___ say . . ."
88 Euripides tragedy
90 It may not need clarification
92 Bobby of the Chicago Eight
94 Level
95 Indian honorific
96 Elevator button
97 Strict Jesuit?
99 Neuron's tips?
100 Peru's El ___ volcano
102 Psychiatrist's urging
103 Ben-Hur, for a time
105 Sign up
107 Univ. paper
108 Extraction
110 Houston pro soccer team
112 Made a case
116 "The Break-Up" co-star, 2006
117 Smart fowl?
120 "The Great ___" (Pat Conroy novel)
121 Shoe store purchase
122 Comeback
123 Cold war jet
124 Word before or after old
125 "Nice!"
126 Less sufficient

DOWN

1 Faction
2 Roman emperor with a three-month reign
3 Speech spot
4 Some movie theaters
5 Commercial end for Water
6 Common pizzeria order
7 Lie detector alternative
8 Precious, to a Brit
9 Reach rival
10 Hungarian
11 A/C meas.
12 Start to weep
13 Bundle of pies?
14 Blue chip, maybe
15 Haberdashery purchases
16 "Mr. Cowell, grab that 'American Idol' contestant!"?
17 Lifeless
18 Intrinsically
22 Relatively recent time
24 Achieved in school athletics
29 One cold symptom
30 Place for couples?
32 Procter & Gamble soap
34 13 years before the Battle of Hastings
35 "Biography" channel
36 Banded rock
37 Fisherman's trap
40 Real-estate ad abbr.
41 Capsized, with "over"
44 "While We're Young" songwriter Wilder
45 Last ruler of the Julio-Claudian dynasty
51 Red Sea port
53 Drawn back
55 Fair-sized plot
58 Cornwall carriage
60 "Take your time"
62 Towel stitching
65 Bully turned Samaritan?
67 1932 Democratic campaign plank
69 Market value of a company's assets divided by their replacement cost
70 Video shooters, for short
71 Eye part
72 House Un-American Activities Committee event?
74 Eschewing help
76 Eyed angrily
78 Something bid
79 Bygone explosion, in headlines
80 Wrong
82 Not take out of the company, say
84 Onetime Movietone productions
86 Veterans
89 A defendant may be tried in it
91 Latch
93 Like most sitcoms
98 Some footballers: Abbr.
101 W.W. II nickname
103 Charley horse, e.g.
104 Roofed patio
106 It ends with a baccalauréat
109 Chinese mafia
111 Cartoonist who created the Tammany Hall tiger
112 Drudge
113 For fear that
114 90° from sur
115 Some game
118 Black bird
119 Transcript fig.

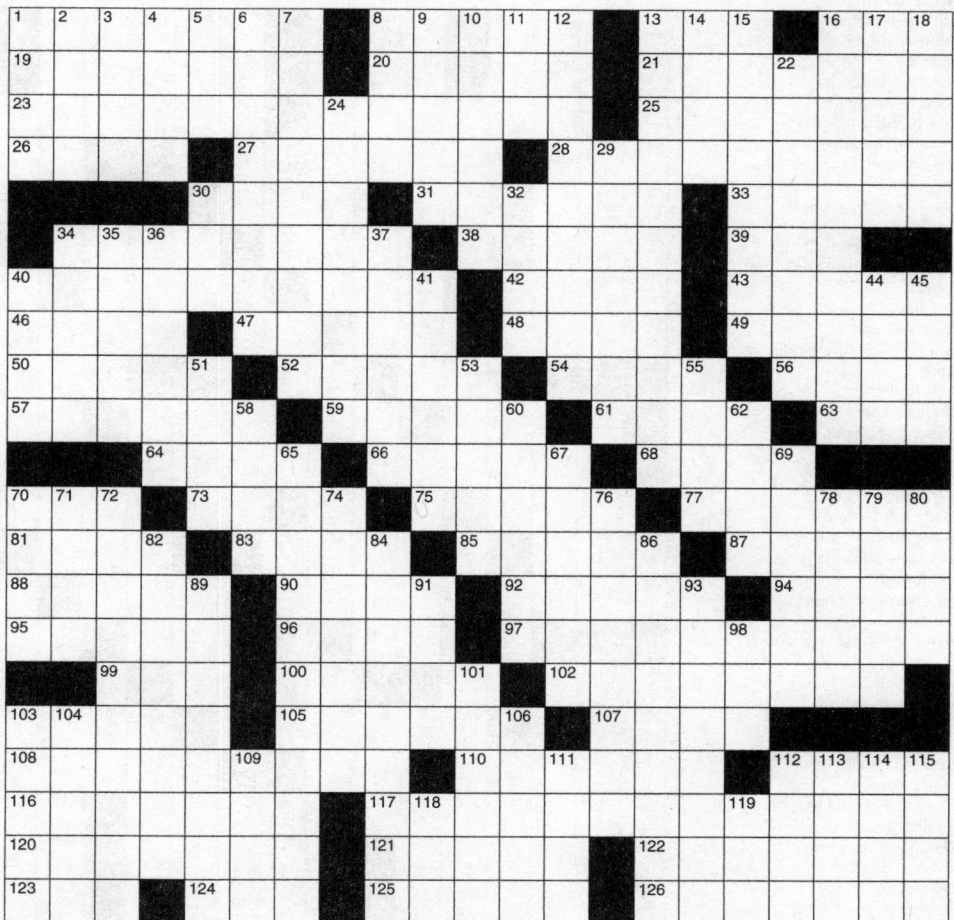

by Brendan Emmett Quigley

ACROSS

1 Pirate spirits
5 Jarhead's rank: Abbr.
8 Author of "Dreams of My Father"
13 Kids may take them to school in boxes
19 Authors' list ender
20 Corn product
21 Japanese apples named for a mountain
22 Like Bollywood films
23 Writer Steel
25 Al's impressions?
27 "What did Bill do to earn this check, anyway?"?
29 Unaided perception
30 Sum in English
31 Protected by law
32 "À la Recherche du Temps Perdu" author
34 1960 Pirates World Series hero, familiarly
35 Vietnam's ___ Dinh Diem
36 First name in beauty products
37 Natural riser
38 Flirt
40 It might make you sick
42 Bit
43 Capital of Lorraine
44 Flavorful seed source
46 Half of an athletic pair
48 Bill's biography?
53 Deutsch article
54 Flair, e.g.
55 Carnatic pieces
56 Sequel's sequel
57 Lonely trucker, perhaps
59 Maestro Toscanini
62 Have a bawl
63 Go postal
64 "And tonight's guest is . . . Ann!"?
68 Old English bard
69 2007 Hall of Fame inductee Ripken
70 Seconded
71 Ages and ages
72 Lou Gehrig's disease: Abbr.
73 Andrea ___
75 "___ time"
76 Ger. neighbor
77 Dance like Rush?
81 Excites
85 "Just ___!"
86 Boring
87 Many a fed. holiday
88 When doubled, a Robin Williams character's catchphrase
89 As a friend, in France
92 Set of Web pages
93 Hawaiian staple vegetables
95 ___-X
96 Chem. unit
97 Rags' opposite
100 Judd of "Numb3rs"
101 Mantel piece
102 Like the era of highest sheet music sales
104 Phoning Phil and hanging up immediately?
106 Don's parting words?
109 Number revealer
110 Disconcert
111 Spinning
112 "Helping doctors help patients" org.
113 Singer Braxton

114 Comes after
115 Laughs heartily
116 Sunday delivery: Abbr.
117 An NCO

DOWN

1 Joe Louis Arena team
2 Tony winner for "Who's Afraid of Virginia Woolf?"
3 Frequent end of an anniversary toast
4 Boo-boo
5 A synthetic
6 Clooney or Rooney
7 Like baseball shoes
8 Iced
9 Power-driven shop tool
10 1977 double-platinum Steely Dan album
11 Clock div.
12 Beginning of a noted political admonition
13 High ___
14 Perturbs
15 Carded
16 The silver screen
17 What Astrophysics and Advanced Calculus probably aren't
18 Reaction to pepper, maybe
24 Overhang

26 Mer filler
28 Snicker syllable
32 Red Rose
33 Triple-header, maybe
37 Magazine exec in a robe, familiarly
39 ___ Lilly
41 Partner of kissed
43 Wee
44 Be a benefactor
45 Ex-Yankee Hideki
47 "The Galloping Gourmet" host Graham
48 Riga resident
49 Roman symbol of power
50 Sheet material
51 Yarn spinners
52 Litter cry
54 Qualifying round, informally
57 Pedicab alternative
58 Back
59 Mushroom with an umbrella cap
60 Wrestler Flair famous for the figure four leglock
61 Where angels come from
63 Hot
65 Word before primaire or secondaire
66 Style with dark clothes and heavy eyeliner
67 Look like a creep?

68 Deplorable
73 Pleasing
74 Hoffman who once backed a pig for president
76 Like human vision
78 Cut-up
79 Hgts.
80 Ajman's home: Abbr.
81 "Tsk!"
82 Arizona state flowers
83 Perfect
84 What the puzzlemaker did to the name in each of this puzzle's theme answers?
87 Position in a rhythm band
89 See 90-Down
90 With 89-Down, historic part of NW Europe
91 Some seal hunters
92 Rabbi's instrument
93 Material for a whitesmith
94 Illustrator Silverstein
98 They may come to une tête
99 A.F.L.'s partner
100 Laughs heartily
103 Set before V
104 Action figure?
105 Some "CSI" figs.
107 Black pride cut, informally
108 PBS supporter

by Ben Tausig

ACROSS

1 Ring regulator: Abbr.
4 State secrets
8 Argosy
14 "The Perfect Fool" composer
19 Cupcake
20 Anise-flavored apéritif popular in Turkey and the Balkans
21 Tan shades
22 Have because of
23 Best Picture of 1954
26 Four-time Indy winner
27 Not turned up
28 Half-Betazoid on "Star Trek: T.N.G."
29 Olympic troublemaker
31 Asian honorific
32 Skin
33 In addition to
37 Boise-to-Billings dir.
38 One whose business is taking off?
40 It's done
41 Burlesques
43 Descry
45 Nursery nappy
47 Doll in "A Doll's House"
48 Biblical name meaning "laughter"
51 "Hollywood Squares" line
53 Six-pointer, perhaps
55 It's spotted on a ranch
58 Swampy
59 High-end version of a product
63 Berenstain of kid-lit's Berenstain Bears
64 L.A. summer setting
65 Took one's first steps
66 Ring Lardner title character
68 "Sweet ___" (1937 Oscar song)
70 Worry
73 "Anne of Green Gables" setting
74 True
76 Looked for
78 First name in chillers
79 Casual denials
80 Singer with the 1996 #1 hit "You're Makin' Me High"
83 Row between houses?
84 Lovers' plight
86 Reign
87 Lose liquidity
88 Topping made with pine nuts
89 It should be even
91 Snap
93 Zigzag
96 French mime
99 Master of the double take?
101 Showy climber
105 Oh of Cologne
106 Role for Alec Guinness and Ewan McGregor
109 Receiver of a brush-off?
110 At birth
111 Transcontinental bridge, e.g.: Abbr.
112 City near Carson National Forest
113 Gut feeling
114 Full speed ahead
116 Broadcast with Baba Booey, with "The"
121 Champagne department
122 French "White House"
123 Jerk
124 Bath suds

125 Starting pay?
126 One on a quest
127 For the second time
128 Key of cartooning

DOWN

1 Cousin of "uh-oh"
2 British hood
3 Buck topper
4 Steep
5 Bar code?
6 Sometimes called
7 Arctic
8 Out of the country
9 Tasteful
10 Salyut 7's successor
11 What "syne" means
12 With Altair and Vega, it forms the Summer Triangle
13 Colt .45s, today
14 Santa's landing site
15 To have and to hold
16 Where to find the Windward and Leeward Islands
17 "A Sentimental Journey" author
18 Disraeli and Churchill
24 Eve's follower
25 Go off
30 One of the Brothers Karamazov
33 Elect
34 Civic center?
35 Voltaire's religious view
36 Heighten
39 Iron pumper's target
42 In film, gradual appearance of an image through an expanding circle
44 Bride in "My Big Fat Greek Wedding"
46 When repeated twice, et cetera
48 Fix firmly
49 Brandy + orange liqueur + lemon juice
50 Fancy salad ingredient
52 Symbols of strength
54 Tuscan treat
56 Sign inside a restaurant
57 Common baseball count
59 Oscar winner as Mr. Chips
60 Copy righter?
61 Annual literary prize since 1946
62 Jazz (up)
65 Salt
67 Physique, slangily
69 Brilliance
71 Boodle
72 Subject of Article I, Section 8 of the Constitution

75 Ample, to Li'l Abner
77 "You're gonna pay!"
81 Moviedom's Massey
82 Back
83 Misses, e.g.
85 Batgirl and Wonder Woman
88 Brit, to an Aussie
90 Soft shots
92 Symbol of strength
94 Neighbor of Greece: Abbr.
95 Kona keepsake
96 Summer topper
97 Block buster?
98 Gives religiously?
100 Tumble
102 Doughboy's topper
103 Oxford pad
104 Stinko
107 Intact
108 Rebuffs
113 Bamboozle
115 Carol ending?
117 Ex follower
118 It's all you have to do sometimes
119 Slice of history
120 Deli slice

by Bob Klahn

ACROSS

1 Award for hanging
7 18th-century Venetian master who painted "Adoration of the Magi"
14 Magnetic induction unit
19 ___ Beach, Calif.
20 How miracle workers walk
21 It may be left holding the bag
22 Up to top physics standards?
24 Flammable gas
25 Time, in Munich
26 Pet lovers' org.
27 Raid target
29 Actress Scala
30 Spinning
32 Recumbent W.W. II general?
37 Punching tool
39 Perry of fashion
40 Zhou ___
41 Substitute (for)
46 First game of a Chinese doubleheader?
50 Inkling
51 Omelette ingredient
53 Yard units
54 Answer, briefly
55 Container for an iron or wedge?
58 Grab
62 Scot's topper
63 Prefix with comic
64 Ludacris's music
66 "Air Music" composer, 1974
68 "I'm not interested in having tea!"?
76 Absolut rival, for short
77 Thing often rolled over, in brief
78 Tiny amounts
80 British rule in India
83 Bureau
86 Where to pick up nuclear supplies?
90 Lago composition
92 Seagoing: Abbr.
94 Small salmon
95 Big rig
96 Crucifix?
101 Like some odes
103 Fabric with a repeated pattern
104 House overhang
106 Green
107 Traveler's aid in South Carolina?
111 Item often cloned
116 With it
117 Burglar's advance man, maybe
118 Goes (for)
120 Bern's river
121 Bakery lures
123 Easily transportable plantation product?
128 Take umbrage at
129 Lawyer, at court
130 Writers Shreve and Brookner
131 "Golden Boy" playwright
132 Wharf locale
133 Schoolyard challenge

DOWN

1 Square
2 Surgical beam producer
3 Texas A&M athlete
4 Nasdaq info
5 Game with Skip and Reverse cards
6 St. Louis's historic ___ Bridge
7 Puccini classic
8 Present at birth
9 Meadow mother
10 Pussy foot
11 Member of the 500-home run club
12 "The Joys of Yiddish" author
13 "Smoking ___?"
14 Call 911, e.g.
15 Sound of satisfaction
16 Facing
17 Seattle cager, for short
18 Word with round or rump
21 Modern music genre
23 Makeup kit item
28 Give two fives for ___
31 "Well, ___-di-dah!"
33 Spa offering, briefly
34 Patron saint of Norway
35 Low cards in pinochle
36 1930s heavyweight champ
38 "Hold on there!"
41 Brief shots?
42 Killed time
43 Prefix with surgery
44 Mountain retreats
45 When repeated, a reproach
47 Eared seal
48 Longoria of "Desperate Housewives"
49 Record letters
52 Fairway cry
56 Baked, in Bologna
57 '60s hot spot
59 Party person
60 William Tell's home
61 Charlemagne's father, dubbed "the Short"
65 Rock and Roll Hall of Fame designer
67 Peak in NE Greece
69 Prince in Ezekiel
70 ___ de France
71 Joe Pesci title role
72 Dada pioneer
73 Figure in a bust
74 Questionnaire category
75 Watts at the movies
79 ___ and Span (cleanser)
80 Coll. dorm figures
81 Questionnaire info
82 Place together
84 Small part
85 Folgers alternative
87 Alley ___
88 Unable to pass the bar?
89 Biography subtitled "Living in the Shadows"
91 Suffix with liquid or fabric
93 "L'Shana ___" (Rosh Hashana greeting)
97 Garage litter
98 Marlins' div.
99 Cong. period
100 Court ruling?
102 It makes MADD mad
105 Not as busy
107 Singer with Xavier Cugat
108 Brought on board
109 A.C.C. team, informally
110 Spaced out
112 It's a dyeing art
113 Photo finish
114 Tourney type
115 Perfume, in a way
119 Con game
122 Ran into
124 Shepherd's locale
125 Child seat?
126 Brouhaha
127 ___ trial basis

by Alan Arbesfeld

ACROSS

1 Immature
8 "___ at Large," 2003 Fox sitcom
13 El ___ (Peruvian volcano)
18 Like Kashmir rugs
20 For all to hear
21 One-dimensional
22 Nebraska town, named after an Indian tribe, featured in "Lonesome Dove"
23 Run away from chewing-tobacco users?
25 Alexander the Great's ambition?
27 Leading the field
28 ___ admin (computer techie, for short)
29 Revolution-era loyalist
30 Black and tan ingredient
31 Mental acuity
34 Glinting flecks in granite
37 Problem for a sweaty-handed Tarzan?
41 Trawler's trailer
42 Much of Anaïs Nin's work
45 Quite often
46 One of the five stages of grief
48 Leaves in hot water
49 ___ de guerre
50 Oil company in a 1999 merger
53 Technique involving thickly applied paint
55 Crumb carrier
56 One who's crazy for a sharp-dressed man?
58 Moved two chessmen in one turn
59 Early collaborator with Eastwood
61 Islamic chieftain
62 Drug ___
64 Bring on board
65 Stole, perhaps
66 Shakespearean prince who's handsome and muscular?
68 Membranous structure
69 Sportswear brand
71 Weekly service
72 Creditor's collection
73 Some hieroglyphic characters
76 At great length
78 Fish-worshiping groups?
81 Insect egg
82 Novelist Jamaica ___
83 You might hear it going up and down
84 Backup singer's syllable
85 Tridactyl bird
86 Scotland's Summer ___
87 Market pessimist
89 Beguiles
91 Powell's "The Thin Man" co-star
92 What a magician might do with a big saw?
98 Theories
99 1978 disco hit
101 Say what isn't so
102 "Good gracious!"
103 Bass part
105 Mr. Bean
107 How to avoid getting tipsy on hard liquor?
113 Designed jeans?
116 Barograph reading
117 DVD box set, possibly
118 "Ready ___ . . ."
119 Flat remover
120 Boxed-off map section

121 Ladies and gentlemen of the jury
122 Producer of the Keystone Cops films

DOWN

1 Part of firefighter attire
2 Ship launched from Iolcus
3 Favoritism
4 Dresses down
5 Tabletop decoration
6 Good news for some prisoners
7 Parade-ground command
8 Thin and crisp
9 Soothes
10 They're not positive
11 Performance that takes a second
12 Some Web site banners
13 Paw
14 Following behind
15 Oil spill?
16 Sealant
17 Schedule-keeping org.
19 Christine of "Chicago Hope"
21 Eton collar material
24 "Man is by nature a ___ animal": Aristotle
26 Long, long time
30 Excitement
32 Show signs of falling
33 Took a big step
34 Bad stuff to microwave
35 One of the Forsytes in "The Forsyte Saga"
36 Macho beer-drinker's outerwear?
37 Seductress
38 Place to hole up
39 Not feeling 100 percent
40 Breaks
43 Gather
44 Sweet talk
47 Lane on Broadway
50 Greek god of ridicule
51 Contemporary of Virgil
52 See 94-Down
54 Do damage to
57 "___ Dance" (David Bowie album)
60 Perceptive person's detection
62 Throw out
63 Pitts of silent film
66 Unable to see much
67 Little green man
68 Figure skater Cohen
69 At a slow pace
70 Popular sleep aid
71 "Excusez-___!"
74 Words mouthed to a camera

75 Leaves gasping
77 Telegraphy signal
78 Short-spoken
79 Take up the entire sofa
80 Nail holder
83 Ginnie ___
88 Iconic Anne Baxter role
90 Gets one's food on a tray, say
93 Fleshy-leaved shrubs
94 With 52-Down, "Symphonie Fantastique" composer
95 Discharges
96 Party to many a civil union
97 Begin using
100 Bandleader Shaw
103 French business partner, maybe
104 "Peer Gynt" playwright
106 What a line of dots may signify
107 Peel
108 Charles Lindbergh's wife
109 Author of "Trinity"
110 Draw in
111 Brisk step
112 Posted
113 ESP, remote viewing, and such
114 Hall-of-Famer Dawson
115 Music genre

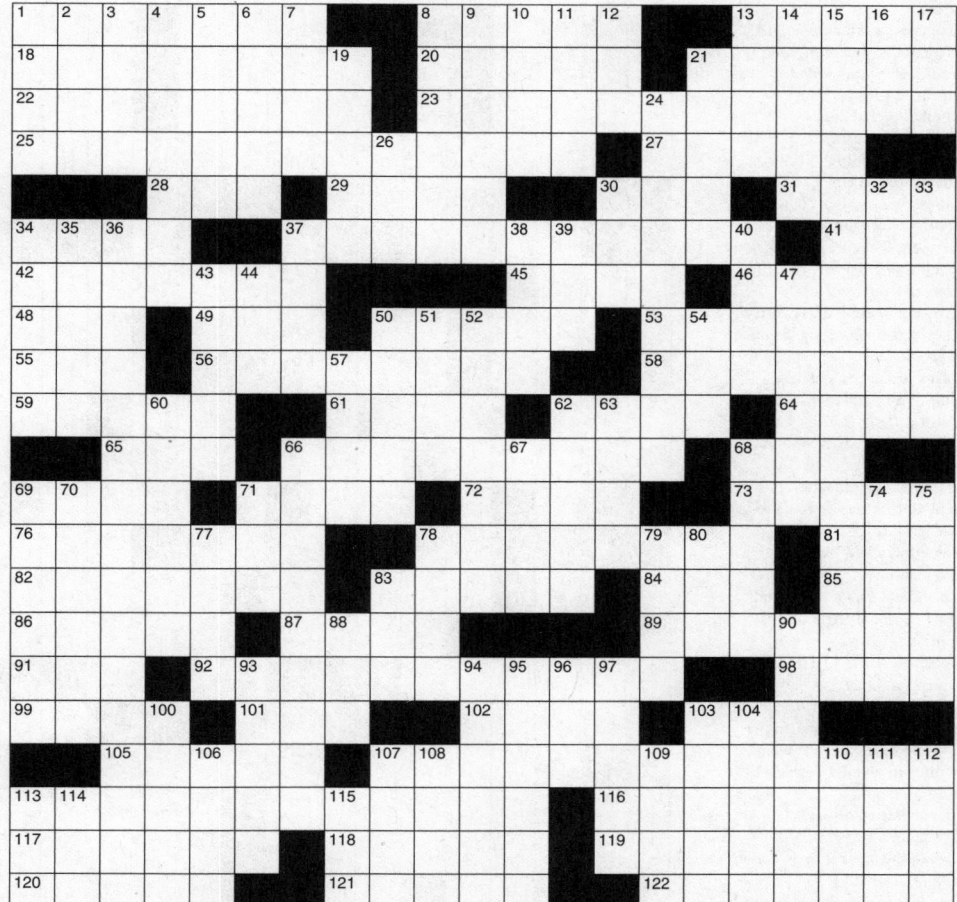

by Patrick Berry

ACROSS

1 Contractors' offerings
5 Rigging technicians
10 Traipse (about)
13 Diamond points
18 Fashion's Tahari
19 Affected
20 Web-based education
22 Between green and black, maybe
23 General assemblies
24 Nonsense about a cocktail?
25 Warning about Mel Gibson on a wrestling surface?
28 Catchy tunes
29 ___ prime
30 Somewhere around
34 Far from perky
35 One who tells it like it isn't
38 Bagel order
39 Skosh
41 Major book about a leader of the lighter industry?
47 Mr. Noodle's friend on "Sesame Street"
48 Ltr. with a period
50 Like most jigsaw puzzles
51 Snow leopard
53 Capital of Honshu
54 French Toaster Sticks maker
55 Work with intaglio
56 Decent
57 Fixes a soundtrack
59 Margaret famous for painting waiflike children with big eyes
62 Japanned metal
63 Climber's challenge
66 Not for the masses
67 Hound, typically?
69 Subject of the film "An Unreasonable Man"
71 Sportscaster Dierdorf
72 He spent 29 years in the Knesset
74 Kind of powder
75 Formerly did
76 Part of making a crossword
78 They travel very long distances
80 X-ray doses
81 Takes too much, quickly
84 Half of an animation duo
85 Verdi's "Don ___"
87 "___ Unleashed!" (cartoon volume)
88 Figure skating maneuver
90 Why horses are attracted to a witch's headgear?
93 Something "realise" lacks
94 Overshadows
96 Chang and Eng's homeland
97 1987 Suzanne Vega hit
99 Join up
100 Berserkly
103 Divers' milieus
106 Why guitar-loving Cooke was blue when his gal named her favorite musical instrument?
112 Witticism about a wrinkly little dog?
115 Flame battler, at times
116 Cover, in a way
117 Part of the answer to 36-Down
118 Tannin source
119 City that lost capital status in 1990
120 Unable to pay the bill
121 1980s video game console, in brief
122 Puzzled (out)
123 ___ Spenlow (Dickens girl)

DOWN

1 Road's shoulder
2 Its first word translates as "wrath"
3 A nitwit liked the loud noise?
4 Apparently do
5 "Eydie Swings the Blues" singer
6 Some tomatoes
7 Find ___ one's heart
8 Gray lines
9 Dominican-born player with more than 600 homers
10 Infection causes
11 Get ___ of
12 Messing of "Will & Grace"
13 Open up, as a topic
14 Whenever
15 "My dear man"
16 Musician Brian
17 Rank below warrant officer: Abbr.
19 Some crosstown trips
21 Word before lock and load
26 Swift's "A Tale of ___"
27 1980s Soviet leader Andropov
31 Count (on)
32 Signed in, say
33 Middle name of "the King"
35 Red-shelled fruit: Var.
36 R.N.'s locale
37 U.S. dance grp.
38 L.A.'s region
39 Having multiple layers
40 German chancellor Merkel
42 "Skedaddle!"
43 Making a curling motion with the forefinger, maybe
44 Frenzied situation
45 Like some jeans
46 To-do pile's place
49 Promote
52 Perfect places
56 Italian saint Philip ___
58 Nut producer
60 In ___ (dazed)
61 Vote in Québec
63 Complicate commercials for woodworking tools?
64 End of a James Bond title
65 Wrote a novel, e.g.
67 Safari spottings
68 Graveyard shift time
70 Aviation-related
73 Doldrums
75 W.W. II American naval cruiser
77 Slangy turndown
79 "Feels good!"
81 Shoppe adjective
82 Temporarily not working
83 Take to the skies
85 William Petersen series
86 "Oh, clever!"
89 Flourish
91 Calls (for)
92 "Symphonie Fantastique" need
95 Show off
98 Feature of some locks
100 Clinton's first defense secretary
101 "___ is just pink trying to be purple": Whistler
102 Exeunt ___ (stage direction)
103 Beurre blanc, e.g.
104 Rider of the steed Babieca
105 Coupon user
107 Two-out actions: Abbr.
108 Plebe's place: Abbr.
109 Home to the Dr Pepper Museum
110 Velcro alternative
111 Her sidekick was Gabrielle
112 Greek consonants
113 New England sch.
114 New Pontiac of 1964

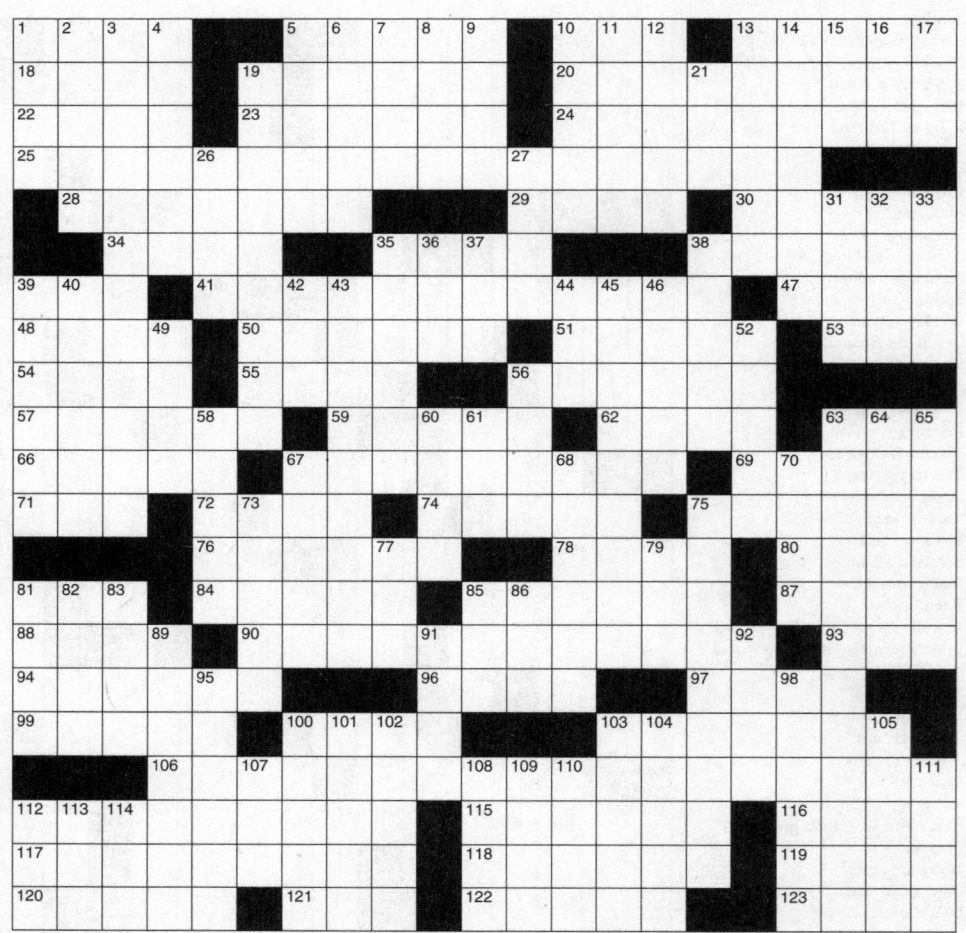

by Trip Payne

ACROSS

1 Marx's collaborator on "The Communist Manifesto"
7 It's beyond repair
16 Abbr. on a food package
20 Await
21 So that one might
22 Fort ___, captured by U.S. forces in 1814
23 Ford purchased online?
25 It's measured in degrees
26 Generic comic strip diner
27 Word with night or right
28 Quick outing on the links
29 Consumes
30 Carrier to Tokyo
31 French spread
33 It's needed to find the right key
36 Like some diets
38 Honda owned by one of the Simpsons?
42 Errs
44 ___ Bien Phu, Vietnam
45 Group of the same race or culture
47 Parts of the lunar landscape
49 Wool source
52 Bump
53 Major oil source
56 Michelin Guide listing
57 "Avast!"
58 City dweller's Acura?
60 Fast www hookup
61 Bring in
62 Kind of kick
63 Lolling
65 Old Jewish villages
67 Standard
70 Home pregnancy checker, e.g.
73 Camera components
75 Bet
77 It's set partly at the Temple of Vulcan
78 When doubled, a much-married celebrity
80 Genuine Isuzu?
83 Like a pop fly
84 Not feel oneself
85 Uncut
86 Made (off)
87 Tots' wheels
88 ___-Roman
90 Traduce
92 Not safe to skate on, say
93 Go downhill fast
96 Tiny Volkswagen?
101 Hanukkah treats
103 Board honcho
104 Wall St. debuts
105 Ore. neighbor
106 Sleep ___
108 O.T. book
110 Broadway's Hagen
111 S. Amer. land
112 All ears
113 One of the first Buicks to roll off the line?
119 Religious statue locale
120 1983 Stephen King thriller
121 Bad way to be caught
122 What a rake may do
123 Party throwers
124 Took home

DOWN

1 He ascended to heaven in a whirlwind, in II Kings
2 Emphatic refusal
3 Stadium cheer
4 Makes (out)
5 Photocopier tray size: Abbr.
6 ___ of God
7 Like nobles
8 Scott Turow's first book
9 Study of poisons: Abbr.
10 Dadaist Jean
11 "Bad" cholesterol, initially
12 Nuevo ___, Mexican state bordering Texas
13 Sen. Hatch
14 They listen to dictators
15 Most upset
16 Space clouds
17 Reliable Suzuki?
18 Booby trap component
19 Second place from the right
24 Big name in stationery
31 Compare the costs of
32 Steaming along, maybe
33 Paved road: Sp.
34 Burning issue?
35 Kidney-related
37 Admirals' commands
39 Emmy winner for "Roots"
40 Size approximation
41 Time long past
43 Without
46 Overdrawn account?
48 Weekly 90-min. show
49 Nails
50 Rachel's older sister
51 Half-assembled Mitsubishi?
52 III preceders: Abbr.
54 Improve
55 "___ to Wake Up," 2006 Oscar-winning song by Melissa Etheridge
58 Oust
59 Prefix with science
62 Either sister starring in 2004's "New York Minute"
64 Kind of contest
66 Exhaust
68 Genoa's Palazzo San ___
69 Sevilla's home
71 What Descartes thought of?
72 Squirts
74 Meager
76 Understanding
78 Turn back
79 Dear ___
81 Cable carrier?
82 Thing of the past
83 Old Dodge
87 Poetic preposition
89 Teeth do it
91 Suffix with serpent
92 Rapper ___ Shakur
94 Rendering, say
95 Question following "Oh, yeah?!"
97 Service charges?
98 Cabalistic
99 Performance artist Anderson
100 Skinned
102 They may have a ball
106 Voiced
107 Pick-up spot?
109 Furrow
110 ___ Reader
111 Ministre d'___
114 Lao-___
115 "___ magic!"
116 Winter autobahn hazard
117 Hamburger's one
118 Wichita-to-Omaha dir.

by Seth A. Abel

ACROSS

1 Feed for cattle and horses
8 River or city of Maine
12 E-5 in the U.S.A.F.
16 Fourth steps
19 Bashes
20 Control ___ (four-wheel-drive system)
21 Vessel lost at Pearl Harbor
22 Piz Bernina or Eiger
23 Yuletide celebration
25 Unwavering
27 Decadent
28 Clearing
30 Hindu queen
31 Not fair at all
32 Bingo call
33 Rock group with the 12-time platinum album "Hysteria"
35 Some martyrs: Abbr.
36 Gorge
37 Swiss ___
38 Music center?
39 Weena's fictional race
40 Marc Antony's love
42 Rolodex abbr.
44 Like Narcissus?
50 Popular Hispanic newspaper name
53 Reposeful
54 Longtime soap actress Jones
55 "Prince ___" ("Aladdin" song)
56 Play analyzer
58 Year England captured Normandy at the Battle of Tinchebray
59 Kind of sweater
61 Fully functional
62 Actor Kilmer
63 Last time?
66 1964 Beatles #1 hit
68 Museum hanging
69 Employee's move, for short
70 Words from a promising individual?
73 Ye follower
74 Samoa-to-Hawaii dir.
75 Spitchcock
76 Starters
77 "Bald" baby
79 Hail
81 Classic outdoor winter toys
84 Uganda's ___ Amin
85 "Climb ___ Mountain"
86 One who's gone but not forgotten
87 Mag magnate
89 ___-plié (ballet move)
91 Personnel person
93 "___ homo" (declaration in John 19:5)
97 Bond's man?
100 Ltr. carriers
101 Quasar co-discoverer Sandage
102 Pope of 452 who met with Attila
103 Red-eye cause
105 Burning
106 Adam Sandler's "Spanglish" co-star
108 Precious cargo of legend
110 Mythical beast
111 Seussian villagers
112 1988 Cy Young winner Hershiser
113 Laundry worker
114 Verb follower?
115 Kind
116 Ophthalmologist's concern
117 Rolls

DOWN

1 Sources of fall color
2 Light, in a way
3 Repetitive exclamation from Shakespeare
4 Sen. Specter and others
5 "Waiting for ___" (Odets play)
6 Bash
7 Certain flake
8 Mushroom stems
9 Silver-colored
10 Songwriter Sammy
11 Santa's reindeer, traditionally
12 Never-failing
13 Rickey Henderson record-breaking stat
14 Beetle juice?
15 Edward O. ___, card-counting author of "Beat the Dealer"
16 Zoological studies
17 Edits
18 Words per minute, e.g.
24 Manx trait
26 Pin spots
29 Eliminate
32 "___ good cheer"
34 Actress Getty
36 Bolt
39 Stumbling sounds
40 13, for Al
41 Air
43 Senior Saarinen
44 Biblical strongman
45 Dropping acid, say
46 Evening person?
47 Go kaput
48 First name in court fiction
49 Hanna-Barbera collectible
51 Redenbacher of popcorn fame
52 Hero's hero
55 Genesis shepherd
57 Forces in the water
59 Grouch
60 Craft often shown landing on three legs
61 Old sports org.
64 Let out
65 Current with the wind
66 Metric foot
67 Geezer
70 Anatomical duct
71 Voluptuous
72 Osaka O.K.
76 Ailey and Toffler
77 ___ effort
78 ___ clear
80 Towering figure in French engineering
81 Carrie Chapman Catt, for one
82 Little wrigglers
83 Baa maids?
87 He-Man Woman-___ Club ("Little Rascals" group)
88 Link, as fingers of the hands
90 Key of Dvořák's "New World" Symphony
91 "Crimes of the Heart" playwright Beth
92 Out of gear
93 Firstborn
94 John of "Rat Race"
95 Constellation between Lynx and Hydra
96 Starts to make a scene?
97 "Life ___ short . . ."
98 Brand under AMC Theatres
99 "We Got the Beat" group
101 "The Night Cafe" was painted there
104 Comic Sahl
105 Frizzy coif
107 "Well, what have we here?!"
109 Big inits. in news

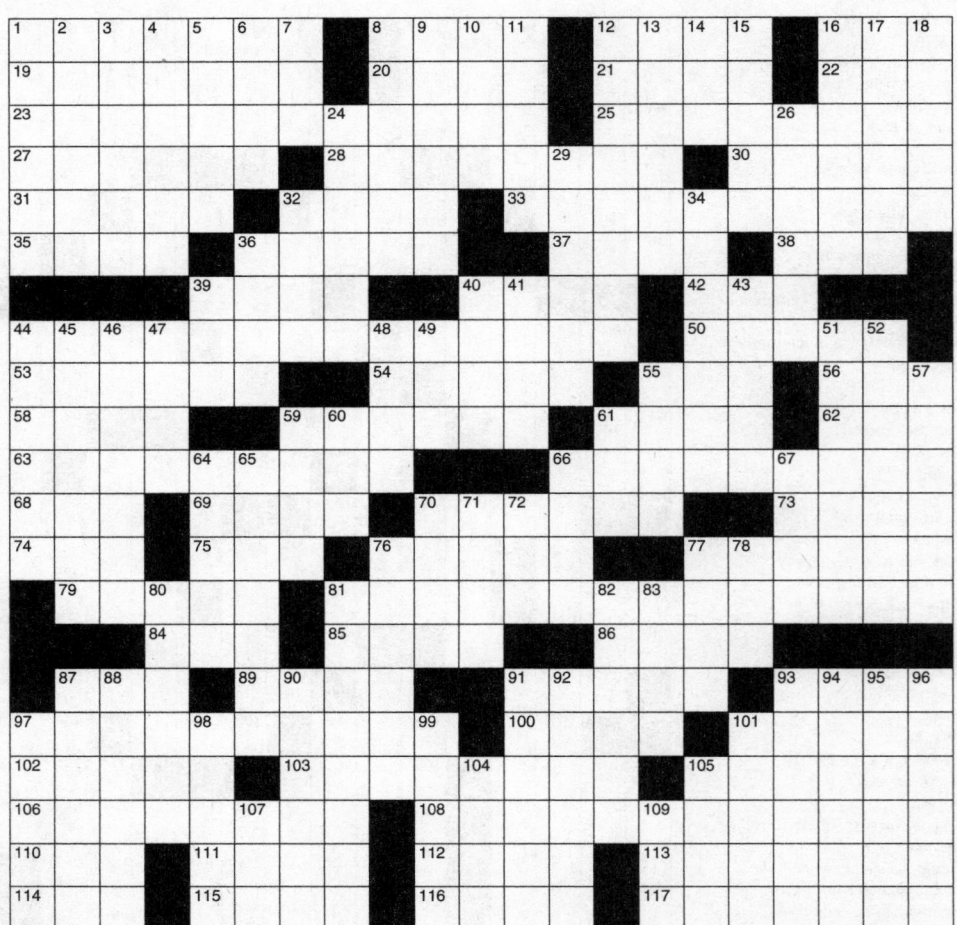

by Patrick Blindauer

ACROSS

1 Current
7 One making a delivery
10 "___ fan tutte"
14 Get set
18 Fished with a baited line
20 Garden figure
21 "Too bad"
22 Cookie introduced in 1912
23 Movie critic Kael
24 Prison movie about a medical miracle?
27 Wine made from the moscato bianco grape
28 O.K.: Var.
30 Global warming?
31 Tim Allen comedy about unionizing seasonal workers?
34 Loser's cry
35 "Born Under ___ Sign" (1960s blues album)
36 Monkey business
38 I.S.P. of note
41 In addition
44 With 95-Down, investigate
45 Court pseudonym
46 Pay to play
47 Home of golf's Sony Open
48 Turn over
50 Prequel to "Reservoir Dogs?"
53 Onetime host of "Classic Concentration"
55 Home of Chennai
58 Airports
59 Judicial cover-ups?
60 "Answer the question"
62 Tuscany city
63 Request to Vanna White
64 Ingmar Bergman classic narrated by Jacques Cousteau?
67 Brick holder
70 Scintilla
72 "Out of Africa" author
73 With 69-Down, not just hard of hearing
75 Positive potential
77 Meal with bitter herbs
78 Cloud of gas and dust
79 Chaplin comedy about a religious migration?
83 Attend
85 On and after
86 Funny Louis and others
87 Conductor ___-Pekka Salonen
88 Game resembling crazy eights
90 Like the letters on a dreidel
92 Kreskin claim
93 Joan Baez's "Farewell, ___," written by Bob Dylan
96 "___ and Janis" (comic strip)
97 Part of the Old World
98 Chiller about glass-climbing reptiles?
104 Stamp
107 Private telephone channel
108 "It's ___" (Pet Shop Boys hit)
109 Tom Cruise action thriller about a nasty argument?
112 Embellishment
114 Thingum
115 Jealous Olympian
116 Skull and Bones member, e.g.
117 One heading down a slippery slope
118 Sonoma neighbor
119 Oaxaca women: Abbr.
120 Red ___ #2
121 Hens, but not roosters

DOWN

1 Parade honoree, for short
2 Refuse
3 Way to go
4 Jazz guitar great Herb ___
5 Laila who dances in and out of the ring
6 Sci-fi movie about gender discrimination?
7 French red
8 Had thirds, maybe
9 Meter or liter
10 Pic taker
11 Suffix with pay
12 Nautical danger
13 "Honest!"
14 Good ones are cracked
15 Home of 1-Down
16 Advanced
17 Expensive box
19 Toothed, botanically
25 1950s TV name
26 Part of D.A.: Abbr.
29 Pops
32 "Delightful!"
33 Creamy color
37 Keystone ___
38 Spoof about the soul of a fraternity?
39 Midwest native
40 Magnifier
41 Singer ___ Neville
42 Bogart/Bacall mystery about serious basement dampness?
43 London Underground, with "the"
44 Intuited
46 Loads
47 Other: Sp.
49 Medieval hymn start
50 Awarded zero stars, say
51 Romeo's last words
52 Goalie's area
54 Chihuahua, por ejemplo
56 Not wanting to fight, say
57 Sister of Queen Beatrix of the Netherlands
60 Itch
61 County of Cooperstown, N.Y.
62 ID theft target
65 Hotfooted it
66 "My ___!"
68 Turned down, in a way
69 See 73-Across
71 Fixes
74 Winter lift?
75 ___ Reader
76 M.D.
78 Lois Lane player of early TV, whose first name is a hint to this puzzle's theme
80 Assemble again
81 Operate
82 Pizzeria in Spike Lee's "Do the Right Thing"
84 Assemblages
88 Not shown
89 With nothing to hide
91 Vampy wear
93 "Like, no way!"
94 Odd shares
95 See 44-Across
96 "Just ___ thought!"
97 Kitchen attraction
99 Pitcher of milk?
100 ___ wagon
101 In reserve
102 Cowboy rival
103 Many Rice grads: Abbr.
104 Victor's cry
105 ___ Hari
106 Get set
110 Disco ___
111 Had a life
113 Clover locale

by David J. Kahn and Steve Kahn

ACROSS

1 Literary slips
7 Lost
14 Grade school administration, maybe
20 Joint
21 Former Acura model
22 Fashion's Bartley
23 Start of a holiday verse
26 Locks
27 10%
28 "___ Gold" (1997 film)
29 Suffix with respond
30 Way overdue to take off?
32 Former Japanese P.M. Shinzo ___
34 "Being and Nothingness" writer
38 About
39 Area for a reupholsterer
43 Comment made with a nod
44 "___ alternative . . ."
45 "Pay ___ mind"
46 Insect repellent
48 Verse, part 2
54 Author Deighton
55 ___ the mistletoe
56 Audibly
57 Expiate, with "for"
58 Nicholas and others: Abbr.
59 Ticks off
60 Church part
61 Intrinsically
62 AAA recommendations: Abbr.
63 Sandwich shop orders
64 Lumber
66 "The Sandbox" playwright
69 "What to do? What to do?" feeling
70 Brown
71 Young amphibian
74 Flora and fauna
75 Some sorority sisters
76 Implied
77 Christmas ___
78 Verse, part 3
82 Archer William
83 Fannie ___ (investing options)
84 Theodemocratic state
85 Up ___ good
86 Porters
88 Popular cuisine
90 Unemotional type, slangily
92 Certain soldier
93 "Little Miss Sunshine" co-star
94 Mentalist Geller
95 Dangerous seepage
99 Decorative gateway in Japan
101 Classic role played by Gérard Depardieu in "The Man in the Iron Mask"
106 End of the verse
111 Jack of "The Apartment"
112 Fruitcake and plum pudding, e.g.
113 Tickles
114 Source of "we three kings"
115 Puts a new bottom on
116 Blocks

DOWN

1 Once, old-style
2 Where the bag of gifts is stowed on a sleigh
3 Auberjonois of "The Christmas Star"
4 Times in classifieds
5 Promo, perhaps
6 Fictional detective Lupin
7 "Mamma ___!"
8 Home of Christmas Lake Village: Abbr.
9 RR stop
10 Of fast times?
11 Discriminating sort, in a way
12 Heated
13 Word repeated in "Now ___ away! ___ away! ___ away . . . !"
14 French pronoun
15 Line former
16 Green-blue
17 "Anything ___?"
18 Blue-black berrylike fruit
19 Whips
24 F.D.R.'s successor
25 Longed (for)
30 Studio sign
31 Uncle ___
33 Univ. QB, perhaps
34 Grammy and Emmy-winning soprano
35 Until now
36 Straps in a sleigh
37 Number of lords a-leaping
38 Grate-ful?
39 Based on ___ story
40 Made a long story short?
41 Title in Toledo
42 Difficult period
44 Big range
45 Stravinsky and others
47 Christmas ___
49 Garfield's assassin
50 Memo starter
51 Initiation rite
52 Kind of artery
53 French-named city on Galveston Bay
60 Mideast desert
62 Like the Christmas story, often
63 What snow shovels may produce
64 Christmas cookie ingredient
65 Cub's place
66 Some
67 Career soldier
68 Peter of "Everybody Loves Raymond"
69 Elbows
70 It's a wrap
71 ___ salts
72 Singer Apple
73 Joint part
75 Will likely
76 "Born ___"
79 "Walk Like ___"
80 Part of Captain Cook's explorations
81 Had
87 Rafting area
88 Big pickle?
89 Out-elbowed?
90 Pressed
91 Group
93 Take for ___
94 News source, for short
95 Move, in Realtor-speak
96 Swear
97 Moore of "G.I. Jane"
98 "Coffee, Tea ___?"
100 Court hearing
102 "Take ___!"
103 Author Shere
104 Lulu
105 Lip
107 Big bang maker
108 Word left off the end of the clue at 13-Down
109 Poor grade
110 Satisfactory grade, in kindergarten

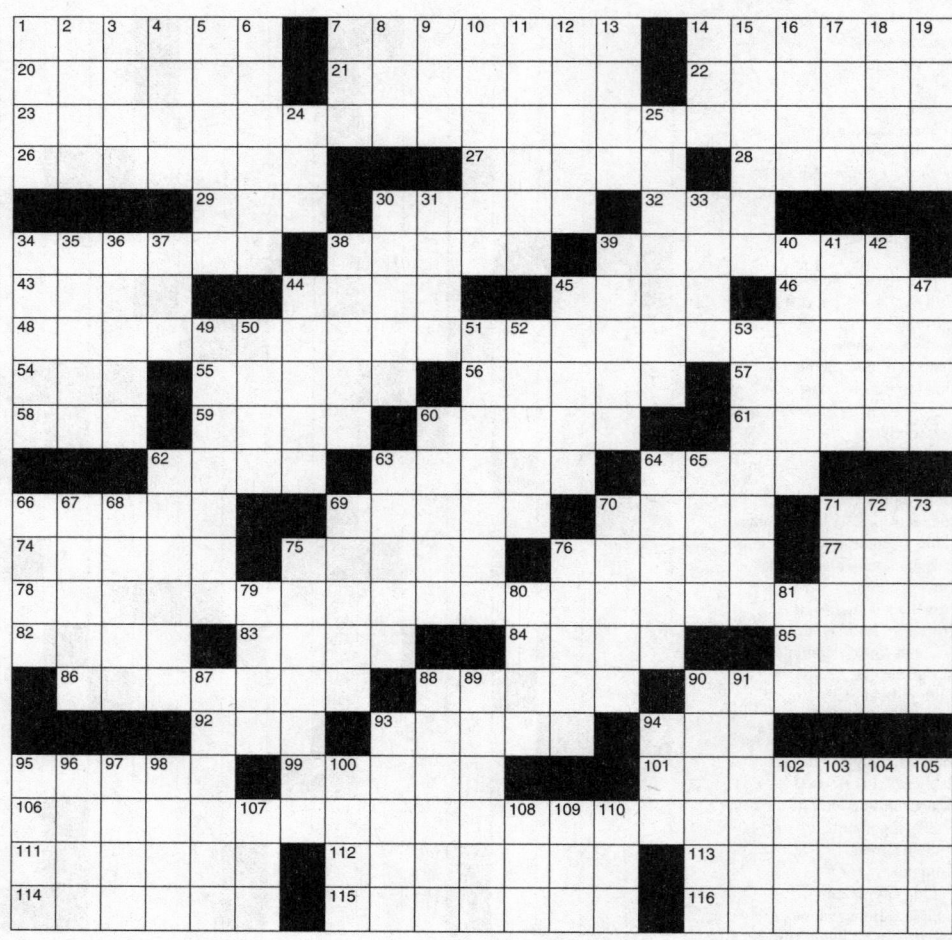

by Adam G. Perl

Note: The 16 circled letters, starting in square #34 and proceeding roughly counterclockwise, ending at #38, will spell the opening lyric of a popular song.

ACROSS

1 Land of 300+ islands
5 Not straight
10 Words: Abbr.
15 Eclipse feature
19 Borodin's "Prince ___"
20 N.F.L. team for which Barry Sanders played
21 "Dancing With the Stars" winner ___ Ohno
22 Shortly
23 Wright wings
24 Playwright Fugard
25 Not familiar with
26 Nuptial exchange
27 Shed some light on?
29 Deli offering
31 Artificial heat?
32 Pull
40 Like some folders
41 Cadaverous
42 Class in factories
44 Oil by the barrel
45 Photographer Adams
47 Avalons, e.g.
48 Have ___ (be innocent, maybe)
50 Date with a Dr.
52 No fancy threads
54 Piece of soap
56 Poker great Ungar and others
59 Breaches
60 Gets a move on
63 Rain forests and grasslands, e.g.
65 R.N.'s locale
66 Ice cream maker Joseph
67 Clarinetist's purchase
68 Scatter
70 Smidgen
72 Cultural funding org.
73 "___ big deal!"
75. 13
78 Dec. holiday plans?
80 Pump room?
82 Five-min. periods, maybe
83 A wee hour
85 Without slack
86 "Jurassic Park" actress
88 Advantages
90 Lord's worker
91 Part of R.S.V.P.
92 Cen. parts
94 Yule ___
95 No longer working: Abbr.
96 Bourg's department
97 Before, in verse
98 Ginger treats
100 Cole Porter's "You Don't Know ___"
102 Hitches
104 Fraternity letters
107 Provider of an old silk hat, e.g. (as depicted at the top of this puzzle)
110 Rugged wheels, briefly
114 Lyric, part 5
119 Rustic setting
120 Ear-relevant
121 State one's views
122 J.F.K. alternative
123 "The Oath" author Frank
125 Horizontal molding pieces
131 Wolves
133 Mountain ridge
134 Lyric, part 3, after "With a"
137 Contents of some scrolls
138 Kind of track
140 Wound (up)
141 Herbal tea
142 Loses ground?
143 Crawl (with)
144 Lord's worker
145 New Year's Eve parties, e.g.
146 Wood measure
147 ___ Accords
148 News agency started in 1925
149 "Endymion" poet

DOWN

1 Holiday party
2 Homes that may have tunnel entrances
3 Lyric, part 2, after "Was a"
4 Cheater hunters, maybe
5 French chef Ducasse
6 Luxuriousness
7 One who can't have everything?
8 Rocker Brian
9 Certain computer connection, briefly
10 Sliding door place
11 "Set ___ the doors, O soul!": Whitman
12 Forage plant
13 Sask. neighbor
14 Leg up
15 Snarl unsnarler
16 Lyric, part 4
17 Arose
18 Kind of kick
28 Giant successes?
30 Shell food?
33 "I beg to differ!"
34 "Kiss my grits" lady
35 Writer Willy who popularized spaceflight
36 ___-Aztecan language
37 "Have some!"
38 Second Amendment advocacy grp.
39 "The ___ Kid"
42 Part of many a test
43 "Here!"
46 Highlands tongue
49 Cardinal's home
50 Favorers of the young
51 Dish with stir-fried rice noodles
53 "Passion" director
55 French treaty city of 1802
57 Accord of 1985?
58 What icicles do
61 Literary inits.
62 Bully
63 It may be fit for a king
64 1945 battle site, for short
67 Long Island Rail Road station
69 Alphabet trio
71 Esoteric
74 End up with
76 Fall (over)
77 "The ___ Cat" (Tom and Jerry short)
79 Pacino and others
81 Banks on a runway
84 Horace contemporary
87 Bobstays, e.g.
89 Kyle ___, "The Terminator" hero
93 Globular
96 When the show must go on
98 Grounded flier
99 "Don't ___ word!"
101 Dietary abbr.
102 Start another tour
103 Animal pouch
104 Feel one's way around?
105 High-hats
106 Timid words
108 Places for tolls
109 1986 Gene Hackman film
111 Not narrow
112 Tramps
113 ½ and ⅓ parts
115 Sprinkler
116 Heavily sedated
117 ___ trial basis
118 Holidayish
124 "Revolutionary" piece by Chopin
126 Harpist, of sorts
127 Nobody
128 Visitor's sleeping spot, maybe
129 "So ___ be on my way/In the early mornin' rain" (Gordon Lightfoot lyric)
130 Sleep problem
132 Old Testament prophet
135 Dr. Octavius, Spider-Man foe
136 Some E-mail attachments
139 Legal conclusion?
141 Shatner's "___ War"

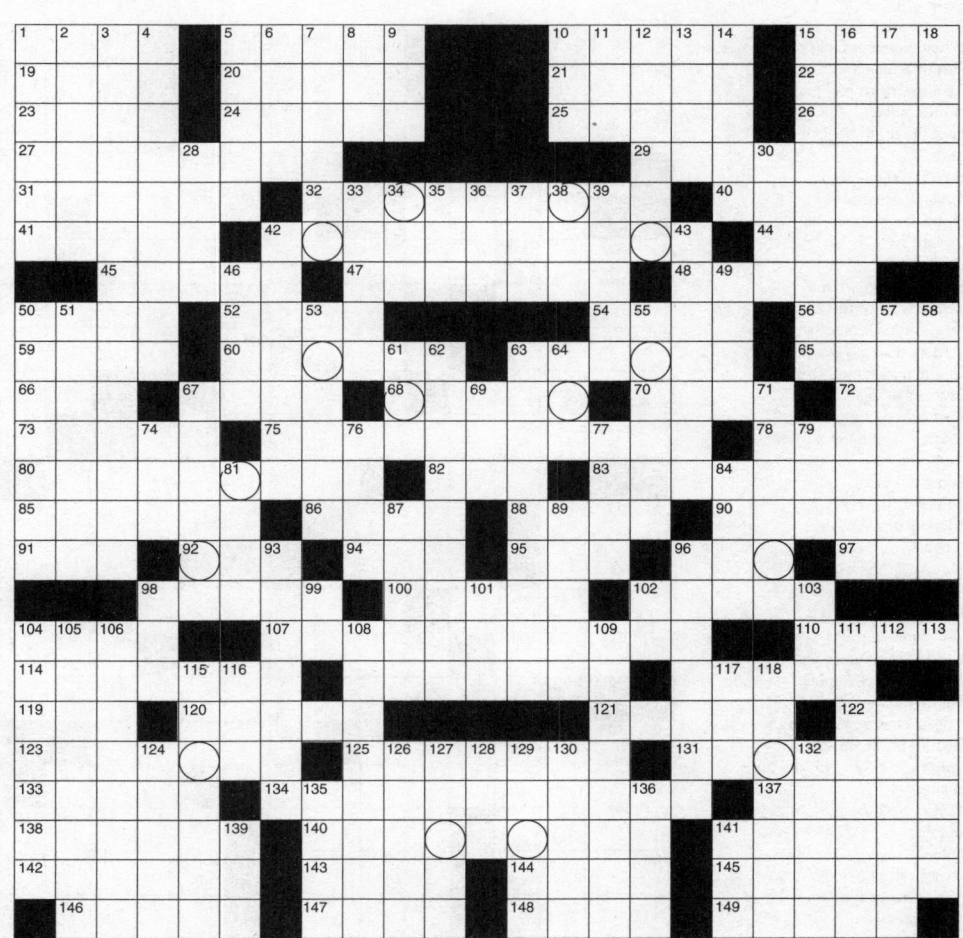

by Elizabeth C. Gorski

ACROSS

1 Kind of court
6 Decorative inlay material
11 Screening
15 Took off
19 Shooter's target
20 Facility
21 What pi may be used to find
22 Much family history, e.g.
23 *Feature of some kids' cereals
25 Shelter supplies
26 Feeling
27 Rita Hayworth title role of 1946
28 Monarch's bane
29 *Regular provider
31 Bollix up
32 Interior look
34 Aniselike herbs
35 "___ dreaming?"
37 *Holder of the world record for the longest ovation on the operatic stage (80 minutes)
41 W.W. II noncombatants
43 Spirit
44 Eremites
45 "The Guns of August" figure
49 Weekend warrior's woe
50 Grauman of Grauman's Chinese Theater
51 Swift gift
52 Reagan attorney general
53 Where you can feel the heat
55 Part of a tennis racket
57 Accusatory words
59 H look-alike
60 *Let the mind believe what it likes
64 Parter of the waters
65 Soyuz destination
66 Governessy
67 Covers up
70 Behind
72 Room sharer, often
74 Group west of the Atlantic: Abbr.
76 *Bastion of brotherhood
80 Uniters with 51-Down
81 Hug and kiss, to a Brit
83 Cracker topper
84 Bird baked in a pie
85 1920s anarchist in a celebrated trial
87 Some cottons
91 Tennis's Shriver
93 Kierkegaard's "The Sickness ___ Death"
94 "My Way" lyricist
95 Mexican revolutionary ___ Hidalgo
96 Brush makeup
97 Earth Day subj.
98 *Elementary school test package
102 Slice of history
103 Approaches aggressively
106 Portrait photographer Arbus
107 Ralph ___, 1974 N.L. batting champ
109 *Dress for the return of cool weather
111 Indeed
113 Overdo it, in a way
115 Requirement for some degree candidates
116 ___ avis
117 *Not even close
120 Dungeons & Dragons figure
121 List ender
122 Ones being shot at
123 Heinrich who wrote "Atta Troll"
124 Moneybags in "The Wind in the Willows"
125 Comfy retreats
126 Unpadded
127 Synthetic fabric

DOWN

1 Grp. influential in campaigns
2 Wide-eyed
3 *Alaskan cruise sighting
4 Midway, e.g.
5 Preliminary events
6 Cowboys' org.
7 Bean who was the fourth man to walk on the moon
8 Gave up at last
9 Ran amok
10 Add instead of subtract, e.g.
11 Some tubes
12 Lover boy?
13 Lights
14 Speeds up
15 It's sour
16 Disney duck
17 Documentary filmmaker Morris
18 Gets off the bottle
24 Title on a child's bookshelf
29 Object of a vain wait
30 Lee who directed "Brokeback Mountain"
33 Pay increase to keep up with inflation, in brief
35 Up to one's ears
36 Former Portuguese colony in China
38 Put right
39 Core groups
40 Piddling
42 Title with a tilde
46 *Wasn't clear, as one's future
47 Where Monferrato wine comes from
48 Behind
51 Uniters with 80-Across
52 Finds at Pompeii
54 Songlike
56 Suffix with sheep or goat
58 Soapstone, e.g.
61 Mideast's Gulf of ___
62 Mauna ___
63 Firecracker parts
68 Cabinet inits. since 1947
69 Show annoyance with
71 Chef's hat
72 Sportsman of the Year co-winner of 1998
73 ___ the Great
75 Like some electronics
77 Politician's projection
78 Seminole's archrival
79 Virulent virus
82 1945 Colette novel
86 Spread some holiday joy
88 Quaint garden fixtures
89 O.K.
90 Where Napoleon planned his Hundred Days campaign
92 Welds
95 Reached the due date
96 Helmsman
99 That: Sp.
100 "Do I have a volunteer?"
101 Company whose production goes in cycles?
103 Going on
104 Load of ships?
105 Santa ___, Calif.
108 Rodeo competitor
110 "The Nanny" actress Drescher
112 Poor returns?
114 Island-dotted lake of Northern Ireland
117 Not fair
118 Food additive
119 ___ Aviv

by Lynn Lempel

ACROSS

1 "Come on . . . be good, kids"
7 Kind of jacket
11 Actor Gulager
14 Occurs to, with "on"
19 Emulate Earhart
20 Bean town?
21 Alley ___
22 Traditional whale hunter
23 Like some titmice
24 Went too far
26 Pretty cool
27 Mark who won the Masters and British Open in 1998
28 The old frontier you and I don't remember?
30 Is covered in dew, perhaps
32 Mahmoud Ahmadinejad, e.g.
33 Longtime Bob Hope broadcaster
35 ___ d'amore
37 Like some traffic
38 Donkey Kong, for one
39 Place to gamble in N.Y.C.
41 Job ad abbr.
43 Center of success?
44 Rap's Dr.
45 Climate that's copy-protected by law?
49 Ralph Nader and Ross Perot
52 Brought on
53 Sound from a fan
54 ___ Tunes
55 U.K. record label
57 Richness
60 Like some grasses
61 Porridge ingredients
63 Scratches (out)
64 Took too many pills, briefly
65 Merlin on an Imax screen?
67 Fall mos.
71 Currency whose symbol is "$"
72 Like Java man
73 Lose one's marbles
78 What to follow in the forest
80 Stat for Warren Spahn: Abbr.
81 Pull out formally
82 F.B.I. director appointed by Clinton
83 Jimmy of DC Comics
87 Bond poster
89 Eyelid moistener at a museum?
93 Some colas, familiarly
94 Small wts.
95 "Well, ___-di-dah!"
96 Asian school of thought
97 U.S.O. show attendees
98 Cuddly sci-fi critter
100 Algonquian tongue
101 Court call
103 Twangy
105 Mover left or right
107 Rouse a beloved English queen?
110 Nocturnal insect
113 Buggy drivers
115 In the world
116 National airline of Afghanistan
117 Coca-Cola trademark
118 Singer Des' ___
119 10-year host of "Entertainment Tonight"
120 Boasts of
121 Seventh-grader, often
122 Many, many mos.
123 Pamplona shouts
124 Tangle up (in)

DOWN

1 Group with a secy. gen.
2 Certain gamete
3 Better half takes the stage?
4 Christmas on Capri
5 "S.N.L." alum Cheri
6 Married in error?
7 Scent maker
8 Add pep to
9 "What ___!" ("This place needs cleaning!")
10 Go-___
11 Able to be followed
12 Bath scrubber
13 So far
14 "Goll-lee!"
15 Many a "Star Trek" character
16 Tush made of shuttle thread?
17 Bit of trail mix
18 Pork place?
25 Grabbed surreptitiously
29 Graduation or confirmation
31 Following
34 Not just ask
35 Florida county seat
36 Not on deck
38 Had something
40 Go "waaaah!"
42 Got things wrong
44 Harriet Beecher Stowe novel
46 Elite
47 Didn't walk or go by subway, say
48 ___ Epstein, Red Sox G.M. starting in 2002
50 Mr. Right, with "the"
51 Enjoy the theater
56 Word before and after "a"
58 Prell competitor
59 Currency exchange abbr.
61 Painter Mondrian
62 Milk source
63 Former Israeli president Weizman
65 3.5, e.g.: Abbr.
66 Actress Papas
67 Viscera
68 Rodeo locale
69 Stick one's foot in Chardonnay?
70 Good winter entree
73 Some toothpastes
74 Where to get a mil. commission
75 Development of amnesia?
76 In ___ (stunned)
77 None too bright
79 Illustrator for Charles Dickens
81 Fabric that needs serious mending?
84 Bequests
85 Circus props
86 Supposed makers of crop circles
88 Suffix with buck
90 Bird whose name sounds like its soft call
91 Tricks
92 Get more soap suds out of
99 Angers
100 Metal that may ignite if scratched
102 Try
104 Dr. J was one
105 Spinning dizzily
106 Part of DKNY
108 Tribal chief
109 "The Simpsons" bus driver
111 They're not good for QB's
112 Nasty wound
113 Back
114 Big mouth

by Stella Daily and Bruce Venzke

134 TRIANGULATION

ACROSS

1 Magazine that features "Alfred's Poor Almanac"
4 I.R.S. form 1099- ___
8 Early pulpit
12 "The Simpsons" character who often refers to himself in the third person
18 Speedy steed
20 "___ tale's best for winter": Shak.
21 Reddish-brown
22 How Mulan dresses in much of "Mulan"
23 Fielder's cry
24 Something to play
26 Numbers game
27 They're left behind
29 Turns in
31 Old infantry spears
32 Saw things
33 "___ Blas" (Lesage novel)
34 "Where ___ go wrong?"
36 Procter & Gamble brand
37 One succumbing to 6-Down
39 Bird: Prefix
40 It might be silver
42 Be in another form
44 "Don't worry about me"
46 Archbishop Tutu
48 Censures
50 Some players in a kids' game
52 Single, for one: Abbr.
53 As quickly as possible
54 Sinai borderer: Abbr.
55 King in a Steve Martin song
56 Star in old westerns
58 Home of Canadian P.M. Stephen Harper
59 Freight weight
60 "Great" boy detective
62 When the sun is directly overhead
64 Combined
67 Facilities
69 Creepy sort
73 Thin-framed, big-footed woman of cartoons
75 Indian bread
77 Lilliputian
78 Chest protector
81 Subject of this puzzle [and proceeding counterclockwise]
83 Summons: Abbr.
85 Words of honor?
86 Thought
87 "Notes ___ Scandal," 2006 film
88 Skateboarder's accessory
90 Rim in which a gem is set
91 Guessing game
95 Flat ___ (some proponents of I.R.S. reform)
96 Big picture?: Abbr.
97 Jazz singer Nina
99 Songwriters' org.
100 Gag reflex?
101 Córdoba kinswoman
103 Bring (out)
104 Bagel topper
105 Strip joints?
108 Buttonholes
110 New York governor Before Paterson
113 Place
115 Drink whose name is Tahitian for "good"

117 Like any points on a circle, from the center
119 X-ray ___, joke shop offering
120 Sandinista leader
121 Pipsqueak
122 Judge, with "up"
123 Went like the dickens
124 Mixed economy advocate
125 Salty septet
126 Disney World transport
127 Galas

DOWN

1 "Speed-the-Plow" playwright
2 Greet the day
3 Whence the line "Into the eternal darkness; into fire and into ice"
4 Medieval weapon
5 "That ___ it should be"
6 See 37-Across
7 PC data reader
8 Three-time A.L. M.V.P., familiarly
9 Pouty look
10 Working out of
11 What those in agreement are said to be of
12 Court figs.
13 Bats
14 ___ Hawkins Day
15 "Seinfeld" character
16 "Catch your breath"
17 "___ pro omnibus, omnes pro uno"
19 1950s stereotype
25 Joan Rivers's daughter and TV co-host
28 Place for surfing
30 Star Wars, initially
33 Flit (about)
35 Highlighted, as text
38 Second showing
40 Wish one could
41 Comprehensive
43 Spanish pronoun
44 Query to the Lord in Matthew
45 Quark-plus-antiquark particle
47 "Love of loves"
49 In the blink of ___
51 Not just hungry
53 Oaf
56 Inebriate
57 See 81-Across
61 Place for a swing
63 Maria Muldaur's "___ Woman"
65 Like some diet colas, in brief
66 Makes up?
68 Power in Hollywood
70 Like things

71 Chest material
72 Listens to
74 "That makes sense!"
76 Bottom of the ___
78 The Owls of the N.C.A.A.
79 "Do what you want"
80 Aggressiveness
82 Played
84 It was passed in May 1773
89 Poop
91 Store on "Sesame Street"
92 Relic
93 Don Juan
94 Put the kibosh on
98 "___ Miniver"
102 When some nighttime news begins
106 Alamogordo's county
107 Makes attractive, with "up"
108 Every which way
109 Wizard
111 Kind of melt
112 Jerry Scott/Jim Borgman comic
113 Anthem part
114 Tabloid twosome
116 "___ in Icarus" (1979 French thriller)
118 How every letter to The Economist begins

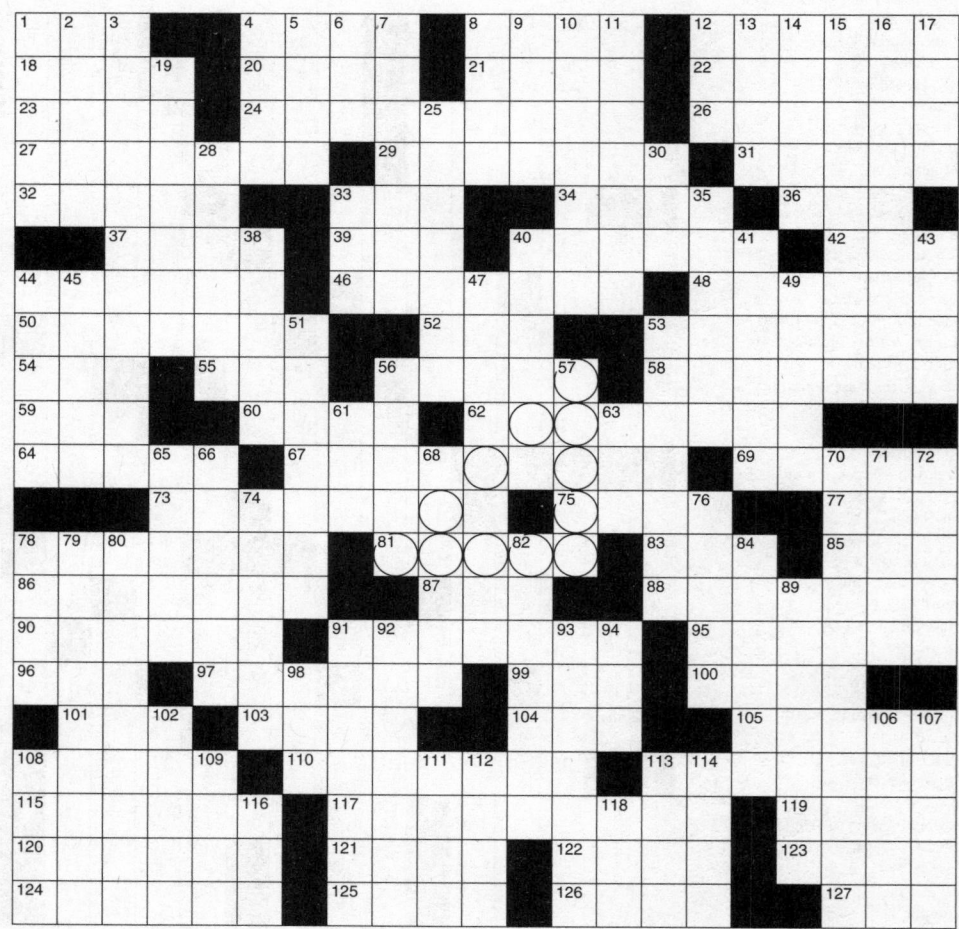

by Natan Last

ACROSS

1 Literary elephant
6 Succeeded in
11 Hot
17 Drag show accessory
20 ——— Stadium, home of the University of Hawaii Warriors
21 Baseball Hall-of-Famer Edd
22 Admonish
23 Suffix with absorb
24 Like a useless photo lab employee?
27 Stephen of "Breakfast on Pluto"
28 Dejected
29 Trespasses
30 Lineage
31 Imported by plane
33 TV oil baron
35 "Let's go, Miguel!"
36 Wally's TV brother, with "the"
38 Take on
39 Offers breakfast to students before first period?
43 Marriage ———
44 Part of N.A.A.C.P.: Abbr.
45 First word of "Jabberwocky"
46 Put a rider on, e.g.
47 It may be false
48 Game stopper
50 Place for a panel
52 Director Anderson
53 Beer sources for genteel guests?
57 Extremely inept person, slangily
59 Sharp turn
62 ——— Arbor
63 Through
64 Cartoonist Bil
65 Sauce thickener
66 Name in a hymn
67 Worthless talk, in slang
69 It may charge you a fee
70 Casino surface
71 Mattress brand
72 Reminder to a forgetful judge on bowling night?
78 Early invader of Britain
79 Esq.
80 Sette minus quattro
81 Utter
82 Give ——— of hope
83 Functions
84 1977 George Burns film
86 Fix
87 Letter addenda, for short
90 Band with the 1989 hit "Stand"
91 Own (up)
92 What talk show guests have before the broadcast?
95 Yowl
96 Playboy's look
97 Sloops' headsails
98 Sported
99 Poker game with four hole cards
102 See 26-Down
104 Ring stats
106 Guest beds, often
107 Sign outside a church lavatory?
113 Stately trees
114 Work units
115 Satirical paper, with "The"
116 They may be scattered
117 Short-hop plane
119 Potential hangar buildup
120 On the safe side
121 Music with jazzlike riffs
124 Ruby ———
125 Where a Monkee changes after a game?
130 "——— Poetica"
131 Handily defeated
132 Church support
133 1964 Quinn role
134 Still
135 Tasty bit
136 PC key
137 Beginning

DOWN

1 Barnyard calls
2 ———-Romeo
3 Laredo or Nuevo Laredo
4 "Now it's clear!"
5 Cereal topping
6 Torts
7 Responses to punches
8 Crackpot
9 Religious retreats
10 1976 horror film whose score won an Oscar
11 Talks from a Rev.
12 Toll hwy.
13 Sports legend whose #4 was retired
14 Day spa accessories
15 Unfold
16 "Finding ———," 2003 film
17 Eccentric friend on "Designing Women"
18 Seldom-used golf club
19 Over
22 1969 Oscar-nominated film role
25 Little job for a body shop
26 With 102-Across, dashboard warning light
32 Loud hits
34 Exert, as influence
35 ——— 1, Yuri Gagarin's spacecraft
36 Jaguar alternatives
37 Seventh-brightest star in a constellation
39 Offer to buy at auction
40 Meteorological effect
41 Steam shovel inventor William
42 Guthrie's follower at Woodstock
43 TV host Kelly
48 Diva's effect
49 Host of public radio's "This American Life"
50 Cubs' protector
51 Survey info
52 Increase, in a way
54 Poland Spring competitor
55 Owen ———, John Irving character
56 "A maid with hair of gold," in an old song
57 Goes it alone
58 Attempt to trick
59 "Beetle Bailey" soldier
60 Analogy part
61 U.S. possession since 1898
65 Kind of hall
66 Schmo
67 Rap enthusiast, in slang
68 Rob of "Melrose Place"
70 Damager of the ozone layer
71 Pouting person's action
72 Bygone leader
73 Fabled race loser
74 Reason for an office visit
75 "——— my fault!"
76 Impulse
77 Paper purchases
83 Turnaround, slangily
84 Bauxite, e.g.
85 "Right Place Wrong Time" singer, 1973
87 Seminar leaders
88 Expensive strings
89 Dict. listings
91 Brothers
92 Beginning, as of an idea
93 Seine tributary
94 Stirred up, as memories
95 Blanket holder
96 Golden Triangle country
99 Prescription phrase
100 "Le Misanthrope" playwright
101 Place for an elbow
102 One pulling in
103 Road bend
104 Italian province or its capital
105 Singer with the #1 country album "80's Ladies"
106 Playful movement
108 Company with a star logo
109 Source
110 "This one's ———!"
111 Physical therapy equipment
112 "Now it's clear!"
118 The first prophet of God, in Islam
119 Awful
120 Feel compassion
122 Kind of beef
123 Part of a Latin 101 conjugation
126 Gridiron units: Abbr.
127 Java
128 Giant born in Louisiana
129 1989 Gold Glove winner Darling

by Mike Nothnagel

ACROSS

1 Artist's digs, maybe
5 Totally accurate
11 Pineapple desserts
17 "___, gorgeous!" (Fanny Brice's comment to herself when looking in the mirror)
18 One of wine's Gallo brothers
19 Autobiographical short story by Edgar Allan Poe
20 Marisa of "What Women Want"
21 1974 Mocedades hit
22 Careful consideration
23 Men's fashion accessories
25 Cork shooter
27 "Biography" network
28 Accelerated
29 Threw off the scent
30 Check list?
31 Canonized mlle.
32 More encouraging
33 Third word of "America"
34 Blue Devils' and Tigers' org.
37 Contact lens solutions
39 They're better than one
44 Elton's johns
45 Blind element
47 Stereotypical reaction to Elvis
49 Magneto's adversaries, in comic books
50 Lugs
52 Spread in a spread
54 Passé
56 Classic Toyota sports cars
58 ___ Bradshaw, "Sex and the City" role
59 Wynken, Blynken and Nod, e.g.
60 Turf, as opposed to surf
61 Dancer Alvin
62 Malodorous
64 Become part of
65 Imp
68 Place to get dates?
69 Fronded plant
70 Fictional submariner
72 Civil rights march site, 1965
73 Family
75 Wise
77 Repeated John Gielgud role
79 Popular song from Broadway's "The Wiz"
81 Titanic message
82 Arctic diver
83 Runs
85 Eponymous German electrophysicist
87 Begets
91 Things on strings
92 Deterge
96 Prefix with -zoic
97 Sitcom title role for Brandy Norwood
98 1997 Jim Carrey film
99 What a man and a woman become in marriage
101 Two-wheeled covered carriage
103 Hops-drying kilns
104 Establishing a business
105 Hero of Bellini's "I Puritani"
106 Anticipate
107 Mary Tyler Moore co-star
108 Seinfeld, for one
109 Feast

DOWN

1 Sainted pope of A.D. 683
2 Ancient Mexican people
3 Evidence of dandruff
4 Facilities
6 Slips
7 Hydrocarbon suffix
8 Execrate
9 Bone formation
10 Mathematical sequence of unknown length
11 ___ Bator
12 A pop
13 Na_2CO_3
14 Dental filling
15 Literature's Lorna
16 Lose little by little
17 U.R.L. lead-in
19 Former Israeli P.M. Olmert
24 They may be funny or bright
25 Neighbor of Switz.
29 Educator Maria
30 Subatomic particle that is a nuclear binder
32 Mideast money
33 Bad dancer's handicap
34 "Enough!"
35 Collected
36 Mistress
38 Bridges in Hollywood
39 The "ten" in "hang ten"
40 Reactionary
41 Flower also called a naked lady
42 Hero maker
43 Old dirk
45 Unblemished
47 Lineage
48 Failings
51 Breezes (through)
53 Quite wrong
54 Business position
55 Word before and after "after"
57 Cross product
58 Geom. figure
61 Disco term meaning "galore"
62 Punch
63 French Sudan, today
64 Raspberry
66 "___ Angel," 1933 film
67 Scratch sheet listings
69 Slams
71 Fannie ___ (securities)
74 Jupiter or Mars
76 ___ Gay, W.W. II bomber
78 Ointment ingredient
79 Subject of the book "Last Flight"
80 Setting for "Driving Miss Daisy"
83 Call, or call on
84 Turkish pooh-bahs
86 Lake ___, third-largest lake in Africa
87 Imagine, informally
88 Sectioned, as a window
89 Prince Valiant's wife
90 Tapestry threads
93 Month before Iyar
94 "Socrate" composer
95 First, in Frankfurt
97 Relig. title
98 Lady's man
100 Anchorage-to-Fairbanks dir.
102 Great ball of fire

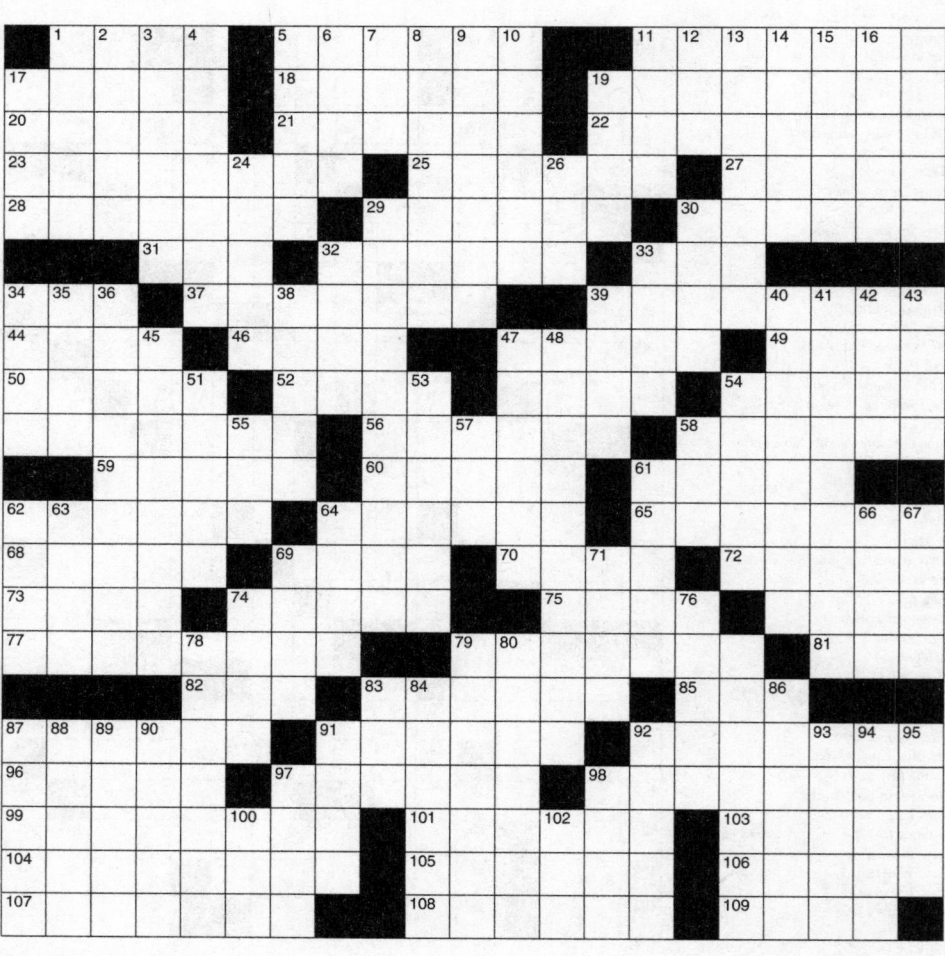

by Matt Ginsberg

ACROSS

1 Inferior
10 Puzzle page favorite
15 S. Amer. land
19 Like some addresses
20 Communist's belief
22 Part of a blouse that touches the waist?
23 The real scoop about lipids?
24 They're better than F.G.'s
25 Portion of a drag queen's wardrobe
26 Bumptious
27 Toy company that launched Rubik's Cube
28 Bad
29 Snowmobile parts
31 Professional with an x-ray machine: Abbr.
33 Underage child of a military officer?
38 Nonsense of a market pessimist?
44 Affirm
45 Oven maker
46 Caught in ___
47 Biblical birthright seller
48 Oscar winner Hunt
50 Glad Wrap competitor
51 Pianist Dame Myra
52 Missy Elliott's "___ What I'm Talkin' About"
53 Toil of a Broadway show?
55 Match for a bad guy?
58 Owns
59 Fine-tune
60 Italian port on the Adriatic
61 Make ___ of
62 Sam's Club competitor
64 Yes
68 Watchdog org.?
72 Fixes
74 Hair behind the ears, maybe
75 E-mail directive: Abbr.
78 What can produce a "boing!"?
82 Ardor of a new employee?
84 Bookstore sect.
85 "Our Gang" affirmative
86 Stop early
88 Botulin, e.g.
89 "___ la Douce," 1963 film
90 Charlie's Angels, e.g.
91 Tally mark
92 Torn
93 Comeback of a Japanese game?
95 Singer Johnny's gallop?
98 It can be measured in gigs
99 So
100 "Yo!"
101 Over
105 Molière's Harpagon, e.g.
108 Prosperity
110 Go the other way
113 Privilege of liberals?
115 Road in Yellowstone?
118 Become level
119 Darlin'
120 Give it ___
121 Say yes
122 Reason to take Valium

DOWN

1 Trampled
2 Accidents
3 "___ Alive!" (1974 thriller)
4 One looking for a lift?
5 Wilts
6 Comic Rudner
7 New Testament book
8 "The way of nature"
9 Popular street name
10 Patriot Putnam of the American Revolution
11 When planes are due, for short
12 Equivocator's choice
13 Child-raiser's cry?
14 Start of a cheer
15 City WNW of Stillwater
16 François Truffaut's field
17 West Point rival, for short
18 ___ nitrate
19 Polo Grounds legend
21 Words sung before and after "is just"
26 Literally, "fish tooth"
28 Rambunctious
29 Lewis Carroll creature
30 Hawaii's ___ Coast
32 Habiliments
33 "Happy Days" character
34 Province of central Spain
35 Villain in "Martin Chuzzlewit"
36 "National Treasure" group
37 Turkish hospice
38 Believers in the spiritual unity of all people
39 Roadside sign abbr.
40 Obscure
41 Gas bill info
42 Roofing items
43 Yearns (for)
49 Refuse holder
54 It's pitched
56 Times gone by
57 Current
60 Be angry
63 It's kept within the lines, usually
65 Sully
66 "At the ___ Core," 1976 sci-fi film
67 Laredo-to-Fort Worth dir.
68 Comparable in size
69 Veep after Hubert
70 Destinations of some limos
71 Perfecto, e.g.
73 One taking a quick look
75 Handyman
76 Squeeze-dry
77 Al ___
79 Must, informally
80 Ukulele activity
81 Playable
82 ___ -totsy
83 Venture
87 Erymanthian ___, fourth labor of Hercules
94 Artist Max
96 Pure
97 Restrained
99 Sports car since '53
101 Italian wheels
102 Moola
103 Miles away
104 ___ -bitty
106 "The Lay of the Host of ___" (old Russian epic poem)
107 Elisabeth of "Leaving Las Vegas"
108 Small warbler
109 Makes (out)
110 Speeds
111 Alamo battler?
112 1,000 smackers
114 Actor Stephen
115 West Coast hrs.
116 Wow
117 "Riddle-me-___"

by Bill Zais

ACROSS

1 Words "beautifully marked in currants" in "Alice in Wonderland"
6 Common ___
9 Make an example of
13 Destination in Genesis 8
19 With 105-Across, what the answer to each starred clue starts with
21 *Again
23 *Baseball's Willie Mays, with "the"
24 *Fiancé
25 Glycerides, e.g.
26 Football Hall-of-Famer Ernie
28 Home of Faa'a International Airport
29 Lie
30 Jury pool
31 Watch-crystal holder
32 Villain
33 Ring results, briefly
34 Bigwig
38 "Awesome!"
41 Next-to-last round
42 Little of France?
43 St. Louis, e.g.
44 Brawl motivator
45 Crunch's title
46 Rod holders
50 Photocopier choice
51 Hollow-point ammo
53 *Metal used for swords
55 Stage awards
56 Butlers and maids
57 Be about to fall
58 *Symbol of rejoicing for someone's long-awaited return
61 *Brownish-orange
65 Lady-in-waiting in "Othello"
66 Lovers of expensive furs may put them on
67 West Coast wine city
68 *Kind of ratio
72 Divine
74 New York's ___-Fontanne Theater
75 Supermarket lines?
76 "We Need a Little Christmas" singer
77 Hoop grp.
78 Alma mater for Neil Armstrong and Pat Nixon: Abbr.
79 Close of day, to poets
80 Gutter locale
81 Thomas Mann's "Der ___ in Venedig"
82 Attempts
85 With 20-Down, airshow activities
86 Jim who wrote "Ball Four"
88 Indy champ Bobby
90 Dentist's concern
91 ___ of vantage (good position for viewing)
96 Split
98 Split
99 Like wiping one's dirty mouth on one's sleeve
100 *Decelerating
102 *Composer's due
104 *Whatever happens
105 See 19-Across
106 Cantankerous
107 Not including
108 Inexact fig.
109 Magazine holders

DOWN

1 Mississippi quartet
2 ___ of thousands
3 "___ Remember"
4 "Real Time" moderator
5 Tip reducer?
6 Variety of leather
7 Exercised power over
8 All the parts of a column except the bottom
9 Stick
10 Accustom
11 Actress Harper
12 Diplomats' place: Abbr.
13 Ball handler?
14 "Not I!" hearer
15 Titular Verdi role
16 Laugh-a-minute
17 Both: Prefix
18 Curling goal
20 See 85-Across
22 Author of the Oprah's Book Club selection "We Were the Mulvaneys"
27 I's opposite on a clock
30 Improvises
31 Bar personnel
32 Light from a headlight
33 Rears
35 Cracker topper
36 What 35-Down may do
37 Jessica of "7th Heaven"
38 Done with
39 Tourist mecca near Venezuela
40 Relinquish
41 Passing remark?
42 Sch. fair organizer
46 Schumacher of auto racing
47 The "E" in H.R.E.: Abbr.
48 Violinist Mischa
49 This, in Havana
50 Cox's call
52 Spot
53 Manhattan street leading to the Williamsburg Bridge
54 Guarantees
56 Sensory receptor in the ear
59 "Mon ___!"
60 Loud, abrupt sound
61 Dog of old comics
62 Denier's reply
63 Aerobics technique
64 Winning
66 +
68 +
69 Impair through inactivity
70 Atahualpa, e.g.
71 It may be + or −
72 Act of kindness
73 Soothsayer's subject
76 "Death in the Afternoon" figures
80 Muse of music
83 Creator of "Hägar the Horrible"
84 Hero
85 Part of many a Halloween outfit
86 Noble partner
87 Fictional TV planet
89 ___ Fleming, central character in "The Red Badge of Courage"
90 Dots on a map
91 Home of 67-Across: Abbr.
92 Top
93 Not so friendly
94 Capital of East Flanders
95 Fits (inside)
96 Reed instrument: Abbr.
97 Pork cut
98 Liver in Lyon
99 Braggadocio
100 "No seats left"
101 FedEx competitor
103 Still

by Henry Hook

ACROSS

1 Theme of this puzzle
9 Accord competitor
15 Is afflicted with sigmatism
20 Emphatic refusal
21 Tulsa native
22 French pen filler
23 Film (1954), actress (2003)
25 Nothing, to Nero
26 Brief
27 Comments around cute babies
28 East ender?
29 "We can't delay!"
30 Visually assess
31 Morsel
33 Fish in fish and chips
35 Isabel Allende's "___ of My Soul"
36 Florence-to-Rome dir.
37 Director (2003), actor (1962)
39 Interject
40 Rests
41 12 meses
42 Low tie
44 Like the Wild West
47 Pen with a cap
48 Abbr. at the bottom of a letter
49 Places for runners
52 Work ___
53 Granny, in Gelsenkirchen
55 China's largest ethnic group
57 Nineveh's kingdom
59 Smeared
61 Film (1992), actor (1958)
64 Follower of weekend news, briefly
65 ___ bran
66 Friend in a western
68 "The Age of Anxiety" author
69 Rent
70 Philosopher Kung Fu-___
71 Actor (1934), actor (1995)
73 Destination of the Bounty in "Mutiny on the Bounty"
76 Comedy club annoyance
78 Olive ___
79 Troll dolls, once
81 Beau ___
82 Milo of "Ulysses"
83 Kind
85 "___ Diaboliques"
87 Big pan
89 Lead role in "La Cage aux Folles"
91 Venezuelan export
92 Object of veneration in ancient Egypt
93 Cool
94 Actress (1986), director (1962)
98 Mail order option, for short
101 Sport jersey material
102 Author Huxley
103 Wallop
104 Kwik-E-Mart owner on "The Simpsons"
105 Pantomime, say
107 Tahoe, e.g., for short
108 Future school?
109 See 113-Down
111 Soil improver
112 Actress (1983), supporting actor (1999)
116 Humble
117 Rebel
118 Checks
119 Surgical aid
120 Jerks
121 Forensic experts

DOWN

1 Investment options, for short
2 Dolls
3 Password, e.g.
4 Reactions to fireworks
5 N.F.L. guard Chris
6 Overawe
7 Santa ___
8 Spin
9 Rus. and Ukr., once
10 Response to "pow!" in cartoons
11 Big name in grooming aids
12 Winter wear
13 Detective superintendent Jane of TV's "Prime Suspect"
14 Knack
15 Jay that chatters
16 At first
17 Film (1993), actress (1987)
18 Ready
19 Three-time French Open champ, 1990–92
24 Household item with a neck
29 One flying over Hawaii
31 Stakes
32 Linda Ronstadt's "___ Easy"
33 Villa in Mexico
34 Like the inside of a sphere
37 Gat
38 ___ alai
40 Slender
43 Org.
44 Basutoland, today
45 World books
46 Song (1942), supporting actress (1994)
47 Capital known as the Venice of the East
48 Swamps
50 Informal eating place
51 More racy
54 Sierra Club founder
56 Prized horse
58 Elated
60 Area between hills
62 Geezer
63 Inspiration
67 Kind of vow
71 Reunion gatherers
72 "Us" or "them" in "It's us against them"
74 "Didn't we just have that?"
75 Global energy company
77 Make the beds, dust, etc.
80 March around camp, e.g.
84 Term of respect abroad
86 ". . . as old as yonder ___": James Joyce
88 Late news?
90 Part of a Latin 101 conjugation
91 Works
93 Mother of Paris
95 One of the Alcotts
96 "It's ___!"
97 Swarmed
98 Tibetan or Afghan
99 First act in a revue
100 Pressure
101 Taj ___
106 Junkie
108 Solicits orders (for)
109 Girl in Tennessee Williams's "Summer and Smoke"
110 Worms, e.g.
112 Jrs. no more
113 109-Across's old radio partner
114 Fire
115 Truck part

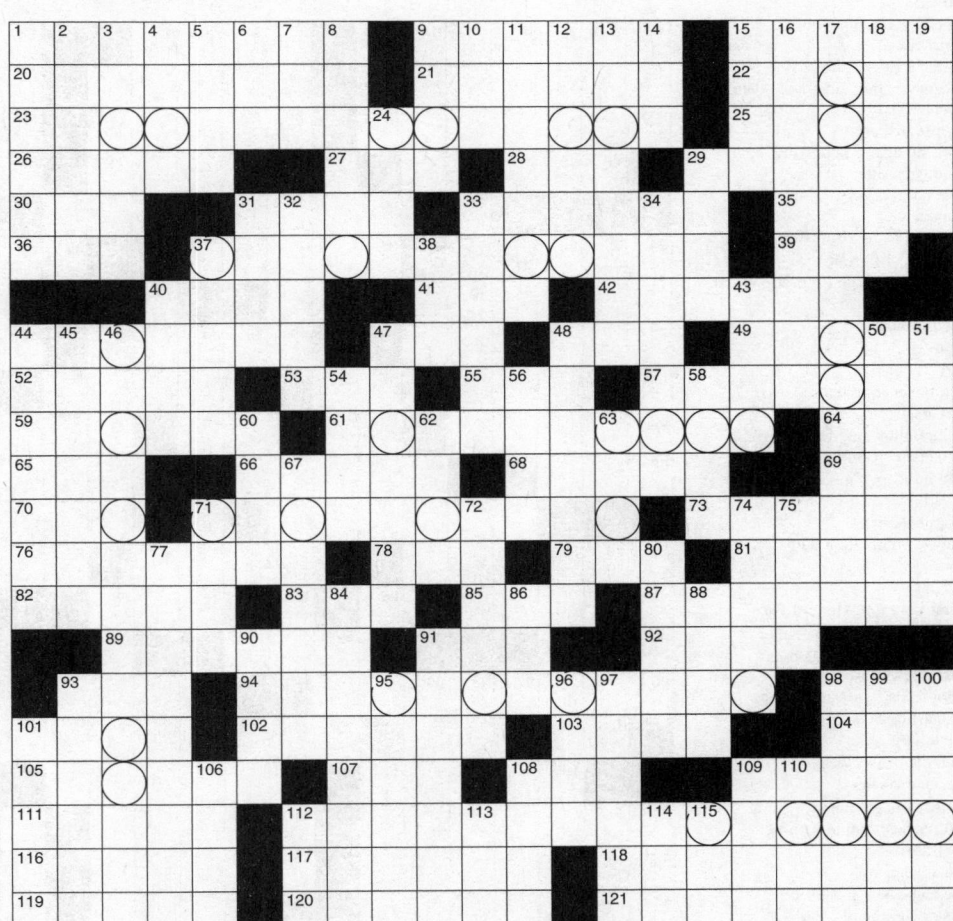

by Nancy Nicholson Joline

ACROSS

1 Offer for an R. J. Reynolds brand?
8 Rules, for short
12 1970 Simon & Garfunkel hit
19 Away from a teaching post
20 Forster's "___ With a View"
22 Joining
23 Cube holder
24 IUD part
25 Realm of Otto von Bismarck
26 1802 acquisition of 25-Across
27 Settles on, in a way
28 Top of a platter
29 Papa pad?
32 Composes
34 Org. that oversees quadrennial games
37 Sporty Mazda
38 Canola and sunflower oil?
41 Best fraternity pledge tormentor?
45 Jack who said "Just the facts, ma'am"
47 Rugged coastline feature
48 "My!"
49 Casual attire
52 Not the most exciting school athletes?
56 Social gathering with the Rockettes?
59 "Like a Rock" singer Bob
61 Cosmetician Lauder and others
62 Get decked out
63 Waste maker
65 Puts up again, as bowling pins
67 Squiggly letter
68 Got sober?
70 Flutter
73 Shows past the doorstep
75 Student of Bartók
76 The lion in "The Lion, the Witch and the Wardrobe"
78 Clap hands on
81 Pan-fry
83 C.I.A. noggins?
85 Hit boxer John with a haymaker?
87 "___ Calloways" (Disney film)
89 "Damien" subtitle
90 Mount Rigi, e.g.
91 Head set
93 Fog in Zürich?
96 How-to films for a dairy farm?
100 ___ nerve
102 First song on "More of the Monkees"
103 ___, meenie, miney, mo
104 Side view of salmon?
109 "Soon It's ___ Rain" ("The Fantasticks" song)
111 Reliquary
112 Temple of Isis locale
116 Facial growths
118 Phrase of agreement
119 Words heard after opening a gift, maybe
121 Hazel, e.g.
122 Ice Cube né ___ Jackson
123 It started around 1100 B.C.
124 Do a mailroom task
125 Professional org.
126 Transcribe some Dickens?

DOWN

1 Colorful carp
2 Enough, for some
3 Plaudits, of a sort
4 "Sure, I'm game"
5 Exposed
6 One of Donald's exes
7 Susan of "Looker"
8 Train storage area
9 ___ Tubb, the Texas Troubadour
10 Nabber's cry
11 Rather, informally
12 Silver prizes
13 Physicist Fermi
14 ___ Real, Spain
15 The "se" in per se
16 The King's "princess"
17 Common pasta suffix
18 Eastern title
21 Like some Sp. nouns
27 "The Sopranos" Emmy winner Falco
30 No man's land, in brief
31 Vladimir Putin's onetime org.
33 Michael of R.E.M.
34 Wagner heroine
35 Extras
36 Mooches
39 It commonly follows a verb: Abbr.
40 Disrespect
42 Salespeople, informally
43 Lukas of "Witness"
44 Sheet music abbr.
45 Locks on a dome
46 Chef Lagasse
50 Cornerstone abbr.
51 Must
53 Winners' signs
54 August hrs.
55 Some football blockers: Abbr.
57 "See ___?"
58 Plane part
60 Signs a lease
64 "Julius Caesar" setting
66 D. J.'s bane
68 Classic soft drink with orange, grape and peach flavors
69 Shad delicacies
70 "So-Called Chaos" singer Morissette
71 Like Niels Bohr
72 Kind of inspection
73 Orch. section
74 Old French coin
76 Means of defense: Abbr.
77 Come across as
78 Canned meat brand
79 "And that's ___" ("Believe you me")
80 Christina in the 2005 revival of "Sweet Charity"
82 Speech stumbles
84 Informal greetings
86 Zoo feature, in England
88 Finnic language
92 Fashion inits.
94 Ring bearer
95 Here, on the Riviera
97 Fife player
98 Dough for tortillas
99 Plywood layer
100 ___ Book Club
101 7, 11 and 13
105 Bologna bone
106 Mandela's native tongue
107 Hijacked cruise ship Achille ___
108 Bar at the bar
110 "I'd hate to break up ___"
113 Having a taste of the grape
114 Run up ___
115 NASA cancellation
116 Econ. measure
117 Your and my
119 Snap
120 Cyrano's nose

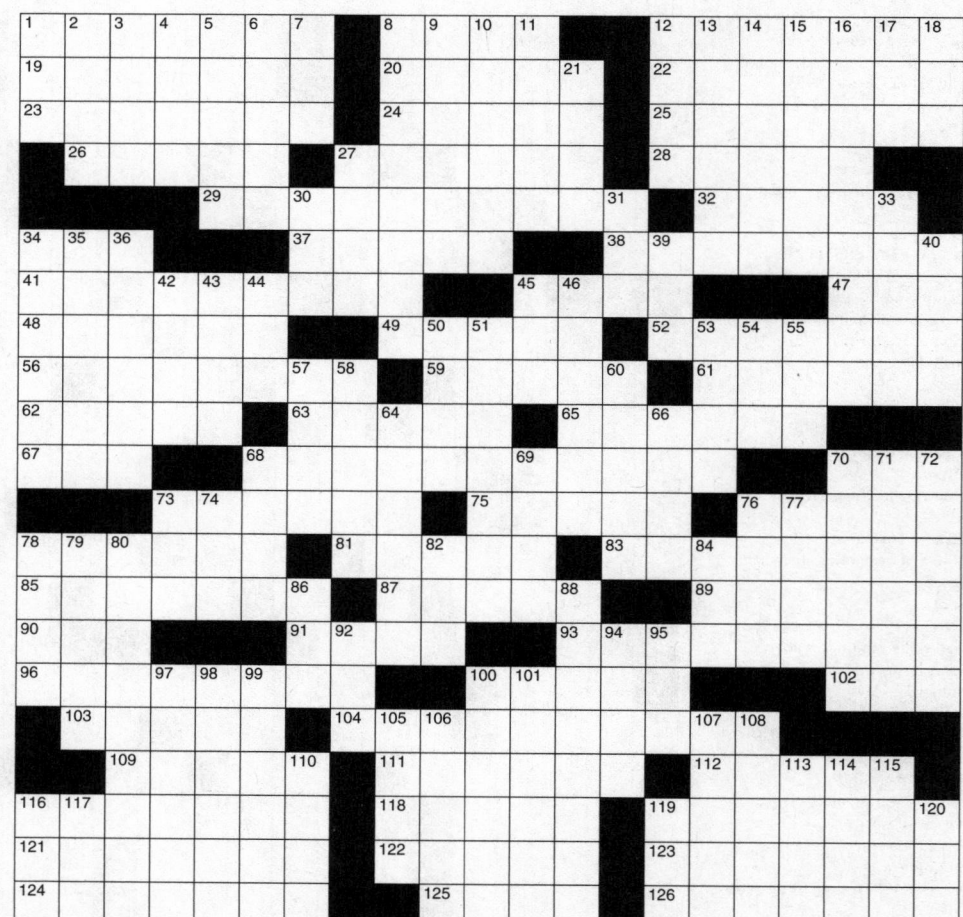

by Patrick Blindauer and Tony Orbach

ACROSS

1 Upper end of a soprano's range
6 Life work?
9 In support of
12 Bishopric
19 Basketballer nicknamed the Diesel
20 Attribute (to)
22 Joins up
23 Concave button
24 "Over my dead body!" / Alert [split]
26 Exchange words? / New beginning [merger]
28 ___ Maria (coffee liqueur)
29 Gift-wrapper's need
30 Strummed instrument
32 "___ my doubts"
33 Animated film character voiced by Matthew Broderick
35 Fine fellow
36 Undecided, you might say
38 Deal (out)
39 Annoying obligations / "No need to check" [split]
42 1980s "NBC News Overnight" anchor / Feared insect [merger]
44 At full speed
45 "Mazel ___!"
46 "The History ___" (Tony-winning play)
47 Harsh
48 Return flight destinations?
52 Off-limits
55 Get down
56 Plant manager?
58 Figure just above the total
59 Black hole's boundary / Despite the fact that [split]
62 Group migration
64 Like Eton attendees
65 Author of the "Earth's Children" series
66 Social reformer Lucretia
67 "Great Scott!"
68 A little cross?
70 Double sugar / Travel freely? [merger]
74 Get dressed (up)
75 "Feh!"
76 Insects found in trunks
77 Takes off
78 Bag
80 In the cooler
81 Unread messages, usually
83 Mountain SE of ancient Troy
85 It has many sides
86 Commuter's source of entertainment / Actor John or David [split]
90 Martini ingredient / Delta site [merger]
94 Burt's "Stroker Ace" co-star
95 "The Seagull" ingenue
96 Water, to Watteau
97 Fictional blue humanoid
98 Aggressive patriot
99 Fishtank accessory
100 Prefix with potent
102 MapQuest suggestion: Abbr.
103 Franz Liszt, e.g. / Didn't go straight, maybe [split]
106 "Come back now, y'hear?" / Park employee [merger]
110 TV journalist Van Susteren
113 Commentator
114 Using company resources
115 Great white ___
116 Took too long, as a meeting
117 Superhero name ender
118 Broke bread
119 Finger-lickin' good

DOWN

1 ___ polloi
2 Overnight site
3 Patrician
4 Della sells hers in "The Gift of the Magi"
5 See 26-Across
6 Keen producers
7 Quarantine
8 Scale's range
9 Taylor's deputy on TV
10 Kimono securer
11 ___ room
12 Gap filler?
13 Occupy
14 Blast furnace input
15 Peacemaker maker
16 #1 hit for Marty Robbins
17 Add surreptitiously
18 Some phosphates, e.g.
21 Observance
25 See 24-Across
27 Modern political acronym
30 Navajo enemy
31 See 42-Across
33 Abrupt increase on a graph
34 Assuages one's guilt
37 Prepares, in a way, as chicken
39 Adult insect
40 California county with Point Reyes National Seashore
41 See 39-Across
43 Origin
44 Complete
47 It's not needed in hydroponics
49 It's clipped at both ends
50 Philippic
51 Game similar to bridge
52 Really appeals to
53 Earthly paradise of Celtic legend
54 Caviar source
55 W.W. II light machine gun
56 See 70-Across
57 Bleeped word
60 Reagan's first secretary of state
61 See 59-Across
62 Pros who practice
63 Violinist Itzhak
66 Four-legged female
69 Napped fabrics
70 "Goodbye, Mr. Chips" star
71 ___ Sea, connected to St. George's Channel
72 It's split
73 At a distance
76 ___ bourguignon
79 See 90-Across
81 1953 3-D film starring Fernando Lamas
82 Earlier
84 Seat separator
85 See 106-Across
86 Stop up
87 Some campaign fund-raisers
88 See 86-Across
89 Cereal grass
90 Himalayan cedar
91 ___ Quimby, girl of children's lit
92 Chinese province bordering Vietnam, Laos and Myanmar
93 Change genetically
94 ___ franca
98 2007 title role for Ellen Page
101 "___ be O.K."
103 Chemistry Nobelist Otto
104 See 103-Across
105 Precinct
107 ___ landslide
108 Country singer McGraw
109 What retroviruses contain
111 Preschooler
112 To some extent

by Patrick Berry

ACROSS

1 Place for bluegrass
7 #1 on the charts
12 Blast
20 Kia sedan
21 Café con ___
22 Certify
23 Broad comedies involving hogs?
25 Like traditional Catholic Masses
26 N.H.L.'s Tikkanen
27 Entertainment center at many a sports bar
28 Where bluejackets go
30 Movement that inspired '60s fashion
31 Good viewing spot for a canyon
32 Bickering
33 Bookcase lineup
34 Beautifully illustrated report of a computer failure?
39 Clark's partner
40 It's put on some houses
41 "It'll ___ you"
42 Stockholm-bound carrier
45 First-year J.D. student
46 Makes eyes at
49 All-time top-selling Atari video game
51 Cake maker's boast?
53 Short-legged, thick-set horse
55 Not badgering, say
56 Flood survivor
57 Nursery rhyme call sung to an old French melody
60 Short breaks
61 French director's comment about his submission to a film festival?
67 Wide-headed fastener
68 Smears
69 Ang Thong resident
70 How some kids spend the summer
73 "Peer Gynt" mother
74 Bird call on a farm?
79 They're developed by a muscleman
82 Lip cover
83 Nebraska county with an Indian name
84 Super Bowl XLII M.V.P. Manning
85 Gen. Lee, in brief
86 Loyal
88 Lobster claw
89 A Simpson without access to his volume of the "Odyssey"?
94 Rocker Morissette
96 Till compartment
97 Succulents that soothe
98 Easy wins
99 Starter starter?
100 Sign that's often lit
101 Film editor's job
104 Most heterogeneous
106 Former Tennessee senator's Halloween costumes?
109 Prestigious
110 Curt
111 Name on some euros
112 Sources of a cosmetics oil
113 King in 1 B.C.
114 Body-sculpting undergarment

DOWN

1 Be down
2 Narrative writing
3 Razor brand
4 Cartoonist Browne
5 Breakfast menu heading
6 Brave words?
7 Mason of a sort
8 Griffin who loved game shows
9 Virginia is in it: Abbr.
10 Cover
11 Redcoat's ally
12 Do for a V.I.P.?
13 South American tuber
14 Creatures with three hearts
15 Opening remarks at a coffee makers' convention?
16 Paying guest
17 "Do ___?"
18 Baseball catchers
19 Time on la Côte d'Azur
24 Banking initialism
29 ". . . to name just a few": Abbr.
31 Not straight
32 Seller's terms
33 Symbol of blackness
34 Coup start
35 Clinton's attorney general
36 Pitcher
37 Give ___ up
38 Also addresses, as with an e-mail
42 Long-necked instrument
43 Opposite of reject
44 Payroll dept. ID's
46 Light wind?
47 Sacred cup
48 Christine of "Running on Empty"
49 French cleric
50 ___ consequence
52 Check holder: Abbr.
53 Monthly charge
54 Couple in a rowboat
57 Tournament passes
58 ___ Boy, classic figure in Japanese anime
59 One of Dumas's Musketeers
61 "___ Inside" (slogan)
62 Louis Vuitton competitor
63 Rat-___
64 Some Wharton alums
66 Tooth holders
66 Hawaiian Punch rival
67 Sticky stuff
71 Where a dope unloads a ship?
72 Words on a deathbed, maybe
74 Bass ___
75 Popular snack cakes
76 Talked-about twosome
77 Part
78 Tree in bloom in a Van Gogh painting
80 Five-dollar bills, slangily
81 Photocopier option: Abbr.
82 Fraternity members
86 Highest grade
87 Was not cooped up
88 Love
89 Whence the line "To sleep: perchance to dream"
90 Stopped fasting
91 Vented
92 Minnesota's St. ___ College
93 Fabrics that shimmer
94 Stood
95 Led Zeppelin's "Whole ___ Love"
99 Norms: Abbr.
100 ___ buco
101 Bloke
102 ___ Reader
103 Bygone autocrat
104 Touched
105 "Didn't I tell you?"
107 Clearance rack abbr.
108 Valedictorian's pride, for short

by Elizabeth C. Gorski

ACROSS

1 Track figure
8 Din-din
12 Nautical line
19 Ally makers
20 Search high and low
22 Like some grievances
23 Home of the newspaper Haaretz
24 *Electrical engineers and news anchors?*
26 *World travelers and wine connoisseurs?*
28 Wrestling locale
29 Cheer greatly
30 Some Millers
31 It may be pinched
32 Zealous
34 Business card abbr.
35 Oriole or Blue Jay, for short
36 Completely bungle
38 Hercules or Ulysses
39 Eyed
42 Classic Hans Christian Andersen story, with "The"
44 *Geologists and music video producers?*
46 Meal crumb
47 Congestion site
48 Some volcanic deposits
52 *College students and mattress testers?*
57 Greeted
58 Outdoor cover
59 Robert who introduced the term "cell" to biology
60 Where the antihelix is
61 Under
64 Itinerary word
65 Choir stands
67 Despicable sort
69 Executed
70 Stop
72 The Gamecocks of the Southeastern Conf.
73 Machinates
76 Prominent D.C. lobby
78 Wallop
79 Twelve ___
81 Supercool
82 *Old West outlaws and aspiring thespians?*
85 Bit of gridiron equipment
87 Obviously sad
88 Boffo
89 *Beat-era musicians and orthopedists?*
91 Show on the small screen
96 Home of the Rachel Carson National Wildlife Refuge
98 PC screens, for short
99 Certain investigators, for short
100 Champ just before 36-Down
101 Tough spot
102 Lavishes gifts (on), say
104 U.N. chief ___ Ki-moon
105 Desex
106 Huge, in poetry
109 Shak. is its most-quoted writer
110 *Fort Knox officials and pop singers?*
113 *Comedians and parade directors?*
116 Defeat in a derby
117 Office newbie
118 "___ joking!"
119 Lettered top
120 Set out
121 Cold war inits.
122 Activity in which spelling counts?

DOWN

1 Like a guardian
2 Kept from home
3 Flew
4 Bay ___ (residents of Massachusetts)
5 Walter ___, author of "The Hustler"
6 Prince in "The Little Mermaid"
7 Answer
8 Mortgagee's concern
9 Sharp
10 Craggy peaks
11 Boulogne-___-Mer, France
12 For all to play, in music
13 With 105-Down, a short play
14 Salon option
15 Cambodian money
16 Florid
17 Stroked
18 Car with an innovative "rolling dome" speedometer
21 Ad-libs and such
25 Honcho
27 Western tribe
32 Stepped aside, in court
33 Gave
36 1976–80 Wimbledon champ
37 Not touch
38 Sounds of anger or jubilation
40 Factory shipments: Abbr.
41 Hurdle for some college srs.
43 Sharpeners
44 Estuary
45 Assist in shady doings
47 Blood ___
49 Extravagant
50 Mournful
51 Sudden floods
52 Much smaller now
53 Exterminator's option
54 Gangster's gun
55 Onetime nickname at 1600 Pennsylvania Ave.
56 Hurried
57 Member of the familia
62 Needing bleach, say
63 Campaign feature
66 Eked (out)
68 Feels indignant about
71 Egg holder
74 Religious pilgrimage
75 Rebounds and steals
77 Hurt so bad
80 Fruit-flavored soda
83 ___ Magica
84 "Essential" things
86 A.T.M. need
87 Without oomph
90 Certain chamber group
91 Oversee
92 Heat-related
93 On
94 Dog after the winter, e.g.
95 How Calvin Coolidge spoke
96 You can say that again
97 Lacking scruples
99 Less accurate
101 Kids
103 Expressed delight
104 Some South Africans
105 See 13-Down
107 Symbol of thinness
108 Attire not for the modest
110 Striped animals
111 Wands
112 Prefix with zone
114 "Imagine that!"
115 Note to be used later

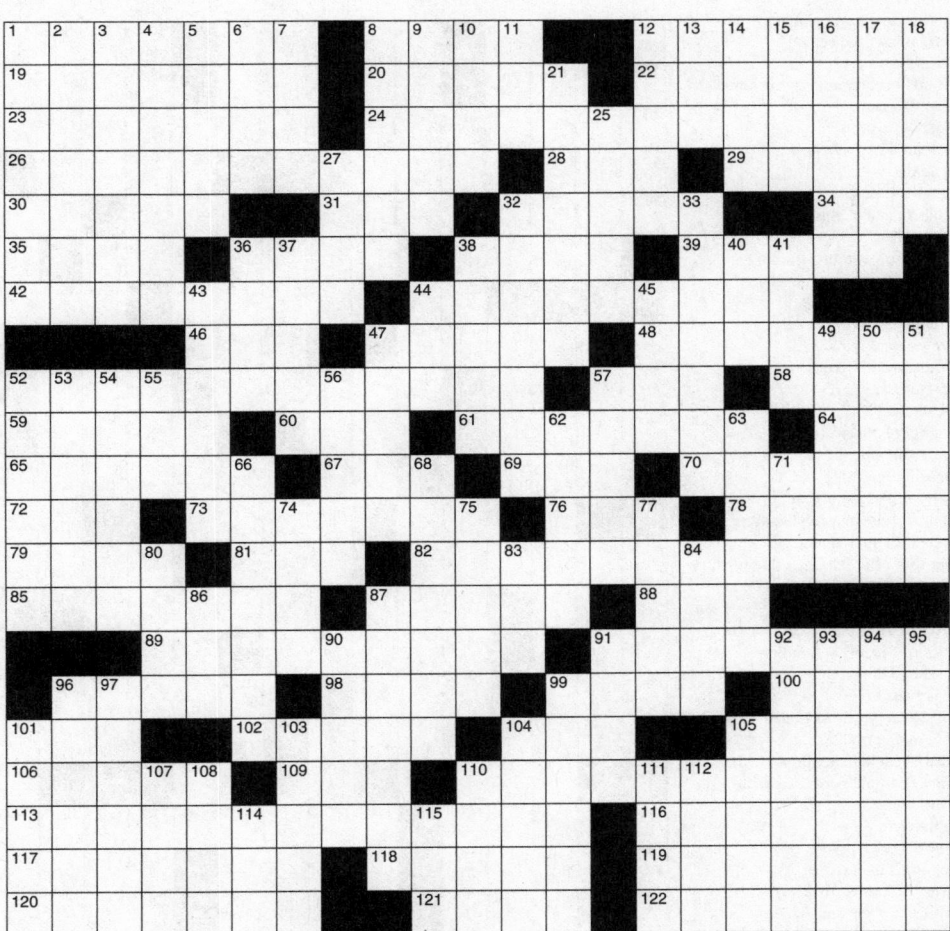

by Robert W. Harris

144 MIXED FEELINGS

ACROSS

1 Lively, in mus.
5 101, in a course name
10 "Little ___ in Slumberland" (pioneering comic strip)
14 One on two feet
19 Literature Nobelist Morrison
20 Word on a wanted poster
21 He's seen on the ceiling of the Sistine Chapel
22 Serengeti grazer
23 Pedicurist's need
26 Antics
27 Zingers
28 Toot one's horn
29 Scrooge's nephew in "A Christmas Carol"
30 Wearer of uniform #37, retired by both the Yankees and the Mets
34 Entered pompously
38 Clears
39 Relating to flight technology
41 Carnival site
42 "Inka Dinka ___"
43 Close overlapping of fugue voices
45 Prince ___, Eddie Murphy film role
47 Caboose, e.g.
48 Frolicking
52 Whispering party game
54 Vardalos of the screen
55 Diva's delivery
56 Holiday celebrating deliverance from Haman
59 Narrow inlet
60 Textile factory fixture
62 ___ fide
63 Lingo suffix
64 Unfortunate development
65 Bone-dry
66 Divider of wedding guests
68 Champion figure skater Irina
72 Leaves for lunch?
75 Author Janowitz
77 Professor 'iggins
78 Picassos and Pissarros
80 55-Across, e.g.
81 Bewitched
83 Penlight battery size
84 ___ radiation
86 DeMille output
87 Early millennium year
88 Manual transmission position
91 French dome toppers
93 Big shot after making a big shot, maybe: Abbr.
94 Kind of question
95 Peter Shaffer play based on the lives of Mozart and Salieri
98 "___-haw!"
99 Make haste
100 Like sugar vis-à-vis Equal
102 H.S. subject
106 Heartbreaking situations
109 Kitchen implement used with a little muscle
112 In the mail
113 K.G.B. predecessor
115 Popular Toyota
116 Users of 118-Across
118 Bats, balls, gloves, etc.
122 False appearance
123 Capital of Italy
124 Annie of "Ghostbusters"
125 Blade of Grasse
126 Lugged
127 Zenith
128 Company-owned building, e.g.
129 Sch. research papers

DOWN

1 Place for a fan
2 Writer Peggy known for the phrase "a kinder, gentler nation"
3 Actually existing
4 Stately dance with short steps
5 Tempts
6 Elite athlete
7 Error indicator
8 Suffix with adverb
9 Hit TV show with the theme song "Who Are You"
10 Port west of Monte Vesuvio
11 Fall setting
12 A, B and C
13 Mantra syllables
14 Come-hither look
15 Coming-clean words
16 Protective mailer
17 Music producer Brian
18 License to drill?: Abbr.
24 Milano of "Who's the Boss?"
25 Carbolic acid
29 Top-rated TV series of 2001–02
31 Consort of 21-Across
32 Capone henchman
33 "They're in my hot little hands!"
35 BlackBerry rival
36 Land of Ephesus
37 Acknowledge tacitly
40 Heads in the Pantheon?
44 Variety
46 Poet Omar ___
48 Rhyme scheme of "Stopping by Woods on a Snowy Evening"
49 "Star Trek: T.N.G." counselor Deanna
50 Some business attire
51 Yellow Teletubby
53 Composer Satie
57 Letters before many a state's name
58 Brush up on
61 Whiteboard cleaner
64 Subj. that deals with mixed feelings
67 Bearing nothing
69 Japanese eel and rice dish
70 "King Lear" or "Hamlet": Abbr.
71 Boxer's measurement
73 Touched down
74 Medics
76 Nonbeliever
79 Classic Dana fragrance for women
81 Representations of a winged woman holding an atom
82 Big name in skin care products
84 Entire range
85 Amazon parrot
89 Opener for a crystal ball gazer
90 Dine at a diner
92 F equivalent
96 Not dis
97 Declaim
101 Estimated: Abbr.
103 Chemical cousin
104 Lug: Var.
105 Online protocol for remote log-in
107 Discontinue
108 Absorb
110 Like lip-glossed lips
111 Deserves
114 Cause for an R, perhaps
116 Badge holder: Abbr.
117 Status ___
118 Main
119 Day ___
120 Dawn goddess
121 Divisions of gals.

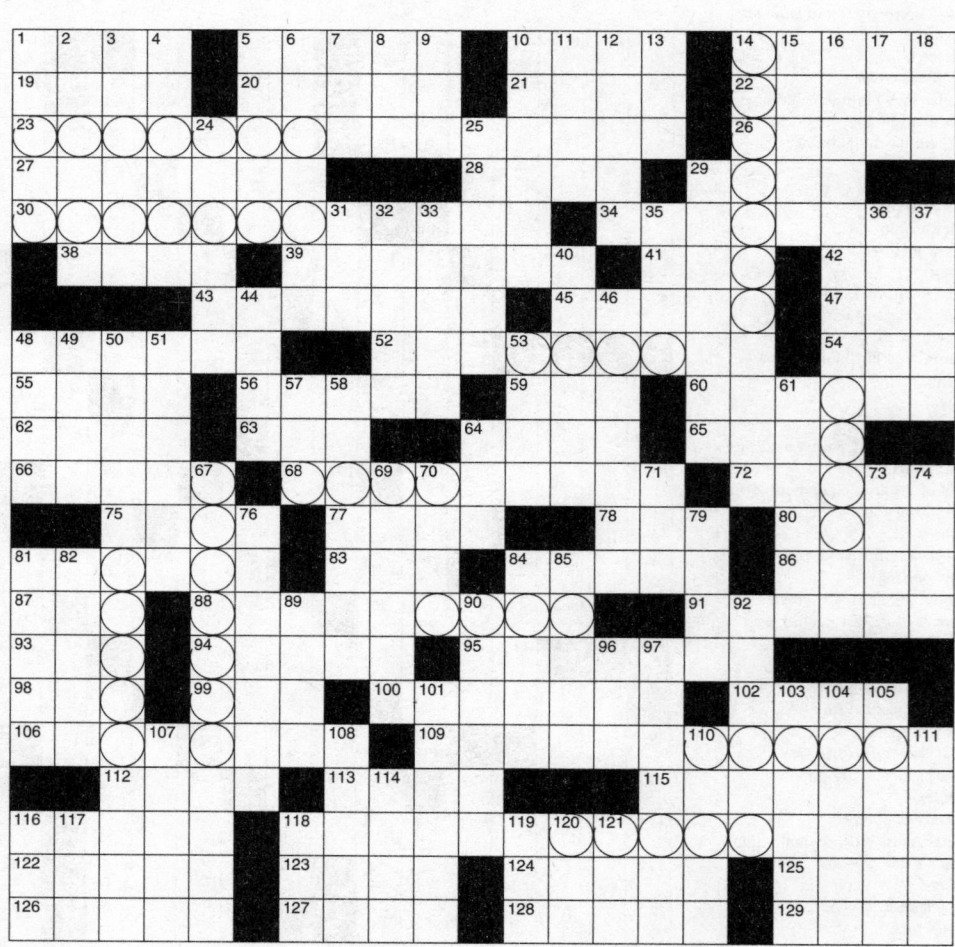

by Paula Gamache

ACROSS

1 Rocker Ocasek and others
5 Dwellers along the Dnieper River
10 "A ___, petal and a thorn" (Emily Dickinson poem)
15 Rtes.
18 1969 self-titled jazz album
19 United We Stand America founder
20 Eastern seaboard rte.
21 Greek discord goddess
23 Tax break for Gumby?
26 Publication read by Drs.
27 "Steady ___ goes"
28 Motor levers
29 Abjures
31 Money replaced by the 49-Down
33 "Bien sûr!"
34 Primitive wind instruments
35 Blessing for a shipboard romance?
40 Without compassion
41 Indisposed
42 Be indisposed
43 Architect whose epitaph says "Reader, if you seek his monument, look around you"
44 It's short for a long car
47 World's longest wooden roller coaster, at Kings Island
51 Battery type
52 "Hawaii Five-O" airer
55 Bridge writer Culbertson
56 Perhaps doesn't believe witty Rogers?
58 "Let's ___!"
59 Like some single-sex schools
61 Near-grads: Abbr.
62 Dinner plate scraping
63 ___'acte
64 "On First Looking Into Chapman's Homer" poet
65 Tribe originally from the Deep South
68 Wood shop device
69 Rigor of a fever
70 "Yoo-___!"
72 "Alley ___!"
73 "Oh, please"
75 Enough to hold a lotta iPod tunes
76 End-game maneuvers?
80 Turncoat
81 Somalia neighbor: Abbr.
82 Modern address
83 Zero interest
84 W.W. II vessels
85 Choice marbles
87 End of some 82-Acrosses
88 "Hands Across the Sea" composer
90 Writer ___ Rogers St. Johns
92 Excavate in the white cliffs?
99 "A Little Bitty Tear" singer, 1962
101 United
102 Flamenco cheer
103 Current gauge
104 1910s–'20s Dutch art movement
108 Like many "Survivor" contestants
109 Short ride
110 Drab Oriental fabric?
113 Word before or after "on"
114 Was a good Samaritan to
115 Rock genre
116 Blink ___ eye
117 Born abroad
118 Musts
119 Plant swelling
120 Communism battler, with "the"

DOWN

1 Summarizes
2 "Maybe"
3 Minor league baseball category
4 Greet someone
5 Hot Springs, e.g.
6 March fast?
7 Metropolitan ___
8 What people are saying, briefly
9 Promotion
10 Apt. overseer
11 Mechanics give them: Abbr.
12 Taro dish
13 Like half of all terminals
14 Leader with a goatee
15 Say "hallelujah!"
16 Sketch sewing-kit stores?
17 British fruitcake
22 Fresh
24 "Same here"
25 Prime minister raised in Milwaukee
30 Snail shell shape
32 Personification
34 "Be a ___!"
36 Kind of alcohol
37 Expressed wonder
38 Hops drier
39 "Apologia pro ___ Sua"
43 Kelly or Whitman
44 Waste of a sort
45 Crooked
46 Clown's parade memoir?
48 Twaddle
49 31-Across replacer
50 Decamp
51 One of the four elements
53 Toweling-off place
54 Urban grid
56 Start to lead?
57 "Holy moly!"
60 Onetime telecom giant
63 Listener
65 Friday, for one
66 Dictionary, often
67 Where private messages may be sent?: Abbr.
68 Delay
70 Towel stitching
71 Olive ___
73 Dear ___ Madam . . .
74 Breath: Prefix
76 1990–'91 war site
77 Shortly
78 Braided
79 Wood shop device
84 Night owl's TV fare
86 "The House of the Spirits" author, 1982
87 Grunts
89 ___ law (early legal code)
90 Cause to blush
91 Criticize harshly
92 ___ Melodies
93 "I ___ appreciate . . ."
94 In installments
95 In hijab, e.g.
96 "L'chaim!"
97 Figure skater Sokolova and others
98 Little stinger
100 Steakhouse shunner
104 Not natural
105 Terminal figs.
106 Leap on a stage
107 Good soil
111 Summer offering
112 20-Across terminus: Abbr.

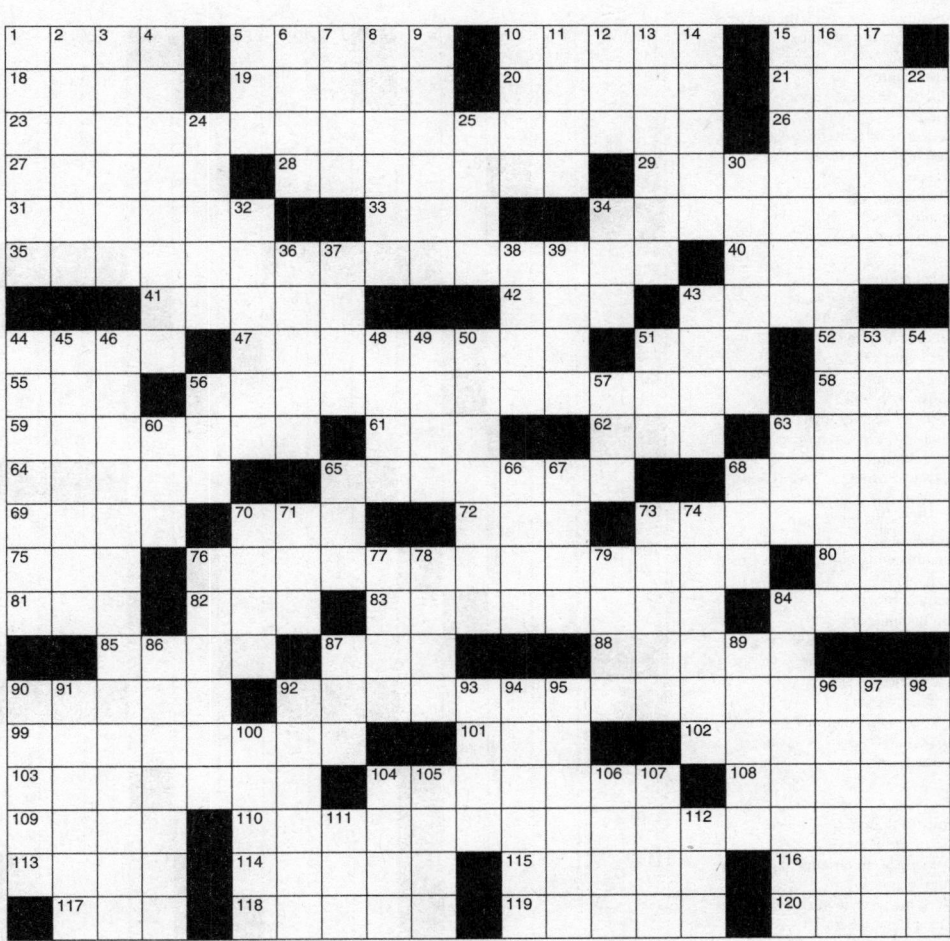

by Daniel C. Bryant

146 HOW INSULTING!

ACROSS

1 Polish Peace Nobelist
7 Story development
10 Tongue of Jung: Abbr.
13 Variety show potpourri
18 Scrubs
19 Head of Great Britain
20 Where "I shot a man" in Johnny Cash's "Folsom Prison Blues"
21 Something to believe in
22 Foul weather condition?
25 1980s U.N. ambassador Kirkpatrick
26 Date
27 Sounded wowed
28 Plume source
29 Child protector?
30 Some moralizing about getting off a balance beam?
34 Quitter's assertion
36 Former Giants giant
37 Saloon door sign
38 "Do your thing, Jack the Ripper"?
43 Provides tools for, as a crime
46 Hefty competitor
47 Matériel
48 Hardships
50 Numbskull
54 Cheerful chorus
55 Wampum
57 Classic soft drink
58 Apartment 1-A resident, maybe
59 Sophistication of clubs like Sam's and BJ's?
62 Wool source
66 Title for Michael Caine
67 Declines
68 Concerns of someone who's choking?
75 Prepare
76 Used a bus, e.g.
77 March master
78 Fraction of a min.
82 Delta 88, e.g.
83 Asian shrine
85 Mid 10th-century year
86 Another, in Andalucía
87 Bruce who played Watson
88 Her Royal Daunter?
91 Eucharist plate
94 Suffix with ball
95 Take off, as a brooch
96 Coleslaw-loving children?
104 ____ nothing
105 Player of filmdom's Mr. Chips
106 With all one's strength
107 Welsh rabbit ingredient
110 Airbus, e.g.
111 Find chewing gum under a desk, perhaps?
114 Passage practices
115 Chihuahua drink
116 Prominent Chihuahua feature
117 Samantha's cousin on "Bewitched"
118 In other words
119 Bygone map letters
120 Hook shape
121 Texas team

DOWN

1 Rolls of dough
2 Broadway Rose-lover
3 Crosses the international date line from east to west
4 Work measurement unit
5 James I and Charles I
6 Northeast state of India
7 1979 film parodied in "Spaceballs"
8 Sonata movement
9 Subordinate person
10 Sci-fi, e.g.
11 Over
12 Swiss dish of grated and fried potatoes
13 Place in Monopoly
14 Continue
15 Doing the same old same old
16 Joint parts
17 Insertion in an operation
20 Just
23 Even if, briefly
24 More humid
31 Bagnold, Blyton, Markey, etc.
32 Postal creed word
33 Some NCOs
34 Rock's ____ Pop
35 Popular pop
39 '50s teen star
40 Incenses
41 Car financing co.
42 "As we have therefore opportunity, let ____ good to all men": Galatians
43 Tommie ____, 1966 A.L. Rookie of the Year
44 Nobel physicist Niels
45 Actor Bana of "Munich"
49 Prelims
50 Import tax
51 Magnum ____
52 "Coming Home" co-star
53 Stacking contest cookie
56 Puzzled (out)
58 Metal refuse
59 Sideless wagon
60 Nonexistent
61 Seals are part of it
62 Do that's picked
63 Advent song
64 More than nudge
65 9 to 5, e.g.
69 Go on too long
70 Venetian V.I.P. of yore
71 Wannabe's model
72 Rx writers
73 Judy Garland's real last name
74 "La ____ Bonita" (Madonna song)
78 Diamond center
79 Efficiency device
80 ". . . ____ saw Elba"
81 Mass. neighbor
83 Worrisome engine sound
84 Highway or Pet lead-in
87 Like a relative notified in an emergency, maybe
89 ____ while
90 Preserves fruits
91 Sans a healthy glow
92 Remove by cutting
93 Porterhouse alternatives
94 Honshu metropolis
96 Banana liqueur drink shaken over ice
97 Old Norse works
98 Magician Henning and others
99 Run up
100 Oral flourishes
101 Starfleet V.I.P.'s: Abbr.
102 Japanese yes
103 "Once You ____ Stranger" (1969 thriller)
108 TV host known for his mandibular prognathism
109 History chapters
112 Word between two surnames
113 Leftover for Rover

by Cathy Millhauser

When this puzzle is done, the letters in the following squares spell a bonus phrase: 7A - 3rd letter, 31A - 5th, 65A - 4th, 104A - 6th, 136A - 3rd, 151A - 1st, 149A - 4th, 133A - 4th, 100A - 1st, 62A - 1st, 29A - 6th

ACROSS

1 Thing in a case
4 1960s–'80s Red Sox legend, informally
7 In the cellar
11 Org. that promotes adoption
15 "Poor venomous fool," in "Antony and Cleopatra"
18 Pumpkin-picking time: Abbr.
19 "Sons and Lovers" Oscar nominee Mary
20 Expected
22 King of comedy
23 Going rate?: Abbr.
24 1941 Henry Luce article that coined a name for an era
28 Barcelona Olympics prize
29 Tevye creator ___ Aleichem
30 Eight-time Norris Trophy winner
31 Protein acid, informally
32 Have ___ to pick
33 Celine Dion's "I'm Your Angel" duet partner
34 Closeout come-on
39 Designated driver's drink
40 Badges, e.g., in brief
41 ___ candy (some pop tunes)
42 Work of Seigneur de Montaigne
43 "Your Moment of ___" ("The Daily Show" feature)
45 Truncated cones, in math
49 Streaming
52 Novel that ends "Don't ever tell anybody anything. If you do, you start missing everybody"
61 Not to mention
62 Atlas section
63 "Roll Over Beethoven" band, for short
64 1990s–2000s English tennis star Tim
65 Rocky Mountains resort
66 Wide-eyed
67 First principles
70 "I'm king of the world!," e.g.
71 Exceeded the speed limit?
72 "Tancredi" composer
75 Artful deception
78 State quarters?
80 Actress Ullmann
81 Suffix with billion
82 1972 Harry Nilsson hit
90 Windsor, e.g.
95 Switch finish?
96 Absorb a loss
97 1984 Heisman winner
99 Orient
100 Chickadees' kin
101 Laughing gas and water, chemically
103 Mess up
104 Lover in "The Merchant of Venice"
106 Genuine: Ger.
107 Prime eatery
111 Sloughs off
113 You can't take it with you
114 Upstate N.Y. sch.
115 Tribute in jest
118 Managed
119 Sneak a peek
121 Boot part
125 Stanley Cup finalists of 1982 and 1994
131 Couple
133 Long-legged wader
134 He played Krupa in "The Gene Krupa Story"
135 "You did it!"
136 Lorenz Hart specialty
137 Pricey sports car, informally
138 Head of a special government inquiry
143 Hard wood
144 Math. class
145 Actress Watts
146 Home on "Gilligan's Island"
147 Inflation meas.
148 On the other hand
149 Charles de Gaulle alternative
150 Varsity QB, e.g.
151 Sign at a smash
152 Possessed

DOWN

1 "Number 10" Abstract Expressionist
2 Made a comeback?
3 "A Streetcar Named Desire" role
4 "Dee-lish!"
5 "These ___ the times that . . ."
6 Closed (in on)
7 Money
8 Botanist Gray
9 Center of many revolutions
10 Certain X or O
11 Subbed (for)
12 Dive
13 Glances
14 "___ takers?"
15 Spanish sherry
16 Offshoot
17 Snap
21 Mother of Judah
25 Popular portal
26 Kupcinet and Cross
27 Application letters
29 Some namesakes: Abbr.
32 Without obligation
35 Change of a mortgage, slangily
36 Paul Bunyan story
37 Ministry of ___, in "1984"
38 Ryder Cup team
40 Time ___
43 Tase
44 When many get a St.-Tropez tan
46 Biblical queendom
47 Joint part
48 Royal Navy foe of 1588
50 Willow used in basketry
51 Hills of Yorkshire
52 Spree
53 Monster hurricane of 1989
54 Libido
55 Lowly workers
56 Do voodoo on
57 Skull and Bones members
58 Latitude
59 Bleeth of "Baywatch"
60 Unabridged
67 Executive's charter, maybe
68 Infiltrator
69 Flat-bottomed boat
73 Despot ___ Amin
74 Lead-in to "the above" or "your business"
76 Like some twins
77 ___ center
79 Mystery element
82 Leaps across the ballet stage
83 "Vega$" star Robert
84 Nick Nolte movie based on a Kurt Vonnegut novel
85 Some advanced researchers, for short
86 Traditional almanac data
87 Bikini blast
88 Sorry sort
89 Parisian "to be"
91 Jean who wrote "Please Don't Eat the Daisies"
92 "So long, dahling"
93 "The fix ___"
94 Virginie ou Pennsylvanie
98 Subject of the book "Many Unhappy Returns": Abbr.
102 ___ Zagora, Bulgaria
104 Infant's food
105 "Certainement!"
108 Mussorgsky's "Pictures ___ Exhibition"
109 Contact lens solution brand
110 Venture
112 ___ Miguel, Azores island
116 Sting's last name
117 "Hannah Montana" star Miley Cyrus, for one
119 32-card game
120 Charges (up)
121 "Into the Wild" actor Emile
122 Home of Gannon Univ.
123 Author of the "Elements," ca. 300 B.C.
124 Past records?
125 Singh on the links
126 Demean
127 Bad guys
128 Name
129 Filmmaker Joel or Ethan
130 Jaded figure
131 2006 neologism meaning "to demote"
132 Author Rand
138 "May ___ now?"
139 Bust
140 ___ Pérignon
141 Comic Philips
142 "___ Father . . ."

by John Farmer

148 Oops!

ACROSS

1 Program executors, for short
5 Miracle-___
8 Tribal council makeup, often
14 Casual attire
19 Like the carol "Away in a Manger," originally
21 Wine sometimes blended with Cabernet Sauvignon
22 Be
23 Turn away
24 Foot, slangily
25 2% alternative
26 *Long, long time
28 Loot
30 Yank or Tiger
31 Half-baked
32 *Stick with a needle, maybe
34 *Absence at a nudist colony?
41 What a Tennessee cheerleader asks for a lot?
42 Stuck
43 Neighbor of Ga.
44 *Bugs
50 Jazzy Jones
51 *Wee
54 Below par
55 X-ray ___
56 "What a moron I am!"
57 Gawk at
58 Whatchamacallit
60 Monterrey mister
62 Suffix not seen much in London
63 Least bold
65 Like the answers to the 10 asterisked clues, more often than any other English words, according to a 1999 study
69 Narrative
71 ___ choy (Chinese vegetable)
72 Contract specifics
73 Luster
74 Tip of the Arabian Peninsula
76 Massage target?
77 Spicy cuisine
81 Debt acknowledgment
82 *Conspicuous
86 Trying period for a doctoral student
87 *Supplant
91 Clean air org.
92 Baseball's ___ league
93 Gen ___
94 *Doggedness
97 *Oblige
103 Commotion
104 Series of rounds
105 Is undecided
107 *Event
113 Root used in perfumery
115 Farmer's ___
117 Attempts
118 T-shirt style
119 Follows
120 Like some pens
121 Swift's "A Modest Proposal," e.g.
122 Plain
123 Alternative to dial-up
124 French noblemen

DOWN

1 Symbol of happiness
2 Long-haired sheepdog
3 Regulated bus.
4 Writer/illustrator Silverstein
5 Mustang competitor
6 Photoshop options
7 Tops
8 Ambulance figure: Abbr.
9 Many August babies
10 Disarming words?
11 Rocker John
12 Violinist's need
13 Pen, to Pierre
14 1950s Braves All-Star pitcher Burdette
15 Relaxes, in a way
16 It's bowed
17 Archipelago part
18 Cubic meter
20 Laredo-to-Galveston dir.
27 "Bro!"
29 Cliff
33 Spanish "a"
34 Karl Marx's one
35 Alphabet quartet
36 Expose
37 Product with TV's first advertising jingle, 1948
38 Word of encouragement
39 QB Manning
40 "Illmatic" rapper
44 Most massive
45 The whole wide world
46 Show up again
47 Judged, with "up"
48 They're seen in many John Constable paintings
49 ___ machine
51 Orator's no-no
52 Restaurant chain since 1958
53 Close, as a relationship
56 Laura of "Jurassic Park"
58 Some shampoos
59 Running mate with Dick
60 Like cotton candy
61 Commercial come-on
62 Type
64 Ticklish one?
65 Freeze
66 Target of many a Bart Simpson prank call
67 Rice-A-___
68 Marmalade component
69 Without adjustments
70 Dynasty of Confucius and Lao-tzu
75 Trendy
77 Olive or apple
78 Goldie of "Cactus Flower"
79 Actor Baldwin
80 "Ah, yes"
83 O.K. mark
84 When Earth Day is celebrated: Abbr.
85 ___ profundo
86 Anthem contraction
88 Rare imports, maybe
89 Crucial sleep stage
90 Cock-a-doodle-doo
92 Examination
94 Opposite of "nod off"
95 Marked permanently
96 Parish priests
97 Previously mentioned
98 Toes' woes
99 Parish priests
100 Matriarchs
101 ___-garde
102 Brusque
106 Ooze
108 Dorm heads, for short
109 "Heavens!"
110 International chain of fusion cuisine restaurants
111 Course after trig
112 Somme times
114 Heavens
116 Literary inits.

by Oliver Hill

ACROSS

1 Craving, slangily
6 Crèche figures
10 Impromptu Halloween costume
15 Spray withdrawn in 1989
19 Try to steal the scene, maybe
20 "Darn it!"
21 Mountain chain
23 Nick name?
24 1977 Dolly Parton song for tree fanciers?
26 Bridal collection
28 Not ___ many words
29 Nominal promotion of a military officer
30 Sugar substitute?
31 Modern pentathlon event
32 Inner circles
33 1965 Yardbirds song for tree fanciers?
39 ___ volatile
40 Bellowing
41 Nirvana seeker
42 World capital, founded in 1538, formerly known as Chuquisaca
44 Suffix with myth
48 Went like a shot
50 1957 Jerry Lee Lewis song for tree fanciers?
53 Outer limits
54 Stand
56 Rush hour sounds
57 Port of Iraq
58 One trillionth: Prefix
59 Rossini subject
60 Air Force athlete
61 1964 Bobby Goldsboro song for tree fanciers?
68 It's spotted in the wild
69 Like a lot of Australia
70 Lay on the line
71 Brain parts
72 Tippy transport
74 Bank deposit?
75 Old-time oath
79 1982 Joan Jett and the Blackhearts song for tree fanciers?
82 Jazzy Nina
84 Altar procedure
85 "Sesame Street" regular
86 Beaufort scale category
88 Neighbor of Chad
89 Flight formation
90 1959 Chuck Berry song for tree fanciers?
92 Source of some coffee
96 Italian bread
98 Source of creosote
99 Sugar or flour
100 Doozy
101 Do police work
107 1978 Linda Ronstadt song for tree fanciers?
110 Palate part
111 Sing "Bye Bye Birdie," e.g.
112 Hurt badly
113 16th-century English dramatist George
114 Badlands sight
115 Exorcist's enemy
116 Red army?
117 Sp. misses

DOWN

1 Witty remark
2 "A Jug of Wine . . ." poet
3 Off-limits item
4 Words of reproach
5 Strand
6 Key fort?
7 Stretch
8 Ashram leader
9 Chemical suffix
10 Teatime treat
11 Theater audience
12 For this reason
13 Dot follower, often
14 Tito Puente played them
15 "Sink or Swim" author
16 Permission
17 Sign of spring
18 Go into hysterics
22 ___ Lad, doughnut shop on "The Simpsons"
25 Cry of dismay
27 Insignificant amount
31 "A Letter for ___" (Hume Cronyn film)
32 ___ Jr., West Coast hamburger chain
33 Discombobulate
34 Mill material
35 Cross
36 Thanksgiving serving
37 Enters cyberspace
38 Dungeons & Dragons character
39 Sing like Fitzgerald
42 Impassive
43 Nut holder
44 "___ else fails . . ."
45 ___ Systems, networking giant
46 Helpful pointer
47 Musical Rimes
49 Underlying meaning
51 Place for an easel
52 One way to be taken
55 R.N.'s station
58 Purple stuff, perhaps
59 Power of film
60 Happy gatherings
61 Play-by-play partner
62 Theodor Escherich's discovery
63 Ledger entry
64 Anacin alternative
65 ___-Poo of "The Mikado"
66 1970s–'80s baseball All-Star Manny
67 Rap star ___ Jon
72 Chick on the piano
73 Rough condition to face?
74 Criticize
75 Eastern ruler
76 Energetic
77 From the top
78 Laura of "Blue Velvet"
80 Ran through again
81 Give the once-over
83 Cliques
87 Prizes
90 Sufficient, informally
91 Dance specialty
92 Dickens title starter
93 Soul singer Lou
94 Via ___ (Roman road)
95 Be noisy
96 Words before bed or rest
97 Not at all familiar
99 E-mail annoyance
100 "The Informer" author O'Flaherty
101 Kind of meeting in "O Brother, Where Art Thou?"
102 Give off
103 Camper driver
104 Something one can never do
105 Salmon tail?
106 Actress Charlotte and explorer John
108 Grand ___, Nova Scotia
109 John's "Pulp Fiction" co-star

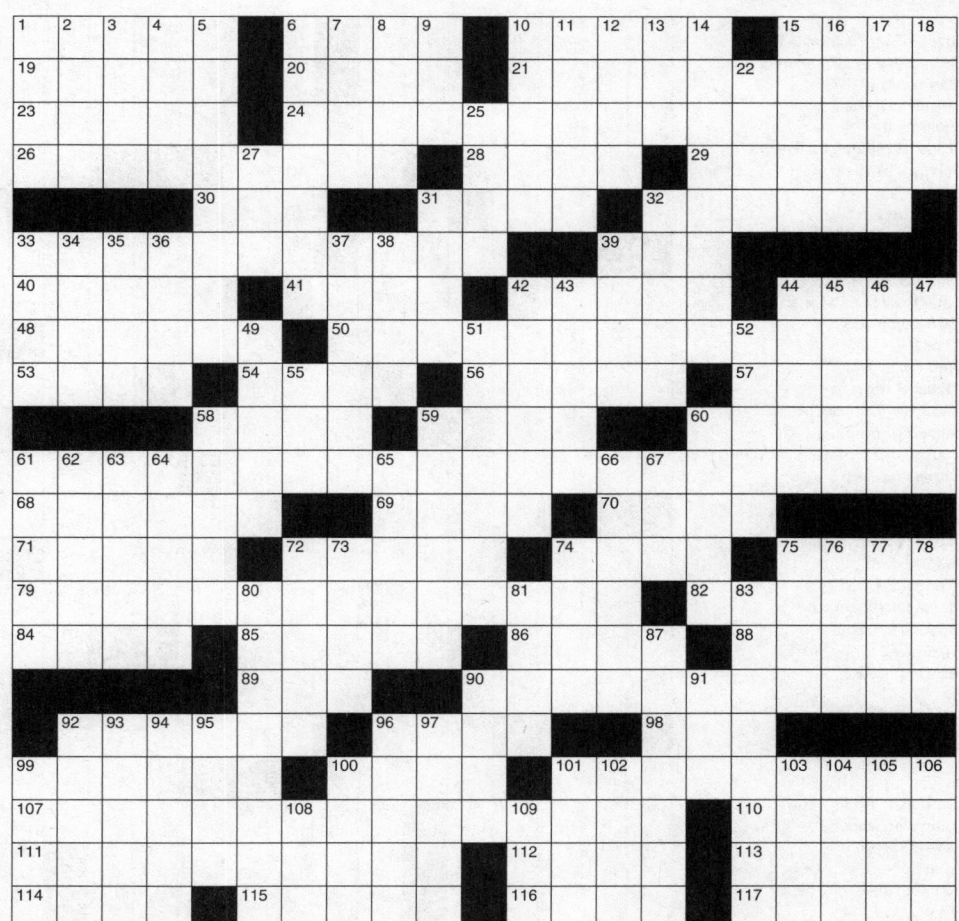

by Richard Silvestri

ACROSS

1 Rooter at the Meadowlands
8 Lean and bony
15 Superman, to his father
20 Common solvent
21 Filled
22 Acid in proteins
23 State of a bottle-fed baby?
25 Woody Allen title role
26 Afternoon hr.
27 Construction bit
28 Bleacher
30 Comme ci, comme ça
31 Was visibly irked with
35 Shower with flowers, say
36 Soft drink brand
38 A platform in front of Elsinore, in "Hamlet"?
44 Contemporary of Duchamp
47 "Doctor Faustus" novelist
49 Jazz virtuoso Garner
50 The toe of a geographical "boot"
51 Massage therapist's office?
55 Like a Rolek watch
57 Fashion designer Bartley
58 Brown alternative
59 "You can ___ horse to water . . ."
61 Sentimentality
62 "Puppy Love" singer, 1960
63 Jawaharlal Nehru's daughter
65 Rouge roulette number
67 Group of yo-yo experts?
70 One willing to take a bullet for Martin or Charlie?
76 Neighbor of Hung.
77 Fixes firmly
79 Shade on the French Riviera
80 Calypso offshoot
83 Actor Alain
86 It has banks in Bern
87 Urban area in a Cheech Marin film
89 1965 Peace Prize recipient
91 Little Bo-Peep's charges?
94 Catty comments?
95 87 or 93
97 Turn on an axis
98 Alphabet trio
99 Musicians at a marsh?
103 Numerical prefix
105 Corrosive chemical, to a chemist
106 Strong and deep
108 Oversight
112 Limo feature
117 "Road" picture partner for Bob
118 "Same here!"
119 "The joke's ___!"
120 St. Paul sixth graders?
125 Indonesian island
126 Victimizes
127 Brewing needs
128 Do
129 Calendar divisions
130 ___ Row

DOWN

1 ___ Kádár, 1950s–'80s Hungarian leader
2 Low-price prefix
3 "The Love Boat" actress Lauren
4 Squash, squish or squelch
5 Head
6 Gloucester's Cape ___
7 Chick
8 Cuban-born jazz great Sandoval
9 Fix
10 3.9, e.g.: Abbr.
11 Final: Abbr.
12 Gift with a string attached?
13 Over
14 Fix-up
15 Buzzers
16 Green card, informally
17 Leslie Caron title role
18 Home of the Chisholm Trail Expo Center
19 Front of a mezzanine
24 ___ big way
29 Casually showed up
31 Land west of Togo
32 The less you see of this person the better
33 Intro to business?
34 Alpine region
37 German biographer ___ Ludwig
39 ___ of the above
40 Romaine
41 Online periodical, for short
42 Warsaw Pact counterforce
43 Automaker Ferrari
44 Key of Elgar's Symphony No. 1
45 Get the class back together
46 ___-boo

48 "Bye Bye Bye" band, 2000
52 Cousin of a camel
53 "Aren't I amazing?!"
54 Skirt type
56 Called
60 Good blackjack holdings
63 Like G8 meetings: Abbr.
64 "There's no such thing ___ publicity"
66 Subdue
68 "My man!"
69 Resort to violence
71 "Three cheers" recipient
72 Ideal sites
73 Like some pyramids
74 Lined
75 Don, as a sari
78 "Luncheon on the Grass" and others
80 Well
81 Baby-bouncing locale
82 Sanyo competitor
84 Words to live by
85 Hornet, e.g.
87 Extracted chemical
88 "___ of Six" (Joseph Conrad story collection)
90 Hrs. on the 90th meridian

92 Addie's husband in "As I Lay Dying"
93 Stretch . . . or a hint to this puzzle's theme?
96 Shop grippers
100 "And I'm the queen of England"
101 Director Mark of "Earthquake"
102 Particles in electrolysis
104 Slide presentation?
107 Amazon ___
109 They might be bounced off others
110 Troubadour's stock
111 Wimp
112 Scribbles (down)
113 Body of troops
114 "Well, I declare!"
115 Summer hangout
116 Poop
118 Seaborne lackey
121 Org. interested in schools
122 Albany is its cap.
123 That's "that" in Tijuana
124 Pro ___

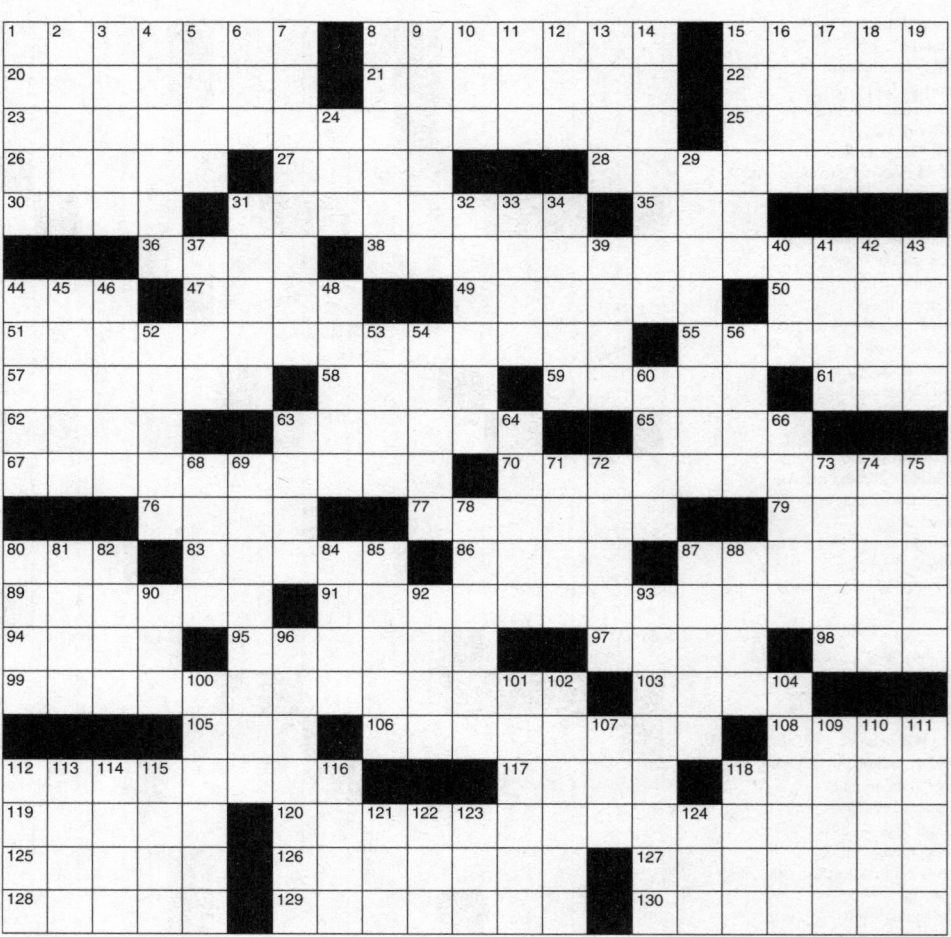

by Tony Orbach and Patrick Blindauer

ACROSS

1 Site of campus workstations
6 Ancient pueblo dwellers
13 Norm of "This Old House"
18 Muse with a wreath of myrtle and roses
19 Together
20 Tell things?
21 Bill formerly of the Rolling Stones
22 Fight imaginary foes
24 Richard ___, 2002 Pulitzer winner for Fiction
26 ___ B'rith
27 Sylph in Pope's "The Rape of the Lock"
28 Pressure, of a sort
32 "Sixteen Tons" singer, 1955
36 Do better than
37 In the capacity of
38 X-ray units
41 Nails
42 Notch shape
43 "Would you like to see ___?"
45 Italian restaurant chain
47 Game pieces
48 Some badge holders
49 "Alice in Wonderland" sister
50 It's a laugh
51 Each
53 "Lawrence of Arabia" composer Maurice
54 ___-doodle
56 Start of the names of some health care plans
58 Daily grind
60 Place for a vine
61 Bent over
63 How headings are often typed
65 Surfing spot
66 Immigrant's class: Abbr.
68 "Survivor" setting, often
69 Blood-typing letters
70 Fire
72 Some M.I.T. grads: Abbr.
73 Buster?
75 Certain T-shirt design
77 Sure application spot
79 Drug-free
80 National Chili Mo.
81 Blue shade
83 "Pearly Shells" singer
85 Refrain syllables
86 Loud laugh
88 Take to Vegas, maybe
90 Valuable find
92 Mideast call to prayer
93 Airport with a BART terminal
95 Steer
97 Kids
98 Kind of score
99 "Deadwood" figure
100 Untouched
101 Meaningless amount
103 Quick stumbles
104 Dealer's handout
107 Starts, as rehab
110 Upper ___
111 Shade provider
114 Outplays
115 Former L.A. Ram who holds the N.F.L. record for most receiving yards in a game (336)
119 Response to "Any volunteers?"
123 Pretends
124 "Back door's open!"
125 Explorer of sorts
126 To date
127 In order
128 Post with a column

DOWN

1 Missal location
2 "Geronimo!," e.g.
3 Escape
4 Defender company
5 Test extras
6 Electrolysis particle
7 Match ___ (tie game, in France)
8 Aardvark
9 ___ Phillips, who played Livia in "I, Claudius"
10 Old film pooch
11 "Fan-tastic!"
12 Suffix in some pasta names
13 Hosts
14 To the point
15 Opening track of "The Beatles' Second Album"
16 Cobbler's tool
17 Eds. read them
19 "No problem!"
20 Oscar-winning Brody
23 Jack of "Eraserhead"
25 Good nickname for a cook?
28 Galley marking
29 Peripatetic sort
30 Einstein subject
31 Short-billed rail
33 Push for more business orders
34 House of Lancaster symbol
35 Jilts
39 Sloping surfaces next to sinks
40 Pacifier
44 Cheese ___
46 Good farming results
48 Klinger portrayer on "M*A*S*H"
52 ___ pro nobis
53 Awarding of huge settlements to plaintiffs, in modern lingo
55 Some greetings
57 Zoologist Fossey
59 Early anti-Communist
62 Mix
64 The Nutmeg State: Abbr.
66 Hug
67 Marathoner Alberto
71 Control: Abbr.
74 Actor James
76 Indian tribe encountered by Lewis and Clark
78 Sign of the cross
82 "Were that so!"
84 Plain as day
87 Excellent debt rating
89 Rappel down
91 Edsel driver's gas choice
93 "Bambi" author
94 Monastery figure
96 Sovereign's representative
99 It's a trap
102 Approves
105 Thicket
106 Faust, e.g.
108 Old Treasury offering
109 Nation of ___
112 Month in which Moses is said to have been born and died
113 Aloe ___
115 Fourth-most populous state, just after N.Y.
116 French article
117 Turkish title
118 Press (for)
120 VII octupled
121 Many a toothpaste
122 Suffix with direct

by Brendan Emmett Quigley

152 SPY GLASS

When this puzzle is done, the seven circles will contain the letters from A to G. Starting with A, connect them alphabetically with one continuous line, and you'll get an image of a 39-Across.

ACROSS

1 How architects' models are built
8 Lou Bega's "___ No. 5"
13 Ottoman V.I.P.'s
18 Foyer item
19 Plug in a travel kit
21 It may give you a cold shoulder
22 Alarming
23 *1969*
25 Auditioned for "American Idol"
26 Italian town known for its embroidery
28 End of a plumb line
29 Law assignment
30 Garbage hauler
32 "True"
35 Neighborhood next to N.Y.C.'s East Village
37 Ecuador and Venezuela are in it
39 [See instructions]
41 Relating to a blood line
45 Sub systems
47 Suffix with urban
48 *1973–85*
50 Moles' production
52 Subj. for bilinguals
54 Like some video, to cable customers
55 Warhol's "___ of Six Self-Portraits"
56 Lambs' kin
58 Aside (from)
61 "Smooth Operator" singer
62 French seas
63 Powder site, maybe
64 First mate
65 "Put ___ writing!"
67 Layer
68 *1987–89*
71 Figures at many a wedding reception, briefly
74 Kite flier's wish
75 Muscle mag displays
76 Sneaky
77 Semitic deity
78 Med. plans
80 Gut course
82 Alexander Hamilton's last act
83 "By the power vested ___ . . ."
84 Aches
86 N.B.A.'s ___ Ming
88 Ventured (forth)
90 Writer born May 28, 1908
93 Speech pauses
95 Surprisingly
96 Brings out
97 Offering from St. Joseph
99 Willy Wonka's creator
100 ___ buco
102 Mexican beer
103 A great deal
105 "Lost" filming locale
108 Global currency org.
110 2003 best-selling fantasy novel by teen author Christopher Paolini
113 Beethoven's third?
115 *1995–2002*
119 New Jersey city, county or river
121 Name-drop, maybe?
122 Least restrained
123 Artist Watteau
124 Ward off
125 Singer Jones and others
126 Piano players' hangouts

DOWN

1 Old propaganda propagator
2 Ocean menaces
3 *1962–67, 1971*
4 Attire with supersized pockets
5 "Exodus" hero
6 ___ 9, first spacecraft to land softly on the moon
7 Deviled things
8 Chairman's supporter?
9 Natl. Poetry Mo.
10 Brief encounter?
11 Programme airer, with "the"
12 Knee sock material
13 Wood shaper
14 Like some wrestling
15 Tennis star Mandlikova
16 Edwards and others: Abbr.
17 Eye doctor's concern
19 Shakes up
20 Hungers
24 On
27 California's ___ Valley
31 "___ #1!"
33 Title for 48-Across and 3-Down
34 Lennon's mate
36 Nears, with "on"
38 "The Allegory of Love" writer, 1936
40 Kurchatov who oversaw the Soviet atomic bomb project
42 Lowly one
43 Composer of "Dido and Aeneas"
44 Spearheaded
45 Sign of approval
46 White-collared thrush: Var.
49 Authorizes
51 Butterfly experts, perhaps
53 March 25, in the Christian calendar
57 It can be fragile
59 Residences, in slang
60 Drs.' org.
64 Ship-to-ship communication
66 In song, "Once you pass its borders, you can ne'er return again"
68 Fights
69 Cable TV inits.
70 Baton Rouge sch.
71 *2006–*
72 Bond common to the answers to the six *italicized* clues
73 Runners' locales
74 It's full of holes
77 Rock guitarist once married to Goldie Hawn
78 Commander
79 Plan for dinner
81 1998 Sarah McLachlan hit
82 Alpha
84 Disapproving cry
85 Bluesy Smith
87 Night lights
89 Rich soil
91 Homeland protection org.
92 Main mailbox locale: Abbr.
94 Sweater flaw
98 Castle and Cara
101 Game played with a 40-card deck
104 "Romanzero" poet
105 Phone co. employee
106 Suffix with billion
107 Jalopy
109 Univ. house
111 Autumn birthstone
112 Second start?
114 Clinches
116 Hanna-Barbera art
117 German direction
118 ___ Na Na
120 Disco guy on "The Simpsons"

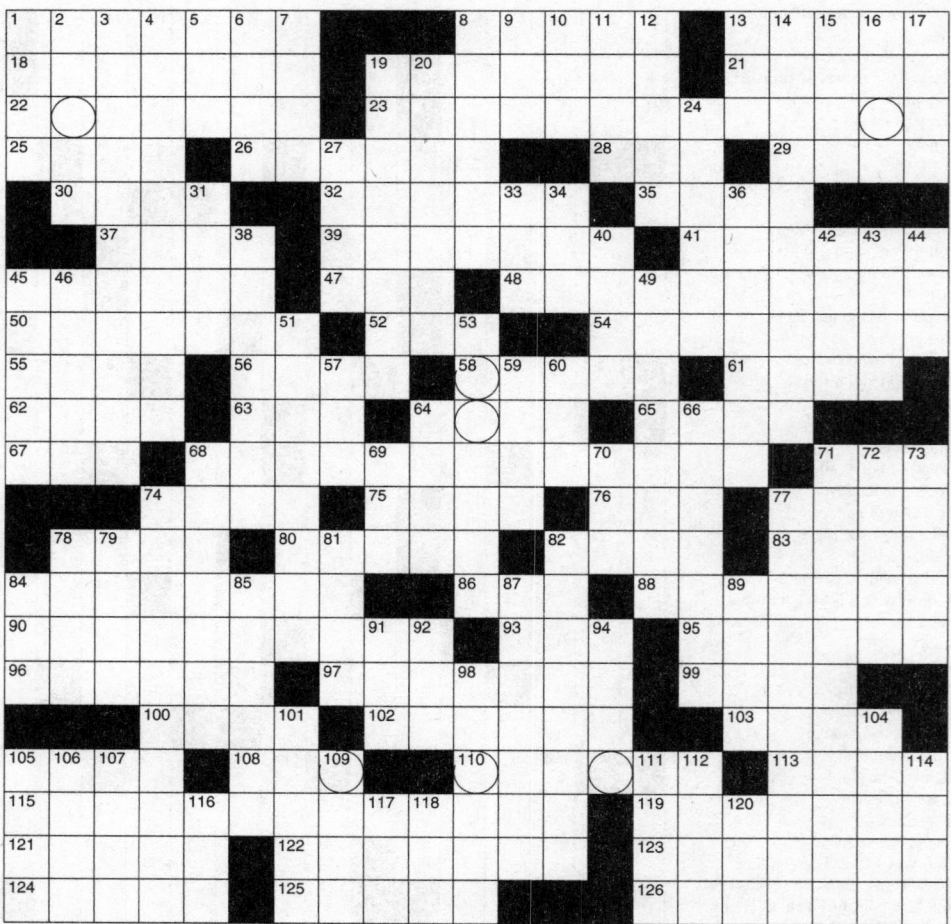

by Elizabeth C. Gorski

ACROSS

1 Diane of "Alice Doesn't Live Here Anymore"
5 Picture holder
10 ___ alai
13 They may be big fellers
17 Prefix with business
18 West African coins
20 On one's ___
21 World capital formerly a pirate stronghold
22 Waistband sold in stores?
24 Issue to avoid
26 Bad things to share
27 Wiser from an ethical perspective?
29 Miller brand
30 Two points?
31 Well-born folks
32 Fighting force trained by Pavlov?
38 Qualifying races
39 Auto superseded by the Rambler
40 Actress Susan of "L.A. Law"
41 Leading man?
45 Some cloisonné pieces
46 Distresses
47 Put through demeaning rituals
49 City just west of Silver Springs
50 Salon selections
51 Kilo- times 1,000
52 Mardi ___
54 Skirts worn by both men and women
56 Freelance autopsist?
59 Renaissance painter Uccello
61 Lady Bird Johnson's given birth name
62 Private
63 Catchy song parts heard on "Name That Tune"?
66 Country with a camel on its coat of arms
67 Sign
68 Captain Hook's mate in "Peter Pan"
69 X3 and X5 maker
72 Pack carriers
73 T. ___ Price (investment firm)
75 Intervals
76 Animation
77 Minus
78 Club wielders' grp.
79 Stud farm visitor
80 Crème de la crème
81 Stones and brickbats?
86 Appointed
90 Attorney general during Reagan's second term
91 "Metropolis" director
92 Store that peddles political influence?
95 Like glass doors, often
98 Its bite is worse than its bark
99 Boiled lobster's feature?
102 Be part of the opening lineup
103 High dudgeon
104 Ankle covering
105 Barrett of gossip
106 Lots of talk
107 Smidgen
108 Only beardless one of the Seven Dwarfs
109 Fall around Christmas

DOWN

1 Testing facilities
2 Flu symptom
3 Washes without water
4 Record keepers, of a sort
5 Mobile phone company
6 Bottom of the barrel
7 Weave's partner
8 Rimbaud's "___ Saison en Enfer"
9 "___ the Wanderer" (1820 gothic novel)
10 Composer Pachelbel
11 Gone from the company, maybe
12 Like many large cos.
13 Evildoer
14 To the rear of
15 It's in the spring
16 Alibi
19 Premium vodka brand, for short
21 N.F.L. star Grier
23 Bug-ridden software releases
25 Miniature
28 Down Under jumper
30 Buchanan's secretary of state
32 Sound of a failure
33 Lifesaver
34 Architect Jones
35 Ornamental piece of drapery
36 Timber-dressing tool
37 Actress Witherspoon
41 Squirrels' cache
42 Word to which a common reply is "Bitteschön"
43 "Tattered Tom" author
44 Ensign holder
46 Bacterium that needs oxygen
47 Submit
48 John of "The Addams Family"
49 Self-descriptive fruit
51 Cheek teeth
52 ___ Park, historic home near Philadelphia
53 Vin color
55 Organic compounds with nitrogen
56 French aristocrats
57 Nudge
58 Founding member of the Dadaists
59 Place to keep Mace
60 Not quite right
63 Get better
64 Slowly
65 Motivate
69 Fighting words
70 Fly-catching aid
71 Depression causes
74 Granola tidbit
75 Willing
76 Appliances with lids
78 Belarus port
79 Think that might is right?
80 It may come with attachments
81 Not just sit there
82 Projected onto a screen
83 Last number in a column
84 Ohm of Ohm's law
85 Queen of mystery
86 2005 Best Picture winner
87 ___ Sorrel (woman in a love triangle in "Adam Bede")
88 Available by the pint, perhaps
89 Rubberneck
93 Alter pieces?
94 ___ Roberts, first inductee into the Romance Writers of America Hall of Fame
95 ___-Ball
96 Inadvisable action
97 Chew on
100 Per la grazia di ___ (by the grace of God)
101 Brand at a gas station

by Patrick Berry

154 Q & A Session

ACROSS

1 Bear-named villainess in Superman films
5 Cause of a full stop for sailing ships
13 Ritzy Rio neighborhood
20 Column on a questionnaire
21 Blasted, with "on"
22 Wreaked havoc on
23 They tremble in the slightest breeze
25 Apple pie order
26 Strip
27 Hoedown sites
28 Geneviève, e.g.: Abbr.
29 Beginning of a cowboy song refrain
30 Loathing
31 "Star Wars," e.g.
32 Parliamentary measure of 1774
35 It's pitched
36 Abbey area
37 Introductory course?
39 Grassy plains
40 Ten-millionth of a joule
41 Too much ink
42 Arctic bird
43 Run out
44 Period in which we live
47 Addams who created the Addams family
51 Drang's counterpart
53 Sidesplitter
54 Word before and after "yes"
55 Reason for lights going out
56 Trio of comedy
58 Takes off
60 "All ___"
62 Mrs., abroad
63 Recoiling from
65 Pursue
68 Hikes
69 Compound that's subject to tautomerism
70 Vending machine tricker
72 Packard's partner
73 Scintillas
75 Chess opening?
77 Canine cry
79 Cries shrilly
80 ___ Mawr
81 "The Spirit of Australia" sloganeer
84 Engorge
86 Wildly
87 Implements using fulcrums
88 Red, e.g., once
91 Credit card magnet
94 Birthstone for some Libras
95 Stage direction
96 Relative of Welsh
97 Daughter of James II
99 Shadow
100 Attacks
101 Tea holder
102 Grasp
103 Teem
105 Washing machine setting
106 Title girl of a Willa Cather novel
109 Graham Greene novel set in Saigon, with "The"
111 Woodworker, at times
112 Without paraphrasing
113 Pig product
114 Backwoods valleys
115 Freezing mixtures
116 Scroll holders

DOWN

1 Two wiggling fingers, maybe
2 Drunkard
3 White-hot
4 Invite to a movie, say
5 Classic 1965 novel set on the planet Arrakis
6 Arts and Sciences major: Abbr.
7 Gypsum variety
8 Amount to take
9 "It Happened One Night" director
10 Mideast city that was once a British protectorate
11 Monocle, basically
12 Members of 82-Down
13 Ready to blow
14 Like forget-me-nots
15 Gardner of "Mogambo"
16 Where G.I.'s fought Charlie
17 "Ararat" director, 2002
18 Doc
19 Mavens
24 Computing-Tabulating-Recording Co., today
28 Slangy greeting
31 Primer pooch
32 Wharves
33 South African who twice won the U.S. Open
34 Hidden drawback
36 El ___ (1942 battle site)
37 Glide
38 "___ House," 1983 Madness hit
41 Is a second-story man
42 Stuffed shirts
43 Really mean
44 What, to Camus
45 Capital on the Dvina River
46 Suffix with zillion
48 Low-cost stopover
49 Stops on le métro
50 Word next to an arrow, maybe
51 Daze
52 Cozy and warm
55 St. Lawrence and others
56 In Harry Potter books, nonmagical offspring of wizard parents
57 Treaded transport
59 Sign of a brake problem
61 Patrick of "X-Men"
64 Place between hills
66 Fruit named for its appearance
67 Fever causes
71 Spray under the sink
74 1973 #1 hit for the Rolling Stones
76 Tour de France stage
78 Close
81 More upset
82 Sawbones' org.
83 Play a sax solo, maybe
85 Hosp. staffer
88 1988 Tracy Chapman hit
89 Just for the heck of it
90 Offers
91 Sport with a service line
92 Seek aid from
93 Many a tux
94 Beginning of all New York ZIP codes
95 Wild animal ID
96 Battle of ___ Bay, 1898
98 Gets warmer
99 Karate-like exercises
100 The Beatles' "And I Love ___"
103 Plaintiff
104 Lean and sinewy
105 Solitaires, e.g.
107 It's well-supplied
108 Palm Springs-to-Las Vegas dir.
109 Home shopping channel
110 Watch unit: Abbr.

by Will Nediger

ACROSS

1 Fills to almost overflowing
8 Unposed photo
14 Search blindly
19 What some shoot in a golf round
20 Decked out
22 Alternatives to Yodels
23 Memo about Stephen King's "Christine"?
25 Bob Marley's "___ the Sheriff"
26 Drop from the invitation list, say
27 Dig in
28 Staple figure in origami
30 Emmy-winning Ward
31 Meeting of the minds?
32 Memo about an inveterate perjurer?
37 Like the Honda Element
38 BBC : Britain :: ___ : Italy
39 Part of ½
40 Want to undo
41 Absentee
44 Kind of line
46 "Now I see!"
48 Memo about a dating guide?
50 Way around Paris
53 Contingencies
54 MSN rival
55 Board
57 An essay may be on one
61 Loon
64 Memo about where tariffs are imposed on incoming ships?
68 In the slightest
69 Mocks
70 Apple gadget
71 Memo about stores for animal appendages?
74 Falls on the border
76 Strategic W.W. I river
77 Mower part
78 Wee bit
79 D.C. bigwig
80 City on the Ruhr
82 Memo about a religious outpost for prisoners?
88 1492 voyager
91 Editorial take
92 Have mercy (on)
93 Bearded beast
94 Source of wool
99 Timecard abbr.
100 Flirtatious sort
101 Memo about why to buy an air purifier?
105 Box office sign
108 Canned
109 Lightly moisten
110 Journey part
111 "Right on!"
112 Ready to roll? . . . or not ready to roll?
114 Memo about a lyricist?
119 Top echelon
120 Ignore the usual wake-up time
121 Clothing chain since 1994
122 It's distracting
123 John James Audubon, e.g.
124 "Ain't gonna happen!"

DOWN

1 Short and often not sweet
2 Some are Dutch
3 Give some zing
4 Hoity-toity type
5 Special ___
6 Fourth members of a musical group
7 At will
8 Inflexible, as some rules
9 Suffix with stock or block
10 Go-ahead signal
11 ___ Malfoy, Harry Potter antagonist
12 Buries
13 Special military assignment
14 4, on a phone
15 "Arrested Development" actress Portia de ___
16 Candy bar whose name is an exclamation
17 It may be used for banking
18 They're left behind
21 1958 hit whose B-side was "La Bamba"
24 Articulate
29 Biggest section in a dictionary
32 Rice-A-___
33 All of a crowd, maybe
34 When repeated, Mork's TV sign-off
35 Prefix with byte
36 Whaling adverb
37 Kid's greeting
41 Threefold
42 Proves otherwise
43 Like Albany or Chicago
44 Low-___
45 Bordering on
47 Frank
49 One of a comedic trio
50 LeBlanc of "Joey"
51 One with a pole position?
52 General on a Chinese menu
56 Long lines on a timeline
58 Turkey is part of it
59 Music players
60 Rule before a revolution, maybe
62 Popular table wine
63 Clay, by another name
64 No longer working: Abbr.
65 Specialized fishermen
66 Grand ___, setting for "Evangeline"
67 HDTV maker
69 King ___ Carlos of Spain
72 Figure-watchers' figs.
73 World Cup cheer
74 Where Forrest Gump did a tour
75 "Gotcha," to a beatnik
78 Boom maker
81 Put (away)
83 K-12 grades, collectively
84 ___ loading
85 How a ringtone may be set
86 Discman maker
87 ___ Ed
88 Like many nonanimated Disney films
89 Banished
90 Having digits
95 Isr. neighbor
96 They do impressions
97 First Ford
98 Invariably
100 Filet type
102 Schiller's "___ Joy"
103 Babydoll
104 Old western actor Van Cleef
105 Makeup applier's boo-boo
106 One of the Canterbury pilgrims
107 Ham ___
111 Years in old Rome
113 Old Ottoman title
115 Univ. in Troy, N.Y.
116 Family nickname
117 Shine, in product names
118 Fingers

by Jeremy Newton

156 CHAIN REACTION

ACROSS

1 Third Crusade siege site
5 Citadel trainee
10 Where houses traditionally have no walls
15 Isn't idle
19 Leeway
20 Like galleys
21 Run ___ of
22 Great Lakes salmon
23 FOOD COURT ___ CIRCUIT BOARD
25 CIRCUIT BOARD ___ ROOM SERVICE
27 Music may come in it
28 Stock market worker
30 Like some sacrifices
31 Stove option
32 Is for a group?
33 Clothing lines
34 Life's partner
37 ___-midi (French time of day)
41 Like many dorms nowadays
42 Laughable
43 ROOM SERVICE ___ LIGHT TOUCH
46 Code unit
49 Covert sound
50 "Beetle Bailey" character
51 What greedy people want
52 Cause someone's insomnia, maybe
54 "Git!"
55 LIGHT TOUCH ___ BELL PEPPER
57 Pet animal of Salvador Dali
58 Sponge
60 Sylvia Plath poem that begins "I know the bottom, she says. I know it with my great tap root"
61 Weightlifter's rep
62 Impassioned
63 Corporate division
65 Fabric border
68 Give up
69 Young newt
70 Some dates have one
71 Long-armed Sumatrans
73 BELL PEPPER ___ BRUSH FIRE
76 Was idle
77 Track take
78 "It's been real"
79 Protection
80 Iota
81 "Father ___," hit 1990s British sitcom
82 BRUSH FIRE ___ SMART CAR
84 Songwriter Carole Bayer ___
85 "Comin' ___ the Rye"
86 French word before deux or nous
87 Dialogue units
88 Bore
92 Third-century year
94 D-Day mo.
95 Tale of a trip to Ithaca
96 Shaped, as wood
100 Julia who starred in "Sabrina," 1995
104 SMART CAR ___ PIANO BAR
106 PIANO BAR ___ TRAILHEAD
108 Composer Thomas
109 Irving Berlin's "___ My Heart at the Stage Door Canteen"
110 Tennessee teammate
111 Final Four game
112 Tomorrow's opposite: Abbr.
113 Send
114 Some seconds
115 Too: Fr.

DOWN

1 Tennis lobs, e.g.
2 Prince Albert, for one
3 Gift that might cut
4 Newly developed, as technology
5 Pullover shirts
6 Dweller along the Mekong
7 Once, old-style
8 Mugful
9 Work of prose or poetry
10 More conservative, as investments
11 In front of, in dialect
12 Farm call
13 Best, in a way
14 Played the enchantress
15 Gulf of Guinea capital
16 Alternatives to RCs
17 ___ park
18 Blisters, e.g.
24 "Stop it!"
26 Place for an opinion
29 Code unit
34 Give insider info
35 Protect
36 TRAILHEAD ___ COUNTERTOP
37 Turkey's tallest peak
38 Read carefully
39 Throw a fit
40 Heaven on earth
41 Vikki who sang "It Must Be Him"
44 Soap plant
45 Some camera lenses
46 COUNTERTOP ___ POST OFFICE
47 Oaxaca gold
48 Hanoi holiday
50 Teahouse treats
52 Cut decoratively
53 Brass
55 Heavy hitter
56 Area around the mouth
57 A tremendous supply
59 2, 4, 6, 8, etc.
63 Calyx part
64 They were seen at Black Power meetings
65 Like Iran's Ahmadinejad
66 Satan is often seen with one
67 Records
70 Bull or Buck, e.g.
71 Make a choice
72 Paris's ___ La Fayette
73 Farm tower
74 Ball in a basket
75 "Syriana" actress Amanda
78 Tote
80 It's in front of a mizzen
82 Something to pop
83 Write on a BlackBerry, maybe
84 Eat noisily
85 Recipe abbr.
88 Fee for many a doctor's visit
89 Put on a pedestal
90 City on the Rhone
91 Key
92 Split
93 Garçon's handout
94 Bordello patrons
97 Channel for interior decorators
98 Buffalo's county
99 Go out with
101 Button next to a *
102 Fictional captain
103 IV ___
105 A way to vote
107 Drivel

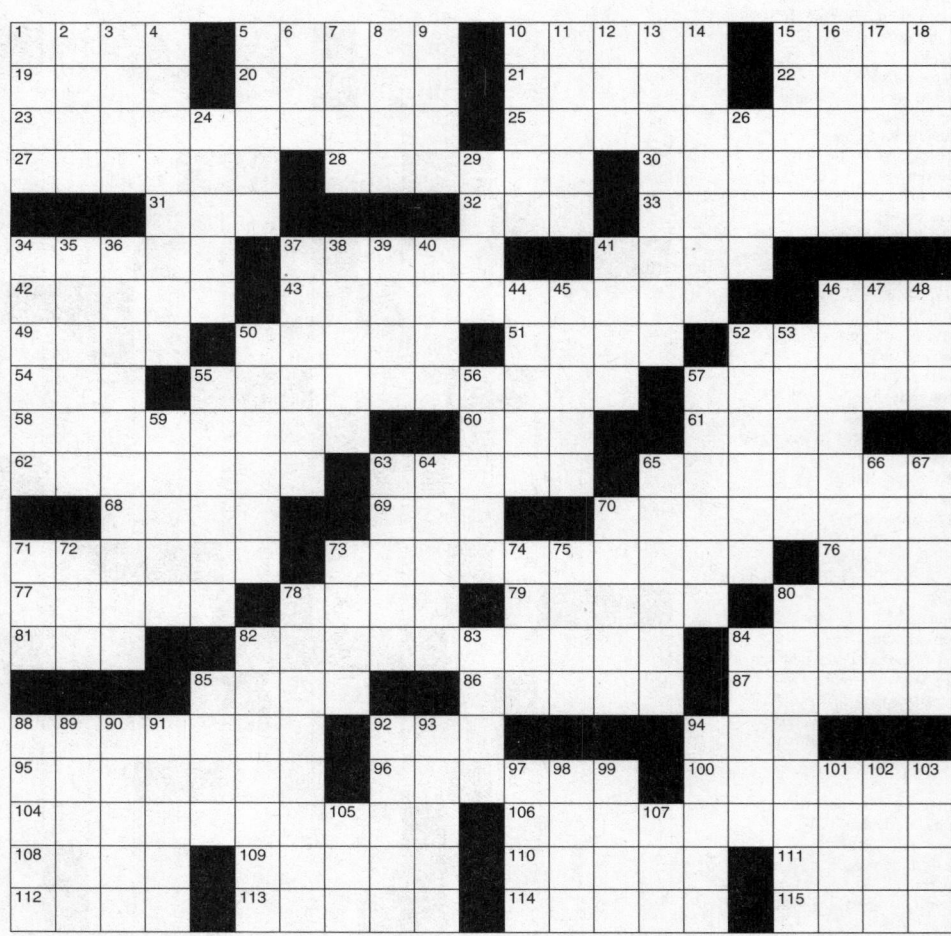

by Pamela Amick Klawitter

ACROSS

1 City once called Eva Perón
8 Jim Belushi's costume in "Trading Places"
15 Cross stock
19 Napoleon's relatives
20 Woo
21 Reform Party founder
22 Impatient kid's plea at a zoo?
24 Minneapolis suburb
25 Four: Prefix
26 Wipe out
27 Animal with an onomatopoeic name
28 More kempt
29 Big name in computer printers
31 Worrisome type at a china shop?
33 X-rated
36 Sea route
39 "That hurt!"
40 Count with a severe overbite
43 Villa ___ (town near Atlanta)
44 Dwellers along Lake Victoria
48 Seeking the right women's tennis attire?
50 Love overseas
51 Maker of the old Royale
52 "Get it?"
53 Insinuating
54 Warning sign on a pirate ship?
57 Gold medalist skier Hermann
59 Miss Piggy's pronoun
60 "Presto!"
61 Source of some inside humor?
67 Name on a plane
69 The dark side
70 Young hog
71 Tree doctor?
75 City WSW of Dortmund
77 Geom. point
80 24-hr. convenience
81 Dope
82 Your basic "So this guy walks into a bar . . ."?
85 Disastrous drop
88 Rabbit's title
89 Certain hand-held
90 ___-majesté
91 Brand-new to the language
93 Gulf
94 Use of steel wool, e.g.?
98 Palate appendage
101 Butch Cassidy, for one
102 ___ crow
103 Peaks
105 Swingers' stats
109 "Be that as ___ . . ."
110 Cheez Whiz you could blow up?
113 What a rake does
114 Thaw
115 Traveler's temptation
116 Once, in the past
117 Hellish
118 Bears witness

DOWN

1 In case
2 Workout aftermath
3 Churchyard unit
4 Jack who wrote the lyrics to "Tenderly"
5 Intend (to)
6 Nursery items
7 Cartoon dog
8 Father of Deimos and Phobos
9 Apple or pear
10 Comedic Philips
11 Punch with a kick
12 Take apart
13 Become blocked, in a way
14 Christie contemporary
15 Took a two-wheeler
16 "A Masked Ball" aria
17 Music for a baseball team?
18 Movie lover's cable channel
21 Have a quick look from the hallway, say
23 Geiger of counter fame
28 Alternative to J.F.K. and La Guardia
30 Rain hard
31 "___ teaches you when to be silent": Disraeli
32 Prepare to chat, maybe
33 Some hand-helds
34 Golden pond fish
35 Be something special
37 Padded
38 Laugh, in Lille
41 Type of eye surgery
42 Practically pristine
44 Thurman of "Kill Bill"
45 "When You ___ Love" (1912 tune)
46 Actress Patricia
47 Concession stand purchase
49 Opera's ___ Te Kanawa
50 Settled (on)
54 Luau fare
55 Converse competitor
56 Holler's partner
57 Use shamelessly
58 Gray area?: Abbr.
59 Co. with a butterfly logo
61 Nature's aerators
62 Nikita's no
63 White wine apéritif
64 Soyuz launcher
65 Lots
66 South Pacific kingdom
67 "Voice of Israel" author
68 Org. with peacekeeping forces
72 Stock ticker's inventor
73 1958 Best Actor David
74 "___ Day" (1993 rap hit)
75 Flush (with)
76 Arid
77 Perfume brand
78 Boxing stats
79 There are 435 in Cong.
82 Seed cover
83 Ben-Gurion carrier
84 Author portrayed in the miniseries "The Lost Boys"
86 Indiana city near the Michigan border
87 Spoils
88 Illegal record
91 Sly
92 Boneheaded
94 Deceit
95 Out-and-out
96 When doubled, sings
97 Something to believe
99 Roxie's dance partner in "Chicago"
100 "___ or lose . . ."
103 Lead-in to girl
104 Battle of Normandy city
106 Streisand, to friends
107 "___ first you don't succeed . . ."
108 Orch. section
110 Wallet items, informally
111 Darth Vader's boyhood nickname
112 Chess piece: Abbr.

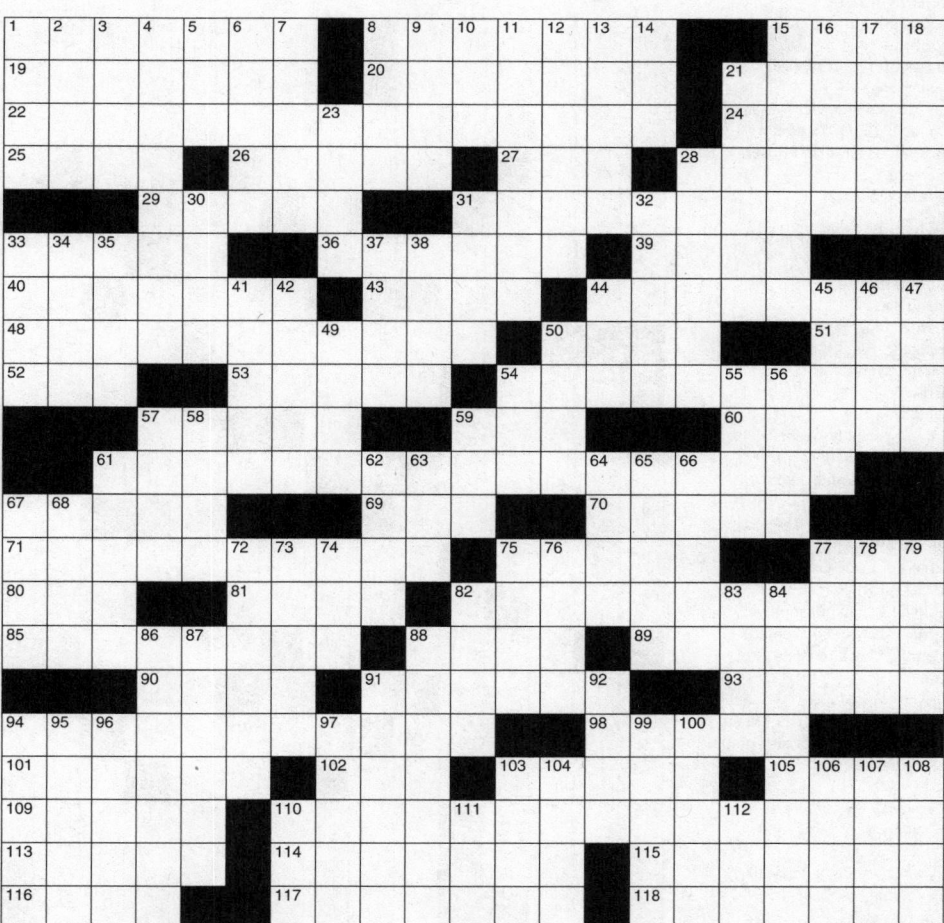

by Tony Orbach and Patrick Blindauer

ACROSS

1 Town at the eighth mile of the Boston Marathon
7 1971 Tom Jones hit
16 Dict. fill
19 Charlie Chan player J. ___ Naish
20 Acted briefly
21 Online activity
22 V.I.P. in a limo?
24 Penn Station inits.
25 Sycophant's reply
26 Articles by nonstaffers
27 Singer Winehouse
28 Glass-enclosed porches
30 1999 film with the tagline "Fame. Be careful. It's out there"
32 Way of the East
33 Open
35 Dirty
36 Stories about halting horses?
39 Kisses, on paper
41 Team building?
42 1954 event code-named Castle Bravo
43 Swedish Chemistry Nobelist Tiselius
45 Detailed, old-style
47 Produce for show
51 Roundabout
53 Corduroy feature
56 Certain guy, in personals shorthand
58 Causes of meteorological phenomena?
60 "Q: Are We Not Men? A: We Are ___!" (hit 1978 album)
61 Eponymous German brewer Eberhard
63 Says, in teenspeak
64 Stir
66 They're in control of their faculties
67 Etc. and ibid., e.g.
69 Unequaled
70 Missile's course
72 Trudge (through)
73 Baton wavers
76 Miffs
77 Iceland?
81 Fully or partially: Abbr.
82 French-Belgian border river
83 Start of a sign on a gate
84 Scatterbrain
86 National League East player
88 Kind of atty.
90 Explorer ___ da Gama
94 MDX and RDX maker
96 National League East player
98 Barrier Ahab stands behind?
102 Literally, "back to back"
104 Lure
106 60-Across producer
107 Long-distance swimmer Diana
108 Something little girls may play
110 Fifth pillar of Islam
111 Body layer
113 Internet address letters
114 "What are you, some kind of ___?"
115 Cry after writing a particularly fun column?
119 Office note
120 Settle
121 Arab League V.I.P.'s
122 Eur. carrier
123 Small plane, perhaps
124 Common town sign

DOWN

1 "Treasure Island" illustrator, 1911
2 Showed delight over
3 River crosser
4 Eng. neighbor
5 U.S.A.F. Academy site
6 One who lifts a lot
7 Little stubble
8 Residence on the Rhein
9 Summer setting in MA and PA
10 Extremely arid
11 In ___ (really out of it)
12 Pitch maker?
13 "___ losing it, or . . . ?"
14 Investigators: Abbr.
15 Goes up and down
16 45, e.g.?
17 Connecticut town where "The Stepford Wives" was filmed
18 Italian road
21 Sen. McCaskill of Missouri
23 "Are you ___?!"
29 Like some good soil
31 Clergy attire
33 Out into view
34 Rock's Richards and Moon
37 Orchestra sect.
38 High, in the Alps
40 Legal suspension
44 Overthrowing, e.g.
46 Lead-in to while
48 Cutting remarks?
49 Slogan holder, often
50 It has a blade
52 Is shy
54 1887 Chekhov play
55 Tomb raider's find
56 Derisive
57 Where ax murderers' weapons are on display?
59 Lines on a musical staff
60 1973 Helen Reddy #1 hit
61 Tylenol rival
62 Troupe org.
65 Calls one's own
67 Ray, e.g., in brief
68 Like the bad guy
71 Phnom Penh money
72 Shaved, in a way
73 Bygone station
74 Part of N.C.A.A.: Abbr.
75 Indication of big shoes to fill?
78 Dip
79 Wishy-___
80 Words with snag or home run
83 Carpenter's supply
85 Dow Jones fig.
87 Blue blood, informally
89 "Flags of Our Fathers" setting
91 Pourer's comment
92 Catfight participants
93 Boot Hill setting
94 Title family name on TV
95 Eye part
97 Tiny laughs
99 One with bad looks?
100 Letters on a cross
101 Polite turndown
103 Best
105 Training staff
109 Fen-___ (banned diet aid)
111 Exhausted
112 Michigan town or college
116 Season for les vacances
117 Little bird
118 Third-century Chinese dynasty

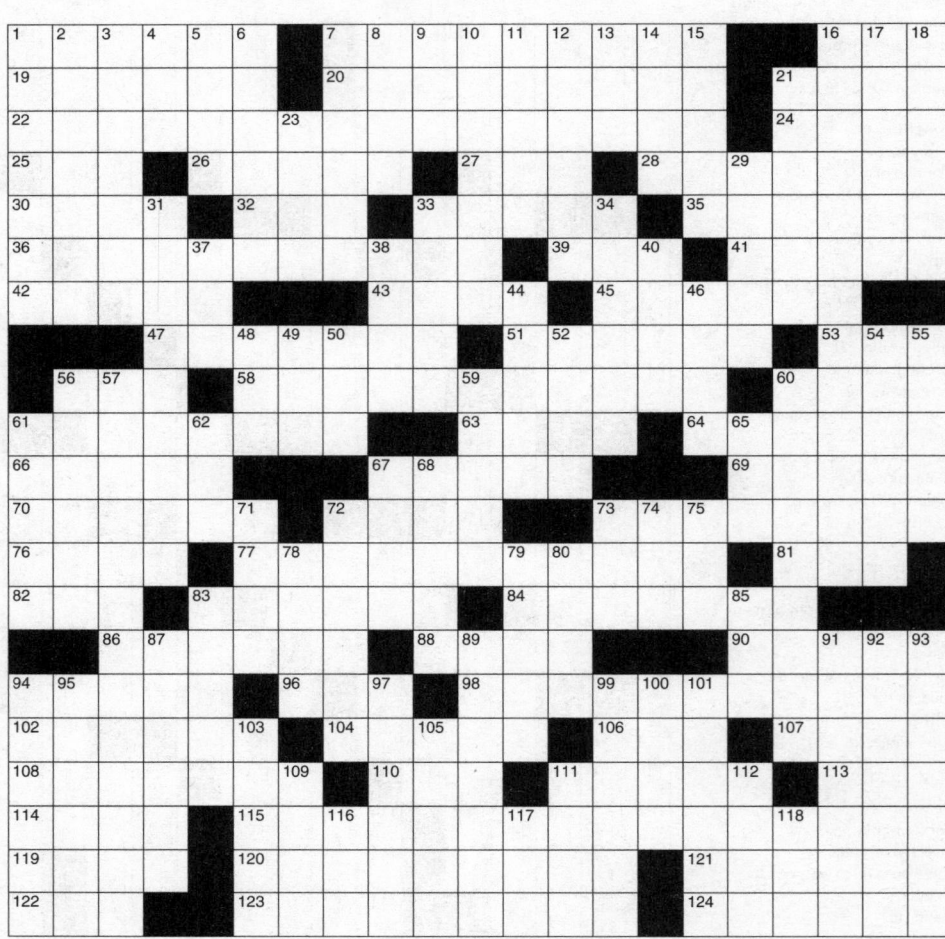

by Brendan Emmett Quigley

ACROSS

1 Having chutzpah
6 Home of the Braves: Abbr.
9 Hale-___ (comet seen in 1997)
13 Take a chance
19 Page facing a verso
20 Arthur Miller play about the Salem witch trials, with "The"
22 Enigmas
23 Take heat from?
24 Downhill racer
25 Poet John who wrote "Lives of X," an autobiography in verse
26 Last request, part 1
29 Rains in Spain
30 Twigs, perhaps
31 Animal more closely related to the mongoose than the dog
32 Inhuman
35 Groundbreaking inventions?
36 Cabinet inits. since 1979
38 Part of a range: Abbr.
39 Records
40 Not maj.
41 Endorsers, typically
44 Election ending?
45 Request, part 2
52 Barney's buddy, In cartoondom
54 Veiled comment?
55 "Sense and Sensibility" author
56 "Thumbs way up!" review
57 Unlike drive, reverse has just one
59 Lord's land
61 With 95-Across, chef whose recipes are used on the International Space Station
63 National Institutes of Health location
65 Request, part 3
66 How good investors invest
68 Profitless
69 Bill
71 On Soc. Sec., typically
72 "The King and I" setting
73 Park ___
76 Disfigure
77 God, in Granada
79 Request, part 4
84 ___ culpa
85 Actress Mimieux of "Where the Boys Are"
86 Supply in a loft
87 Alludes (to)
89 Lambert airport's home: Abbr.
92 "___ pig's eye!"
93 Created
95 See 61-Across
96 ___ ballerina
98 Salma Hayek, for one
101 1970s Renault
102 End of the request
108 European carrier
109 Part of many an autobiography's author credit
110 Morticia, to Fester, on "The Addams Family"
111 Gander : goose :: tercel : ___
112 More chic
113 Clothing retailer Bauer
114 Erica Jong's phobia, ostensibly
115 "Yonder window," according to Romeo
116 Uno + due
117 Actions

DOWN

1 Very dry
2 Only female attorney general
3 Sch. known for its discipline
4 Having grooves
5 'Hood inhabitant
6 Existing
7 Crowd in Calais?
8 Grease up
9 Propaganda technique introduced by Hitler in "Mein Kampf"
10 M.D.'s who deliver
11 What dead men don't wear, per a 1982 film title
12 Tasty tubes
13 Suggestive
14 W.W. I's so-called "U-Boat Alley"
15 Reptilian, in a way
16 ___ Abdul-Jabbar
17 Tab, e.g.
18 "Shogun" sequel
21 Soft
27 Not exactly
28 One of two title roles (in the same film) for Spencer Tracy
32 Bellyache
33 Peppy
34 Desire, for one
35 Sign in the stands
37 Noted bunny lover
40 Jason's jiltee
41 Matador's move
42 Social worker
43 Scattered (about)
46 Pirate whose treasure is recovered in Poe's "The Gold-Bug"
47 Keeper of a flame?
48 Total
49 Dickens's shortest novel
50 Bad guys
51 Count (on)
53 Benin, until 1975
58 Matter of law
60 Lassitude
62 Deep bleu sea
63 Bigmouth, for one
64 Pollen producer
66 Hair-raising
67 Ein Berliner, often
69 "Picnic" playwright
70 Clarifying words
74 ESPN sportscaster Dick
75 Treebeard, e.g.
78 Manuscript encl.
80 Ace's specialty
81 Slaves
82 Spinachlike plant
83 Won back
88 Unseen part of the moon
89 Marijuana cigarette, slangily
90 Like some Afghan leaders
91 In the cards
93 Ecological groupings
94 Not AWOL
95 Poe poem that ends "From grief and groan to a golden throne beside the King of Heaven"
97 Word of thanks
99 Quickly
100 Edison rival
101 Cubic decimeter
103 Spend time (with)
104 Cut, say
105 Give up
106 Aspirin, e.g.
107 Roger who won the Best Actor Tony for "Nicholas Nickleby"

by Matt Ginsberg

ACROSS

1 Demanded without reason
7 Leader of Lesbos?
13 Unlikely attenders of R-rated films
19 Honor
20 Injustice
21 Feel remorse for
22 November 5, in Britain
24 Not remote
25 Thin as ___
26 Depression
28 Humans last lived there in 2000
29 Wild sheep of the western United States
36 Mocks
37 "La Gioconda" mezzo-soprano
38 Flies over the Equator
39 Salt Lake City player
40 Annual Sunday event, with "the"
43 Breezes (through)
44 Best Actor of 1991
49 Treat like a hero, maybe
52 In direct opposition
53 Gaudy jewelry, in slang
54 Broad
55 Alphabet quartet
56 Trail to follow
58 Ring figure
59 It's quite different from the high-school variety
66 Transfix
67 Eurasian ducks
68 Climatic scene in "Hamlet"
69 Parrying weapon
70 Blackmore's Lorna
72 City 70 miles SSW of Toledo
76 ___ state
77 Viking, for one
81 La Scala cheer
82 Events registered by seismometers, in brief
83 Resident: Suffix
84 Foamcore component
87 "Doctor Zhivago" role
89 Deserving a lower insurance premium
91 Army supply officer
96 Spigoted vessel
97 Italie et Allemagne
98 Single-handedly
99 Equitable way to return a favor
102 Egg roll topping, perhaps
109 Thatched
110 Perfume ingredient
111 Mrs. Woody Allen
112 It may be bilateral
113 Belgian city with an 1854 manifesto
114 Like shorelines, often

DOWN

1 Lose strength
2 Prefix with pressure
3 Standoffish
4 Give bad marks
5 Signs of a bad outlet
6 "Venice Preserved" dramatist Thomas
7 Part of U.N.L.V.
8 Natural bristle
9 Year that Michelangelo began work on "David"
10 One desiring change

11 National flower of Mexico
12 Illinois city, site of the last Lincoln-Douglas debate
13 Favorable
14 TV pooch
15 FedEx rival
16 Moon of Mars
17 Unabridged
18 Rudder locations
20 Move, to a real-estate broker
23 Kipling novel
27 Procure
29 Batting average, e.g.
30 ___ citato
31 ___ Bator
32 Quaint "not"
33 Caboose
34 Some deodorants
35 Abbr. after Cleveland or Brooklyn
36 Fair
40 Four Holy Roman emperors
41 Bazaar units
42 Iowa college
43 Go rapidly
45 Charge for cash
46 Large chamber group
47 Ancient Greek coins
48 Pickup attachment
49 Start of something big?

50 Shooting star, maybe
51 Mad magazine cartoonist Dave
54 Spoonful, say
56 Bygone blades
57 Kitten "mitten"
58 Second string
59 Bossman or bosswoman
60 Stinky, as gym clothes
61 Pizza place
62 Capri, e.g., to a Capriote
63 Magazine founded by Bob Guccione
64 ___ of Nantes, 1598
65 "Super Duper ___" (anime series)
70 "Forty Miles of Bad Road" guitarist
71 Flip over
72 Some offensive linemen: Abbr.
73 Port near Nazareth
74 Purveyor of chips
75 Open court hearing
77 ___-à-porter
78 "And ___ thou slain the Jabberwock?": Carroll
79 Spillane's "___ Jury"
80 Within striking distance
81 "It's c-c-c-cold!"
84 Pipsqueak
85 Word with page or wood

86 ___ Stadium, opening of 1923 and 2009
87 Feeling evoked in drama
88 Basketball datum
89 Security system component
90 Playground retort
92 Prefix with economics
93 Celtic speaker
94 ___ beetle
95 "Don't even bother"
100 Sun Valley locale: Abbr.
101 Invoice amount
103 Once known as
104 Untold millennia
105 Half brother of Tom Sawyer
106 Moreover
107 Manhattan part
108 Impersonated

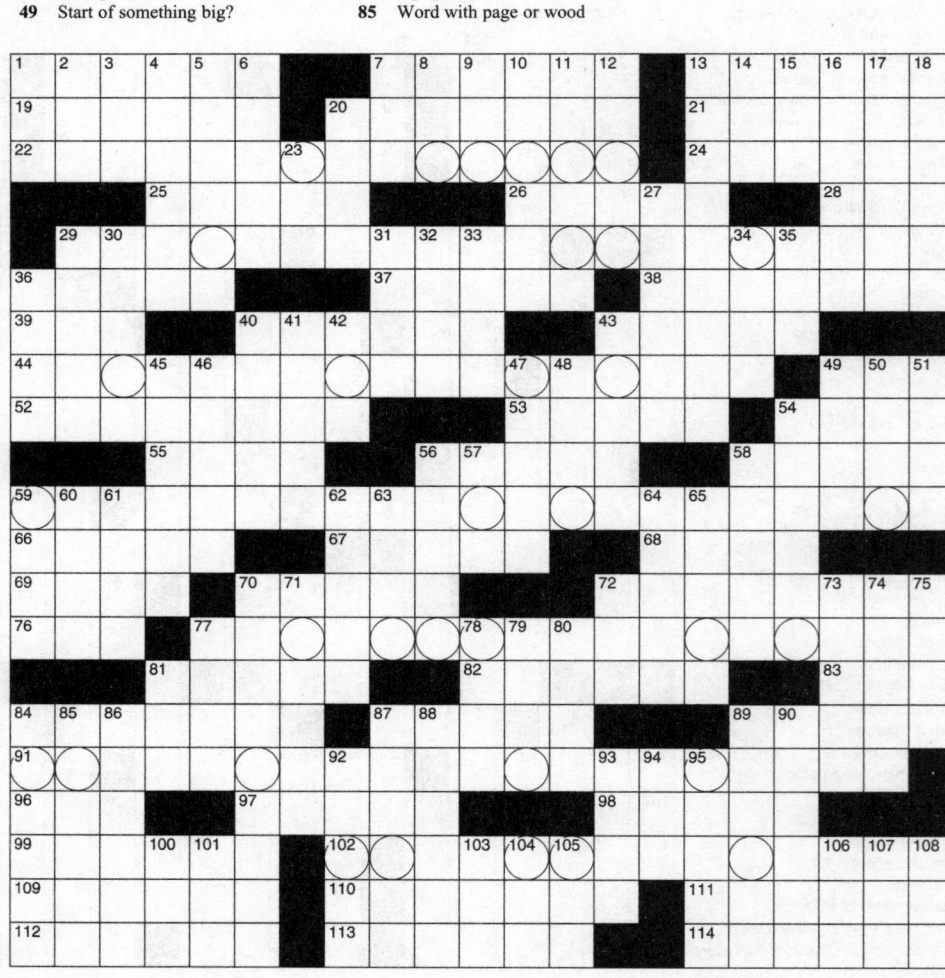

by Barry C. Silk

ACROSS

1 2003 Stanley Cup champions
7 Portrays
12 It's found in many pockets nowadays
16 Command to an overfriendly canine
20 Genus of poisonous mushrooms
22 Brewing
23 Pasta used in soups
24 Actress Polo
25 Nickname for a bodybuilder
26 Flip
27 Junior in the N.F.L.
28 Bunch
29 Popular 1970s British TV series
32 Bug
34 Fraternity letters
35 Dungeon items
37 "Now you're talking!"
38 Took the risk
45 From ___ Z
47 Radiate
51 When a second-shift employee may get home
52 City that overlooks a bay of the same name
53 Opening screen option on many an A.T.M.
56 "Think big" sloganeer
57 One inside another
59 Spot alternative
61 Fine-tunes
62 Split
63 Abbr. in a real-estate listing
64 Creator of the Tammany Hall tiger
66 Tic-tac-toe plays
68 Warner Brothers shotgun toter
69 "Whose woods these ___ think I know": Frost
71 Liberals
73 Actor Brynner
74 ___ rut
75 Keats, e.g.
76 Ilk
77 It may have two doors
79 Ralph who co-wrote "Have Yourself a Merry Little Christmas"
81 Cartoonist Keane
82 "The Praise of Folly" writer
84 Cause of unemployment
86 It might follow a slash mark
90 "Amen!"
91 Club alternative
92 Slangy street greeting
94 Ball with a yellow stripe
95 Arrangements
98 Four-star hotel amenity
99 J.F.K. info: Abbr.
101 Football defensive line position
102 Old musical high notes
103 Deuce beaters
104 Where to pick up pick-up sticks
106 Viking Ericson
108 Summer Mass. setting
109 Bug
110 "We ___ please"
111 Nativity scene figures
114 ___ Mae
116 Stead
117 Like most apartments
119 A hyperbola has two
121 Having stars, say
122 Deliver, as a harsh criticism
124 "Star Trek" TV series, to fans
125 Exasperated teacher's cry
128 Shade of blue
130 Kids drink from them
132 Comedian Margaret
133 Part of a shark's respiratory system
137 Missing glasses' location, usually
145 Genesis son
146 Issue
148 The second "R" in J. R. R. Tolkien
149 Wrinkles
150 Fan mag
151 Pixar fish
152 Africa's ___ Mountains
153 A super's may be supersized
154 Result of pulling the plug?
155 Overflow
156 Unesco World Heritage Site in Jordan
157 Gives in return

DOWN

1 Block
2 Birds that can sprint at 30 m.p.h.
3 Extensive
4 One of a people conquered in 1533
5 French orphan of film
6 Camper's aid
7 Miss
8 "___ first . . ."
9 Arrangement of 40-Downs
10 "Ain't gonna happen"
11 Commercial prefix with foam
12 Cyclades island
13 Before: Abbr.
14 Longtime Boston Symphony conductor
15 Hollow center?
16 Barely fair, maybe
17 Sugar source
18 Read aloud
19 Exclamation of surprise
21 In itself
30 Went from second to first, say
31 Fasten with a pop
33 Will Ferrell title role
36 Erect
38 Not brought home
39 Off
40 See 9-Down
41 Awake by
42 Bootleggers' bane
43 Son-in-law of Muhammad
44 Go-ahead
46 Common hockey score
48 Proposed "fifth taste," which means "savory" in Japanese
49 Keeps
50 Put forth
54 "Do you want me to?"
55 Tasmania's highest peak
58 Z-car brand
60 International oil and gas giant, informally
62 Benedict III's predecessor
65 Misses, e.g.
67 Negative
70 Sentiment suggesting "Try this!"
72 Secured, in a way, with "on"
78 Cipher org.
80 T or F, e.g.: Abbr.
81 Construction project that gave rise to the Ted Williams Tunnel
83 Sphagnous
85 Some taters
86 Over
87 Building component?
88 Shrinking, perhaps
89 Took it easy
91 Gone bad
93 Frog legs, to some
95 Hold off
96 TV puppet
97 Precept
98 Pal of Kenny and Kyle
100 Tach reading
105 Common entry point
107 Alpine sights
112 Behind
113 Happen, slangily
115 "I'll pass"
117 Plush
118 Connoisseur
120 Pawned
123 Head counts?
126 Tristram's love
127 More gloomy
129 Singer Mann
131 "That's ___!"
133 Look
134 Footnote abbr.
135 Impart
136 Player's call
138 Behind
139 "Bridal Chorus" bride
140 Bazooka Joe's working peeper
141 Ground cover
142 Early Chinese dynasty
143 Choice word
144 E-mail, e.g.: Abbr.
147 Cartoon feline

by Mike Nothnagel and David Quarfoot

ACROSS

1 Swarm
5 Lots
10 11th-century year
14 Audibly shocked
19 Hot rod rod
20 One of the Four Seasons
21 German article
22 Glow
23 "Will the long-winded ___ ___ his sermon?"
26 Philosopher Kierkegaard
27 Puts on
28 Power brokers
29 "Let me tell you . . ."
30 Mark, Anthony and others: Abbr.
31 "Tasty!"
32 "The majority of British ___ ___ policy coming to fruition"
34 Left over
36 Shoot out
37 Took care of
40 Washington State airport
43 Amaze
44 One of five Norwegian kings
48 "I noticed you use the ___ ___ often than the tarnished one"
51 Promised
52 Ties a second knot
53 Habit
54 Human ___ Project
55 Alphabet quartet
57 "The driver's crew decided to make the ___ ___ priority"
60 "Life ___ beach"
63 Welcome at the door
65 Crossed one's i's and dotted one's t's?
66 Promgoers: Abbr.
67 "The parishioners ignored the ___ ___ meat on Friday"
71 Understands
74 Train head
75 Work hard
76 Ultimatum's end
80 It might lead to a cloud formation, for short
81 "The judges put the names of each ___ ___ for the M.C. to read"
86 Pusher catcher, for short
87 Shoe letters
88 Retinue of Pan
89 YouTube offering
90 Baloney
92 Teacher: Var.
94 "As one member of the crew ___ ___ co-worker leaned on his shovel"
101 Nigerian export
102 Any ship
105 Company bought by Chevron in 2005
106 Dig
107 Box-and-one alternative
109 Mushroom variety
110 "You won't find any ___ ___ Turner album"
112 Wilder and Hackman
113 Wash. neighbor
114 Potato pancake
115 Race pace
116 Daisy type
117 It's frequently stolen
118 Calm
119 Tom Joad, e.g.

DOWN

1 Bad-weather gear
2 Apply
3 Dwellers in Middle-earth
4 Cross
5 Park in New York, say
6 Australia, e.g.
7 Automotive pioneer
8 It may come from a barrel
9 Take up wholeheartedly
10 Deserve
11 Deceive
12 Central
13 Like some boxes on ballots
14 Franciscan home
15 Relics of the Wild West
16 ___-ground missile
17 Derisive look
18 Copper
24 English portraitist Sir Joshua
25 1994 and 1997 U.S. Open winner
29 Green shade
32 Bucket of bolts
33 Grove in many an English churchyard
34 Pure
35 Your: Fr.
37 Lat. or Lith., once
38 Ursine : bear :: pithecan : ___
39 Amaze
41 Al's is almost 27
42 Place to hang your hat
43 Lady ___, first woman to sit in British Parliament
45 Sacks
46 Mail for a knight
47 Johnson and Johnson, e.g.
49 Kind of sale
50 "___ Nous" (1983 film)
51 Having all the money one needs
54 Bible distributor
56 Milk
57 Attach, as to a lapel
58 Cuisine choice
59 Many a pirate's appendage
60 "That is to say . . ."
61 Receiver of lists
62 Tick off
64 Actress Holmes
68 Record holder
69 About which the Bible says "Consider her ways, and be wise"
70 Confederate
72 "Hairspray" actor
73 Baseball bigwig Bud
77 Top
78 Beijing-to-Shanghai dir.
79 Ike's W.W. II domain
81 Broadcast signal
82 Compromises
83 Tore
84 Minister's deg.
85 Japanese-born Hall of Fame golfer
87 Daredevil Knievel
91 Poker call
93 Deseeded, as cotton
94 "Hasta ___"
95 Incorporate into a city
96 Fess Parker TV role
97 Greek marketplace
98 Folk percussion instruments
99 Old enough
100 Break down
102 Smarmy smile
103 Red River city
104 Related on the mother's side
107 ___ Hari
108 Football Hall-of-Famer Graham
110 Melodramatic response in comics
111 Jazz cornetist Adderley

by Peter A. Collins and Joe Krozel

ACROSS

1 Big name in baked beans
8 Neighbor of Oakland
15 Gilberto's partner on "The Girl From Ipanema," 1964
19 Earsplitting
21 Cicero or Publius
22 Light shade
23 21
25 Neighbor of a Georgian
26 Filled out
27 Exchanged vows
28 Knocker's request
30 Off-road wheels, for short
31 Vespasian's successor
33 Command ctrs.
36 One of an old film trio
37 Way out
40 Los ___
43 Anna of "X-Men"
45 Humans, e.g.
47 Like a butterfingers
48 Temperaments
49 Rock's ___ Folds Five
50 Cries of agony
52 Viva-voce vote
53 Pastry shop treat
54 Conductors' aids
57 Quick expression of gratitude
58 Gets better
59 Natty dresser
60 Grant-giving org.
61 Butterfly relative
63 "___ She Lovely"
64 Cereal killer
66 Rather inclined
68 Breakfast spot, briefly
71 "Vissi d'arte" singer
73 "N.Y. State of Mind" rapper
75 Yossarian's tentmate, in "Catch-22"
76 Curl performer
77 Part of some three-day weekends: Abbr.
79 Number one
82 Athos's arm
83 Ontario, par exemple
84 "Generations of healthy, happy pets" sloganeer
85 Small songbird
86 Chopsticks eschewers, informally
87 Razor handle?
89 The ___ Band, with guitarist Little Steven
92 Choir supports
93 He played 2,130 consecutive games
95 "Sire"
97 The Desi of Desilu
99 Middle of summer?
100 Certain people buried in Westminster Abbey
101 Black-and-white broadcast?
104 Divine epithet
106 Cut made by a saw
107 Gilpin of "Frasier"
108 Sticks (out)
109 Ignore, as a problem
115 Assist in evil
116 Freaky
117 Dimming
118 They may be revolutionary
119 The very beginning
120 1967 pop sensation, with "the"

DOWN

1 Europe's longest river
2 Turn aside
3 Beersheba's desert
4 Sticking point
5 Unilever detergent
6 Chic, in the '60s
7 People who no what they like?
8 Emulates a reporter
9 Kona keepsake
10 Brashares who wrote "The Sisterhood of the Traveling Pants"
11 Zine
12 And others, in a list
13 Old Venetian officials
14 Self-titled album of 1980
15 St. Peter, e.g.?
16 High-school gym feature
17 Chance to play
18 Ringo's drummer son
20 Styled
24 Mr. Potato Head features
29 Infamous 1999 computer virus with a woman's name
31 Woes, to a Yiddish speaker
32 More aloof
33 Target, with "on"
34 Marmalade ingredients
35 Stop: Abbr.
37 On a par with
38 Barbecue order
39 "Watermark" vocalist
41 Brightly colored fish
42 Charon's workplace
43 Wears out the carpet?
44 Declaration of August 14, 1941
46 Activity in which people get their kicks
48 NuGrape competitor
51 Call letters on 1970s–'80s TV
54 Pet cat, in British lingo
55 "Once ___ midnight dreary . . ."
56 Betray, in a way
59 Soda shop order
62 Single malt, for instance
64 Rachel Carson's sci.
65 Hissy fit
67 Joule division
69 Raspberries
70 Takes, with "for"
72 Legs
74 Their business is going downhill
76 Explodes
77 Aggressively promote
78 Put the pedal to the metal
80 Promising
81 Couple
82 Dampish
86 Not burdened by
88 Record list
90 Nail site
91 Not live
94 "Great" guy
96 Superman's father
98 "Holy smokes!"
101 Place with an eagle's-eye view
102 Someone who just got out of a long bath, facetiously
103 Jason of "American Pie"
104 International baseball powerhouse
105 Former shah ___ Pahlavi
106 Banjo supporter
107 Executive's extra
108 Paleontologist's discovery
110 Musician's gift
111 Active leader?
112 Subject of a Keats ode
113 Couple
114 Egg source

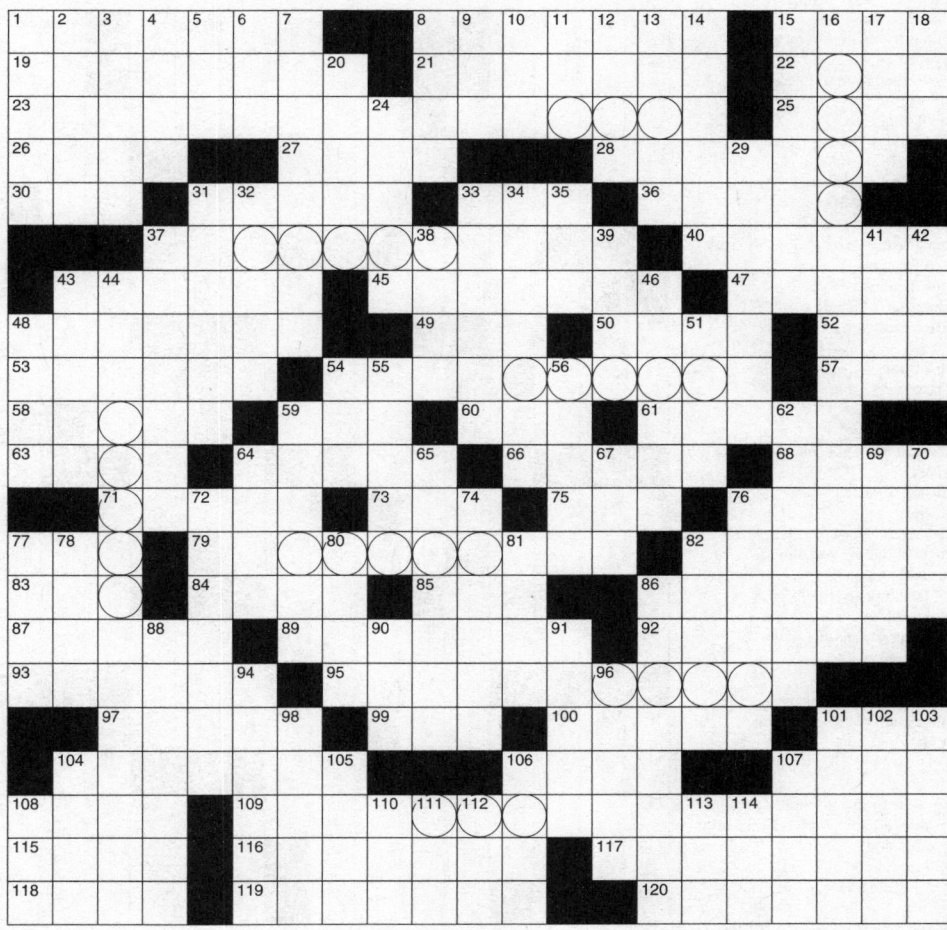

by Will Nediger

ACROSS

1. Edges at the track
5. Scores 100 on a test
11. Mother and wife of Uranus: Var.
15. Suffix with electron
18. It surrounds a lens
19. Sugar in tea, e.g.
20. Pointer on a poster
22. Seat site
24. Movie about a "Sopranos"-like actress from the Mediterranean?
26. Many a Turk
28. Simile part
29. Oscar and Tony winner Mercedes
30. Movie adaptation of "L.A. Law"?
34. The original Jefferson Airplane, e.g.
35. Rift
36. Back-to-work time: Abbr.
37. Hardware store section
39. Movie about a time-share?
48. Add or delete, say
50. 2000 title role for Richard Gere
51. English 8-Down
52. Popular movie house name
53. Middle of many German names
54. As a friend, to François
56. Comparable to a beet?
58. Crowd in Berlin?
59. Movie about the coming of difficult times?
63. Nearest the heart
65. Notes from short people?
66. Spike TV, once
67. Former Voice of America org.
68. Together
71. Movie about one of Dumbo's parents?
77. Room in la casa
78. Meat Loaf's "Rocky Horror Picture Show" role
81. Highest score achievable by a single dart in darts
82. Der Blaue Reiter artist
83. Polo alternatives
85. Recovery grps.
86. I, to Claudius
87. Advertiser's "magic word"
88. Movie about a narco's worst dream?
95. Bank quote
96. "The Matrix" role
97. Person in a tree: Abbr.
98. Bagel topping
102. Movie about a bus. on Rodeo Drive?
110. Causing a ruckus
111. Job spec.
112. Canonized Norwegian king
113. Movie about the zoo's most punctual simian?
118. ___-jazz (music style)
119. Goes wild
120. Upholsterer's sample
121. Rock's end
122. Linguistic suffix
123. They connote disapproval
124. Information technology giant
125. Pull (in)

DOWN

1. Rapper with the 1996 nine-time platinum album "All Eyez on Me"
2. Trump's first
3. Kind of colony
4. Didn't make a move
5. Moving
6. George who was nicknamed "the man who owned Broadway"
7. 1985 Peter Yates-directed movie
8. Latin 51-Across
9. "Make ___ double"
10. Abbr. on a business card
11. "Saturday Night Live" has a new one every week
12. Handle, in archaeology
13. Whack
14. Like a picnic
15. Cay
16. Pirate's secret
17. Young salmon
21. French waters
23. Until now
25. Mai ___
27. Canter
31. Actress Adams, star of 2007's "Enchanted"
32. Cry when going down?
33. One in Oaxaca
34. Neighbor of Nor.
38. Words of woe
39. Turner of records
40. Writer Buchanan and others
41. Strong cart
42. Screen sites
43. Angle
44. One who's out
45. "I, Claudius" role
46. Impersonates
47. "I'll do that right away!"
48. "Deliver Us From ___" (2003 film)
49. "Dumb, dumb, dumb!"
54. Bring out
55. Words before dark or black
56. Keats's "The Eve of St. ___"
57. Gossiping
60. Oil capital
61. Get into
62. Like Bruckner's Symphony No. 7
64. Actress Vardalos
67. "Oil!" author Sinclair
68. ". . . as it ___ heaven"
69. "Casablanca" extra
70. Toil
71. Nickname on "The Addams Family"
72. Schreiber of "The Manchurian Candidate"
73. W.W. II vet, e.g.
74. "Gone With the Wind" setting
75. Soldier's food, for short
76. Impersonate
79. Potty
80. Meeting planners
84. Lost Persian, e.g.
87. Toppled
89. Regatta trophy
90. P.O. delivery
91. Novelist Harper
92. Super finish?
93. Expression for the Joker
94. Buildup around the mouth
98. Take in
99. ___-pocus
100. Author who wrote "Did you ever stop to think, and forget to start again?"
101. Those, in Tijuana
103. Always, poetically
104. Aspiring attys.' hurdles
105. Old TV's "___ Derringer"
106. Thrills
107. Ballot listing
108. "Oh, pretty please?"
109. Time and again
111. "Star Wars" critter
114. Tour de France units: Abbr.
115. The Wildcats of the Big 12 Conf.
116. Not lease, say
117. Vessel for Thor Heyerdahl

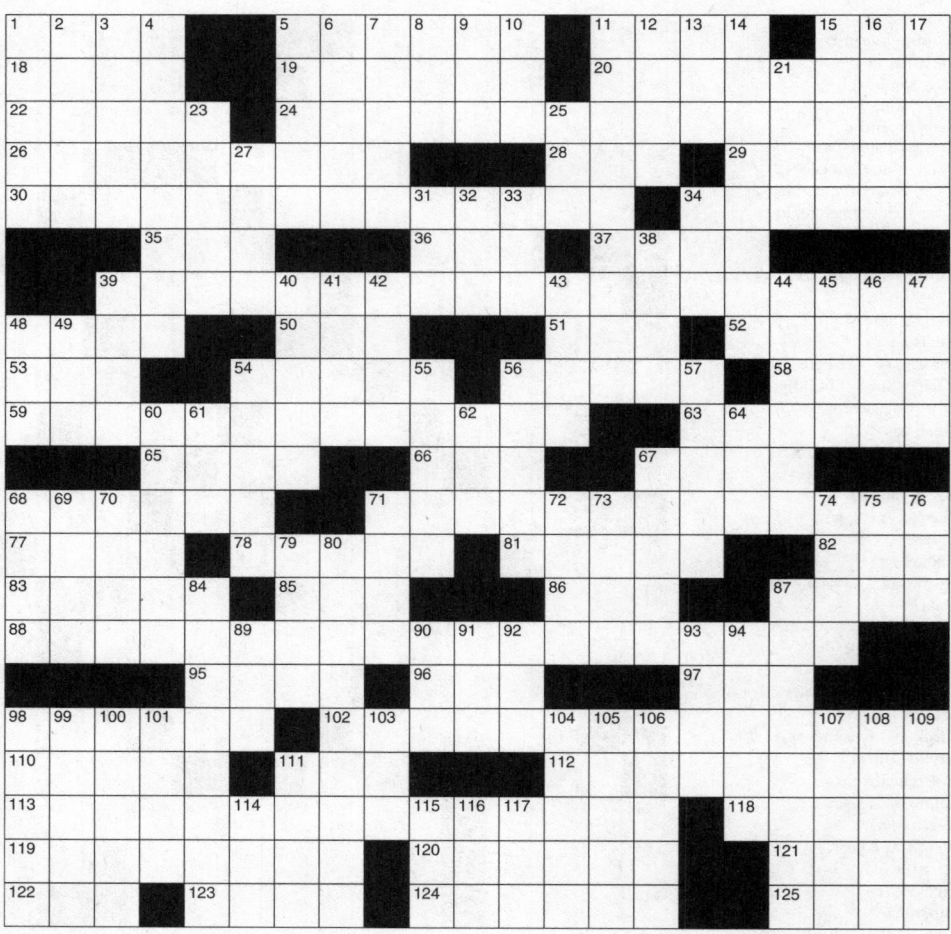

by Caleb Madison

ACROSS

1 Dish that's often roasted
5 U.K. counterespionage agcy.
8 Belonging to
13 July holiday, with "the"
16 Spell caster
20 Declare
21 PC key
22 Silents star Bara
23 Agent Gold of "Entourage"
24 Teensy bit
25 Think the world of
27 "Now I remember"
28 Leaves in the kitchen
30 Start of instructions for what to do when this puzzle is done
33 "Moving forward" sloganeer
34 Galilee's locale
35 G.I. addresses
38 Soft-shoe, e.g.
41 "___ in cat"
43 Something to go in . . . or on
47 ___-de-sac
48 With 67- and 97-Across, second part of the instructions
57 "___ won't!"
58 Sequoyah, for one
60 Victim of Hercules' second labor
61 Given directly
63 Ones caught in a maze?
64 Little squirt, maybe
65 Lachrymose
66 "___ et manus" (M.I.T.'s motto)
67 See 48-Across
72 Brag
74 Digs
75 In and of ___
76 Most liable to sunburn
77 Call on a pitch
78 Need for the winner of a Wimbledon men's match
81 Young 'un
82 "___ Ba Yah" (campfire song)
83 It follows the initial part of a procedure
85 Beethoven's Third
88 Forecast for improved weather
92 College ___
94 Religious image: Var.
95 Seasonal activity
96 Capital of Italy
97 See 48-Across
103 Baby kangaroos
104 Start of a counting rhyme
105 BlackBerrys, e.g., for short
106 Blackthorn pickings
108 Request for Vanna
109 Staples of early education
110 "The War of the Worlds" invaders, briefly
113 How one must win in Ping-Pong
115 "Rubbish!"
116 Some corner stores
119 Orange and green fruits
123 Rock candy, essentially
126 Einstein's birthplace
127 Common hockey power play
129 Author mentioned in the Beatles' "I Am the Walrus"
130 Trillionth: Prefix
132 Study of the heavens: Abbr.
133 Bias
135 Collaborative Web document
138 Final part of instructions
145 Something you later might think better of
146 Consumer
147 "Death in Venice" and "Of Mice and Men"
148 Machine used to maneuver manure
149 Slay somebody
150 Thoreau, e.g.

DOWN

1 Head
2 With: Fr.
3 A small one helps the indecisive
4 QB Favre and others
5 Like corn bread
6 Childish retort
7 Costing a nickel
8 Rat-___
9 "Zip it"
10 Cyclops' feature
11 Experimented too much?
12 Burkina ___
13 Structure of Chekhov's "The Cherry Orchard"
14 Court figure
15 "Broom-___"
16 ___ Bay, 1898 battle site
17 Memo abbr.
18 2007 Peace Nobelist
19 Subgenre of punk rock
26 1990s Indian P.M.
29 Mugful
31 Commerce treaty starting 1947
32 "Oh, pooh!"
35 Big Ten rival: Abbr.
36 "Stupidest thing I ever heard!"
37 Poisonous shrub
39 Sound at a sauna
40 Remove with effort
41 Assume the fetal position
42 Ottoman big shot
44 Opened, as a flag
45 Skating jumps
46 Suffix with planet
48 Pro
49 Safari sight
50 Unleash upon
51 "Avast!"
52 Pantheon head
53 Respect
54 Copycats
55 Succeed effortlessly
56 Bygone TV control: Abbr.
59 62-Down carriers: Abbr.
62 Gridiron grp.
66 File on an iPod
68 Access the contents of, say
69 Mother, slangily
70 Invents
71 Let slip
73 1940s conflict: Abbr.
79 Hoity-___
80 Punjabi believers
83 "A Little Princess" heroine and others
84 Internet forum rabble-rouser
86 Iowa college
87 Brings to a boil
89 Audible pauses
90 Greeting to Gaius
91 Necessary: Abbr.
92 "___ Wedding," Alan Alda film
93 Overseas O.K.
97 Prefix with sphere
98 Sine qua non
99 Dos' followers
100 Pick up
101 Western wolf
102 Some hand-raisers
103 Alternative to a cross
107 "___ Cried" (1962 hit)
109 N.Y.C. time when it's midnight in L.A.
110 Emissions org.
111 ___ chi
112 Thesaurus offering: Abbr.
114 Like a team that's ahead by a safety
117 Trick-taking game
118 Girl's name that's Latin for "fame"
119 Walk
120 "I concur"
121 Behind
122 Hubbub
124 Black-eyed legume
125 Comic Charles Nelson ___
127 Highest-rated, as a hotel
128 Like the majority of Interstate highways
130 Tire (out)
131 "Like ___ not . . ."
132 Bide-___
134 Monterrey kin
136 Many-armed Hindu goddess
137 Old actresses Claire and Balin
138 Traveler's aid, for short
139 Funny
140 Kung ___ chicken
141 In accord (with)
142 Eastern Canadian prov.
143 Campers, briefly
144 Id ___

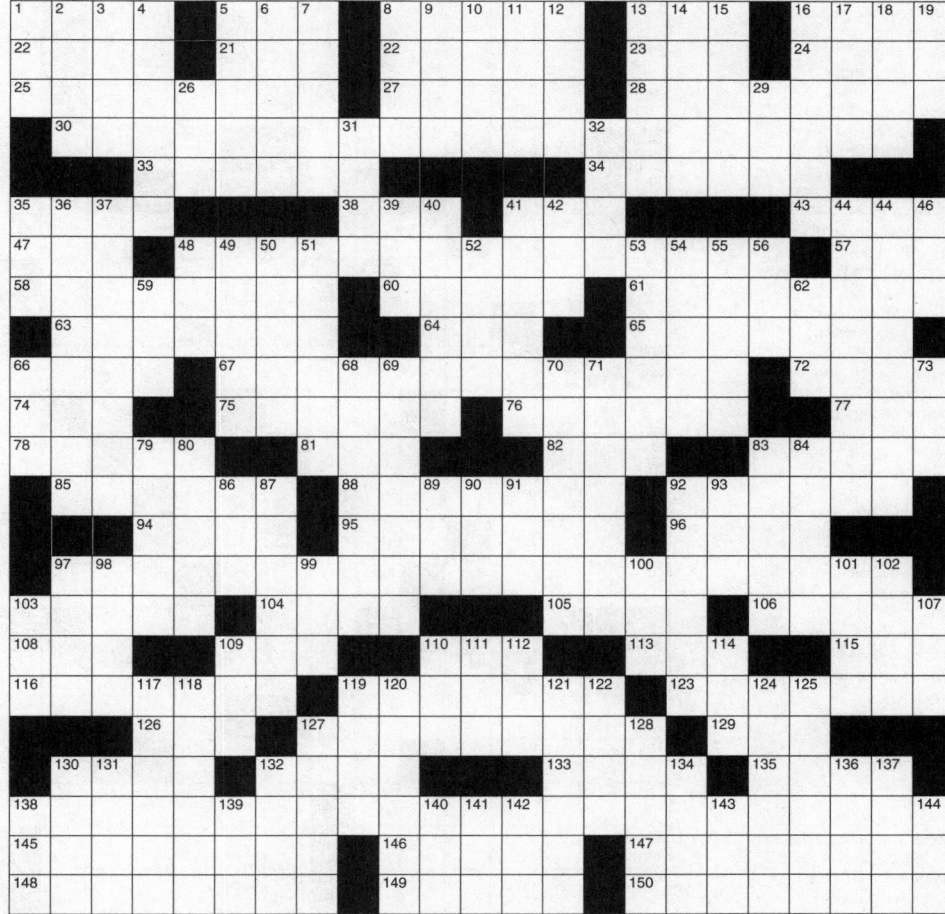

by Kevin G. Der

ACROSS

1 Pep rally shout
7 Sics on
13 More than a favorite
20 Program begun under Kennedy
21 Digs
22 Single advancement
23 Plea made to a chimney sweep?
25 Holding one's own
26 Topic in a golf lesson
27 Pancho's pal
29 Colonial John
30 Moving
32 ___ hole in (corrodes)
35 Graduation deliveries
37 Jobs for some underwriters, for short
38 Distribute equal amounts?
41 "The Daughter of Time" novelist, 1951
42 Friendliness
44 "___ Mucho" (1944 #1 hit)
45 1968 live folk album
47 Humorist Sedaris
48 Sub
51 Maximum extent
53 Pushover
56 Vote involved in a 15th wedding anniversary?
59 Recipient of a lettera amorosa
60 Missile Command maker
63 Floors
64 Sounds from a hot bath
65 Subject to loss on a laptop
67 Follies
69 Genetic letters
70 Have no accomplices
71 Done
72 Three times a day, on an Rx
73 Thurman of "The Avengers"
74 Title role for Streisand
75 Mire
76 Narrow-minded affairs?
80 Kitchen appliance brand
82 When doubled, an old sitcom sign-off
83 Blasts from the past, briefly
84 Payroll fig.
87 N.B.A. star Lamar ___
89 Act as a go-between
91 Main lines
93 Peter Pan rival
95 Teacher's pet?
99 Commercial prefix with jet
100 One making an impression
102 Poet who wrote "She walks in beauty, like the night"
103 Belong
104 Blacksmith, often
105 Race of Norse deities
108 Picks up
110 More like a bubble bath
112 Stop to admire one's pillaging?
117 Hams
118 World capital said to have been founded by King Midas
119 Muse of astronomy
120 "Hmmm . . ."
121 Theater annoyance
122 Manages

DOWN

1 Oomph
2 W.W. II agcy.
3 Movie with the repeated line "To infinity, and beyond!"
4 Snobbery
5 Site of many kisses
6 Sound from a dungeon
7 Hereditary
8 Around 1,000, e.g.: Abbr.
9 Word repeated in Emily Dickinson's "___ so much joy! so much joy!"
10 Winter vehicles with treads
11 Yours, in Nemours
12 Day care charges
13 State in the Sierra Madre
14 Game with Wild Draw Four cards
15 Runs the hose over again
16 Stopping place in a Carlo Levi title
17 Sexiest bell ringer?
18 Ancient Jewish ascetic
19 Lilliputian
24 Home of the world's northernmost capital: Abbr.
28 "I Never Played the Game" writer
30 Sanyo competitor
31 ___ blocker
33 "This Boy's Life" author Wolff
34 Nerve material?
36 Health org.
38 Stern cry?
39 "Very funny!"
40 Oscar winner Jannings and others
43 Again and again?
46 Spots
49 Showed hospitality at the door
50 Bygone muscle cars
52 They have substantial bills
54 Sen. Lott
55 Mountain air
56 Got started, with "up"

57 Alternative to a hotel, briefly
58 Cable channel whose first showing was "Gone With the Wind"
60 John Wayne film, with "The"
61 "Swan Lake" garb
62 Part of a Beckett play?
66 Makes an assertion
68 Tchaikovsky's Symphony No. 6 ___ minor
69 Mass, for one
70 Gallic girlfriend
72 "Pagliacci" clown
73 Guam, e.g.: Abbr.
77 Aplenty
78 Take back
79 Ministre d'___
81 You can count on them
84 Texas toppers
85 Delhi wrap
86 Bygone Dodge
88 Early 12th-century year
90 What turned-out pants pockets may signify
92 Slicker accessory
93 Toastmaster General of old comedy
94 Bury
96 Last ride?
97 Hungarian playwright known for "Liliom"
98 Like a line, briefly
101 Pauses

103 Partner in a French firm, maybe
106 Hunk
107 Actress Skye
109 Put ___ in one's ear
111 Prior to, in verse
113 Select
114 We may precede this
115 Ad ___
116 Box on a calendar

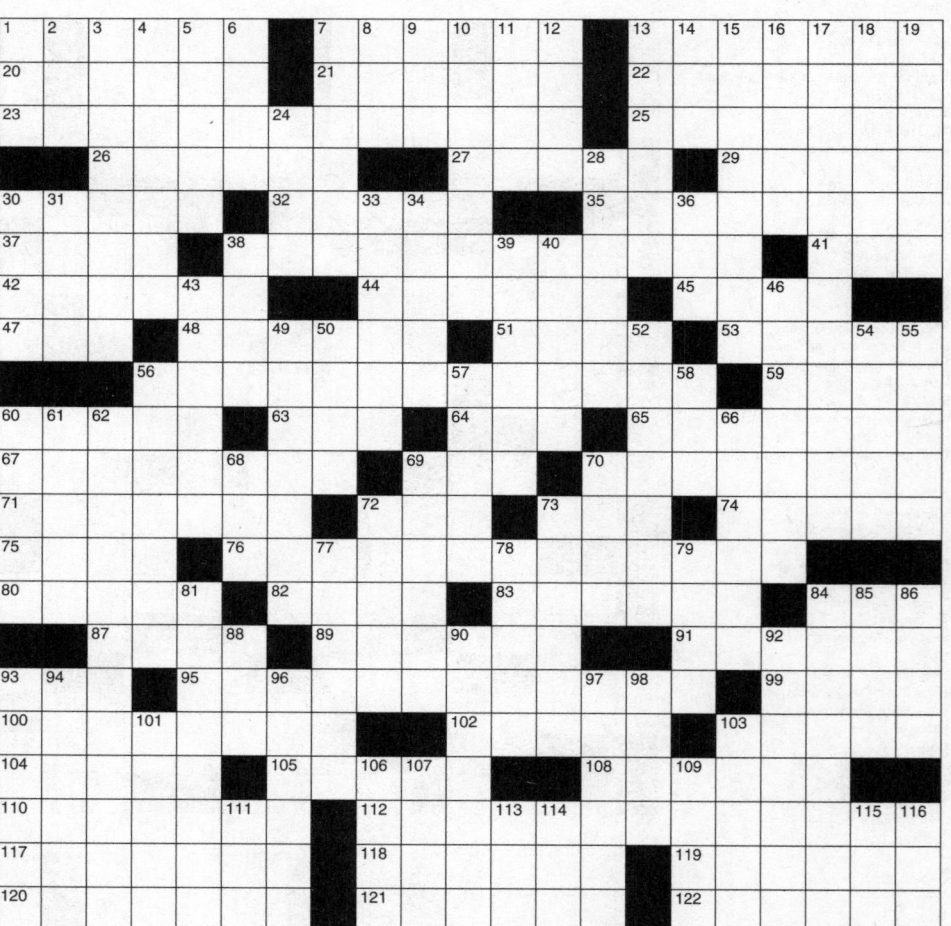

by Alan Arbesfeld

ACROSS

1 Goes on TV
5 Kublai Khan and others
12 Barkeep's supply
18 Transports, in a way
21 Place to make an omelet
22 Studio behind the original "Star Trek"
23 Protected
24 Program on which pundits talk about marinara and such?
26 Easily makes the hole with, in golf
27 Trapper's ware
28 Walloped, quickly
29 Hydroelectric org.
30 Venice's Bridge of ___
32 Program on which pundits say dumbfounding things?
37 You might not be able to stand this
39 Big winner at the casino
41 Home of 14-Down
42 All: Prefix
43 Bass ___
44 Possessor of many rings
45 Late bloomer
47 Suffix with viol
49 Easily concealed weapon
51 Program on which pundits talk about hangings?
56 Sulu player on "Star Trek"
57 "The Wild Duck" dramatist
59 Got dark
60 At all
62 Leave rubber, with "out"
63 Indians play it
65 Exasperated exclamations
66 Program on which pundits express indignant surprise?
71 Kwik-E-Mart clerk
73 Earring type
74 Afternoon hour
75 Personal ad abbr.
76 Kind of winds
79 Tuscan province
80 Old Dodges
84 Program on which pundits slug it out with reporters?
87 Passed out in a bad way
90 Start of a Vol. 1 heading
91 I do's
92 Whence Zeno
93 Life overseas
94 Brooding sort
96 Pollster Roper
97 Analyze
98 Wood for bows
99 Program on which pundits kvetch?
104 Buffoons
106 "Who ___?" (song from "Les Miz")
107 Mens ___ (criminal intent)
108 Works at a museum
110 Worrier's words
113 Program on which pundits deride the power of the federal government?
118 Old cash register key
119 Answer the call
120 It may be a lot
121 Waxes
122 Commentator Myers
123 Have
124 Would-be J.D.'s exam

DOWN

1 Words after hard or keep
2 ___ Thomas, the Soul Queen of New Orleans
3 Cut of beef
4 "Pardon me, Pasquale"
5 Sticker abbr.
6 Michael of "Caddyshack"
7 Nabisco ___ wafer
8 Ostentation
9 Commercial suffix with Motor
10 Med. country
11 The Cards, on scoreboards
12 Has way too much of, slangily
13 ___ double life
14 Cyclones' sch.
15 A role some people play
16 Control surface on a plane's wing
17 NPR newswoman Stamberg
19 Program on which pundits talk about Camelot?
20 Lady of Brazil
25 Just makes, with "out"
31 One who says "See you in court!"
33 In the stomach
34 Govt. gangbusters
35 Lifesaver, e.g.
36 ___ max
37 History
38 Michigan college
40 Not quite good enough for the majors, say
45 Addled
46 Nonkosher food
47 Actor Jason of the Harry Potter films
48 Volleyball action
50 Matriarch of six of the 12 Tribes of Israel
52 One of Chekhov's "Three Sisters"
53 ___ before
54 180
55 Map lines: Abbr.
58 Attention getter
61 Start of a pirate chant
63 Miler turned congressman
64 Many ski chalets
66 Sushi staple
67 Improve
68 Loamy soil
69 Program on which pundits talk for 48 straight hours?
70 "All ___" (Tomlin film)
71 State dept. figure
72 Dupin's creator
77 Strong position
78 Giant star of the 1930s and '40s
79 Big East's ___ Hall
81 Specialists in special ops
82 "Why would ___?"
83 Dither
85 Sport with a 4½-ounce ball
86 Cine- suffix
88 "The most beautiful woman ever to visit Casablanca"
89 Years on the diamond
94 Decent
95 Isolate
96 Time online, for example
97 Harshly bright
99 Cut a cord, say
100 Present itself
101 Musical matchmaker
102 Certain caucuser
103 Beatrice, to Leonato, in "Much Ado About Nothing"
105 Subject of the book "Disaster in Dearborn"
109 Tube lineup
111 ". . . and to ___ good-night"
112 What's left
114 Covered up
115 Big load
116 "Double Fantasy" singer
117 Safety equipment

by Randolph Ross

ACROSS

1 Portraitist of George Washington
7 Robot maid on "The Jetsons"
12 Sorority chapter
17 Leader of a flock
18 Do away with
19 Spreader of holiday cheer
21 Singer who said "At least I had that, one guy understood me"
22 Possible punishment for steroid use
23 Enhance
24 When Cannes heats up
25 Native tongue of R&B singer Rihanna
26 Bow to
27 Wise guy
28 Ear part
29 "Esq." titleholders
31 Keep an eye out for
33 Meager
34 Prefix with sphere
35 Fuming
38 Daring
39 Alvin and the Chipmunks, e.g.
40 Experts at exports
43 Genre explored by Run-D.M.C. and Aerosmith
44 Diurnally
45 "Hop ___!"
46 Mexican mouse chaser
48 Inner circle
51 Proust title character
53 Job interview topic
57 Sioux tribe member
58 State capital on the Colorado River
61 Economy-size
63 Langston Hughes poem
64 Cry at sea
66 Cancún resident, once
68 Farm call
69 Hall's partner in pop
70 "This is how it's done"
71 Worth mentioning
72 Pattern for light or sound
74 Soft hat materials
76 Actors Max and Max Jr.
78 See
79 ___ Taylor, co-host of "Make Me a Supermodel"
80 It appears when things go bad
82 Boils down
85 Thrill seeker
91 "If you ask me," online
92 The "A" of James A. Garfield
94 Some exams for joint pain sufferers
95 Litigant
96 Symptom of catarrh
97 Focused (on)
99 Brisk pace
100 Cavs, on a scoreboard
101 Nativity figure
102 "Was it ___ I saw?" (classic palindrome)
103 Samuel L. Jackson's character in "Pulp Fiction"
106 Were present?
107 It might run in the rain
109 Filled (with)
110 Part of a serial
112 Eroded
113 It's usually said with the eyes closed

114 Wig
115 Egg holders
116 Kind of skill
117 Farm machine

DOWN

1 Weightlifter's helper
2 Have a break at 4:00, say
3 Troop troupe: Abbr.
4 Basic travel path
5 First name in gossip
6 Paris was part of it
7 Equips with new clips
8 Small African antelope
9 It's darn likely
10 "My, my, old chap!"
11 Dusk, to Donne
12 Unlikely event for puritans
13 MADD member
14 Foe of Spider-Man
15 Like some modern maps
16 Coffee table item
19 Mustang rivals
20 Gene who sang "Back in the Saddle Again"
21 Cause of many uprisings
27 Members of the bar?
30 Biker's add-on
32 Early Chinese dynasty
33 Admit defeat, in a way
34 Lucratively
36 Polite disclaimer
37 ABC a.m. show, briefly
38 Last resort in poker, often
41 Doesn't waver
42 Euripides drama
43 G.P.S. suggestion
46 Bottle opener's surprise
47 Vegas openings?
48 Untangles, in a way
49 Cyberball maker
50 Pop singer who appeared in the movie "Sgt. Pepper's Lonely Hearts Club Band"
51 It's called in a political convention roll call
52 Undercover device
53 Campaigns for
54 "Quite possibly"
55 Surface-___
56 Singles and jingles
59 Sub with sauerkraut?
60 White wine from Verona
62 W., e.g.: Abbr.
65 Professional with many contacts?
67 Lords and ladies
73 Is past?
75 Scrape (out)

77 Like some professors
79 Sask. neighbor
80 Drinks in frosted glasses
81 Married
82 Hit Sony product introduced in 1984
83 Model after
84 American, Swiss, etc.
85 Design feature of many a viaduct
86 Lookout, maybe
87 "OMG, that's sooo funny!"
88 Kind of bar
89 Squared away
90 First name in cosmetics
92 Now, in Nogales
93 Wages, before overtime
97 Beer serving in a pub
98 "Yippee!"
101 Jabbers
102 U.S. gas chain
104 Triple-edged sword
105 Part of a horse's genealogy
108 Cool ___
109 Genealogical grp.
111 S, on a French compass

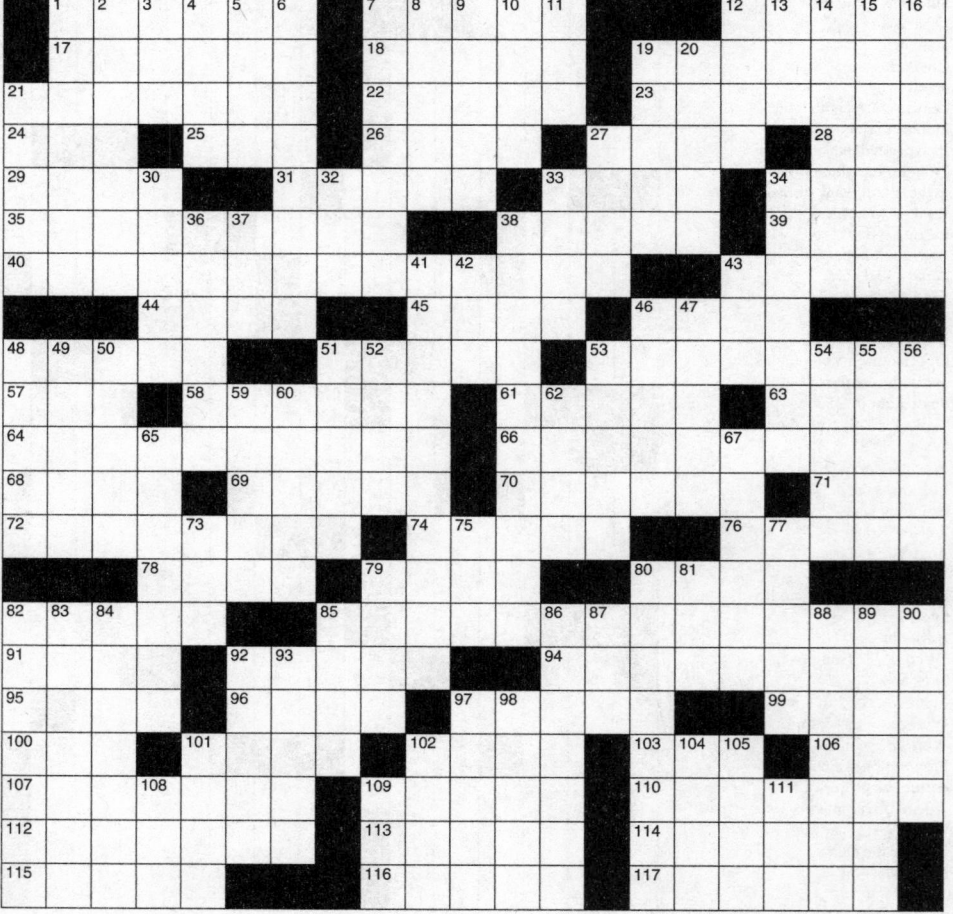

by Jeremy Newton

ACROSS

1 Drapery material
7 Lumber supplier
14 Item marked in pounds
20 City and county of central California
21 Rushing
22 Hair color
23 School in Madison, N.J.
25 Cause of worry lines
26 Poet whose last words were "Of course [God] will forgive me; that's his business"
27 "Beau ___"
29 Coup d' ___ (quick glance)
30 Bank postings
33 Don't believe it
37 Seward-to-Fairbanks dir.
38 ___ rancheros
39 Levelheaded
40 Raw bar offering
42 Officer in "Alice's Restaurant"
43 Launches
45 Classic theater name
46 "The Divine Comedy," for Dante
49 1950s–'70s TV host
51 Petrol purchase
54 It's often punched on a keypad
55 Reader's goal
56 Online reading
58 Redeem
59 Wife, informally
61 Fraternity member
62 Difficult situation
63 Sitting with one's hand on one's chin, e.g.
66 Track-and-field event
69 Google results
70 Duds
72 Record producer who published the diary "A Year With Swollen Appendices"
73 Appetite whetter
75 Favored one side or the other
76 Kon-Tiki material
78 Turned right
79 What eds. read
82 Get divorced
83 ___ avis
84 Dropped off
87 More spooky
89 Work site?
91 German river
92 Trig angle
94 Salad morsel
95 "On Language" columnist
97 Mens ___ (guilty mind)
98 Pantry array
102 Enzyme in some yeasts
103 There's one for dance
105 Prefix with centric
106 Only U.S. vice president born in Maryland
107 San Luis ___
109 Ones in charge of a case . . . or a literal hint to the eight other longest answers in this puzzle
116 Vacation arrangement
117 Big name in auto parts
118 French subjects?
119 Alarm clock button
120 Psychiatric visit
121 Major diamond exporter

DOWN

1 Mil. authority
2 Laugh start
3 Suffix with cyan-
4 City with the world's first telephone directory (1878)
5 Loyally following
6 Nuts
7 Had work looming?
8 Combined
9 Blade in sports
10 The shakes
11 "The Da Vinci Code" scholar Sir ___ Teabing
12 Novelist who wrote "The Gravedigger's Daughter"
13 No-tell motel visit
14 Italy's Reggia di ___ (royal palace)
15 Pizza
16 River that rises in Cantabria
17 Beloved figure in England
18 Bearlike
19 Eve ___, "The Vagina Monologues" monologist
24 Connections
28 Quaint letter opener
30 Eating sound
31 Persian Gulf emirate
32 Cover many subjects?
33 Extremely pleasing, in slang
34 Occupied
35 Word with smart or mind
36 Upbraid
39 Biological dividing wall
41 Being debated
43 Kind of fin
44 Dumped out
45 Singer Corinne Bailey ___
47 Longtime news inits.
48 Potato choice
50 Egyptian crosses
52 Yemeni money
53 Tolkien creatures
57 Nobodies
58 Southern legume
59 Scoundrels
60 Window washer's boo-boo
62 Unlikely to be Miss America
63 Ghostlike
64 Big tournament
65 Card game played to 61
67 China's Zhou
68 Loose overcoat
71 Condense again, as an article
74 The Mormons, initially
76 High jump need
77 Certain photo caption
79 Broadcasters, e.g.
80 Predictors
81 Brief indulgence
83 "Malcolm in the Middle" boy
85 Cy Young candidates' stats
86 Liberal
88 Behind
90 Larry O'Brien Championship Trophy org.
92 Safeguards
93 Deli order
95 Sacred places
96 Winning hand in blackjack
99 Stewpots
100 Certain flower girl
101 "The Grapes of Wrath" family
102 T-shirt size: Abbr.
104 "___ perpetua" (Idaho's motto)
106 Lots
108 Opposite of guerra
110 Paris's Parc ___ Princes
111 Sixth-century year
112 Prefix with freak
113 Letters on a brandy bottle
114 Marine predator
115 Org. that has its benefits

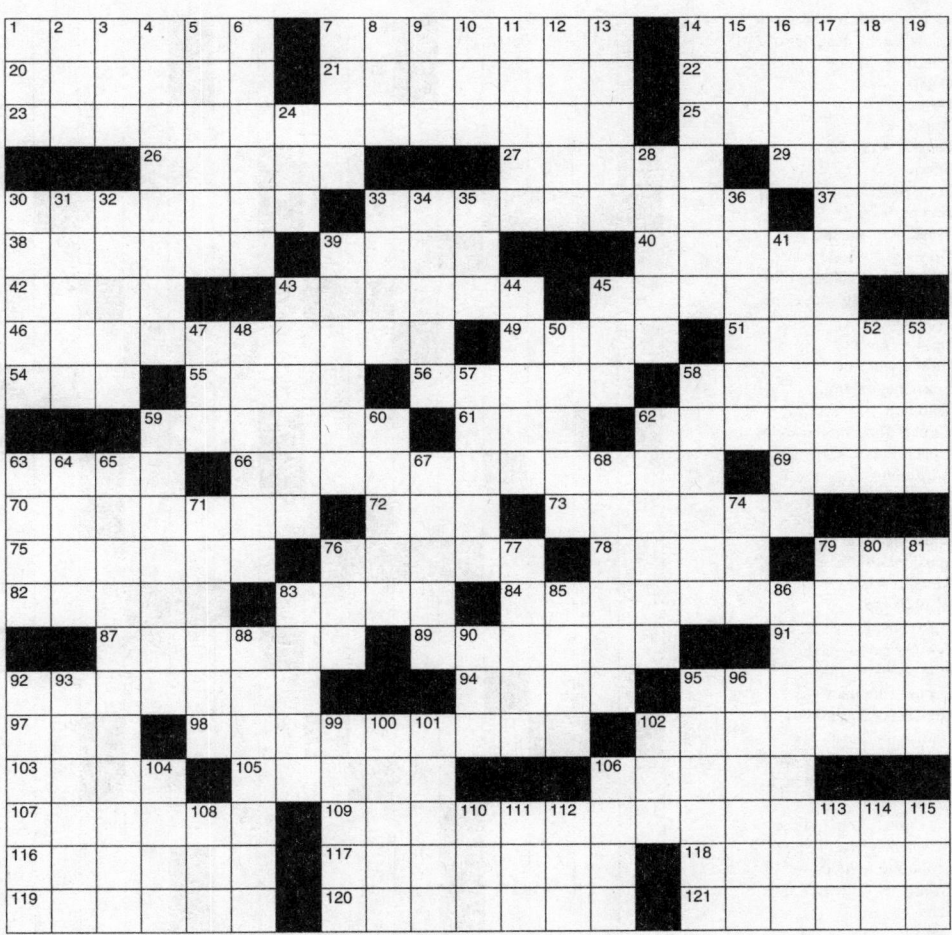

by Brendan Emmett Quigley

ACROSS

1 Butcher shop purchase
6 Some foreign pen pals
10 Photo paper option
15 [How dare you!]
19 Song sung by Gwen in Broadway's "Chicago"
20 Radio host/pianist John
21 Greek market of old
22 "The Lion King" lioness
23 When jerks come out?
26 X out
27 Pertinent to the discussion
28 Kind of dialysis
29 Novice
31 "A Doll's House" wife
32 Wishes undone
33 Some people or food at parties
34 Nonkosher sandwiches
38 String around a cake box?
41 City near Tel Aviv
44 Moistens again
46 Once-in-a-lifetime exchange, maybe
47 Texas county, river or forest that's a girl's first name
49 Vinegar: Prefix
50 AOL alternative
52 Bridge
53 Men or women who pinch?
58 "New Look" designer of 1947
59 Charity's urging
60 Orbital point
62 Dope
64 Appeal to
66 Penseur's thought
67 Speck
68 Prefix with -crat
70 Hair stuff
71 Mushroom stalks
73 Dress-up costume piece
75 Month in a Faulkner title
77 One of Woody's stock at Woodstock
78 Nerd's essence?
82 Unlikely to run
87 Legal eagles' org.
88 Come up
89 Capital of South Australia
90 French Polynesia constituents
93 Lauds
94 Thrice, in prescriptions
95 Roast the other side of the marshmallow?
99 Novelist's need
100 W.W. II gun
101 "Let's just leave ___ that"
102 Teri Garr's "Young Frankenstein" role
104 Certain celebrant
107 Legislative assemblies
108 "Praise the Lord!"
112 A leveret is a young one
113 Discouraging comment to a cloner?
117 ___ Center, home of the New Jersey Nets
118 Pertaining to hair
119 "Almighty" title role for Steve Carell
120 Caustic
121 Eye part
122 Desirable places
123 Kind of difference, oxymoronically
124 "Land ___!"

DOWN

1 Monitor type, for short
2 Jolly laugh
3 Yak pack
4 Big East Conference team, for short
5 Attach, as a patch
6 Invitation information specification
7 Gathering points
8 Suffix with book
9 Like some eggs or cloth
10 They're attractive, but not necessarily to each other
11 Shocked
12 Awl, for one
13 Play about Capote
14 Salary
15 Bamboozles
16 Gyro meat
17 "Others" in a Latin phrase
18 Crown
24 Apple pocketfuls
25 Transmitter starter?
30 Fencing swords
33 The Flintstones' pet
34 Uncouth youth
35 Poland's Walesa
36 Moth, perhaps?
37 Altercation
39 Trig ratio
40 Sun Tzu's "The Art of ___"
41 Fabric that really breathes?
42 Low tie
43 Strawberry of note
45 Off-campus local
48 City near Milan
50 Outback buddy
51 Shooting sport
52 Second-century year
54 St. Louis's ___ Bridge
55 Nagpur noble
56 Fern germ
57 These, to Juan
61 Rusty on the diamond
62 Utah's lily
63 Pitcher of a perfect game, 9/9/65
64 "Vigilant ___ to steal cream": Falstaff
65 Walked with a purpose
69 Wahine's dance
72 Shooting game
74 Addams family cousin
76 Spaghetti ___
79 Hops kiln
80 Analogy phrase
81 Battery part
83 A large number
84 JPEG or text
85 Score just before victory, maybe
86 Fall mo.
90 Weeping
91 Rimes with the 1996 hit "Blue"
92 Subjects of many legal battles
93 Goad
96 Garage container
97 Native American home
98 Waiting at the bank, say
100 Beginnings
103 Localities
104 Dr. with advice in O magazine
105 Level
106 Monopoly game token
107 Whine
109 Place to play b-ball
110 Give orders like a drill sergeant
111 "Night" author Wiesel
114 Fact finisher
115 Hydroelectric org.
116 Mormons, initially

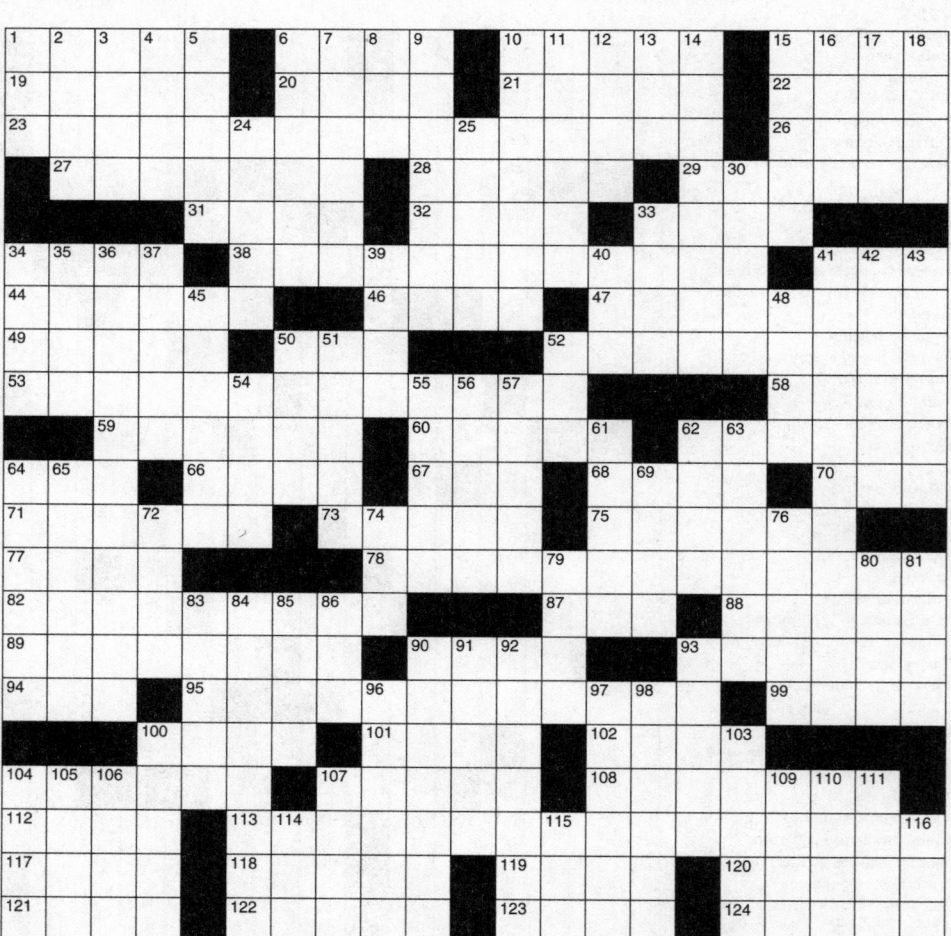

by Cathy Allis Millhauser

ACROSS

1 Seafood dishes
8 ____ the board
14 Certified
22 Socrates or Pythagoras, e.g.
23 Mangle by mastication
24 Perfunctory
25 Lower part of a duet
26 Showing concern?
27 Hanging over many a mantel
28 *Common Guernsey bull
31 Flower parts
32 West Flanders site of three W.W. I battles
33 Lid attachment
35 "Ally McBeal" co-star Lucy
36 Composer Charles
40 Ones being tested
41 *1968 firm featuring a murderous cheerleader
46 *Urban farce
48 Studio supporter
49 Destination for Mary and Joseph
50 Stainless steel, for one
51 ____ ear
52 Whopper topper
56 See 47-Down
57 Hiccup
58 Life
59 Hwys.
60 Shore birds
61 *Where stars can be seen fluffing and folding
64 Kensington kiss
65 Hair line?
66 Verdant stretches
67 ____ Beach, Fla.
68 Gallic toppers
71 *What theaters play
73 One of Luther's 95
75 Look lasciviously
76 Skye of "Say Anything . . ."
77 What "matar" means on an Indian menu
78 Great Trek trekker
79 *Bean, e.g.
83 Russian diet?
84 Badge awarder: Abbr.
87 Region including Texarkana
88 Mexican waterways
89 G.I.'s
91 Serve well
92 Goes on "Wheel of Fortune"?
94 Snail variety whose name means "small gray"
95 Bygone P.M. with a palindromic name
96 "Ville d'Avray" painter
97 *Onetime regal status of Shanghai or Canton
98 *Get blankets
102 Presides over as a judge
103 Pizzeria chain, familiarly
104 "Is that ____?"
105 Apple cores?: Abbr.
106 Pulitzer-winning journalist Seymour
107 "Swept Away" director Guy
111 *Novice in an ad campaign
120 Home of the Cadillac Ranch
122 Word with aunt or voyage
123 "Heavens to Betsy!"
124 Computer information path
125 "Rama Lama Ding Dong" singers, with "the"
126 Broke out
127 Thomas Gray and others
128 Drug company once headed by Donald Rumsfeld
129 Fixed motor parts

DOWN

1 Events gone by
2 From square one
3 "____ homo"
4 Columbia athlete
5 Mardi Gras follower
6 Roy Rogers sidekick Devine
7 "Pipe down!"
8 Precision
9 Takeout option
10 Tears
11 Wilson of "The Darjeeling Limited"
12 Sport for rikishi
13 German wine made from the late harvest
14 "Killer" program
15 Showcase item
16 Some shapes in topology
17 New newts
18 Ilk
19 Ski runs, e.g.
20 Designer Pucci
21 Old car with the slogan "We are driven"
29 Sunroof and spoilers, e.g.
30 Gourmand
34 N.L. Central team: Abbr.
36 Less welcoming
37 Strongly green
38 Short jackets for boys
38 Roget offerings: Abbr.
40 Short jackets for women
41 *Bad drivers back them up
42 1 to 10, say
43 Godliness
44 Available
45 On easy street
47 Kind of examiner 56-Across was
51 Like xenon
52 Little foxes
53 Snaps back?
54 Places to develop
55 Ones who are always starting something?
57 Chilling: Var.
58 Apothecary container
62 Swells up
63 Vintage autos
64 Complete, as a Senate term
65 Pub order
68 Jacket material?
69 Start of a counting rhyme
70 Clinton's first labor secretary
71 Terse order
72 Chihuahua change
73 Small birds, in British lingo
74 Robust
76 Getaway locale
78 "Pass the Courvoisier" rapper
80 Key shade
81 Juice
82 Rap sheet listing
83 How the Great Sphinx looks
84 The fifth element
85 Gerald's predecessor
86 Staff members: Abbr.
90 Forerunner of the K.G.B.
92 Absorb, in a way
93 Takes for granted
94 Make ready for the dishwasher
96 Filch
97 2000 Jennifer Lopez thriller
98 Weekly with 30+ million circulation
99 ____ instincts
100 Shift, in volleyball
101 Monkey predator
106 Playground quarry
108 Escarpment
109 Spinner for the Spinners
110 They're no good
112 Invited
113 Alaska senator Murkowski
114 Mole, e.g.
115 1977 flick with the tagline "Terror just beneath the surface"
116 "Git!"
117 What each starred clue—and its answer—contains
118 Part of FEMA: Abbr.
119 Cabernets, e.g.
121 Little yelps

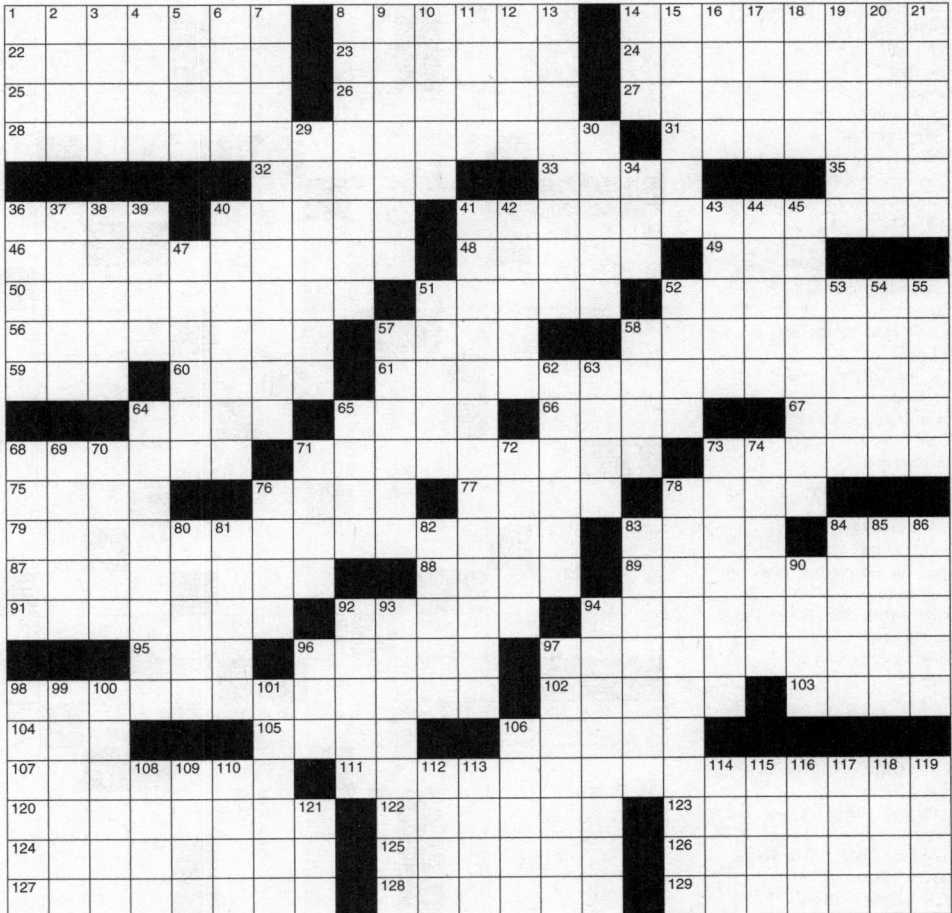

by Byron Walden

ACROSS

1 Sudden increase
6 Jacks, e.g.
10 Wallop
14 Fancy footwear
19 Up in the air
20 Object of a mil. search
21 Deserve special perks, say
22 Georges who wrote "Life: A User's Manual"
23 Low-budget films about hearty European meals?
26 Even things
27 Conductor ___-Pekka Salonen
28 Page with views
29 Organ repair sites, briefly
30 Some crew members
32 Hip-hop's ___ Kim
33 Where hermit painters retire?
36 "Impossible" response to the question "Are you sleeping?"
39 "I'm not quite done yet"
41 Bone: Prefix
42 Biography of Odin, e.g.?
46 Traffic directors
50 Say without saying?
51 One to one, e.g.
52 Bring (in) abundantly
54 Pinza of "South Pacific"
55 Bones that support tibiae
56 German beef?
58 Family dinner
62 Eva's half sister?
63 Fingered
64 Zinger
66 Say A is not A, say
67 College cohorts
69 Place to go for kitchenware?
73 Ivory or Coast
75 Grp. that includes Canada and Colombia
76 Hardware fastener
77 It's taken by some coll. seniors
80 It may be stroked
81 Used
84 A little extra burnishing, maybe, in brief
85 E.R. part: Abbr.
86 Ltr. holders
88 Picard's counselor on "Star Trek: T.N.G."
89 Narrow inlet
91 Supermarket section
92 Recital list
95 How beatniks raise kids?
99 Decide to take part
101 Make more tempting, as a deal
102 Worked (up)
103 Étagère with a single tiny shelf?
108 Be in a cast
109 Frequent drivers
110 Butt
111 Protester
112 Semi-attached compartment?
115 Stash
116 Where citrus trees grow in small groups?
121 Richards : Moore :: Grant : ___
122 Slate, for one
123 "The Virginian" author Wister
124 Hardly laid-back
125 Mythical enchantress
126 Explodes
127 Agent with many girls
128 White and wet

DOWN

1 Nigerian-born singer with five Top 40 hits
2 Grade elevator
3 Wee bit
4 "Original or crispy" offerer
5 Study of natural animal behavior patterns
6 Drop leaf support
7 Staggered
8 Take some off the top?
9 Skull and Bones meeting attendee
10 Rapper with a professional title
11 Mrs. Gorbachev
12 4×4, briefly
13 Infatuates
14 Less dense
15 Place to find a long-term companion, maybe
16 Oven emanation
17 Precept
18 Embarrassing outbreak
24 Like cacti
25 Chamber work
31 Fictional clue sniffer
33 California city where A & W root beer was born
34 Skater Brian
35 Chicago journalist Mike
36 Last Supper question
37 Rashad of football
38 City NW of Minneapolis
40 Lepidopterous movie monster
43 Moves quietly
44 Once around
45 Hardest to get
47 13-time Gold Glove-winning shortstop
48 Learned
49 In order (to)
53 Sharp scolding
56 Something very tough
57 Cover in a layer
59 "How can ___?"
60 Ceylon's capital?
61 French pronoun
65 Soothe, in a way, as a burn
68 "American Pie" songwriter
70 Queue before Q
71 Banker's worry
72 Ready to run later
73 When repeated, "Out of the way!"
74 Latin lambs
78 Raptor's roost
79 Date not marked on a calendar?
82 Circular gasket
83 Inundate
87 With no adverse consequences
90 Old TV's "___ Three Lives"
91 Numbers, at times
93 Subject of a 2004 F.D.A. dietary supplement ban
94 Disturbance
96 Missouri feeder
97 Done
98 Straight: Prefix
100 Marching smartly
103 Archaic Irish script
104 Hanger?
105 Kenyan grazer
106 Deep-six
107 1970s–'80s supermodel
111 "So be it"
112 Family head
113 Over
114 Celebration time, for short
117 Grp. with a co-pay
118 High ball
119 Noted war photo site, briefly
120 Reagan adviser Nofziger

by Rich Norris

ACROSS

1 Titles for some monks
5 Litter unit
8 Wind with a wide range
12 Fashion
18 Tony's cousin
19 Paul Anka's "___ Beso"
20 "Too rich for my blood"
21 Carbohydrate-binding protein
22 Be fooled
24 Is completely hamstrung
26 Cold sufferer's complaint
28 Completely cover
29 Fool
30 Contradict
31 Stream bank sliders
33 Mad workers: Abbr.
34 Old printing process, for short
35 Big bore
38 And more: Abbr.
40 Musical set in Berlin
43 Dept. head
44 Stomach section
46 Way off
50 Ballet's Markova or Alonso
51 "WarGames" org.
53 Photographer's request, maybe
56 Opposite of comico-
57 Part-time players
59 Some playground shoes
60 Cut
61 Confines
62 Cooking meas.
63 Phlegmatic
65 Public persona
67 Hospital procedure, for short
69 IV to III, maybe
71 Part of a bedroom suite
73 Pigskin pickoff: Abbr.
74 Little bits
77 Title of some 2004 Summer Olympics preview shows
81 "O.K., play!"
82 Not quite boiling
83 Security agreements
84 Spanish Harlem grocery
85 Kitties
86 Double ___
88 Have a date, say
89 It's not a silk purse source, it's said
90 Tennis center?
93 Cousin of "Voilà!"
95 Mixed bag
96 You may have a nightcap when you're in these
99 Like some salons
101 Platform introduced in 1981
103 1969 Nabokov novel
106 Certain feeds for horses
108 Atlantic City casino
112 Perjure oneself . . . or what can be found six times in this puzzle
114 Batted the ball too high, perhaps
115 Punish by fining
116 Cast iron, e.g.
117 "Yes"
118 Victim of Pizarro
119 Lessee
120 Ominous time of old
121 ___ gestae
122 Poetic adverb

DOWN

1 Inflexible teaching
2 Toes the line
3 Catcher's collection
4 Clockmaker ___ Thomas
5 Sri Lankan export
6 Wear out, potentially
7 Producer who discovered and married Loren
8 Poet known as "the Tentmaker"
9 High society
10 Make greater strides than
11 LAX listing: Abbr.
12 Eau ___
13 Opportunity to go beyond the first grade?
14 Come back
15 Suffix with form or inform
16 Like forks
17 Many Rice grads: Abbr.
20 Hosp. area
23 Kind of rice used in risotto
25 Hooray for Jorge
27 Child's attention-getting call to a parent
32 Like some customs
34 Bigot, of a sort
36 Prefix with business
37 Cast events after filming is done
39 Showed up
40 Wine vessel
41 How a ship may be turned
42 Cardinal's residence
45 Some Venetian Renaissance paintings
47 Be perfect
48 They're often drawn
49 Defendant in court: Abbr.
51 Fresh
52 Slip a Mickey to
54 Belgian treaty site
55 It doesn't really represent change
57 Left
58 Nugget holder
60 Distiller ___ Walker
64 1960s baseball All-Star Blue Moon ___
65 Cousin of equi-
66 Square ___
68 Reply to "You couldn't have!"
69 Pull up
70 Cry of exasperation
72 Loses one's shirt?
73 Ties
75 New York City racetrack, informally
76 Macy's logo
78 Surge
79 2006 N.B.A. champs
80 Put away, in a way
81 Concerned wife's question in the E.R., maybe
84 Western wear
87 Like a home that's no risk to the builder
89 Soap-making solution
91 Subtlety
92 Former late-night TV host
94 Blow out
96 ___ opposite
97 Longtime Philippine archbishop ___ Sin
98 One of the Dutch Masters
100 Suffix with vapour
102 As yet
103 Priest's urging
104 Two for some hand holders
105 Preacher's post
107 Offended
109 Siouan people
110 Rationale
111 Ruler of the Aesir
113 Italy's equivalent of the BBC

by Joe DiPietro

ACROSS

1 Titles are often put in it: Abbr.
5 Scarlett O'Hara, e.g.
10 Like Arnold Schoenberg's music
16 1990 Literature Nobelist Octavio ___
19 Singer Winans
20 Certain bulb
21 Smooth and shiny
22 Actress Thurman
23 Switch in an orchestra section?
26 "Take the filly in the fifth," e.g.
27 Pressing need?
28 Union member since 1896
29 Wise men
31 Emmy category
34 You can make one for yourself
37 North Carolina university
38 Negative north of England
40 Pilgrim?
45 86-Across's alma mater: Abbr.
48 Got cozy together
50 Beau ___
51 Scare off
52 Stumble ___
53 Kipling's "Follow Me ___"
54 Came about
56 Something near many a checkout line
57 Neolithic outlaws?
63 Bank offering, for short
64 Beckett's "Endgame: ___ In One Act"
65 "Crazy Legs" Hirsch of the early N.F.L.
66 Parented
68 How dastards speak
71 Rabbit's home, maybe
72 Major-league manager Tony
73 Be Circe-like
74 Alfred E. Neuman visages
75 Cut
76 Sch. group
77 Invisible lost dogs?
83 Sheet music abbr.
84 Do some tune-up work on
85 First Shia imam
86 Gen. Robt. ___
87 Swag
89 Some photo files, in computer lingo
92 Signifying
95 Internet initialism
96 Gets fat?
98 Org. for 86-Across
99 Composer Dohnányi
101 Blackthorn
102 Author Zora ___ Hurston
104 African nation founder Jomo ___
108 Inside pitch?
111 Traditional symbol of friendship
114 Devon river
115 Go-go club?
120 Turn down
121 Hero pilot
122 Result of some sandbagging
123 Whistler's whistle, maybe
124 Trough site
125 Key of Bach's best-known Mass
126 J.F.K.'s "Why England ___"
127 They ring in a ring

DOWN

1 Clinches
2 Bible reading
3 Let win
4 Franz who composed "You Are My Heart's Delight"
5 French approval
6 Part of E.S.L.: Abbr.
7 Stead
8 Spoils
9 ___ terrible
10 Bermuda hrs.
11 Swab
12 Milo's title partner in a 1989 film
13 El ___
14 One opening up a can of worms?
15 Everyday disinfectant
16 Add new connections between floors?
17 Whitaker played him in a 2006 film
18 Nukes
24 Menotti role for a boy soprano
25 Actress Belafonte
30 Pout
32 Curly conker
33 "The Naked and the Dead" star, 1958
35 All the rage
36 Longtime D.C. delegate to Congress ___ Holmes Norton
38 PX users
39 Spider-Man's ___ May
41 "Delish!"
42 Graf ___
43 Loaded with fat
44 "The Time Machine" people
46 Distances in Canada
47 Force in the ocean
49 Costume designer Danilo ___
51 Another name for 28-Across
55 Soda fountain supply
58 Gourmet
59 Gene variant
60 Word origin: Abbr.
61 Crepes
62 Kid's comeback
67 Meadows of comedy
68 Certain Himalayan
69 Anatomical cavity
70 Dieter?
71 Needing a lift?
72 Reveal to, as a secret
74 Grouse
75 Serf
78 W.W. II Axis leader
79 Leman and others
80 American suffragist honored with a 1995 stamp
81 Desires
82 Genesis creator
88 Cowboy actor Calhoun
90 Jug capacity: Abbr.
91 A deadly sin
93 Saturn S.U.V.
94 Les ___-Unis
96 Cry upon an arrest
97 Is honest (with)
100 Old Indian V.I.P.
103 Numbers game
104 Some sneakers
105 Way out
106 ___ Polo of "Meet the Fockers"
107 Galway Bay's ___ Islands
109 Explorer Tasman of Tasmania fame
110 Messenger of Noah
112 "Rule, Britannia" composer
113 Sleep indicators
116 "Baudolino" author
117 Thrice, in Rx's
118 "You betcha"
119 Collector's goal

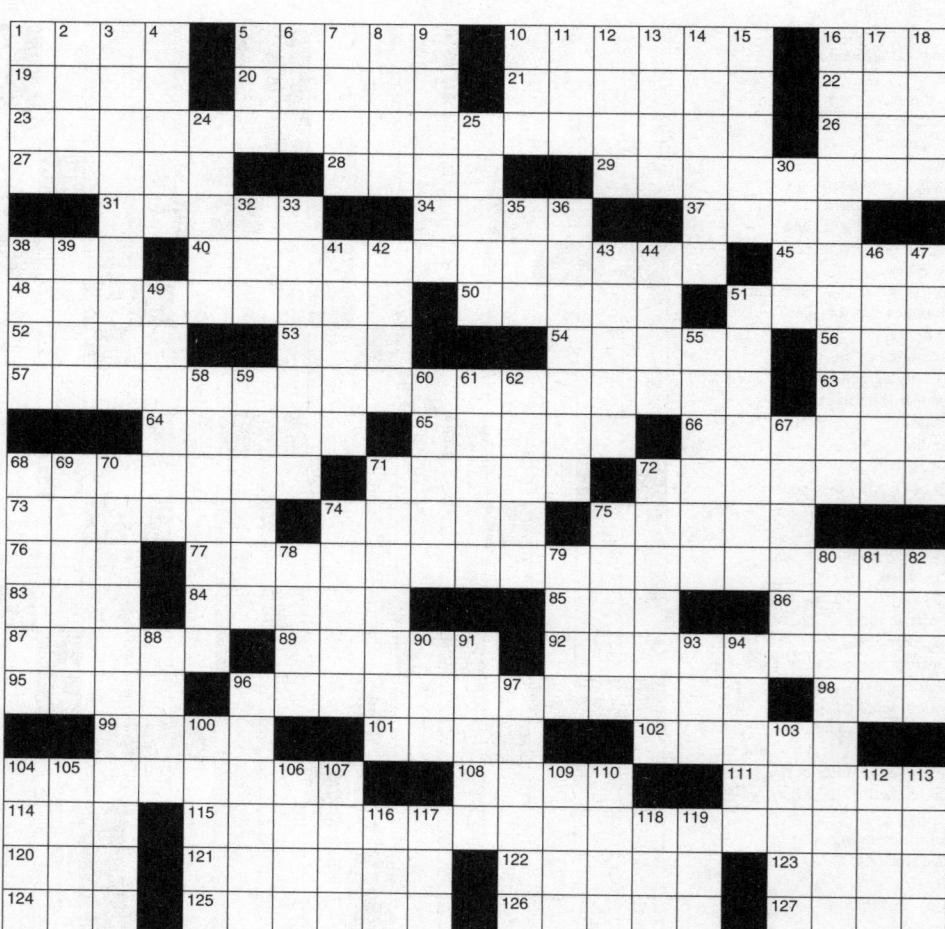

by Daniel C. Bryant

ACROSS

1 Precipitate
7 Amplifier jack letters
10 Liveliness
16 "Sort of" ending
19 Full assembly
20 Nabokov heroine
21 Falafel sandwich sauce
22 Never, in Nürnberg
23 They work on Steinways
24 Where you might see 115-Across
27 They're hidden in a Hirschfeld sketch
28 Others, in Latin
29 Tie followers, briefly
30 Rubber that meets the road
31 Coffee order
34 Deceive
36 Consumers
38 Pumpkin bomb-throwing enemy of 115-Across, with "the"
40 Scottish cattle breed
42 "Show me!"
43 Gibson's "Ransom" co-star
44 Prominent stars in constellations
49 What's more
50 Food writer Rombauer and others
52 Related to base eight
56 Royals abroad, maybe
58 "___ see"
60 Go (for)
61 Bandleader Puente
62 Scratch cause
65 Leaves behind
68 "London Fields" author
69 Taliban leader
70 Way overseas
71 French goose
72 Mess up
73 Plant with tendrils
74 Selfish cry before and after "all"
75 Sight from the Bering Sea
77 Astrologers' work
79 Geraint's beloved
80 Vintage wheels
81 System of beliefs
83 Baby carrier brand
84 Dress lines
86 Singer Lauper
88 Legal org.
91 Plus
92 Loathing
94 Shoelace ends: Var.
97 Handel opera based on Greek myth
100 Film star who played 38-Across
105 Resemble
106 Wish granters
108 The planet Venus
110 Memo starter
111 Lux. locale
112 "___ fool . . ."
114 Identify from memory
115 Theme of this puzzle
119 Lighthearted
120 Suffix with puppet
121 Extremely
122 Pupil's spot
123 It's covered by a sleeve
124 Hosp. staff
125 Learn easily
126 Beam
127 Firewood measures

DOWN

1 10-G, e.g.: Abbr.
2 Laundry whitener
3 Actor Jeremy of "North Country"
4 Nervousness
5 Run down
6 Some intellectual property: Abbr.
7 Chewy cookie
8 Immunity ___ on "Survivor"
9 Monet painting also known as "The Woman in the Green Dress"
10 And more: Abbr.
11 Wooden shoe
12 115-Across's day job
13 They run through South America
14 Publicity
15 Peculiarity
16 Visible
17 California's High ___
18 Joan of Arc's crime
25 Visual presentation of what gave 115-Across special powers
26 Tentacled enemy of 115-Across
32 Economics fig.
33 Indian fort locale
35 ___'acte
36 High ways?
37 To boot
39 Drawers in a laundry room
41 Hardly luxurious
44 Looks good on
45 Assay
46 Largest moon of Uranus
47 Film star who played 26-Down
48 Quattro + due
51 Comfy shoe
53 Stopwatch info
54 All excited
55 Goes ballistic
57 Company leaders: Abbr.
59 Bouquet
63 Mohawk, for one
64 Film star who played 115-Across
66 White-glove affairs
67 Sp. matrons
76 Big time?
78 Modern test subj.
82 "Scenes From a ___" (Woody Allen film)
85 Home of Rapid City: Abbr.
87 Setting of the painting "Washington Crossing the Delaware"
89 Natural sweetener
90 "Don't look ___ that way!"
93 Suffix with glass
95 Dim perception
96 Old campus grp.
97 Let up
98 Stake attachment, maybe
99 Takes in, say
101 Small program
102 Girl's name meaning "happy"
103 Person with a public address
104 Swindle
107 Young business partner?
109 Beginnings
111 Book before Daniel: Abbr.
113 Water brand
116 Intersected
117 Glamorous Gardner
118 Sticky stuff
119 Abbr. in a real estate ad

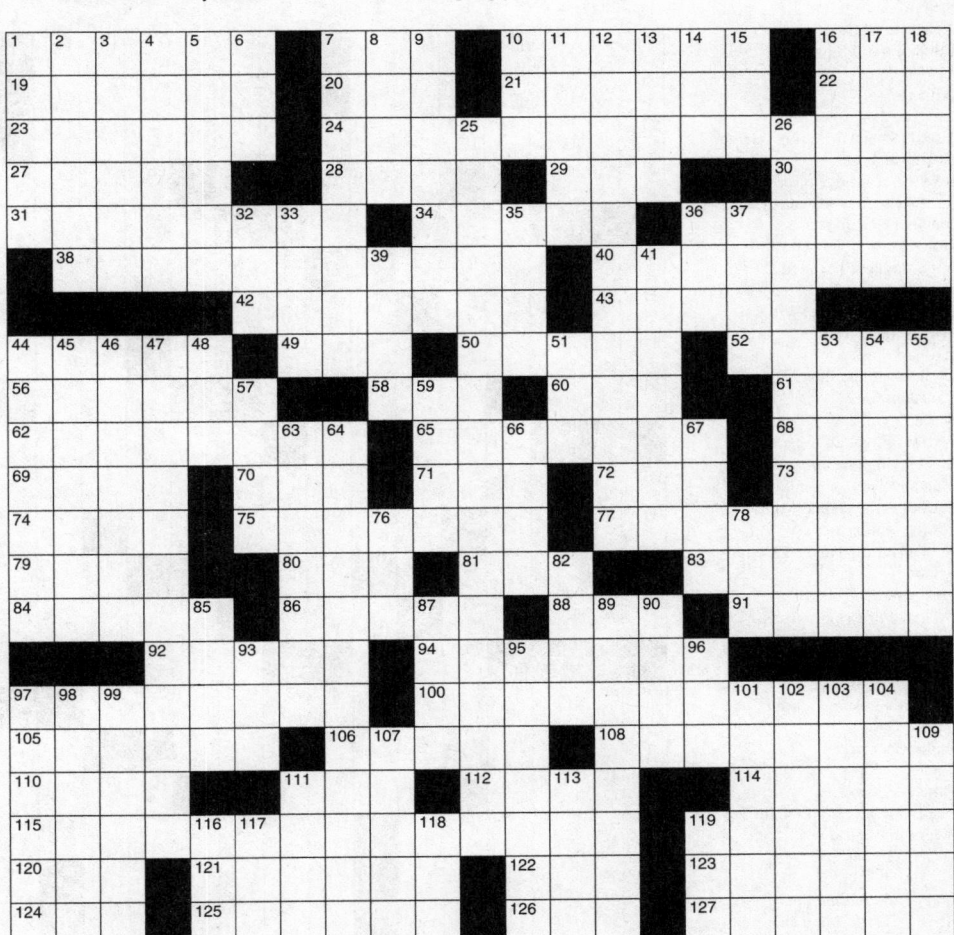

by Elizabeth C. Gorski

ACROSS

1 18th-century Venetian fresco painter
8 Gets with the times
14 Pellet shooters
20 It's lighter than air
21 Site of two ecumenical councils
22 "Capeesh?"
23 Question to a paralegal?
25 ___ Sea, west of New Zealand
26 Type
27 Hoods
28 Overhead shot
30 "Sugar Lips" trumpeter
31 What if, informally
33 Figure in an Edmund Spenser poem
34 Inner: Prefix
35 Ancient name for Great Britain
38 Red Sox franchise?
41 Three-time Masters winner Nick
42 Bogus
44 Symbol on the back of a dollar bill
45 Warning sign outside of Br'er Rabbit's home?
47 Classic cowboy name
49 Not on good terms (with)
54 Pigeon
55 Sire
56 Neighbor of Switz.
57 London's ___ Square
58 Brown shade
59 Affiance
62 Imagine that
63 Useful advice for a ring referee?
68 Botanical angle
69 Science of the ear
70 ___ Davis, first African-American to win a Heisman
71 How-to
73 It's more than a stretch
74 CB radios, once
75 Some batteries
78 "Don't make ___!"
79 Juilliard deg.
80 Clinician in the 'hood?
83 Canadian prov.
85 Knife
86 Ancient Egyptian kingdom
87 Silicone implant companies?
93 Man and ape
94 Start of some choice words?
95 Parting words
96 Hoops Hall-of-Famer Thomas
98 Brink
99 Low person on a staff
100 "Marshal of Cripple Creek," e.g.
102 Sure target
106 Beloved of Pyramus
108 Matzo mover?
111 Georgia's Lake ___, behind the Buford Dam
112 Underwater trap
113 Connect with
114 Timeless, in verse
115 One living month to month, say
116 Weeks in Madrid

DOWN

1 Fancy shooting marbles
2 "If you ask me," in a chat room
3 Matter of life and death: Abbr.
4 It's left on a ship
5 I

6 Boxer nicknamed "The Bear"
7 Promising words
8 Uncommon blood type, informally
9 Childish claim
10 Horizontal: Abbr.
11 Chum
12 Abounded
13 Hunt overseas
14 Incidentally
15 Wrap around the neck
16 Overdoes the accolades
17 Philly money maker
18 Almost at
19 Forwarded
24 Lemon or orange
29 Vicks nasal decongestant
32 Hero of New Orleans
33 Be outscored at the end
35 Jet locales: Abbr.
36 Doctor Zhivago's love
37 Sound on classic Pong
38 Rhythm
39 Play with machines
40 French for 44-Across
42 Score the winning point in cribbage
43 Renounce
46 "Chill!"
47 Twist

48 For initiates only
50 Bête ___
51 ___ Bing! (go-go bar on "The Sopranos")
52 Over
53 Exclamation with a handshake
56 "This is not ___" (warning label)
57 "The Lion King" character voiced by Whoopi Goldberg
58 Slightly above average
59 Invitation stipulation
60 Brain scan letters
61 Homeland of Orpheus
63 Sutra
64 Bar ___
65 Die Zeit article
66 "Essays of ___"
67 Periods between Winter and Summer Olympics
72 Egyptian symbols of royalty
74 U.S.N. officers
75 French cleric
76 Duller than dull
77 With the intent
79 Botch
80 Architect ___ van der Rohe
81 Musket end?
82 Bliss
84 Stand for things

85 Lice and mice, e.g.
87 Automotive comeback of 1998
88 Cardinal's topper
89 Power source
90 Cry with a salute
91 French engineer Gustave
92 Sobieski who played Joan of Arc
93 Duffer's accomplishment
96 Suffix with social
97 Butt abutters
100 Wind in a pit
101 Uffizi Gallery hanging
103 Singing partner of Brooks
104 Numerical prefix
105 Old theaters once owned by Howard Hughes
107 Jerry's partner
109 Festoons with Charmin, informally
110 Pro ___

by Paula Gamache

ACROSS

1 Doodled, e.g.
5 Elvis film "___ Scarum"
10 Attorney's favorite sweets?
16 Reign
17 "Loverboy" actress who made the cast sick?
20 It's love, in Lille
21 Séance-loving crime writer?
23 Adjustment means on a radio
24 Yards, e.g.
25 Obi-Wan Kenobi, for one
26 Uris hero ___ Ben Canaan
27 Market closing?
28 Abbr. after Ted Kennedy's name
29 Kind of tape
31 Earthquake
33 Meshed foundation in lace
35 Exclamation from a blockhead
36 Show too much feeling?
39 "O.S.S." star, 1946
40 Hall of Fame golfer who invented the all-plastic club?
45 Alla ___ (pasta style)
48 Planned site of the Geo. W. Bush Presidential Library
49 Piece that gets riveted
50 Young wife (age 18) of Charlie Chaplin (age 54)
51 Restraints
52 Egg ___ yung
53 All-telling gossip queen who repeats everything she hears?
55 Letters of commerce
56 Laying-on of hands?
59 "You're such ___ for helping"
60 Ronny & the Daytonas hit
61 Eccentric
62 Acapulco gold
63 Long (for)
65 Letters of sizes
67 Yul Brynner died the same day as ___ Welles (odd fact)
69 Relatives of TV host Tom
71 Everest setting
72 Avant-garde composer who sat around a lot?
76 Linger in the hot sun
77 Loses on purpose?
78 Y-axis, for one
79 Handy places to shop
80 Army type, for short
81 Prima donna Norman
82 Passionate tennis star?
85 Yaw relative, on an aircraft
86 Some etiquette rules
87 Online address
88 "Rats!"
91 Regular writing
94 York, e.g.: Abbr.
95 Hollywood's Téa
97 Eye the bull's-eye
99 Trip-planning org.
100 Option for a sandwich
103 Lower than: It.
104 Disney pirate, 1953
105 Moscow V.I.P. who liked to cook on a ship?
110 Eban of Israel
111 "I have no face cards" actress?
112 Near Eastern port
113 Easter ___ (period up to Pentecost Sunday)
114 European resort Monte ___
115 Driving alternative in S.F.

DOWN

1 Explorer Francis
2 Destroyer
3 Author Leonard
4 Hall of Fame coach Ewbank
5 U.S. president after Grant
6 Noriega's weapons
7 Delgado's rivers
8 Rear admiral's org.
9 Extremely upset
10 Detestable one
11 Former Dodge
12 Operated
13 Reason for overtime
14 Top Chinese Zhou
15 Your future is their business
17 Freeboot
18 Old I.B.M. offering
19 Useful article
21 Red Roof rival
22 Lip
28 Entertainer Martin and others
29 Teutonic name part
30 Tenor, perhaps
31 Enos Slaughter's team for 13 yrs.
32 Roo's donkey friend
34 Slope
35 "Wagon Master" actress Joanne
36 Heaven on earth
37 Assigner of G's and R's: Abbr.
38 Tuba sounds
40 Wild
41 Action on Wall St.
42 Swamps
43 Monstrousness
44 "You dirty ___!"
45 Patrick Macnee's 1960s TV co-star Diana
46 Opus with singing
47 Interstate sight
48 Nonmatching item, maybe
52 Toy store ___ Schwarz
54 Add-on for Gator
56 Guy who digs fossils, slangily
57 American Beauty pest
58 Inspiration for Keats
61 Nails but good
63 Old aviation magazine ___ Digest
64 Have a bawl
66 Reshape a cornea, say
68 Items for knitters
70 Gallantry-in-war medals: Abbr.
71 House of Representatives divider
72 Tree with serrate leaves
73 Big name in tea
74 Ocho minus cinco
75 US Airways datum: Abbr.
77 Vacation destination for sandwich lovers?
80 It's void in Vichy
81 English duke ___ Gaunt
83 Runner Sebastian
84 Odd morsel
85 Rummaged
89 Sorority letter
90 Iron Man co-creator Larry
91 Mythical piper
92 Pullman supports
93 "Song of the Islands" co-star Jack
94 Old Testament king
95 Not express
96 Intro with centric
98 Connoted
100 Hit by Marty Robbins, "El ___"
101 Eager beaver's assertion
102 Really test
103 Ilse's "very"
104 Swedish import
106 Hell ___ handbasket
107 Y. A. Tittle scores
108 Org. with a five-ring logo
109 United competitor: Abbr.

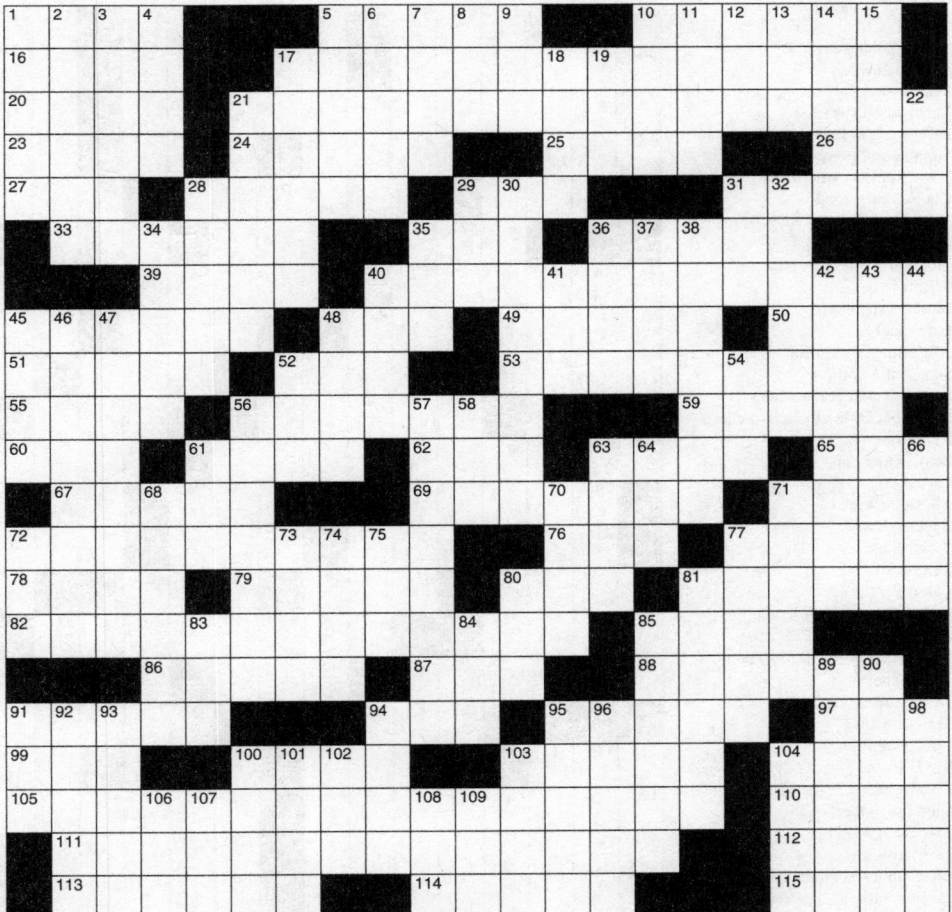

by Merl Reagle

178 PICTURE THIS

ACROSS

1. Dr. Seuss character with a red hat
7. Train stop?
12. Not useless, as clothing
20. British noble, for short
21. Football Hall-of-Famer coach Greasy ___
22. Earmarked (for)
23. Leader of the Fauvist movement
25. Title of a work by 23-Across
26. Publicity
27. Fictional spread
28. Hip in the '60s
29. Hideout
30. Agcy. overseeing reactor safety
31. It's deep
33. Winter protection
35. Metric weight
36. Vegetable with yellow pods
38. Nurse
39. Intense aversions
44. Somewhat reduced
47. Academic area
50. Debate (with)
51. Whirling
53. Nabokov novel
54. Flying grp. since 1918
56. ___ Accords of 1993
57. Workout target
58. "On&On" singer Erykah ___
61. Special ___
63. Say "Final answer," say
65. Will be now?
66. Double-layer breads
67. First name in spydom
69. Paris's ___ la Paix
70. Suppliers of greetings
73. What Ramona wore in a 1966 Chuck Berry song
76. Year Super Bowl XXXVII was played
77. Ziegfeld Follies designer
79. Scuffles
80. Morning deposit
81. Individual
83. Al Kaline, in uniform
84. Son, at the Sorbonne
85. It's cultivated in the Andes
86. Stone in a 2008 Olympic medal
87. Rejections
89. Invoice amount
91. Carted off
93. Auspices: Var.
94. Cushion user?
98. Brags about
99. More cool
102. Canterbury can
103. Boardinghouse boarders
105. Florence attraction
107. Musical for which Ben Vereen won a Tony
108. Those, to Muñoz
112. See 106-Down
115. Nobelist Pavlov
116. Big D player
117. Visiting the U.S. capital
119. Sportage maker
120. 25-Across, e.g.
122. 23-Across, e.g.
125. Factor in a restaurant rating
126. Skylit areas
127. Like the return of swallows to Capistrano
128. Cupid, e.g.
129. Fiber-yielding plant
130. Volleyball position

DOWN

1. Old term of respect
2. Concert venue
3. Otter cousins
4. Home of the Ramon Crater: Abbr.
5. Scuffling
6. N.Y.C. cultural event
7. Brightest star in Scorpius
8. Tiki bar offering
9. Devil's home?
10. Onetime political columnist Joseph
11. Sax player's need
12. Cleanup hitter, e.g.
13. Like the earliest Olympic festivals
14. Animal oddity
15. Had a big laugh
16. Long-distance letters
17. Revolutionary 1930s bomber
18. Duke of Cornwall's father-in-law, in Shakespeare
19. Part of H.E.W.: Abbr.
24. Show horse
32. Like the mathematician Euler
34. Fond du ___, Wis.
35. Personal quirk
37. Horned viper
38. Reply to irritably
40. Compound variant
41. How 25-Across appeared at a 6-Down in 1961
42. Kipling short story, with "The"
43. Low-cost accommodations, briefly
44. Reddish purple
45. Angrily crusading
46. Styles of 25-Across and the like
48. Ancient land near the Dead Sea
49. Pouch
52. Spain joined it in 1982
55. How long 25-Across was 41-Down before being noticed and fixed
59. Be bold enough
60. Web browsers
62. Unreasonable, pricewise
64. Oozy mixtures
66. Fraternity letters
68. Prefix with chemical
71. Most urgent
72. Well-oiled
74. Concert venue
75. Brings around
78. Brad and 86-Down, e.g.
82. San Francisco's ___ Hill
85. Touch off
86. See 78-Down
88. "The Laughing Man" author
90. Prospering ones
92. ___ es Salaam
95. Make a slip
96. "Alley ___"
97. Current
100. Worked on a Life sentence?
101. Coulee
104. Ho Chi ___
106. With 112-Across, Okla. military area
107. First installment
109. Get around
110. Bridal path
111. Butterfly variety
112. On ___ with (equal to)
113. Celebrity
114. Andersson of "Wild Strawberries"
116. Some 6-Down curators: Abbr.
118. Canadian natives
121. "Ladders to Fire" writer
123. Long in films
124. Make lace

by David J. Kahn

ACROSS

1 Like tests and dirt roads
7 Web programmer's medium
11 Deadens
16 Adolphe ___, musical instrument inventor
19 "Honestly, man!"
20 It may be gray
21 Economist Janeway
22 Open someone else's e-mails, maybe
23 Not accented
24 Will's opposite
25 Poker player's wear
26 Brynner of stage and screen
27 Sale sweeteners
29 Helpful comment to a judge?
32 "Stripes" actor, 1981
34 Imago, e.g.
35 Brunch time
36 Maine, e.g.: Abbr.
39 "Also Sprach Zarathustra" hitmaker, 1973
41 A cadet might be asked to pick it up
43 Insurance paperwork
46 Snowy ___
47 Fruit flies?
52 Dirty radio sitcom?
55 Given to showy affectation
56 Put to use
57 Monastery office
58 Polonius's hiding place
60 Bank holding
61 Do some grapplin'
65 Makes a muffler, e.g.
66 Weapon in the Charge of the Light Brigade
67 Jokey question to a Verizon technician?
71 Summer swarm
72 With regard to
73 Beauty spots
74 Line at a track
75 Cowgirl Dale
76 Chinese brew
80 Output of une législature
81 Bull: Prefix
82 Darius the Scamp?
88 Pot-smoking cleric?
91 Raccoon relative
92 Endor inhabitants
93 The story of the aftermath of Oceanic Flight 815
94 Read the riot act to
96 The Tigers, on scoreboards
97 Donnybrook
100 Engine problem
101 One who may give you a shot in the arm
105 Result of excessive rowing?
109 Makes clear
113 Hairy TV cousin
114 Shade of pink
115 ___ Torrence, American sprinter who won three gold medals at the 1992 and 1996 Olympics
117 Make merry
118 Casbah wear
119 Set of keys?
120 Suffix for a collection
121 Henry Fielding novel and heroine
122 Fix, as fritters
123 Form beginning
124 Cell suffix
125 Beth, for one

DOWN

1 Sound like an angry dog
2 Saying again and again
3 "Get ___" (doo-wop classic)
4 Libyan money
5 1979 Broadway hit with the song "On This Night of a Thousand Stars"
6 X
7 Turn to the left
8 Home-run run
9 Herringlike fish
10 Point near the deadline
11 Evolve
12 Celebs as a group
13 Drops in the air
14 "Fiddlesticks!"
15 Like spandex
16 Watch furtively
17 One of the ABC Islands
18 Plant circulatory tissue
28 Joined forces (with)
30 Line at a track
31 Scuba venue
33 Genesis creator
36 "True blue" and gold team
37 No neatnik
38 Volvo rival
40 Scepter topper
41 Tropical drink embellishment
42 Variety show lineup
44 Turkish inns
45 Cousins of cockatiels
48 Singer Kitt
49 Voice a view
50 Send to the Hill, say
51 Lang follower
53 Big Board: Abbr.
54 Tolled
59 Criticizes in no uncertain terms
60 Knocks down
62 Spring Jewish holiday
63 Historical Scottish county
64 On a plane?
65 Chess piece: Abbr.
66 Poe poem that ends "From grief and groan to a golden throne beside the King of Heaven"
67 Compound conjunction
68 r's, in math
69 P.D. rank
70 When shadows are shortest
71 Green activity
75 Grub
77 Hymn start
78 Microwave
79 Adventurous deed
81 Kind of storm
83 Environment-related
84 Bed on wheels
85 In the dumps
86 Inventory unit
87 Backed up
89 Mathematician Turing
90 Miss Havisham's ward in "Great Expectations"
95 Fleet member
97 Spruce (up)
98 Provide the spread
99 Posh
100 Fossil-yielding rock
102 Windshield attachment
103 Part of Caesar's boast
104 Desire
106 "Don't look at me"
107 1982 Disney film
108 Setting for many a reception
110 Dummkopf
111 War of 1812 battle site
112 Celeb
116 Paisley denial

by Richard Silvestri

180 "HEY!"

ACROSS

1 Nailed
5 ___ diagram
9 Is in the Vatican
12 Stubborn response
19 Contact sport with a purification ritual
20 Jobs offering of 1998
21 Start of the seventh century
22 Paws
23 *Distinguishes
26 Languished
27 Little fingers
28 Brightest star in Auriga, from the Latin for "little she-goat"
30 Plant with two seed leaves
31 Literary wrap-up
33 *Does a hostler's work
36 ___ onto
37 Bar product
38 Make a choice
39 Sharp rebuke
40 "Taking Heat" memoirist Fleischer
43 Played out
45 San ___, locale just north of Tijuana, Mexico
47 "The Story-Teller" storyteller
48 *Participates in a bear market
51 Word of dissent
52 English actor Sir ___ Jacobi
53 Suffix with disk
54 Burn cause
55 Card's insignia
56 Formal
57 Like many root vegetables for the winter
61 Home of the Wright Brothers Natl. Memorial
63 It may be illegal to hang one
64 Start of an announcement . . . or a hint to what's hidden in the answers to the six starred clues
70 Empty (of)
71 Landscaper's locale
72 Free of mistakes
74 Dutch artist Theo
78 TV pooch with a temper
79 Alley-___ pass
81 Ancestor of a banjo
82 President-___
83 Cross shape
84 *Plays at a pond, in a way
88 Speak carelessly
89 Ellen of "Grey's Anatomy"
91 "Dune" director David
92 Emerson's "jealous mistress"
93 When said three times, a 1970 film
94 "___ Mutual Friend"
95 Seasonal time, in store signs
97 Provokes
99 *Engages in some mutual gossip
102 Loser of a footrace with Hippomenes
106 "Christopher Robin went down with ___": Milne
107 Queens neighborhood near La Guardia
109 Subjects of many bets
110 Clique
112 *Commits knitting boo-boos
114 Actress Annabella of "The Sopranos"
115 Brit's oath
116 Conceited
117 Sticker?
118 Most grinchlike
119 Merino mother
120 Worrisome engine sound
121 "___, how love can trifle with itself!": Shak.

DOWN

1 The Beatles' "___ Why"
2 Give a hint
3 Correct
4 Olympics no-no
5 Scoreboard side
6 911 respondent
7 Busters?
8 Sweet 16 org.
9 How to put a coin in a coin slot
10 Lugs
11 "A Visit From St. Nicholas," e.g.
12 "___ a living"
13 Entertains, as a child at bedtime
14 Accept a bad defeat, in slang
15 Chicken dish
16 Medium of OPEC transactions
17 Some landlocked bodies of water
18 Vacation time in Valois
24 Silvery salmon
25 ___ facto
29 Lacking limbs
32 Give off
34 Moving easily
35 Like Bart Simpson's hair
37 Cabinet head: Abbr.
40 Summer drinks
41 Like some dirt paths
42 "___ old for this!"
44 Residential sign
46 "He-e-ere's Johnny!," e.g.
49 Equatorial land
50 Pulitzer winner for "Russia Leaves the War"
52 Load bearer?
55 Caved in
56 Proofreader's mark
58 Québec traffic sign
59 Barbara of "Mission: Impossible"
60 Co. name ender
62 Midpoint: Abbr.
63 Bygone TV inits.
65 Examine covetously
66 Brisk
67 Guthrie with a guitar
68 Sweater's place
69 Make a record of
73 Try
74 Isn't serious
75 Stipend
76 Pain along the course of a nerve
77 Junkyard junk
78 Strict disciplinarian
80 Bribes
83 Ballyhoo
84 Seconds, say
85 Temper tantrum
86 Removing, as paint
87 Everything
89 Frauds
90 Plane seating specification
96 Right away
98 Retreats
100 Make it home safely
101 Fingerprint feature
102 Very, in music
103 Nothing
104 "Lady T" singer ___ Marie
105 Lunkheads
108 Answer, shortly
110 Doctrine
111 Overly rehearsed
113 ___ soldier

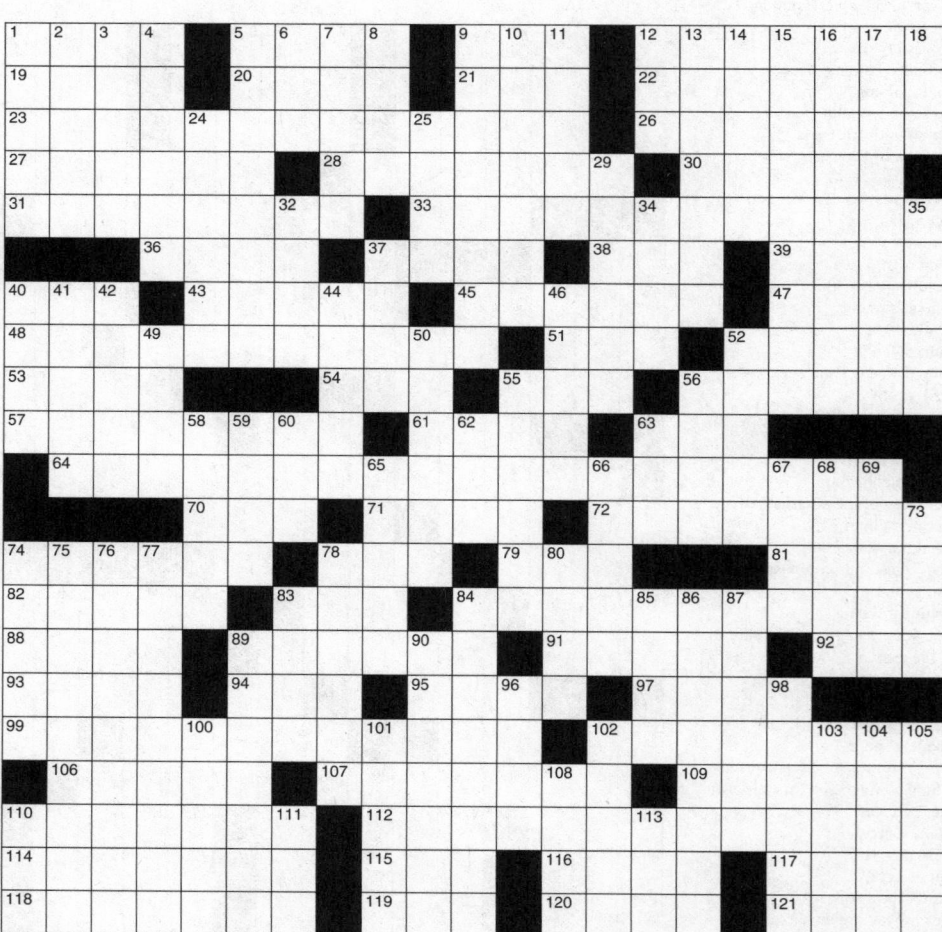

by Jim Page

ACROSS

1 Small amount of power
5 Where opposite sides meet
11 Fireplace tool
16 Be bold enough
20 Eponym of a North Carolina "-ville"
21 Skeptical response
22 Use TurboTax, perhaps
23 Particular
24 Mother of Cronus
25 Like Rudner's audiences after a good joke?
28 "Stormy" seabird
30 Zool. or ecol.
31 Drama that uses masks
32 Supremely macho
33 Treat for Damone?
37 Northern star?
39 Drool catchers
40 Volkswagen coupe convertible
41 Runners may round them
42 Like fries, typically
43 Sunlit ledge
44 Google search result
45 Delhi-to-Madras dir.
47 Author Dinesen
49 Exist
50 Attack vigorously
52 Where Paul stays when performing in New York City?
58 Carol ending?
59 Hindu honorific
61 Once known as
62 "Heroes" actress Larter
63 It's said for stress
67 Chewed out
69 Comes in dramatically, like West?
72 Baghdad's ___ City
73 More furtive
75 Threshold
76 Needing air freshener
77 Better-suited
79 Funny frame
80 Largest U.S. movie theater chain
83 "___ Millions" (Eugene O'Neill play)
86 The rite place?
89 Black, in a way
91 "The Neverending Story" author
95 McAn's favorite novel?
99 Astronomical collision results
101 Tyrrhenian Sea port
102 Dict. tag on "tzar"
103 It may be radical
104 Duped
105 Op. ___
106 Odds of Alda winning an Oscar?
110 Take on
112 Piece of software, for short
115 Patron saint of goldsmiths
116 Sign of a champ
117 Unwrap, in verse
119 Sound
120 Knave
123 ___ a customer
126 Gilbert and Sullivan princess
127 Tinnitus causes
128 Kiss on the cheek, perhaps
129 Putting in a row, like Sampras's rackets?
133 More affordable
135 Conductance unit
136 Suffix with fail
137 Person of learning
139 Court case where Ripken is one of many plaintiffs?
143 Trickle
145 ___ tape
146 Don't fold or call
147 Banishes to Elba, e.g.
148 Light brown
149 Spotted
150 Nautical measure
151 Recipients
152 Having similar genetics

DOWN

1 Boxer's approval
2 "Quickly," quickly
3 Horror film enjoyed by Turner?
4 It holds a service
5 More whimsical
6 Fish with toxic blood
7 Trees with soft wood
8 ___ curiae (friends of the court)
9 Mixer
10 Official lang. of Mauritius
11 Roy Orbison and Marvin Gaye, e.g.
12 Musical that inspired Redding?
13 Agcy. with the Office of Disease Prevention
14 Scintillate
15 It's on the back of the $1 bill
16 Bleak
17 Home of the world's largest aquarium
18 What a stamped hand may allow you to do
19 Typography units
21 Cologne trio
26 Viracocha worshiper
27 Rick's love, in film
29 Bedside workers, often: Abbr.
34 Relax
35 Hairstylist José
36 P.D.A. part: Abbr.
38 Humorist George
39 Woman in "Othello"
42 Sidestep
43 Cheese with eyes
44 Turmoil
45 Say "#@%!"
46 Try to unearth
48 Spelling clarification
51 -like, alternatively
53 "Take a Chance ___" (Abba song)
54 Tripod, sometimes
55 Banned chemical
56 Skin layer
57 Shoulder frill
60 Going nowhere
64 Half 19-Down
65 Fill in (for)
66 "The Daughter of Time" author
68 Choking spot
70 ". . . if ___ saw one!"
71 Tulip chair designer Saarinen
74 "Dies ___"
78 Standard partner
79 Accord rival
81 Clearly impress
82 Take turns?
83 Parts of a range: Abbr.
84 "The light has dawned!"
85 Seminary subj.
87 Flower typically given to Neeson?
88 Brand of nonstick cookware
89 "W." director
90 "This can't be!"
92 How Goldin and her rivals finish in photography competitions?
93 Boring things
94 Cosmetics magnate Lauder
96 Available, in a way
97 Dirty
98 Levitate
100 Mathematician Lovelace
107 The Gang's leader
108 ___ lady
109 Sarah Palin's husband
111 Taiwan's setting
112 Mean: Abbr.
113 One just out
114 Georgia or Virginia, e.g.
118 Dupes
121 Teacher's teaching
122 Airport monitor info, for short
124 Comes back the same
125 Common noun ending
126 Really existing
127 Part of R&D: Abbr.
129 State tree of Texas
130 Organic fertilizer
131 Physicist Schrödinger
132 Trotter fodder
134 Brownish songbird
138 Actress Polo
139 Contents of jewel cases
140 Uncle, in Uruguay
141 Played a heart, say
142 Little: Suffix
144 86-Across, e.g.

by Trip Payne

ACROSS

1 Hog lovers
7 Cheesy snack
11 Bad sport
20 Kind of valve in the heart
21 Potato source
22 Begin
23 Like some chocolat
24 Prefix with -logy
25 Witnesses giving written testimony
26 Barbecue sound
27 Wrap up by
29 Round dances
31 Bother no end
32 Symbol of strength
34 Repeat calls?
36 N.F.L. coach with a perfect 17-0 record in 1972
38 Like preowned cars
40 Spin-producing tennis shot
41 Like Silly Putty
44 Neat as ___
46 Oslo's land: Abbr.
47 Wave off
49 Fulminate (against)
50 Gets ready to go out in the cold
53 Book in which the destruction of Samaria is foreseen
54 Gang brawl
56 Violent behavior, in British slang
57 It means a lot to Jorge
59 Oktoberfest souvenir
61 Candied holiday serving
62 Former Toyota
64 Pacific salmon
66 Invited to one's penthouse, say
68 "Hooked on Classics" record company
69 Cry when a surprise guest arrives
73 Stuck, after "in"
77 Having bristles
79 View from a beach house
80 Elizabeth Ann and others
82 With 83-Down, early learning aid
85 Greases
87 Egypt's Mubarak
89 Like some fireplaces
90 Warm blanket material
92 Virile
94 Answered the phone
97 G.M. or G.E.
98 Top-Sider, e.g.
101 1501, on a monument
102 TV's Science Guy and others
103 Abscond
105 Sound: Prefix
106 Memorable parties
108 Cracks up
109 Regis Philbin, e.g.
111 Stretchy
114 Admit
116 Bug-B-Gon maker
117 Beginning
119 Code-cracking org.
120 Without delay
123 Venerable
125 Georges Braque, for one
127 Fruitcake flavorings
128 Wanderers
129 Throat soother
130 Boot camp pals

131 Landing spot for 74-Down
132 Plumbers' drain openers

DOWN

1 Banquo in Verdi's "Macbeth," e.g.
2 2008 documentary about the national debt
3 December 25 answer to 69-Across?
4 U.F.O. fliers
5 Choir supports
6 Act opener
7 Basketry palm
8 "We've got ___!"
9 Rum Tum Tugger, for one
10 Greeting from 74-Down
11 Tabs in the fridge?
12 Buried treasures
13 Open indelicately
14 Maniacal leader?
15 Schedule of TV programs
16 Mild chili designation
17 Song whose subject is encouraged to "hurry down the chimney tonight"
18 Singer James
19 What remains
28 Apollo's birthplace
30 Towers' attachments

33 Grape graspers
35 Includes in an e-mailing
36 ___ Na Na
37 Rustic excursions
39 Bongo, e.g.
41 Wrap fully
42 Country singer McCann
43 K-6 sch. designation
44 By surprise
45 Sound of the Northwest
48 D.D.E. opponent
51 ___ cit. (footnote abbr.)
52 One reaching a goal?
55 "Burma Looks Ahead" author
58 Bossy types?
60 Listener
63 Mass production figure?
65 C.I.S. members, once
67 Whom psychiatrists see
70 Stick in the water?
71 Pops
72 Three French ___
74 December 25 answer to 69-Across?
75 Anoint with sacred oil, old-style
76 Early PC interface
78 QB Manning
81 Archaic verb ending
82 Javelins and Hornets, e.g.

83 See 82-Across
84 Father ___
86 Succeeded at musical chairs
88 Poet's foot
91 Paintbrushes and such
93 It's worth 100 smackers
95 Lays off
96 Manners of speaking
99 Cries of pain
100 U.S.N. rank
104 A couple of people may work in it
107 Subject for Galileo
109 Leaves for a buffet?
110 Ring figures
112 Joe Jackson's "___ Really Going Out With Him?"
113 Phoebe of "Gremlins"
114 Neeson of "Rob Roy"
115 Single-named supermodel
116 Siouan speaker
118 It's closed on Dec. 25
121 "Let's call ___ night"
122 Lawyer: Abbr.
124 "Aladdin" monkey
126 Neck wrap

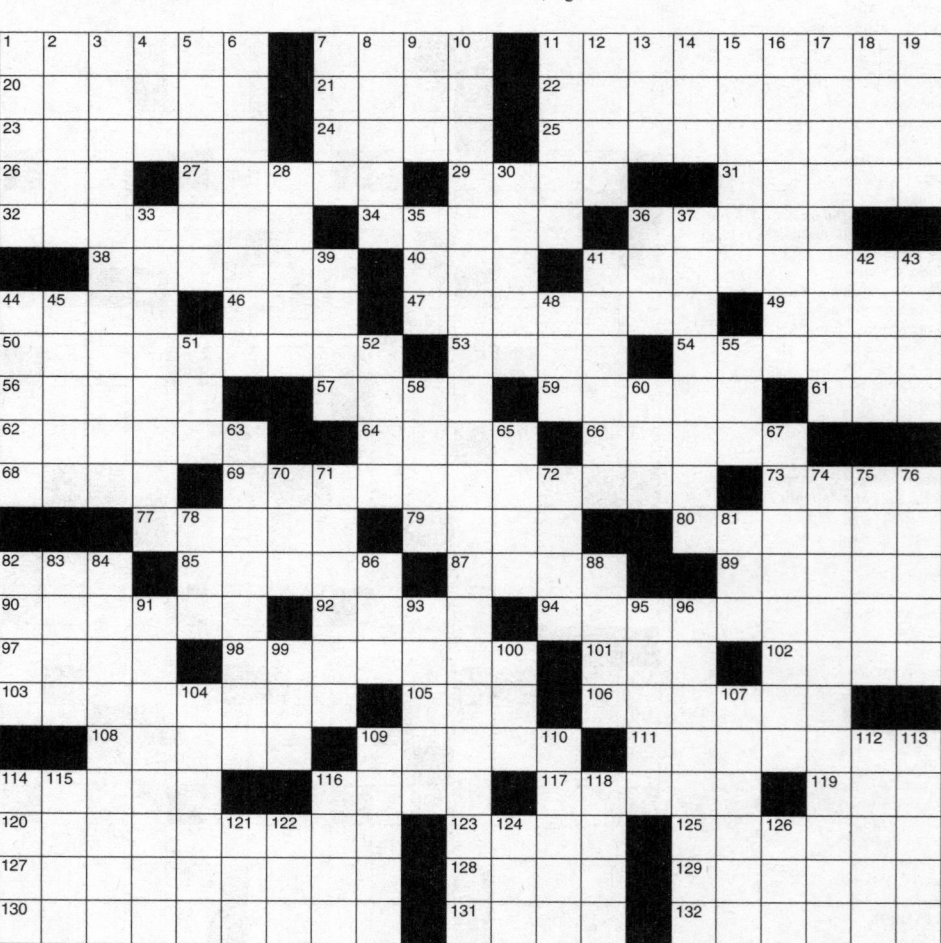

by Elizabeth C. Gorski

ACROSS

1 Harry's pal at Hogwarts
4 Hit 2004 film with many sequels
7 What this puzzle's eight concentric rings (uncircled and circled) represent
13 Wooden peg
18 Pressed for time
20 1968 N.B.A. All-Star Dick
22 ___ Adler of Conan Doyle's "A Scandal in Bohemia"
23 Georgia's Fort ___, site of an 1862 surrender
24 Malevolent look
25 Rubber gasket
26 Gratis
27 Lincoln Town Car, for one
28 Patriots' Day mo.
30 Big ox
31 Prefix with political
32 ___ dance
33 Six-Day War combatants
35 Entrance
38 Actress ___ Dawn Chong
40 "Nascar Now" channel
42 Medevac worker
43 Way to go
44 Dog biscuits and such
47 Formulator of the Three Principles of the People
52 Gopher-wood construction
53 Submarine egress
54 Ruination
55 Infra's opposite
56 King famous for frightening people
59 Like some campaign ads
62 Pomeranian's bark
63 Sic ___ (bibliographical term)
64 Elementary particle
65 Actress/model Connie
68 On land
70 Appropriate center for this puzzle
71 Frozen food company
72 Exterior decorator?
74 Beautify
76 Let one's anger show
79 E-mail address ender
80 Treasure sought in "Titanic"
82 Heavy metal band?
83 Stuck in the mud
86 Storm
87 No longer working
89 Cuff feature
90 Satisfies, as baser instincts
92 Husband, in Hidalgo
93 "___ 911!" (comedy series)
94 Fed. purchasing org.
95 Long-range weapon, briefly
97 According to
98 The Auld Sod
99 Childhood skin affliction
103 Goes around
106 Where a pin may be made
108 Greenwich Village campus, for short
109 Poorly
110 Volkswagen model
111 BBC panel show regular Phill
115 Brand of basketball
117 Something it's not always wise to share
119 Generally
120 Grace ___ ("Jane Eyre" character)
121 1960 Bobby Rydell hit
122 Electricians
123 Ready to play, you might say
124 One of these can be found reading counterclockwise somewhere in each concentric ring
125 Behave
126 Go down

DOWN

1 Philbin's "Live" co-host
2 Responsibility
3 Simba's mate in "The Lion King"
4 The Everly Brothers' "Wake Up Little ___"
5 Make impossible demands
6 Little bit
7 Scale-busting
8 "Gaspard de la Nuit" composer
9 Tack room items
10 Veneer patterns
11 First-time driver, often
12 Porker's pen
13 Museum displays
14 Yossarian's tentmate in "Catch-22"
15 "Mack the Knife" songwriter
16 Lassitude
17 Pantyhose brand
19 Worn out
21 Bigelow beverages
29 Rodent, to a raptor
32 Red food dye source
33 All together
34 Roman rebuke
35 Comprehend
36 Trunk in your trunk
37 Plays
39 Ireland's ___ Islands
41 Exam for H.S. jrs.
45 Retin-A treats it
46 Region near Mount Olympus
48 "In a pig's eye!"
49 Controversial 1987 exposé by ex-MI5 agent Peter Wright
50 Cartman's first name on "South Park"
51 Bay Area county
54 Oatcakes popular in Scotland
57 Discreet attention-getter
58 Exclamation in "The Farmer in the Dell"
60 Semisoft cheese from Holland
61 Tunes that might make you want to get out on the floor?
64 Romeo's reckless friend
66 Legal claim on property
67 Writer Ferber
69 Hull scrapers
72 Desk-borrowing worker
73 Top 10 hit for Sarah McLachlan
75 Harvest
77 Nicholas Gage memoir
78 Possessor?
81 Ray a k a the Hamburger King
82 Poet's inspiration
84 Sharpness
85 Preordained
88 Bursts open
91 Pedestrian safety feature
92 What Mr. Spock suppressed
93 Leave one's post, possibly
96 Lee with the 1960 #1 hit "I'm Sorry"
99 Bungling
100 "Skip to ___"
101 Hoax
102 ___ stick (trick-or-treater's accessory)
104 Make up (for)
105 Painter of a Zola portrait
107 In different places
110 Jack's partner in rhyme
111 Cloak-wearing "Star Wars" race
112 Rolaids rival
113 Big-screen beekeeper
114 Propelled
116 ___ Miss
118 Domino dot

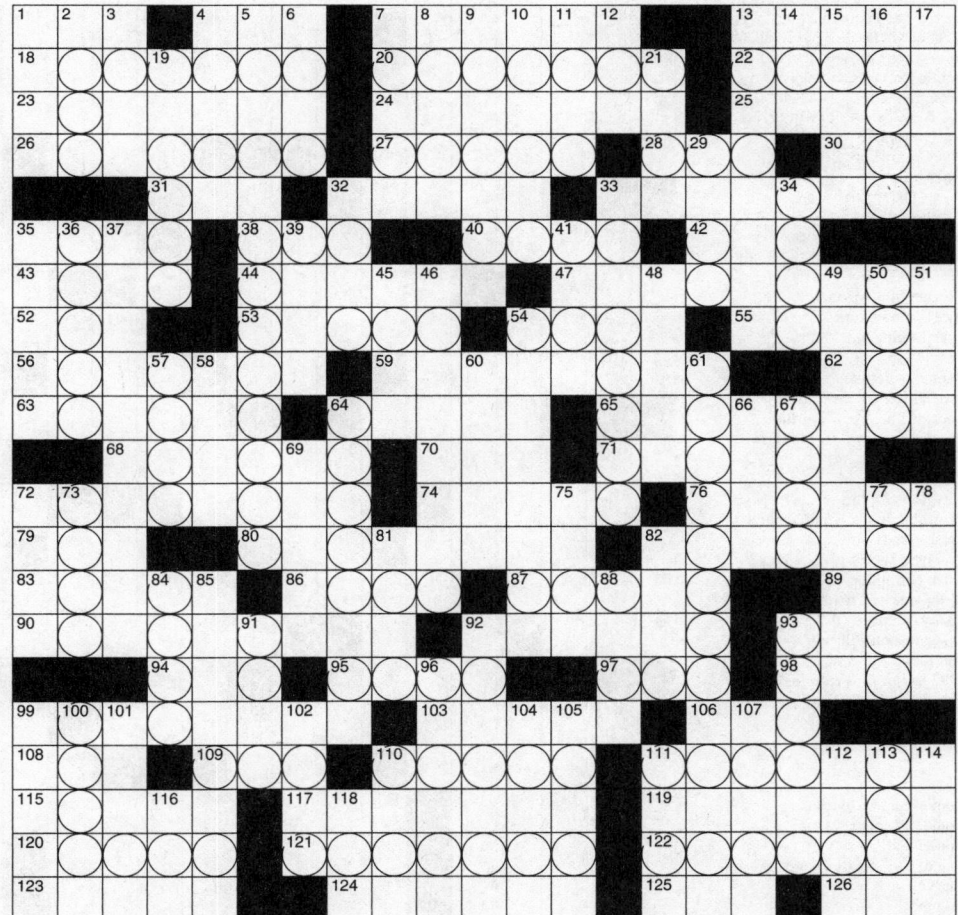

by Patrick Berry

184 WHEN IN ROME

ACROSS

1. Emmy-winning actor Powers ___
7. Like Polk, among U.S. presidents
15. Arizona state birds
20. Experiment runner?
21. Oliver Twist's request
22. Having new tenants
23. Many a fish story
25. Run up
26. Word shouted to start a party
27. Place to sojourn
28. Duds
29. Nobelist Walesa
30. Stubble
34. Took steps
37. Zoo heavyweight
39. Pop maker?
40. Slangy turndown
41. Gabs
43. Rubbed raw, say
44. Nickelodeon's "Kenan & ___"
47. Last film directed by Cecil B. DeMille
52. "Later!"
53. Not going anywhere
54. Was up
55. Film speed no.
56. Newspaper section
58. Like Australia's Outback
60. A
62. Carol opener
63. 1976 #1 hit whose title follows the words "There must be . . ."
70. Mandel of "Deal or No Deal"
71. Auto whose name is derived from a Zoroastrian deity
72. Rheinland city
73. ___ Blake, player of Miss Kitty on "Gunsmoke"
75. Many-armed org.?
76. Make a bow
79. "I can't hear you!"
83. Puppeteer Tony
84. Gabriel García Márquez best seller
88. "Further . . ."
89. Vintage film channel
90. Wisconsin city on Lake Michigan
91. "Tour" grp.
92. Batman's domain
95. Like shower rooms, often
96. Lopsided postseason result
98. Event first won by a Marmon Wasp
102. Prefix with distant
104. Playground retort
105. Charlottetown's home: Abbr.
106. Clear brandy
110. One who hardly gives a hoot?
111. Salad bar option
115. Birthplace of Charles De Gaulle
116. Nassau native
117. Takes responsibility for
118. Bad look
119. 1997 horror film with the tagline "If you can't breathe, you can't scream"
120. Price qualifier

DOWN

1. Nonkosher sandwiches
2. Home of Mount Ka'ala
3. Upper: Ger.
4. One of Ty Cobb's record 295 in the A.L.
5. Odium
6. Work ___
7. Renaissance family name
8. Camp seat, maybe
9. Music genre derived from punk rock
10. Ex-fighter
11. It might have an attachment
12. "Simmer down!"
13. A dangerous thing to fall into
14. "Yo!"
15. Showed pain, in a way
16. Many a lake cabin
17. 11th-century military hero
18. It comes before surgery
19. Scatter
24. Religious retreat
28. Gauge
30. Curriculum ___
31. Nonstop
32. Appliance attachment
33. Go-___
34. Bucking
35. "Call Me Irresponsible" lyricist
36. Mother of Helios
38. Web code
41. Untagged, say
42. Word said before someone snaps
44. Russian ballet company
45. Wonderland cake message
46. Deadbeat
48. Activity at the dentist's
49. Blasted
50. Glimpse
51. Manhattan neighborhood
52. Nondairy milk source
57. Hoi ___
59. Suffix with serf
60. Gardner of the silver screen
61. Arctic diver
63. Asian capital whose trains offer oxygen masks
64. One with two X's
65. Tony, e.g.
66. Sprinter's assignment
67. Book before Nehemiah
68. "It was ___ and stormy night . . ."
69. University of Missouri campus site
74. Bank info: Abbr.
76. Author Morrison and others
77. "Too rich for me"
78. Latin 101 verb
80. Bamboozle
81. Leg up
82. Harvest
85. Jewish youth org.
86. "The X-Files" grp.
87. "Goodness gracious!"
89. Countertop item
92. Supermodel Bündchen
93. Rome's ___ Way
94. Brandy's TV name
96. Afternoon serial, informally
97. "Night" writer
98. Golden calves
99. Kind of situation
100. Milan's Santa Maria ___ Grazie
101. Light purple
103. Chili con ___
106. Mystery writer Buchanan
107. Shop device
108. QB stats
109. Inflated heads
111. Wall St. credential
112. Te ___
113. Diarist Anaïs
114. Old man

by Daniel A. Finan

ACROSS

1 Box in many dens
5 Insignificant
8 Rap
14 Second-largest city of Rhode Island
19 "___ Majesty's Secret Service"
20 "This round's ___"
21 Set, as a gem
22 Art shop offering
23 Flier to Omsk
25 Song with the lyric "We salute him, one and all"
27 Most coll. applicants
28 Thrown for ___
30 Suitable for service
31 Wyoming senator Mike
32 More petite
34 Exhaustive
38 By means of
40 Drop a brick
41 Green's songwriting partner in old musicals
42 Reddish-brown horses
46 With 90-Across, what the 28 circled squares in this puzzle represent
52 See 45-Down
53 Compass heading
54 "The Great Ziegfeld" co-star, 1936
55 Organic compounds
56 Patriotic displays
59 Record holder?
61 Alice's cat in "Alice in Wonderland"
62 Jazz Age figure
63 Kid's rejoinder
65 White House family of the 1840s
66 First U.S. chief justice
68 Butterfly's title
74 Rock salt
77 Like many campgrounds at night
78 Source of late election returns, with "the"
83 Seat of Ward County, N.D.
84 White House tour highlight
86 Daly TV role
87 Pilot, e.g.
88 Oslo Accords grp.
89 Zaragoza's river
90 See 46-Across
97 James Joyce short story
98 "Running on Empty" actress
99 Nobel physicist Tamm
100 Youngster
101 "d" preceder
103 Debater's ploy
107 Over-the-shoulder wrap
110 Kitchen tool with a tube
112 Favored, with "on"
114 Old German rocket
115 Political insider
120 N.F.L. coach with the most career wins
122 Plumbing, e.g.
123 Some college donors
124 "The Simpsons" character whose last name has 18 letters
125 Lying, in a way
126 "Family Ties" mom
127 Behind
128 Citizenship Day mo.
129 Citi Field team, starting in 2009

DOWN

1 A goner
2 Possible answer to "Where are you?"
3 Chapter's partner
4 First word of Montana's motto
5 Pre-election workers
6 Set adrift
7 Some Security Council vetoes
8 Snicker sound
9 Member of an empire that ended in the 16th century
10 Dr. ___
11 Hang one's ___ (trust in)
12 "Sesame Street" tune, with "The"
13 Fountain in New Orleans
14 Corduroy ridge
15 Quaker Oats product
16 Outside's opposite
17 At the home of: Fr.
18 Diplomat Annan
24 Laissez-___
26 Devastation
29 Pits
33 Former big name in browsers
35 Popular film Web site, briefly
36 Spanish monarch
37 Schubert's "Symphony No. 8 ___ Minor"
39 Put out
41 Workplace for Reps. and Dems.
42 Decline
43 Like heaven's vault, in a Shelley poem
44 Song syllables
45 With 52-Across, what angels pray for
46 Mine part
47 Opportune
48 Like some chambers
49 Sport
50 Possible location for a back door
51 Etymologist's interest
57 "Talk of the Nation" airer
58 Camal subject
59 Certain engine
60 Reagan-___
64 "___ babbino caro" (Puccini aria)
66 Islamic spirit
67 "___ be in England": Browning
69 Lab noise?
70 Some exiles
71 Out
72 Introduction to economics?
73 Used as a dining surface
75 Energized
76 Tells it like it isn't
77 Arctic sight
78 Country singer Black
79 Inauguration recital
80 Yearn (for)
81 Newly sprouted trees
82 Impatient sort
84 Numbers?
85 Frankie with a falsetto
91 Parts of forearms
92 Where a torpedo may be made
93 Turner of note
94 By way of: Abbr.
95 Cheer
96 "OMG!," quaintly
101 The Wizard of ___ Park
102 Io's guardian, in Greek myth
103 Not wait for the parents' blessing, say
104 Bit of I.C.U. equipment
105 Barn young 'un
106 PBS policy
107 Elbowroom
108 Ear part
109 Give back
111 West Virginia resource
113 ___ touch
116 Kicker's aid
117 Old Dodge
118 Suffix with Caesar
119 Quick rule?
121 Something often cured

by David J. Kahn

ACROSS

1 In a fog
7 Fattening sites
12 School founded by a brewer
18 Comic Judy
19 Fusilli's shape
20 Delta, for one
21 John Knowles book about the tortoise's winning strategy?
23 Paper launched in 1944
24 Its setting is a setting
25 Color close to aqua
26 Makes sound
28 Slumber party guest
29 Public outcry
32 Frasier's brother
35 Debate position
36 Diamond corners
37 John Kennedy Toole book about a desert union?
41 Luke's sister
42 "Whip It" singers
43 Wrong
44 Parkers plug them
46 Peruvian coin
47 Musical based on "La Bohème"
48 "___ So Fine"
51 Discussion groups
52 Sine, cosine and tangent
55 Recess
57 Duke is part of it, for short
58 Henry James story about a mutiny?
62 Minimal swimwear
65 Tour-planning org.
66 Island ring
67 Islam's largest branch
68 Jane Austen book about Rosa Parks?
74 Moral misdeed
75 Ring combo
76 Patch sort
77 Strasberg subject
80 Was a pioneer
81 Door feature
84 Horror director Craven
85 Kite-flying need
86 Be cyclical
87 Writer Tarbell and others
89 Superwide shoe specification
90 Thomas Hardy book about a taxpayer's deductions for groceries?
96 Prophets
97 City on Guanabara Bay
98 Pianist Peter and family
99 Doughy snack
101 Robust
102 Start of many Latin American place names
104 Dubai native
106 Filing asst.
107 It's not wall-to-wall
109 John Grisham book about fashion show critics?
114 Ordinary
115 Sheathe
116 Frosh topper
117 Sudden contractions
118 TV event of January 1977
119 Baseball card number

DOWN

1 Harts
2 Coin replaced by the Euro
3 Lacking in substance
4 Trophy
5 Pilot's projection: Abbr.
6 Blowgun ammo
7 Relieved
8 Service award
9 401(k)'s kin
10 Singly
11 Happy colleague
12 Competes
13 Radius setting
14 Campaign poster inscriptions
15 Gary of "Forrest Gump"
16 Guitarist Segovia
17 Cassette parts
19 Sobersided
20 1984 Steve Martin/Lily Tomlin film
22 Dido's love
27 Like appreciative fans
30 "Jefferson in Paris" star
31 Use a prie-dieu
33 1974 foreign-language hit
34 Knowledge, in France
36 Stirs
38 Historic event
39 Upended umlaut
40 Alice's cat
44 Kind of shop or language
45 Prepared for transmission
48 Meddles
49 Vespers time
50 Ross's forte
51 Recon unit
52 Win
53 "Computers for people" company
54 Old five-centesimi coin
56 Heart ward, for short
59 Swindled
60 Sinn ___
61 Behavioral quirk
63 Clear
64 Rubbernecks
69 Time being
70 Field marshal Rommel
71 Actor Baker
72 Precarious
73 Corroded
78 Floorboard sound
79 Soundtrack album, e.g.
82 Scandal reaction
83 Bobby Orr, from 1966 to 1976
85 It has its ups and downs
86 Enjoys a favorite book
88 "Die Fledermaus" composer
90 Shred
91 "All's Well That Ends Well" heroine
92 Cad
93 "Deed I Do" singer
94 Andean beast
95 Morale
96 Pillow covers
100 He introduced the Easter egg roll on the White House lawn
102 Stars
103 Cry of despair
105 Rum cake
108 Fishes-Bull go-between
110 "The Island of the Day Before" author
111 Snitch
112 In addition
113 Quick punch

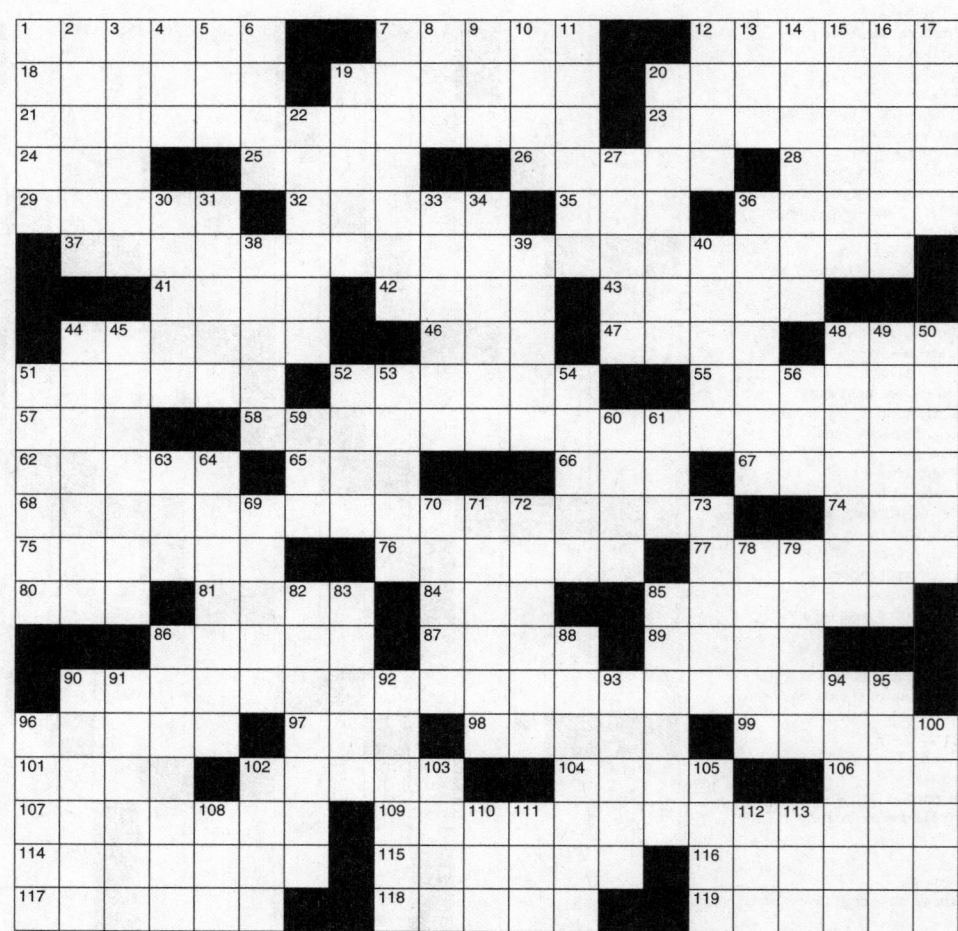

by Mike Shenk

ACROSS

1 March event
7 ___ law (i = v/r)
11 They may appear in the long run
16 "The Phantom of the Opera" star, 1962
19 Appear
20 TV actress Spelling
21 Sound from the bleachers
22 She played Sarah in "The Bible"
23 Hardly Mensa material
25 Kind of session
26 Understanding
27 Hard rock, maybe
28 Suburb north of Seattle
29 Mole, for one
30 Directional suffix
31 Warhol icon Sedgwick
33 Medit. nation
34 Tricked
35 Stem joint
36 "The ___ Adventure" ("Star Wars" spinoff)
37 Group of planes
39 Bitsy beginning
40 Like
41 "Gilligan's Island" actress
43 1974 hit subtitled "Touch the Wind"
45 Composer Prokofiev
46 "Exodus" role
47 John of York
48 Pizzeria patron
49 Property of housepets?
50 Tackled
51 Hay morsel
52 Reassurer's words
54 Animation
55 Perfect
57 Ending with blind or broad
58 Kilowatt-hour fraction
59 Congratulations, of a sort
60 Decline
62 Bereavements
64 "It Happened One Night" producer
67 Violinist Jean-___ Ponty
68 Dosage amts.
71 Diamond of records
73 Nigerian language
74 Book stores?
76 Cozened
77 First Lady of 1900
80 Magazine that debuted 2/17/33
82 Cheer
83 ___ Darya (Asian river)
84 When repeated twice, a 1964 pop hit
85 Botswanan problem
86 Go-getters
88 Portray
90 Grenoble's river
91 Battle of Coronel admiral, 1914
92 Drunk's woe, with "the"
94 "The Dark at the Top of the Stairs" playwright
95 Better than never?
96 Pancreas, e.g.
97 Time to look ahead
98 First name in spydom
99 "___ only knew"
100 Intersecting street
101 Sammy Davis Jr. had one
103 Drop the ball
105 Small songbird
106 Come about
107 Site of Chief Big Foot's last stand
109 Clockmaker Terry
110 ___ citato
111 Not well-done
112 They're not in the nuclear family
113 Matter for a judge
114 Thrills
115 "My Way" songwriter
116 Sensible to the nth degree

DOWN

1 ___ Fjord (inlet of the Skagerrak)
2 Preview programs for computers
3 Contract
4 Transfix
5 Possible change in Russia
6 Not lethargic
7 Idle
8 Center of a roast
9 Rocky Lane spoke for him
10 Tom Sawyer's half brother
11 One letting go
12 Couch potatoes, often
13 "The Furys" novelist James
14 Wrapped up
15 School reward
16 Lausanne lies on it
17 Is intemperate
18 Quirks, say
24 "These Dreams" singer, 1986
29 Maniacal
32 Guitar-picking pioneer Everly
35 Math calculation
36 North Holland seaport
37 Delicate
38 In a difficult position
40 Tackle
42 Open tract
44 Drip site
45 Ethel Merman and Jack Benny, e.g.
52 "Children of the Albatross" author
53 Conductor ___ Klas
56 Hold
57 Logging-on need
59 Sorority letter
61 Torpedo
62 A.M.A. members
63 Disgusted
64 .6102 cubic inch
65 Frederick Forsyth best seller, with "The"
66 1975 James Taylor hit
68 Euripidean work
69 Angler's hope
70 Chaldeans
72 The maximum, often
74 ___-majesté
75 Turns away
76 Put to use
78 Duds at work
79 Pot grower?
81 To be, in Bordeaux
87 Cave
89 Inlet
91 Oscar Madison, for one
93 Donald's daughter
96 Bellyache
98 Kind of hound
100 U.S.N. personnel
101 Enter
102 Itchings
104 Unwind
107 Depression-era inits.
108 Resource to be tapped?

by Frank Longo

188 FAMILY TIES

ACROSS

1 Cry of relief
7 Actress Campbell of "Martin"
12 Greenery
19 Stainless
20 Bony
21 Mammals like camels
22 Minnie's mama
24 Amount of fun
25 James Whitcomb Riley's "___ I Went Mad"
26 Make waves, for short?
27 Request for permission
29 A small one is white
30 Jodie's mom or dad
34 Unmannered
38 Changing places
41 Tops
42 Lawn mower maker
44 Where area code 813 is: Abbr.
45 Pad, so to speak
46 Zip
47 Partridge locales?
49 Side-channel, in Canada
50 Mel's daughters
54 Farm females
55 Tentativeness
57 Synthetic fiber
58 Mawkish
59 Life's strange turns
60 Throws off
61 Not esto or eso
62 Univ. grant source
63 Member of Glenn's family
67 Elemental ending
70 Competitor of Bloomies
72 Part of a candlelight ceremony, maybe
73 Where zebras and giraffes graze
75 They travel on foot
77 Subatomic particle
78 Unruffled
80 Soprano in "Louise"
81 Michael J.'s kids
83 Understand
84 Gym equipment
86 One for Juan
87 Kind of alphabet
88 Hurricane heading: Abbr.
89 '50s–'60s teen idol
90 French bench
92 Hoarder
94 Side in a Euro conflict
96 Jasmine's family member
99 Uranians, e.g.
101 Kind of exhaust
102 Provide, as with legal authority
103 Lizard, old-style
106 Hitched
110 Member of Joyce's family
114 Sautéed fish dish
115 Lots of potatoes
116 Designer Pucci
117 Follows a sidewalk preacher
118 First name in cosmetics
119 Holds off

DOWN

1 Tip
2 God with iron gloves
3 Midnight or beyond
4 Hair color
5 Initial instruction
6 Cherished name in Calcutta
7 Kitchen meas.
8 Suffix with Manhattan
9 "Able" one
10 Capital once known as Salisbury
11 Masefield's "___ That Pass By"
12 Testing site
13 Ben-Gurion carrier
14 Liqueur flavor
15 Traveler
16 Close friend, in slang
17 Hoedown date
18 Squiggly shape
20 "What's to become ___?"
23 Dog bowl bits
28 Investor's concern
30 Certain camera shot
31 Union demand
32 Charles's game
33 ". . . ___ a good-night!"
35 Anita, Bonnie, Ruth and June
36 Sore labour's bath, to Shakespeare
37 Flip, in a way
38 Return, as chips
39 Doubleday et al.
40 Donna's sons
43 Penn Sta. traffic
46 Big Apple's 30 Rock occupant
47 Ship commanded by Martin Pinzón
48 Caboose

50 Highlanders
51 ___ many words
52 "Give me an example, smarty"
53 Bar's partner
56 Sounds of time passing
58 Allen or Martin
60 He played Robin and Don Juan
61 Tracks
64 "Braveheart" setting
65 Bridge positions
66 Tropical spot
68 Nervousness
69 Climbing plant with a dye-yielding root
71 Burnoose wearer
74 Straddling
75 Deliveries to a butcher
76 Cut back
77 Silvers role
78 Shell
79 Tic-tac-toe failure
81 Football Hall-of-Famer Ford
82 Candid Allen
85 Fortification
87 Spring part
90 S.A.T.'s
91 Solvent
92 Stress, for one
93 Tousled

95 Old Texaco star
97 Broadway salute to Blake
98 Times to call, in classifieds
100 Elated
103 Vogue rival
104 So-so
105 Terrible time
106 Vandalize
107 Honest name
108 Grammy category
109 Paris's Parc ___ Princes
111 Not just any
112 Ground breaker
113 Tiny carp?

by Randolph Ross

ACROSS

1 Routine responses?
6 Least amiable
12 One who sets up shots
18 Make ___ for
20 Radiators and such
22 Camden Yards player
23 One of the Beverly Hillbillies
24 The World ___
25 Lab vessel
26 View surreptitiously
28 Concubine's room
29 Tart
30 How the celebrity's mom and dad survived?
37 Contemptible one
38 Theme park transport
39 Hit man, so to speak
40 Novelist Nin
42 Name of three English rivers
43 Be against change
47 How the case of commercial espionage is halted?
52 ___ du Diable
53 Cry of delight
54 Bitter, to a Brit
55 Chatter
56 Nonplussed
58 Birchbark
60 Bowling game
63 Commute overseas regularly?
68 Quit
69 Top
70 More monumental
71 Short test for brains?
72 Base figure: Abbr.
73 Annual hoops event, familiarly
74 Taste
77 Evening hours, to Larry King?
87 Ready for a vacation
88 Sundance's girl
89 Pour ___ troubled waters
90 Where the Via del Corso runs
91 Elath resident
94 Small toymakers: Var.
95 President Bush writes part of his autobiography?
101 Andretti, for one
102 1920s White House nickname
103 Greenish-yellow hue
104 Sit in on
106 "King Rat" novelist
110 Birdie of Broadway's "Bye Bye Birdie"
113 Diving instructions, maybe
114 Barely perceptible
115 Heavy hammer
116 Lay hold of
117 ___ vérité
118 Krupp family city

DOWN

1 Muslim pilgrimage: Var.
2 Cousin of a lemur
3 Weekly radio program
4 Heatless
5 It can go in brackets
6 Angry words
7 Animator's sheet
8 Words before and after "what" for Popeye
9 LAX abbr.
10 Counterpart for madame
11 Wall Street figure
12 Stole
13 Hardware
14 Chutists' needs
15 Keen
16 '80s TV divorcee
17 Strapped
19 Arizona native
21 Mayo Clinic test
27 S.A. country
30 Master
31 Not dissonant, musically
32 Beat it!
33 Emulate Tyra Banks
34 Agassi, at times
35 Challenger of Stalin
36 Sign of damage
41 Mollify
43 When repeated, cry at a celebratory party
44 Intimidate, with "out"
45 "To fetch ___ . . ."
46 Combining the ideal characteristics of its variety
48 Nipped, with "out"
49 1973 World Series stadium
50 Reached in amount
51 "The Time Machine" people
56 Letters on a telephone bill
57 Redressed, with "for"
58 Williams title start
59 "So then what?"
60 Specter
61 Left and right, maybe
62 Midpoint: Abbr.
63 Camp vehicles
64 Strain
65 Big name in golf
66 Light: Prefix
67 Tax-free bond, briefly
74 Banking game
75 "See ya!"
76 English 101 subject
78 Most gamesome
79 Having equal angles
80 Salinger dedicatee
81 Interpret
82 She had a "Tootsie" role
83 List ender
84 Tpkes.
85 "Das Rheingold" locale
86 Telephone connections
91 Leaning to the right
92 Corned beef alternative
93 Important sports org.
95 Exams for advanced study, briefly
96 Noted stationer
97 "Coffee ___?"
98 Churchly: Abbr.
99 Some office equipment
100 Élève's place
105 Letters after Sen. Jeanne Shaheen's name
107 Sportscaster Scully
108 Compass heading
109 Thrash
111 Sensitive subject, often
112 Stereo site

by David J. Kahn

ACROSS

1 Kindergarten stuff
5 Deduce
11 Like some socks
14 Outdoes
19 Loser in an upset
20 Part of the iris bordering the pupil
21 Implant
22 Grammar subject
23 Dancer's apparel?
26 Money substitute
27 Preacher's apparel?
28 Factory worker's apparel?
30 Florida's ___ National Forest
31 "Cheers" setting
33 Start of many criminal case names
34 The universe on day one
37 Unexpected blows
39 Actor Peter et al.
43 Home, to Hans
44 Psychiatrist's apparel?
49 Brutally dismiss
50 Suffix with disk
51 Kansas town
52 Amount to be raised, maybe
53 A regular type
54 Cable network, briefly
55 Miner's apparel?
59 Burns's partner
60 "Ditto"
62 Send
63 Earthy deposits
64 Conners
65 Saki, really
66 Author Marsh
68 Separates, in a way
70 Now
71 Election times
74 ___ as a pig
75 Projectionist's apparel?
77 One of the 13 orig. colonies
78 Rhineland town heavily bombed in W.W. II
79 Apt family name in "The Wizard of Oz"
80 Constellation animal
81 "___ cost to you!"
82 Suffix with special
83 Entomologist's apparel?
87 Silent actress Naldi
88 Highly seasoned stew
90 TV Mr.
91 Joyous hymn
92 Country
95 Govt. intelligence org.
96 Meeting room staple
99 Referee's apparel?
103 Pro athlete's apparel?
107 ___ friends
108 Lawyer's apparel?
111 Compact matter
112 Elevs.
113 Flower part
114 Mountain known locally as Mongibello
115 Kind of skill or home
116 Luggage marking
117 Restful
118 Onetime barrier breakers

DOWN

1 1956 Peck role
2 Island south of Borneo
3 Plagiarize
4 Free
5 Nero's successor
6 Dizzy
7 Edison contemporary
8 Holler's partner
9 Polar worker
10 Snitch
11 Fed. watchdog
12 Opportunities, so to speak
13 Resided
14 1956 Marilyn Monroe film
15 Collectible Dutch print
16 Hindu garment
17 Letters of rejoicing
18 Library Card Sign-Up Mo.
24 Gumshoes
25 Sealy competitor
29 Ivy Leaguer
31 Fella
32 "___ Lay Dying"
34 Castle locale
35 Kind of yoga
36 Mechanic's apparel?
37 One of the Marianas
38 Become suddenly aware
40 Engineer's apparel?
41 Shine
42 Penn and others
44 Certain office worker
45 Surf sounds
46 Composer Siegmeister
47 Old dagger
48 Paper size: Abbr.
53 Highlander's pride
55 Treasure site
56 Day after mercredi
57 Skeletal parts
58 Saint ___ College of California
59 Stock up
61 Form of Spanish "to be"
65 Continue
66 Sip
67 Intimate
68 Master
69 4 × 4 name
70 E-ZPass payment
71 One of the Monkees
72 Nosy one
73 Longtime G.M. chief Alfred
75 Evil, to Yves
76 1884 literary hero, informally
79 Physicist Ohm
81 Lab reports
83 Son's designation, with "the"
84 Hollywood's B.D. and Anna May
85 Certain H.S. teams
86 Good bond rating
89 Yankee
91 Anne McCaffrey's dragon land
93 Don Marquis character
94 Airs
96 Wonderland message
97 "Men in Black" menace
98 River at Lyon
99 Malt liquor yeast
100 South Seas adventure story
101 Delete
102 Onetime athletic org.
103 Lasting effect
104 Belt-tightening
105 1971 Grammy song "___ No Sunshine"
106 Child welfare grps.
109 It's got your no.
110 Downed

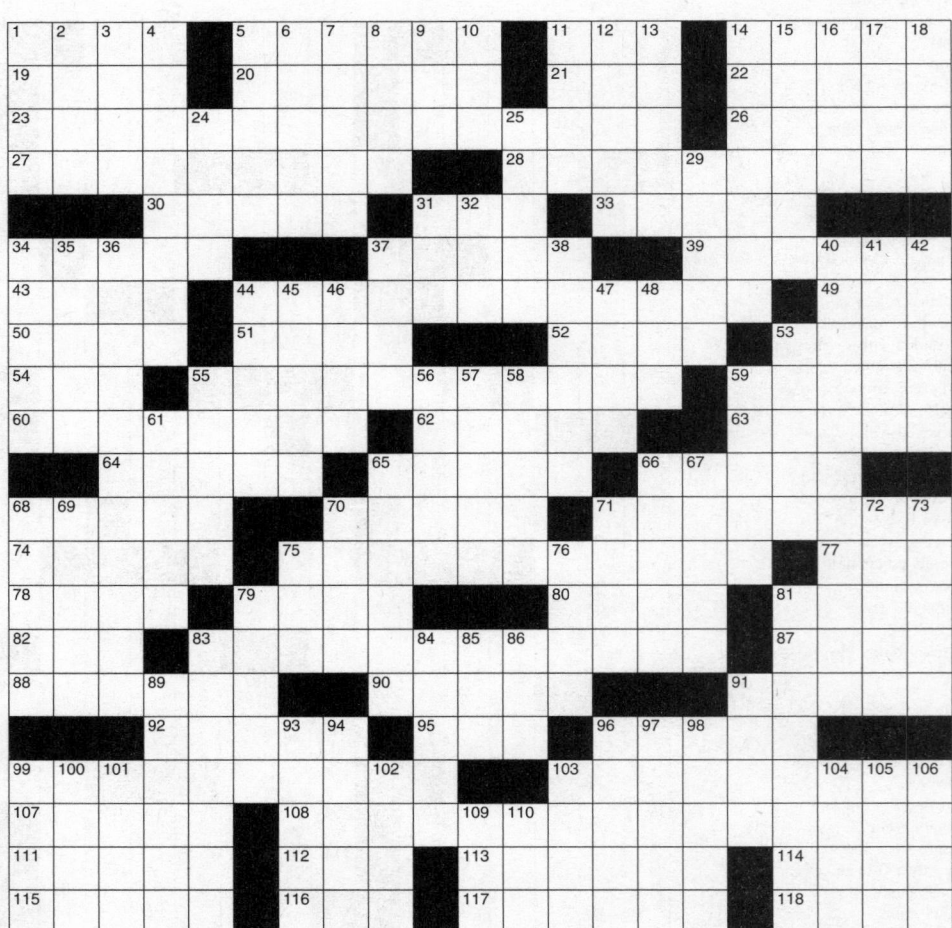

by Michael S. Maurer

ACROSS

1 Mailing supply
7 Leaves of metal
12 Coped
19 A Musketeer
20 Cliched movie ending
21 Better
22 Most ghastly
23 Hose-wielding serf, perhaps?
25 Slangy acumen
26 1977 film killer
27 "The Clan of the Cave Bear" author
28 Charlotte's web site
29 Developmental period
30 Trumpeter Ziggy
31 Rabin's successor
33 Fact about unladylike habits?
37 Chow
41 Cries akin to "Shucks!"
42 Clingmans Dome locale: Abbr.
43 T or F, e.g.: Abbr.
44 Overhauled
46 Charleston dancer
49 "This means ___!"
51 Expert witness at a trial
52 Samplers
53 Ones peeking at rams and ewes?
56 Winter Palace dweller, once
57 Loser to Braddock, 1935
58 Emollient source
59 Rent
60 Famed Chicago boat?
65 Invitation word
69 "Help!" in France
70 Pilgrim's pronoun
71 Blood: Prefix
75 Long-winded oration of Andrew, e.g.?
78 Heavenly host
81 Bureaucratic stuff
82 John Dos Passos trilogy
83 Pass in some bowls
84 Yak in the pulpit
85 Qt. couple
87 More than chuckle
89 The Nittany Lions: Abbr.
90 Early pulpit
91 Stifling of a happy bird?
96 Hotfoot it
98 Refreshing spot
99 Get nosy
100 Vacation sites
104 Ancient Roman wheel
105 Lt. Kojak
106 Prefix with -graph
109 Seedy place?
112 Live, as a game ball
113 Pen
114 Habituates
115 The Green Wave
116 Popular Christmas gift
117 Like Batman
118 Volcano, e.g.

DOWN

1 Napkin holders
2 Composer Khachaturian
3 Back talk, to one prophet?
4 Crop up
5 Conversation starter
6 Onetime J.F.K. jet set
7 1995 cop on the spot
8 Like some garages
9 Montreal, for one
10 Guitar designer Fender
11 Buckle up
12 Stephen King title
13 Capacious
14 Member-supported org.
15 Abu Dhabi denizen
16 "Naked Maja" painter
17 By any chance
18 Laura or Bruce of film
20 Hot
24 Political debates, often
30 Washstand toppers
32 Palmists, e.g.
33 Go with the wind
34 Certain fledgling
35 Suffix with hoop
36 Magazine formerly known as Modern Maturity
38 Emulate Mia
39 Thomas Mann's "___ Kroger"
40 Mean grin
44 Event for those who know the ropes
45 Irish offshoot
47 Frmr. Span. coin: Abbr.
48 Short wave?
49 Coaster rider's cry
50 Makes bubbly
51 Swamp critter
53 ___ law (ancient code)
54 Worked with alfalfa
55 Additionally
57 Hecklers' chorus
61 Nobel-winning Bunche
62 Captain Hook's sidekick
63 Ostrich cousin
64 Sharpen
65 Kvetch
66 Kind of hat or house
67 Web user's need
68 Cornerstone abbr.
72 Afore
73 Irish side dish?
74 Humble
76 Guadalajara lunch
77 "Tom Thumb" star Tamblyn, 1958
78 Kind
79 Ruin
80 Cast aspersions on
85 It's a snap
86 Huge
87 Mended
88 ___ Hound (Canis Major)
91 Low-frequency speaker
92 Tallies
93 Pakistani city
94 Unfold
95 Big hit
97 Hag
100 Bursae
101 Fore-and-after's fore
102 Tops
103 Remote location
106 Rests
107 Silver hair
108 ___ and terminer
110 Weimar "with"
111 Spanish queen until 1931

by Cathy Millhauser

ACROSS

1 Buzzing
6 Billiard stroke
11 Name in computer software
16 Hinder
21 Oscar Madison's secretary
22 Hero of the first opera written for TV
23 Ain't right?
24 Leaf
25 GREEN
27 GREEN
29 Bank deposit
30 Keep for oneself
31 Concert finale
32 ___ League
33 Kansas city
35 Raiders' chief
38 Subjects of modern mapping
39 Bitty's partner
40 V-chips block it
42 Column couple
44 Trojan War figure
46 GREEN
52 Corsair and Citation, for two
56 ___-a-porter
57 Feature of Roy Lichtenstein's art
58 Genealogist's abbr.
59 Eastern attire
61 Dit's partner
62 Come to
65 Kind of testing
67 Novarro of silents
69 City on the Mohawk
71 Jimmy Dorsey's "___ Mine"
72 Watering holes
74 GREEN
77 GREEN
79 George ___
80 Stretch
81 Colleen
82 Detergent
83 French toast portion?
85 Easily handled, as a ship
87 Lhasa ___
90 Beethoven's "Choral" Symphony
93 Service station offering
94 GREEN
98 GREEN
101 Commencement
102 Voyage preceder
103 1993 N.B.A. Rookie of the Year
104 "Forget it!"
105 Where firings take place on a daily basis
107 Spicy stew
109 Mineral suffix
110 Gospels follower
112 Commuters' ways
114 Financial aid criterion
116 Dexterity
117 What some fans do
119 GREEN
123 Smoking container
126 Foam at the mouth
127 Petitions
128 Pulitzer dramatist Connelly
131 Ancient city in 2-Down
133 Food item usually picked wild
136 Abases
140 Jerusalem's Mosque of ___
141 Aristocracies
143 Arm
145 Granada greeting
146 GREEN
148 GREEN
150 Reason for 55-Down's rebellion
151 Underground worker
152 Petitions
153 Math measurements
154 Blackthorn fruits
155 Colonel's insignia
156 Digression
157 To wit: Lat.

DOWN

1 Out of place
2 Aleppo's land
3 Coloratura's specialty
4 Provoke
5 Bowl sound
6 County in NW Ireland
7 City once called Philadelphia
8 One born on a kibbutz
9 Most likely to collapse
10 Annex
11 Victoria, e.g.
12 Rubber gasket
13 With 15-Down, some chains
14 Outfoxed
15 See 13-Down
16 Newt
17 Costly sweaters
18 Say suddenly
19 Target
20 1955 film robot
26 Lewis of children's TV
28 Rankle
34 Go-ahead
36 Takeoff, approx.
37 The Lone Ranger's real identity
41 It may be living or dead
43 She's still with Stiller
45 Ignominy
46 Squarely
47 ___-Detoo
48 Some Balts
49 Lonesome George of early TV
50 Address nos.
51 Shades
53 Woman on TV's "Ab Fab"
54 They're fit to be tied
55 1786 Springfield insurrectionist
59 Lounge
60 Assumed names
63 Off
64 Vietnamese port
66 Populous place
68 Team V.I.P.: Abbr.
70 Flat sign
73 Discerning
75 Shoptalk
76 Hole enlarger
78 Sicilia, for one
79 Shipmate of Starbuck
84 Panzer
86 ___-tat
87 French 101 verb
88 It's spotted in westerns
89 Driving hazard
91 Sgts., e.g.
92 Service station offering
94 Private
95 Sub
96 Rally
97 Record
99 Winged
100 Film used for recording tapes
101 Dairy aisle buy
106 Bush leaguers
108 Advances
111 Tall player
113 Sting
115 Pat
118 Grow together
119 Babbling
120 Id moderator
121 Pasta go-with
122 "Yuck!"
124 Banned Wilde drama
125 Desdemona's faithful servant
128 Shapes
129 Film director Jon
130 Sly character
132 Celebrate
134 Name in Chinese politics
135 Actor Christopher
137 The world according to Arp
138 Object of frequent sightings
139 "___ Isn't So" (Hall & Oates hit)
142 Desiccated
144 Language that gave us the word "whisky"
147 C.I.A. forerunner
148 Tax pro
149 Calendar abbr.

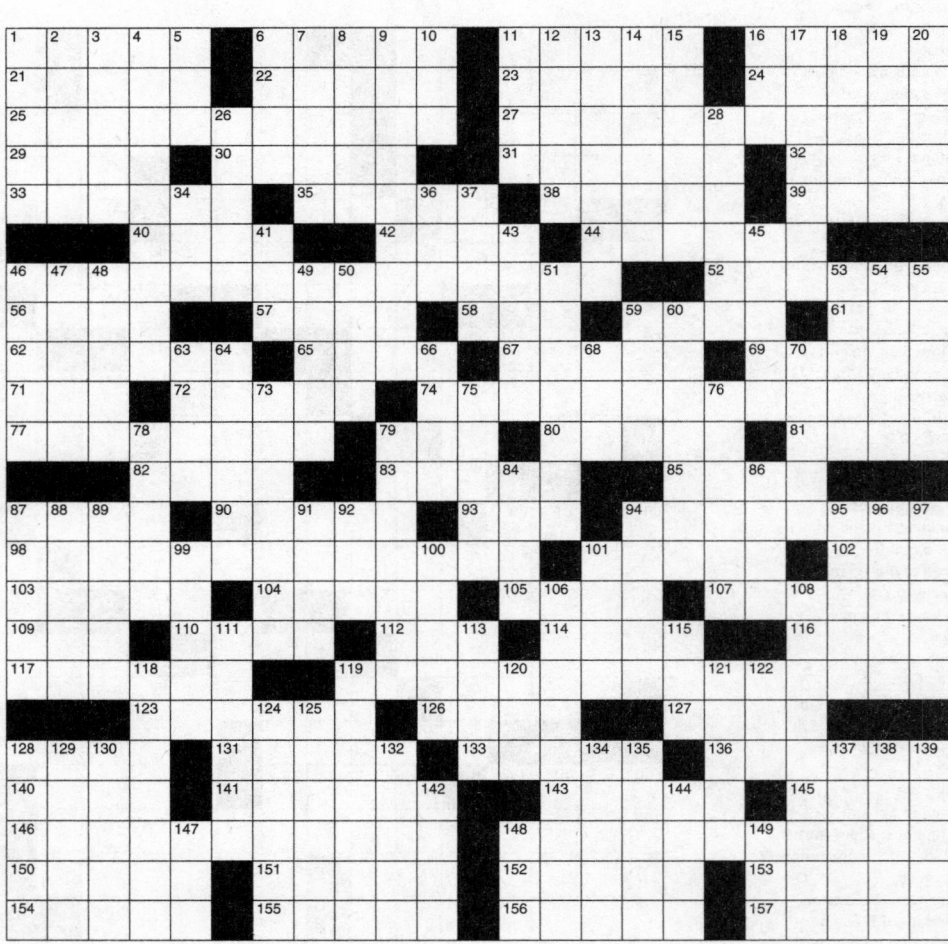

by Nancy Nicholson Joline

ACROSS

1. Like putty in one's hands, maybe
7. Teen's woe
14. Rum cocktail
20. Rockville ___, L.I.
21. Musical instrument with finger holes
22. Tigers' school
23. Soup ingredient
24. Start of a quip by 67-Across
26. Backgammon impossibility
27. Tab topic
29. Ring thing
30. It has a red coat
31. Quipu maker
33. It might be sung on one's birthday
37. Skins
39. Part 2 of the quip
44. Exploits
45. Hot
46. Say further
47. Place, as a bet
48. Traveller's check
49. Lucky draw
50. Drudge
52. Sharp taste
53. With 56-Down, city near Knoxville
56. See 72-Across
59. Withdraws
61. Part 3 of the quip
65. Trouble
66. Show stoppers
67. Author of the quip
69. Bumbling beast
72. With 56-Across, like some shares
73. Part 4 of the quip
75. Zones
79. Ball girls
80. Downing and others: Abbr.
81. Some W.B.C. outcomes
82. Briny
83. Suffers from
85. Examines, with "over"
86. Prado treasure
87. Charles, e.g.
88. Norwegian king
92. Beet variety
94. Part 5 of the quip
101. '50s TV comedian
102. Concurred
103. Pig
104. ___-humanite (crime against humanity): Fr.
105. Historic grp.
107. Airport line
109. Alert, for short
110. End of the quip
115. Elusive subject, familiarly
117. Deep-frying need
118. Ex-con, maybe
119. Rubber ring
120. Ticket order
121. Jacks or better, in poker
122. Blurs

DOWN

1. Nova follower
2. Spelling
3. What pronouns refer to
4. Local org.
5. Skater Heiden
6. Struck out
7. Shalikashvili's predecessor
8. '90s brew
9. Warp, say
10. It comes before adolescence
11. "___ Darlin'" (1957 hit)
12. Sphinx
13. Copy to a floppy
14. Enthusiastic exclamation
15. They're boring
16. In the same place
17. Deli option
18. Composer Khachaturian
19. A keeper may keep it
25. Ties up
28. Contact, perhaps
32. Hanging clear of the bottom
34. A.M. TV offering
35. Mythical bird
36. "___ questions?"
38. Relief
40. Female octopus
41. "Pillow Talk" actress
42. 1993 Kevin Kline comedy
43. Choice beef cuts
48. Bust, so to speak
49. Bleated
50. Fugitive's trail
51. "Jurassic Park" girl
52. Its slogan was once "The things we do to make you happy"
53. Wrinkle-resistant fabric
54. Govt. agent's employer
55. Opera's ___ Te Kanawa
56. See 53-Across
57. Biting
58. Pea stabbers
60. Olympics great Janet
62. He doubted God's ability to bring water out of a rock
63. Wards (off)
64. Film director Buñuel
68. New York ___
69. Popular dessert
70. "The Dukes of Hazzard" spinoff
71. Jour. staff
72. Airline to Karachi
74. Attacks
75. It might have the shakes
76. Tannish
77. TV pal of Mary and Rhoda
78. Ought to have, informally
84. Certain look
85. Accelerator
87. Map abbr.
88. Saturn's wife
89. ___ Fresnos, Tex.
90. Black and tan ingredient
91. Bordeaux business owner
92. Popular cereal
93. Stashes
95. Absentee
96. Where the Tagus flows
97. Cap attachment
98. Conditions of equilibrium
99. More silly
100. ___ Field
104. British emblem
106. ___ Snaps (dog treats)
108. Petticoat junction
110. "Name him!"
111. England's Isle of ___
112. Before, in poetry
113. Sun follower?
114. Big cheer
116. Compass dir.

by Peter Gordon

ACROSS

1 Steady
6 Sauteed dish
10 Edison's middle name
14 Dessert item
19 Silver Ghost, informally
20 Lohengrin's love
21 Activist
22 Up
23 Title for a cleric's book?
25 Teen fantasy?
27 Do type
28 Gone
29 1995 Pitt flick
30 Product of the press?
32 Quickly apply
37 Goodfellow ___, Tex.
40 It may be black or green
41 Deep bell sound
42 Mr. Hyde, e.g.
44 Cybernetics pioneer ___ Wiener
46 Firm
48 Pinochle combo
49 "Dirty dog," for one
50 City discussed at the 1954 Geneva Conference
52 Senate support
54 Cows, maybe
55 Opposite of baja
56 Black spot
58 Kind of expression
60 They cross the line
62 ___ one
64 Bank deposit
65 Sewing tool
66 Masseuse's target
67 "Was ___ blame?"
68 Program
70 Ring org.
73 70-Across weapon
75 Miss America attire
77 Dweller across the strait from Singapore
79 Stadium sight
81 Horrible
84 Prefix with mechanics
85 Thick fog, in slang
86 "___-Man" (1974 spy/sci-fi film)
88 Center of activity
89 Wit
90 Part of a W.W. II exclamation
91 Search for x
93 Bit of business attire
96 Kind of apparel
99 Foreign refusal
100 Shower with flowers
101 Certain model railroads
102 Ardent and then some
103 Cavern, in poetry
105 "Backdraft" concern
107 Old piece
109 Wedding locale in a Crosby film
112 Anorexic?
116 Simple beachwear?
119 Provide, as with some quality
120 For fear that
121 Split, so to speak
122 Pen patter
123 Not thinking straight
124 Douay prophet
125 Heart of the matter
126 Desert drainage basin

DOWN

1 Support ___
2 Former Virginia senator
3 Lily relative
4 Hints
5 Artsy one
6 Engage in a food fight at KFC?
7 Out of this world
8 Onetime sight at Dulles
9 "That'll show you!"
10 Deem
11 Screw (up)
12 Hero-worship
13 Like Australia's western plateau
14 Famous Tuesday Club member
15 ___ bark beetle
16 Actress Myrna
17 Repeatedly
18 Ultimate
24 Fin
26 Bounce
30 Do a salon job
31 Hitchhiker from Calcutta?
33 Hammer in manufacturing
34 Tiny Christmas decoration?
35 Was coquettish with
36 Auction actions
37 Cochise player Michael in '50s TV
38 Succeed
39 Unbearably hot holiday?
41 Quite a thrill
43 Capriole
45 Small fastener
47 Foreign refusal
51 Jerks
53 1953 title role for Rita Hayworth
56 Treat
57 Talk fondly
59 "Field of Dreams" setting
61 What a padlock may fasten
63 Org.
67 Where Mt. Carmel is: Abbr.
69 Kindly spirit?
71 Spanish Harlem, for one
72 Current terminals
74 Disable
76 With bated breath
78 Small fastener
79 City ESE of Bombay
80 Water ring
82 Chilling
83 Go up and down the dial
85 Budge
87 Whitens
92 It might come out of a summit
94 Rose-red dye
95 Stove workspace
97 Fictional ghost
98 It passes between decks
104 Clangor
105 Be ready for
106 It meant nothing to Caesar
108 Capital of Manche
110 North or South district in Hawaii
111 Black
112 Drops outside
113 Musician Brian
114 Hubbub
115 Procter & Gamble soap
116 Oomph
117 Year in Nero's reign
118 Agcy. overseeing Fed. records

by June Boggs

ACROSS

1 Favorite Degas subject
8 Behave
11 ___-Ball
15 It often has its arms out front
18 Gorged oneself
19 Classified
21 "Windsor Forest" poet
22 Dinner offerings
24 Services, in a way
25 "Mr. Basketball" Holman et al.
26 Gray remover, maybe
27 "Suzanne" songwriter
28 Orbital point
29 "The Simpsons" tavern
31 Show of affection
33 Backgammon piece
34 Oater affirmative
36 Engine conduits
37 Hits errantly, in golf
38 Impassioned
41 State to be in
42 Word with ready or shy
44 Reef
45 Hair-raising site?
47 Undercover operation
52 #2 at the 1994 U.S. Open
54 Swing voter: Abbr.
55 Lodge
56 CD-___
57 Ice cream parlor order
59 "La vita nuova" poet
60 Captures, in a way
63 Rachmaninoff's "___-tableaux"
64 Indian stringed instruments
65 Make up
66 Like some muscles
67 Poop
68 Impetuous
69 Listen: Sp.
70 British noble, briefly
72 "___ in my memory lock'd": Ophelia
73 Certain berth
76 Kind of pie
79 Community spirit
81 Majors in acting
82 Ruling groups
83 Farm resident
84 Part of a split personality
86 Orchestral works
88 Considerable irritant
91 Word in many business names
92 "Star Trek" role
93 Soup kitchen offering
97 Taradiddles
100 Puffball relative
101 Release upon
102 Hotfooted it
104 Clock sound
106 Make money
107 Health care group
110 Sews up
111 Reserved
112 Totals
113 Christie contemporary
114 Musical syllables
115 Never, in Nuremberg
116 Least irrigated

DOWN

1 Butler's expletive
2 Col. Hannibal Smith's group
3 Cool
4 Relative of an agate
5 Plumbing piece
6 Chancel entrance display
7 Collar inserts
8 Collar
9 Animator's unit
10 Parcels
11 "___ Is Love" (1962 hit)
12 They provide prayer support
13 Brings in
14 1997 U.S. Open champ
15 Long-term pollution concern
16 Data transmission path
17 Actress Armstrong and others
20 Tend the hearth
21 Toaster treat
23 Couple or so
28 Word before and after "to"
30 Parasol
32 Quite a while
35 Fund-raising grp.
37 Seemed funny
38 Sit-up benefactors
39 Squeal
40 Travels of Shane, e.g.
41 Locale
42 Mention
43 Breeze through
46 Items in sync?
47 Imaginary
48 Chaplin and others
49 Mil. transports
50 "Are you nervous?" response, à la Don Knotts
51 Diamond execs
53 Gist
58 Hairsplitters
59 Pronouncements
61 Charge with
62 Bribe money, in slang
63 Chacon of the 1962 Mets
64 Still-life subject
65 Hasty
66 Pocket item
67 Holiday purchases
68 Diamond target
71 Company that made Photophones
72 Ford sobriquet
74 Sniggler's quest
75 Fam. reunion attendee
77 Castle features
78 "Paper Moon" actor or actress
80 Breakfast orders, briefly
83 J.F.K. posting
85 Emulated Mme. Defarge
86 Kind of meeting
87 Prize
88 Aquarium acquisitions
89 Track and field events
90 Secure
93 Topps rival
94 Gaucho gear
95 Mil. address
96 Longtime Guy Lombardo record label
98 City on the Oregon Trail
99 Dumbarton denizens
103 New Look designer
105 Measure of speed
107 Presidential monogram
108 Star Wars, initially
109 "___ dreaming?"

by Rich Norris

ACROSS

1 Cutaneous
7 Rock group that sang "Let's Go"
14 Splendid
19 Conductor Toscanini
20 Like some shoes
21 Grammy-winning single of 1958
22 Groundskeeper's bagful at an Atlantic City newspaper?
24 Armpit
25 Companion
26 Oregon ___
27 Playboy Khan
28 Library ref.
29 Where "Falstaff" premiered, 1893
32 Start of a string of 13 popes
34 Dish alternative, maybe
36 Loudness measure
37 Musician who co-starred in "Trespass"
38 Descartes conclusion
39 Horse owned by a Boston newspaper?
42 Hired hands at Microsoft
44 Sponsorship
46 Camera since 1924
47 Bank sitters
49 Some picture frames
52 Used rubber
56 Garden, in a way
57 Correspondence to the editor of an Allentown newspaper?
60 Allan-___
61 Obviously sleep-deprived
63 End of a Burns title
64 Prepare to get juice
65 Madonna's "La ___ Bonita"
67 Kind of law
69 Yeshiva product
71 Off, so to speak
72 Drink with 87-Across
74 Concert memento
76 Like a clover leaf
78 Take over, in a way
79 Columbia, S.C., newspaper's security department?
81 Vane dir.
84 Like a mule
86 Mars, to Aries, in astrology
87 Ingredient in a 72-Across
89 Thunderstruck
91 ___ facto
93 Like Chippendale furniture
94 Way into the bathroom at a Macon newspaper?
99 Start to function?
101 Snake oil, purportedly
102 Hungary was a member of it
103 Suffix with sect
104 Named before
106 Do some roadwork
107 Automobile sticker fig.
108 Jack-in-the-box part
109 I.Q. recordholder Marilyn ___ Savant
111 Prize
113 Associated
115 Shell shot at a Harrisburg newspaper?
120 Come
121 Nobel physicist Becquerel
122 Frank
123 Rather awkward
124 Mouthing off more
125 Crackers

DOWN

1 Skip, as a stone on water
2 Muff
3 Hwy.
4 Sweet wine
5 Some insurance fraud
6 ___ Tay, Scotland
7 Part of an old Greek fleet
8 In the know about
9 Subject of a psych. experiment
10 Do
11 Permanent-magnet alloy
12 Seize again
13 '60s campus grp.
14 Popular theater name
15 Bulldog
16 Big goon
17 '50s–'60s "What's My Line?" panelist
18 Beginning of a tape
21 Harper, for one
23 "Come Back, Little Sheba" wife
27 Edits
29 Book before Nahum
30 Likeness: Prefix
31 Come-on at a Lakeland newspaper?
33 "Enough!"
35 Handsome, as Henri
36 Carmichael classic
38 Sharon, for one
40 Attorney-to-be's exams
41 In base 8
43 Shipping dept. stamp
45 Pupil's reward
48 Roy Rogers's real surname
50 A great dist.
51 ". . . and last in the American League" team
53 Recruiter at a Wichita newspaper?
54 Inter ___
55 Say it ain't so
58 ___ squares (statistical method)
59 Malcontent
62 They're full of beans
64 A bobby pin may hold it
65 "Look at me, ___ . . ."
66 Start of some Italian church names
68 Tutsi foe
70 ___-a-brac
73 Cutting down
75 Misrepresent
77 Eddie Rickenbacker's 94th ___ Squadron
79 Alaska air base
80 Great Fire of London diarist
82 Pelvic bones
83 Tempter
85 Acting Day
88 Gets via computer
90 Prefix with 1-Across
92 Name dropper?
94 Gong in an orchestra set
95 Run out
96 Hybrid cats
97 Humidor item
98 Fife player
100 "As You Like It" servant
105 In unison
106 "Jurassic Park" mosquito preserver
108 Roman historian
110 Some B'way shows
112 Bird whose male hatches the eggs
114 Bad-mouth
115 Stage setups, for short
116 "Superman ___"
117 ___ bind
118 Baseball's Dykstra
119 Before, once

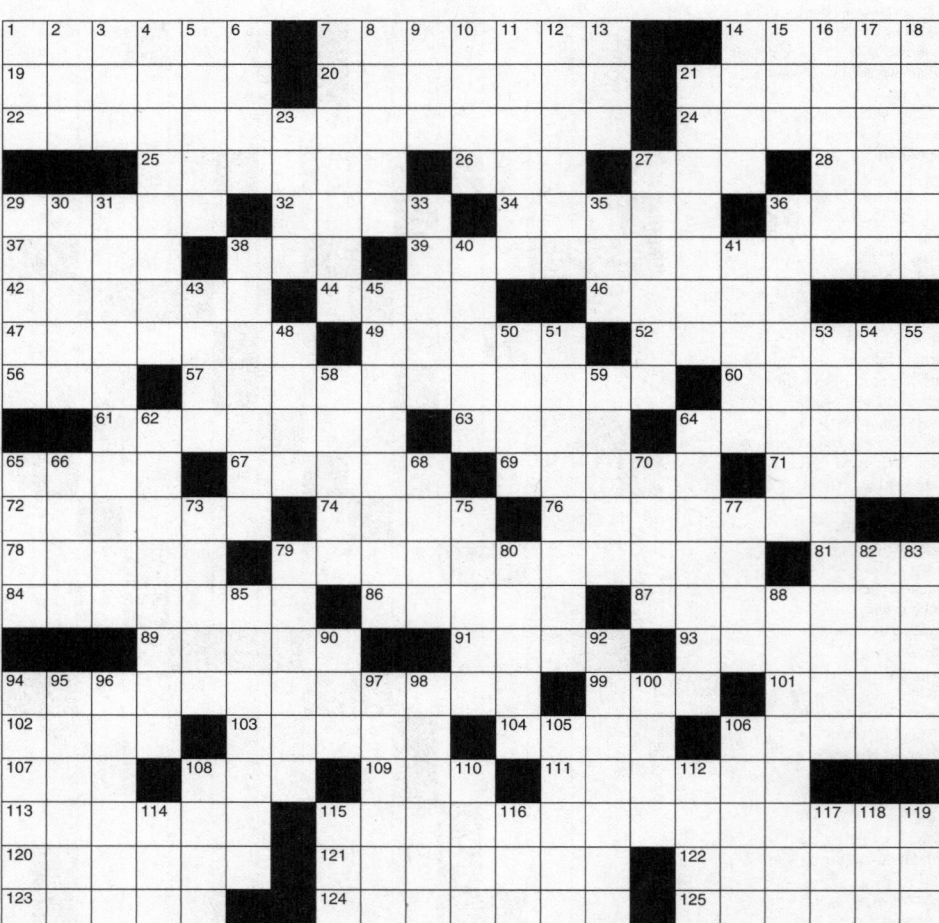

by Fred Piscop

ACROSS

1 It comes in a scoop
5 Small club, say
9 Underlying
14 Essential parts
19 Butcher's cut
20 Luxembourg town where George Patton is buried
21 Daughter of William the Conqueror
22 On ___ (reveling)
23 First name in mystery
24 Grand
25 Tree knots
26 ___ Domingo
27 Seat setting
28 Seven-time Stanley Cup competitor
31 Unexplained skill
32 Harried
33 Scraps
34 "Little House on the Prairie" co-star Karen
35 Counts, e.g.
37 '20s–'50s papal name
38 Transfer and messenger materials
39 Yoga practitioner
40 Film maker Gus Van ___
41 What to call a lady
42 Letter trio
45 F-4's
48 Former Toronto pitching ace
50 Noted name in civil rights
51 Dark times, briefly
52 Good cheer
53 Where Europe was divided
54 Sales worker
55 Country name, 1937–49
57 With 17-Down, a temporary urban home
58 Characters in "Julius Caesar" and "The Merchant of Venice"
60 Stadium sounds
62 Close one
66 Spa: Abbr.
67 Like a prize-winning witch's costume
69 Rightful
70 Financial page inits.
72 ___ kwon do
73 Reams
74 Zip
75 Former Eur. carrier
77 Like very few games
79 Aldrin's craft
80 Strength
83 Lao-___
84 Sugar ___
85 Somewhat
86 Kick
87 Handful, maybe
88 It may be laid on thick
89 Scythe handle
90 Ogle
94 Word with pepper or paper
95 Covering
96 Intl. group since 1948
99 Voltaire, e.g.
102 Color of some hummingbird throats
103 Noted Civil War biography
104 First name in daytime talk
105 Start of a cheer
106 Site of a '70s revolution
107 "___ my case"
108 Violate a treaty, perhaps
109 Land of literature
110 One of the Ringling Brothers
111 They run in the blood
112 Pick up
113 Depilatory brand
114 Throw off

DOWN

1 ___ France
2 Charles and others
3 They have suns and red, white and blue fields
4 Small roll
5 Title site in a Sondheim musical
6 Tippy canoe area
7 Microphone inventor Berliner
8 Place to play b-ball
9 Charter Baseball Hall-of-Famer
10 "___ only"
11 They're bound to work
12 "___ Have to Do Is Dream"
13 Pasta dishes
14 Turkish pooh-bahs
15 W.W. II Axis members: Ugh Abbr.
16 Prizes for Tommy Tune
17 See 57-Across
18 Outlet
29 Accomplishments
30 A pusher may push it
32 Give more medicine
36 ___'acte
37 Annoyance
38 Recherche
39 Try
40 Basic Halloween costume
41 Breakfast offering
42 Divisions politiques
43 King called "le Bel"
44 Be rewarded at work
45 Ring around the end of a post
46 1996 biography "Citizen ___"
47 Spelling on TV
48 Med. nation
49 Hounds
56 Conditions
57 Any vessel
58 Coll. course
59 Ahas
61 Edge
63 Horace, for one
64 Sheepdog with fine matted hair
65 Wrong for the situation
68 Yacht's dir.
71 Catch slyly
74 Reply from Boris
75 Dins
76 This and that
78 "Step ___!"
80 Headdress, maybe
81 1974 hit by Chicago
82 Unaware
84 Bric-a-___
87 ___ Reader's Encyclopedia (classic literary reference)
88 N.H.L. team from Alberta
89 Rock guitarist ___ Ray Vaughan
90 Shoot
91 "Voila!"
92 "I Love a Parade" composer
93 "Touched by an Angel" co-star
94 Where to see "The Last Supper"
95 Lit
97 Decrease
98 Bishops' group
100 Beat it
101 Broiler
102 Guadalquivir and others

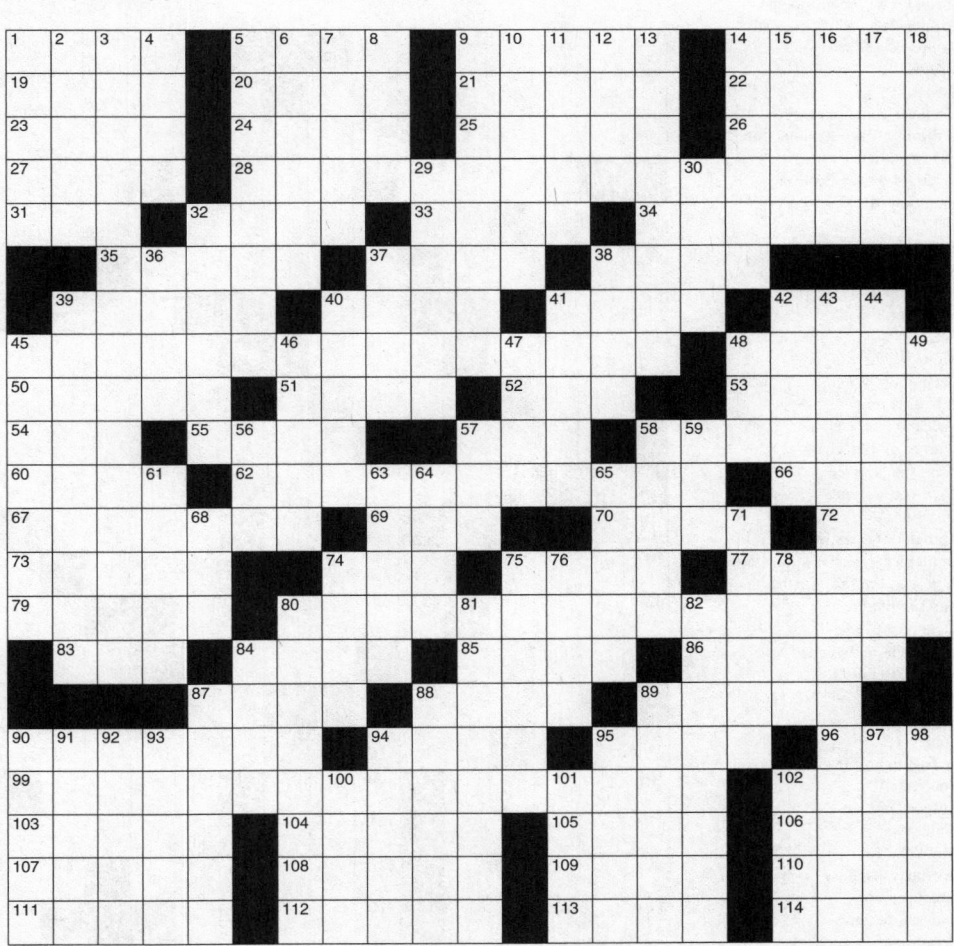

by Robert H. Wolfe

ACROSS

1 Unrehearsed
8 Clear, in a way
13 Two-time U.S. Open champ
18 Showing again
20 Starting again
21 Jump for joy
22 MAC
24 Action star Jean-Claude Van ___
25 Tear down, in England
26 Taro root
27 Mom's specialty
28 Palette color
29 ___ Na Na
31 HARD DRIVE
35 White-tailed bird
36 Site of the Outback Bowl
38 One
39 One-___
41 Baseball's Moises
42 Theater group, for short
43 Lugubrious
46 Asian open sedan chair
49 Wipe the floor with
50 With 87-Down, early commercialists
51 "Happy" first name
53 Place for a cashier, maybe
54 Author Auletta
55 Coups de grâce
56 BACKUP
58 Test killer
59 Vermeer contemporary
61 It means "place without water" in Mongolian
62 Wide shoe specification
63 Interviewed
64 CHIP
68 Some cuts
71 Anthem contraction
72 TV Maverick
73 Words on a quarter
76 Fire ___
77 MOUSE
79 Technique
80 A.C.C. team
82 Volcano near Catania
83 Warner on horseback
84 Press into service
85 "Are you ___ out?"
86 Discuss
88 Roman or Greek, e.g.
89 Not a picky specification
90 A year in the life of Attila
91 Tic-Tac rival
93 "The Last Supper," e.g.
96 "Somewhere in Time" actor
97 Har-___ (tennis surface)
99 WEB SITE
103 Legal point
104 Took on
106 Le Figaro article
107 Contender
108 Author Dinesen
110 Limber
111 NETWORK
116 Recruit's response
117 Luncheonette
118 Radiator features
119 Certain Art Deco works
120 Show off
121 Traveled by double-ripper

DOWN

1 Ball
2 Not agin
3 BIT
4 ___ run of bad luck
5 Bristle, botanically
6 Second-generation Japanese
7 Pol. designation for Sen. Jeanne Shaheen
8 Mark
9 Envelope abbr.
10 "The Young Man From Atlanta" playwright
11 Tracks
12 Nabber's cry
13 Noted ice cream maker
14 Conclusion of a term
15 HACKER
16 Bugs's foil
17 Grave
19 Not as accomplished
20 Shakespearean verb with thou
23 Soaking
29 Cheerless
30 Lunar phenomena
32 People of influence
33 Auto with Teletouch transmission
34 Eight is enough for this
37 Fix
40 Surrounded (by)
44 Executor, sometimes
45 Word in some magazine titles
47 ___ arch
48 Square
50 Church receptacle
51 FLOPPY DISK
52 "Mermaids" actress
55 Florida vacation spot, with "the"
56 Blackmailer, e.g.
57 1860s White House name
60 Get ready to fly
61 Shin armor
63 Scads
65 Bind, so to speak
66 Direct ending
67 Menace
68 Film director Nicolas
69 Doing
70 DIGITAL MONITOR
74 PRODIGY
75 Unfold
77 Soup for a cold
78 '40s–'50s TV drama sponsor
79 "Do ___ like"
81 Early spring sign
84 Opens
85 Word with bag or cap
87 See 50-Across
89 Best seller "Angela's ___"
92 Speaks impertinently to
94 Fall back
95 Uplift
96 Kind of price
97 Macduff was one
98 Hardship
100 Bad luck, old-style
101 "Cool!"
102 Kind of hemp
105 Mario of the N.B.A.
109 Not much
112 Suffix with bow
113 Up, as a vote
114 Tpke.
115 Either of two books of the Apocrypha: Abbr.

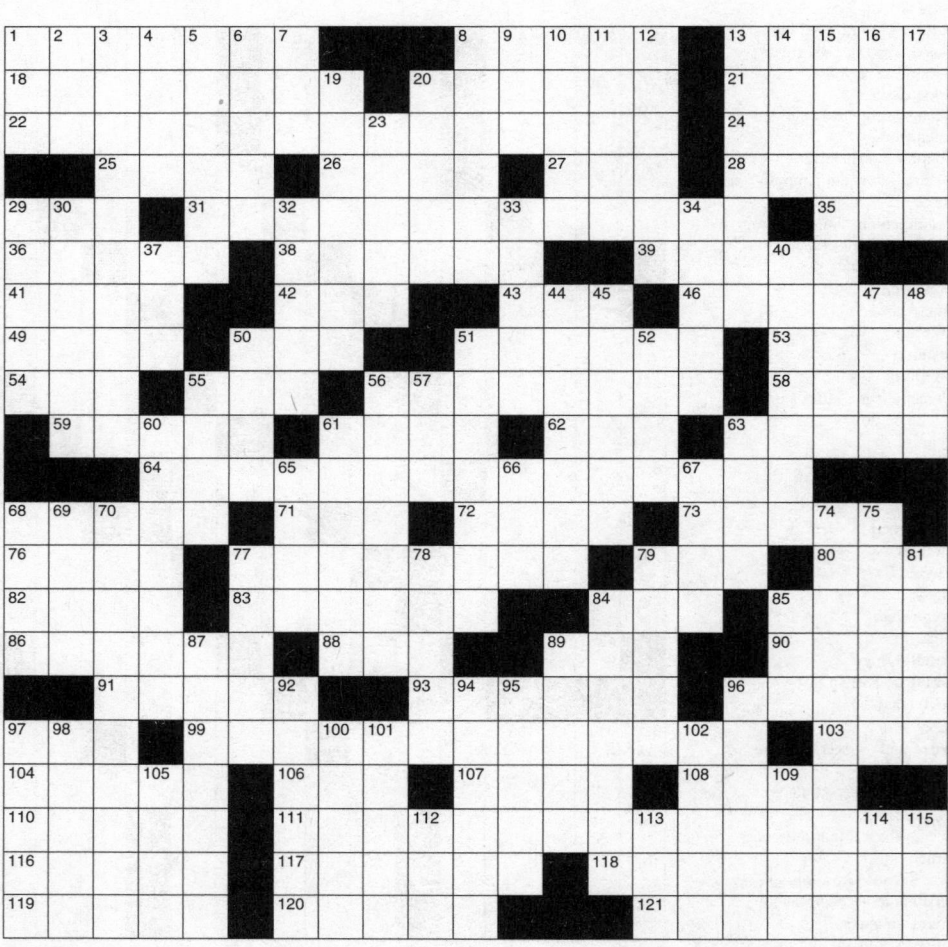

by David J. Kahn

ACROSS

1 Sleeping spots
7 Rats
12 Mark of official approval
18 White-knuckled
20 Pointless
21 Breathing aid
22 1944 film
25 See 45-Down
26 With 60-Down, bid
27 Blasted a hole in
28 Boots
29 "The Road Runner" background sights
33 "___ mud in your eye!"
35 Pitcher Fernandez
37 Fan letdown
38 "The First Wives' Club" members
40 Latin clarification
42 Make an outstanding design?
45 1965 film
51 Skirt
52 English churchyard features
53 Dealer in piece goods
54 Literally, "goddess"
55 They're toasted at luncheons
56 Shooting match
58 Domingo y lunes
62 Word of encouragement
63 City of northern Finland
64 Certain drop
65 Singer Jackson
67 1986 or 1994 film
72 Habituates
73 "James and the Giant Peach" author
74 Dole's Senate successor
75 Intl. air hub
76 Big name in video games
77 Golden ___ (seniors)
79 Ball throwers
80 It played the Platters' platters
81 Hoglike animals
84 Auto with models 900 and 9000
85 Locale of ancient Ur
86 1951 film
91 Unfair shake
92 Relaxation in 63-Across
93 Exciting experience, in slang
94 En-graved letters?
95 "That feels good!"
97 Was in knots
100 Recesses
103 If A = B and B = C, then A = C, e.g.
106 "Serpico" author Peter
108 Glass-___ Currency Act, 1913
110 Impolite reply
112 1948 film
118 Helmsman
119 Like some walks
120 Successful person
121 Bootlicker
122 Theroux's "The Happy ___ of Oceania"
123 Bay, county or city of Ireland

DOWN

1 Super Bowl XIV participants
2 Late bedtime
3 Daisy variety
4 Request to a guest
5 Kenyan independence leader ___ Mboya
6 Look for damages
7 Former Chief Justice Harlan ___ Stone
8 Breaks
9 More than nod
10 Contentious political assembly
11 Antivenins
12 British F.B.I.
13 First name in folk
14 Third Chinese dynasty
15 Two-time president of Texas
16 Snob
17 Actress Harper and others
19 Computer game ___ City
21 Isao ___ of the P.G.A.
23 Slangy turndown
24 Coming up
30 Crayola color
31 Canceled
32 Questionnaire datum
34 Author LeShan
36 "Edward Scissorhands" star
39 Strait of Messina menace
41 Iron: Prefix
43 "The Simpsons" bartender
44 With 111-Down, vulture or hawk
45 With 25-Across, voiced an opinion
46 Satanic moniker
47 Southern swarmer
48 Lull
49 Sympathetic sounds
50 A Turner
55 Pays the price for
56 Namesakes of a son of Adam
57 Swiss theologian Barth
59 Site of a famous flag-raising
60 See 26-Across
61 Real-life sailor on whom Crusoe was based
63 Words of praise
64 Paul I, e.g.
65 Pot contents
66 18, 19 and 20 of a series
68 Henry Clay, for one
69 West-central Texas city
70 Double fold
71 Challenger of the dragon Smaug
77 Boost
78 "The Pelican Brief" author
79 Case workers, for short
80 Arches
82 '90s film autobiography subtitled "My Story"
83 Bear of literature
84 Fish that sings when mating
85 Bit
86 Embodiment of impractical chivalry
87 They make calls from home
88 They're bright and full of energy
89 The Tar Heels: Abbr.
90 Mouths
91 Loud and rude
96 1944 Bing Crosby hit
98 Cuddly film creatures of 1983
99 Opium ___
101 Jostle
102 Historic rival of Florence
104 City near Provo
105 Vidal's "___ Breckinridge"
107 Prefix with -vert
109 Riot-stopping grps.
111 See 44-Down
113 Mid.
114 Wheaton of "Stand By Me"
115 Seasonal drink
116 Actress Thurman
117 Country singer McDaniel

by Matt Gaffney

ACROSS

1 Must
6 Dispute
10 Strip name
14 Thrash
19 Make suit, as a suit
20 Noted São Paulo-born athlete
21 Pastoral pipe
22 "God ___ refuge . . .": Psalm 46
23 Wingding
24 Jive men
25 Golf pro?
27 Play 18 holes of miniature golf?
30 Place for a lace
31 It's a matter of pride
32 Mr. ___ (old mystery game)
33 Rodents, jocularly
35 Weekend golfer's club?
41 Golf course?
45 ___ Chicago Grill (fast food chain)
46 Sunken treasure locale
47 Bouquet ___
48 French biography
49 Prepare garlic, perhaps
52 Victimizes
54 Stamps
56 Go quietly
57 Dino, to Fred and Wilma
58 Canaanite's deity
60 Bird holder
61 ___ del Corso, Rome
63 1770 patriot Attucks
66 The stuff of folk tales
67 Divots, for instance?
72 "___ gut" (German praise)
74 Nonets
75 ___ Gabriel
76 Where the action is
78 Recognizes
79 Overseas relative
82 Word before and after "of the"
86 Fails to
88 Preppy, e.g.
91 Robert Devereux's earldom
92 Woodworker's tool
93 Lacking fresh air
95 Approaching
97 Kind of scores
98 Golfer's coverup?
100 Nostalgic for golf?
103 "Slithy" creatures
104 Fine, informally
105 Staff
106 "King Solomon's Mines" plot line
109 Like some bad golf shots?
116 L.P.G.A. player?
120 Haphazard collection
121 Spotted animal
122 Corn
123 Hollow
124 Ivy League member
125 Daughter of William the Conqueror
126 "Er . . . um . . ."
127 Less than solid
128 Laze in the tub
129 Introvert

DOWN

1 Instrument held between the knees
2 Baseball brothers' name
3 Copy of a photo, briefly
4 Like a Car and Driver car
5 Spanish essayist ___ y Gasset
6 Abbreviation for a pound
7 Oviform : egg :: pyriform : ___
8 Quarter of a quartet, maybe
9 Check the boundaries again
10 Teacher, frequently
11 Federal agcy., 1946–75
12 Lexicographer's conclusion
13 Pother
14 Many a Beijing commuter
15 Out
16 Music category
17 Couch potato's passion
18 At one time, at one time
26 ___ pain
28 Rogers and Clark
29 Basic ___
33 Wharton degree
34 Swimmer's stopper
35 Arithmetic homework
36 Condo
37 Have ___ of (not allow)
38 "Ed Wood" star, 1994
39 Not easy to find
40 "Oh, right!"
42 The Land of the Blessed
43 Exactitude
44 New Hampshire college town
47 Grind
50 Popular tourist attractions
51 "Essays of ___"
53 Parting words
55 Ancient money
59 Act like
62 Last word of Shelley's "Adonais"
63 Take it easy
64 Mail abbr.
65 Graduating class: Abbr.
67 Old joke
68 Waiting
69 Storm dir.
70 Whiteheads, e.g.
71 Rest
72 Time's 1977 Man of the Year
73 Slowly destroy
77 Rather and Jennings, e.g.
79 Sri Lankan exports
80 Cross inscription
81 Memo starter
83 Org.
84 Furniture wood
85 Office phone nos.
87 Mrs. Walton of "The Waltons"
89 Wedding
90 Work areas
94 Blvds.
96 Brute
99 Verse part
100 By and large
101 Diet
102 Enthusiastic yes
106 Ventura County's ___ Valley
107 Composer Khachaturian
108 Pâte basé
110 It melts in your mouth
111 One of the Sinatras
112 Sign of impatience
113 Kind of mitt
114 Drop
115 Award of merit
117 First name in dictators
118 Meaning, for short
119 Brownie

by Karen Hodge

The New York Times

SMART PUZZLES
PRESENTED WITH STYLE

Available at your local bookstore or online at www.nytimes.com/nytstore

 St. Martin's Griffin

Crossword Solutions

1

```
AZALEA  ALABAMA  MILSAP
RETIES  SOMINEX  ONEIDA
PROVES  SWINGSETMISSES
 ONE  ARE   EASE  THINS
 HEADSETTAILS   ASIA
HOSTESS  ARMS   CANTBE
SUB  SITATOP  HASAT IRV
TREK  NOSES  BOLERO CIA
 CRU  CARETDRIVER  KON
DIKES  KPS  EASTER  RECD
ICEBAG   ANY    SEETHE
VATS  LACTIC  JLO  WAFER
INC  BALLETCHAIN   ELL
NSA  EZPASS  UNMAN  MEOW
EEL  LIONS  TRIEDON  AVE
DELETE   BLOC  ALIASES
 SSRS   ROCKETROLLER
WAIST  LEAH    REN  NAH
UNDERLOCKETKEY  GUISES
SEENAT  REMAINS  ESCORT
SWEEPS  USEDPOT  ROONEY
```

2

```
OLAV  APSE   AUTISM  CUR
PUNCHLINES  TRICIA  ANY
EXTRACTORTRAILERS  LTD
SEESTO  WOUK   TAUT  LIE
   STDS  COLEEXPORTER
ANDS  TRUCK  ETRE   DUH
PEACE  AIL  GETS  ONEAL
EXLAXATTITUDE  MONOCLE
TEMPI   NESS  LIV  NOLO
PER  MIST   AIRES   POS
QUICKEXCHANGEARTIST
PUN  TIKIS  TOON   TIC
AIDE  SEV  COEN  AMANA
SEERESS  GARLICEXPRESS
STRIP  CARY  SHA  YULES
SKI  MRED  STATE  SLAW
EXPATPAULSEN   TADS
NEE  HIND  LOIS  GOBACK
ANN  EXTENSIONHEADACHE
MOD  TILSIT  PROTRACTOR
INS  SEETHE  EWES  HEWN
```

3

```
COHOST  AGNATE   PATRON
AVANTI  DRIVER  ESSENCE
REVEAL  DININGALACRATE
AREAL   MOST    WATER
FRAMERINTHEDELL  NORSE
EAN  REN  GAD   STROLL
NED  AGAMEOFDRATS  LAS
 RASP  BIN  TIETO  ELLE
IPANA   EAST  ECON  DIO
DEFENDS  OURS  ANI ONME
ORO  GOTOWRAPSPEED  GIA
SERA  SEN  EDIT DRAGONS
GMT  ARAP  EDER  ROUGE
ARUM  GOLEM  ELI  ANET
SIS  WELLREGRADED  STD
ANIMAS   IRA   GAO  HEF
PECOS  ILLEGALRAMSDEAL
 RHINO   BEAN   METRO
PRATINGCOMPANY  SOURER
CORONAE  PRESTO  ENCASE
STINGS   SIPHON  ADEPTS
```

4

```
GUESTFEES  SADE  ABBOTT
ANAHEIMCA  CRIT  GOALIE
PIRATESOFTHECARIBBEAN
  POL  EBOOK  INSO
 TENDER  AOLERS  LOAMS
RIIS  WEB  LANCE  ENROL
ENV  EXECUTE  SATED TUO
INORDER  SERB  ORD  LST
COLONS  IFS  AIR  GENIE
EVITA  FRAT  BRET  RANK
SEGA  HARI  YEAH  SKEW
NARD  ATEE  FADE  MALTA
TRYIT  ESS  ODE  EILEEN
BID  SOO  TROY  WRESTED
ROE  NOTER  ADORERS TRA
ANNEE  TREVI  UAR  MESS
ESSAY  AIDING  MESMER
 SLAW  ZELIG  WIT
INDIANAJONESADVENTURE
TALENT  INNS  ONEDOLLAR
THIRDS  BEAS  LATETEENS
```

5

```
ELECTRA  OLEG  EMISSIVE
SAMOYED  NOTA  ACTUATED
SUBURBANBLAZERVENTURE
ODOR  ABAR  LEM   ROPER
 SWIG  REA  BIGHAIR
CIVICACCORDINSIGHT
HEW  JIG  KOO  SATIE OID
UTE  OSLO  MUS  NIL BVDS
SABLECOUGARMYSTIQUE
TOBE  OIL  TEAK  NORRIS
LIENORS  ANSEL  MEMENTO
ENDORA  BRAY  TIA  AMIN
FRONTIERSTANZAQUEST
EPEE  LAP  ATO  NOVA NSA
LIE  VALET  ESL  LIT TOG
INTREPIDRAMCARAVAN
ITSASIN   ASA   ROBO
BUBBE   MOM  AREA  JUNO
ESCORTMUSTANGEXPLORER
REDSAUCE  CYAN  PEEKSAT
GREENBAY  HOYA  ORDEALS
```

6

```
UMPS  PAVAROTTI   FALL
CERT  OVULATION   ILEA
STOOP  KEEPSATIT  OSIER
DESPISER  SHY  LEATHERS
RAPPORTS    MERSENNE
SMILEY☺  HORDE  ☺CREAMS
PACERS  MINIONS  HOTTIE
CIA   ENROUTE    OCT
ADLIB  SWEATBAND  LARKS
 NOPE  SMELL  IRON
COWSLIP  PRY   DUSTBIN
EVE  DATA   RIDE   ENE
DEI  ☺FACTS  FUNNY☺ LTR
ERGS   HICCUPS   BLED
WHITE☺  MAULS  ☺SAVER
HATCHET☺  REL  ☺POWDERS
OTT  CLOCK☺  ☺VALUE PAN
BERG  SWAM  ANAP  COCA
BRAID  ERAS  SSGT  FAQIR
LEILA  LDRS  TELE  USUAL
EDNAS  SSTS  USES  REELS
```

7

```
ATTACHE  PENPAL   CAPGUN
BOOSTER  EMERGE   ARIOSO
URBANDEODORANT    RIPSAW
SEAN   BAR   WEBPAGES
ERG  NEUROCONSERVATIVE
DOODADS  ALS   EAT  PET
ENE  MOPE   KEYNOTERS
THECURRYINGGAME   ERA
AURA   EEL   OUTRAGE
ENOLAGAY  SHEA   MENSCH
LCD  BUREAUBRIDGES   HOO
SHEILA   PROS   FASTTALK
PERCALE   ALI   OKIE
MSS  HOURLYMATRIMONY
COLONIALS   SEAT   ONE
ONO  OCS   JAL   NUDISTS
TOWNWITHOUTPURITY   OOH
PIONEERS   SIP   SLUE
MEAGRE  ALTEREDSTATURE
ACCESS  LOSETO   AERATED
STERES  SPOKEN   TRAGEDY
```

8

```
RECT   ARTIST   SKID  JAW
LOBAR  JEANIE   TYRO  UTE
AMERICANPINKCROSS   LOI
PERPLEXES   HUT   PING
DOTELL  WILLIAMOFPEACH
ITI  NOEND   OUNCES
SETPOINT  AEC   OGRISH
LEMONCREAMJACKETS   IOU
ERAS   ENV   EST   SILOS
DONTGO  SALMON   MAANDPA
MISTERMINTJEANS
PALAVER  INDIRA   ATHAND
SCONE  OTC   AVA   OLEO
SUV  AZURECOLLARWORKER
ERRATA  CMA   SPECTATE
INPAIN  TIARA   SST
MOODPERIWINKLE   TAMARA
POTS   ENO   IRRIGATES
IDI  ULTRALAVENDERRAYS
SLO  PERU   URANIA   AGLET
HEN  COON   VERSES   MELS
```

9

```
ACME   ARCA   CZAR  ATBEST
SLAPSDOWN  HUTU   LARDER
PARACHUTEPANTS   BRIDLE
ISR  HOG  MARINEMAMMALS
CHIT  CHAIS   RNA
AHI  PASTPARTICIPLE
AGENDAS  IWERE   ASSAIL
ADELAIDE  VITALE   ACNE
DAMASKS  MASSMARKETING
ABASH   BUTT   PLEX   FEY
THESTAGE   MASERATI
ESE  LEEK   PARE   MOCHA
PARALLELPARKS   TOPSPIN
SNIP   MARCIE   HALLPASS
OKAPIS  VIRAL   ORDEALS
MALLMANAGEMENT   SRI
ARI   VOLGA   ESSE
PAJAMAPARTIES   RUE  ATM
LIONEL  MAYFLOWERMADAM
ODENSE  ISPS  AABATTERY
TALESE  SHOO   PRES  ASKS
```

10

```
TATARS  SONATA   HMO  GEORG
OMELET  ARAGON   URI  RIVER
NEXTTONOTHING   NIL  ARENA
STERNO   STYES   LATERON
REEDS   ADLER   ALI   HUT
DIANA  HASTO   AIRMAN   ANE
ATBAT  FOLLOWINGUP   PUCE
DUCT  OLEGS   NCOS   TOILES
APSE   PARE   AFTERSHAVE
KEG  RETRO   IMPARTED
LIFTING  IRAE   PEAS   CONE
IDLERS   AMNESIC   BRETON
MOON  ETNA  MMES   TASSELS
ALPACINO   FAUST   ART
BEFORELONG   ACHE   ZETA
SCULLS  APER   STOOD   ALAS
ORNE  AHEADOFTIME   EPOCH
LID  SENSES   PLACE   LANKY
OTE  PEG   SERIO   ROGET
MERRILL   SONOF   REMISS
ORDER  EGO  BESIDEONESELF
NIOBE  REX   ORISON   UNTRUE
SAGAS   SEX   TSETSE   STATED
```

11

```
BRAG   DEBUG   CASK   CPAS
LUEGO  AROSE   ALEE   RODE
ISLEOFMANET   YANG   ILEX
NIA  APSE   SCENT   ITISI
DEPRESSED   TAN   RACISTS
ASSENT   JOHNNYCACHET
STENT   FETE   NEE   UMA
ROLAIDS   PATELLA
SHAY  PERSIANLAME   MATT
HONOREES   LAYLA   HASTA
ARGUED   ALINE   LISTEN
DROVE   CAPON   AMASSING
YORE  HYDEPARQUET   ENDO
RAGDOLL   SAUNTER
ORA  ASS   NOTE   OMITS
DOCTORFILLET   MARNIE
ALAMODE  AIL   STAIRSTEP
REBEL  LENTO   MADE   ORT
RAIL  CLAD   POISONPENNE
ERNE  HOSE   ENTER   FLEET
NYSE  EWER   DEERE   CODY
```

12

```
GOOGLE   ROUST   LAURA
PUTRID   EQUATION   ENRON
ARTIFICIALRESPIRATION
DETENTES   TIGERS
OVO  NOES   MECHANICAL
NIPPER   THEFIRST   ELLA
ATEAT  WEANED   GUNROOM
LARDS  WINCE   CLOSE   DUB
AMA   KINDA   MAEWEST
BITMAP   SYMBOLIN   SHIRT
ENOUGH   PAT   LIENEE
LARGE  TOGETONA   YENFOR
SOBERED   RIFLE   ORR
MBA  LOREN   VOTRE   MARIA
EARLDOM  PILEIN   OLMEC
SINE  POORMARK   INSANE
HOOTENANNY   AINT   LTD
DRAPES   DEPARTED
MAJORMEDICALINSURANCE
CROWE   RATIFIES   REHEAL
SPEND   YEATS   NYLONS
```

13

```
DNA  LUSH    SLEW  METTLE
RUG  ASSET   PARE  ALOHAS
ODERINTHECOURT    REDACT
LINED  SHROUDS    RICOTTA
LETSBE  ERNS   MINT  OAT
   CANIHAVESOMME   NITE
MATURED    SADLY   WISE
TEHEE   SOFA  SEX   TETE
GRAM   LORDHAVEMERSEY
    MEG  HINGE   BAZOOKA
SHE  AVONTOBEALONE  GEM
NOSTRIL    UNMAN    RRR
LETSGOYANGTZES    OOPS
 HALL  GIN  OXEN  HUSSY
 GERE  SONAR   ONASSIS
SUBS   GOGETEMTIGRIS
TAR  RELO   BURN  ARENAS
ONEFOLD  DIECAST  DAILY
LIAISE  CATCHMEIFYUKON
INKJET  ALEC  SADIE  ONO
DESIST   PIMA  MENS  NED
```

14

```
MASTER  ICUS   OPT  DRAKE
OCTANE  SPRAINED   RELET
SHALLOWBUSINESS   IDLES
EON   PAN  ANDIE   UPDOS
YODELER   TINTER   AWHO
  DONTHAVEACALLOWMAN
SCAGGS  UPI  HSI  ANENT
CERES  ALPACA     HST
ACTSO  BALLADMOUTHING
REF  NAB   RISE   ESPIES
FLIT  WALLETNURSE  SRTA
SILICA  ETYM   UPN  VAL
 AMERICASCALLUP  ORATE
    ETA   KNEELS  PANAM
MEADE  RTS   NNE  GROANS
 IMDALLYINGTOSEEYOU
GAMY  OSCARS    EMBLEMS
NIGEL  TRITT  MOC  PEA
CURAD  BALLROOMCLOSETS
SEEME  SCALABLE  UNSERS
ALDEN  AST  PEDS  BASSEY
```

15

```
 SNUFF   CATER   EPS  NEIL
 TAPIR   UTILE   RAT  ONME
BRIDGETJ[ONE]SSDIARY  FRAG
RELO  ENOS   ATTN   LOGO
EAT  IST  THELOVELYB[ONE]S
AKIND   WUHAN    EZER
MYPOINTANDIDOHAVE[ONE]
SONICE  LITERAL    GAS
L[ONE]SOMEDOVE SEARLE EVA
ALIAS   EGG   ROLE   LAY
LIMP  THENOSPINZ[ONE]  DALI
ANI  BOOR   ARF   SETON
LEA  ATRISK  [ONE]TRUETHING
ARN  RESCUES   HASBRO
 ANDTHENTHEREWEREN[ONE]
 URDU   DEANE    ENNEA
AROOMOF[ONE]SOWN  CAP  COD
TSAR  LISP   IVAN  RONA
BURN  METALKPRETTY[ONE]DAY
ALEE  ERE  AFROS  ISLET
YARD  COP  SCENT  CLYDE
```

16

```
MOPED  ONESEC   GIRL   MRI
OCULI  RECALL   ADIA   YEN
BALLETBARRIO   PLAYGOLF
INLETS   TUG  SWEETIEPIE
LATS  HRE   TEE   ANTICS
EDA  ZIONMASTERS  TOAST
 ABSORB  ELKS  ALOOF
 TOTEBAG   AHAB   FLAP
SLAM  ROLAIDS   BERMUDA
SPAT  GTO  ROTE  RAYGUN
CURIOFORTHECOMMONCOLD
ARIOSO  SEAN   BAN  ASTA
LOANERS  STEPDAD  PSIS
ANTI  CPAS   LORELEI
 STEEL   REEL   FANOUT
ANGLO  CAMERALIONS  SOT
MORAYS   ODE  ARD  SHAH
EVENSTEVEN  FOG  RATEDR
LEADROLE  OLDGRAYMARIO
INT  UNIT  SAILED  ALIEN
AAS  SEAS   EXCEED  TENSE
```

17

```
CAPRA  SABOT   ATMS  REAP
OSIER  PIANO   CROC  EASE
MATTE  IDLER   HAMOFFRYE
ONHANDREMARK   PARALLEL
 LAUER   LENA    CRO
TAOISM   FLYOFFTHEWALL
ARIA  ALII   BREWED  REA
RENTS  ATRIA   WAR  SIAM
TAKEONTHEGLOVES  BLADE
 CITE  NADIR   SEINES
MANACLE  POSED  FERMENT
ABASES   FORKS   ERLE
NOSIR  RELEASEDOFFBAIL
ILSA  HID  NAKED  TRIPE
ALA  SOCIAL   ENOL  ALSO
CAUGHTONGUARD   ORISON
 RAW  ERNO   SWAIN
DESOLATE  KNOCKOFFWOOD
ONPUTTING  AMEER  LARVA
NYET  EDIT  LINED  ESSEN
SAWS  REDO  SETTS  SHONE
```

18

```
SOBERS   LAKME   AGELINE
ALANON   ONION   COLANUT
FINDSABOTTLEONABEACH
AVI  SKIPIT   LEDA  BLEU
REST  INE   EDGE   DOERS
ISHALLGRANTYOUONEWISH
  RAY   LISP   SPUN
ASTI  LOOS   FEEL  PSAS
PEACEINTHEMIDDLEEAST
ROAN  LSU   LAV   RANTO
ELF  AMAPOFTHEAREA  JIG
POESY   PRO   CUR   FOGY
IGRANTYOUANOTHERWISH
NYNY  REMS   UBER  ABET
 GIAN   PITA   UKE
THECUBSINAWORLDSERIES
HOURS   ASOF   OOH  SNAP
OLGA  DINT  DOGNAP  TSE
LETMESEETHATMAPAGAIN
ONEILLS   LATTE   EVOKED
WESTIES   CLEON   DETERS
```

19

```
SALUTE  CULT    SODDEN
PRESENT BRIEFS SPRUCE
INTENSIVESCARE SPOTON
NOTDO BARA BANS ONCLE
   RAIN KAPOW NEH
CASA MASKINGPRICE CIE
ATPLAY ELISE PANDORA
CHILLSTREET BENTOVER
HOROL REPS PLUS JEST
ESOTERIC TAOS ISONTO
   GAMESHOWGHOST
CACHET ISUP HURRAHED
OBOE UVEA BMOC AMOCO
BELLROPE FRIGHTFIELD
OLDDEAR EELER REDRAG
LES BROOMSERVICE ESTE
   CDE ABITE LAYS
MOREL RENI IMIN APSES
OTELLO SEVENYEARWITCH
WHALER EMAILS LETTUCE
NOMADS LSAT MOANED
```

20

```
BIOLAB SNOB CASH EFS
IGNORE AURA ASTI DOWD
COERCE AMAN LEAN SUER
  THESTATENISLANDFERRY
ECON NCR SKI ILOVE
THU MANHATTANTRANSFER
CARROL ILIE ONUS
  OWES GRINSAT IRE
ABRONXTALE GIS ENNEAD
REEF ORO DOC TURISMO
RUNTHENEWYORKMARATHON
ALERTLY EAT JAM SONG
SAGEST SLY PROMQUEENS
  HEE OOHLALA ITLL
  OREO ARCO REFITS
FIVEBOROUGHCOURSE NOS
ENERO NED NTH AARE
ATREEGROWSINBROOKLYN
TOON LEVI DORA AEGEAN
SINO APES AGIN KNEADS
  TAW DONE HOOK SORROW
```

21

```
JAMESFOX TILLAGE QTRS
ADAMSALE AMOEBAE WRAP
NORTHWESTPASSAGE EAVE
IRT AKA AIRES ARLEN
SNIPPET UNITEDWESTAND
  RESEAT OREILLY
JAPED BEDE STLO SHE
IHOP AMERICANCHOPSUEY
GEL SPAY PORT EARLE
SMELLARAT LIESTO RPMS
  VIRGINWOOLSWEATER
LIAM EATING TIPTOEING
ETUIS COIF NEET SOO
DELTABLUESSINGER LEVI
AMT LIEN TROI AIDAN
  ALFATAH OTITIS
SONGOFSOLOMON MRMAGOO
OXBOW ELENA POE ERN
LIAR CONTINENTALDRIFT
ODEA PROTEAN ALLATSEA
SERE ROBERTO RESTSTOP
```

22

```
  BRAGS ADELA IPOD JESTS
PIEMAN LUMEN MERE UPTON
ULTIMO EMBODIMENT GIJOE
SKIDMOREBANANAPEEL SOLE
SENSATE BRA CCS REACHER
ERAT LAE RAU SECONDS
SSE SEAPLANE LEE RIPS
  NAVYBLUEBLAZER DAWNS
BYGONES SWASTIKAS LOON
LEADEN BASE DEO RNA
TATI OAFISH BLACKTOP
  COLGATETOOTHPASTE ESSE
LIBELERS DRAGON
ORR ANI WOO ARTE TOPTEN
LAOS ASCENDANT POPEYED
LEWIS HUNTERGATHERER
  NDAK ETH TERRAPIN PCS
LABELED ELY YDS CLAP
AMASSER PLO ORT ISRAELI
REGT NOTREDAMEHUNCHBACK
INGER WEAVESAWEB ROADIE
ADEPT SADE ANOSE INLETS
TERSE ETAL PINER MEADE
```

23

```
RABBIT COMESTO SCALD
ELLERY SHRAPNEL ELDER
TAILOR HIGHTOPSOCIETY
AMMAN SERA BEER MAMA
POPTOPWARNER ENNOBLED
  ERRORS GEE APE
REDDEER BOXTOPTURTLE
OUR ZEBRAS TRUES VAT
ALAST MIS GAIL IROC
RAGTOPPICKER SLAPDASH
  SARAH HELIO UBOLT
GOTRIDOF TIPTOPONEILL
INRE NOUS PIS ERNIE
LEI SUERS JESUIT GMS
LAPTOPDANCER HOLYSEE
  ORT AUD SPORES
SHOWBOAT BIGTOPKAHUNA
YARN IDYL RALE RAKES
BLACKTOPBEAUTY INPAWN
ILLAT BEAMMEUP SEESTO
LEERS EARFULS ODDEST
```

24

```
BOOTH OWL VENUE SUPERB
RABBI XII EXERTS ANDREI
ATEAM YDS LOUISA LOSETO
GEL IGET RRS RIMS LOM
ANIMATE WACO IAGO TORE
  CHINACABINETCONTENTS
NCAA IBARS PIER RAG
FOOTBALLCHAMPIONSHIP
ALL NES STNS ATOLLS
DOASIDO ADAGIO PRETEEN
  TOR ACELA MOOED DEAL
THOROUGHFAREINNEWYORK
SEEP MASSE BIZET REM
SCALPER RHONES OUTEATS
ESPIED HERE FEN RAH
  GRAVEYARDINDODGECITY
AHS EARL ODEON OOZE
OLDTELEVISIONANTENNA
NEDS EPEE TROT MYSTICS
AVE MASH MAC OPEC FLA
BINGED OCULAR JAR STEAL
ENDURE SINISE ALI TEARS
TEASER VICES ILL PARKA
```

25

```
REFITS  TURBAN  MDC EKG
EMILIO  OREIDA  AIRBALL
LIFEOFMYLIGHT   CROATIA
RINGTOSS  OTB   ECHOED
  EAST    PACEOFCHANGE
USM  HIATAL  ROUTE
PLACEOFPRIDE    ESTATES
PYRITE  SALADOIL  TOLE
ELIDE LEMS ITA  CORNER
RYE RIO   ATOM  ENIGMA
  CENSUSOFTHEBUREAU
CAUSAL  ABLE   MTV  ELF
HURTLE HIE GELS  OTTER
EDIE  ALTEREGO  STRIVE
FIESTAS  RATOFTHEYEAR
  AGNES  MANTRA   DRE
BATTLEOFHEAT    AKIM
WREAKS  FEE   ALIENATE
ACACIAS  ARRIVALOFTIME
NESTEGG  RIOTED  FEELER
ADE  SOT  SEDERS  FRYERS
```

26

```
SOARS  SPAT  TRAM  LISAS
ATRIA  TOUR  HALE  EVERT
SOAPY  ALDA  ORCA  MANIA
HOMEWORKISDUEONMONDAY
ALI  HOT  THO  ASIN  INE
YES  EZRA  TYRA  INTONED
  INEEDAVOLUNTEER
AJAR  KIN  USDA   ATEST
COBALT  ETTU  IBMS  OATH
ANYQUESTIONS  SALE  REE
DESIRED  CODAS  YODELER
ESS  EMAG  NEXTTIMETYPE
MEET  SKIP  REAR  ONHOLD
ESSEN  BENS  RIA   ONES
  SEEMEAFTERCLASS
BEASTLY  SLAB  KITH  TOM
ATM  CASK  NBC  ENO  EPA
YOUDONTNEEDTOKNOWTHIS
SILAS  EENY  IDEA  BARAK
ALERT  RENE  DENT  IRATE
TETES  YSER  ERTE  ZONED
```

27

```
WHOSWHO  GDANSK  THOMMCAN
AREAS  RUBATO  SEARCHME
SAINTNICHOLAS  TARTARUS
ACNE  ASTRAY  TASS  TILT
TEESHOT  SCALE   SEE
  BOUGHSOFHOLLY  ETTA
HOOHAS  TRUFFLE  ADAMS
BRAN  HEAROF  MARINA
OILINESS  ERRING   SHA
COLONY  APHORISMS  USED
ALENE  CHOCAHOLICS  ONHOLD
MELS  HORSESHOES  PURPLE
PSU  AMENDS  TEAROPEN
  JAMESI  HORRORS  BEND
SANTE  ATLARGE  PERES
HOCHI  CHOOCHOOTRAINS
LUC  AWING  ASLOPE
ETHOS  AGED  ROASTS  ERAS
STRAPSIN  HAPPYHOLIDAYS
ULULATES  AMIENS  HOGTIE
PESETAS  TSETSE  PEENS
```

28

```
LAPSES  AMBLED  RAMPAGE
ICEAXE  SERIES  IMMOVED
REPROACHMOTEL  PEDXING
ASSAD  LEON  RON   LIE
  HUMANITARIANREPAID
ERA  SOP  RESORT   ARA
RIFF  OPS  SWEET  IMSET
GOTTAREPEATANDRUN  ONE
STEMS  DUMB  NAXOS  FUSE
RECT  RAIN   LETINON
REPAIRINGDIRTYLAUNDRY
ACADIAN   LOWE   SPAS
CARE  CASCA  BORA  ALGER
EST  REPLACETABLECLOTH
RHYME  TIRED  AFT  YORE
  IBM  DETEST  AUK  DEA
REPLAYSITONTHELINE
ATE  FUN  PELF  IVANI
THEMOON  REPELSALVADOR
SATUPON  BERTIE  SEDATE
ONEMPTY  SWEEPS  USERID
```

29

```
SECT  ADOLPH  TILL  CARB
ELLA  SONORA  ISAY  ALOU
RAISETHEPOT  ENTRENOUS
BLOTTO  FEEDTHEKITTY
  ERUPTS  SRI   SEN
USC  ENSILE  ONCE  DEBTS
NIA  DIVAS  SWAMI  SUET
MELDS  SOLTI  IRONS  CPU
AGLOW  ORNATE  SHAKEN
NETGAIN  MATCHTHEANTES
  HENNAS  GRE  SIRRAH
BREAKTHEHOUSE  STOKEUP
REBREW  RONDOS  NIOBE
IVE  ROWEL  EVADE  ANDOR
NUTS  SANYO  ELATE  DAM
GESTE  DATA  REMAIL  STS
  EDS  OHO  NELLIE
DRAWTHEFLUSH  ENTERS
MESAVERDE  CUTTHECARDS
VEER  ENID  AMAZON  IMAN
SLAT  POCO  REBUTS  LASS
```

30

```
ALLAT  HEMIC   DAPPLE
MEANER  PACINO  PAPERER
INTONE  IRONON  IMPROVE
DIVINGBELLE  TAKES  SAC
NIN  IOTA  PORE   PENT
FIAT  SWINEFLUE  SPLATS
CTN  ATEE  SEARS  CAEN
CESARE  SATAN   ARCADES
  CIRC  BORNEFREE  CAT
APRIL  OAR  ELATED  ORR
LAUD  SUMAC  ROSIN  ANTA
PEN  STRADA  ITS  FISHY
HAN  CASTELOTS  TALL
ANIMATE  CARET  RASCAL
NAPE  WRITE  RASP  HCL
ANGLES  EITHERORE  REED
SOLE  BPOE  ETON  AST
SRA  PRATT  WESTWARDHOE
EMPEROR  AVIATE  LINING
TASTERS  CALVED  STEREO
SLEAZY  TYLER   TRESS
```

31

```
WAIF  SETTO   CRAB  LENT
ALTI  AFOUL   SHULA CLAY
IDENTIFIEDITASAGSHARP
TORNADO STRIPES LANCE
   THRO OAF    ROI
WROTEITDOWNFROMMEMORY
EUROS  DAN  INON   TAO
ESTD FIST SANER SATYR
USEOFTWOHANDSANDANOSE
NEG  IRON  YODEL  ENT
STANDON LUCID HASIDIM
  AGO MASON RARE ONO
WHILEPLAYINGBILLIARDS
HADAT ADORE ABLY REOS
OIL  USAF  SLO  SAMOA
AREQUIEMFORHISPETBIRD
  UTE  MAI  ELAL
CLEAN MOANING AREARUG
BYTHEROLLINGOFTWODICE
EROO EDGES LOTTA ZEST
RANG PEAS  ESSEX ENDS
```

The Mystery Person is WOLFGANGAMADEUSMOZART

32

```
FONTS SUPS  DRAB   TOSS
INOIL THAT  OENO  DARNS
CINCO YOGACLASS  OXBOW
HOCKTHEHERALDANGELS
ENESCO  STRIDE   USA
   ALKA OAS  PLOWMEN
AFRAIDOFTHEDOCK   ERO
DCL  DOFF  DISH   HANS
ACA INRI BRUSH  AUDIT
LEWISANDCLOCK  ECHOER
SAN VIP AEC ALE    WPA
HITMEN MAKESPOCKSFLY
OLMOS POLYP RACE   DOL
TAOS  COMO  MESO   ICE
AMC  GREATWHITESHOCK
TAKEAIM HES   STEM
   LUC COACTS  WISETO
BOCKSUPTHEWRONGTREE
GRAPH AIRSTREAM  OATES
PAREE BNAI  EDYS STENT
AWED  UGHS  DESK HESSE
```

33

```
OLAF  YUP  BARO  SHE SRA
MASERATI OVERSEAS   HED
NOSYORINQUISITIVE   AMO
IST DRLAURA  GONE  SPAR
  CEO FIN MIDEASTERN
WINDOWCOVERINGS   KOOKS
ODORS  HRE  ISAY    INF
ESSO TIER POL  ORDEALS
   MSEC WALKEUNE   ABIE
ISH TAKERSOUTPOSTGAME
SCOREPADDISTAUNPEELED
LATEWORDNCERUPEON   LYS
ALEC TEYNNERS   KNOB
MELROSE SWF PEND  RAGE
 FUN  HTML OTE   GABLE
STOIC HEADOFTHEPRISON
CARTESIANS  APE  LAD
ANDS CARD STIRSUP  ATT
RKO DOTSINTHENIGHTSKY
EEG BLUENILE  EMISSION
DDS LDS SHOR TIN   EASE
```

34

```
CANE  MENSA BRAVA  AGAR
ARAT  ICAHN RUPEE  MERE
SIGH NOPRIORESSRECORD
ASSISI  UMM  DETOX  MED
BEACHCOMBINE    BITES
ANT EAVE SIEG   RISOTTO
CARESSMANUFACTURER
SRA SNOW  YEOW     RYES
PEEPS NATO  SODAS
REVOLTS PIPETTESQUEAK
EYETOOTH VID  SAYUNCLE
PALETTEAROUND  LEAFLET
  HEAVE  MAAM   TRACT
ETNA  LEIA ROSA    ETS
GREGORIANCHANTEUSE
GETEVEN STOP ORTO  WOW
SCRUB  SUPERBOWLINE
APO LOADS REV   BSIDES
MASSEUSEHYSTERIA  BETS
ASTI NEMEA IRISH  ELEE
PSST DAISY TYSON  LYNX
```

35

```
SAMOSA SLAPDASH  AGITA
PEAHEN NILEBLUE  TONES
ANDMAKEITSNAPPY  ENACT
REA SLEPTON HESS  ESSO
TIM CENSER  TAR   CUSP
ADELA RACY    FINELY
 APOP SNAPPER   ONION
BIGDEAL NEHRU    ITGO
EVIL SAVEME ANIN  LSAT
LOVES YAXIS  RETIREE
TRE PAINTS HASSLE  CEL
INASTIR QUOTA    PROVO
ACTI ISLA UPHOLD  ONEG
NASL ALCEE   ARIADNE
ALOES FATLESS  DENS
 IMSURE ARPA    ATRAS
ECRU SSN AGORAS   AVE
ASTR MICA ANILINE  DEA
ILIAD DEFICITSPENDING
LIMNS ONETASTE  ASIAGO
STEEL LESSTHAN  REELED
```

36

```
 CHARTER  THAT   INUSE
THENERVE  HOLE   NIGER
WRONGTOEVERSPLITTHEM
OUR LOIS  GOTO THE PIU
KEEPER  BONE  BEERCANS
ISTOBESELDOMLYUSED
AEC  JAL   ROSE    RTS
ISMOREORLESSOK    AAA
GUINNESS WHONEEDSTHEM
UNREAL READERS   LEOVI
ADA SOSO   OSLO    PES
NETTY SPORTIN  GIJANE
AREIMPORTANT CARRACER
MAR  ARENTNECESSARY
CSI ELIO  LOO    CBS
TOENDSENTENCESWITH
ELEGISTS LEAR  LOAFER
OLD EKE ATAD IDLE  AYE
ALLTIMEWORSTMISTAKES
RESET SORE  ANNEALED
STUDS PLOD  NOTEPAD
```

37

ERITREA ITSLATE PAGES
VETOERS NATASHA AROMA
INCOMETAXRACKET SIDED
COHN UNSER FOSSE LEI
TIESINTO TAO HOMERS
SRS THENOELPRIZE ASST
TEL KNEE DOALLS
GRIM CHIT SAIN ETAS
ORIN CHEESEURGERS MUS
MANHOLES WIT DISSECT
ANKARA SPRITES SOURCE
HOOTERS HUN TEENSIER
ALF LOOMINGDALES ICEE
ADES CELS ICON MEAD
IDEALS OHOH SEQ
SISI LEAKFORECAST RDA
GOATEE NFL LOWSPEED
TDS NEATO LOPER ACED
MATTE FATHEROFTHERIDE
ATEAM ALTERER AMMETER
JERRY RESTSON SOIREES

38

WNBA GERE ACME MOMENT
OEUF OLIN SLIP AMALIE
WARRENFACTIONS RACINE
SPRITE SRI POT CHOSEN
CAAN YES LESHAN
BATTENPRACTICE WYES
ICON GIT LLANOS HARA
MINSTREL AMA NABOKOV
ATE RAVENMANIAC YOUDO
MYDEAR ION VUE APTER
TIERACK CASSINI
ITSON AGE FAN TOEING
SHANE PARTONSHOTS COM
LANDERS ALA ALOEVERA
ANDI ATBATS ATL IRAN
MESS CARRIONCHARGES
OVERIT MET SOMN
ESCROW ECO HIE DANIEL
STADIA FISSIONLICENSE
SORELY ENTO NOON SOPS
OPERAS REED SSTS ERNS

39

(P)WATCH OPENSEA HOT(P)
SAHARA ERRATUM OLAV
ISOMER NOTRARE OSTE
ZOOMS MOVEIT REHEAT
ENTITLE ESTE ICANSO
ASA AMOCO
SPERMBANK ARA ESPO
CACAO SNAPOPEN ZHOU
ALOTOF ASOF LEGREST
GENERIC BOFF NEARTO
REVISAL LEGO REF
(P)PCS EIGHTBALL AIR(P)
KIA EMIT ALTOIDS
NEPALI SABE ISEENOW
ICERINK FLAP HAVETO
FERN UNCLETOM NEVIN
ESSO TOO SPICERACK
GETIT ENS
POINTB FOOD DATSUNS
INDOOR FEVERS HANOI
COLD EDUCATE YELLED
KNEE AERATED ETOILE
(P)ERS KEEPERS PANTS(P)

(P) = POCKET

40

PLEBE CLANG FRET SAP
DONALD EIGER LETO PLO
QUAKIERSTATE OSCULATE
BECK NOAHS HOI CARAT
ALTER DRESSIERDRAWERS
CLERIC LINDY EON
HAD COSBY OLDEST ORES
FORTE SWEATIERVEST
TOO DOGMA RYAN CESTA
TRIG OLEARY PARTON
HULL BITTIERPILL BOND
IMPALA NARNIA URIS
SPUME POCK TOANY YEA
BUMPIERCROPS WEEKS
EPPS RETIRE KERRI FED
SLO MENDE STEELY
COCKIERSPANIELS SUDAN
AVAIL DOS ONEUP RONA
COSMICAL BOXIERSHORTS
TIE COIF BRINK IMPART
IDS ANNA SONGS MESAS

41

ALEWIFE FLEWIN MARLIN
RENAMES IOLANI EROICA
IANTHETERRIBLE GABLER
ONETOTEN NCAA BABIYAR
SEAS ETD ISTOO NOGO
ODD HOMEOFTHEBRAE FEW
COO ROO INHEAT
MADISON NEPAL EYESHOT
AGRA LONESOMEDOE TERI
ARI FARO ROTI SPRAIN
NEEDY ALBATROSS GOLFS
DERAIL TOME CHAS LIT
POEM OPENINGMOES DECA
ANDORRA EDDIE SPRAYER
UNHAND LES EON
SAC ENDINGMACHINE WCS
TRAM AFIRE EAT SHIH
OCTOPUS COMA KASHMIRI
OHIOAN YOUONLYLIEONCE
GEORDI ELNINO ILLTELL
ERNEST HEDREN CODERED

42

HIDEHO LATERON PRESSURE
OCELOT EXOTICA ROTHIRAS
WENTSTRAIGHTUP OBEISANT
ESTOP AHS LESS AANDE
NINNY SAWASLIGHTLOSS
SCH TUG APGAR OTOES
TOOKABEATING PLURALS
AVRIL MONIES FOAL EDIT
SEAT ASAN SPRINT SPOSA
INCHEDAHEAD FELLSHARPLY
SSE PELL DOH BEY EMOTES
MOST WEREHOT ALIS
ONEACT CAL PAZ TAPA CRI
LEDTHERALLY GOTHAMMERED
OASTS RAKEIN OISE SOTO
GLEE BANS PILATE ASCII
YELLSAT GAVEUPGROUND
CRETE SEGOS LEM SAO
REACHEDANEWLOW DANSE
ANNUL LORE IAN DEERE
SUSPENSE GAINEDMOMENTUM
PREPPIES ORVILLE MAINST
SELASSIE TSETSES CLEATS

43

```
RAILSAT  DRILL   APOGEES
ALTOONA  EASES   CAROUSE
DISGUSTOFWIND    CLAIROL
SAYIT   LILT    REACT
  CHARLESINDISCHARGE
AHS  ESTAS   COPSE   LAOS
NOTONCE   QTIPS    NONUS
GOLFDISCOURSE    IRONORE
SHUT    AVIA    PRETENDS
TAKE  SIRENS    ARIAS
  SERMONONTHEDISMOUNT
   ANILS   EXUDES   LEAP
APOSTATE   SAME    NANA
LIFTERS   TRUMPDISCARDS
INGOD   REAPS    SPORTED
SNAP  FAIRY   OSLIN   OME
TABLEOFDISCONTENTS
   INSTS   ODEA   ACTAS
CIAGATE   BLOODDISCOUNT
TIGHTER   BERRA   ROTUNDA
RIOTERS   SASSY   ECSTASY
```

44

```
LIFTS  ALGA  AGAPE   USSR
APRIL  SEES  REPOS   SOLO
BOOTEEINTHEBEAST    ADOS
   LEAF   SEC   TSOS  AVE
THEPRINTSONTHEPOPPER
SEEDY  COO   UEY   PHONE
ACR  CAN  MKTS   GSHAPED
THETAURUSINTHEHAIR
  SABLE   TROY  MADE  POT
CHASED  GREW  RILE  GOBI
LITTLEREADWRITINGHOOD
OKIE  SONY  HUNS  DOOLEY
PEP  MAYO  AITS  MIDST
  JACKANDTHEBENSTALK
ISAIDSO  AWES  ALG  BAA
MAMBA   DNA   MRT  MOLDY
THEEMPERORSNUKELOWES
HAN  SEXY   HOE   DIRE
ERIS  RUMPLEDSTILTSKIN
RATE  PLOTS  ALEC  ATONE
ENYA  STPAT  TINE  LONGE
```

45

```
ARI  ELIO  WHAM   SHEDD
SULA  MINX  HILO  SCARE[ON/OFF]
PILLSBURYBAKE[ON/OFF] PALACE
INTOTO  EMOTES   DINESIN
REREADS  OKA   INTRUDE
EDY  PIKER  DATIVE   RES
  WHEEL[ON/OFF]ORTUNE C[ON/OFF]ERS
AUDI  SEN  SANTE   BIC
CREPT  TOBAGO   FENDED[ON/OFF]
TAPER[ON/OFF] RAG  ISAAC  LIE
ENO  USETHE[ON/OFF]SWITCH  URI
DIS  SPUES   HAS[ON/OFF]ENDER
[ON/OFF]CENTER  TEASET  SEES[ON/OFF]
   AMC  BEECH   NIE  ISTS
LARGE  SAWN[ON/OFF]SHOTGUN
ECO  LAREDO   ORLOP   SWF
[ON/OFF]CAMPUS   MOM  EMPOWER
ARREARS   BAILEE   AEROBE
RUSTLE  DESSERTANDC[ON/OFF]EE
DEARER[ON/OFF]SET  ETUI   HERS
OSTER   STAS  DADA   DST
```

46

```
EPOPEE   NED   TEETHES
MARINES  ICES  POWERADE
QUICKCENTURY   AGELIMIT
ULNAE  QURANDURAN   PRES
AVG  AUTO   RES   PLA
DISABLE   SCAN   NEEDLE
  QUILTBYASSOCIATION
OCCURS  RESTS  DON  SOTS
PARA   TOAT   HOTEL
QBERTANDROEPER   VIABLY
ROPIEST  OLDER  SEABLUE
STEAMS  QUESTBATHROOMS
   PIVOT   NAPE   LIEN
INIT  SIP  IMAGO  CRISTO
QEDHOTCHILIPEPPERS
SALEMS  POTS   RESHOOT
OSS  MOO   LEIS   URU
RAVI  QANDABEARS  OATER
APERTURE   QUITYOURSELF
MITERING  INRE  NASTASE
AGONIZE   TEX   ROOTED
```

47

```
PRIEST  BOSS   EVER  WOK
RONDOS  CRATE  DELAWA(R)E
UNCELEBRATED   IRISHSEA
DIOR  TAO  RAMBO   HIHAT
ENG(L)ISHCHANNEL  SOLIDS
  ERE  KEN   STEELMEN
BRR  ASSERT   NOODGES
AHEM  ORBITS  SCAN  TAU
CELIBACY  C(H)ICKEN  ROSE
HAYFORK   ELOI   AUNTS
   FAMOUSCROSSINGS
MOSES   SOHO   NAUTICA
APED  TAGTEAM  HANNIBA(L)
GEL  AIDA  EDISON   CARP
ICEDTEA   SHOERS   RDS
  CO(L)UMBUS  EEK  UPI
CATNAP  ONEARMEDBANDIT
ORION  ORALB  DOI  SOME
ABORTIVE  JULIUS(C)AESAR
CONSIDER  USURP  OTTERS
HRS  CANS  KEGS   NESSIE
```

48

```
CUSS  LOKI  ABOMB  KAFKA
OSHA  IWIN  RANEE  ILIAD
DEARSANTA   THEANSWERIS
  BRITISHWAITINGLINE
YESES  EFS   AYS   WAH
   NOES  ATRIAL  PALE
SECONDPERSONSINGULAR
EEEE  STAY  ISH  EUCLID
ARYL  VNECK   PROWSE
TAOIST   OOLA  AMAT  WES
OPRAHWINFREYSMAGAZINE
NEE  TOTE  KILO  EVONNE
  MIRAGE  NANCY   WOES
CALICO  ATA  ITOO  INAT
DRINKWITHJAMANDBREAD
LOVE  MENACE   SASE
IDE  BRA   COM   ENATE
  WORLDWIDEWEBPREFIX
RAINYSEASON  NONVERBAL
BORIC  INLET  SHOE  OILY
ILENE  TEARS  ARMS  SATE
```

49

```
ASEA  RIDER   SHARE  ABIT
SENDSANOTE    HONOR  CONE
PROJECTMANHATTAN     CRUX
CUR  NIH  STARTER   DEIST
AMMO  EEL   SPIN    MOSSES
       DISCOUNTSENIORS
LAMENTABLE    ANTI    PAO
AMISS  NEEDLES    TETHERS
PARSEC  DESERTCOLORADO
      AAH    ALERT    ECOL
ESL  MINUTENEWYORK    ERE
ATTN   ILOSE        DEP
RECORDBADTRACK    STUPOR
PROVERB   DESPOND   TRADE
SNL  CALX   PLURALIZED
      SAKEFOROLDTIMES
DAPPLE  APOP   EPH   TEAR
RURAL  ICETEAS   FEM  DIO
ARID  ENTRANCESERVANTS
MAZE  CROAT   TAKESPLACE
ALES  TERSE   STADT   ASHY
```

50

```
INAWE  SOS  ALES    TOPPS
NASAL  IRA  LUCY   FACEIT
SITTINGBULLION     SKEWER
TRIEDON   DEIGN   THEATRE
      RET  MISSIONMANNERS
SEAL  AFUSS    ACRO    RES
CABOOSES    AUNT    PPP
RUNOFTHEMILLION    RANAT
ADE  FER  AIMAT   CHICAGO
MERIT   OLIO    GOSSIPED
       MOUNTAINPASSION
MRPEANUT   DELA    NOISY
PARAGON  GIJOE  TUE   NHA
STENO  NOTIONFORPROFIT
      TOG  NOSY   SETSFREE
ADO  DALE    AMISH    FADS
DEPOSITIONSLIP      EWE
OMITTED   RIPEN   GRANDMA
BEATAT  PONYEXPRESSION
EATERY   INTO  EGO   TEMPT
SNERT    COHN  SAW   ESSES
```

51

```
AFRO   MRMOM   ICAN   OJOS
SEARS  OUTIE   NAME   VINO
KRYSTALBALL    STABLEMEN
TAE  ORDER   MIEN   ARSON
OLDFOGY  ANNAGRAMM   HUE
      AGO  BRIOCHE  LAMONT
WARRENPEACE   TREX   ORCS
ELI    RETELL    SVELTE
BIGGREEN    OSSA     NEZ
EVERETT   JERRYRIGGS
RELICT   PALERMO   RAKISH
    DOUGGRAVES   DIGINTO
RID  LAST    BASENJIS
DOREMI   ESPRIT     UNE
PESO  AMOR  PAIGETURNER
EVENTS   RECEIVE    APE
TAB  SKIPTOWNE   APRICOT
SLUNG  SHIN   RADIO   ABA
HESITATER   APRILRAINES
ORCA  ROUE   TRADE   ROAST
PAHS  POSE   METER    ULEE
```

52

```
BESTS  JAMB  SEND   TOILS
ASCOT  APER  HUES   UPLIT
STANDUPSTRAIGHT    RHONE
EEL  NAES   DREI   SNIVEL
REPOMAN    EDEN   GETREAL
MIR  ANDS   EPOCH    IGA
CLEANMYPLATE    ANTEATER
ELAND   ANEMONES    OOF
NAS  MINERS   DESERTROSE
TNT  YOGAS   YOKEL   HINNY
REELOUT   SEW    ELECTEE
ARROW  ZEROS   RACER   HEB
LOSANGELES   CULTIC   ERA
   NBA  EVAGABOR   HAGEN
READUPON   DOMYHOMEWORK
ELS  SEDAN   NASA     EEO
SEAFIRE   OBEY    BAKLAVA
PARENS   GRUB   MOEN   LEW
ENURE  SETMYSIGHTSHIGH
COLDS  PROP   UCLA   DUBAI
TREES  YENS   VEER   STINT
```

53

```
GLO  GOALS   STEAM    DIN
REV  ALLIE   STRATI   ARNO
ASE  LILAC   TIARAS   MITT
MARIAVONTRAPP      PREVUE
MBAS  EWE  ALES   PRICERS
ARRAS   VIAL    WEIGHIN
REMODELLING     HANSEN
    IMEASY  SPORT    TUB
BACK  MANE   SEEM   EOCENE
ADAR  ADA   ACES   DAHLIA
DORAL   SINGAPORE   SALTS
ENDUED   OILY  ELS   FEET
MAITAI  POLE   ASIT   ERRS
SIN  CHOKE    ALOHAS
AWAKEN   OFFDUTYCOPS
  CLAMMED   EPOS    MANIC
DECRIAL   OVER  SAC  SEER
ISOMER   HEREFORDSHIRE
PSAT  TIRANA   ALERT   OCA
INCH  INURES   CANOE   TEM
NAH   NAMED    TRAMP   ADS
```

54

```
APBS  STAMP   BANCO   WISP
SHEP  LIBERTYBELL    ENTR
PONE  AMELIORATED    IDEE
INJECTED   CEN   SAMISENS
READIER   SYNES   TENSPOT
ATM  ASSAI    ASSNS    EPI
TRI   UNPLUGS        NAG
EEN  PANS   REN  WNER  DDE
DEFLATE   NOTSO   ICELESS
RISER    SOFTY    NOTIN
TOADS   AFROS     EPCOT
ANN  BNUP  SEP  ANS   EMU
RFK  YODA  PEP   SMUT  HEB
MIL  SOG   IDA   SAP   ALE
ALIST   NOPROBLEM   ABLER
CENTEN   DAIMLER   NBOLTS
  NED   ASTNENT    DUN
DAT  TOP          BIT   ESS
ACHIEVABLE    ONIONTARTS
ICANRELATE    ROSEGARDEN
STRESSMARK    OVERSLEEPS
```

55

```
BEGUMS ESCUDOS SAPPHO
ARARAT PAISANO POURED
COLADA EDGARALLANPONY
KILLERBEANIE IRE TBS
ECO AMA TAR TREK BEAS
RAP NAIL MEAT DEANE
CONTEMPTOFCOURTNEY
ROBOT IDEALLY RAH
ERASERS XACTO DICESUP
WITHOUTACLOONEY LENA
ROT FEES ANEW ASP
ALES THEKARATEKIDNEY
PENPALS XANAX SEDUCER
ERA PITCREW ELENI
REMEMBERTHEALIMONY
IPODS JOEY TART BUS
TIVO LEWD PRO ICH ENT
AGE ROC FROMONHEINIE
LOOKOUTBOLOGNA IGNITE
INUITS IHAVEIT DAGGER
NETPAY TOYOTAS SPENDS
```

56

```
ILIAC AFTS PUMA IMACS
WANNA GAZE OREL TARRY
IVANTHETERRIBLE SRTAS
NANANANA ARAB INTENT
ARTHURCONANDOYLE
VSHAPES TOOT LOUR
ETON AUTO OMENS QBS
NAPOLEONBONAPARTE ULE
NYE ACUTER LTRS SAIN
GTOS HAIG ATKINS
SAMUELTAYLORCOLERIDGE
PIUSXI LEAP OSIS
ARCH ELAM ADJOIN ADD
TEK ELVISAARONPRESLEY
EDS TAINT CBER APSE
MASC THOR TOPTHIS
CHRISTOPHERREEVE
PUEBLO RAIN NEATIDEA
ROLLE LAURENCEOLIVIER
AMOUR ELLS PERF TENET
TOTES OBIT ROOF ESTES
```

57

```
PRES MOROS GUN MORK
AESOP SAINT ONESEASON
RAMBLINROSE PASTELHUE
AMEBAS STPAUL TOOLATE
EYRE EDNA ONCE
SNERD CANCERCURE AGER
LAX ACUTE DIES DEBONE
OPIATE WAC PSIS BLOTS
TATLER IRATE ACCREDIT
EASE LENO ORO ORE
OWNS BALDINGPATE BLED
NIM SRS GIRL SWEE
TEAMMATE CAVED TIEBAR
ISSUE OLEO ESE ENROBE
MESSED SAME TRADE YEN
ELEC OVEREXPOSE GESTE
ALTI COPA SALE
STATUES ANIMAL SALAMI
LAMEBRAIN RESUMESPEED
APPLESEED ELITE SORRY
BESS DRY DANZA TOLL
```

58

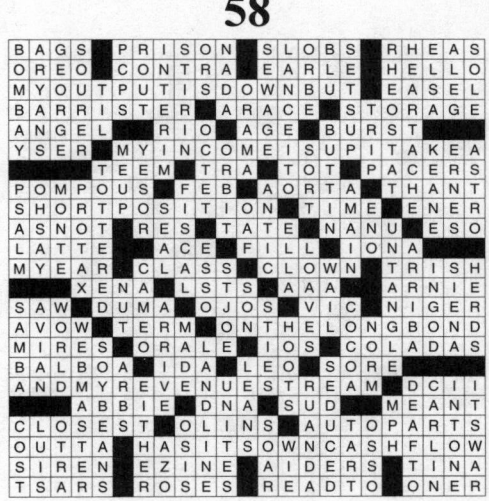

```
BAGS PRISON SLOBS RHEAS
OREO CONTRA EARLE HELLO
MYOUTPUTISDOWNBUT EASEL
BARRISTER ARACE STORAGE
ANGEL RIO AGE BURST
YSER MYINCOMEISUPITAKEA
TEEM TRA TOT PACERS
POMPOUS FEB AORTA THANT
SHORTPOSITION TIME ENER
ASNOT RES TATE NANU ESO
LATTE ACE FILL IONA
MYEAR CLASS CLOWN TRISH
XENA LSTS AAA ARNIE
SAW DUMA OJOS VIC NIGER
AVOW TERM ONTHELONGBOND
MIRES ORALE IOS COLADAS
BALBOA IDA LEO SORE
ANDMYREVENUESTREAM DCII
ABBIE DNA SUD MEANT
CLOSEST OLINS AUTOPARTS
OUTTA HASITSOWNCASHFLOW
SIREN EZINE AIDERS TINA
TSARS ROSES READTO ONER
```

59

```
MAN SCALPS ACTIII COG
ELI ALLSET FLACON ARR
NUT BEAUTYPROTEST REE
UMPIRE ILL MAP RIDGE
INASTATEOFPROFUSION
ROCS EEL DWI PADRONE
OAKUM ADO EEE NEA
THELIBRARYOFPROGRESS
HURTLE GAP IANS LOAF
ANA ART STE RINGO
ABSENTMINDEDCONFESSOR
FACTO ASI DEO DAS
BNAI AILS TAP SEAMUS
GROSSNATIONALCONDUCT
LOS MSS LEA TESLA
SKIAREA NIN ESS LIAR
CONTESTANTWORKETHIC
OASES HUE ASH REECHO
FLU PROFESSIONBOX ION
FAR ONMEDS ENROBE TSE
SSE THEUSA REAPED YES
```

60

```
ASSIST SLED SPITON
QUELQUECHOSE HOOKNOSE
TDWATERHOUSE OKCORRAL
SINGE SIR EMCEE ISTO
SLEETY HLMENCKEN
ABATE FIE AREOLAE
AMFM CSLEWIS SNOG PTA
REGISTRY NEDS SUGAR
PROTEUS LANCE INAPTLY
OYER PERK NINOTCHKA
MCD EZBAKEOVENS IAN
CORNBREAD EWER TBAR
CHINESE TAPER FAUSTUS
ONCEA CODE BULLPENS
OSH URDU JREWING CELT
STBARTS GAG IVANV
MXMISSILE OLDSAW
ARUN MINSK TOO BUGLE
YATITTLE UNRESOLUTION
EYESORES SECRETAGENTS
DEPART SEAS HISSAT
```

61

```
ABBA  OPERA  SNEAD  BUSS
FLAN  DUPED  TITLE  APET
CUDDLEFISH  ANTIMADDER
REROOFS  ESTEE  ARMADA
ORNE  ESTER  CREATED
PALIN  DAVIES  CLEANER
SPADES  NAVE  PLUS
AIDS  PODDEDPLANTS  KAI
TAD  OBOE  HUSK  ATILT
EASIER  ATOMS  STUDIO
TARDILY  PLANE  STANDIN
HODADS  RAINY  GURNEY
ANAME  AARE  TREE  HAT
TEY  BUDDINGHEADS  MAXI
NIAS  RUMP  SPEWED
MALODOR  HAMPER  ANKLE
SERAPES  RATIO  ASCH
ATONER  TONED  APPEASE
SHUDDERBUG  OFFPUDDING
HONI  ABASE  RARER  EROO
ADDS  TIRED  SNORT  NEST
```

62

```
LABEL  HASTE  BEEFS  MRE
ENURE  USURP  UNCUT  OER
IDONTLIKEYOURTONE  LPS
SAYSHITO  NETS  NESTEA
TAP  VINYL  AILMENT
ALF  LONESOMEDOVE  ANTZ
LEAF  ERAT  ONAROLL
ATLANTA  ADDICTS  SLAKE
MOSQUITOCOAST  TELAVIV
ONESIDED  BLOC  TODATE
IREST  AROAR
COOKIE  SCOT  SNAKEPIT
CAREERS  EBONYANDIVORY
STANS  TINYTIM  LEXICON
NOTAONE  ECCE  LUNA
EGGS  LOVINGCARESS  SSN
TOEHOLD  ARESO  EOS
HAZARD  ASTO  UPGRADES
ILE  DONTTOUCHTHATDIAL
CIS  ENEMY  NIMOY  OTERO
SET  REESE  DAMNS  FOUNT
```

63

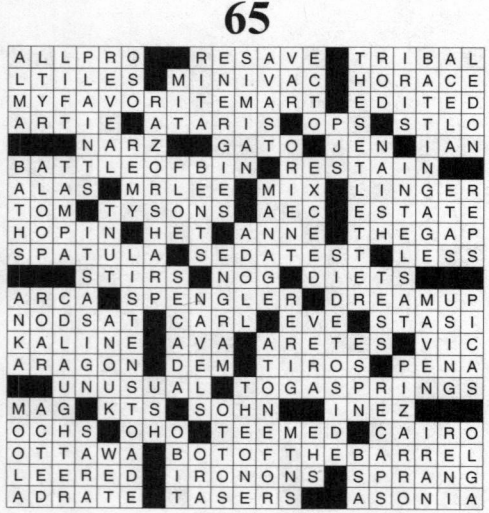

```
PASTED  AWAKEN  ATTACHE
INCODE  CALICO  BRONZED
KNOWSFOURGNUS  MASTERY
EARN  TWAS  SEM  DEICES
ESO  ETHOS  RETEACH
ABC  BAREINNMINED  BRO
BRACER  POLENTA  ASIAN
EARLYISH  NGO  GRAMPS
DUDE  MISTRESS  ORNATE
FEDERICO  ATEALOT
AMY  MEATBUYCHANTS  ERS
POUTIER  APOSTATE
POLAND  GOPLACES  AWAY
ALEROS  ENO  CYNICISM
LABOR  BOONIES  ETHNIC
SHE  BORNETWOLOOS  DNA
ENLARGE  EELED  YAP
MEMOIR  ESA  AVES  ROPE
ABILENE  WRYBREDFLOWER
HASTIER  AMELIE  PAMELA
INTENSE  YENTAS  DWARFS
```

64

```
METS  STAFFS  PAD  HIM
HANOI  INDIAN  OLDJEANS
ANION  SUITCOMPLAINING
LUSTALITTLEBIT  YGOR
SALVIA  SYD  LAM  STYLI
LEE  SPA  INBED  EGAD
GATINSTYLE  SAG  OLE
DEEM  NACHOS  ASWANDAM
SEATAT  SHERA  RANSOM
ITSAJOB  IRK  FIG  XSOUT
ARIB  PURSESAIDES  ETNA
MENLO  LEM  TAC  SIOBHAN
GENTLE  FUNKY  PRYERS
HOTSTUFF  ODDLOT  WARM
UNH  ORR  RAYPERVIEW
TIED  FOCAL  EAN  HAP
STJOE  GAD  ISO  DRIVEN
ONLY  MISSINGCOUSINS
DRINKOFDISASTER  SKATE
JANEEYRE  NATANT  SERAC
SET  OON  SCAPES  ORYX
```

65

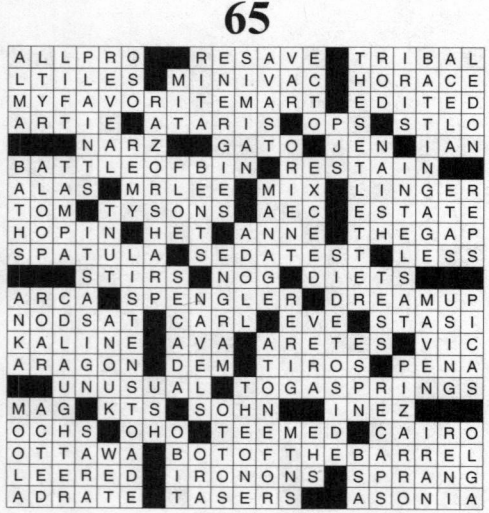

```
ALLPRO  RESAVE  TRIBAL
LTILES  MINIVAC  HORACE
MYFAVORITEMART  EDITED
ARTIE  ATARIS  OPS  STLO
NARZ  GATO  JEN  IAN
BATTLEOFBIN  RESTAIN
ALAS  MRLEE  MIX  LINGER
TOM  TYSONS  AEC  ESTATE
HOPIN  HET  ANNE  THEGAP
SPATULA  SEDATEST  LESS
STIRS  NOG  DIETS
ARCA  SPENGLER  DREAMUP
NODSAT  CARL  EVE  STASI
KALINE  AVA  ARETES  VIC
ARAGON  DEM  TIROS  PENA
UNUSUAL  TOGASPRINGS
MAG  KTS  SOHN  INEZ
OCHS  OHO  TEEMED  CAIRO
OTTAWA  BOTOFTHEBARREL
LEERED  IRONONS  SPRANG
ADRATE  TASERS  ASONIA
```

66

```
OSCAR  ARMS  INGE  PERU
HOOVER  TOIT  NEOPHYTES
MYLIFE  OGRE  CATHARTIC
SAD  INAMERICATHEYOUNG
CELEB  TONI  LSD
AREALWAYSREADY  REDACT
KERR  ETE  MRX  LAMINAR
ILE  CRETAN  DIME  ISSUE
TIARA  TOGIVETOTHOSE
ATLAST  PELF  AAA  ONES
WHOAREOLDERTHAN
SABU  PLO  AURA  UBOATS
THEMSELVESTHE  ERNIE
ASABC  BOSC  SIGURD  NEA
LINEAGE  AHA  UTE  NATO
ENORME  FULLBENEFITSOF
TSE  EDAM  NOCHE
THEIRINEXPERIENCE  WOO
VERSATILE  NINA  USNEWS
PRIEDOPEN  TUES  SAMLET
GONE  NERO  EMMY  WILDE
```

67

```
MONTERO ■ WOWEDEM ■ TERRA
AROUSER ■ OOHLALA ■ ALOES
DEBTOFASALESMAN ■ HOOPS
AGUT ■ CEDAR ■ ALAMO ■ TEE
MOTOROLA ■ EXS ■ YELLAT
ENS ■ THERATOFKHAN ■ EELS
■ SEM ■ RONA ■ ENACTS
SSGTS ■ TBAR ■ CARE ■ ATSEA
APIP ■ USEBOATHANDS ■ PAS
FIVEONES ■ COM ■ DUSTERS
ACETIC ■ SECURED ■ RIVOLI
RUBELLA ■ NUT ■ ROASTPIG
ILE ■ WELTCREATION ■ ALEN
SERTA ■ IBLE ■ CAPP ■ APERS
■ TRYSTS ■ ADES ■ HUE ■
ESTA ■ POPULARMITTS ■ DRY
UTOPIA ■ ELM ■ COSTFREE
REA ■ FRANC ■ PLIER ■ LADS
ALBEE ■ TAKEMYBRETTAWAY
ILONA ■ ONEVOTE ■ AVARICE
LAYER ■ PARAPET ■ TALENTS
```

68

```
ITALIC ■ SIMPER ■ IONESCO
NOVENA ■ AZALEA ■ TEESHOT
LEADINGLADIES ■ COMPOST
EST ■ TAO ■ ARA ■ PAH ■ ENOTE
AHAS ■ PACKINGSLIPS ■ TAR
FORETELL ■ DTS ■ LEOI ■ ISS
■ ESTO ■ SAC ■ TRUSTSIN ■
■ UDO ■ NARC ■ OPTS ■ MGMT
DUMPINGGROUNDS ■ YESSIR
APA ■ EMO ■ OPPOSES ■ LOTSA
EDT ■ FEUD ■ ICE ■ TYRE ■ ACC
MACRO ■ POLEAXE ■ NOV ■ RUT
OTHERS ■ WORKINGCLASSES
NEIL ■ TANG ■ ETTE ■ ETA ■
■ NOMATTER ■ SIN ■ OWAR ■
RIG ■ ORTO ■ MAB ■ COURTIER
RAP ■ DRAWINGROOMS ■ ORSO
AGAPE ■ INN ■ EER ■ SAT ■ DIO
TRILLIN ■ RUNNINGBOARDS
EERIEST ■ EVADES ■ LIPOUT
DESERTS ■ MASALA ■ ELOPES
```

69

```
ATALOSS ■ CROCI ■ OCANADA
SHRIVEL ■ ALTHO ■ LOWERED
PENNAME ■ RESAW ■ DALLIED
SOOT ■ IDOLS ■ RELAX ■ LAPS
■ GUYS ■ DYES ■
MARG ■ BESS ■ OATS ■ SLUE
GLORIA ■ TIS ■ EUP ■ EMISMS
MAKEST ■ EMOSTOF ■ NASDAQ
■ ART ■ ROSSANO ■ ANT ■
GRATAE ■ SNARLER ■ TOEING
TENDER ■ EARTED
EASILY ■ VANESSA ■ SMITES
■ VIP ■ APOGEES ■ EAN ■
ROSITA ■ LARGERT ■ ANLIFE
POWDER ■ ORN ■ AVA ■ TOATEE
THEE ■ KART ■ IRES ■ WONG
■ MEMO ■ BETH ■
TOAD ■ EMMET ■ ATEIN ■ FOPS
INRANGE ■ NETWT ■ LOLITAS
NUCLEAR ■ TRADE ■ LAYSOUT
ASSIGNS ■ SONYS ■ SHEKELS
```

70

```
HDTV ■ USAF ■ OBJ ■ ROSEHIP
AREA ■ PAIL ■ NAE ■ ACETONE
JOLLYMRROGERS ■ STATUTE
ILLSAY ■ CREPTUP ■ AMUSER
SLYER ■ MOIRA ■ RIDS ■ IRA
■ GOODMRDEEDS ■ SNAG
CEREBRAL ■ STINTS ■ INGLE
ANOMIE ■ AGA ■ SWAMIS
ISAID ■ BRANDMRX ■ COPRA
RUSSE ■ YOWEE ■ BANDB
NETS ■ MRINBETWEEN ■ RUST
■ EASED ■ RIPEN ■ TABOO
■ CDROM ■ MODELMRT ■ EGBDF
SIMILE ■ AMO ■ STOLAF
AGREE ■ DROPIT ■ FINENESS
LAPS ■ MYBOYMRBILL ■
ERE ■ REEL ■ MILNE ■ ADAYS
SCALER ■ EUGENIA ■ IMFREE
MANIACS ■ SPRINGMRCLEAN
ASUNDER ■ PAS ■ KLUM ■ ATRA
NETZERO ■ SSE ■ SEGA ■ TENT
```

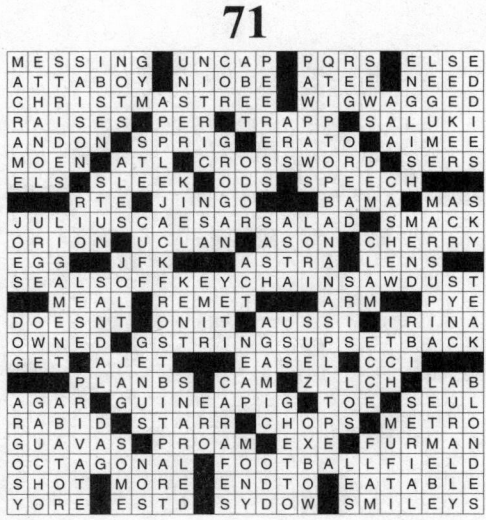

71

```
MESSING ■ UNCAP ■ PQRS ■ ELSE
ATTABOY ■ NIOBE ■ ATEE ■ NEED
CHRISTMASTREE ■ WIGWAGGED
RAISES ■ PER ■ TRAPP ■ SALUKI
ANDON ■ SPRIG ■ ERATO ■ AIMEE
MOEN ■ ATL ■ CROSSWORD ■ SERS
ELS ■ SLEEK ■ ODS ■ SPEECH ■
■ RTE ■ JINGO ■ BAMA ■ MAS
JULIUSCAESARSALAD ■ SMACK
ORION ■ UCLAN ■ ASON ■ CHERRY
EGG ■ JFK ■ ASTRA ■ LENS ■
SEALSOFFKEYCHAINSAWDUST
■ MEAL ■ REMET ■ ARM ■ PYE
DOESNT ■ ONIT ■ AUSSI ■ IRINA
OWNED ■ GSTRINGSUPSETBACK
GET ■ AJET ■ EASEL ■ CCI ■
■ PLANBS ■ CAM ■ ZILCH ■ LAB
AGAR ■ GUINEAPIG ■ TOE ■ SEUL
RABID ■ STARR ■ CHOPS ■ METRO
GUAVAS ■ PROAM ■ EXE ■ FURMAN
OCTAGONAL ■ FOOTBALLFIELD
SHOT ■ MORE ■ ENDTO ■ EATABLE
YORE ■ ESTD ■ SYDOW ■ SMILEYS
```

72

```
MANTAS ■ RACY ■ WEBS ■ PUMA
OREIDA ■ OLEO ■ IMAM ■ INON
REVEAL ■ SINGAPORESLING
PNEUMATICTIRE ■ AALTO
HARP ■ MINE ■ SUGARMAPLE
■ NIL ■ STOPIN ■ ORRIS
METROSTATION ■ VISA ■ ITS
OREOS ■ SPASM ■ WEST ■ ACHE
PUNCHCARDS ■ EWER ■ TESS
ECO ■ OAT ■ IONIA ■ IDO
STREWN ■ BREWERY ■ AIMSAT
■ USA ■ RESEW ■ STU ■ CUE
PAAR ■ SCUD ■ MOTHERLODE
ANNO ■ THIS ■ MOIRA ■ NOWIN
PIT ■ KAOS ■ BOWLINGALLEY
AMISH ■ RELOAN ■ AOL
WASHATERIA ■ EONS ■ SODA
■ TEENA ■ GREENPASTURES
FORESTPRESERVE ■ IAMBUS
BRUT ■ ETUI ■ LION ■ PUMICE
ISMS ■ RAGA ■ SKIS ■ STATES
```

73

```
ICIEST  KANSAS  MALACHI
MODELA  ILOILO  ONESHOT
AMERICANLITER   RAGTIME
REA  POND  SEETHE   ICON
ETTAS   ELMO    UNLINK
THESHOWERMUSTGOON    ELI
     POW  DEMISE  URANUS
TLC  DENTE   AMPS  VERBAL
YEAS  SOBERSISTER   TRUE
PAULO  DADAS    SERIO
EDGER  ERST  COAT  ASTRO
     HABLA  FORGE  YAHOO
FUTZ  OLIVELOAFER   NEAP
ALIENS  NINE  TAMIL   RMS
SENSEI   ANGELO     GER
TEA  ANYPORTERINASTORM
     FERGIE   TYNE  SEPIA
OLIN   ETALII  UMPS   PST
LIBERAL  BUTTEROFAJOKE
EMERALD  ENABLE  CLOSER
SARONGS  SALEMS  STEEDS
```

74

```
AERO  CZAR  ILOILO  PUSS
TREY  LINE  NOIDEA  ENTE
TOPS[ERG]EANT  FOLIESB[ERG]ERE
IDOTOO   IRONS   STAYMAN
RESET  ACRE  STP  SYN[ERG]Y
EDER  ISLES   OAS   STE
      BETT[ERG]ETMOVING   NAP
THEYSAY  OOZEDOUT    CMA
RHODES   ANTZ    SATYRS
OER   OAKY  HIVES  NOFAT
AMIGO  POLT[ERG]EIST  GEODE
DOZEN  IDAHO   ALSO   RIO
MOONED   ROIL    BEACON
ARN  SIGNPOST  IVORIES
PST  FOULWEATH[ERG]EAR
     AHH  DNA  SHOES  BAIT
FLOOR  NYC  COPS   HULCE
TAMALES  ALTAR   DUBLIN
EV[ERG]REENTREE  EDGARB[ERG]EN
ARES  LASERS  AUEL  LESE
MERE  SPEAKS  UGLY  ENTR
```

75

```
GONG  SWARMS  ACED   TRIP
ISEE  LENDEE  MARE   REMI
SUBSTANDARD  EPIC   OPAL
      TINT  CONNOTATIONS
RADARGUNS  NOD  UGH   IAN
ABELE  POOLAREA   ORANGE
POSTDATING  ADMINISTER
TWI   SOREAT   OVALS
     CVII   OIL  ALLOWED
EXCOMMUNICATION    NILE
AMANA  NEMO  BARK  BASIN
SANT  COUNTERBALANCES
ESTRADA  SKI    INTO
     ATEST  TINEAR   NBA
PROPORTION  SUPERVISOR
HELPME  ONELITER   ONINE
AVE  ILA  GLO  SEAPLANES
SEMICIRCULAR    TAGS
ERIN  COLA  DISLOCATION
RISK  TSAR  EMIGRE  IOWA
SESS  SEND  RECESS  RULE
```

76

```
GELS  GIRL  BESS  RAPIDS
EXAM  ADUE  ROAN  ACUMEN
ETTA  SONATASTANDSTILL
RECUT   RUS   UFO    ANI
JACKSONINTHEPULPIT
ALA  ENID  TEN   ASIMOV
BARBS  VENISONVIDIVICI
BREA  RENO  TWOON   EATS
AGED  ENTER   SLATY   MEA
REREAD  SONNETPROFITS
      GRASS  TIE  STOLI
VIRGINMASONRY   UKASES
ONE  ATIME   DAMUP   SNAP
ICAN  TOWAR  MOLE   CARA
CARIBBEANSEASON  POKER
ENSTAR   OPE  CASE   EDS
PARSONFORTHECOURSE
LEI   AVE  RIO    ANNIE
WATCHYOURSTEPSON  IVAN
OINKED  LOOT  PORT  TELE
ERASES  ESSO  SUEY  ERST
```

77

```
NIP  BOSOM   SKICAP   PTL
EMI  ATONOF  CANADA   OWE
OPENSESAME  HOARDS   LIT
NAPES   TE[ND]OWN   ITSON[ME]
GCLEF  GENERA  PRE   OAST
ATA  [ID]OLATRY  QUA  S[NY]DER
S[OR]T  DRAMAS  PUMICE   STY
SEALIN   TREASONS
     BEECH  LAOS  [IN]STEREO
CARNE  LEOTOLSTOY  TRUER
BELLAS  WEA[KS]POT  LO[VA]BLE
ONEAM  ALLTHERAGE   NESS
TERR[AZ]ZO   SHOR   YACHT
     DOORSTEP   GHOSTS
GAY  NOTFAR  PASSER   HAD
OMITS  APR  DILATORS  ROY
TREE  FED  FINNAN   ELOPE
SALTII   DUVALL   [FL]EWAT
ODD  BLEWIT  TAKESISSUE
FIT  MEXICO  ADELIE   ILS
TOO  STOLEN  DRIPS    NOT
```

78

```
ATPEACE  JANDJ    FULCRA
BORSCHT  ELICIT   ALPHAS
ORESTES  SLEIGHDRAGONS
RESEAM  CUE  ISEE    ALOU
TREX  LAOS   AWLS    LUC
SON  LAVA  PEEWEEWREATH
     TRIBAL  ILK  BTEAM
OASES  SPIELED  IASIMOV
PLOT  GTOS   INOR    ANE
OFFICE  RATTEDON  TAKEN
SIMEON  TIMELAG  DOREMI
SEISM  REDCROSS  AVISOS
URN  FERN  EONS    OTRO
MIDTERM  OUGHTNT  ASHEN
     IDEAS  SNO  WEENIE
LOBSTERCLAUS  OSSA  FOP
EXE  SKYE   SOTO    MIRE
AFRO  ETNA  MUD   BARRIE
DONNERTHEDEAD  SELLFOR
TRIUNE  EXALTS  ESTELLE
ODESSA  AMITY  MOSEYED
```

79

```
RCA   IDARE   UND   ACTFOR
LEAN  BARBER  LIE   EOSINE
SEVENSAMURAI  TNN   GUAVAS
TOES  OLIGARCHIES  INRE
ANNUALS   HAMMIEST  EEE
FOURSEASONS  ROOTS  DEANE
FREAK  ELATED  NIP  ORSON
SAS  SIXWEEKS  STEN  WRYLY
   AORTA  SACHS  MNOP
BROGUES  MAL  TAS  HAIRIER
RANAT  DREAMON  KERN  EMU
ODES  TENTOMIDNIGHT  ICON
NIH  TINA  LEADERS  BRETT
COOKING  TIN  SRA  BRAISES
   UOMO  WHATS  BOUTS
THROE  YARN  TWOJAKES  CIO
BOWLS  UTE  SPIRIT  MOOGS
AMISS  REEVE  EIGHTMENOUT
RET  QUIRKILY  RENEWAL
   HAUL  BILLMELATER  ENNE
CAYMAN  INE  HAPPYNEWYEAR
CHOPRA  RGS  ARGENT  HERS
CAUSES  DST  SNARE  YDS
```

80

```
MEDAL  ARIAS  SAFEHA(V)EN
AMINE  ROONE  ALEXAND(R)A
YESYOUR(X)(L)(N)C  DOMIN(I)O(N)S
ARCTIC  YALL  SEATO  OOH
   HIST  EURO  IGN
BALI  BURNEDIN(F)(E)(G)  ADAS
UCONN  NUS  ENGAGE  SERA
(L)(N)(D)GENERES  RANSOMER
BEE  REDACT  LOAN  PLATO
   AVRIL  ECARD  GAINON
SEALION  (X)(P)(D)(N)C  CORNDOG
ALLIES  SKIED  TOTHE
LICES  BTEN  AMARNA  IAM
ICANTSEE  UNKNOWN(N)(T)(T)
NITE  NARITA  EEE  KORAN
ETRE  (L)(M)(N)TARYMATH  REDS
   ASP  SOMA  SEAT
LAZ  EARTO  LBOS  ATHENA
A(S)(S)ERTION  O(B)(C)(T)PROBLEM
MAKESROOM  AETNA  LAMIA
APP(L)EISLE  DROSS  LYONS
```

81

```
TESLA  AVON  CASS  ALIBI
OCEAN  BILE  IMHO  JOKES
SHAKO  BEAU  NOEL  ANNAL
SOLEDDOWNTHERIVER  ENA
   BEST  REMAKES  TWIN
ATTEST  ANIMALS  TILTED
HOOD  ARENA  YECCH
AFL  HOLEDONESNOSE  EEL
BULGARIA  STAR  STYNE
   ERNST  GOESAPE  KUDOS
MADEDO  DOGLEGS  WAFFLE
ARIEL  AIRLINE  MOTTO
MATTE  TAME  BAKESALE
ALL  BOWLEDASBRASS  LOT
   IDAHO  WIRES  TENT
ANKARA  APRICOT  DREDGE
DEED  RETHINK  BIEN
RBI  GETTINGCOALEDFEET
OUTDO  AILS  AHME  CORKY
ILIAD  ILIE  LIME  AUGER
TASKS  LAPD  LOOP  PROSE
```

82

```
GLIDE  MAC  TIPPY  LAUDS
REDISTILL  ADORE  ERNIE
ANASTASIA  PEROTCHOICE
FALCONCARESSED  LASTED
   UMPS  EDITS  SEVE
TAPAS  SATIN  WAR  BSA
ERIN  BARRETTEMAVERICK
REN  WYLIE  OSCINE  ESAI
NAOMIJUDD  ELAN  STERN
   ALOT  GETAT  DEICES
DERIVEINRESTAURANTS
TRALEE  NOIRE  SOLO
OUTER  EARL  DIANELANE
AMEN  ANNALS  EBBED  REX
DURESSREHEARSALS  RISE
SPY  WHO  LEERY  TESTS
   LEON  METAL  FAST
ACHIER  DERIDEAPRICOTS
SOULTERRAIN  CLEOPATRA
ADLAI  DANCE  TENGALLON
PEACE  ABYSS  SET  NEEDS
```

83

```
SPEWS  OSIER  GIBB  OOPS
TOSIR  CADRE  OTRA  DRAT
ALLNIGHTERS  GUARDDUTY
   GLAREDAT  OPERAS
PROBATE  TIA  SENHORA
LINEN  STARSKY  TOOLED
STEAK  SLO  FAUST  EDGE
STARTINGPITCHER  SIN
APO  CAMEOUT  CASHEWS
TOWNCAR  DEN  DAM  ELITE
MONEYS  MUSCLES  BISTRO
ERWIN  FOP  HAG  SENECAN
   HELIPAD  SERRATE  HRS
SOI  CLIENTSCASEFILE
LUGS  ALLIE  DTS  VIRGO
ASHPAN  SNIFTER  ETONS
PETITES  NAH  RAGTOPS
   EUCLID  TEENIDOL
HANDBRAKE  WISDOMTEETH
BRIO  EVER  ASSAD  IMAGO
OMAN  WEAN  SMOKE  TEPID
```

84

```
VNECK  TBONESTEAK  AONE
CONDE  HUBBAHUBBA  POEM
HOTSY  ERECTORSET  EZRA
INE  HARPY  HONES  TREVI
PERFORMS  LETON  CHISEL
   ELIS  SOREN  TOAT
INBRED  EVER  WHATISIT
MOORS  HARE  SHEL  FEAR
AREA  NONE  BATES  USAGE
CARRIESON  GYRATOR  LOX
   INITIALINITIALS
EDT  SLENDER  KICKSTAND
BRETT  STEAL  EEKS  ACAD
ANNI  USED  LOSS  ATRIA
YODELLED  MAIN  STEELY
   SOAS  TITLE  SAHL
OSBORN  BADLY  BELLYRUB
ROUND  MALTA  SLATE  ANS
IDLE  MILLENNIUM  TAMMI
NOGO  AFTERTASTE  INBED
GMEN  IFORMATION  CNOTE
```

85

```
AGATE  MAMA  EFGH  AGATHAS
LITHO  YSER  ARIA  TITHERS
BRAES  ♥ILY  TEAR  ♥BREAKS
ALL♥   SWAT  MOUNDS  BY♥
NIKOLAI  ♥LAND  ♥IES  OMSK
  FULL  SITE  LEGS  FOAM
  LTCOL  MUSCADET  SARDS
♥IER  GREAT♥ED  PURPLE♥
BOXEDOUT  IONIA  ARAISE
RUNACROSS  NUT  FERNWOOD
PRESEEN  BAT  MARYANN
SNL  SOIL  GARR  MSU
♥OFGOLD  LOX  DIS♥ENS
LETLOOSE  HOE  WOODTONES
ENRICO  GUESS  POWERFUL
GRAVIDA  SHEDEMON  EDEL
DRONE  ♥ANDSOUL  ♥BEAT
REBS  ERIA  NTSB  ENTR
JEEP  ADOG  DECAY  DESKJOB
  LIZ  NEWISH  JUNG  NAZI
EQUALTO  RED♥  POSE  BESOT
FUNNIER  INIT  EVES  ASONE
TIETACK  ATNO  WEDS  ASNER
```

86

```
TBONE  MUIR  AEONS  SLED
AARON  ATNO  RELEE  COPA
ETATS  REFS  GREATBRAIN
BITINGCROSBY  OPULENCE
ONECAR  ORIOLE  SPEE
  ERES  NOEND  SUNOCO
DEADLYSITIN  VII  EULA
UNS  STLO  SHORTCIRCUS
RENEW  SOON  AIKMAN  HET
ARETHA  SLAIN  ANTI
NOWYOUSEEITNOWYOUDONT
  MODE  LEACH  ERENOW
SHA  PIRATE  HEIL  NOTSO
SUNVISITORS  ASEA  HIP
RANI  FAR  HUNTINGPERM
SCENEV  BARON  SOIR
  ETAL  HORSES  DROWSE
AREYOUOK  ONEARMEDBAND
TITANLINES  ATTA  ELSAS
ASTR  TREAT  TMAN  RETIE
TEED  SEERS  SESS  SMELL
```

87

```
FUNGO  CLOTS  DAFT  SPA
ONION  THELAW  ELLA  TON
EAGLE  MADAMIMADAM  END
  PEDDLES  INAROW  HWYS
BARB  ANE  BAERS  STOAT
BRIEFS  FROM  TAE  OPRAH
STARRS  IONIZING  YETIS
  GAO  ECO  ONTOP  SILT
CCCVI  ILK  ERMA  ARPS
AURAL  CDC  MBA  CARLAS
STYRENE  OSCAR  SATIATE
ASSISI  RAE  ICU  INNIE
  TATA  SNEE  EAR  OGDEN
FRAT  SAWIN  CTR  ONS
BELIE  DESSERTS  CAESAR
INGOT  DAH  CIAO  ELTORO
  TANDY  THROB  NBA  ELAN
DAZS  ALBEIT  CONTROL
ACE  GREENGOBLIN  ANISE
MAR  EDNA  ONSITE  DANES
ERS  ESTD  READY  ALGAE
```

88

```
DITTO  ANTED  TRAC  ESPN
ONEAL  HEAVE  RAUL  GRIT
ONEBELOWPAR  UNDEROATH
FATS  ERAS  AGELIMIT
UTE  LSAT  TIETO  ENIGMA
SERBIA  FOLLOWINGSUIT
  RAGWEEDS  STOMATA
BEFOREHAND  VAGUE  VEL
ODIC  IRS  IAGO  AWARE
EDNABEST  ADLIB  FRI
RANDOMHOUSEUNABRIDGED
  EDS  ELISE  CRAPGAME
ABYSS  ANAT  OKA  ELIE
DRU  LORAN  ABOVEBOARD
DASBOOT  DRONESON
OVERSUBSCRIBE  POSING
NOFAIR  TOONS  MAIN  MOO
  LEANONME  MIME  AGRO
AFTERWARD  THELASTWORD
BOOS  LIMO  TOTES  MANIA
EXES  SLYS  EVERS  CREST
```

89

```
INFRA  BALI  RWE  CHEESE
COLOR  REINDEER  AORTAS
KNACKFORGROWINGPLANTS
  SAMEHERE  SOIL  ASE
AMCS  COOT  MAC  ATAT
SALAMI  TIVO  BANGLE
SPECIALFORCESSOLDIER
ALA  SLURPEE  MAUI  ARE
DENT  MOPE  MINT  CSPAN
  HARES  TEAS  EATING
DOCUMENTFORIMMIGRANTS
OROMEO  APIN  APODS
CLUBS  HICS  SOIR  HERB
SES  PORT  CARNAGE  PEE
SIGNALTODRIVEYOURCAR
  SNOOPY  RIAL  TRIODE
  AVES  YET  ERBE  STET
SOL  OREM  DISLOYAL
WHATTHEMOONISNTMADEOF
ANDREA  LOWGRADE  CARLA
MODEST  INN  ESOS  KNEES
```

90

```
NCAR  THAI  ADEAD  MOAN
ROOM&BOARD  DOWN&DIRTY
INREBUTTAL  ABANDONEES
CONN  RAH  YEMEN  TOSEE
ONEDOLLAR  A&E  IKEA
HOT  RAU  ETTE  ARIDNESS
  DEPP  SHIVAREE  AWE
EMAILS  OPENERS  LARSEN
GINAS  NIB  FOP  HAYES
OXYGEN  TROAS  NAUSEATE
M&M  ACHES&PAINS  S&L
AMICABLE  SPECS  SAMPLE
NANNY  VCR  LAT  VAIOS
ITUNES  HERALDS  RENEWS
ACT  EPISODEI  MEDE
CHECKSIN  DORA  ADO  MAB
  RISK  R&R  NETINCOME
PATIO  BERET  NIA  REST
CROSSBRACE  ATALLCOSTS
BLACK&BLUE  CURDS&WHEY
SODO  BIKEL  TEMA  WEAL
```

91

```
BLAMES  SADCASE  CUERVO
RAMONE  CLERKED  ALLIED
EMBRACEABLEEWE   LEANTO
SELECTOR  TALENT  IGOR
TRENT  NIB  MAR  IRANI
     ESP  NOUS   PRETEND
SUBS  RIGHTONQUEUE  GIT
PRUSSIA  REDOUT  PUTTER
AGR  HEMO  RATA  SPORTY
TENNISSHOO  ARMS   MUS
     ENTAIL   TOUSLE
TNT  MODS  MOUNTAINDO
PROWAR  BETA  EDEL  OED
TATTLE  SATEEN  ENABLED
SPH  IDONTHAVETWO  RODS
     PISCOPO  REMO  SAO
NTEST  BRA  ONA  DWARF
GAGA  SERAPE  GREENPEA
ANGLEE  RUNAROUNDSIOUX
INNEED  ATTRITE  ETERNE
LAUDED  SESTETS  RESTED
```

92

```
TWOS  OVENS  BOPS  UPBOW
HALO  BASIN  EDIT  PUPAE
ACDC  ALLBASSETSAREOFF
WOEISME  SPOTTY  DAREST
     EVANS  SLIT  BAIT
CRETE  SHUTTLECASSOCKS
LARYNX  INOIL  ANTE  HAT
ARIP  AURA  ENGR  WISE
META  XKE  PRATT  APACHE
PRUSSIA  SIESTAS  OSKAR
     SASSINGTHEBLUES
DORAG  EMIGRES  INTAILS
COOGAN  SPYON  CDC  IMIT
COVE  EMUS  DUEL  LIMA
ALE  OWAR  COEDS  ELINOR
BAREFACEDLASSIE  ANGST
     ANGE  RITT  PANDG
CRUSOE  PAPERY  TOYWITH
CULTURALMORASSES  ADAM
LINOS  DIAN  DEARE  LENO
INANE  MESS  AROSE  LAGS
```

93

```
CERAMIST  CARAT  BAILIFF
AMARANTH  OXEYE  BEINGFAT
DISARMER  OLDEN  ENTRAINS
     TRIMESTER  THRICE  MGM
LBJ  INSET  SUNPORCH  BIBI
ORATED  BOT  MOONIE  DOGIT
POSED  GOMAD  ULEE  EIGHTH
     MASKEDAVENGERS  ROUTE
AMIR  ITY  ELIAS  DORS
MONOSKI  WREST  GRIDS  TKT
BLESSINGINDISGUISE  ARES
LOGES  IRE  OAF  PLUNK
ECUS  UNDERCOVERFBIAGENT
SHY  SPEED  OBESE  ACCEDES
     LIED  SAONE  SSE  BELK
GWENN  SECRETADMIRERS
ELEVEN  HAUS  ISAAC  NAIAD
NIMES  METRES  TYR  BGIRLS
TBAR  CABERNET  ATEAR  ELL
END  BINARY  CARNELIAN
BEERIEST  OFUSE  NERVEGAS
BSINGLES  FORTE  UNDERONE
ESTADOS  FREED  PASSFAIL
```

94

```
AGASP  ESTOP   MAITREDS
TOSIR  THEWEB  ONTHESEA
PLACECHEESEONTOSEESAW
ADM  TAE  KNEESOCK
RAISESLITCANDLE  LEGS
     TNT  ORATE   LUDENS
CDCASE  NES  THETAB  NEA
AERIE  FINAL  ANON  SELF
NAIR  HEATSUPTEAKETTLE
DTS  SAT  STER  TAI
WHISTLEJOLTSDOZINGCAT
SAL  ASIF  ESA  CIR
TIPSOVERAQUARIUM  BODY
HMOS  ADOG  LEEDS  BIDES
AMI  CRUDES  OHO  ARREST
DINGHY  MANET  PET
XTRA  FLOODSMOUSEHOLE
INLIEUOF  SEZ  REX
BUILDABETTERMOUSETRAP
ARTLOVER  HECTOR  BOISE
GLOSSARY  SAVOY  YENTL
```

95

```
MAJOR  BUSLANE  IAMS  TMEN
ADOBE  ONEIRON  SWAK  HILO
LIKEFISHIFITS  MARIGOLDS
ONEARM  SEEOUT  STRAND
     HYATT  FRESHITSGOOD
ALE  TURKIC  EPA  OSAGE
LILAC  RAINES  INCASH  TRE
TRUTHINITSSUNDAYCLOTHES
SALOON  THEUSA  CARLO
     PRAM  TRAVAIL  WEAR
OBI  IRISH  ANECHOASKINGA
HORIZONTAL  CONTENTION
SHADOWTODANCE  PEETE  DDT
OREL  LABELER  ETES
     ERNIE  SAYIDO  EPILOG
THEDEIFICATIONOFREALITY
WON  EPINAL  MRKITE  DONOR
ORRIN  MLI  ESSENE  DEO
ANACTOFPEACE  NEARS
     GARBLE  NEWBIE  SALLIE
ONINYEARS  BEINGNOTDOING
DONS  SIKH  ALLGONE  OMEGA
ERGO  ELSE  GLEANER  NOSED
```

96

```
JOLT  TRAD  ETHER  ATBAY
ARIA  AUTO  NOISE  VIOLA
MARKSPITZ  JUNEPOINTER
SLEEPIN  IHOPE  ABASHED
     SING  NOYES  RETE
FAINT  AGREE  VASELINE
DONNYOSMOND  JIBES  CUR
ERN  IFFY  DUEL  FIDO
AGES  GRAF  KENJENNINGS
RESTORER  JACKO  AINGE
     ARES  FORKS  PIKE
MARIE  AILES  CELESTAS
MERVGRIFFIN  SRAS  TORO
ADEE  RATE  SPUR  RIO
SEE  PERCY  ETHELMERMAN
CALLEDIT  LAPEL  ANEEL
     ONIT  CESAR  BIGD
ATLANTA  HAITI  ELECTRA
FREDASTAIRE  CARLLEWIS
TOTEM  EARNS  ARGO  LACK
SWORE  DURST  LEST  LYES
```

97

```
CREES   ICEAGES   SLAP
HEAVE   FANWAVE   AWARE
MENSAWEARDEPARTMENTS
HOC  INNS  RUSE  GRIDDLE
ANKLES  CAIRO  SEA  RAT
WOEIS  THREEMENINATUBA
SCRATCHER  EXE  SLR
ELEM  ROWERS  HABITABLE
RED  FIRSTAIDAKIT  COAL
PILES  FOILED  MITZI
CRANES  REFUGED  DANTES
HOSTA  TALIAS  LINGO
UPTO  INDIANAOCEAN  MAC
BEATINGIT  STRAIN  ELIA
ARC  ACT  ACCEPTERS
AWALKINTHEPARKA  ROSSI
RET  SEE  NOBEL  JONSON
CATSHOW  TATA  ELON  PUG
ARIVERARUNSTHROUGHIT
ROLEX  RATTIER  CLEAT
ONAN  KISSERS  HEDDA
```

98

```
SASHED  ADAMS  ABE  GRIT
IMPALA  SADAT  BELGIANS
TURNSTOSTONE  ISSUANCE
ASIDE  SHA  SEALE  TNG
REGS  THESCARLETLETTER
ATO  EER  ANSE  ARAT
SHOWHOWITSDONE  TENURE
TEL  ELEV  SLO  SATES
REALM  LANE  ENT  URE
ADFEE  ONEND  REPLACE
DEIS  SHOVEOVER  THEA
RISESTO  BRIER  HEARD
ESO  EEK  TITO  ARNIE
GUSTO  DIS  OLDS  DEL
HENSON  SIMPLEPLEASURE
ITBE  YEAS  AAA  ATH
PAINTINTOACORNER  AMBS
ATE  GENRE  FAO  ATYOU
ELSINORE  MARLINLINEUP
STEADMAN  AGOAL  EDERLE
ADDL  EMS  SEEPS  VERSES
```

99

```
SKAT  MOCHA  GRASSO  SNARE
INGA  AXIOM  RICHER  HAREM
COURTTOTRYBEATINGVICTIM
SWAMI  INTENSIVE  ONLINE
AGOG  ANA  ECOL  SST
MARCHPLANNEDFORAUGUST
AGO  TRACT  SAAB  TARP
EARL  ADEEP  LOOM  GIVES
TEACHERSTRIKESIDLEKIDS
EMIR  STEEN  SCARE  EDEN
RUED  REST  ATEAM  AMS
FEDSDISCOVERCRACKINLA
TOR  HIPPO  EREI  KYRA
ELAL  TSARS  TONGS  TVMA
CITYSHOMELESSCUTINHALF
HOOCH  SAIL  HILDA  LILO
RAHS  NOOK  DEANA  IAN
LAWYERSGIVEPOORADVICE
ASI  AXEL  EVE  ESAI
ATOAST  LITERALLY  MAJOR
MANGETSYEARINVIOLINCASE
CLEFT  COSMIC  INGOT  OVAL
OLLAS  INTAKE  STABS  MAYO
```

100

```
APSO  TRACHEA  HIHO  AFT
PLAX  NICHOLS  IDEA  LAO
BAREFOOTINTHEPORK  ELK
STAYAT  DOOR  MEASLE
THEMERCHANTOFVENISON
EAU  DAIS  MAWS
THEBURGERSOPERA  BEND
EUROPEAN  TIED  GEDDES
SMITTEN  BALL  MARGARET
HENSON  WURSTSIDESTORY
GOAL  TREE
PORGYANDBISQUE  NUTMEG
AVERAGES  NOUN  FISHERY
RELACE  DRNO  PASSESON
RANK  ABIESIRISHROAST
ASTI  TYKE  YET
CHITLINSOFALESSERGOD
CAVEIN  FLOE  WEARER
ODE  AHAMFORALLSEASONS
SOT  RAGU  STPETER  UNIV
TWO  STEM  SATIRES  POMP
```

101

```
AMINOR  SECANTS  BOOHOO
SATIRE  TAPROOT  ENRAPT
STOCKCHARACTER  TEASET
THREATENS  SLED  GLARE
SNOW  SHOOTINGSTAR
LEAH  SOTTO  OTRAS
ABSORB  FRITOPIES  MARS
MASTEROFARTS  ANODAL
AYN  HORSY  ISLAM  EDINA
MAAM  APIARY  SEEDY
WIZARDOFID  ACEOFCLUBS
AMEND  LOMEIN  SOIT
YALIE  URALS  CHILE  ORE
ORIANA  LIGHTNINGBUG
FIGS  BARBEDWIT  OTOOLE
PIXAR  REAPS  LEER
COMPUTERICON  ARIL
ARIEL  LEGO  BARELYSEE
NINEPM  BALLPARKFIGURE
DOTTIE  IDIOTIC  ICEDIN
ONSETS  TENDSTO  THESKY
```

102

```
ACHE  OGPU  ARGOT  POSTS
CHUM  MIEN  MIRTH  ELIOT
CAMPAIGNPROMISE  CIGAR
ERA  STORIES  NERO  ONME
PINCH  LOLA  GAPS  HOS
TOPO  MODERNPROMETHEUS
STRODE  MAUI  COARSE
EPISTLE  UNPEG  KLEES
EMT  JASONPRIESTLEY
GIZMO  ENGLUT  TOE  APSO
GREENE  GRO  IGO  STRUTS
SOLS  PUB  PAVANE  EDSEL
SEASONPREMIERE  HMO
SAPID  DWELT  YAKUTSK
TRIAGE  IOUS  SHIISM
MANHATTANPROJECT  ONTO
OPS  ROWS  NELL  INPEN
RADS  NIPS  TIEBEAM  RRS
IHOPE  SILKSCREENPRINT
TOWER  TROOP  ERST  AZUR
ZENER  SEEDS  RTES  NEMO
```

103

```
LIBELS  HEWS  ASKS  THEM
ANORAK  ARIA  CHIA  HEMA
DANGCARROTS  TALLORDER
IFSO  TRICKDOWNTHEORY
DIA  BLEACH  ENL  MENSA
AXILLA  HAYES  SESSION
SEMS  SODIUM  CNN
BREADANDBUTTERPICK
SEXT  SARAN  OAK  LOOSES
IPASS  KABUL  DISSENT
DEC  THETEMPOFDOOM  ARI
ENTREES  SCREW  OSLIN
STAINS  VHS  TULSA  SACK
BOOGIEWOOGIEBUGBOY
MOT  URCHIN  RAFT
INHASTE  POSED  FOSSIL
SPORE  ALE  ERECTS  ANO
FAMILYSTYDINNER  ALTO
IPSOFACTO  THEJUNGBOOK
LEOS  LAIN  SOSA  SIENNA
ERNE  ENCS  ARTY  ALLSET
```

104

```
AKITAS  ENDED  KARL  RHO
HENRIK  RAISA  ANTE  OED
SECURITIESANALYST  TAI
INASENSE  CULL  SLATE
NEST  LASSO  ELONGATE
MER  MUSICALCOMEDY
AMINOS  CANED  NEO  PILE
FAMOUSLASTWORDS  SONYS
TYPES  UGHS  IOS  OEO
ROULETTE  FDA  IVANKA
ART  THEDOCTORISIN  HTS
SEARED  PHD  MASERATI
MAY  CEO  SANA  TIKIS
ATEUP  SHRIMPCOCKTAILS
WEAL  CIA  CARET  ILLSAY
WATERSOFTENER  ACE
DETAINEE  ABACK  DAIS
FARSI  AMAD  ERODIBLE
ANI  DEPARTMENTOFLABOR
ICE  ELAL  SIREN  FINEST
LES  DIME  TESLA  SIESTA
```

105

```
ASPIRATORS  STIMULANT
ELIMINATED  OPERASERIA
FIELDTRIPS  PARKRANGER
PDA  SOS  2ND ED  LUG
SATBY  AFTS  NBASTAR
OTTER  CAIRO  LGA  AHSO
MRE  RAINMAN  SARA  ISON
SERB  DIK  MOLDIER  EINE
KARATS  ADENO  ONTARGET
METH  SRA  EER  EOS  NYS
3RD ESTATE  WHOSON  1ST
ASA  SIR  ARM  EHS  ARTI
FORGETIT  GOBAD  SPURNS
ELMO  EARLOBE  ETS  NACL
WOOD  STYE  INVADES  COO
NUDE  EME  LEHRS  ASKME
GRENADE  DETS  STOMP
SIP  GO HOME  SKY  MEL
GRASSSKIRT  GROUNDBEEF
NOVELETTES  SILHOUETTE
POSSESSES  UNENDORSED
```

106

```
SOLACE  MAPLES  CHOWDER
IRONON  THEASP  RATHOLE
LUSTINAMERICA  ATTIMES
TINED  ROD  AFC  RONI
ROCCO  SINNININTHERAIN
UNA  PRONE  TORTE  TSR
HAUS  ARF  HONI  DOA  INI
RISQUEBUSINESS  BILGES
REUP  NIT  SHORELEAVE
EONS  KID  HAY  ATEE
THENAUGHTYPROFESSOR
DIAZ  GIL  ELO  EDIE
ALLEGATION  OTC  GOIN
NELSON  BROADCASTNUDES
EDU  DOT  ALTS  RHO  TOME
CIO  RELIT  APING  NEW
SAINTMISBEHAVIN  ESTAS
PUNS  APT  ELI  ENIAC
ORATORS  THEBAWDYGUARD
CATERTO  ORNERY  PEDROS
KEEPSIN  REDEYE  DRIEST
```

107

```
SAGES  CASABA  DUH  ISM
KNICKS  ELINOR  ENTENTE
INVOICEOFDOOM  NAMEDAY
TEE  LAP  INSTILLLIFE
AFIRE  BON  ARI  AFR
INDIFFERENTSTROKES
MEANT  EDISON  ELMERS
AIRS  ASPIC  LOP  SAXON
CNN  INCOMETOTHERESCUE
ERGO  ONEDGE  HOSE
CRIMSON  BONGS  GREENER
RUNE  RELACE  MEAD
INCREASERESISTANT  CAR
STAIR  SOL  GLINT  DOME
POSTIT  JOPLIN  SALMA
INVOCATIONALSCHOOL
AKA  SRO  AOK  OPALS
INTENTPOLES  RON  STU
MESSIAH  INTUITIONFEES
ELECTRA  SIERRA  RESUME
ETA  SSN  ADRIAN  DUMPS
```

108

```
MARYANN  CRAIGS  ROAST
ALOEVERA  REDCAP  ANKHS
JAMAICANMECRAZY  BERRA
ADE  TOP  ENE  INOUR
YOUDBESETONSTUNNING
SEAMY  BOOTSY  NOSE
AMELIA  CEE  ENC  THOS
ORISITJUSTYOU  SHIFT
ARC  NIC  CHACHA  OFA
KARL  HHH  LAUREATE
YOUREOUTOFTHISWORLD
COLORADO  ASS  NAES
APT  LITTLE  SSN  RBI
DEWEY  CANIHAVEYOURS
IRON  MLB  AXE  ICETEA
ARFS  MOESHA  SCOTT
YOURETHEONLYTENISEE
SCORE  OCT  EAU  NCO
NOTIE  YOUREMMMMMMGOOD
AMEND  TVROOM  POPSICLE
PORGY  DEEDEE  SHUSHED
```

109

```
PINGPONG  MAANDPA  HAM
EMOTICONS OFFYEAR  ILE
NOTONESCUPOFTEETH  GIG
DUE ELY BOCA  TEACHER
STRATO MEMOIRS  TAWNY
 CATHODEWRAITH  DATA
PTER ELIS SIGHED  YON
MOHR SLIT  NOMEAT
ISO BAIN HAMLET  AMORE
SSR ESCAPEKEITH  RAHAL
SLOVAK TRILL  ATHENA
IQUIT DOUBLEYOUTH  ATT
SSGTS ENISLE TSOS  LEE
 HAMILL LOOP  CTRS
JEB ENVOIS SOON  AAHS
AARP SEATTLESLEUTH
CREAM NOSIREE  NANANA
KHAYYAM ITIS LAN  LOC
MAD BOTTOMOFTHEWEALTH
ART ANGELOU  ORIENTATE
NTH DESCENT  SADDENED
```

110

```
PETULA BRAN SHAD  CPAS
ARISEN IDLE COSI  LANA
NIGHTINGALEHAWKSLARKS
ACE SOIE USER  FRESCAS
MARTINPARROTSCOOTS
 ANS TEEN  ARBORDAY
RASP DENS GRIME  IOLA
OBI INERT BEENE  ANGER
LOGICAL ACTI  PIGGED
FINCHDUCKSCUCKOOS
ELSE IGNIS GHOST  PLEA
 WRENSWALLOWSRAILS
SENSES SECY  AIMLESS
HUEYS FLEES BALES  GIA
ALEC BOOST COLD  SEEM
HADATALK WHOA  CMI
 MERLINROOKSBOOBIES
YESORNO AERO KART  NUI
SPARROWGULLSCARDINALS
EINE NEAT DERN  ELOPES
RCAS EROS SRIS  DESTRY
```

111

```
 SHINING SONTAG  ETHIC
CHEMICAL MONACO  RHODE
NEWAGEMOVEMENTS  GETIN
NANCE WEEP TIEA  CPOS
 ROWEL HARVESTHOME
ACHE WORDS RAE  TROTS
QUARTERSTAFF  ERES
UPLOADS WASH  ROPETOW
ASFIT TOADY EAR  ANODE
 ACEY BLUELAGOON  TEE
UCLA MOOGS IVORY  SHAD
ROO PAPERTIGER  EPEE
GRADE ESE BANAL  EMMAS
ENFIELD NEAT  EELPOUT
 SKIS CRESCENTROLL
LATIN MST DARCY  ENDO
WAXINGSALON  LEHAR
ARIL OONA OVUM  EMILE
NILLA FULLMETALJACKET
DALEY TROYES  TOODLEOO
STARE CEMENT  ELYSIAN
```

112

```
SOFAR SPAGHETTI  DIMES
MARIE PATROLMAN  ENEMY
UTURN INTELLECT  CPLUS
 IVEBEENAMINERFORA
STAGERS SAO  TARRING
TABLEAU TENTS  AUSSIES
OLAV LUAUS TAUNT  OTTO
ASTEROIDS  DRAWSNEAR
DAS OMOO ALI AMAT  STE
 AUDEN BRAUNS  ARRAU
EBSEN READIED  MIDST
PAYTO SEN DEA  PIERO
UTNE AUPAIR NASSAU TVAD
PEEN DIRGE EKING  SEMI
UNI SIRENS CAREER  NSC
 LAGOON ERRANT
ISYET DEGAULLE  GOYAS
SPONSOR RATIO  BIENNIA
TRUE HEARTOFGOLD  FIST
LINA ONTOE TILDE  ANNA
EGGS HEARS SNAGS  TEEN
```

113

```
EMBLEM IMAC  BACKBAY
BORAXO ACIDY  EXHALED
BOOSTERCHAIR  GLAZERS
RATATAT DIS  ROE
RADON FISCALPERIODS
UGARTE OARS AGES  ITT
SEXY SANTA PROAM  NEO
 SPA YAMS  RAGGED
PUB WEBBROWSER  OHNO
CRETIN LONE  APPLE
BLARNEYED  HEYERDAHL
 REESE MUON  NEARBY
SCTV NANOSECOND  TOE
NIHILO SOME  INA
AVE ADOPT SIPON  SLIP
GIB YORE HUSH  TATAMI
LUNARECLIPSES  RETAG
RAS TOP  RETAPED
REDPINE CHINESEBOXES
FREEDOM HOPED  CLUEIN
DENSEST SPOT  SETSTO
```

114

```
MAINST OMEGAS  TABASCO
OBLATE BEARDS  ORALLAW
PULPITFICTION  TELLALL
 ENCL CONN  SANKIN
ANDTHEBANDITPLAYEDON
EGO YUL SIR  DELE
REMAT RUNAT PINOT  REO
ALARUM FICHU  NOREASON
SITINSOFTHEFATHERS
EMT AGO MOPE  MINT
DIE OTOMIS SERGEI  EHS
 TRON EDAM RMN  WOE
FREETOBITEYOUANDME
PICAYUNE UTERO  SLEEPS
ENL ERGOT ALOUD  SALSA
EROS ROZ TEA  HOW
PITIEDPIPEROFHAMELIN
 HEROIC NOPE  TOTO
EPIGONE KITINGHENRYIV
BREEDER ATONCE  BANANA
WORSENS THREES  ASAMAN
```

115

QANDA SPASM DATUM MEG
EQUUS CANTO IRATE ADO
DUNST HITUP SORELOSER
ANTIPERSPIRANTS LAND
RAM YESES RADII
ASTA RAF HATCHETFACE
SHAD STASH DELUXE
HARDHEARTED REST LIMB
KATIE ROYAL OSOLEMIO
SENOR SAL BOZ ERODING
HAT IFTHESHOEFITS TOG
ALUMNAE SEA REN SPARS
DELUGING ENSOR PEETE
EGAD SCAN DRIVERSSIDE
WAITON INIGO COIL
SHESALLTHAT DOZ INNS
TONED ONEAL TAB
INTL HIPPOCRATICOATH
NOOFFENSE HEXES ONEUP
GUM CEDAR INERT SERAI
ORB CLOTS EARNS TWICE

116

BANJO WHAT KANJI JAGR
EBSEN EIRE DROOL ALAI
EBERT ASTARLINGISBORN
RACEHORSE EASE KABOBS
MEDO MINE DEFENSE
SQUIDINKLING DRYER
TUVALU ION DINO AAA
DIED MILITARYCOUPLING
STASI MTN PILE HASTE
SIPE LPGA CHAPLIN
WITHALLDUELINGRESPECT
AMIABLY LAID LUXE
NONCE INRE GOD STACY
DUCKLINGANDCOVER ALOE
ATT NOOR AWE EELING
RISER TOWNDUMPLING
SILENTL REVS SAIS
POINTA AONE DEEPSIXED
UNDERLINGARREST OZONE
RIDE LATEN BETA DEUCE
NAYS SNERT IMAX ESTER

117

BEGUN PAIN GALA SOAPS
BUONO RENO OLES TOTAL
BROKEFORGO DLII AMANA
DEVITO KEEPSFORPLAY
BROMINE FAR REALMS
COMPLIMENTSFORFISH
DUET BEE RES COS
EEN THEBESTFORWORKOUT
OWEN TELS NUNCIO
JUMBOSIZE NOAHS NIKON
UPTO ADAYFORKING GLUE
GROIN SKEIN APARTHEID
GOSSIP ODES PAST
LOSTTIMEFORMAKEUP PET
ETA VON ELO WALK
KNOWLEDGEFORTHIRST
BASALT TET ORESTES
APPLESFORBOB POINTE
SERIA AJAR ALLFORFREE
TRANS HADI JOIE YURIS
ASYET DYES AXED ILENE

118

EDEN BOAS OSHA THROAT
DEMI LYNN ROOM ROARER
GAMEMISCONDUCT AUNTIE
ANACIN HOPES RIDS HOE
RESECT OKRA FACETIOUS
AZUR LOOKEDON
HALFSERIOUSLY INTACT
OLEO NTWT ELEVS ELOI
PATROL ENERGETIC RIDE
INS MAS ERE ANOINTED
GATHERINGCLOUDS
INCAREOF DOE SNL FLA
DAHL NETRESULT TEDIUM
ETUI ISSEL LIVY ODAY
DOGLEG WANDERINGSOUL
ETHYLENE APER
TAKEITOUT PEAT GETSBY
ACE EHUD SHARI AEOLIA
STANNO WATERINGTROUGH
SUNUNU ISAW OGLE LEGO
OPENER GAGS TSOS ESSO

119

DILATOR ALBUMEN FERAL
INALINE LOOPERS IVANA
ACHENES TUPPERWA[REP]ARTY
[DEM]ARCATED REEKS TIDIES
ONORDER ATTEND
REA[DEM]ANDWEEP ACTI
ARGON EMS CA[REP]ACKAGES
FIRSTBORN SIRED AROMA
TEA OAR AGATE TYCOON
INTERNET BLO HUTS
LEN DONTM[IND]IFIDO ETE
MILT ASS ONLOOKER
OLEARY BALKY PIX OBS
MANNA SNAIL FLATPANEL
ACA[DEM]YAWARD UIE ADELA
NAME INSTANT[REP]LAY
SPRAIN ENTHUSE
SILENT PINTO SPA[REP]ARTS
I[DEM]ANDARECOUNT IRONOUT
SANER BEETRED STRIPED
INAWE INTENDS HOTNESS

120

ILSA LUCITE ISMS FREI
LAND UNISON ATOP REDO
IDAHOPOTATO MAYIGONOW
ALKENE RAISINGARIZONA
DEERE PUCE ROE ELEVE
ESSES MATCH ANAIS
SEETHED ISIN RUE TLC
EXMOOR ESQS TELLS ELI
STP TENNESSEEWALTZ
ERIK NOG INC AAHS
ARIVERRUNSTHROUGHIT
SERA PAS ISP NSEC
IMFROMMISSOURI SEE
MSN PROSY PHAT ONCALL
OTO YSL SPUN ROTATES
PARMA HOSNI GATOR
LEONA FOO SPRY TONYA
ALABAMAJUBILEE VALIUM
POLITICOS BAKEDALASKA
BULL GERE INONIT LEON
STYE ODDS STEEPS TINA

121

```
SODAPOP   TOMBS    PAT  SIP
ETAMINE   WRATH    ANILINE
CHICKENLEAGUE      STEAMER
TOSS  STEELY   DETECTORS
      ALOT   BAZAAR   LENTE
  MAGRITTE    RETRY    IDS
BLANKCHEEK   SEAS    PAEAN
SINE  EARLE  TACH   STILE
MIDIS LEPEW  RHEA    EZER
TIESUP DOLAN EACH    ECO
   SERA  TENOR   FREQ
CUR ZAGS  DEREG   ERRANT
AVER MOON  DUPLO   SADTO
MEDEA OLEO  SEALE   TIER
SAHIB  DOWN  HARDPRIEST
   ENS  MISTI  LETITOUT
SLAVE ENROLL  DISS
PARENTAGE  DYNAMO  PLED
ANISTON  EDUCATEDGEESE
SANTINI  LACES   RIPOSTE
MIG AGE  SWEET   SCANTER
```

122

```
RUMS PFC  OBAMA   JUICES
ETAL OIL  FUJIS   INDIAN
DANIELLE  FRANKENSENSE
WHYPAYMAHER   NAKEDEYE
IAM VESTED  PROUST   MAZ
NGO ESTEE   HEAT   TEASE
GERM  TAD  METZ   DILL
SNEAKER  LIFEOFOREILLY
   DER PEN  RAGAS   III
CBER  ARTURO   SOB  SNAP
YOUREGETTINGCOULTER
SCOP CAL  ECHOED   EONS
ALS DORIA  ITS   BEL
DOTHELIMBAUGH  FIRESUP
   ASEC BLAH  MON  NANU
ENAMI  SITE  TAROS  GEN
MOL RICHES  HIRSCH  URN
PRERADIO  DONAHUEDARE
IMUSBEOFFNOW  CALLERID
RATTLE  AREEL  AMA  TONI
ENSUES  ROARS  SER  SSGT
```

123

```
WBA  BLAB  ARMADA  HOLST
HON  RAKI  BEIGES  OWETO
ONTHEWATERFRONT   UNSER
ONLOW  TROI   ERIS   SRI
PEEL  OVERANDABOVE   ENE
STRIPPER  DEED   SATIRES
   DETECT  DIDY  NORA
ISAAC  OOO  STAG   PINTO
MIRY  DELUXEMODEL   STAN
PDT TODDLED  ALIBIIKE
LEILANI  ANGST   AVONLEA
ACCURATE  AWAITED   LON
NAHS  TONIBRAXTON   FEUD
TROTH RULE  GEL   PESTO
   KEEL  FOTO  SLALOM
PIERROT  NOAH  CLEMATIS
ACH OBIWANKENOBI   LINT
NEE ISTH  TAOS   SENSE
AMAIN  HOWARDSTERNSHOW
MARNE  ELYSEE  YOYO  ALE
ANTES  SEEKER  ANEW  TED
```

124

```
PLAQUE   TIEPOLO   GAUSS
LAGUNA   ONWATER  TEAPOT
ASGOODASNEWTON   ETHANE
ZEIT  SPCA   ROACH   GIA
AREEL  PATTONONTHEBACK
   AWL ELLIS  ENLAI
PINCHHIT  CANTONOPENER
IDEA OEUF  FEET   RSVP
CLUBCARTON  SNAPUP   TAM
SERIO  RAP   ROREM
DONTGIVEMEANYLIPTON
   STOLI   IRA   IOTAS
RAJ AGENCY  PROTONSHOP
AGUA  NAUT  COHO   SEMI
SEXTONSYMBOL  PINDARIC
   TOILE  EAVES   RAW
CHARLESTONATLAS   IBMPC
HIP CASER   OPTS   AARE
AROMAS  ROLLAWAYCOTTON
RESENT  PLEADER   ANITAS
ODETS  SEAPORT  MAKEME
```

125

```
BABYISH   WANDA    MISTI
ORIENTAL  ALOUD   LINEAR
OGALLALA  FLEESPITTERS
TOSLAYTHEEAST   ONTOP
   SYS  TORY  ALE   WITS
MICA  VINYLSLIDING   NET
EROTICA  ALOT   ANGER
TEA NOM  MOBIL   IMPASTO
ANT FOPLOVER   CASTLED
LEONE  EMIR  CZAR   HIRE
FUR STUDLYHAL   SAC
PUMA MASS  IOUS   ANKHS
ONANDON  CODCULTS   NIT
KINCAID  MUZAK  OOH  EMU
ISLES  BEAR   LEADSON
LOY HALVETHEGAL   ISMS
YMCA LIE  EGAD   FIN
   ORSON  PACEYOURBELTS
PLOTTEDPANTS   PRESSURE
SERIES  ORNOT  TIREIRON
INSET  PEERS   SENNETT
```

126

```
BIDS  GRIPS  GAD   BASES
ELIE  TOOTOO   ELEARNING
RIPE  ARMIES  ROBROYROT
MADMAXMANMAYMARMAT
DITTIES   USDA    CIRCA
DOUR  LIAR    SHMEAR
TAD BIGBICBIZBIO   ELMO
INIT DIECUT  OUNCE   YEN
EGGO ETCH   NOTBAD
REDUBS  KEANE   TOLE  ALP
ELITE  FOEFORFOX   NADER
DAN EBAN  ONION   USEDTO
   CLUING  UFOS   RADS
ODS HANNA  CARLOS   ODIE
LOOP HAGHASHAYHAT   ZED
DWARFS  SIAM   LUKA
ENROL  AMOK   SEABEDS
   SADSAMSAWSALSAYSAX
PUGPUPPUN  CANUCK   PAVE
INTENSIVE  ACACIA   ADEN
SHORT  NES  DOPED   DORA
```

127

```
ENGELS    TOTALLOSS   NTWT
LOOKTO    INORDERTO   ERIE
INTERNETEXPLORER      BURN
JOES   ALL      NINE   USES
ANA  PATE   EAR   NOSALT
HOMERSODYSSEY    STRAYS
   DIEN  ETHNOS    MESAS
ALPACA  JAR  ARABIA   INN
CEASE  URBANLEGEND    DSL
EARN   ONSIDE    ATEASE
SHTETLS  GAUGE   TESTKIT
   IRISES    RISKED  AIDA
ZSA  REALTROOPER   ARCED
AIL  ENTIRE  RAN  TRIKES
GRECO   MALIGN   THIN
  SCHUSS  MINIATUREGOLF
  LATKES  CEO  IPOS  CAL
ONIT  EZEK    UTA   ECUA
RAPT  TWENTIETHCENTURY
APSE  CHRISTINE   INALIE
LEER  HOSTESSES   NETTED
```

128

```
ALFALFA   SACO    SSGT  FAS
SOIREES   TRAC  UTAH   ALP
TWELFTHNIGHT   RESOLUTE
EFFETE   OPENAREA   RANEE
RAINY  BTEN  DEFLEPPARD
STES  FEAST   MISS   ESS
     ELOI   AMOR  TEL
SELFREFLECTIVE   ELSOL
ATEASE  RENEE   ALI  REF
MCVI   PULLON  ABLE  VAL
SHELFLIFE   IFEELFINE
OIL  RELO  ISHALL   OLDE
NNE  EEL  ATEAM   EAGLET
  GREET  FLEXIBLEFLYERS
   IDI  EVRY   AWOL
HEF  DEMI   HIRER   ECCE
IANFLEMING  ENVS   ALLAN
STLEO  INSOMNIA  ARDENT
TEALEONI  GOLDENFLEECE
ORC  WHOS  OREL  PRESSER
OSE  SORT   STYE  ROSTERS
```

129

```
STREAM    MOM   COSI   JELL
TROLLED   EVE  ALAS   OREO
PAULINE  DEADMANWAKING
ASTI  INDORSE   DETENTE
THESANTACAUSE    RATS
    ABAD  TRICKERY   AOL
  ATTHAT  SEE  ROE  ANTE
OAHU  CEDE   PUPFICTION
TREBEK  INDIA    DROMES
ROBES   YESORNO  SIENA
ANI  THESEVENTHSEA  HOD
  GRAIN  DINESEN  STONE
UPSIDE   SEDER  NEBULA
THEGODRUSH   GOTO  ASOF
NYES  ESA  UNO  HEBREW
ESP  ANGELINA   ARLO
  ASIA  SNAKESONAPANE
IMPRINT   TIELINE  ASIN
WAROFTHEWORDS   GILDING
ITEM  HERA  ELI  SLEDDER
NAPA  SRAS  DYE  LAYERS
```

130

```
ERRATA    MISLAID   IQTEST
REEFER    INTEGRA   LUELLA
SANTASHADANEASYSEASON
TRESSES     TITHE   ULEES
    ENT  OBESE   ABE
SARTRE  ANENT   ARMREST
ISEE   ASAN   ITNO   DEET
LYINGINHISBIGRECLINER
LEN  UNDER  ALOUD  ATONE
STS  IRES   SPIRE  PERSE
   RTES  PITAS  PLOD
ALBEE   PANIC   SEAR  EFT
BIOTA  IOTAS   TACIT  PIE
IFYOUASKHIMFORAREASON
TELL  MAES   IRAN   TONO
  REDCAPS  CAJUN  ICEMAN
   ANT  ARKIN   URI
RADON  TORII    PORTHOS
EVERYTOYISMADEINCHINA
LEMMON  EDIBLES   ELATES
ORIENT   RESOLES   DETERS
```

131

```
FIJI  ARCED    VOCAB  HALO
IGOR  LIONS   APOLO  ANON
ELLS  ATHOL   NEWTO  IDOS
SOLARIZE     PASTRAMI
TOYGUN  INFLUENCE  TABBED
ASHEN  PROLETARIAT  CRUDE
  ANSEL  TOYOTAS  ANOUT
APPT  RAGS   CAKE   STUS
GAPS  SCOOTS  BIOMES  HOSP
EDY  REED  STREW  IOTA  NEA
ITSNO  BAKERSDOZEN  RANDR
SHOESTORE  OTS  ONEOCLOCK
TAUTLY  DERN  PROS  VASSAL
SIL  YRS  LOG  RET  AIN  ERE
  SNAPS  PAREE  RIDES
PSIS  HABERDASHER  ATVS
ANDTWOEYESMADEOUTOFCOAL
LEA  AURAL    OPINE  LGA
PERETTI  FASCIAS  MASHERS
ARETE  CORNCOBPIPE  TORAH
TENURE  TIGHTENED  TISANE
ERODES  TEEM  SERF  EVENTS
  STERE  OSLO  TASS  KEATS
```

132

```
PAPAL   NACRE   MESH  FLEW
AGATE   FLAIR   AREA  LORE
COCOAFLAVOR   COTS  AURA
  GILDA  NET  GASSTATION
   FLUB   DECOR  FENNELS
AMI  PLACIDODOMINGO
WACS  ELAN  LONERS  TSAR
ACHE  SID   SATIRE  MEESE
SAUNA  GRIP   ETTU  ETA
HUMORONESELF   OAR  MIR
  PRIM  SHROUDS  LATE
SIB  OAS  MASONICLODGE
OVA  SNOG   EDAM  SQUAB
SACCO  LISLES  PAM  UNTO
ANKA  MIGUEL   SAGE  ECOL
  READINGBATTERY  ERA
ACCOSTS  DIANE    GARR
FALLOUTFIT   YEA  EMOTE
ORAL  RARA  WORLDSAPART
OGRE  ETAL  ENEMY  HEINE
TOAD  DENS  TERSE  ARNEL
```

133

NOWNOW · FLAK · CLU · DAWNS
AVIATE · LIMA · OOP · ALEUT
TUFTED · OVERSHOT · NIFTY
OMEARA · WESTWEFORGET
· GLISTENS · IRANI · NBC
OBOE · THRU · APE · OTB · EOE
CEE · DRE · PATENTWEATHER
ALSORANS · LEDTO · WHIRR
LOONEY · EMI · OPULENCE
AWNED · PEASE · EKES · ODED
· GIANTWIZARD ·
OCTS · PESO · ERECT · GOMAD
FOOTPATH · ERA · SECEDE
FREEH · OLSEN · BAILSMAN
ARTWINKWETTER · RCS · OZS
LAH · ZEN · GIS · EWOK · CREE
LET · NASAL · ARROWKEY
WAKEVICTORIA · EARWIG
AMISH · EXISTENT · ARIANA
FANTA · REE · TESH · VAUNTS
TWEEN · YRS · OLES · ENMESH

134

MAD · MISC · AMBO · DIS[COS]TU
ARAB · ASAD · ROAN · ASAMAN
MINE · CA[TAN]DMOUSE · SUDOKU
ESTATES · REDEEMS · PIKES
TEETH · GIL · DIDI · ERA
[SIN]NER · AVI · LINING · ARE
IMFINE · DESMOND · BLAMES
SEEKERS · SYN · SOONEST
ISR · TUT · BADG(E) · ALBERTA
TON · NATE · A(T)MIDDAY
INONE · REST(R)(O)(O)MS · LETCH
OLIVEOY(L) · NAAN · WEE
RIBCAGE · (T)(R)(I)GO · CIT · ODE
IDEATED · ONA · KNEEPAD
COLLET · HANGMAN · TAXERS
ENL · SIMONE · BMI · HAHA
TIA · TROT · LOX · CA[SIN]OS
AC[COS]TS · SPITZER · SITUATE
MAITAI · EQUIDIS[TAN]T · SPEX
ORTEGA · RUNT · SIZE · TORE
KEYNES · SEAS · TRAM · DOS

135

BABAR · WONAT · STOLEN · BOA
ALOHA · ROUSH · REPROVE · ENT
AFRAIDOFTHEDARKROOM · REA
SAD · SINS · ROOTS · FLOWNIN
EWING · VAMOS · BEAV · HIRE
BRINGSHOMEROOMTHEBACON
RITES · ASSN · TWAS · AMEND
IDOL · TILT · DAIS · WES
POWDERROOMKEGS · SPAZ · ZIG
ANN · VIA · KEANE · ROUX · JESU
BILGE · ATM · FELT · SERTA
THEBALLSINYOURCOURTROOM
SAXON · ATTY · TRE · SPEAK
ARAY · USES · OHGOD · JAM · PSS
REM · FESS · GREENROOMPARTY
CRY · LEER · JIBS · WORN
OMAHA · AJAR · TKOS · SOFAS
NORESTROOMFORTHEWICKED
ELMS · ERGS · ONION · ASHES
AIRTAXI · FUMES · ALEE · SKA
DEE · DAVYJONESLOCKERROOM
ARS · ACEDOUT · TITHE · ZORBA
YET · MORSEL · ENTER · ONSET

136

LOFT · DEADON · UPSIDEC
HELLO · ERNEST · ELEONORA
TOMEI · ERESTU · HARDLOOK
TIECLIPS · POPGUN · AANDE
PICKEDS · MISLED · PAYEES
STE · ROSIER · TIS
ACC · SALINES · TWOHEADS
LOOS · SLAT · SWOON · XMEN
LOUTS · OLEO · TEEF · STALE
ALREADY · SUPRAS · CARRIE
TRIAD · STEAK · AILEY
SMELLY · JOININ · GREMLIN
OASIS · FERN · NEMO · SELMA
CLAN · DLEIF · SAGE · WING
KINGLEAR · EASEONT · SOS
AUK · SPATES · OHM
SPAWNS · PEARLS · CLEANSE
PALEO · MOESHA · LIARLIAR
ONEFLESH · HANSOM · OASTS
SETTINGS · ARTURO · AWAIT
EDASNER · STANDC · DINE

137

THIRDRATE · REBUS · ECUA
ORATORICAL · UTOPIANISM
TOPSBOTTOM · FATSSKINNY
TDS · BOAS · PUSHY · IDEAL
REP · SKIS · DDS
MAJORSMINOR · BEARSBULL
AVOW · AMANA · ALIE · ESAU
LINDA · SARAN · HESS · DATS
PLAYSWORK · HEAVYSLIGHT
HAS · HONE · BARI · AMESS
COSTCO · ASSENT
ASPCA · RIGS · MANE · FWD
SPRINGSFALL · HIRESFIRE
BIOG · OTAY · ABORT · TOXIN
IRMA · TRIO · NOTCH · RENT
GOSRETURN · CASHSCHARGE
RAM · VERY · HEY
AGAIN · MISER · WEAL · ZAG
LEFTSRIGHT · PARKSDRIVE
FLATTENOUT · SWEETIEPIE
ATRY · AGREE · TENSENESS

138

EATME · ERA · CITE · ARARAT
SCRAMBLED · ONEMORETIME
SAYHEYKID · HUSBANDTOBE
ESTERS · NEVERS · TAHITI
STORY · VENIRE · BEZEL
BADDIE · KOS · NABOB
RAD · SEMIS · PEU · ROI
IRE · CAPN · RETINAE · SIZE
DUMDUMS · DAMASCUSSTEEL
OBIES · HELP · TEETER
FATTEDCALF · TERRACOTTA
EMILIA · AIRS · UKIAH
PRICEEARNINGS · FORESEE
LUNT · UPCCODE · MAME · NBA
USC · EEN · EAVES · TOD
STABS · FLY · BOUTON
RAHAL · TARTAR · COIGN
CLOVEN · FORKED · GAUCHE
SLOWINGDOWN · ROYALTIES
RAINORSHINE · PRESIDENT
ORNERY · LESS · EST · FORTS

139

```
THEOSCAR SONATA LISPS
NONONONO SOONER ENCRE
ONTHEWATERFRONT NIHIL
TERSE AWS ERN NOTIME
EYE BITE PLAICE INES
SSE PETERJACKSON ADD
SITS ANO ONEALL
LAWLESS BIC ENC SLEDS
ETHIC OMA HAN ASSYRIA
SLIMED UNFORGIVEN SNL
OAT AMIGO AUDEN LET
TSE CLARKGABLE TAHITI
HECKLER OYL FAD GESTE
OSHEA ILK LES ROASTER
RENATO OIL IBIS
HIP MARLEEMATLIN COD
MESH ALDOUS BELT APU
ACTOUT SUV ROE ABNER
HUMUS SHIRLEYMACLAINE
ABASE RISEUP EXAMINES
LASER SPASMS DEBATERS
```

140

```
KOOLBID REGS CECILIA
ONLEAVE AROOM UNITING
ICETRAY INTRA PRUSSIA
ESSEN ELECTS SIDEA
DADDYSHACK CALMS
IOC MIATA GOODFATS
STARHAZER WEBB RIA
OHDEAR DENIM JVDRIPS
LEGPARTY SEGER ESTEES
DRESS HASTE RESETS
ESS NIXEDDRINKS ADO
SEESIN SOLTI ASLAN
SNATCH SAUTE SPYBEANS
POPRUIZ THOSE OMENII
ALP EYES SWISSMIST
MILKDVDS OPTIC SHE
EENIE LOXPROFILE
GONNA SHRINE ASWAN
GOATEES SOAMI PUTITON
NUTTREE OSHEA IRONAGE
PRESORT ASSN COPYBOZ
```

141

```
HIGHC BIO FOR DIOCESE
ONEAL ASCRIBE ENROLLS
INNIE NOTIFICANHELPIT
TRANSLATE TIA TAPE
UKE IHAVE SIMBA SIR
TIED METE IMPOSITIONS
ELLERBEE AMAIN TOV
BOYS STARK NESTS
TABOO BOOGIE HOE TIP
EVENTHORIZON DIASPORA
MALE AUEL MOTT EGAD
PLUSSIGN DISACCHARIDE
TOG UGH BORERS FLEES
SNARE ONICE SPAM
IDA FEAST CARRADIO
DRYVERMOUTH LONI NINA
EAU SMURF JINGO NET
OMNI RTE HUNGARIAN
DONTBEASTRANGER GRETA
ANALYST INHOUSE HERON
RANLATE MAN ATE TASTY
```

142

```
MEADOW SMASH GOODTIME
OPTIMA LECHE ACCREDIT
PORKERFARCES LATINATE
ESA LCDTV ASEA OPART
AERIE ATIT SPINES
PRETTYCRASHACCOUNT
LEWIS LIEN COST SAS
ONEL OGLES ASTEROIDS
TORTEBRAG COB SOFTON
NOAH BAABAA NAPS
IGAVEITMYBRESTSHORT
TNUT LIBELS THAI
ATCAMP ASE CROWCHIRP
PECTORALS GLOSS OTOE
ELI ROBT TRUE CHELA
HOMERAWAYFROMHOMER
ALANIS TENS ALOES
ROMPS SELF ONAIR CUT
MOTLIEST FRISTFRIGHTS
ESTEEMED TERSE ESPANA
TEATREES HEROD SHAPER
```

143

```
TIPSTER EATS TOWROPE
UNITERS SCOUR UNAIRED
TELAVIV CURRENTEVENTS
EXOTICPORTS MAT ELATE
LITES TOE RABID TEL
ALER BLOW HERO OGLED
REDSHOES ROCKBANDS
ORT SINUS BASALTS
SPRINGBREAKS MET TARP
HOOKE EAR SEDATED VIA
RISERS CUR DID DESIST
USC SCHEMES NRA BASTE
NOON RAD STAGECOACHES
KNEEPAD TEARY HIT
HIPJOINTS TELECAST
MAINE CRTS FEDS ASHE
JAM DOTES BAN ALTER
ENORM OED GOLDRECORDS
STRAIGHTLINES OUTRIDE
TRAINEE YOURE DREIDEL
SALLIED USSR SORCERY
```

144

```
ANIM BASIC NEMO BIPED
TONI ALIAS ADAM ELAND
TOENAILCLIPPERS DIDOS
INSULTS HONK FRED
CASEYSTENGEL STRODEIN
NETS AVIONIC RIO DOO
STRETTO AKEEM END
ATPLAY TELEPHONE NIA
ARIA PURIM RIA DYEVAT
BONA ESE PITY SERE
AISLE SLUTSKAYA SALAD
TAMA ENRY ART SOLO
ENRAPT AAA GAMMA EPIC
MII THIRDGEAR BERETS
MVP YESNO AMADEUS
YEE HIE NATURAL HIST
SADCASES POTATOMASHER
SENT OGPU COROLLA
SQUAD SPORTSEQUIPMENT
GUISE EURO POTTS EPEE
TOTED APEX ASSET RPTS
```

145

```
RICS  SLAVS   SEPAL   RDS
ELLA  PEROT   USONE   ERIS
CLAYMANEXEMPTION   JAMA
ASSHE  TAPPETS   DISOWNS
PESETA   OUI   PANPIPES
SEALOVEAPPROVAL   ICILY
   LOATH   AIL   WREN
LIMO  THEBEAST    CBS
ELY  MAYDOUBTAWILL  EAT
ALLGIRL  SRS  ORT  ENTR
KEATS  CHOCTAW   LATHE
AGUE  HOO  OOP  SPAREME
GIG  KEYPAWNMOVING  RAT
ETH  URL  NODESIRE  LSTS
   TAWS  GOV  SOUSA
ADELA  MINEDOVERMATTER
BURLIVES  ONE  OLEOLE
AMMETER  DESTIJL  ISLED
SPIN  GRAYTOILEOFCHINA
HOLD  AIDED  METAL  OFAN
 NEE  NEEDS  EDEMA  WEST
```

146

```
WALESA  ARC  GER  SKITS
ABORTS  LOO  RENO  TENET
DISGUSTINGWINDS  JEANE
SEE  AAHED  EGRET  APRON
 SERMONONTHEDISMOUNT
ICANT   OTT   GENTS
GODISFIGURE   ABETS
GLAD  ARMS  RIGORS  DODO
YAYS  BEADS  NEHI  SUPER
 DISCOUNTERCULTURE
ANGORA   SIR   SAYSNO
FOODANDDISLODGING
READY  RODE  SOUSA  MSEC
OLDS  PAGODA  CMLV  OTRO
 NIGEL  DISMAYQUEEN
PATEN   OON   UNPIN
CABBAGEDISPATCHKIDS
ALLOR  DONAT  AMAIN  ALE
PLANE  DUCKANDDISCOVER
RITES  AGUA  EAR  SERENA
IDEST  SSR  ESS  ASTROS
```

147

```
RES  YAZ  LAST  SPCA  ASP
OCT  URE  USUAL  ALAN  MPH
THEAMERICANCENTURY  ORO
SHOLOM  ORR  AMINO  ANIT
RKELLY  EVERYTHINGMUSTGO
SODA  IDS  EAR  ESSAI
  ZEN  FRUSTA  AFLOW
THECATCHERINTHERYE  ALSO
EUROPE  ELO  HENMAN  VAIL
AGOG  AXIOMS  BOAST  ODED
ROSSINI  SMOKEANDMIRRORS
  DORM  LIV  AIRE
JUMPINTOTHEFIRE  NECKTIE
EROO  EATIT  FLUTIE  EAST
TITS  OXIDES  ERR  PORTIA
ECHT  FIVESTARRESTAURANT
SHEDS  ESTATE  RPI
 ROAST  RAN  SPY  HEEL
VANCOUVERCANUCKS  PAIRUP
IBIS  MINEO  YAY  LYRICS
JAG  INDEPENDENTCOUNSEL
ASH  GEOM  NAOMI  HUT  CPI
YET  ORLY  BMOC  SRO  HAD
```

148

```
CPUS  GRO  ELDERS  LEVIS
LUTHERAN  MERLOT  EXIST
ALIENATE  TOOTSY  WHOLE
MILLENIUM  SPOILS  ALER
  DOPY  INNOCULATE
EMBARASSMENT   ANE
INAJAM  ALA  HARRASSES
NORAH  MINISCULE  ILL
SPEX  DOH  OGLE  GIZMO
 SENOR  IZE  MEEKEST
IMPROPERLYSPELLED
ACCOUNT  BOK  TERMS
SHEEN  OMAN  EGO  THAI
IOU  NOTICABLE  ORALS
SUPERCEDE  EPA  PEEWEE
 XER  PERSEVERENCE
ACCOMODATE  STIR
BOUT  WAVERS  OCCURENCE
ORRIS  MARKET  HASAGOAT
VNECK  ENSUES  ERASABLE
ESSAY  STEPPE  DSL  DUCS
```

149

```
JONES  MAGI  SHEET  ALAR
EMOTE  CRUD  CORDILLERA
SANTA  HEREYOUGUMAGAIN
TROUSSEAU  INSO  BREVET
  HON  EPEE  CADRES
FIRYOURLOVE   SAL
AROAR  YOGI  SUCRE  ICAL
ZOOMED  GREATBALSAFIRE
ENDS  RISE  TOOTS  BASRA
 PICO  TELL  FALCON
CEDARFUNNYLITTLECLOWN
OCELOT  ARID  RISK
LOBES  CANOE  SILT  EGAD
OLIVEROCKNROLL  SIMONE
RITE  ERNIE  GALE  NIGER
 VEE  ELMOSTGROWN
ARABIA  PANE  TAR
STAPLE  LULU  KEEPORDER
PAWPAWPITIFULME  UVULA
ALLITERATE  MAIM  PEELE
MESA  DEMON  ANTS  SRTAS
```

150

```
JETSFAN  ANGULAR  KALEL
ACETONE  REPLETE  AMINO
NOWEANSITUATION  ZELIG
ONEPM  TNUT  PEROXIDE
SOSO  GLAREDAT  WOO
 NEHI  ORIGINALSCENE
ARP  MANN  ERROLL  OMAN
FEELINGSTATION  ERSATZ
LUELLA  YALE  LEADA  GOO
ANKA  INDIRA  CINQ
TEAMDUNCAN  SHEENGUARD
 AUST  EMBEDS  AZUR
SKA  DELON  AARE  EASTLA
UNICEF  ABANDONEDSHEEP
MEWS  OCTANE  SLUE  CDE
PEATORCHESTRA  OCTA
 HCL  RESONANT  MISS
JUMPSEAT  BING  SODOI
ONYOU  MINNESOTATWEENS
TIMOR  PREYSON  TEABAGS
STYLE  SEASONS  EMBASSY
```

151

```
P C L A B   A N A S A Z I     A B R A M
E R A T O   I N U N I S O N   A R R O W S
W Y M A N   T I L T A T W I N D M I L L S
  R U S S O   B N A I   A R I E L
I N S I S T E N C E   E R N I E F O R D
T O P   Q U A   R A D S   A C E S   V E E
A M E N U   S B A R R O   M E N   F E D S
L A C I E   Y U K   A P O P   J A R R E
  D I P S Y   M E D I   R U T   A R B O R
  A S T O O P   I N C A P S   C R E S T
E S L   I S L E   A B O   S A C K   E E S
N A R C O   I R O N O N   A R M P I T
C L E A N   O C T   A N I L   D O N H O
L A L A S   R O A R   W E D   T R O V E
A Z A N   S F O   A D V I S E   J I V E S
S A T   E A R P   A S I S   S O U   E R S
P R I C E L I S T   C H E C K S I N T O
  V O L T A   E A V E   B E S T S
F L I P P E R A N D E R S O N   I L L G O
L E T S O N   G O A R O U N D   C A V E R
A S Y E T   A R R A Y E D   E M I L Y
```

152

```
T O S C A L E     M A M B O   A G H A S
A R E A R U G   A D A P T E R   D R A F T
S O A R I N G   G E O R G E L A Z E N B Y
S A N G   A S S I S I   B O B   C A S E
  S C O W   I T I S S O   N O H O
  O P E C   M A R T I N I   A O R T A L
S O N A R S   I T E   R O G E R M O O R E
T U N N E L S   E S L   O N D E M A N D
A S E T   E W E S   A P A R T   S A D E
M E R S   W I G   A D A M   I T I N
P L Y   T I M O T H Y D A L T O N   D J S
  G U S T   B O D S   S L Y   B A A L
H M O S   E A S Y A   D U E L   I N M E
F E E L S B A D   Y A O   S A L L I E D
I A N F L E M I N G   U M S   N O L E S S
E D U C E S   A S P I R I N   D A H L
  O S S O   C O R O N A   M U C H
O A H U   I M F   E R A G O N   D R E I
P I E R C E B R O S N A N   P A S S A I C
E R A S E   R A S H E S T   A N T O I N E
R E P E L   E T T A S   L O U N G E S
```

153

```
L A D D   A L B U M   J A I   S A W S
A G R I   L E O N E S   O W N   R A B A T
B U Y A B L E B E L T   H O T P O T A T O
S E C R E T S   M O R A L L Y S A F E R
  L I T E   C O L O N   G E N T R Y
T H E S A L I V A T I O N A R M Y
H E A T S   N A S H   D E Y   A D A M
U R N S   A I L S   H A Z E   O C A L A
D O S   M E G A   G R A S   S A R O N G S
  C O R O N E R O N T H E M A R K E T
  P A O L O   C L A U D I A   I N N E R
H U M M A B L E B E G I N N I N G S
E R I T R E A   O M E N   S M E E   B M W
A S S E S   R O W E   G A P S   B R I O
L E S S   P G A   M A R E   E L I T E
  R I O T I N G I M P L E M E N T S
C H O S E N   M E E S E   L A N G
R E N T A S E N A T O R   S L I D I N G
A T T A C K D O G   R E D S K E L E T O N
S T A R T   I R E   G A I T E R   R O N A
H Y P E   T A D   D O P E Y   S N O W
```

154

```
U R S A   D E A D C A L M   I P A N E M A
N O E S   U N L O A D E D   R A V A G E D
Q U A K I N G A S P E N S   A L A M O D E
U N R O B E   B A R N S   S T E   Y I P
O D I U M   S A G A   Q U E B E C A C T
T E N T   A P S E   S O U P   L L A N O S
E R G   B L O T   S K U A   O U S T
  Q U A T E R N A R Y A G E   C H A S
S T U R M   R I O T   S I R   S H O R T
S T O O G E S   G O E S   R I S E   S R A
Q U A I L I N G A T   Q U E S T A F T E R
U P S   E N O L   S L U G   H E W L E T T
I O T A S   C E E   Y E L P   W A U L S
B R Y N   Q A N T A S A I R W A Y S
  G L U T   A M O K   O A R S   F O E
S T R I P E   O P A L   E X I T   M A N X
Q U E E N A N N E   T A I L   H A S A T
U R N   S E E   S W A R M   G E N T L E
A N T O N I A   Q U I E T A M E R I C A N
S T A I N E R   V E R B A T I M   L A R D
H O L L E R S   C R Y O G E N S   A R K S
```

155

```
T O P S O F F   C A N D I D   G R O P E
E V E N P A R   A D O R N E D   H O H O S
R E P O S S E S S E D A U T O   I S H O T
S N U B   E A T   C R A N E   S E L A
E S P   R E L Y I N G O N I N S T I N C T
  B O X Y   R A I   S L A S H   R U E
T R U A N T   C O N G A   A H Y E S
R E P A I R M A N U A L   M E T R O
I F S   A O L   M E A L S   T E S T
N U T C A S E   R E P O R T F O R D U T Y
A T A L L   J E E R S A T   C O R E R
R E T A I L O U T L E T S   N I A G A R A
Y S E R   B L A D E   T A D   S E N
  E S S E N   R E C O N M I S S I O N
P I N T A   S L A N T   G O E A S Y
G N U   L L A M A   H R S   M I N X
R E M O T E P O S S I B I L I T Y   S R O
A X E D   B E D E W   L E G   A M E N
T I R E D   R E V E R S E E N G I N E E R
E L I T E   S L E E P I N   O L D N A V Y
D E C O Y   A R T I S T   N O S I R E E
```

156

```
A C R E   P L E B E   S A M O A   A C T S
R O O M   O A R E D   A F O U L   C O H O
C A S E C L O S E D   F O O T L O C K E R
S T E R E O   T R A D E R   S U P R E M E
  G A S   A R E   C R E A S E S
T I M E S   A P R E S   C O E D
I N A N E   R O A D H A Z A R D   D O T
P S S T   S A R G E   M O R E   S N O R E
O U T   S C R E E N D O O R   O C E L O T
F R E E L O A D   E L M   C U R L
F E R V E N T   S A L E S   S E L V A G E
C E D E   E F T   C H A P E R O N
O R A N G S   S P R A Y P A I N T   S A T
P U R S E   C I A O   A E G I S   M I T E
T E D   W A L L S T R E E T   S A G E R
  T H R O   E N T R E   L I N E S
C A L I B E R   C C X   J U N
O D Y S S E Y   L A T H E D   O R M O N D
P O O L P L A Y E R   G R A P H P A P E R
A R N E   I L E F T   T I T A N   S E M I
Y E S T   E L A T E   V E E P S   T R O P
```

157

```
LAPLATA  APESUIT    PENS
ECLAIRS  ROMANCE    PEROT
SHOWMETHEMONKEY     EDINA
TETR  ERASE  GNU    NEATER
     EPSON   TRIPLEKLUTZ
PORNO   STRAIT   OWIE
DRACULA  RICA   UGANDANS
AFTERASKORT   AMOR   REO
SEE   SNIDE  PLANKAHEAD
   MAIER   MOI   VOILA
  WINKWINKSITUATION
ENOLA    YIN   SHOAT
BARKTENDER  ESSEN   CTR
ATM   DIRT  AVERAGEJOKE
NOSEDIVE  BRER  PALMTOP
   LESE  COINED   ABYSS
GUNKCONTROL   UVULA
UTAHAN   EAT  ACMES  RBIS
ITMAY  INFLATABLEKRAFT
LEERS   DETENTE  MINIBAR
ERST   STYGIAN   ATTESTS
```

158

```
NATICK   SHESALADY    WDS
CARROL   HADACAMEO   CHAT
WHEELEDAUTHORITY    LIRR
YES  OPEDS  AMY   SOLARIA
EDTV  TAO  FRANK  SOILED
TALESOFWHOA  XES   ARENA
HTEST    ARNE   ITEMED
   TROTOUT  ROTARY   RIB
SWM  WEATHERWHYS   DEVO
ANHEUSER   GOES  THECAN
DEANS    ABBRS    ALONE
VECTOR   PLOD  MAESTROS
IRKS  ISLEOFWHITE   ADV
LYS  BEWARE   AIRHEAD
   MARLIN  DIST   VASCO
ACURA  MET  WHALINGWALL
DOSIDO  DECOY  ENO  NYAD
DRESSUP  HAJ  DERMA  WWW
ANUT  THEEDITORIALWHEE
MEMO  DETERMINE  AMEERS
SAS   ONESEATER  MAINST
```

159

```
BRASH  ATL  BOPP  RISKIT
RECTO  CRUCIBLE   ARCANA
UNARM  TOBOGGAN   CIARDI
TODIEQUIETLYINMYSLEEP
   AGUAS  TINDER   HYENA
BESTIAL  HOES  HHS  MTN
ENTERS   MIN   PAYEES
EER  LIKEMYGRANDFATHER
FRED   IDO  AUSTEN   RAVE
GEAR  DEMESNE    EMERIL
BETHESDA   NOT  SHREWDLY
ATCOST   INVOICE   RETD
SIAM  AVENUE  MAR   DIOS
SCREAMINGINTERROR  MEA
   YVETTE   HAY  REFERS
STL  INA   BORN  LAGASSE
PRIMA  LATINA   LECAR
LIKETHEPEOPLEINHISCAR
IBERIA   ASTOLDTO  NIECE
FALCON   CLASSIER  EDDIE
FLYING   EAST  TRE  DEEDS
```

160

```
SAIDSO   LAMBDA   PRUDES
ACCEPT   RAWDEAL  REPENT
GUYFAWKESNIGHT  ONSITE
  ARAIL   GLOOM    MIR
ROCKYMOUNTAINBIGHORN
JAPES    LAURA  TSETSES
UTE   OSCARS   SAILS
SIRANTHONYHOPKINS  MOB
TOETOTOE   BLING   DAME
   MNOP  SPOOR   BOXER
PROFESSIONALWRESTLING
RIVET   SMEWS   DUEL
EPEE  DOONE   LIMAOHIO
ZEN  PUBLISHINGCOMPANY
   BRAVA   ATESTS   ITE
STYRENE  PASHA   SAFER
QUARTERMASTERGENERAL
URN   ETATS    ALONE
INKIND  CHINESEMUSTARD
REEDED  ROSEOIL  SOONYI
TREATY   OSTEND   ERODED
```

161

```
DEVILS  LIMNS  IPOD  ↓BOY
AMANITA  AFOOT  ORZO  TERI
MUSCLES  SASSY  SEAU  HEAP
↑STAIRS↓STAIRS   VWBEETLE
   NUS   IRONS   ALL→
←IT↑↑TOCHANCE  ATO  EFFUSE
ONEAM  HILO  ESPANOL  IMAX
NESTED  FIDO  HONES  LEAVE
BRS  NAST  XSANDOS  ELMER
AREI  THE←  YUL  INA  ODIST
SORT  SEDAN  BLANE  BIL
ERASMUS  ↓SIZING  DIVISOR
→ON  SPADE  S↑DOG  NINE
SET↑S  SPA  ARR  →END  ELAS
TREYS  TOYSHOP  LEIF  EDT
ANNOY  AIMTO  MAGI  GINNIE
LIEU  ONLEASE  FOCI  RATED
LETRIP  TNG  SIT↓ANDSHUT↑
   AQUA  TEATS  CHO
GILLSLIT  →WHEREYOU←THEM
ABEL  EMIT  REUEL  CREASES
ZINE  NEMO  ATLAS  KEYRING
EDDY  TEEM  PETRA  REPAYS
```

162

```
TEEM  ALOAD  MLIX  AGASP
AXLE  VALLI  EINE  SHINE
REVERENDEVEREND   SOREN
PRETENDS  ELITE   LISTEN
STS  YUM  HISTORYISTORY
   UNEATEN     EMIT
SAWTO  SEATAC  AWE  OLAV
SPOTLESSSPOTLESS  SWORE
REWEDS   WONT   GENOME
   RSTU  PITSTOPITSTOP
ISA  ASKIN  ERRED   SRS
MANDATEANDATE    GETS
ENGINE  TOIL   ORELSE
ATEST  FINALISTINALIST
NARC  EEE  NYMPHS  VIDEO
   JIVE    PEDAGOG
LABOREDABORED  OIL  SHE
UNOCAL  GOFOR  MANTOMAN
ENOKI  SONATINAONATINA
GENES  OREG  LATKE  TROT
OXEYE  BASE  STAID  OKIE
```

163

```
VANCAMP   ALAMEDA   GETZ
OVERLOUD  SENATOR   AQUA
LEGALDRINKING(AGE)   TURK
GREW   IDOS   LETMEIN
ATV  TITUS  HQS  SHEMP
  ESCAPEROUTE   ALAMOS
 PAQUIN  SIMIANS  INEPT
NATURES  BEN  YOWS  NAY
ECLAIR  MUSIC(CRACKS)  THX
HEALS  FOP  NEA  CRAWL
ISNT  ERGOT  STEEP  HOJO
 TOSCA  NAS  ORR  BICEP
FRI  TO(P)RANKING  MUSKET
LAC  ALPO  TIT  FORKERS
OCCAM  ESTREET  RISERS
GEHRIG  YOURMAJ(ESTY)
 ARNAZ  EMS  POETS  APB
 CREATOR  KERF  PERI
JUTS  SWEEP(U)NDERTHERUG
ABET  BIZARRE  LOWERING
WARS  YEARONE  MONKEES
```

164

```
TIPS  ACESIT  GAIA  ICS
UVEA  SOLUTE  UNCLESAM
PANTS  THEMALTESEFALCO
ANATOLIAN  ASA  RUEHL
CALIFORNIASUIT  SEXTET
  GAP  MON  SAWS
 THREEDAYSOFTHECONDO
EDIT  DRT  IAM  ODEON
VON  ENAMI  ASRED  DREI
AHARDDAYSNIGH  INMOST
 IOUS  TNN  USIA
INSYNC  THEELEPHANTMA
SALA  EDDIE  SIXTY  ARP
IZODS  AAS  EGO  FREE
NIGHTOFTHELIVINGDEA
 RATE  NEO  REL
SHMEAR  BEVERLYHILLSCO
NOISY  EOE  SAINTOLAF
ACLOCKWORKORANG  AVANT
RUNSAMOK  SWATCH  ETTE
ESE  TSKS  UNISYS  REIN
```

165

```
LAMB  MI5  AS1OF  4TH  MAGE
AVER  ESC  THEDA  ARI  ATOM
VENERATE  AHYES  CILANTRO
CUTALONGTHEDOTTEDLINE
 TOYOTA  ISRAEL
APOS  TAP  CAS  AUTO
CUL  FOLDTHROUGHEACH  NOI
CHEROKEE  HYDRA  SPOONFED
LABRATS  OIL  TEARFUL
MENS  PAIROFNUMBERS  CROW
PAD  ITSELF  PALEST  LOW
3SETS  TAD  KUM  STEP2
EROICA  CLEARER  BOARDS
 IKON  HARVEST  EURO
INTHEGRIDSEQUENTIALLY
JOEYS  EENY  PDAS  SLOES
ANE  3RS  ETS  BY2  BAH
BODEGAS  PAPAYAS  SUCROSE
 ULM  5AGAINST4  POE
PICO  ASTR  TILT  WIKI
GOTHROWTHEPAPERAIRPLANE
POORIDEA  EATER  NOVELLAS
SPREADER  DO1IN  ESSAYIST
```

166

```
GOTEAM  LETSAT  SUREBET
APOLLO  ISINTO  ONEBASE
SAYITAINTSOOT  NOWORSE
 STANCE  CISCO  ALDEN
ASTIR  EATSA  ORATIONS
IPOS  ALLOTTHESAME  TEY
WARMTH  BESAME  ARLO
AMY  HOAGIE  HILT  SOFTY
 CRYSTALBALLOT  CARO
ATARI  KOS  AHS  UNSAVED
LUNACIES  RNA  ACTALONE
ATANEND  TID  UMA  YENTL
MUCK  BIGOTBUSINESS
OSTER  NANU  NTESTS  SSN
 ODOM  LIAISE  AORTAE
JIF  SCHOOLMARMOT  AERO
ENGRAVER  BYRON  FITIN
SHOER  AESIR  LEARNS
SUDSIER  LOOTANDBEHOLD
EMOTERS  ANKARA  URANIA
LETSSEE  BEEPER  GETSBY
```

167

```
AIRS  MONGOLS  OLIVES
TRUCKS  SKILLET  DESILU
IMMUNE  RELIABLESAUCES
TAPSIN  PELT  KOD  TVA
 SIGHS  FAZETHENATION
PAT  HOUSE  AMES  OMN
ALE  TREE  ASTER  IST
SMALLARM  THENOOSEHOUR
TAKEI  IBSEN  LATENED
 ANY  PEEL  RAGA  OYS
 THEOHREALLYFACTOR
APU  HOOP  FOUR  SWF
MONSOON  SIENA  OMNIS
BEATTHEPRESS  MISDEALT
 ATO  OATHS  ELEA  VIE
 HEN  ELMO  ASSAY  YEW
SUNDAYMOANING  ASSES
AMI  REA  OILS  OHDEAR
WASHINGTONWEAK  NOSALE
ENLIST  ONEACRE  SWELLS
DEEDEE  NOTNEED  LSAT
```

168

```
 STUART  ROSIE  OMEGA
 PASTOR  ERASE  CAROLER
YOKOONO  LI(FEB)AN  AUGMENT
ETE  BA(JAN)  OBEY  S(MAR)TY  COB
ATTS  AWAIT  POOR  ATMO
SEEINGRED  GUTSY  TRIO
TRA(DEC)OMMISSIONS  R(APR)OCK
 ADAY  TOIT  GATO
CADRE  SWANN  BENEFITS
OTO  AUSTIN  GIANT  ITOO
MA(NOV)ERBOARD  ANCIENT(MAY)AN
BRAY  OATES  LIKESO  BIG
SINEWAVE  FELTS  BAERS
 DATE  NIKI  MOLD
DEC(OCT)S  ADRENALINE(JUN)KIE
IMHO  ABRAM  BONESCANS
SUER  HACK  DWELT  TROT
CLE  JO(SEP)H  ARAT  (JUL)ES  ARE
MASCARA  FR(AUG)HT  EPISODE
ATEAWAY  ACHOO  PERUKE
NESTS  MOTOR  SEEDER
```

169

```
CHINTZ   WOODLOT   CHEQUE
MADERA   ONATEAR   AUBURN
DREWUNIVERSITY      STRESS
     HEINE    GESTE    OEIL
CDRATES   FISHSTORY    NNE
HUEVOS   SANE    STEAMER
OBIE    DEBUTS    RIALTO
MAGNUMOPUS   PAAR   LITRE
PIN  PART  EZINE  CASHIN
    MISSUS   ELK  HOTSEAT
POSE  HAMMERTHROW   URLS
APPAREL   ENO   SAMPLE
LEANED  BALSA  GEED   MSS
ENDIT  RARA  FELLASLEEP
    EERIER  INTRAY   EDER
ARCSINE   BEAN   SAFIRE
REA  MASONJARS  LACTASE
MUSE   HELIO     AGNEW
OBISPO  LEADDETECTIVES
RENTAL  ACDELCO  TENSES
SNOOZE  SESSION   ANGOLA
```

170

```
CHOPS  AMIS  MATTE  SLAP
ROXIE  TESH  AGORA  NALA
THETWITCHINGHOUR   OMIT
ONTOPIC   RENAL   NEWBIE
    NORA   RUES   DIPS
BLTS  DESSERTTWINE   LOD
REWETS   IDOS   ANGELINA
ACETO   MSN   CROSSOVER
THETWEAKERSEX     DIOR
    DONATE  APSIS  SKINNY
ASK  IDEE  JOT  THEO  GEL
STIPES   TIARA   AUGUST
ARLO   THESOULOFTWIT
COLORFAST   ABA   ARISE
ADELAIDE   ILES   EXALTS
TER  FLIPONESTWIG   PLOT
    STEN   ITAT   INGA
PRIEST  PLENA   GLORYBE
HARE  YOUCANTTWINEMALL
IZOD  PILAR  EVAN  ACRID
LENS  EDENS  SAME  SAKES
```

171

```
PAELLAS   ACROSS   ATTESTED
ANCIENT   CHEWUP   PROFORMA
SECONDO   CINEMA   PORTRAIT
TWENTYPOUNDNOTE    PISTILS
     YPRES    LASH     LIU
IVES  BETAS  PRETTYPOISON
CITYPOLICE   EASEL    INN
IRONALLOY   INNER   KETCHUP
EINSTEIN   SNAG   VITALITY
RDS  ERNS  CELEBRITYPOKER
SNOG  PART  LEAS     VERO
BERETS   DIRTYPOOL   THESIS
LEER  IONE  PEAS     BOER
UNIVERSITYPOST   DUMA   BSA
RICEBELT    RIOS   USTROOPS
BEHOOVE   SPINS   PETITGRIS
UNU   COROT   TREATYPORT
PARTYPOOPERS   HEARS   UNOS
ANO    CPUS    HERSH
RITCHIE   PUBLICITYPOSTER
AMARILLO   MAIDEN   MERCYME
DATAFLOW   EDSELS   ESCAPED
ELEGISTS   SEARLE   STATORS
```

172

```
SPIKE  GAME  DRUB  SPATS
ALOFT  AWOL  RATE  PEREC
DUTCHSTEWINDIES    ATONE
ESA  OPED  ORS   OARSMEN
    LIL   LONEARTSSTATE
IAM  ONEMORE    OSTEO
SHAGGYGODSTORY   ARROWS
IMPLY  TIE  RAKE    EZIO
TALI  ACH  RIBROAST  ZSA
IDED  BARB  LIE  ROOMIES
   GENERALPOTSOFFICE
BARSOAP  OAS  TNUT  LSAT
EGO  PREOWNED  TLC  EMER
ENVS  TROI  RIA   DAIRY
PIECES   INCOOLPARENTIS
    OPTIN   SWEETEN   HET
ONETHINGSTAND     ACT
GOLFERS   CIG   ANTI  CAB
HOARD  THREELIMEISLAND
ASNER  EMAG  OWEN  TYPEA
MEDEA  POPS  BOND  SNOWY
```

173

```
DOMS  PUP   OBOE   CREATE
OBIE  ESO   IMOUT  LECTIN
GETTAKEN   CANTDOATHING
MYTHROATHURTS    LIEOVER
ASS  BELIE   OTTERS   EDS
    ROTO   YAWNER   ETC
CABARET   MGR   PIT  AFAR
ALICIA   NORAD   BIGSMILE
SERIO   SEMIPROATHLETES
KEDS  HEW   PURLIEU   TSP
    STOIC   IMAGE   ANGIO
SON  DRESSER   INT   DABS
THEROADTOATHENS    HITIT
ONSIMMER   LIENS   BODEGA
POTS   DIP  EAT   SOWSEAR
    ENS   PRESTO   OLIO
PJS  UNISEX   MSDOS   ADA
OATHAYS   SHOWBOATHOTEL
LIEUNDEROATH    FLIEDOUT
AMERCE   ALLOY   AYE  INCA
RENTER   IDES   RES   NEER
```

174

```
ITAL  BELLE  ATONAL  PAZ
CECE  ONION  SATINY  UMA
EXCHANGEOFSTRINGS   TIP
STEAM   UTAH   SOLOMONS
    DRAMA   NAME   ELON
NAE  HOLYSTROLLER   USMA
CUDDLEDUP   IDEAL   DETER
ONTO   OME   AROSE   ATM
STONEARMEDBANDITS   IRA
    APLAY   ELROY   REARED
NASTILY   BRIER   LARUSSA
ENTICE   GRINS   HEWED
PTA  ULTRAVIOLETSTRAYS
ARR  REOIL   ALI    ELEE
LUCRE   JPEGS   CONVEYING
IMHO  GOESALLSTOUT   CSA
    ERNO   SLOE   NEALE
KENYATTA   TVAD   TOPAZ
EXE  WHERETHEBOYSSTARE
DIM  AIRACE  LEVEE  TUNE
STY  BMINOR  SLEPT  OLES
```

175

```
ABRUPT  MIC  ESPRIT  ISH
PLENUM  ADA  TAHINI  NIE
TUNERS  COMICBOOKCOVER
NINAS  ALII  OTS  TIRE
ONESUGAR  LIETO  EATERS
GREENGOBLIN  GALLOWAY
PROVEIT  RUSSO
BETAS  AND  IRMAS  OCTAL
EXILES  SOI  OPT  TITO
CATFIGHT  DITCHES  AMIS
OMAR  TAO  OIE  ERR  VINE
MINE  SIBERIA  READINGS
ENID  REO  ISM  SNUGLI
SEAMS  CYNDI  ABA  ASSET
ODIUM  AIGLETS
ATALANTA  WILLEMDAFOE
BELIKE  GENII  HESPERUS
ATTN  EUR  IMNO  PLACE
THEAMAZING*MAN  BLITHE
EER  EVERSO  EYE  RECORD
DRS  TAKETO  RAY  STERES
```

176

```
TIEPOLO  ADAPTS  BBGUNS
AMMONIA  NICAEA  YOUSEE
WHERESTHEBRIEF  TASMAN
SORT  THUGS  SMASH  HIRT
SPOSE  FAERIE  ENTO
ALBION  BRANDINBOSTON
FALDO  PSEUDO  EYE
BRIERBEWARE  TEX  INBAD
SAP  BEGET  AUS  SLOANE
COCOA  BETROTH  IDEA
KEEPYOUREYEONTHEBRAWL
AXIL  OTOLOGY  ERNIE
MANUAL  FIB  CRAZE  AAS
AMESS  MFA  MEDICINEBRO
PEI  PIERCE  NUBIA
BREASTSELLERS  BIPEDS
EENY  ADIEUS  ISIAH
EDGE  GOFER  OATER  ODOR
THISBE  FLATBREADTRUCK
LANIER  EELPOT  TIEINTO
ETERNE  LESSEE  SEMANAS
```

177

```
DREW  HARUM  TORTES
RULE  MARISAPTOMAINE
AIME  RAYMONDCHANNELER
KNOB  AREAS  JEDI  ARI
EER  DMASS  VCR  SEISM
RESEAU  DOH  EMOTE
LADD  ARNOLDPOLYMER
ROMANA  SMU  IBEAM  OONA
IRONS  FOO  RONAPARROT
GATT  BACKRUB  ADEAR
GTO  KOOK  ORO  ACHE  SML
ORSON  SNYDERS  ASIA
ERIKSETTEE  FRY  DIETS
LINE  MARTS  NCO  JESSYE
MONICAZEALOUS  ROLL
NONOS  URL  OHHELL
PROSE  SGT  LEONI  AIM
AAA  PITA  SOTTO  SMEE
NIKITACRUISECHEF  ABBA
LINDSAYLOWHAND  ADEN
SEASON  CARLO  BART
```

178

```
SAMIAM  ALTAR  WEARABLE
ARISTO  NEALE  ALLOTTED
HENRIMATISSE  LEBATEAU
INK  TARA  MOD  LAIR  NRC
BASS  EARLAP  TONNE
WAXBEAN  SIP  ODIUMS
LOWISH  SCIENCES  SPAR
INASPIN  ADA  RAF  OSLO
LATS  BADU  OPS  COMMIT
ARE  PITAS  MATA  RUEDE
CARDSTORES  TIGHTDRESS
MMIII  ERTE  FRAYS  DEW
PERSON  SIX  FILS  COCA
JADE  NOS  NET  LEDAWAY
EGIS  BANKSHOT  VAUNTS
NEATER  LOO  ROOMERS
DAVID  PIPPIN  ESAS
AFB  IVAN  MAV  INDC  KIA
PAINTING  FRENCHARTIST
AMBIENCE  ATRIA  YEARLY
REINDEER  SISAL  SETTER
```

179

```
GRADED  HTML  DAMPS  SAX
NOJIVE  AREA  ELIOT  PRY
ATONIC  WONT  VISOR  YUL
REBATES  THERESTHEROBE
RAMIS  ADULT  TENAM
USS  DEODATO  PACE
CLAIM  EGRET  PEACHFOES
LOAMANDABNER  ARTY  PLY
ABBACY  ARRAS  LIEN
RASSLE  KNITS  LANCE
AREWEHAVINGPHONEYET
GNATS  ANENT  SALONS
ODDS  EVANS  OOLONG
LOI  TAUR  PERSIANROGUE
FRIARTOKE  COATI  EWOKS
LOST  SCOLDED  DET
SCRAP  STALL  MEDIC
PAININTHEBOAT  DECODES
ITT  CORAL  GWEN  CAVORT
FEZ  ATOLL  IANA  AMELIA
FRY  LINEA  CYTE  LETTER
```

180

```
ACED  VENN  EST  IREFUSE
SUMO  IMAC  DCI  TEARSAT
KEEPSSTRAIGHT  SATIDLE
MINIMI  CAPELLA  DICOT
ENDNOTES  SWEEPSSTALLS
GLOM  SOAP  OPT  SLAP
ARI  TRITE  YSIDRO  SAKI
DUMPSSTOCKS  NAY  DEREK
ETTE  LYE  STL  DRESSY
STORABLE  NCAR  UEY
YOURATTENTIONPLEASE
RID  YARD  INERRANT
JANSEN  REN  OOP  LUTE
ELECT  TAU  SKIPSSTONES
SLUR  POMPEO  LYNCH  ART
TORA  OUR  XMAS  IRES
SWAPSSTORIES  ATALANTA
ALICE  DITMARS  PONIES
INGROUP  DROPSSTITCHES
SCIORRA  GOR  VAIN  TINE
MEANEST  EWE  PING  ALAS
```

181

```
WATT  DEBATE  TONGS  DARE
ASHE  DREAMON  EFILE  ITEM
GAEA  ROLLINGINTHEAISLES
PETREL  SCI  NOH  ALLMAN
VANILLAICECREAM  SANTA
BIBS  EOS  BASES  SALTED
SILL  URL  SSE  ISAK  ARE
WADEIN  LOWEREASTSIDE
INE  SRI  NEE  ALI  IREPEAT
SCATHED  MAKESANENTRANCE
SADR  SLIER  VERGE  MUSTY
APTER  CEL  REGAL
MARCO  ALTAR  SOOTY  ENDE
THEHOUSEOFMIRTH  CRATERS
SALERNO  VAR  ION  HAD  CIT
ASLIKELYASNOT  TACKLE
APP  ELOI  VEE  OPE  HALE
VARLET  ONETO  IDA  DINS
GREET  PLACINGENDTOEND
ONSALE  MHO  URE  SAVANT
CLASSACTIONLAWSUIT  SEEP
DEMO  RAISE  ENISLES  ECRU
SEEN  KNOTS  DONEES  AKIN
```

182

```
BIKERS  NACHO  SORELOSER
AORTIC  IDAHO  ORIGINATE
SUISSE  PATHO  DEPONENTS
SSS  ENDAT  HORAS  EATAT
OAKTREE  ECHOES  SHULA
RESOLD  CHOP  SHAPABLE
APIN  NOR  SHOOAWAY  RAIL
BUNDLESUP  HOSEA  RUMBLE
AGGRO  MUCHO  STEIN  YAM
CELICA  COHOS  HADUP
KTEL  LOOKWHOSHERE  AJAM
SETAL  SHORE  SETONS
ABC  LARDS  HOSNI  TILED
MOHAIR  MACHO  SAIDHELLO
CORP  BOATSHOE  MDI  NYES
SKIPTOWN  PHON  BLASTS
SLAYS  COHOST  ELASTIC
LETIN  ORTHO  ONSET  NSA
IMMEDIATE  HOARY  CUBIST
AMARETTOS  HOBOS  TROCHE
MESSMATES  HOUSE  SNAKES
```

183

```
RON  SAW  ORBITS  DOWEL
INARUSH  BARNETT  IRENE
PULASKI  EVILEYE  ORING
ASAGIFT  SEDAN  APR  LUG
GEO  BELLY  ISRAELIS
GATE  RAE  ESPN  EMT
ROAD  TREATS  SUNYATSEN
ARK  HATCH  BANE  SUPRA
STEPHEN  NEGATIVE  YIP
PASSIM  MESON  SELLECCA
ASHORE  SUN  OREIDA
TATTOOER  ADORN  VENTED
EDU  NECKLACE  MANACLE
MIRED  FURY  KAPUT  HEM
PANDERSTO  ESPOSO  RENO
GSA  ICBM  PER  ERIN
IMPETIGO  ROAMS  MAT
NYU  ILL  JETTA  JUPITUS
ELTON  OPINION  ASARULE
POOLE  WILDONE  WIREMEN
TUNED  PLANET  ACT  SET
```

184

```
BOOTHE  ELEVENTH  WRENS
LABRAT  SOMEMORE  RELET
THEITHATGOTAWAY  INCUR
SURPRISE  INN  ATTIRE
LECH  VOCLOCKSHADOW
ACTED  RHINO  WEASEL
NAH  NATTERS  RED  KEL
THEXCOMMANDMENTS  CIAO
INARUT  LED  ISO  SPORTS
ARID  ALPHA  OCOME
LWAYSTOLEAVEYOURLOVER
HOWIE  MAZDA  KOLN
AMANDA  NRA  TIE  LOUDER
SARG  CYEARSOFSOLITUDE
AND  TCM  KENOSHA  PGA
GOTHAM  TILED  SWEEP
INDIANAPOLISD  EQUI
DOESSO  PEI  EAUDEVIE
OWLET  MISLANDDRESSING
LILLE  BAHAMIAN  SEESTO
SNEER  ANACONDA  ORLESS
```

185

```
TIVO  PU(NY)  HIPHOP  (WA)R(WI)CK
O(NH)ER  O(NM)E  E(NC)HASE  LITHO
AEROFLOT  HA(IL)TOTHECH(IE)F
SRS  ALOSS  ONEA  ENZI
TEENIER  TIRING  VIA
ERR  CO(MD)EN  SORRELS
STATESWONBYBARACKOBA(MA)
HITS  ENE  LOY  ENOLS
A(ME)(RI)(CA)N(FL)AGS  FELON  DINAH
FLAPPER  ARETOO
TYLERS  J(OH)(NJ)AY  MADAMA
HALITE  FIRELIT
COAST  MINOT  O(VA)LOFFICE
LACEY  PEN  PLO  EBRO
(IN)THEPRESI(DE)NT(IA)LELEC(TI)ON
THEDEAD  LAHTI  I(GOR)
LAD  MAITRE  EVASION
SARI  ICER  S(MI)LED  (VT)WO
(CO)(NV)ENTIONGOER  DONSHULA
PI(PA)GE  ALU(MN)AE  APU  ABED
ELYSE  LOSING  SEP  METS
```

186

```
SPACED  STIES  VASSAR
TENUTA  SPIRAL  AIRLINE
ASEPARATEPACE  LEMONDE
GEM  TEAL  HEALS  GIRL
STINK  NILES  PRO  BASES
ACONFEDERACYOFDUNES
LEIA  DEVO  AMISS
METERS  SOL  RENT  HES
PANELS  RATIOS  ALCOVE
ACC  THETURNOFTHECREW
THONG  AAA  LEI  SUNNI
RIDEANDPREJUDICE  SIN
ONETWO  IRONON  ACTING
LED  KNOB  WES  STRING
RECUR  IDAS  EEEE
THERETURNOFTHENAIVE
SEERS  RIO  NEROS  KNISH
HALE  SANTO  ARAB  CPA
AREARUG  THERUNWAYJURY
MUNDANE  ENCASE  BEANIE
SPASMS  ROOTS  ATBATS
```

187

```
OSCARS  OHMS    ACHES   LOM
SHOWUP  TORI    CHANT   AVA
LAMEBRAINED     QANDA   KEN
ORE LY(NNW)OOD  TU(NNE)LER  ERN
EDIE    ISR     WILED   NODE
EWOK    FLEET   ITSY    GOFOR
DA(WNW)ELLS  ERESTU  SERGEI
ARI LOO EATER   TAM(ENE)SS
MET AWN NEVERFEAR    VIM
HONE    SIDED   ERG PATS
WORSEN  GRIEFS
COHN    LUC TBSPS   NEIL
EDO LIBRARIES   HAD IDA
NE(WSW)EEK   ELATE   AMU FUN
TSETSE  TIGERS  REPR(ESE)NT
ISERE   SPEE    SPINS   INGE
LATE    GLAND   EVE MATA
IFI CRO(SSW)AY  GLA(SSE)YE  ERR
TIT PIVOT   WOUNDEDKNEE
ELI OPERE   PINK    NIECES
RES SENDS   ANKA    SAGEST
```

188

```
ATLAST  TISHA   LEAFAGE
CHASTE  OSTEAL  ALPACAS
MOTHEROFPEARL   BARRELS
ERE PERM    MAYI    LIE
FOSTERPARENT    CRASS
CABANAS AONE    TORO    FLA
ABODE   NIL PEARTREES
SNYE    GIBSONGIRLS EWES
HESITANCE   ARNEL   SAPPY
IRONIES EMITS   OTRO
NSF CLOSERELATIVE   IUM
SAKS    CAROL   SAVANNA
SPURS   BOSON   COLLECTED
IRMA    LITTLEFOXES READ
DUMBBELLS   UNO MORSE
ENE ANKA    BANC    AMASSER
SERBS   ONEOFTHEGUYS
ETS DUAL    VEST    EFT
MARRIED BROTHERSINLAW
ABALONE IDAHOS  EMILIO
REPENTS ESTEE   DETERS
```

189

```
HAHAS   ICIEST  BARMAN
APITCH  HEATERS ORIOLE
JETHRO  ALMANAC AMPULE
PEEPAT  ODA     ACRID
STARWIREDPARENTSMONEY
WORM    GYROCAR ICER
ANAIS   OUSE    STANDPAT
MADCONSUMERREPORTSSPY
ILE OOH ALE YAP
ATSEA   CANOE   BOCCIE
JETTHEATLANTICMONTHLY
EXITED  OUTDO   HUGER
EEG NCO NIT BIT
PREMIEREINTERVIEWTIME
STRESSED    ETTA    OILON
ROMA    ISRAELI ELFS
GEORGEDETAILSHOMELIFE
MARIO   CAL ACACIA
ATTEND  CLAVELL CONRAD
TOESIN  LIMINAL SLEDGE
SNATCH  CINEMA  ESSEN
```

190

```
ABCS    GATHER  ODD BESTS
HARE    AREOLA  SOW USAGE
ALITTLESOFTSHOE SCRIP
BIBLEBELT   EARLYSHIFT
OCALA   BAR STATE
CHAOS   GUSTS   LORRES
HAUS    FREUDIANSLIP    AXE
ETTE    IOLA    ANTE    PICA
SHO CLAIMJUMPER ALLEN
SAMEHERE    ELATE   MARLS
USERS   MUNRO   NGAIO
SIFTS   TODAY   TUESDAYS
ASFAT   MOVIESHORTS DEL
HULS    GALE    URSA    ATNO
IZE YELLOWJACKET NITA
BURGOO  NOVAK   PAEAN
RURAL   NSA EASEL
BOXINGRING  SALARYCAP
AMONG   CLASSACTIONSUIT
ROUGE   HTS STAMEN  ETNA
MOTOR   YSL SERENE  SSTS
```

191

```
LABELS  FOILS   MANAGED
ARAMIS  SUNSET  IMPROVE
PALEST  THELORDSPRAYER
SMARTS  ORCA    AUEL    BARN
AGE ELMAN   PERES
WOMENSWEARDAILY EATS
AWS TENN    ANS REDONE
FLAPPER WAR CORONER
TESTERS SHEPHERDSPIES
TSAR    BAER    ALOE    TORE
MRSOLEARYSCOW
COME    AMOI    THEE    HEMA
APOSTLESCREED   CHERUBS
REDTAPE USA LATERAL
PREACH  PTS ROAR    PSU
AMBO    WHISTLERSMOTHER
SCOOT   OASIS   PRY
SPAS    ROTA    THEO    SEISMO
AROOMOFONESOWN  INPLAY
CONFINE INURES  TULANE
SWEATER CAPED   SPEWER
```

192

```
ASTIR   MASSE   LOTUS   EMBAR
MYRNA   AMAHL   ARENT   FOLIO
IRISHSYMBOL KINDOFTHUMB
SILT    HOARD   ENCORE  ARAB
SALINA  NADER   GENES   ITTY
GORE    ITEM    NESTOR
SALADINGREDIENT EDSELS
PRET    DOTS    DAU SARI    DAH
ATTEND  BETA    RAMON   UTICA
NOT OASES   SLANGFORMONEY
GOSIGNAL    III CRANE   LASS
SOAP    SANTE   YARE
APSO    NINTH   GAS IMMATURE
VILLAGECOMMON   ONSET   BON
ONEAL   NOWAY   KILN    RAGOUT
ITE ACTS    ELS NEED    EASE
ROTATE  PLACEFORAPUTTER
CENSER  RAGE    BEGS
MARC    TAMAR   MOREL   SHAMES
OMAR    ELITES  INLET   HOLA
LIMEOROLIVE COLOROFENVY
DEBTS   MINER   PRAYS   RADII
SLOES   EAGLE   ASIDE   IDEST
```

193

```
SHAPED  PIMPLES   MAITAI
CENTRE  OCARINA   AUBURN
OXTAIL  WERELIVINGINAN
TIE CELEB  GEM   EDAM
INCA TELEGRAM  PARES
AGEWHENLEMONADEISMADE
DEEDS  RACY  ADD   LAY
REIN       BYE  SLAVE
TANG OAK RATA  SECEDES
WITHARTIFICIAL    VEX
ADS ALFREDENEUMAN  BEE
PRO  INGREDIENTSAND
REGIONS DEBS STS TKOS
OCEAN  HAS        GOES
ORO  ROI  OLAV  CHARD
FURNITUREPOLISHISMADE
GOBEL  ASSENTED  SLOB
LESE  DAR  TAXIS   APB
WITHREALLEMONS  NESSIE
HOTOIL  PAROLEE  GASKET
ONEWAY  OPENERS  SMEARS
```

194

```
BRACE  HASH  ALVA  MELON
ROLLS  ELSA  DOER  ALOFT
ABOUTFAITH  JUNIORMYTH
BEEHIVE     USEDUP
SEVEN  CIDER   SLAPON
AFB TEA  BONG  ALTEREGO
NORBERT  ALDENTE  MELD
SLUR  HANOI  YEAS  AWES
ALTA  DISGRACE  PAINED
ROADHOGS   NOTA  LODE
AWL ACHE ITO SHOW  WBA
FIST  SASH  SUMATRAN
POMPOM  GRUESOME  AERO
SOUP ROBO  MECCA  CARD
TORA  ALGEBRA  NECKTIE
INTIMATE  NEIN WOO HOS
RAHRAH  ANTRE  ARSON
ROSCOE     WAIKIKI
DEADLYTHIN  PLAINTHONG
ENDUE  LEST  EXIT  OINKS
WOOZY  OSEE  PITH  PLAYA
```

195

```
DANCERS  ACT  SKEE  PUB
ATEALOT  PERSONAL  POPE
MEATLOAFPLATTERS  OILS
NATS  DYER  COHEN  APSIS
MOES  SWEETKISS  STONE
YUP  HOSES  SHANKS
ARDENT  ZEN   CAMERA
BAR SALON  POLICESTING
STICH  IND  HOSTEL  ROM
FRAPPE  DANTE  LASSOS
ETUDES  VINAS  RECOUP
FLEXED  FACTS  MADCAP
OIR  ARISTO  TIS  UPPER
BOSTONCREAM  ETHOS  LEE
JUNTAS  ANT  JEKYLL
SCORES  THORN  SON
UHURA  FREEBREAD  FIBS
MOREL  LETAT  SPED  TOCK
MINT  HEARTASSOCIATION
ICES  SETASIDE  COMESTO
TEY  TRAS  NIE  ARIDEST
```

196

```
DERMAL  THECARS   REGAL
ARTURO  RESOLED  VOLARE
PRESSCLIPPINGS  AXILLA
COHORT  FIR  ALY   OED
MILAN  LEOI  CABLE  SONE
ICET  IAM  GLOBETROTTER
CODERS  EGIS   LEICA
ANGLERS  OVALS  RETREAD
HOE  CALLLETTERS  ADALE
REDEYED  SYNE  PLUGIN
ISLA  LEASH  RABBI  SLAY
MAITAI  STUB  TERNATE
ANNEX  STATEPOLICE  SSW
STERILE  RULER  CURACAO
INAWE  IPSO  ROCOCO
TELEGRAPHKEY  MAL  CURE
AXIS  ARIAN  SAID  RETAR
MPG  LID  VOS  STAKES
TIEDIN  PATRIOTMISSILE
ARRIVE  ANTOINE  WIENER
MESSY  SASSIER  INSANE
```

197

```
INFO  TREY  BASAL  PITHS
LOIN  HAMM  ADELA  ATOOT
ERLE  EPIC  BURLS  SANTO
DAIS  FILADELFIAPHLYER
ESP RODE  ORTS  GRASSLE
PEERS  PIUS  RNAS
HINDU  SANT  MAAM  EFG
FANTOMPHIGHTERS  STIEB
EVERS  EENS  OLE  YALTA
REP  EIRE  SRO  PORTIAS
RAHS  FOTOPHINISH  SPRS
UGLIEST  DUE  NYSE  TAE
LOADS  NIL  BOAC  NOHIT
EAGLE  FYSICALPHITNESS
TSE  BEET  ABIT  GRIPE
BRAT  OLEO  SNATH
STAREAT  MILL  ATOP  OAS
PHRENCHFILOSOFER  RUBY
RELEE  ELLEN  VIVA  IRAN
IREST  REARM  ERIN  OTTO
GENES  SENSE  NEET  SHED
```

198

```
OFFHAND   DEFOG   SELES
REAIRING  DENOVO  EXULT
BRITISHRAINCOAT  DAMME
RASE  EDDO  TLC  UMBER
SHA  TIGERSTEESHOT  ERN
TAMPA  UNITED   ACTER
ALOU  REP  SAD  TONJON
ROUT  FUR  FELICE  CAGE
KEN  KOS  CARLIGHT  ACER
STEEN  GOBI  EEE  ASKED
MYTHREESONSROLE
RUMPS  OER  BRET  GODWE
OPAL  BLACKEYE  ART  UVA
ETNA  REVERE  USE  INOR
GOINTO  ERA  ANY  CDLI
CERTS  FRESCO  REEVE
TRU  AHAUNTEDHOUSE  RES
HIRED  UNE  VIER  ISAK
AGILE  CHAYEFSKYSATIRE
NOSIR  EATERY  SEALANTS
ERTES  SPORT  SLEDDED
```

199

```
ROOSTS   FINKS   CACHET
ANXIOUS  INANE   AIRHOLE
MEETMEINSTPERIODLOUIS
SAY   MAKE  SANK  OUSTS
 MESAS  HERES  SID   TIE
  EXES   IDEST  EMBOSS
HELPEXCLAMATIONPOINT
AVOID  YEWS   DRAPER
DIVA  BLTS  SKEET  DIAS
OLE  OULU  TEAR  BROWNE
NOBODYAPOSTROPHESFOOL
ENURES  DAHL  LOTT  JFK
SEGA  AGERS  DEBS  HIFI
  TAPIRS   SAAB  SUMER
QUOVADISQUESTIONMARK
BUMRAP  SAUNA   TRIP
RIP  AAH  ACHED  APSES
AXIOM  MAAS  OWEN   LIP
SORRYCOMMAWRONGNUMBER
STEERER  BRISK  SOMEONE
YESMAN   ISLES   GALWAY
```

200

```
HASTO  SPAR  GAZA  BASTE
ALTER  PELE  REED  ISOUR
ROAST  CATS  ACEOFCLUBS
PUTTERAROUND    EYELET
   EGO   REE  MEECE
SUNDAYDRIVER  BALLPARK
UNO  SEABED  GARNI  VIE
MINCE  PREYSON  POSTAGE
STEAL  PET  BAAL  TALON
   VIA  CRISPUS  LORE
WEARINGOFTHEGREEN
SEHR  ENNEADS    SAN
ARENA  SEES  TIA  STATE
DOESNOT  STUDENT  ESSEX
ADZ  CLOSE  NEARTO  SAT
TEESHIRT  MISSINGLINKS
  TOVES  AOK   ROD
SAFARI   INTOTHEWOODS
IRONMAIDEN  OLIO  CIVET
MAIZE  DELL  PENN  ADELA
IMEAN  IFFY  SOAK  LONER
```

Celebrate the 100th Anniversary
of the Crossword Puzzle!

Available Summer 2013

Also Available from The New York Times

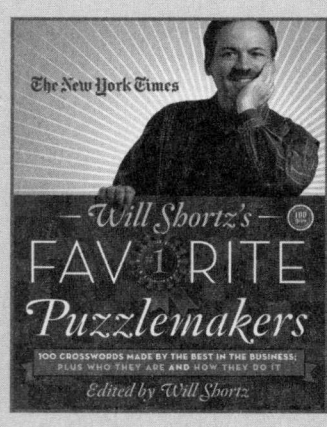